IDIOT'S GUIDE®

of ts

a

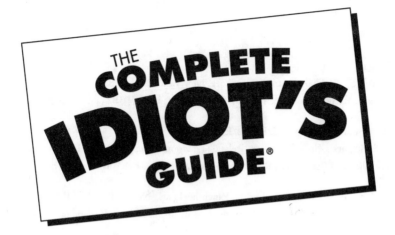

THE
COMPLETE
IDIOT'S
GUIDE®

Big Book of Needle Arts and Crafts

by Laura Ehrlich, Gail Diven, Mary Ann Young, and Lydia Wills

ALPHA

A member of Penguin Group (USA) Inc.

ALPHA BOOKS

Published by the Penguin Group

Penguin Group (USA) Inc., 375 Hudson Street, New York, New York 10014, U.S.A.

Penguin Group (Canada), 10 Alcorn Avenue, Toronto, Ontario, Canada M4V 3B2 (a division of Pearson Penguin Canada Inc.)

Penguin Books Ltd, 80 Strand, London WC2R 0RL, England

Penguin Ireland, 25 St Stephen's Green, Dublin 2, Ireland (a division of Penguin Books Ltd)

Penguin Group (Australia), 250 Camberwell Road, Camberwell, Victoria 3124, Australia (a division of Pearson Australia Group Pty Ltd)

Penguin Books India Pvt Ltd, 11 Community Centre, Panchsheel Park, New Delhi—110 017, India

Penguin Group (NZ), Cnr Airborne and Rosedale Roads, Albany, Auckland, New Zealand (a division of Pearson New Zealand Ltd)

Penguin Books (South Africa) (Pty) Ltd, 24 Sturdee Avenue, Rosebank, Johannesburg 2196, South Africa

Penguin Books Ltd, Registered Offices: 80 Strand, London WC2R 0RL, England

International Standard Book Number: 1-59257-280-4
Library of Congress Catalog Card Number: 2004110013

06 05 04   8 7 6 5 4 3 2 1

Interpretation of the printing code: The rightmost number of the first series of numbers is the year of the book's printing; the rightmost number of the second series of numbers is the number of the book's printing. For example, a printing code of 04-1 shows that the first printing occurred in 2004.

Printed in the United States of America

Note: This publication contains the opinions and ideas of its authors. It is intended to provide helpful and informative material on the subject matter covered. It is sold with the understanding that the authors and publisher are not engaged in rendering professional services in the book. If the reader requires personal assistance or advice, a competent professional should be consulted.

Publisher: *Marie Butler-Knight*
Product Manager: *Phil Kitchel*
Senior Managing Editor: *Jennifer Chisholm*
Senior Acquisitions Editor: *Renee Wilmeth*
Development Editor: *Ginny Bess Munroe*
Production Editor: *Janette Lynn*

Copy Editor: *Keith Cline*
Cartoonist: *Chris Eliopoulos*
Cover/Book Designer: *Trina Wurst*
Indexer: *Angie Bess*
Layout: *Ayanna Lacey*
Proofreading: *Mary Hunt, Jamie Fields*

Contents

Note: Chapters with an * are projects that teach you how to create your own artistic pieces.

22 Embroidery Project: The Art of Monogramming   271

23 Combining Stitches and Special Effects   279

Introduction

This book is divided into several sections, one on each type of needle craft: quilting, embroidery, needlepoint, knitting, crocheting, and sewing. In each section, you'll find basic information, instructional material, and fun facts. As you learn new techniques, you can test them using the projects interspersed throughout this book.

Learn how to create a quilt like your grandmother, stitch color into your napkins and pillows, knit a sweater or scarf for a friend, and sew simple buttons or curtains and pillows for your living room. As you work your way through this book, your confidence will grow, and soon, you'll want to put your signature on the crafts you make. Yes, you'll even learn the art of signing your work.

Extras

Before you get started, review the following sections and learn about the extras strategically placed throughout this book. These tidbits will serve you well as you learn the fine art of crafting.

The following sections describe the features pertinent to each type of craft.

Quilting Features

Making a quilt requires many steps. This book is designed to make it as easy as possible and help you avoid any problems. Sidebars are scattered throughout the book and highlight what is important for all quilters to know. These sidebars are …

Scraps and Pieces

This box offers a variety of different quilt stories, historical tidbits, or just interesting information about quilting.

Quilt Talk

Quilters seem to have a language of their own. Any new and unusual words are explained.

Don't Get Stuck!

Throughout my many years of teaching beginner quilters, I have discovered many different pitfalls that may occur. The hints in these boxes will help you avoid these problems.

Quilting Bee

Sometimes there is an easy way of doing something, and these tips are ones that you would learn at a quilting bee.

Embroidery and Needlepoint Features

Some of the best, simplest, and most important ideas about embroidery and needlepoint are scattered throughout the book in notes. Some of these are necessary for every needleworker to know, some are helpful tips, and others will warn you against pitfalls. A description of each follows:

Needlework 101

These boxes contain definitions that will help you speak needlework lingo.

A Stitch in Time

Needlework tips to keep you on your toes can be found in these boxes.

Decorator's Do's and Don'ts

These warnings from a decorating pro will keep you from design and practical disasters!

Clever Crafter

Clever Crafter boxes hold extra information of interest

Knitting and Crocheting Features

The following stitching tips, definitions, historical anecdotes, and pitfalls to avoid will help you master the art of knitting and crocheting:

Pointers

Is there a better way to do something? Are there variations to the common instructions? Check out the Pointers, where you'll learn valuable hints and tips to make your stitching more enjoyable.

Yarn Spinning

Knitting and crocheting have enjoyed long histories filled with interesting anecdotes. You'll read some of these compelling stories in the Yarn Spinning notes.

Needle Talk

So many definitions are thrown around in the stitching world: gauge, dye lot, half-double crochet.... Look to the Needle Talk notes for simple definitions.

Snarls

Danger! Warning! You potentially could hit a bump in the road if you don't watch out for these common errors.

Sewing Features

The following hints and details—the kind that make the difference between something that looks handmade and something handmade that looks designer—will help you turn your machine into a sewing diva:

Sew Far, Sew Good

These tips make your sewing experience "seam" much more pleasant.

Sew You Were Saying ...

Find definitions of those key sewing terms to make it all "sew" simple here.

Noteworthy Notions

These interesting facts and helpful hints add flair and zip to any sewing project.

Stitch in Your Side

These warnings help you steer clear of needle and thread catastrophes.

Trademarks

All terms mentioned in this book that are known to be or are suspected of being trademarks or service marks have been appropriately capitalized. Alpha Books and Penguin Group (USA) Inc. cannot attest to the accuracy of this information. Use of a term in this book should not be regarded as affecting the validity of any trademark or service mark.

Part 1

Quilting

In this part, you'll learn how to make a quilt from start to finish. You'll learn about the components and construction of a quilt along with the tools and techniques to create the quilt you envision. You will learn how to plan the quilt, buy the materials, piece the quilt top, quilt and baste, and then sign your work of art. As a project, you'll create your own quilt, start to finish.

Time to Plan Your Quilt

In This Chapter

- ◆ Understanding the decisions you will make in planning your quilt
- ◆ Learning how the quilt top is set up
- ◆ Surveying pattern designs and choosing your pattern

Where do you start? To determine which type of quilt you should make, you must ask yourself many questions. When you've decided, your decision is not written in stone. One of my students wanted to make a small crib quilt and started piecing blocks together. She enjoyed the process so much that her crib quilt ended up as a queen-size quilt! That's the beauty of the block method—you can add or subtract squares to suit your need.

When you have decided on the size of quilt you intend to make, you have to pick out the quilt patterns you want to tackle. I have drawn out all the designs for the patterns that are included in this book at the end of this chapter.

This is where we really begin!

Decisions, Decisions, Decisions!

You have to think about several things before starting your quilt. Let's take them one by one.

What's Your Quilt's Use?

First of all: What do *you* want to make? Almost everyone wants to make a bed-size quilt to show off her workmanship. I do *not* suggest you do this. A quilt of that size is a huge undertaking and could take more than a year to complete. I have found that beginners are much happier working on a project that they can finish quickly. You need the positive reinforcement of accomplishment—a wall hanging or *lap quilt* is a perfect small project.

> **Quilt Talk**
>
> A **lap quilt** is a small quilt put together with 6 to 9 blocks, usually 60 by 60 inches square. I like to drape one over a sofa or at the base of a bed.

Another important question to answer is this: Who will use this quilt? If you want to make a crib quilt or a quilt for a young child, you may have to change your ideas about colors and patterns. Children love colors and bold patterns. Be sure to use fabrics that are durable and totally washable. Don't make something that is so difficult and time-consuming that you will be offended if something happens to it—kids will be kids.

Will Your Quilt Be the Center of Attention?

Look around the room that your quilt will live in. Do you want it to be the focal point of the room or blend with the surroundings? Bright dynamic colors will ensure that everyone's eyes are on your masterpiece. Whereas a Scrap quilt may fit in with your colonial décor, a Danish Modern may not. Look through quilt books. Check out the room décor—a dramatic quilt can pull together an eclectic room.

See how Edith Bihler's Pineapple table cover pulls the elements of the room together?

What Do You Like?

Everyone has preferences. Do you like rounded shapes or angular? Flowers or geometrics? Many men do not like the floral motifs of appliqué quilts (and not just men—several of my women students hate those rounded, fussy patterns). Quilts can look either modern or traditional, masculine or feminine. Find out the names of quilt patterns that you are drawn to. I hope you will find many of the patterns you like in this book. When I started quilting, I wanted to make a Dresden Plate quilt with all pastel colors. I didn't start with that block, but I took a class to learn about quilt basics.

Be Realistic

After you have tried a variety of patches in a small quilt, you can tackle a large project. The Sampler quilt is a challenge to coordinate; that's part of the fun.

Here are several suggestions that I have found to be helpful in avoiding problems that beginners have. Be sure you know the parts of the quilt and the terminology. Be realistic about your abilities. Check out the difficulty of the quilt patterns. A hint: The smaller the pieces in a block, the more time-consuming to make; the larger the number of pieces in a block, the more work you have to do. The 12-inch-square block of the Churn Dash pattern has 17 pieces, and the Bear's Paw has 53. That's a big difference! Creating a quilt using only one quilt pattern may be aesthetically pleasing, but it may also become monotonous. Piecing 20 patches that are all the same is not as challenging or as creative as stitching 20 different blocks.

The Quilt Setup

It's important to understand the language of quilting. Before you start planning your quilt, look at the diagram of a quilt and learn the parts of the quilt. Understanding these terms is important because I will be discussing their construction for the quilt top throughout the rest of the quilting chapters of this book.

Parts of a quilt.

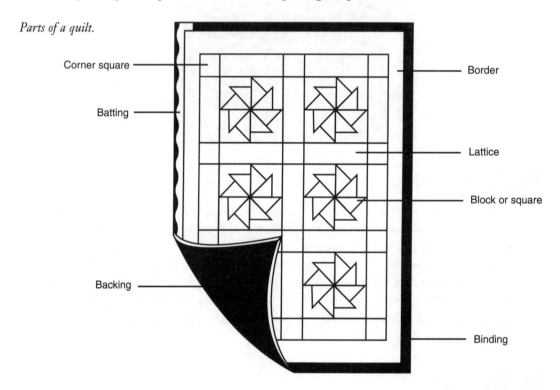

Block

A block is a square of pieced or appliquéd patchwork, also called a square, that is put together with other blocks to make a quilt.

Lattice

A lattice is a strip of fabric that frames each block in a quilt. The strip can be a solid strip, or it can have small squares at the corner of each block. The lattice is also sometimes called sashing. I discuss this part of a quilt in Chapter 14.

Border

A length of fabric that frames the outside edge of the quilt top is the border. Borders can be as simple as solid strips of fabric or as complex as intricate geometric patterns or appliqués. You'll learn about borders in Chapter 14.

Batting

The batting is the inner lining between the top, or face, of a quilt and the bottom layer, or backing, that gives the quilt its fluffiness and warmth. Back in the "good old days," stuffing or filling was anything to fill the middle layer in a quilt. It could be cotton picked in the fields and stuffed into the quilt, or the cotton could have been carded or combed to smooth it out. Sometimes old, worn-out quilts were used as the middle layer, or old, discarded men's suits were cut up and used. Cotton batting purchased in a store was used for many years in the early twentieth century. Polyester batting bought either in packages or from a giant roll dates from the 1970s.

Backing

The bottom part of a quilt that sandwiches the batting with the quilt top is called the backing. It is often considered the "wrong" side of the quilt.

Binding

The binding is the folded-over backing or a long strip of bias fabric that finishes off the edge of a quilt.

Now let's start planning which designs to create for your quilt.

Quilt Designs

Now that you know the parts that make up a quilt top, find the blocks that appeal to you. Pattern blocks are divided by method of piecing and arranged in the order of difficulty. Just remember to match your capabilities to the difficulty of the block.

The first set of blocks are where a beginner should start. Easy pieced blocks have few fabric pieces, and the shapes are easy to assemble. Full-size patterns and instructions are found in Chapter 9. The easy pieced blocks are Double Nine Patch, Churn Dash, Ohio Star, Eight Point Star, Dutchman's Puzzle, Weathervane, and the Rolling Star.

Beginners should start with one of the easy pieced blocks.

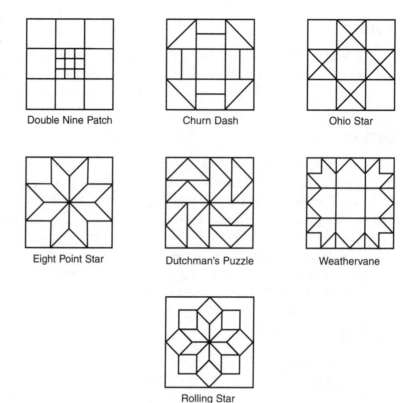

Double Nine Patch

Churn Dash

Ohio Star

Eight Point Star

Dutchman's Puzzle

Weathervane

Rolling Star

Examine the challenging pieced blocks in the next figure. You can see that there are many pieces and the designs are more elaborate. Before a beginner tackles one of these blocks, you should read Chapter 10 to learn special cutting and piecing know-how. Challenging blocks are Drunkard's Path, Pinwheel, Virginia Star, Mexican Star, 54-40 or Fight, Flying Geese, Clay's Choice, and Bear's Paw.

Our quilting ancestors developed blocks that combine both piecing and appliqué techniques in the same design. In some blocks, pieces of fabric are sewn together and the patch is appliquéd onto a background of fabric, as in the Dresden Plate and Grandmother's Fan. There are also blocks that are made in just the opposite way, by piecing the base of the block and then appliquéing specially shaped fabric pieces, such as with the Honey Bee's wings and the Peony's stem and leaves. Check out Chapter 11.

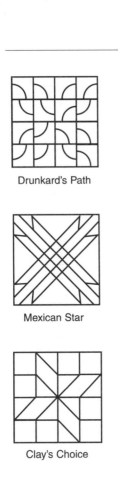

Drunkard's Path

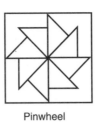

Pinwheel

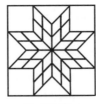

Virginia Star

These blocks will challenge your cutting and piecing ability.

Mexican Star

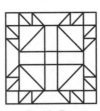

54-40 or Fight

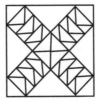

Flying Geese

Clay's Choice

Bear's Paw

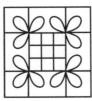

Dresden Plate

Honey Bee

Blocks that are pieced and appliquéd.

Grandmother's Fan

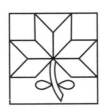

Peony

Traditionally appliquéd blocks have separate pieces of fabric that, when positioned in a specific pattern, form a picture or design. The blocks found in this book are Hearts All Around and Tulips. Chapter 12 contains patterns and instructions.

The last category of blocks in this book is for those people who love and know how to use their sewing machine. The Rail Fence and Log Cabin blocks can be joined by using the hand-piecing method, but they also can be sewn quickly and accurately by using the sewing machine.

Appliqué and machine-pieced blocks.

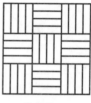

Hearts All Around   Tulips   Rail Fence

Log Cabin

These are just drawings of the blocks you can make from the instructions found in this book. It's up to you to add the color and visual texture with your fabric, which brings us to the next stop: shopping!

The Least You Need to Know

- Choose a project that will be easy to finish. Be honest about your abilities.

- Decide who will use the quilt, what your preferences are, whether you want the quilt to be the focal point of the room, and how you will use it.

- The parts that make up the quilt top are blocks, lattice, and border.

- Survey the quilt designs in this book and choose patterns that you like and that match up with your know-how.

- A Sampler quilt is the best learning experience for a beginner.

2

Tools of the Trade

In This Chapter

- ◆ Finding the basic supplies you really, really need
- ◆ Choosing the materials that best help you
- ◆ Supercool gadgets to spark creativity

This chapter is about the supplies that every quilter needs to make a quilt. Some items listed are necessities. But because everyone has different preferences and abilities, I give you many options and suggestions. Some supplies you will need right now, some you will need at a later time, and others you may want but are never a necessity.

The Necessities: Supplies You Need Right Now

You will be able to find many things listed here right around your house. Look at the list, and see what you can find before you go out to the store. Some things may seem very strange, but I will address each item and explain it.

- Pencils (number 2 lead and a variety of colored pencils)
- Ruler (12 or 18 inches)
- Straight pins
- Paper scissors
- Fabric scissors
- Quilting needles (betweens and embroidery needles)
- Quilting and regular thread
- Poster board or oak tag
- Rubber cement
- Medium sandpaper
- Seam ripper
- Thimbles

Quilt Talk

A **template** is a pattern of the exact size of each design element, usually made with cardboard or plastic. A block may have several shapes of templates incorporated into the square; for example, the Ohio Star block is composed of two templates—a square and a small triangle.

Pencils

Number 2 lead pencil: Quilters use this type of pencil to draft *templates* and trace these patterns onto the wrong side of the fabric. Do not use a softer pencil because you will be forever sharpening it. This pencil can also be used to lightly mark your quilt designs onto the right side of the quilt top.

Colored pencils: Many fabrics are dark in color (navy, red, and especially black) or have a design so busy that a pencil mark does not show. If this is the case, turn your fabric to the wrong side and try whichever colored pencil shows the best. Colored pencils are also helpful in planning the colors of your quilt blocks.

Rulers

I usually use a variety of rulers. The best all-around ruler is one that is see-through plastic, 12 or 18 inches, and has parallel lines running the length, marking every quarter inch. This will be very useful in marking long seam allowances on your fabric and testing to see if your borders or lattices are even. I sometimes also like to use a small plastic 6-inch ruler because it is easier to maneuver around the templates. Other rulers are optional and are discussed later.

Straight Pins

I use regular old straight pins (1-inch-long pins used by dressmakers) when I am piecing my patches. For pin-basting your quilt top, we will discuss other options (see Chapter 15).

Paper Scissors

Paper scissors are necessary when we make the templates. Templates are made from cardboard and sandpaper, or a plastic sheet. If you use good fabric scissors on the template material, they will not be good for long.

Quilting Bee _____

My favorite scissors are Ginghers, and they can be purchased at most quilt stores or through dressmaker catalogues.

Fabric Scissors

There are many different types of scissors or dressmaker shears that you can purchase. Fabric scissors are sharper than paper scissors and are usually made of lighterweight steel. Prices vary greatly. As a beginner, do not buy really expensive scissors. Eventually, if you become addicted to quilting, you will need scissors that cut through the fabric easily—when working on large projects I've had blisters pop up on my fingers as my scissors got dull. Some scissors can even cut through several layers of fabric at a time.

A pair of small thread-cutting scissors is also useful. The best practice is to hang them on a ribbon around your neck. It makes them easier to find while you are working.

Bent dressmaker shears with a protective nylon sheath and thread nippers are your best bet for scissors.

Needles

Quilters use "between" needles to piece their projects. A between needle is short and has a small round eye. The larger the number, the smaller the needle size. Size 10 is smaller than size 6. I had one student who said that compared to quilting needles, her needle was like a crowbar!

When you get experienced, there are also quilting needles that are even shorter than betweens.

Quilting Bee _____

Beginners should buy a package of between needles containing a variety of sizes. You can decide which is the best needle for you, and as you get used to quilting, you may go for the smaller size.

These are specifically used for quilting. Quilters have learned that the smaller the needle, the smaller and more durable the quilting stitches. Occasionally you will need to use embroidery needles when basting your quilt together, decorating your appliqué block with embroidery stitches, or tying your quilt. (Sometimes knots can be used instead of quilting stitches to hold together the three layers.)

Thread

For piecing or quilting, use a cotton-covered polyester quilting thread. This thread is superior to the 100 percent polyester thread that is usually on sale. Quilt thread is heavier and does not tangle or knot. Try to purchase a color that blends well with your fabrics. For example, if your background fabric is muslin, purchase a thread that is ecru; if your background is white, use a white thread; or if the background is navy, buy a navy quilting thread. If you can't match the color with a quilting thread, you can use a regular cotton-covered polyester thread. To keep this thread from tangling, run each length of thread through beeswax.

> **Quilting Bee**
>
> Buy beeswax that is in a holder, because the holder will make it easier for you to run the thread through the beeswax and will keep it neat and clean.

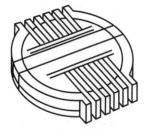

This container of beeswax makes it easy to run your thread through it.

Poster Board or Oak Tag

You can purchase poster board or oak tag paper at stationery, craft, or drug stores. This weight of cardboard is the best for making templates. I've even used gift boxes in a pinch. Just don't use thick cardboard; it is difficult to cut accurately.

Rubber Cement

Rubber cement is used to make templates and for gluing together the poster board and sandpaper. Do not use white school glue or craft glue because it makes your templates ripple and they will not dry flat.

Sandpaper

Not all templates need sandpaper, but it helps beginners trace around the pattern accurately. Buy a medium-weight sandpaper that is approximately 8 inches by 10 inches in size. This will be used for the backing of your templates.

Seam Ripper

I hate to even mention ripping seams, but everyone makes mistakes, and seam rippers remove your boo-boos quickly and safely. A seam ripper is a small penlike tool that allows you to put a sharp point under the "bad" stitches, carefully breaking the thread. Look for a medium-size seam ripper. When a seam ripper is too small, it gets lost in the shuffle. If it is too large, it is harder to manipulate under the line of stitches.

Thimbles

Most quilters or seamstresses insist on using a thimble. A lot of people do not like the needle pricking their finger every time they take a stitch. Unfortunately, I have never felt comfortable wearing one. Many quilters wear a thimble on the third finger of the hand that holds the needle. Some wear thimbles on both hands. There are many types of thimbles. The most common is the metal thimble. Try one out and see how it feels. If it is uncomfortable, try one of the newer types of finger guards available. One very popular type is a leather thimble.

Don't Get Stuck!

One of my quilting students has a problem because her dog loves to chew her leather thimble, so she has to buy several! Keep them out of reach and with your sewing equipment.

These are both thimbles. The right is the traditional, metal thimble; the left is a leather finger guard.

Things You Will Need Later

You will need the items on this next list after you have completed your quilt top. You have pieced or appliquéd, then set the blocks together and framed them out with borders. Certain supplies will be necessary for joining together the three layers of the quilt. Never purchase your batting until the face of the quilt is complete—you may get carried away and your quilt plan may grow.

♦ Batting (The thimbles types and specific amounts of batting needed for your projects are discussed in Chapter 15.)

♦ Marking equipment (Don't buy these yet!)

♦ Quilt stencils

♦ Quilt hoop (Many types are available, and everyone has different dexterity and preferences. Hoops are discussed in Chapter 16.)

Sometimes you have to see the finished quilt top to decide on the type of quilting you want and the pattern of the quilting stencil. As you learn to handle fabrics, you will discover what equipment works for you. Different types of hoops are available. The hoop is necessary to hold the quilt in place and smooth while you quilt. I suggest purchasing your hoop after you are more experienced, and by the time you're ready to quilt, you will be experienced! (Marking and quilting equipment are discussed in detail in Chapter 16.)

Optional Supplies That Are Neat

Through my years of experience, I've found the items on this "neat" list to be helpful. They are not really necessary for a beginner to own; if you become a serious quilter, however, these tools and supplies may assist you with certain projects.

♦ Graph paper (four squares to the inch)

♦ Quilter's quarter

♦ Rotary cutter

♦ Cutting mat with grids

♦ Ruler with a lip

♦ T-square ruler

♦ Quilting pins

Now for an in-depth discussion of each gadget and how you use it.

Graph Paper

Graph paper is helpful when making patterns or templates that have right angles: squares, rectangles, and triangles. It will help you see if your template is true to shape. Be sure to purchase graph paper that has four grids to the inch. It is easier to compute enlarging or transferring patterns. It's much easier to calculate ¼ increments than ⅕-inch grids. Try to fold anything into five sections!

Quilter's Quarter

A quilter's quarter is a ¼-inch by ¼-inch by 8-inch piece of plastic used to mark the ¼-inch seam allowance on your fabric. This tool makes marking very quick and accurate, so beginners like to use it.

Quilting Bee

Be sure to purchase a quilter's quarter that is made of colored plastic. I have searched many an hour trying to find a clear quilter's quarter in my sewing supplies.

Rotary Cutter

A rotary cutter is a great tool for cutting straight lines on your fabric. It looks very similar to a pizza cutter. If you are very careful, it can cut through several layers of fabric at a time. The rotary cutter is used mainly when you are making a quilt that is strip-pieced by machine and can be used when you are cutting lattices and borders. One drawback: You can't cut on curves, and you always need a ruler to guide the rotary blade.

Don't Get Stuck!

Be careful—rotary blades are very sharp. Be sure to always close your cutter as soon as you've finished each and every cut.

Rotary cutter.

Cutting Mat with Grids

Rotary cutters should always be used with a cutting mat that is "self-healing." The plastic mat is strong enough not to be damaged by the sharp blade. These mats are marked with ¼-inch hash marks on the sides and also 1-inch grids over the whole surface. There should also be two bias diagonals over the grid. Buy a mat that is at least 18 by 24 inches. I have just discovered cutting mats that have a handle opening cut right into the plastic. It makes it easier to carry!

Ruler with a Lip

Many see-through plastic rulers with grids are heavy enough to withstand rotary cutters. Rulers come in all sizes and shapes, and the one you purchase will depend on the quilt you are making.

I personally like a plastic ruler with a lip for use with the rotary cutter. It has a clear plastic piece under the ruler that allows you to wedge it against the cutting mat so your cut is accurate.

T-Square Ruler

A metal or heavy-duty plastic T-square is used for squaring off the patches.

Quilting Pins

These pins are 1¾ inches long and have brightly colored heads. They are really great for pin-basting your quilt top, batting, and backing together, and many quilters feel they are a necessity when assembling a quilt.

The Least You Need to Know

- Check over the supply list and look around your house before going shopping.
- Get all your necessary materials before starting your project.
- Experience piecing blocks before buying specialty gadgets.

Chapter 3

Materially Speaking, How Much Do You Need?

In This Chapter

- ◆ Popular quilt sizes
- ◆ How to calculate the amount of fabric needed for a pattern piece
- ◆ Estimating fabric amounts for a particular part of a quilt
- ◆ Table for computing the amount of fabric to buy for an entire quilt

Two theories apply to making quilt: You can either (1) plan, plan, plan, and get all your fabrics before you actually start (which is the preferred method); or (2) you can let your quilt evolve as you go along. One of my beginning students wanted to make four placemats. After constructing two patches, she was hooked and bought enough fabric for a lap quilt. A few weeks later, she decided to make a full-size quilt, so back to the store she went. At the end of the session, she had made a terrific full-size quilt top. This was a success story, but be warned: If you don't purchase enough fabric at the start, when you go back to get more, it's often gone! Let's figure out how much fabric you need.

Your Quilt's Dimensions

It's important to know the size of a finished quilt. I had a student who made a twin-size quilt, but it wasn't quite large enough. She had an antique bed that stood high off the floor and, therefore, the quilt was too short. Please don't let that happen to you. Choose a quilt size, and check your dimensions carefully.

Lap Quilt

A lap quilt can have many purposes. It's a great size for a baby's crib quilt, for hanging on the wall, or, my favorite, for putting over your lap when you're cold.

- Finished size: 40 inches by 56 inches
- 6 blocks: 12-inch squares
- Lattice: 3 inches wide
- Corner squares: 3 inches
- Border: 4 inches wide

Twin Size

- Mattress size: 39 inches by 75 inches
- Finished size: 68 inches by 94 inches
- 15 blocks: 12-inch squares

Full Size

- Mattress size: 52 inches by 75 inches
- Finished size: 80 inches by 103 inches
- 15 blocks: 12-inch squares
- Lattice: 4 inches wide
- Corner squares: 4 inches
- Border: 14 inches, broken down into 6 inches and 8 inches

Queen Size

◆ Mattress size: 60 inches by 80 inches

◆ Finished size: 83 inches by 103 inches

◆ 24 blocks: 12-inch squares

◆ Lattice: 3 inches wide

◆ Corner squares: 3 inches

◆ Border: 10 inches wide

King Size

◆ Mattress size: 72 inches by 84 inches

◆ Finished size: 100 inches by 116 inches

◆ 30 blocks: 12-inch square

◆ Lattice: 4 inches wide

◆ Corner squares: 4 inches

◆ Border: 8 inches wide

How Many Pieces Can I Get from a Yard?

There will come a time when you will have to calculate how much fabric you need to purchase for a quilt project. One quilt block may have many pattern pieces that fit together to make the 12-inch square. The following strategy will help you calculate the amount you need for each pattern piece in a quilt block. If you are creating a quilt that repeats one type of block, you will have many similar pattern pieces (for example, when making a Double Nine Patch lap quilt, pictured next). It has four 4-inch squares of the dominant color and four 4-inch squares of the accent color. Let's figure out how much fabric you will need of each fabric.

1. Count the number of pattern shapes you need for one block. Measure and add on the ¼-inch seam allowances to get the true size. (For each Double Nine Patch, you need four 4½-inch squares of the dominant color and four 4½-inch squares of the accent color.)

A Double Nine Patch lap quilt.

2. Determine how many of these pattern pieces you need for the entire quilt. (There are 4 squares of dominant colors in each block of the Double Nine Patch, and there are 6 blocks in the quilt, so you'll need 24 4½-inch squares.)

3. Measure the width of your fabric. Usually it's 44 inches.

4. Find out how many pattern pieces (with seam allowances added on) will fit across the fabric width. Divide the fabric width by the width of the pattern piece. (That is, 44 inches divided by 4½ inches of the Double Nine Patch square is 9.7—but wait—you can only fit 9 whole square pattern pieces in the width.)

5. To determine the length of fabric needed and how many rows are needed to fit all the squares in, first divide the total number of pattern pieces by the number of squares that fit across the width of the fabric. (Remember, we need 24 squares for the lap quilt, and 24 divided by 9 is 2.6 rows. You'll have to allow for 3 whole rows of fabric.)

6. Then multiply that number of rows by the length of the pattern piece, including the seam allowance. (Multiplying the 4½ inches of the Double Nine Patch square by 3 rows yields 13½ inches.)

7. To figure out how many yards are needed, divide the total inches by 36 inches (for the yard). Add on a 4- or 5-inch "fudge factor" to allow for mistakes. (For the Double Nine Patch, 13½ inches are needed for the rows plus a 4-inch fudge factor to equal 17½ inches. So approximately 18 inches divided by 36 inches equals half a yard. You will need half a yard of the dominant color and half a yard for the accent color.)

See how many Double Nine Patch squares will fit on the fabric.

Do Your Math: Calculate the Right Amount

Now that you know the fabric yardage you need to buy for a specific pattern piece or template of your quilt, let me show you how these amounts can be put together. You can dovetail your patterns with borders and lattices to save fabric. I try to use every scrap of my material. It is difficult to estimate the exact amount of fabric for a sampler quilt because each patch is different. The following table gives you an educated guesstimate for fabric yardage. Backing and batting are not included, but those are discussed in Chapter 15.

Fabric Guesstimates to Purchase for an Entire Project

Quilt Size	Color	What Is Included	Fabric Yardage*
Lap	Dominant	Blocks, lattice	2
	Contrast	Blocks, borders	2
	Blenders	Blocks (two fabrics)	½ each
		Blocks and corner squares (one fabric)	¾
	Background	Blocks	1

continues

Fabric Guesstimates to Purchase for an Entire Project (continued)

Quilt Size	Color	What Is Included	Fabric Yardage*
Twin	Dominant	Blocks, lattice, border B	4
	Contrast	Blocks, border A	3½
	Blenders	Blocks (two fabrics)	¾ each
		Blocks and corner squares (one fabric)	1
	Background	Blocks	1¾
Full	Dominant	Blocks, lattice, border B	4½
	Contrast	Blocks, border A	3¾
	Blenders	Blocks (two to four fabrics)	¾ each
		Blocks and corner squares (one fabric)	1
	Background	Blocks	1¾
Queen	Dominant	Blocks, lattice, border B	5
	Contrast	Blocks, border A	4
	Blenders	Blocks (two fabrics)	1
		Blocks and corner squares (one fabric)	1⅝
	Background	Blocks	2
King	Dominant	Blocks, lattice, border B	5½
	Contrast	Blocks, border A	4½
	Blenders	Blocks (two fabrics)	1¼ each
		Blocks and corner squares (one fabric)	1¾
	Background	Blocks	2½

Remember, these are estimates—not everybody cuts wisely.

Sometimes it's necessary to know the amount of fabric to purchase for a specific part of your quilt. I can't tell you how many times I've had to go back to the store and buy a different fabric for a lattice or border because the one that I purchased wasn't quite right. Occasionally some quilters wait to see how the patches look before choosing the border fabric. In case that happens to you, I've calculated how much fabric you'll need for each section of your quilt.

To use this table, locate the section of the quilt that you need to purchase fabric for—perhaps it's the lattice. Then look for the quilt size you are making, let's say full size, and determine the yardage you should buy.

Yardage for a Specific Part of a Quilt

Part	Quilt Size	Number Needed and Size	Yardage
Lattice	Lap	17 (3" × 12")	¾
	Twin	38 (3" × 12")	1½
	Full	38 (4" × 12")	2
	Queen	58 (3" × 12")	2¼
	King	71 (4" × 12")	2¾
Corner squares	Lap	12 (3" × 3")	¼
	Twin	24 (3" × 3")	½
	Full	24 (4" × 4")	⅝
	Queen	35 (3" × 3")	⅝
	King	42 (4" × 4")	¾
Borders	Lap	4"	1
	Twin	10" or	2½
		A: 4"	1½
		B: 6"	1¾
	Full	14" or	3
		A: 6"	1¾
		B: 8"	2½
	Queen	10" or	3½
		A: 4"	1¾
		B: 6"	2
	King	8" or	3½
		A: 3"	2
		B: 5"	2½
Background fabric	Lap	6 blocks	1
	Twin	15 blocks	1¾
	Full	15 blocks	1¾
	Queen	24 blocks	2
	King	30 blocks	2½

continues

Yardage for a Specific Part of a Quilt (continued)

Part	Quilt Size	Number Needed and Size	Yardage
Blenders	Lap	2 or 3 fabrics	$\frac{1}{2}$–$\frac{3}{4}$ of each
	Twin	3 fabrics	$\frac{3}{4}$–1 of each
	Full	3 to 5 fabrics	$\frac{3}{4}$–1 of each
	Queen	3 to 5 fabrics	1 of each
	King	3 to 5 fabrics	$1\frac{1}{2}$ of each

In your quilt, you may have several blender fabrics. One blender fabric should include all the colors of your color scheme. Others will be of different values of the dominant and accent colors. You can have as many blenders as you want; I've suggested the minimum.

The Least You Need to Know

- ◆ Know the dimensions of the finished size of the quilt.

- ◆ Measure the width of the fabric to calculate the number of templates that will fit.

- ◆ Check the charts and plan the amount of fabric needed, but remember, you may need more.

- ◆ Be realistic—start small.

4

Time to Purchase Your Fabric

In This Chapter

◆ Understanding the type of fabric appropriate for making quilts

◆ Knowing which fabrics to avoid

◆ Choosing fabrics with variety in scale and pattern

◆ Finding fabric to blend in with your color scheme

Purchasing the appropriate fabric for your project can be intimidating, but this chapter sets out guidelines to follow to make it easier. Today we are fortunate to have a variety of sources to obtain fabric. We take fabric for granted, whereas our ancestors used their fabric with reverence, using every scrap. Let's start our modern-day quest for the perfect fabric, and you may become a "fabriholic," too.

What Type of Fabric?

Without a doubt, the best type of fabric for beginners to use is 100 percent cotton. Cotton has been proven through the test of time to be easy to work with and also durable. The material shouldn't ravel or stretch, because these characteristics make it difficult to work with. Your fabric should be colorfast and washable. To check out your fabric, look at the end of the *bolt* in the store.

Quilt Talk

A **bolt** is the fabric that is rolled around a cardboard base. The end of the bolt has a great deal of information: fiber content, colorfastness, finish (permanent press), and, of course, the price.

Synthetic fabrics, such as polyester, are more difficult to control. The fibers themselves are slippery and stretchy, and the cloth frays easily—three very problematic factors. Many quilters will use polyester fabrics when the fibers are blended with cotton. Be sure there is an equal or greater percentage of cotton to polyester. The fabric should be called cotton/polyester, not polyester/cotton. The end of the bolt will state the exact percentage of cotton to polyester, so be sure to look. You can also buy fabric from precut yardage found folded on tables in manystores, but be sure to ask a salesperson for the fabric's fiber content.

Beginners should avoid certain fabrics. Knits, corduroys, ginghams, stripes, and fabrics with *nap* or one-way designs are all difficult-to-handle materials. Fabrics with tulips all standing in a row are just more complicated to cut and sew together into blocks. If you are not careful, some tulips will be on their sides or upside down, or if you are lucky, they will be standing up straight.

Quilt Talk

Nap has nothing to do with sleeping. It's the short, fuzzy ends of fibers on the surface of cloth. The nap usually falls in one direction, as it does on velvet. When you look at velvet one way, it's one color; turn it around, however, and the color darkens depending on the way the fibers are brushed. I extend this definition to include patterns with one-way designs, such as tulips all in a row.

Even though I tell you to avoid these fabrics, quilters do make quilts using these fabrics with great success. I just think that beginners should stick with basic cotton.

Where to Get Your Fabric

Where do you get your fabric? There are plenty of ways to acquire your material. Of course the best place for a beginner to go is to a fabric store that specializes in quilting fabric. The shopkeepers are only too anxious to help beginners plan their quilts. I have a favorite fabric store where the staff helps you choose the fabric, cuts swatches from each piece and pins it on a sheet of paper, and lists where you will use it. Now that is service. Quilt shows offer great selections of fabrics and even have special lengths of fabrics called *fat quarters*, used just for small accents in your quilt.

Now for some unconventional ways to get fabric: There are catalogues that sell supplies and fabrics, so you can buy from your own home. I love to feel the fabric, so I usually don't use catalogues to buy fabrics. They do have an assortment of selections, and the quality is top-notch. When you need small amounts of a fabric, it's fun to have a swap with your friends. Garage sales and rummage sales are also good sources for fabric, although unfortunately you won't know the fiber content in most cases.

Lastly, before you go fabric shopping, look around your house to see what you already have. Remember, you can use fabric from old projects or garments as long as the fabric is cotton and the right weight.

Quilt Talk

A **fat quarter** is one quarter of a yard of fabric. However, instead of the salesperson cutting ¼ yard the normal way across the width of the fabric (9 inches by 44 inches), she cuts the yard in half lengthwise and then across the width (18 inches by 22 inches). These pieces are great because you can fit larger pattern templates on them.

Put Your Fabric on a Scale, Then Do a Background Check

Very few quilts are created from only solid fabrics. There needs to be patterning to make your quilt visually interesting. Let's examine how you can add variety to your fabrics. One of the most important dimensions, besides the color value of a fabric, is the scale of the design. Prints that are all the same size are dull and boring. Little calico prints are nice in small doses, but choosing five calicos of all the same design is monotonous. You should choose small-, medium-, and large-size prints for your quilt. Pin dots and little flowers are examples of small-scale prints—I've even bought fabrics with little spools of thread. Small-scale material appears almost solid. Large-size prints have motifs of 3 or 4 inches in size, and the large design patterns can be an overall floral or paisley or any other large figure.

Look at the motif of the fabric, and keep in mind who will use the quilt. One of my students spent all her time making patches for a baby quilt. When her quilt top was completed, she found a really cute, colorful, frog fabric for the backing. Of course her nephew loves the back of the quilt, not the front that she toiled over. You can see that fabric patterns are a crucial consideration when buying fabric for your quilt.

Look at the variety of scale and how it is more interesting than fabric with a one-size scale.

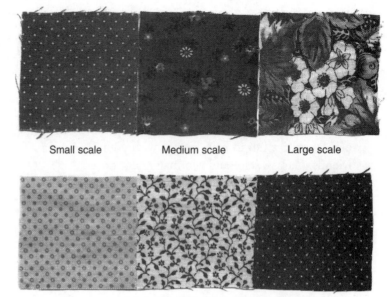

Small scale   Medium scale   Large scale

All one scale

There is one more important factor in purchasing your fabric: the background of a fabric. The background or ground color of the material is the hue on which the design is placed. For example, a fabric may have red and pink hearts on a white background, or you may have red and white hearts on a pink color—same colors, different fabric appearance. Be sure that the background coordinates with all your fabrics. For example, if all of your fabric motifs but one are on an ecru background, a white one will stick out like a sore thumb. The value of the background hue will help blend with your other fabrics.

Quilt Talk

The term **calico** today is used to describe quilt fabrics that are 100 percent cotton or cotton/polyester blends. At one time, calico pertained to a process of printing designs on a cotton fabric by using a roller. The patterns were usually small florals.

Blending Your Fabric Together: Dominant and Contrasting

Now it's time to select your fabric. Most fabric stores have their cottons, many times advertised as *calico*, in one section with all similar hues arranged together, almost like a rainbow.

I start by going to the row that has the dominant color I'm looking for. Let's say I've chosen a color scheme of red and blue, with blue being the dominant color. I first try to find a fabric that blends all the colors of my color scheme—in other words, red and blue. It should be in a large-scale overall pattern. This is the blender fabric.

Scraps and Pieces

Be sure the blender fabric is really the color you want. Many times beginners are so close to the fabric that they see one color, but from afar it may appear a different hue. If the fabric design is red and blue flowers with green leaves, be sure the fabric gives a red and blue look, not green. Do what I call the "squint method." Stand back from the fabric bolt, look away, then turn back and squint at it. The first impression of color is how it will appear in your quilt.

After this blender fabric has been chosen, I then pull out bolts of the dominant- and contrasting-colored fabrics that coordinate with the blender fabric. Next, decide on a lighter or darker value of the dominant and contrasting colors. That brings your fabric total to five, which is perfect for beginners. Lean your bolts of fabric against a wall, one next to another. Step back and do the squint method to evaluate your fabrics. Is there variety in the values of light and darkness of the fabrics? Do you have a good mixture of patterns and scale of designs? Most important, do you like it? This quilt will reflect your personality—can you live with it? If the answers are yes, let's pick out the background fabric.

The background fabric is the material that surrounds the main design of a patch. For example, in the Eight Point Star, the star motif is made up of the dominant, contrasting, or blending color and appears to be laying on top of the background. This background fabric traditionally was a solid color so it would not detract from the pattern. You have to decide on the intensity of the background: Do you want a white, ecru *muslin*, or even a hue of the dominant color?

Remember that a plain white fabric makes a strong contrast against your color scheme. Sometimes a neutral-color muslin makes your quilt colors appear softer. Recently quilters have started using a solid print for the background. This material should have a motif so

Quilt Talk

Muslin is a plain-weave cotton fabric, generally used as the background fabric for your patches or appliqué. Muslin comes in a variety of different shades of beige (unbleached is ecru or beige), and if the manufacturer bleaches the muslin, it will appear whiter. Today there is even a permanent-press muslin that will not wrinkle. Because muslin comes in a wide range of weights, be sure to buy a good quality.

small that from a distance it appears solid, but as you get closer the fabric adds texture to your patch. The white, tan, or gray fabric may have swirls, flowers, or a paisley motif in the same subtle shades of neutral colors. These are known as white-on-white fabrics.

Notice how each star motif looks distinctive with different background fabrics.

  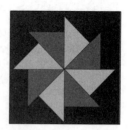

Don't forget that you can also use a color or black for the background. Amish quilts with black backgrounds are extremely dramatic.

Now that I've given you some guidelines to help in your quest for the perfect fabrics, choosing your fabrics should be exciting and fun. Buy the best fabric that you can afford. We want this to be a family heirloom and last a lifetime. Now go out and buy.

The Least You Need to Know

◆ Do not choose fabrics with all the same scale of patterns.

◆ Avoid problem fabrics such as corduroy, ginghams, napped fabrics, one-way designs, and striped fabrics.

◆ Line up all your fabric bolts, step back, and squint to be sure the colors blend.

◆ The best source for beginners to purchase fabric is a specialty quilt shop where you will get the most help.

◆ Buy the best fabric that you can afford.

Knowing and Taking Care of Your Fabric

In This Chapter

- ◆ Preparing your fabric before you start your quilt

- ◆ Organizing and storing your fabrics

- ◆ Understanding the terminology of woven fabrics

I like to prepare and organize my fabrics first. Fabric has to be preshrunk and tested for colorfastness before you can start working with it. Then you need to have an orderly and systematic approach to storing your collection. As you create more and more quilts, you will have additional fabric to store.

Don't Forget to Wash!

As soon as you get home from the store, wash your fabrics! Two qualities of fabrics may give you difficulties: (1) shrinking and (2) fading or running when washed. Both have to be addressed before making your quilt. A friend forgot to wash a red fabric, and after making 15 patches and stitching them together, she started to quilt. Then she wanted to take off a little stain. Unfortunately, as she applied water, the stain got worse—the red fabric started bleeding into the white background fabric. She had to wash the entire quilt and the white background turned a pale shade of pink.

Check to see if your fabric is colorfast. Even if the bolt at the store says that it's colorfast, don't trust it. I divide my fabrics into darks and lights and soak them in a sink of warm water to see if they run.

Quilting Bee

Small, quarter-yard cuts of fabric will get tangled in the dryer, so let them line dry.

Scraps and Pieces

Sometimes when you take your fabric out of the dryer, the fabric is very stiff and wrinkled. If you use this same fabric in your quilt, after washing your quilt, it will have this same appearance. You may not want to use this fabric. Remember, quilts cannot be ironed until they are completed—the inner puffy batting will compress and flatten.

Keep changing the water until it remains clear. After four times of doing this, if the dye still comes out, then desperate measures need to be taken. I soak the fabric in a sink filled with very hot water that has 2 cups of white vinegar added to it. Keep the fabric submerged for about 30 minutes. Then try the colorfast test again, soaking your problem fabric with a scrap of white fabric. If after several times of doing this the color is not set, I would advise not using the fabric.

Besides being sure that the colors are set, let's preshrink the fabric. All fabric has some residual shrinkage. To prevent shrinkage, treat your fabrics as you would a finished quilt. I put the fabrics in warm water and even throw them into the dryer.

If one material shrinks and the others don't, then the quilt top will pucker wherever that fabric is used. Actually, some people like that puckered look, because they feel that it gives their quilt an antique look.

Keep Your Fabrics Dry!

I always have wistful feelings when I read quilt books with chapters on planning your quilting studio. If you are like me, you can only wish for a separate room for your projects. But no matter how small your working space, organizing your fabrics is a necessity.

To keep your fabrics "healthy," be sure to store them away from light and dampness. There is nothing worse than thinking you have leftover scraps of the perfect fabric only to find that it faded or has that moldy smell. Keep fabrics more than half a yard folded with similar colors. Stack these folds of fabric in full view on shelves, so you can easily see your stash. If you don't have a spare closet or bookcase, store similar colors of fabric in those clear plastic boxes that fit under a bed. Avoid storing fabric in the basement or any place with high humidity. Mildew and a musty odor are almost impossible to remove.

The Straight- and Narrow-of-Grain Line

Have you noticed the different ways that fabric feels, drapes, and reacts? Certain characteristics of fabrics will determine how you use them. The most important factor is the fabric *grain*. This determines how your fabric reacts and needs to be handled.

There are several types of grain. When fabric is pulled in different directions, it reacts differently. Each grain or direction has a specific name and characteristic.

Quilt Talk

Grain is the direction that the threads are woven into fabric. Fabric is made up of threads that run perpendicular to each other on a loom. There is a **lengthwise grain**, which runs the length of the fabric, and a **crosswise grain**, which is woven at a right angle to the lengthwise thread.

The threads that run the whole length of the fabric are called the *lengthwise grain* and need to be very strong to endure the weaving proc-ess. Because of their strength, they have very little stretch. The direction that runs parallel to these threads is called the *crosswise grain.* The crosswise threads are not quite as strong and have some "give."

Where the crosswise threads turn around the outer side of the fabric is known as the *selvage* or selvedge.

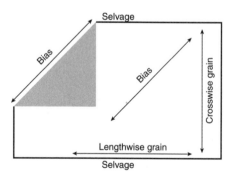

Look at the directions of the different lines of grain.

Because the selvage is thicker and has a denser thread count than the rest of the fabric, it reacts differently. The selvage shrinks and puckers and is very difficult to sew through. Many quilters cut off the selvage as soon as they wash the fabric, but

Quilt Talk

The **selvage** is the outer finished edge of your fabric. It is the edge that doesn't ravel and is more closely woven than the rest of the fabric.

I like to keep it on so I can tell the lengthwise grain. The lengthwise grain is also known as the straight of the grain, because it runs parallel to the selvage.

The tried-and-true technique has templates (quilt patterns) put in a particular direction so that the fabric is easy to handle. The straight of grain is the strongest direction, and each template will have a straight-of-grain arrow that should be placed parallel to the selvage.

Illustrated are several templates with the straight-of-grain arrows indicated.

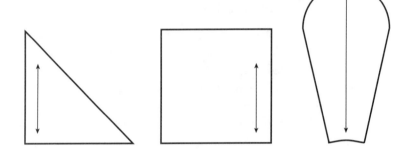

The last type of grain is known as bias. Bias is the diagonal direction of fabric. True bias is at a 45-degree angle to the grainlines.

The bias direction has quite a bit of stretch and is more difficult to handle. Some blocks have a bias piece on the outside edge, and if you are not careful when ironing, it will stretch out of shape. Quilters use bias for preparing the outer binding, because the binding needs to conform to the outer curves, and bias strips make it easy.

The Least You Need to Know

◆ All fabrics have residual shrinkage.

◆ Wash your fabrics to check for shrinkage and colorfastness.

◆ Lengthwise grain is stronger than crosswise grain, and templates should be put on the straight of grain.

◆ The bias direction is stretchy and more difficult to handle but is useful in making bias tape.

Chapter 6

Words to Live By: Templates Are the Patterns of Success

In This Chapter

- ◆ Learning about the different materials for making templates
- ◆ Transferring templates from books
- ◆ Preparing templates for hand- and machine-quilting

In a quilt like the Trip Around the World, how do you cut all those squares neatly? Quilters use templates. A template is anything you draw around to mark pattern pieces for your quilt. Templates can be made of many different materials. Appliqué quilts can use heart-shaped cookie cutters for templates. I've even used a quarter to mark a center of a flower.

Now that you've chosen a quilt block to piece, you're ready to start the quilting process. You can draft the templates yourself, but it is very tedious and time-consuming. When I first taught beginners, I had them draft a Double Nine Patch made of 2 squares: a 4-inch square and a $1\frac{1}{3}$-inch square. Even using graph paper, it took almost the entire two-hour class. That's why all the patterns in this book are full size and ready to copy.

Machine-sewn quilts use different templates than handmade quilts, and both are discussed. Templates can also be purchased from quilting catalogues or specialty quilt stores. Let's find out how to make our patterns of success.

Materials for Making Templates

A template or pattern must be made for each shape in your quilt block.

These three shapes make up the Eight Point Star block.

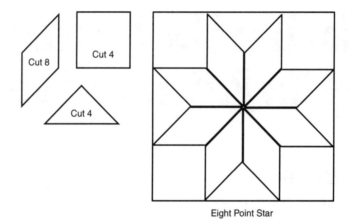

Eight Point Star

Patterns for quilts are totally distinct from patterns with which you sew clothing. If you are used to sewing clothing, quilt patterns or templates may seem very unusual. Commercial clothing patterns are made from printed tissue paper with seam allowances marked on each pattern piece. Quilting patterns have to be extremely accurate to have the parts of the block fit together like a jigsaw puzzle, so the templates are made the exact size of the shape in the hand-pieced block. We will add the seam allowances on the fabric later in Chapter 7.

Because many quilts have hundreds of pattern pieces to draw, templates must be durable. Usually templates are made of cardboard or plastic sheeting. You can find cardboard around the house: file cards, gift boxes, even cereal boxes you cut apart. Optimally, oak tag or poster board are the best weight—easy to cut but durable. As you mark your fabric by drawing around these templates, the points on cardboard templates tend to wear away. If you know that this may be a problem, you might try plastic sheeting. The plastic sheets can be found in craft stores. A student who was a nurse used exposed x-ray sheets for templates.

Accuracy Counts

If one patch is crooked, then your whole quilt is out of alignment. Does that frighten you? It need not. If your templates are precise, then your quilt will be, too. The best type of templates for beginners are made from cardboard and sandpaper. Here are some guidelines to help in the quest for accurate templates.

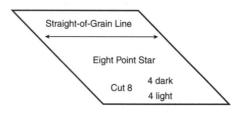

This is the diamond template from the Eight Point Star. It is important to include the name of the block, the number of pattern pieces you need to cut, and the straight-of-grain arrow.

1. Choose a block. (That's easy enough!)

2. Copy each pattern of the block. Either use tracing paper to redraw the patterns or carefully photocopy the page. Be sure to mark the name of the block, the number of blocks you need to cut, and the straight-of-grain arrow.

3. Use rubber cement to affix medium-weight sandpaper to the cardboard. Be sure to apply the rubber cement to the smooth side of the sandpaper.

4. Glue copied patterns onto the cardboard/sandpaper with rubber cement. The template has the copied pattern on top and the rough sandpaper on the bottom.

5. Now it's time to cut very carefully around the outer edges through all three layers—pattern, cardboard, and sandpaper.

6. Test for template accuracy by putting your template over the book's pattern. If it is inaccurate, carefully recut it.

7. Store all your templates for each block together. I like to use zippered plastic bags for each individual block. Be sure to label the block name—you do not want to mix them up!

Quilting Bee

I know you are asking, "Why glue sandpaper to the template?" The sandpaper keeps the template from sliding around while you are marking the fabric.

Don't Get Stuck!

Be sure to use rubber cement and not any other type of glue because only rubber cement dries flat and won't make the cardboard ripple. If your template is not flat, it will not be accurate.

Remember, accuracy counts. The outside of these templates will mark the sewing lines on your fabric, and when sewn, these pieces must fit together perfectly like a jigsaw puzzle.

That doesn't seem too hard, does it?

Quilting Bee

Sometimes when you try to cut small slivers off the templates, you only make it worse by cutting too much. To straighten an uneven edge, file it down with sandpaper or an emery board. You have more control.

Templates for Machine-Piecing

Templates for machine-piecing are slightly different from those for hand-quilting. The ¼-inch seam allowances are included in the template. The cutting line is drawn on your fabric—not the sewing line.

When machine-sewing quilts, you'll pin together and align the cutting edges. The seam line is determined by the sewing machine's ¼-inch presser foot, not by a line drawn on the fabric as in hand quilting. Accurate cutting is extremely important for machine piecing.

A template for machine piecing has the ¼-inch seam allowance incorporated in the template.

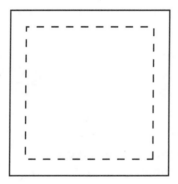

Sometimes machine-sewn quilts have multiple templates (templates that are drawn in a long line). It saves time to mark and sew multiple templates rather than marking and sewing each separate template. The Trip Around the World and Lone Star quilts are examples of quilts with multiple templates. Although I have taught how to make them many times, it still seems like magic when all these templates come together. Several books deal specifically with this method.

These multiple templates drafted together in a row save time.

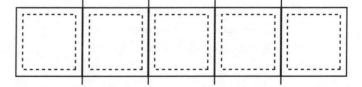

Many machine-made quilts don't have special templates (for example, the Rail Fence). A fabric strip of the correct width is cut from selvage to selvage and sewn together in the *strip-pieced* method, and then cut apart and resewn to form a block. The blocks are sewn together to form the quilt top. (The Rail Fence and Log Cabin blocks are discussed in depth in Chapter 13.)

Remember, no matter whether you are hand- or machine-quilting, you must be sure your templates are exact. Any deviation will cause your quilt not to line up. Check all templates for accuracy against the patterns in the book, and use a T-square ruler for testing right angles in squares and rectangles.

Quilt Talk

Strip-piecing is a method of creating quilts by sewing together long strips of fabric in a set sequence. This newly combined material is then cut apart and resewn to form a part of a quilt.

Be sure to keep templates sorted by blocks. I always have at least one student who tries to put a Double Nine Patch square into an Eight Point Star corner. The templates may look the same, but they are ¼ inch different in size, and there is no way they will fit. So keep them separated in envelopes or my favorite—zippered plastic bags.

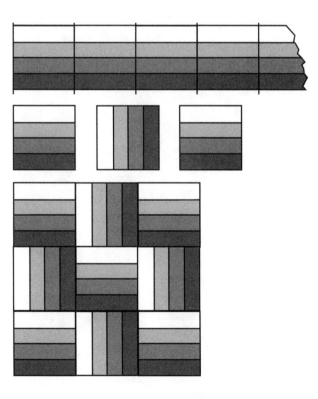

Notice how the strips are sewn together, cut apart, and then resewn to form a Rail Fence block.

The Least You Need to Know

◆ Templates for hand-piecing are pattern pieces that are the exact size of each element in a block.

◆ Templates for machine-sewn quilts have the ¼-inch seam allowance included so that only the cutting line is drawn on the fabric.

◆ The best templates for beginners are made from cardboard and sandpaper glued together.

◆ All markings must be transferred to the templates—be sure to include the name of the block, cutting directions, and straight-of-grain arrow.

◆ Draw and cut templates accurately; then check them for preciseness.

Chapter 7

On Your Mark, Get Set, Cut!

In This Chapter

- ◆ Choosing the correct equipment to mark on fabric
- ◆ Tracing around the template carefully
- ◆ Economizing on fabric
- ◆ Cutting out the pattern pieces
- ◆ Organizing and storing fabric pieces

We've spent a long time making perfectly accurate templates, and now it's time to transfer those shapes onto the material. Can you believe that we draw right on the wrong side of the fabric? Using the correct equipment will help your "markability."

Templates for hand-sewn quilts have no seam allowances. The traced shape is the exact sewing size. We need to draw them onto the fabric after the template is marked. Proper placement of the patterns will help economize the fabric. With all these marked lines, you should think before you cut. Think twice, but cut once.

In short, templates make fabric pieces, those pieces make up a block, and blocks make up a quilt. If only one block is repeated throughout your quilt, there may be hundreds of cut pieces of fabric. How do you keep them all together and not lose them? Keep reading, and you'll find out.

Equip Yourself

You must consider several things before marking your fabric. Choose a tool that is easy to see, marks finely and accurately, and does not run or bleed into the fabric. A number 2 pencil is usually best. Because the wrong side of the fabric is a lighter color than the right side, lead pencils make terrific fine, visible lines. If the fabric is a dark color or has a busy pattern, you may have to use a white, silver, or yellow pencil for the lines to be seen. I usually keep a variety of colors with my supplies to test which color pencil is best.

Quilting Bee

I really prefer an artist's pencil over the ones made for marking quilts. Some pencils are too waxy, make a line too thick, break easily, and need to be sharpened too often—you know, like eyebrow pencils. Avoid those pencils.

Some quilters use ballpoint pens for marking. Be very careful to test whether the pen markings are permanent. Avoid them if they bleed when wet—the color will stain a light-colored fabric.

Be sure your pencil is sharp! You don't want a thick line. Even that small difference multiplied over hundreds of pieces will change the alignment of your quilt. Keep your sharpener handy.

Quilting Bee

It is easy to tell the wrong side of a printed fabric—the design is fuzzier and lighter in color. With solid fabrics, both sides seem to be the same color. There may be a slight difference in values, so be sure you use the same side consistently. I sometimes put a pin or masking tape on the wrong side to remind me of which side I chose.

Your templates should be lined up parallel to the selvage of your fabric. Draw dots in each corner of the template.

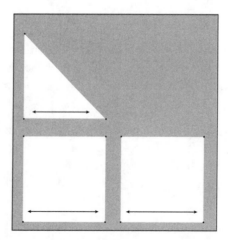

It's as Easy as Drawing from Dot to Dot

It's time to mark your fabric! Here are some simple steps to follow:

1. Be sure the fabric is preshrunk and colorfast.

2. Choose the template and the fabric. Turn the fabric to the wrong side.

3. Find your selvages—these finished edges are your guidelines to pattern placement. Place the straight-of-grain arrow parallel to the selvage. This makes your quilt more durable and the fabric easier to work with when placing it on the lengthwise grain.

4. Start by placing a template ½ inch away from the selvage and parallel to the straight-of-grain arrow.

Don't Get Stuck!

Do not use the selvage—it continues to shrink after the rest of the fabric has been preshrunk and will make your quilt pucker. Also, because selvage is thick, it is extremely difficult to sew and quilt through.

5. Put a dot in each corner of the geometric shape of the template. You will use the dots to help maintain accuracy. This is very important—so make those dots!

6. Carefully draw around the outside edge of the template, connecting the dots. Take care not to press down too hard with the pencil because it drags the fabric and the markings will be out of shape. Lift the template and check for accuracy. Redraw if necessary.

One template down, how many to go?

Cut Between the Sewing Lines

Now that you have drawn your sewing lines, let's draw the cutting line. Don't forget to add the seam allowances onto the outer edge of the markings. Seam allowances for hand-pieced quilts are ¼ inch (not ⅝ inch, as typical in commercial clothing patterns).

There is a perfectly logical reason for a ¼-inch seam allowance. The ¼-inch seam allowance is enough to keep the quilt from raveling, but is not too large that you would have to quilt through it. Those pioneer women really thought this through.

Quilt Talk

The **quilter's quarter** is an 8-inch-long, 4-sided rod of plastic that is ¼-inch wide. It is very easy for beginners to line up this ruler with the seam line to draw the cutting line.

Before you cut, you must make some additional marks on your fabric:

1. Draw a line ¼ inch around the marked seam line. Beginners sometimes use a colored pencil to mark all the cutting lines. This way there is a real visible difference. Use a ruler or *quilter's quarter* to measure the quarter inch.

Look how the cutting line is drawn ¼ inch around the seam lines.

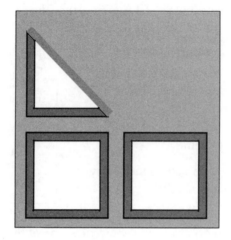

2. Place the next template on the fabric, being sure to leave enough room for the seam allowance.

3. Check that you drew the correct number of pattern pieces, and be sure you drew all the seam allowances.

4. Cut out fabric pieces on the cutting lines. Use sharp scissors to avoid blisters on your hands.

There are strategies to marking fabrics that help you economize fabric usage. The first approach is to start at the selvage side and mark the patterns side by side, only half an inch apart. If you start marking in the middle of the fabric and then place the other templates in no particular order, you waste much of the fabric. Be methodical, and mark across the fabric from selvage to selvage or up the side of the selvage.

You may want to mark up the side of the selvage if you need the length of the fabric for borders. Another idea is to dovetail pattern pieces. Dovetailing means fitting odd-shaped pieces like triangles or wedges into one another. Remember: Plan ahead.

If you are preparing a quilt with repeated blocks, make one patch before you cut out the rest of the quilt. Sometimes you decide to change the color combination or move their placement in the block. When the block is perfected, it's time to cut out the rest of your blocks.

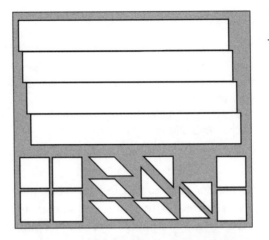

You can utilize all your fabric by thinking ahead.

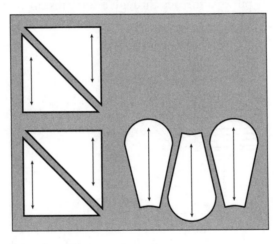

Pattern pieces can be dove-tailed to save fabric.

Stack and Store

There are two methods of storing fabric pieces. For example, an Eight Point Star has three pattern shapes—a diamond, a square, and a triangle. Some quilters keep fabric pieces of each template shape in separate plastic bags—one bag for the diamond, a second for the squares, and a third for the triangles. Other quilters like a plastic bag with all the fabric shapes for one block together. If you are making a lap quilt, you may have six plastic bags that contain the diamonds, squares, and triangles that will be pieced together for one block. This is great if you want a portable project. Pick up a bag and take it with you—all the pieces you need are in one bag.

Quilting Bee _____

All patterns for templates in this book do not have the seam allowance included. In other quilting books, sometimes the ¼-inch seam allowance is included in the drawn template, and sometimes it has to be added. Templates with included seam allowances usually have a dotted line indicating the ¼-inch seam line. If done consistently, it won't matter in the templates or cut pattern pieces.

If you don't like the bag method, you can baste your fabric pieces together. Thread a needle with a long piece of thread with a knot on the end, and stab this through a stack of similar pieces. Don't knot both ends. You can just pull off one piece at a time as you need it. I usually put two threads through a stack just in case one breaks!

You can stack and store all pattern pieces by basting them together.

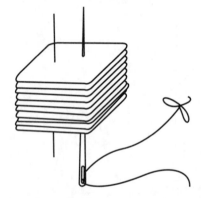

If you are making a Sampler quilt, each block will be different and created one at a time, so patches will be cut and sewn as you go along.

The Least You Need to Know

- A number 2 pencil is best for transferring templates onto the fabric, but try a different color if the pencil line is hard to see.

- Mark on the wrong side of the fabric.

- Place templates with the straight-of-grain line parallel to the selvages.

- Put a dot in each corner of the template and then connect the dots.

- Hand-sewn quilt templates do not have seam allowances; you must add ¼ inch all around the outside for the cutting line.

- Check twice and then cut on the cutting lines.

Chapter 8

Do Be a Sew and Sew

In This Chapter

- ◆ Sewing the piecing stitches and appliqué stitch
- ◆ Understanding how fabric pieces are seamed together
- ◆ Strategies of piecing blocks
- ◆ Pressing quilt blocks

Depending on the type of quilt you have chosen, you may have hundreds of fabric pieces to assemble or as few as 13 pieces for one block. If you are a novice, please let me remind you to start small and cut out pieces for one block only.

It's time to sew your pieces of fabric together! Certain procedures make piecing logical and easy. We'll start with just two pattern pieces and learn to sew them together effortlessly. Continue sewing until a row is formed, then seam the rows together to form a square block. When you have completed your block, it's time to give your patch the professional look by giving it a real press job. Get your needle and thread—let's start.

Know Your Stitches

We'll examine hand-piecing stitches and the appliqué stitch. When these blocks are sewn, the resulting patches are contrasting in appearance.

Piecing Stitch: Know the Ins and Outs

Beginners are always amazed that the stitching for hand-pieced blocks is so easy. It's a simple running stitch where the needle goes in and out of the fabric. Start with a quilting needle and quilting thread. Remember to choose the smallest-size needle that you can work with confidently. Our quilting ancestors discovered that smaller needles made smaller stitches. Be sure to use quilting thread—it's thicker, more durable, and doesn't tangle.

> **Don't Get Stuck!**
>
> Don't make the type of knot that I use for making hems (wrapping the thread around my finger and rolling it back and forth till it forms a massive ball of a knot). If you make a knot like that, it may rub against the fabric of your quilt and wear a hole. We want our quilts to be heirlooms.

1. Cut quilting thread about 2 feet in length. Any longer and it's awkward and tiring to pull the thread through. Any shorter and you have to constantly rethread the needle, and that gets annoying.

2. Put a single knot in the end of the thread. I make a loop with the thread, put the needle through the circle, and pull it through. It should form a little knot with a ¼-inch "tail." The tail keeps the knot from unraveling.

Make a loop with the thread and pull the needle through, leaving a small knot with a tail.

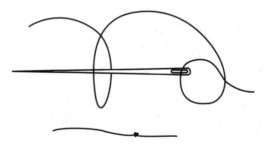

3. Place the two fabric pieces, right sides together, matching the sewing lines. This is it—our first piecing stitch. Poke the needle down through the fabric right on the sewing line and then up through the fabric about ⅛ inch down along the seam line. It's simply a running stitch using an in-and-out motion that is sewn right on the seam line.

Running stitches used for the piecing stitch are very small.

Draw a pencil line on the wrong side of a scrap of fabric and practice the piecing stitch. In and out—it's easy.

Scraps and Pieces

Quilts have a rich history of superstitions. The most universal bit of folklore confirms that each quilt should have a small mistake in it, either a piecing or appliqué mismatch or a quilting *faux pas*. My theory is that after a quilt was completed and the quilt maker discovered the mistake, she developed the idiom that "the quilt is supposed to be like that because only God is perfect." Of course I do not recommend making mistakes in your quilt, but this does make a great explanation.

Appliqué Stitch

Beginners also need to learn the appliqué stitch. In appliquéd blocks, a fabric motif is cut out, layered, and stitched invisibly onto the background of another fabric. Several different techniques make these stitches almost invisible to the eye. In true appliqué, we want to see only the design, not the stitches.

Scraps and Pieces

There has recently been a revival of folk art. The quilt is the most popular example of traditional American crafts. Quilters used the medium of fabric to make pictures of their world. This was the original folk art. Pioneer women would appliqué stylized people (Sunbonnet Sue), animals, flowers, and farm scenes in a primitive style. In these homespun-style quilts, the appliquéd pieces are embroidered with a decorative blanket stitch.

This is the appliqué stitch that I was taught, and it has worked for me. I'll illustrate how to appliqué a heart motif. The appliqué stitch leaves a small, visible dot of a stitch.

Quilt Talk _____

Basting is a large, temporary running stitch that is sewn to hold down the raw edges or hold two pieces of fabric together. You should use a contrasting color so it is easy to see and remove after you have finished appliquéing.

1. Start with your quilting needle and knotted quilting thread in a color that blends with the appliqué motif.

2. Prepare the design by _basting_ under the raw edges.

3. Baste the fabric motif into position on the background fabric. Now let's appliqué.

4. Start with the needle under the background fabric. Push it up through the background and the edge of the appliqué motif. Pull the thread through.

Only a dot of stitch is seen. The needle goes down through the background fabric and up into the edge of the appliqué piece.

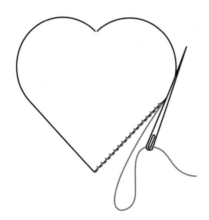

5. Position the needle right next to where the thread came up but on the background only. Take a ⅛-inch stitch through the background, and come up at the edge of the appliqué motif.

Don't Get Stuck! _____

Be sure to mark the dots at each corner of your templates so you know where to start and end your seam lines.

6. Continue appliquéing stitches all around the fabric design, ending underneath the background on the wrong side. Knot off.

The appliqué stitch does seem more time-consuming. The first appliqué block that a beginner creates is a slow go, but you soon develop a rhythm of stitching that makes your block sing.

How Does It Seam?

"Where do I start?" is a question all beginners ask. The answer is with just two fabric pieces, three pins, and your needle and thread. We're going to seam the pieces together using the hand-piecing stitch. Let's take two pieces and turn them right sides together so the penciled seam lines can be seen on both sides of the pieces.

The dots marked at each corner of your templates will be the beginning and end of your seam lines. Stab a pin right into the dot of the top piece into the dot of the bottom fabric. Both dots are matched. Match up and pin the dot at the other end. Put another pin in the seam line in the middle of the pencil line.

Get out your quilting needle and thread, and make a knot. Put the needle in the seam line ⅛ inch from the right-hand dot (if you are right handed, the left-hand dot is just the opposite), and take a *backstitch* into the dot. Then sew the piecing stitch along the seam line.

Continue sewing to the end of the seam line, bringing the needle right into the end dot. Take a backstitch ⅛ inch in reverse and back into the dot. I do not knot this end (knots can rub against and wear out material); instead, I take a 90-degree turn into the seam allowance, make two stitches, and cut off the thread.

Don't Get Stuck! _____

Check for accuracy before you sew. Gather several stitches on your needle, but don't pull the thread through. Turn the piece over and check to see whether your needle is exactly on the line—if not, take the needle out and shift the seam line.

Quilt Talk _____

A **backstitch** is a stitch taken backward from the direction you are sewing to reinforce the seam.

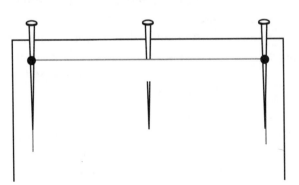

Sew right on the seam line with the hand-piecing stitch.

Pin each end dot of the seam line, and place one pin in the center of the seam line.

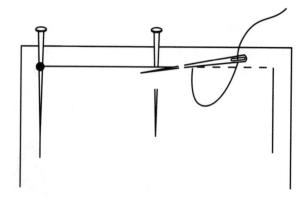

Take a backstitch into the dot at the end and then take two stitches into the seam allowance.

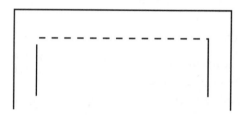

Put Your Blocks Together: Sew Row by Row

Didn't that "seam" easy? Certain strategies make it easier for you to piece your block. First, lay all your block pieces on the table in front of you. Put them in the same position as your finished block. Doesn't it look great? It is easy to decide where to start sewing and then to check whether you've pinned correctly.

Each block has specific directions on sewing procedures, but here are some hints. Start by sewing the smallest pieces together to form a larger unit. Those small scraps of fabric are very easy to lose. Stitch pieces together into rows. One student sewed pieces across and then down in an L-shaped angle instead of sewing rows. She came to me and asked, "How do I put in the middle piece?" Don't sew yourself into a "jam." Sew row by row.

Let's learn how to sew rows together. It is important to have the seams match at intersections. Do not start sewing from one end of the row to the other side. Be sure that the seams align, sewing from the middle out. Pin the dots at each end of the row and at each seam intersection.

Quilting Bee

One student often had to put her work away then set it up again, so she laid out her pieces on a piece of felt or flannel. It was easy to fold up her work, then pull it out again later. The fuzzy nap of the felt kept the pieces in place even when the felt was folded up.

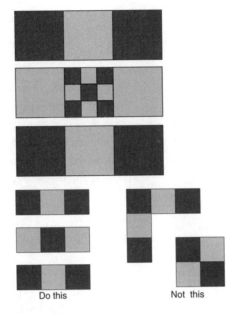

It's easy to sew rows together, but difficult to sew a piece into an angle.

Do this   Not this

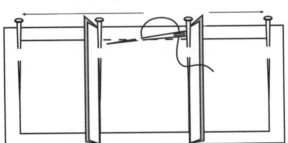

The pins are placed into the dots next to the seam allowances. Check out the direction you should sew.

Don't pin or sew down the seam allowances—you'll need to press them in any direction. Start at one of the center seams, backstitch into the dot, and sew to the end of the seam line. If you have to cross a seam line, sew right up to the dot but stand the seam allowance up and pass the needle through it and continue stitching to the end of the row. Backstitch into the dot and take two stitches into the seam. Sew all of the rows in the same manner, and "Hooray," you have a block.

Ironing Out Your Mistakes

When your block has been pieced, it's time to press it to get a professional look. Wait until the patch is completed to see the optimum way to press. I like to use a steam iron set to either cotton or the synthetic setting, depending on the fabric type.

Here are some guidelines to follow for pressing your block:

1. Iron on the wrong side of the block, with all seams pressed to one side—*not open*.

Don't Get Stuck!

Even if only one of your fabrics is a cotton-polyester blend, press your block at the lower, synthetic setting to prevent scorching it.

Quilting Bee

The seam allowances are pressed to one side, not open as in dressmaking. When seams are pressed together, they are stronger.

2. Press the seam toward the darker color. If you press in the direction of the lighter color, a dark shadow will appear on the quilt top. Sometimes the weight of a fabric will force you to press the seam in one direction, no matter how you try to press it the other way. In this case, let the fabric win.

3. If there are any puckers or your block seems out of alignment, use a wet press cloth to smooth it out.

Be careful to move the iron, lifting it up and down. Sometimes pressing back and forth causes the edges of the patch to stretch. Use a light touch. Many times my students come to me with wrinkled patches and are amazed how terrific they appear after pressing. You can definitely iron out your mistakes.

The Least You Need to Know

- Thread your needle with quilting thread and make a single knot at the end.
- Pin into the dots at each end of the seam line and pin the seam line in the middle.
- Use the hand-piecing stitch for pieced patchwork blocks and the appliqué stitch for appliqué blocks.
- Sew your blocks together row by row.
- Don't sew down intersecting seam allowances; this way you can press them in any direction.
- Press seams to one side, not open.

Chapter 9

Easy Pieced Patchwork Blocks

In This Chapter

- ◆ Learning to identify easy blocks
- ◆ Piecing nine- and four-patch blocks
- ◆ Understanding how to make seams match
- ◆ Piecing an easy block

Pieced blocks are designed in different ways: four equal sections called a four patch, nine sections called a nine patch, five rows called a five patch, and some blocks defy rows and are sewn on an angle.

Each section of the block can be divided into smaller squares, triangles, rectangles, or even shapes that are not nameable.

Four ways blocks can be designed.

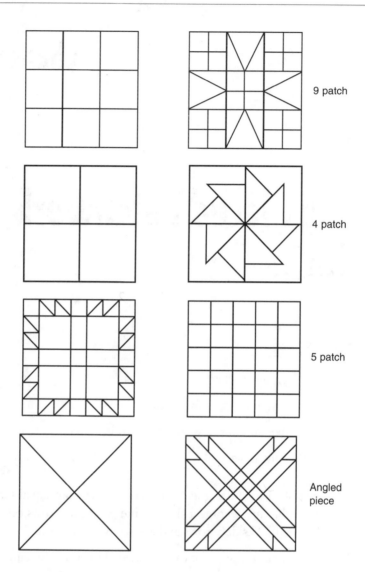

9 patch

4 patch

5 patch

Angled piece

Double Nine Patch

The Double Nine Patch is a good start for beginners—it has only two pattern pieces and they are both squares, the easiest shape to work with because they are cut on the straight of the grain and there is little stretch. Only 17 pieces make up the block.

Why is it called Double Nine? Look at the picture of the block. It is made up of nine 4-inch squares. The middle square is divided into nine 1⅓-inch squares, therefore Double Nine. See, it does make sense! It's easy to plan the colors. You can use two to four different fabrics. After the squares are cut out and laid out on the table, you can flip-flop them to have the block look like a plus or a square (see the Double Nine Patch figure).

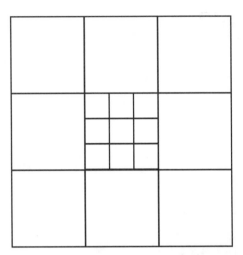

Double Nine Patch block.

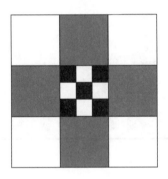 

You can vary the color combination of the Double Nine Patch to create different patterns.

Let's start the step-by-step directions and make our first block:

1. Prepare the templates.

2. Decide on your color combination. Traditionally, the large squares are cut from four dark and four light fabrics. The small squares are cut from four light and five medium tones of fabric.

Don't Get Stuck!

Remember, if you have hand-piecing templates, add on the ¼-inch seam allowances!

Quilting Bee

Don't rip out and resew seams that do not match exactly. This can make the fabric stretch out of shape, making the block look worse. Turn your block over, step back, and look at the errant seam. If it's not obvious, don't take your block apart. If it makes you crazy, carefully take out the stitches, shift your pins, and resew.

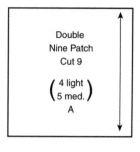

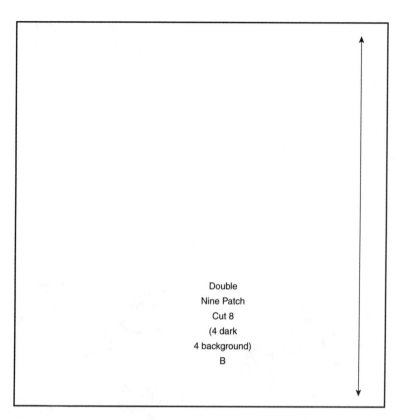

Double
Nine Patch
Cut 9

(4 light)
(5 med.)
A

Double
Nine Patch
Cut 8
(4 dark
4 background)
B

Double Nine Patch templates.

3. Mark around the templates on the wrong side of your fabric.

4. Cut out fabric pieces ¼ inch from the traced seam lines. Beginners, please use a drawn cutting line.

5. Lay out the block on the table in front of you.

6. Sew the 1⅓-inch squares (template A) together in rows to form the center 4-inch square.

7. Sew the block together starting with the top row of three squares.

8. Sew the middle row of the Double Nine Patch by sewing a B template to each side of the center square (see Figure a).

9. Sew the bottom three 4-inch squares.

10. Sew the rows of blocks together, stitching from the inside out, and don't sew down seam allowances (see Figure b).

11. Press.

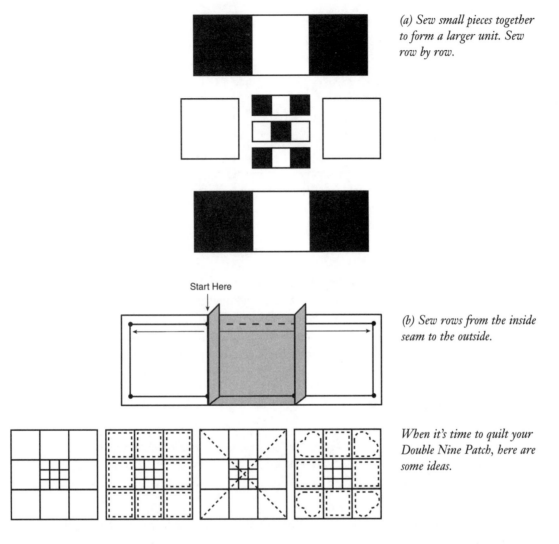

(a) Sew small pieces together to form a larger unit. Sew row by row.

(b) Sew rows from the inside seam to the outside.

When it's time to quilt your Double Nine Patch, here are some ideas.

Remember, you should have the seams of your block match. If they are out of line, it gives your block an unprofessional or sloppy look. You are the boss of the fabric. Pin right into the dots next to the seam allowances of both pieces of fabric you are sewing together. When you pin and stitch accurately, your seams will match.

Churn Dash

The Churn Dash is a nine patch similar to the Double Nine Patch block. It is also called the Monkey Wrench or Sherman's March, depending on what part of the country you live in.

Churn Dash block.

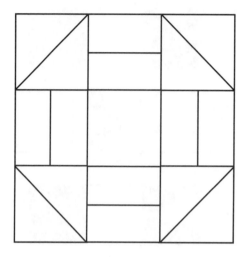

It's a simple patch—great for beginners. There are three major pattern pieces: a 4-inch square, a 2-inch by 4-inch rectangle, and a large triangle—17 pieces in all. You can use either two, three, or four fabrics. The dark fabric is traditionally the inner rectangles and triangles to form a "churn dash" motif. However, once I made this patch with the dark fabrics on the outside, giving it a totally different look.

Scraps and Pieces _____

Legend has it that a pioneer woman who was preparing butter in her churn inspired this patch. It is said that she looked down and saw the shape of the churn blade, known as the dash, and was "stirred" to design this energetic patch.

On your mark, get set, go! Do the Churn Dash, and you will win the race by following these directions:

1. Prepare the templates.

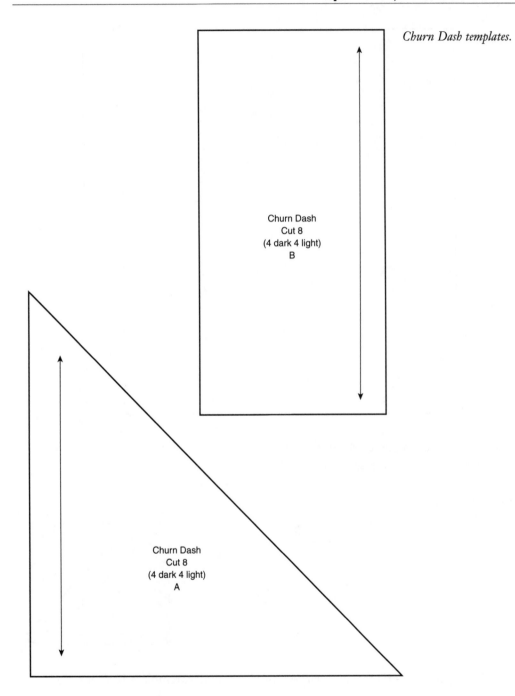

Churn Dash templates.

Churn Dash
Cut 8
(4 dark 4 light)
B

Churn Dash
Cut 8
(4 dark 4 light)
A

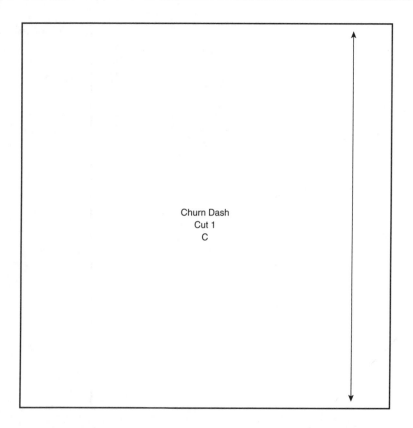

Churn Dash
Cut 1
C

2. Pin and sew together the dark and background triangles (template A) to form a 4-inch square (see Figure a).

(a) Triangles sewn together to form a square.

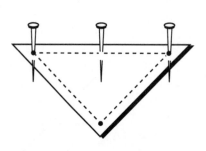 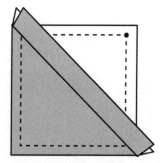

3. Sew together the light- and dark-colored rectangles (template B) to form a 4-inch square.

4. Sew together the top row, the middle row by using rectangles and template C square, and the bottom row (see Figure b).

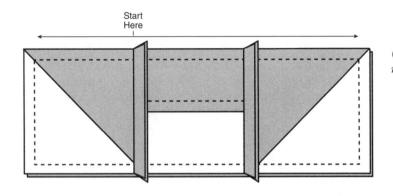

(b) Sewing direction for rows.

5. Sew the rows together starting with the middle square's dot and working across the center square to the outer dot. Then sew from the center square's dot to the end in the opposite direction.

6. Press the finished block.

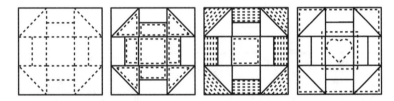

When it's time to quilt the Churn Dash, here are some ideas.

Don't forget to pin carefully, check to see if the piece fits into the block laid out in front, and then sew. Be precise and systematic. Here's to never needing your seam ripper!

Ohio Star

The Ohio Star is a nine-patch design with the star motif built around a central square. This is one of my favorite blocks. It has such a clean look and can be harmonious with either modern or traditional decor. The Ohio Star has two pattern pieces: a 4-inch square and a small triangle. (The 4-inch square is divided into 4 triangles.) There are 21 pieces in the Ohio Star block.

You can use the traditional two colors, giving your patch a very definitive star motif. You can also create it with three colors, making the center square a different fabric. To add another color, change the color of the four inner triangles to make the fabric total four. You can go off the wall and make hourglass shapes by altering the placement of the darkest fabric.

![Quilting Bee]

Quilting Bee _____

Because the nine-patch blocks have similar pattern pieces, you can avoid confusion by making a set of templates for each block and storing them in separate zippered baggies. That way you can find the right triangle as soon as you need it!

Ohio Star block.

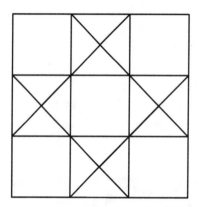

See how different placement of fabrics can change the look of the Ohio Star block.

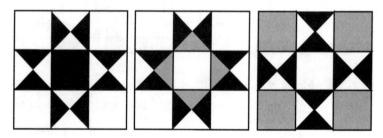

Let's create an Ohio Star block:

1. Prepare the templates and decide on the colors (two, three, or four fabrics).

2. Mark around the outside of the templates, and add the seam allowance onto the wrong side of the fabric.

3. Cut out 21 pieces, and lay out the design.

Don't Get Stuck! _____

Be sure to pin the seam of the small triangles and open the pieces up to check. It is so easy to pin the wrong side of the triangle or, if you've chosen several colors, to pick up the wrong color. I can't tell you how many times I've done this.

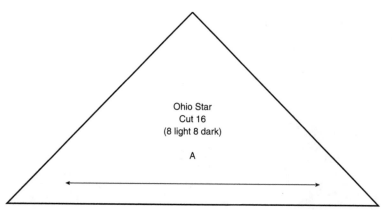

Ohio Star templates.

Ohio Star
Cut 16
(8 light 8 dark)

A

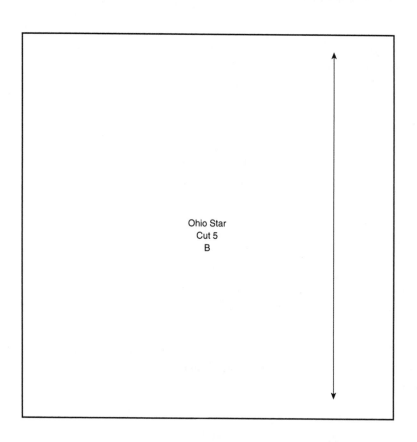

Ohio Star
Cut 5
B

4. Sew together two small triangles (template A) to form a larger triangle (see Figure a).

(a) Sewing the Ohio Star triangles together.

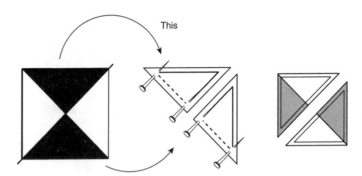

5. Sew two sets of triangles together to form 4-inch squares. Make four squares made up of the triangles (see Figure b).

(b) Sewing seams of triangles together to form a square.

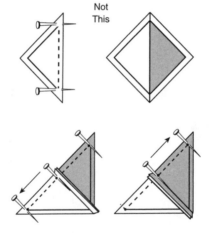

6. Sew together each row of the Ohio Star, being sure that the colors of the triangles are in the correct positions. Stitch the rows together from the inside to the outside dots (see Figure c).

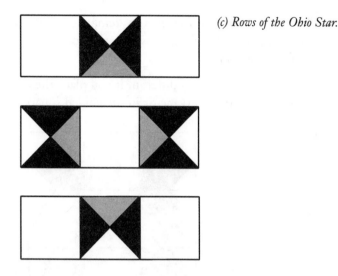

(c) Rows of the Ohio Star.

7. Press.

Weathervane

I first discovered this nine patch when I was making a quilt for my brother, who is a meteorologist. I not only liked the look of the block but also thought the name was appropriate. The blocks are starting to get a little more intricate—this one has 37 pieces.

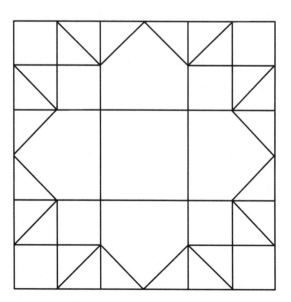

Weathervane block.

The Weathervane has four pattern templates. There is one central 4-inch square, 4 pentagons, eight 2-inch squares (4 dark and 4 background), and 24 triangles (8 dark and 16 background).

This block can look very different if you place the emphasis color in the "arrow" position of the Weathervane or in the angled square.

Notice how different these two Weathervane blocks look.

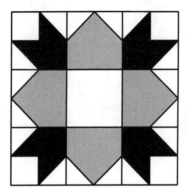 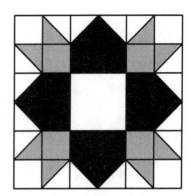

Quilting Bee

I sometimes play with scraps of fabric to determine the color placement. Cut fabric the shape of the block's pattern and lay it over the diagram of the block. Change the colors around and decide which design is best for you. I sometimes draw the pattern with colored pencils, but using scraps is better.

If you use the dark color as the arrows, then your eye is drawn in an X pattern. When the pentagons are a bright accent color, then an angled square is the dominant shape. Decide which is the look you like. Let's let the winds blow us to the directions.

1. Prepare the templates, and decide on the colors.

2. Mark, add on the ¼-inch seam allowances, and cut out the fabric pieces.

3. Lay out the fabric pieces in front of you.

4. Sew the dark triangles to the background triangles (template A) to form a square (see Figure a).

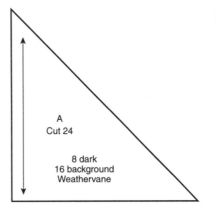

Weathervane templates.

A
Cut 24

8 dark
16 background
Weathervane

Weathervane
Cut 4 dark
Cut 4 light
B

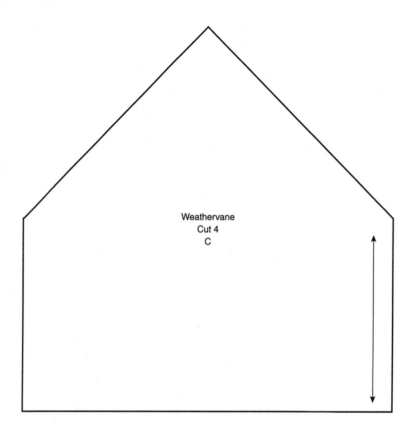

Weathervane
Cut 4
C

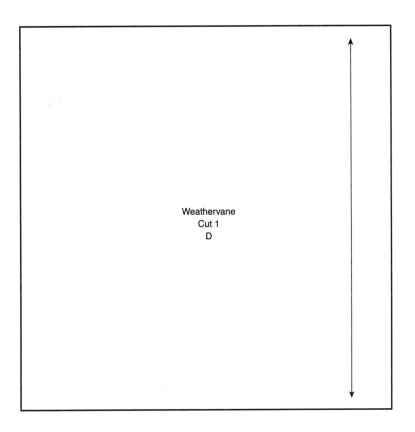

Weathervane
Cut 1
D

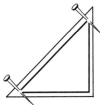

(a) Triangles sewn together.

5. Sew the small square (template B) to the square made up of the triangles. Sew these together in rows, being sure that the position is correct. It really is easy to sew the wrong pieces together (see Figure b).

(b) Squares sewn together.

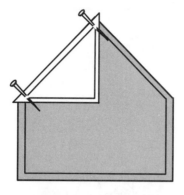

(c) Horizontal rows of the Weathervane.

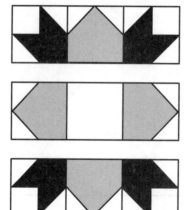

Quilting Bee

Beginners sometimes get nervous because it appears that the seams don't match and the ends of the triangles hang off the sides of the pentagons. Don't fear, only the dots have to match.

6. Sew the triangles (template A) to the pentagon shapes (template C) being sure to pin into the dots (see Figure b).

7. Sew each horizontal row together.

8. Sew rows together from the inside seam to the outer dots (see Figure c).

9. Press.

Dutchman's Puzzle

I don't know the history behind the name Dutchman's Puzzle, but I like the spiral pinwheel effect of the block. It is our first four-patch square; this block is divided into four sections. There are 2 pattern pieces, a large and small triangle, and 24 pieces in all. This block is not a puzzle—it is really fun to create.

Dutchman's Puzzle block.

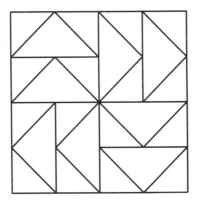

1. Prepare the templates and decide on the color combinations.

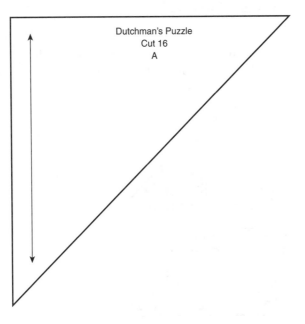

Dutchman's Puzzle
Cut 16
A

Dutchman's Puzzle templates.

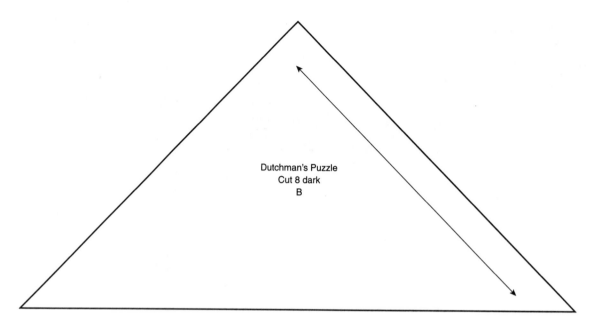

Dutchman's Puzzle
Cut 8 dark
B

2. Mark the templates on the fabric, add ¼-inch seam allowances, and cut out fabric pieces.

3. Lay out the pattern pieces in front of you.

4. Pin together the longest side of the small triangle (template A), to the smallest side of the large triangle (template B). Does that sound confusing? I hope not. When the three triangles are combined, they form a 6-inch by 3-inch rectangle (see Figure a).

(a) Sewing triangles for Dutchman's Puzzle.

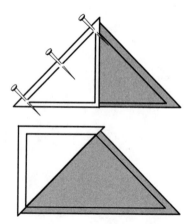

5. Put two sets of the rectangle together to form a 6-inch square. Make four of these square units in the same manner. They appear different in the block because you turn each one a one quarter turn (see Figure b).

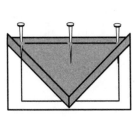

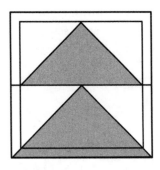

(b) Sewing rectangles of Dutchman's Puzzle.

6. Put horizontal rows together, being sure they are in the correct position (see Figure c).

7. Press.

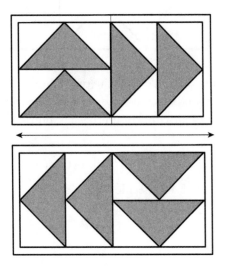

(c) Sew from the inside out.

Eight Point Star

This is the first block that is not sewn together in rows!

The Eight Point Star is drafted with eight diamonds sewn together to form a star. Squares and triangles are alternately sewn around the diamonds to square out the block. There are 3 templates, and you need to cut out 16 pieces in total.

Eight Point Star block.

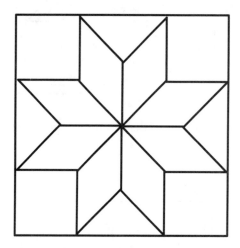

This block can be made with two coordinating fabrics and a background fabric—three altogether. Some students have used five fabrics (one fabric is used for the background, each remaining fabric makes up the star, cutting out two diamonds) to give the star a pinwheel look.

Be a stargazer and make this patch—you'll love it.

1. Prepare the templates and decide on the colors.

2. Mark and cut out the fabric pieces, and lay out the block in front of you.

Eight Point Star templates.

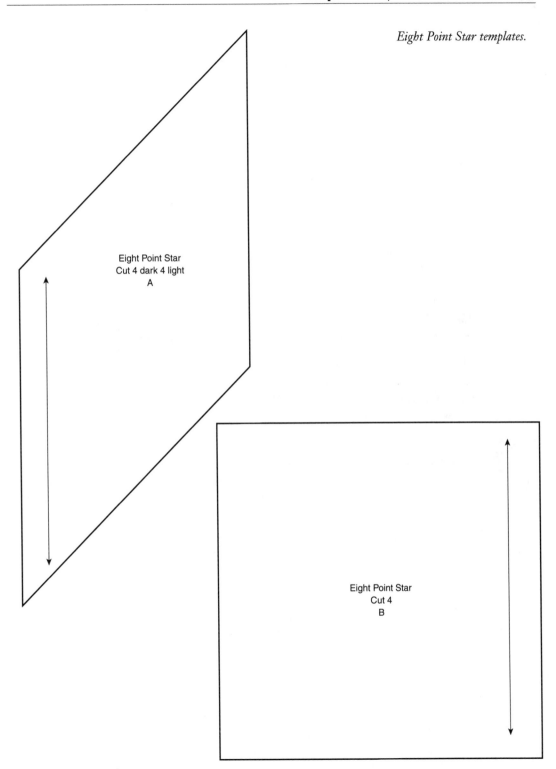

Eight Point Star
Cut 4 dark 4 light
A

Eight Point Star
Cut 4
B

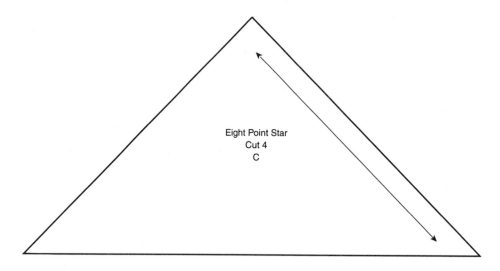

Eight Point Star
Cut 4
C

3. Start by picking up two diamonds (template A) next to each other. Flip over one diamond so the right sides are together. Pin into the dots of one side of the diamond (one fourth of the diamond). Sew between these two dots.

4. I like to sew all the diamonds together to form the star. Be extremely careful to match the dots perfectly, and always replace the pinned pieces to check that you pinned it correctly (see Figure a). If you pin the diamond to the wrong part of the star, you will end up with a herringbone zigzag. That's not a star.

Don't Get Stuck!

Be sure to sew only between the two dots; I can't tell you how many beginners end up sewing the entire half of the diamonds together forming a nice little pocket.

Be sure to alternate the squares and the triangles; otherwise your patch will be a very weird shape.

5. Alternate sewing squares (template B) and triangles (template C) around the star. While the star pieces are in front of you, flip a square over a diamond so the dots match up with the right sides together. Pin into the two dots. Stitch from the widest part of the diamond to the tip of the star. Replace the block on the table, and flip the other side of the square so that it matches the diamond it is next to. Pin and sew from the widest point to the tip of the diamond (see Figure b).

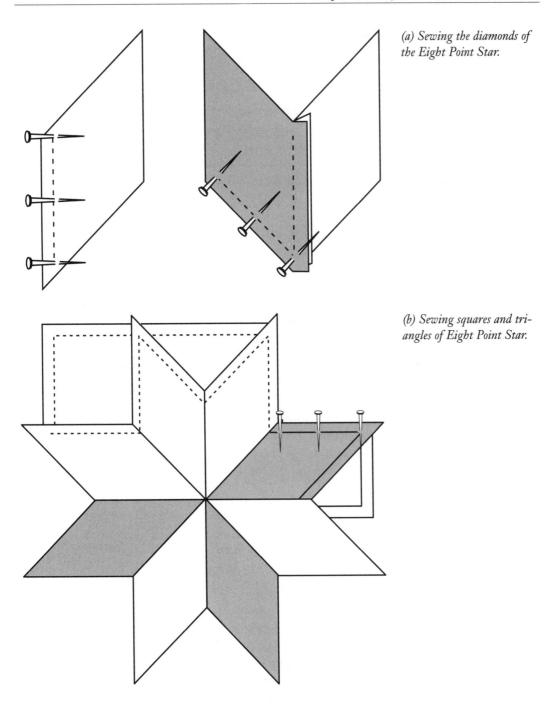

(a) Sewing the diamonds of the Eight Point Star.

(b) Sewing squares and triangles of Eight Point Star.

6. Press all seams of the star in one spiral direction. I like to press the seams of the squares and triangles toward the star, because it makes the star stand out as if it is stuffed. The center of the star may have a small hole, but this will usually press out. To press that mass of seams at the center of the star, put the point of the iron right into the middle and press them flat, spreading them out like petals of a flower (see Figure c).

To reduce the bulk, you may want to clip off some long ends of the seam allowances; be sure not to trim too close, however, because the fabric may ravel. Turn the block over and press the right side.

(c) Ironing the Eight Point Star.

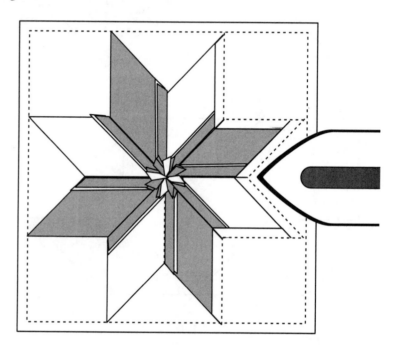

Rolling Star

If you want to take Eight Point Star "up a notch," you should make the Rolling Star. This block has a small central eight point star, but instead of alternating squares and triangles, there are only squares. Remember how I said your Eight Point Star block wouldn't be squared off if you didn't alternate squares and triangles? This central part of the patch then has an octagonal shape and needs to be squared off with a background fabric to complete the 12-inch square.

There are three basic pattern pieces: a diamond, a square, and a four-sided shape that squares off the block. You will be cutting out 24 fabric pieces in all. This block always coordinates nicely into your quilt project because it combines three fabrics from your color scheme and the background. Be sure to use the darkest or brightest color in the part of the block you want to emphasize, either the diamond or the star or the squares.

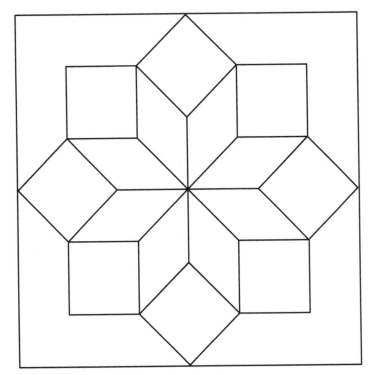

Rolling Star block.

Notice how the placement of the dark color changes the appearance of the block.

If you like the Eight Point Star, go one step further. Check out the instructions and pictures for the Rolling Star. Then let's get rolling on the Rolling Star:

1. Make the templates and decide on the color combinations.

Rolling Star templates.

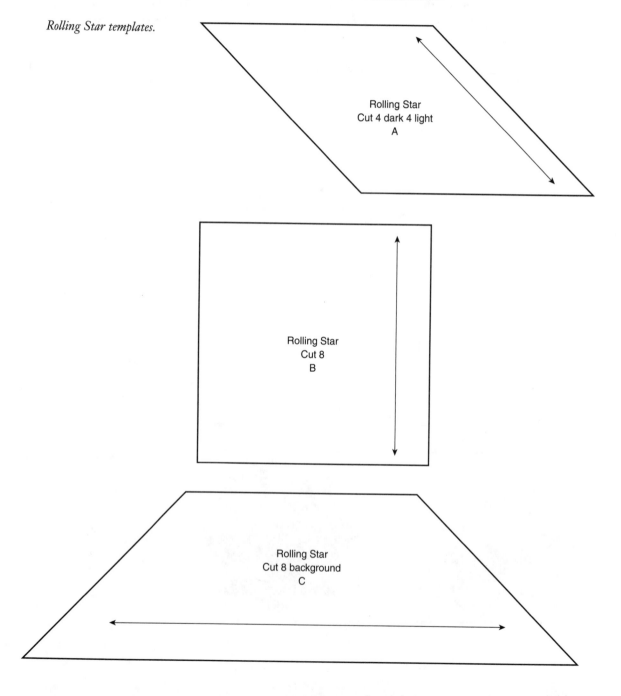

Rolling Star
Cut 4 dark 4 light
A

Rolling Star
Cut 8
B

Rolling Star
Cut 8 background
C

2. Mark, adding on seam allowances, then cut out the fabric pieces and lay out the block in front of you.

3. Start by picking up two adjacent diamonds (template A). Flip over one diamond so their right sides are together, and pin the dots. Sew from dot to dot only (see Figure a).

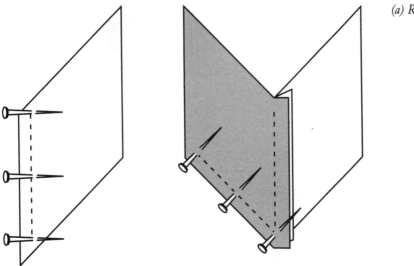

(a) Rolling Star diamonds.

4. Sew all the diamonds together being sure to pick up the correct color diamond and pin it in the right position.

5. Sew the squares (template B) into the diamonds. Turn the square over the diamond with the right sides together. Match the dots. Sew from the widest part of the diamond out to the tip of the star. Sew in all eight squares (see Figure b).

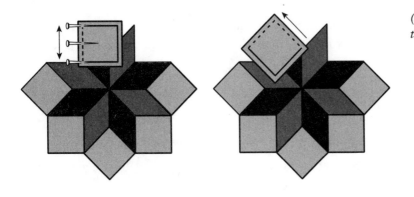

(b) Put squares all around the Rolling Star.

6. Now for those weird-shaped trapezoids. Flip template C so that the "top" of the shape matches one side of the square (see Figure c). Pin and sew only between dots. There will be unsewn ends at each side. Don't worry, we'll sew them next.

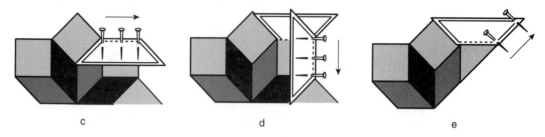

c   d   e

Sewing the background for the Rolling Star.

7. Fold the square in half onto itself, and pin one end of the background to the adjacent square. Sew from the inside dot to the outside of the block (see Figure d).

8. Pin and stitch the center of another rectangle to the next square. Now we have to attach the two ends of the background that are hanging loose. Fold the square in half at an angle so that the background ends meet. Pin the dots and sew from the inside to the outer part of the block (see Figure e).

9. Sew in all the background pieces.

10. Press the inner star in the same way you would press the Eight Point Star. Iron the star and square seam allowances toward the background pieces to reduce bulk.

The Least You Need to Know

♦ Lay the cut-out fabric pieces in front of you and pin two pieces together; be sure to lay the pieces back into the design to check for accuracy and then sew.

♦ Sew small pieces together to form a larger unit.

♦ Pieces of a block are sewn together horizontally in rows or sewn into units that are pieced on the diagonal.

♦ Be sure rows are sewn from the inside seam line to the outer edge.

♦ Perfect your hand-piecing technique by making an easy block before you tackle a more complicated pattern.

Challenging Pieced Patchwork Blocks

In This Chapter

- ◆ Learn what makes a block challenging
- ◆ Special cutting techniques for mirror-image pieces
- ◆ How to sew curved seams
- ◆ Handle challenging blocks with ease

This chapter covers patchwork blocks that will make you think. You will fine-tune your piecing ability, learn how to mark and cut strange shapes, and sew many, many, little pieces together. Each of these blocks has an unusual peculiarity to it. Beware of the number of pattern pieces and templates that have special peculiarities. Blocks with curves are always a threat to beginners. Let's take up the challenge and defy these blocks by knowing what to expect and how to avoid problems.

What Makes a Block Difficult?

You can just look at some blocks and know they will be hard to piece. If the pieces are small, you can be sure you will need many of them to fill up your 12-inch square. I feel that more than 40 pieces make a block a challenge—it is more time-consuming to mark, cut, and sew that many pieces, let alone keep track of them all. The Virginia Star has 40 pattern pieces, whereas the Churn Dash has 17 pieces. That's a big difference. But what visual diversity the Virginia Star has!

A block can be obstinate because there are so many seams to match up. Five patch blocks require you to align 25 seams! Look at the Bear's Paw block in this chapter—when you start sewing the rows together, you will appreciate four patch quilts (the Dutchman's Puzzle, for example) and nine patch quilts (the Ohio Star, for instance). Patchwork blocks that have many pieces or seams are only time-consuming, not troublesome.

Pieces such as squares, rectangles, equilateral triangles, and diamonds are easy pieces to cut and sew. However, some shapes will cause problems. Any asymmetrical shape could give you a headache if it is cut incorrectly. My class once made appliquéd Santa wall hangings. All of the pieces were nonreversible. One student traced and cut out all her templates backward. We ended up with 12 Santa wall hangings facing left and one nonconformist Santa wall hanging facing right. The student was lucky—she made all her templates wrong, but at least she was consistent, because they all fit together. Nonreversible pieces are asymmetrical in shape, and you must be careful to prepare the templates correctly.

Look what happens if one piece is cut wrong! No matter how you move it, it doesn't fit!

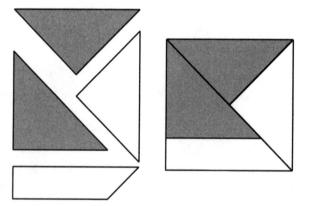

Many times I have cut the outer trapezoid of the Pinwheel block in the wrong direction and all the other pieces in the right direction. With nonreversible pattern pieces, be sure your patterns are marked and cut out accurately. Backward pieces will not fit into your block. If a template says "This side up," believe it.

Mirror Images

Several patchwork blocks have pieces that are called *mirror images*. That means there are left and right sides to the patch. If you look at the 54-40 or Fight block, you will notice a mirror-image template. The long, narrow triangle is asymmetrical, and if you cut the pieces all the same way, half the blocks will not fit. The template will specify if the pieces have to be cut in a mirror-image way. (Cut four regular and four mirror image, totaling eight fabric pieces from one template.)

Quilting Bee

To cut in the **mirror-image** method, first trace around your template the normal way. Then flip it so that the sandpaper side is facing up, not down toward the fabric. Trace around the template for the remaining pieces.

Slow Down on Curves

The last and probably the most difficult piecing problem is sewing curves. We're used to flipping over our fabric pieces so that right sides are together. When that is done with curves, it looks like there is no way they will match. Take it step by step, and it will be easy. When marking curved templates, be sure to make a small mark in the middle of both rounded edges of the seam line. It will be indicated on the template.

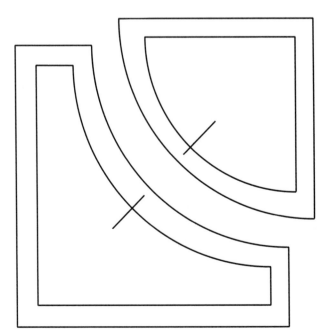

Make a small mark in the middle of the seam line on both pieces.

I start by flipping the pieces right side together. Don't panic. Then pin the curved seams right into that center mark on the seam line. Move the top fabric piece so the dots at one end match up. Pin. Shift the top fabric to match the dots at the other end of the seam line.

How do those pieces fit? Pin the centers and shift the top fabric to pin the ends.

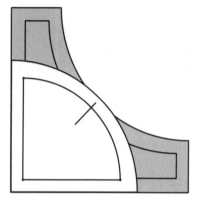 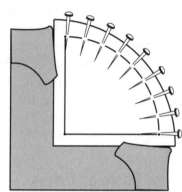

Quilt Talk

A **clip** is a small cut that you make in the seam allowance. A clip or two in a seam allowance enables you to open the seam up and press it flat. Be sure not to clip too far, or you will cut into the seam and make a hole.

Don't Get Stuck!

All quilters should mark the templates clearly with their letters, because pieces can look very similar. With the Bear's Paw, be sure you use template B for the corners, template C for the end of the cross, and template F for the center of the block.

I like to use about nine pins in the seam line to hold the curve into place. Start with a backstitch into the dot at one end, and stitch using your hand-piecing stitch, removing pins as you sew up to them. Ease the fabric as you go so there are no tucks. Press the seam in one direction, usually toward the concave piece, and in most cases you do not even have to *clip* the seam allowance to void puckers.

The Bear's Paw, Clay's Choice, and Virginia Star blocks all have many pieces for assembly. The Pinwheel block has a nonreversible pattern template. Mirror-image cutting techniques are used in the 54-40 or Fight patches. Lastly, the Drunkard's Path (I love that name) consists of pieced curves. The templates in this chapter are the size you need for each design—but remember that all the blocks are 12-inch squares and that seam allowances must be added on when you are marking.

Bear's Paw

This block looks like a bear's four footprints, even with toenails. There are 53 separate pieces in this patch and 6 templates. It is a five patch, which means there are many intersecting seam allowances that must be matched. It is a real challenge. Take it slow and row by row.

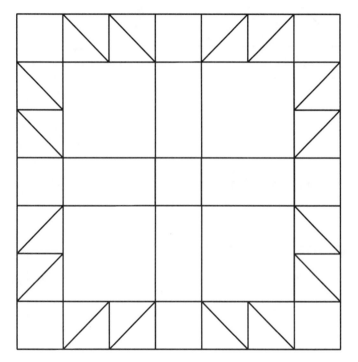

Bear's Paw block. Can you see the four paw prints?

Scraps and Pieces _____

The Bear's Paw is four dark footprints on a light background, but the name is changed if the colors are shifted. It is called Duck's Foot in the Mud when the colors are reversed, with a light-colored fabric on a dark background. Can't you see the pioneer women being inspired and naming this block? Quakers in Philadelphia did not name this block after animals as the quilters in the wilderness did, but called it the Hands of Friendship.

Bear's Paw templates. Remember to add seam allowances!

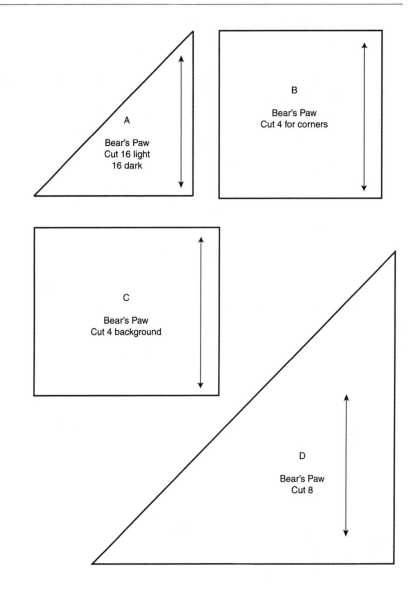

A

Bear's Paw
Cut 16 light
16 dark

B

Bear's Paw
Cut 4 for corners

C

Bear's Paw
Cut 4 background

D

Bear's Paw
Cut 8

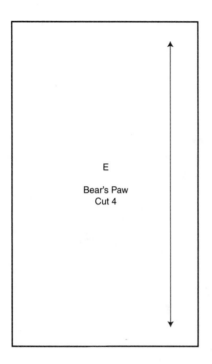

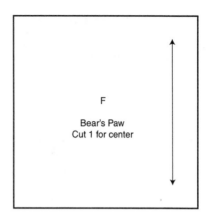

1. Make the templates and decide on the color scheme.

2. Mark and cut out the fabrics, adding on seam allowances.

3. Lay out all the fabric pieces in front of you.

4. Pin the longest side of the triangles (template A) and sew them together. Piece a dark triangle to a background fabric triangle so that it forms a square (see Figure a).

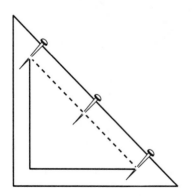

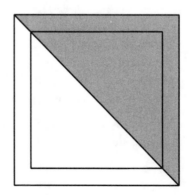

(a) Sew triangles together.

5. Piece the top horizontal row together, using template B for the corner, two combined A triangles, template C, two combined A triangles, and the corner template B (see Figure b). Make another row exactly the same for the bottom row. These form the toenails.

(b) Three rows of Bear's Paw. Just like fitting puzzle pieces together!

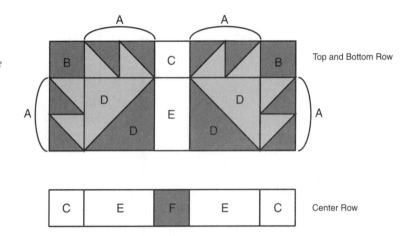

6. Pin and stitch the next row. This row is several pieces thick and forms a unit that combines two triangle A units of the nails, two combined large triangles (template D), rectangle E, then another set of D templates, and the small triangle A nails (see Figure b). Make two of this row.

Sewing the rows of the Bear's Paw block.

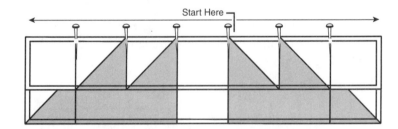

7. Sew together the center row. Piece together rectangle C and rectangle E to center square F, then to piece E, and end with rectangle C.

8. We now have pieced five rows! Wow! Pin and stitch the rows together one at a time, sewing from the inside out. Pin each dot where the seam lines intersect.

9. Press. With so many seam allowances, try to press the rows from the outside to the inside pieces where the pieces are larger.

Clay's Choice

This block was Clay's Choice, and I hope it will be yours. It is a 4 patch, with triangles and squares that form 16 squares. These squares are joined into four 6-inch-square units.

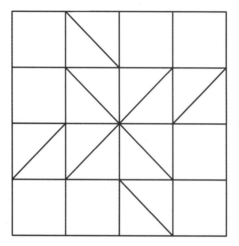

Clay's Choice—a politically inspired block!

There are only two templates, triangle A and square B, but the color placement can make it appear as if there are diamonds. Plan out where you want your colors, because changing the dark color placement will make the patch appear extremely different.

Look how different Clay's Choice can appear by re-arranging colors.

I like the spiraling pinwheel effect this block has; so try out different color schemes.

1. Make the templates and choose the color combination.

2. Mark and cut out the fabric. Then lay the design out in front of where you are working.

Clay's Choice templates—
only two!

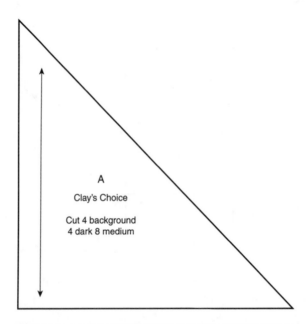

A

Clay's Choice

Cut 4 background
4 dark 8 medium

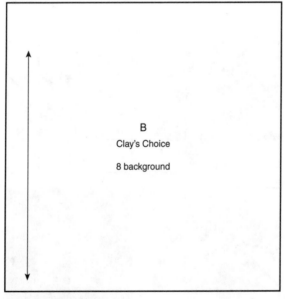

B

Clay's Choice

8 background

3. Pin and sew two A triangles together to form a square. Be sure to pick up the correct color triangle—it is so easy to sew these incorrectly. Pin and check by fitting them into your laid-out pieces.

4. Make the left top unit by sewing the triangles into squares (see Figure a).

5. Stitch two units into the top row, then two units into the bottom row.

6. Sew the rows together (see Figure b). Don't forget to sew from the inside of the center seam to the outside.

7. Press.

Quilting Bee

When sewing two rectangular units of triangle pieces together, flip a unit so that the point of the triangle you are going to seam is on top. Hold up that middle seam allowance, and put a pin in the dots in each side of it. Sew from the inside out. This will make the point line up perfectly.

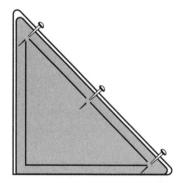
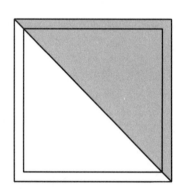

(a) Sew triangles into units.

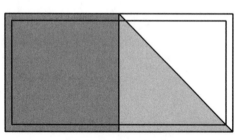

(b) Sew squares into units.

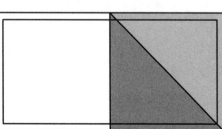

Scraps and Pieces _____

I'm sure you are asking the question, "Who was Clay, and what was his choice?" My husband, the history major, gave me the scoop. Henry Clay was a popular statesman from Kentucky, who actually ran for and lost the presidency three times from 1824 to 1844. He was instrumental in drafting the treaty after the War of 1812 and in attempting to avert the Civil War. His "choice" was probably trying to negotiate between the North and the South. Politics were inspirations for quilters.

Virginia Star

Now for another version of the Eight Point Star. When you look at the block, notice that each diamond is divided into four smaller diamonds.

There are three templates: a small diamond (template A), a square (template B), and a triangle (template C). In all there are 40 pieces. After assembling the diamonds, review the construction of the Eight Point Star in Chapter 9. This patch is also known as the Eastern Star or Blazing Star. I love the way you can select colors that make this block blaze. If you like this block, then you are ready for the largest variation—the Lone Star—but instead of 40 pieces, it may have a thousand!

Virginia Star block. The colors can make it look like a sunburst.

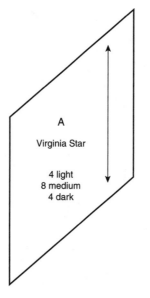

Virginia star templates.

A

Virginia Star

4 light
8 medium
4 dark

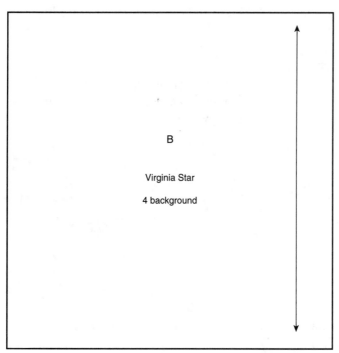

B

Virginia Star

4 background

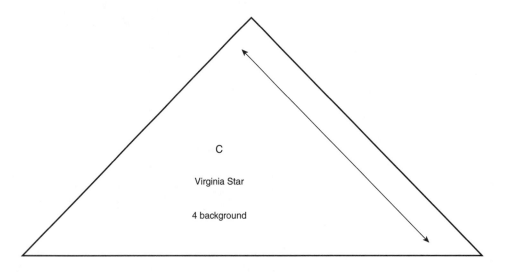

C

Virginia Star

4 background

✰ **Don't Get Stuck!** ___

Be sure you pin into the dots. Don't worry that the seam allowances do not match at the end; it's the dots that count.

1. Make the templates and choose the colors.

2. Mark and cut out the fabrics, adding on seam allowances.

3. Lay out the fabric pieces in front of you.

4. Piece the diamonds together. First flip the tip diamond one to the center diamond two. Pin and sew dot to dot forming a row (see Figure a).

(a) Sewing the small diamonds together into a large diamond unit.

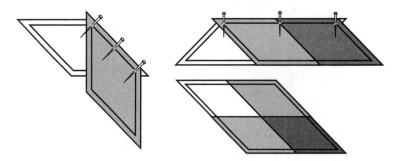

5. Flip, pin, and sew diamond three to four forming another row. (Diamonds two and three are the same color.)

6. Turn the right side of the diamond right sides together with the left side. I know this sounds confusing, but look at Figure b. Sew from the inside seam to the outside.

(b) Press seams in one direction. It will be easier to quilt if the seam allowances are pressed consistently.

7. Sew all diamond units together like the Eight Point Star. Pin two diamonds, right sides together, matching seams of smaller diamonds (see Figure c).

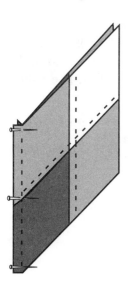
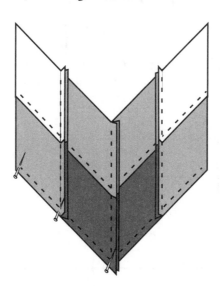

(c) Sewing diamond units together in an Eight Point Star.

8. Sew the square template B around the star alternately with the triangle template C (see Figure d).

9. Press the background seam allowances of the squares and triangles toward the diamonds. Now step back and you can gaze at your star.

(d) Sewing squares and triangles onto the Virginia Star.

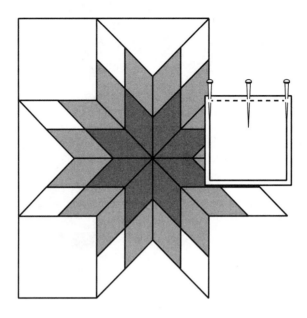

Quilt Talk

A nonreversible template is one that is asymmetrical. If the nonreversible templates are made upside down, the piece will not fit in and is not usable.

Pinwheel

Don't get your head "spinning." This is a great patch but be careful—it's the first block with a *nonreversible template.* If you put a line down the center of the shape, each side of the line is different.

Pinwheel block. These spinning blocks are great for a child's quilt.

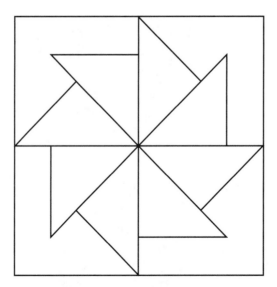

Some students have traced the templates and by mistake drawn the template upside down. When they try to piece the block, they are baffled that the pieces don't fit. I like to cut one of the tricky templates and be sure that it fits before cutting the rest.

This patch has only 16 pieces, so it can be assembled quickly. There are two pattern pieces: a triangle A and the nonreversible trapezoid B. Don't get turned upside down—follow the directions for success:

1. Prepare the templates and choose the colors.

Don't Get Stuck!

With all blocks, remember to match up the dots, not the seam allowances. The seam allowances will hang over the edges. Don't worry, that happens with all triangles and diamonds.

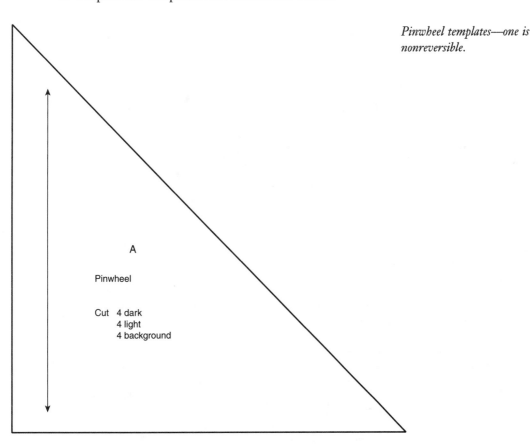

A

Pinwheel

Cut 4 dark
4 light
4 background

Pinwheel templates—one is nonreversible.

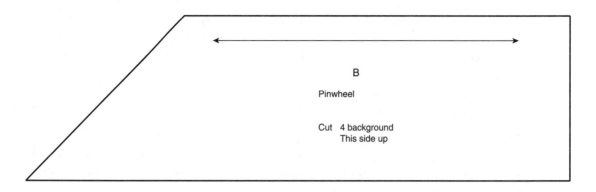

2. Mark and cut out your fabrics, adding on seam allowances.

3. Lay out the pieces in front of you, making certain that the trapezoid pieces fit.

4. Sew the colored triangle A to the trapezoid B, matching the dots. Then pin and stitch (see Figure a).

(a) Sewing a triangle to a trapezoid (templates A and B).

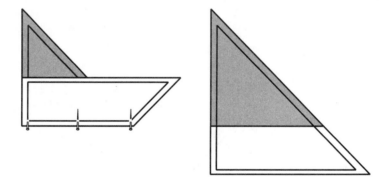

5. Sew a colored triangle A to a background piece A. Match the short sides together, pin into the dots, then fit the pieces into the laid-out pieces on the table. Check that the colored triangle is in the correct place; otherwise your pinwheel won't spin (see Figure b).

(b) These triangles (template A) make up the rest of the Pinwheel block.

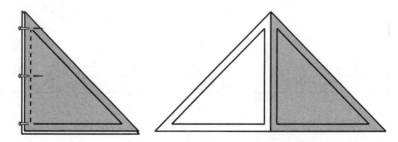

6. Sew these two-pieced triangles (from Figures a and b) together to form a 6-inch square (see Figure c).

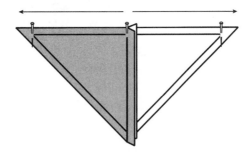

(c) Making 6-inch squares of the Pinwheel.

7. Sew the top two 6-inch squares together, then the bottom two squares to form rows (see Figure d).

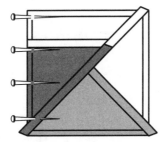

(d) Sew rows together to create the Pinwheel.

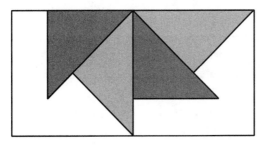

8. Pin the top row to the bottom row, matching the center seam. Sew from the center seam to the outside.

9. Press.

54-40 or Fight

I know you are wondering, so I will tell you—this block was named after a political slogan popular during the 1830s and 1840s. It was a rallying call to support the United States in a border dispute with England over the Oregon territory. Obviously the United States won, because Oregon and Washington are both states.

When you examine this block, it is really only a nine patch, which means nine 4-inch squares are assembled in rows of three.

It is a simple block to piece after the 4-inch square units are assembled. The problem comes when marking your fabric. This is the first block that has mirror-image cutting, necessary when a block has a fabric piece that needs to be duplicated in a reverse fashion.

54-40 or Fight block, a
politically correct block.

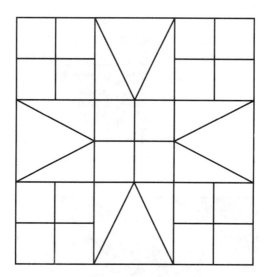

Look at triangular template A. If you try to fold it in half vertically, each side is different, and if you cut out the templates all the same way, half of them will not fit.

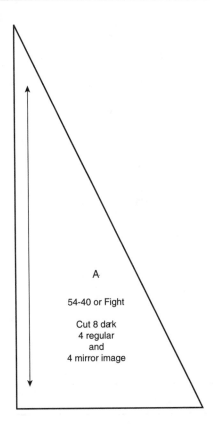

A

54-40 or Fight

Cut 8 dark
4 regular
and
4 mirror image

*54-40 or Fight templates—
one is a mirror-image
template.*

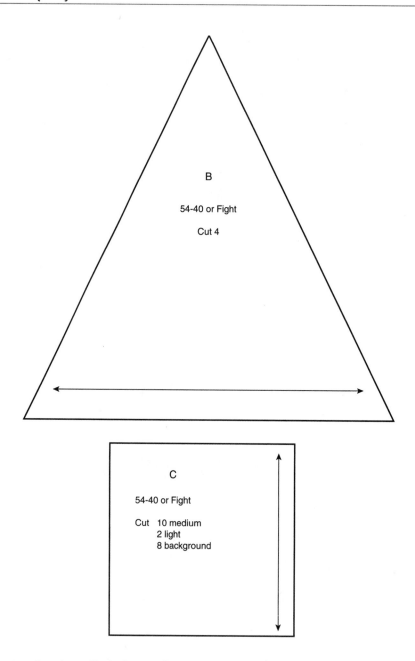

B

54-40 or Fight

Cut 4

C

54-40 or Fight

Cut   10 medium
        2 light
        8 background

The templates usually indicate if any pieces need to be cut in a mirror image. But not all patterns do, so analyze your block for any abnormal-shaped templates.

This block has 3 templates, with 32 pieces in all. You can use three or four different color fabrics. Let's start a rally of our own, but don't fight with this block—it is truly fun to do.

1. Prepare the templates and choose the fabrics.

2. Mark all fabrics, adding on seam allowances. Be certain to cut template A with four pieces cut the normal way and four cut with the sandpaper side up using the mirror-image method.

3. Cut out the fabric, adding on seam allowances, and lay out the patch in front of you.

> **Don't Get Stuck!**
>
> When you trace around a template while the sandpaper side is up, it may slide around, making your markings inaccurate. Be careful to hold the template in place, draw the dots first, and then connect them.

4. Pin the longest side of triangle A to one side of triangle B. Open up the pinned pieces to be sure the correct side is pinned and then sew from dot to dot. Sew the mirror-image piece onto the opposite side of triangle B. This forms a 4-inch square (see Figure a).

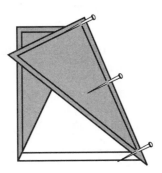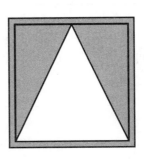

(a) Pin and sew star points for 54-40 or Fight.

5. Pin and stitch four C squares together into two rows to form the corner and center 4-inch squares of the block (see Figure b).

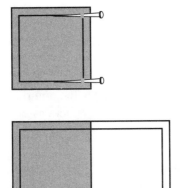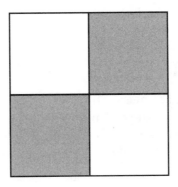

(b) Sew the squares together.

6. Sew the top three 4-inch square units together to form a horizontal row. Then repeat for the middle and bottom rows. There should be three rows of three squares (see Figure c).

(c) Rows of 54-40 or Fight.

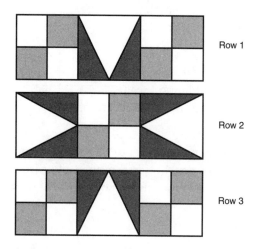

Row 1

Row 2

Row 3

7. Pin and sew the rows together, starting from one of the center seams to the outside, ensuring that the seams align (see Figure d).

Start Here

(d) Top and middle row sewn together.

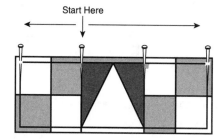

8. Press and give a cheer.

Drunkard's Path

This block is not for beginners! Stitching curves is probably the most challenging of piecework. But I know that you have been marking, cutting, and piecing blocks as you read through this book. If you are comfortable with hand-piecing, maybe now is the time to break away from the straight and narrow.

*Drunkard's Path block—
impossible to walk a straight
line.*

The Drunkard's Path is a very versatile patch. It is created from two templates, an L-shaped template A and an arced wedge B.

Drunkard's Path templates.

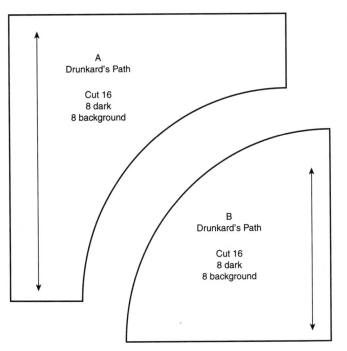

A
Drunkard's Path

Cut 16
8 dark
8 background

B
Drunkard's Path

Cut 16
8 dark
8 background

These two templates fit together to form a 3-inch square. Four of these square units are put together into four rows, making it a four patch quilt. It is really amazing how many variations these templates can create. Books are written just about the Drunkard's Path and its mutations. Pictured are two of my favorite variations: Baby Bunting and Fool's Puzzle.

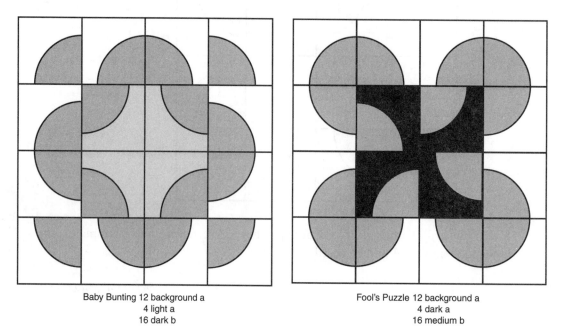

Baby Bunting 12 background a
4 light a
16 dark b

Fool's Puzzle 12 background a
4 dark a
16 medium b

Baby Bunting and Fool's Puzzle variations.

Fabric choices are usually limited to two colors for the Drunkard's Path and possibly three fabrics for the Baby Bunting and Fool's Puzzle. Follow the directions carefully:

1. Make the templates and choose your fabrics.

2. Mark templates onto the fabric, marking the center of each seam line with a dot. Add on the ¼-inch seam allowances, and cut out.

3. Place the L-shaped piece A and the wedge-shaped piece B right sides together. Match the center dots and pin (see Figure a). It doesn't look like it will fit, but don't worry, it will.

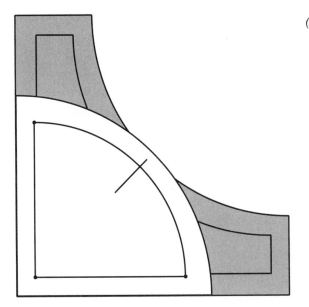

(a) Match the center dots.

4. Move the top wedge, forcing the end dot on one side to match. Pin into the dot. Re-adjust the pieces until the dots at the other end align and pin. I put nine pins into the seam line to hold the curve in place (see Figure b).

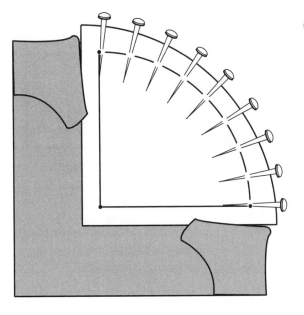

(b) Pin the seam line.

5. Start sewing about ⅛ inch away from the dot on one side, first stitching a back-stitch into the dot. Using the hand-piecing stitch, sew on the seam line, removing pins as you sew. Be careful to ease the fabric so there are no folds in the seam (see Figure c). Make all 16 square units.

(c) Curve sewn and pressed toward the concave curve.

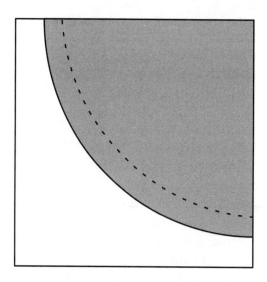

6. Press the curved seam allowances of the wedge toward the L-shaped square (see Figure d).

(d) Rows of Drunkard's Path.

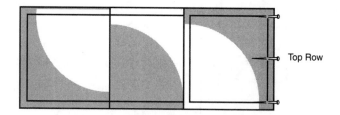

Top Row

Quilting Bee

Some people like to start sewing in the middle of a curved seam where the dot is and then stitch to the end of the seam.

7. Lay out all the squares on a table to form the pattern of the block.

8. Sew all squares in the top horizontal row together and then sew each of the other remaining three rows.

9. Pin and sew the rows together to make the block.

10. Press.

The Least You Need to Know

◆ Take extra care when making asymmetrical-shaped templates; they are nonreversible.

◆ Some patches have mirror-image pieces that are similar but exactly reversed.

◆ Some blocks are pieced on the diagonal.

◆ Curved piecework is difficult—match up the dots, pin, and sew the seam line to prevent tucks and folds.

11

Combination Pieced and Appliqué Blocks

In This Chapter

◆ Understanding combined, pieced, and appliquéd blocks

◆ Steps for applying fabric motifs to your blocks

◆ Learning to make some of the most popular combination appliqué and pieced patterns

In this chapter, we ease into appliqué with blocks that start with piecing the pattern, and finish with some appliqué.

Appli-What?

Appliqué is a French term that means to apply or lay on. In appliqué quilting, small pieces of fabric or a pieced unit are cut into a specific design that is then stitched by hand or machine onto a background fabric.

Quilt Talk _____

In **reverse appliqué**, you layer one or more fabrics under your block and cut designs away from the top of the block to show the bottom color. The fabric is then held in place by the appliqué stitch.

Appliquéd quilts can be either graceful and sophisticated or cute and folksy. The patterns can range from elegant flowers to stylized designs of animals, birds, houses, or almost anything else. There are several different methods of tackling appliqué. You can appliqué individual motifs (the teardrop shape in the Honey Bee), pieced units (the plate of the Dresden Plate), or use the totally different method called *reverse appliqué*, where small amounts of a fabric show through your patchwork.

Let's Learn the Basic Steps of Appliqué

Several steps are involved in making an appliqué block. You may want to skip some of these steps, but please don't.

1. Cut out the fabric pieces, mark, and sew together if necessary.

2. Sew a line of *stay stitching*, a small basting stitch, on the sewing line using a contrasting color.

3. Pin under the raw edges and, for beginners, baste these outer seam allowances down. This will prevent the edges from raveling.

4. Press using an up-and-down motion. Because fabric is so pliable, be sure not to use a side-to-side motion because it might stretch your motif out of shape.

5. Pin your appliqué piece into position.

6. Baste your appliqué piece onto your background fabric.

Quilt Talk _____

Stay stitching is a line of small basting stitches that hold the fabric in its proper shape and make it easier to turn the raw edges under. Be sure to use a contrasting color thread so it is easy to see and remove later.

7. It's time to use the appliqué stitch discussed in Chapter 6. Try to invisibly stitch your motif securely into place.

8. Take out all basting stitches so that the beauty of your block will show.

9. Press.

Beginners sometimes avoid appliqué because they think it is difficult. Don't let yourself be scared off.

Dresden Plate

The Dresden Plate is one of the most popular appliqué blocks. It is believed that this patch was named for a china plate made by a factory in Dresden, Germany. This patch became popular in the 1850s. You can almost see a pioneer woman, needing a quilt pattern take one of her dishes, trace around it, and then cut it into wedges. Instant quilt templates!

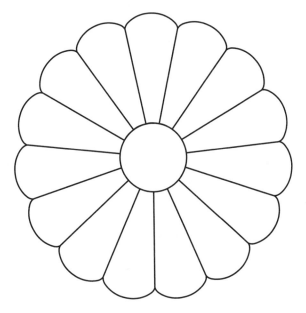

Dresden Plate with 15 wedges. Does this look like your china?

The Dresden Plate can be made in many different sizes and styles. I've seen as few as 12 wedges and as many as 20. The patches can be 10 inches to 24 inches in size. The colors can range from 2, so that the plate looks like spokes of a wheel, all the way up to 20, with each wedge in a different fabric. Wedges can be rounded or pointed. If you have more than one type of Dresden Plate in your template collection, be sure to keep them separate. You don't want to confuse them and try to fit a 20-wedge plate for a 24-inch square onto a 12-inch block.

Our pattern for the Dresden Plate is 12 inches square and the plate has 15 wedges of either 3 or 5 different fabrics. There are two templates: a wedge A and center circle B.

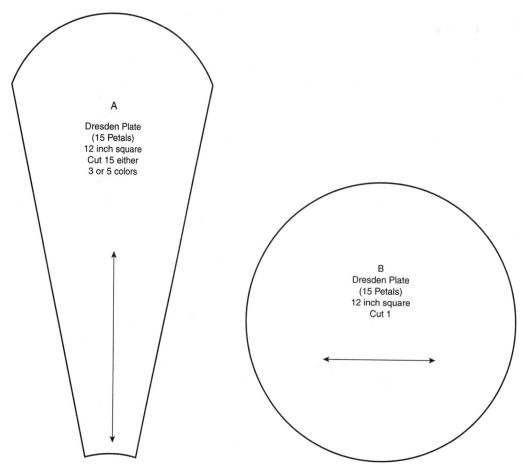

Dresden Plate templates. Cut your fabric carefully.

Quilting Bee

Before you start to sew, lay out your pieces on a square of flannel or felt as discussed in Chapter 8. You will avoid picking up the wrong piece when it is sitting right in front of you. And you will be able to clean up your work quickly by simply rolling up the flannel with your pieces safely clinging to it.

1. Prepare your templates made out of poster board and sandpaper as discussed in Chapter 6.

2. Cut a generous 12½-inch square out of your background fabric.

3. Mark and cut the wedges, adding on the seam allowances. If you are using three fabrics, cut five of each fabric; if you are using five fabrics, cut three of each one.

4. Lay the plate out on the table in front of you. Decide on the correct placement of your fabrics. There should be a set sequence in the

progression of fabrics; for example, a yellow, green, and blue wedge, then repeating yellow, green, and blue wedges in the same order all around the plate.

5. Pick up two wedges that are next to each other and put their right sides together. Pin into the dots you marked at each end. Put the pins right into the dots perpendicular to the seam line (see Figure a).

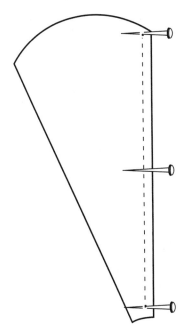

(a) Pinning the wedges together.

6. Sew from dot to dot, backstitching at each end. Do not sew the right-hand turn that goes through the seam allowance. This is one of the few times when the seams are pressed open.

7. Put the wedges back down onto your plate pattern and pick up the next wedge, pin, and sew. It is so easy to pick up the wrong wedge or pin it on the wrong side.

8. Sew the wedges all around, like spokes of a wheel, to form the plate.

9. Press the seams open. You should press these seams open because the square background fabric adds stability (see Figure b).

Don't Get Stuck!

Remember, before you sew your Dresden Plate, check that you pinned correctly. Put the wedges back into the plate to make sure. If the color pattern is not correct, repin the wedge.

(b) Press the seams open and baste on the outer seam line.

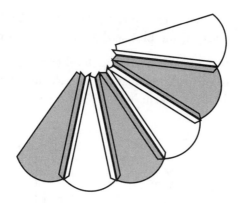

10. With a contrasting thread, baste along the outside rounded seam line. Your basting will show where to turn the raw edges under. Turn the edges under to prevent raveling, and then baste.

11. Center the plate on the background block. You can easily find the middle by folding the block diagonally in both directions and finger pressing. If you hold or pinch the fabric, it will temporarily press it and an X should appear at the center of the open part of the plate.

12. Baste with a large stitch through the middle of each wedge up to within an inch of the outer edge. This will hold the plate securely in place to the background.

13. Now it's time to appliqué. Use lots of pins to hold down the rounded outer edge. I usually use at least five pins for each wedge. Turn under the seam allowance of one wedge and pin under each end where the dots are. Be sure to turn under right on the basting line. Then pin the center of the wedge at the top of the arc, and put one or two more pins on each side. Pin only two wedges at a time (see Figure c).

14. Appliqué around the entire block. Refer to Chapter 8 to review the appliqué stitch.

15. Cut the center circle B. Be sure to add the seam allowances. The center circle can be any of the colors of the plate or the background fabric.

16. Baste on the sewing line with a contrasting color thread, and then turn the seam under and baste again. Pin into position, and baste the circle onto the plate so it will not move. Appliqué around the center.

Don't Get Stuck!

Be sure to use a contrasting thread when basting. It will be easy to see when you have to take the basting stitch out. Nothing's worse than ripping out your appliqué stitch by mistake!

Quilting Bee

Try to take away any points on your rounded edge by pushing them in with your needle as you sew.

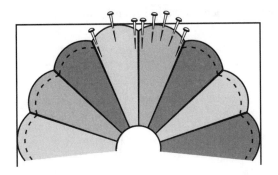

(c) Pin your plate to the background.

17. Remove all the basting threads.

18. Press.

The Dresden Plate is a wonderful block that uses both piecing and appliqué techniques. Many antique Dresden Plate quilts use the wedge-shape pieces side by side around the border, giving the appearance of cones surrounding the quilt, hence the name ice cream border. Can you imagine piecing hundreds of the wedges for a border? When you see the scalloped-edge results, you will appreciate the workmanship even more.

Grandmother's Fan

The Grandmother's Fan is an easy appliqué pattern that has 6 wedges positioned in the corner of a 12-inch block. The fan was very popular during the Victorian era when it was made with velvets, satins, and brocade fabrics. It was decorated with lace and elegant embroidery. It can also be successfully made with pastel fabrics for a crib quilt.

Quilting Bee

Grandmother's Fan is a great pattern for using up all your scraps, because it is made with a variety of colors and fabrics.

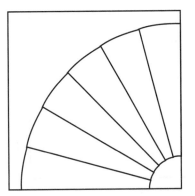

Grandmother's Fan block. Do you have a fan like this in your attic?

This block has two pattern pieces: a wedge A and a quarter circle for the corner piece, template B.

Grandmother's Fan templates.

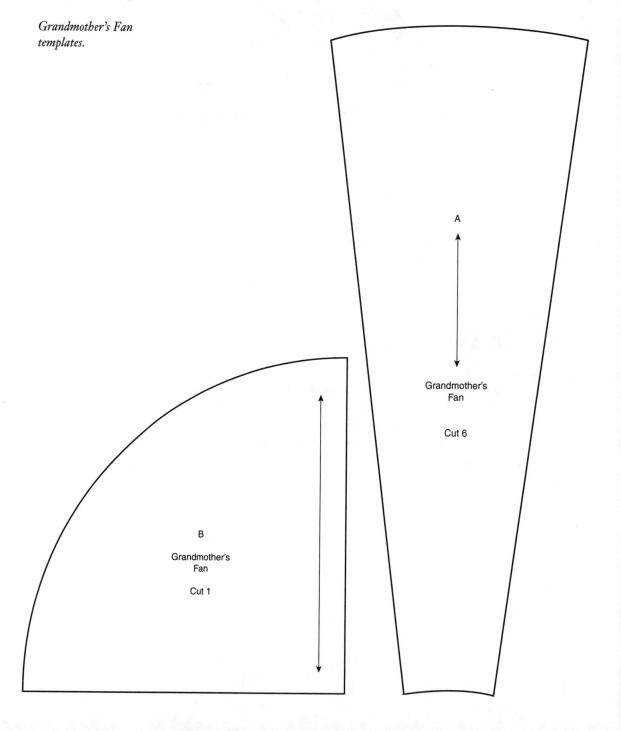

A

Grandmother's
Fan

Cut 6

B
Grandmother's
Fan

Cut 1

Following are step-by-step directions:

1. Prepare the templates.

2. Cut a generous 12½-inch square out of your background fabric.

3. Mark and cut out six A wedges from your fabrics and one corner piece, adding on the seam allowances.

4. Lay out wedges in a pleasing progression of colors.

5. Sew together the pieces of the fan.

6. Press the seams open; the background fabric will add stability.

7. Turn the ¼-inch seam allowance under on the wide part of the fan. Baste with a contrasting-color thread, turning under the seam allowance as you sew (see Figure a). This will prevent fraying edges.

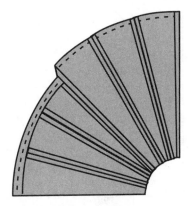

(a) Press the seams open.

8. If you want to put lace or piping on your Grandmother's Fan, this is the time. Baste the lace or piping to the edge as you baste the seam allowances under.

9. Pin the fan into the corner of the square and baste down the center of each wedge.

10. Appliqué the fan onto the background.

11. Now for the corner piece template B: Turn the ¼-inch seam allowance of the curved edge under and baste it down. Pin it in the corner and appliqué it to the fan.

12. Press.

If you are making a quilt out of only Grandmother's Fans, there are many interesting ways to arrange the blocks. You can attach the blocks with or without lattices.

Honey Bee Patch

The Honey Bee block is a nine patch within a nine patch with bee bodies and bee wings appliquéd on top. It is different from the previous appliqué blocks because the base of the patch has to be completely pieced before you appliqué the teardrop bee pieces.

There is a checkerboard in the center of the pieced patch with the outer square forming the head of the bees. This patch has four pattern pieces and can be made with either two, three, or four different fabrics. I once had a beginner student who loved this pattern and made a whole quilt with 30 Honey Bee blocks. The first few blocks were fun, but by number 30, she dreaded those bee wings. We figured there were 30 blocks and 12 teardrops on each block, so that added up to 360 teardrops appliquéd onto her patches!

Honey Bee block: Look at the four "bees."

Honey Bee templates.

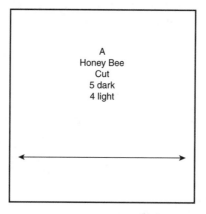

A
Honey Bee
Cut
5 dark
4 light

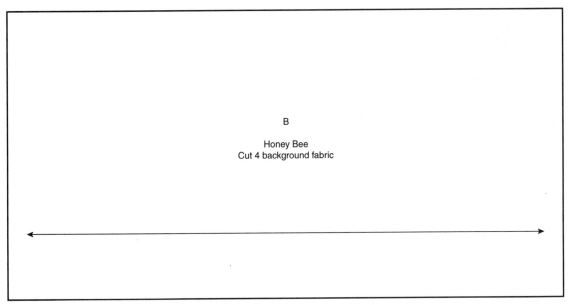

B

Honey Bee
Cut 4 background fabric

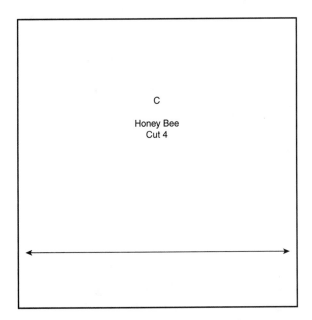

C

Honey Bee
Cut 4

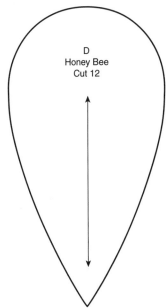

D
Honey Bee
Cut 12

Here are the steps to follow for making a Honey Bee block:

1. Make the templates.

2. Mark and cut out the pattern pieces, adding on seam allowances.

3. Using piece A, assemble the middle checkerboard by sewing squares together row by row, as discussed in Chapter 8.

4. Sew the rectangles to each side of the checkerboard.

5. Sew the top and bottom rows together using template C, (two large squares) to template B. Then sew rectangle B to each side of the checkerboard center. Sew three rows together to form the pieced base of the block (see Figure a).

(a) Sew rows of Honey Bee together.

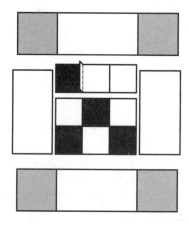

Quilting Bee

Remember to start sewing the middle sections of a row first, and then sew out to the ends of the patch. We want to make sure that the seams that form the corners match. Always sew from one of the middle seams to the outside edge.

6. Sew the rows together forming the 12-inch square base. Pin into the dots at each end of the row and pin at each intersecting seam.

7. Now it's time to sew on the bees. Baste on the seam line of the teardrops to make a line of stay stitching. First turn under the tip of the teardrop, then turn under the raw edges on your basting line and baste this seam down.

8. Position bee pieces. Pin and appliqué.

9. Press.

Look at how different the Honey Bee can appear by varying the positions of the colors.

Peony Patch

What does this block remind you of? If you study the Peony block you will notice that it is very similar to the Eight Point Star discussed in Chapter 9. We even use the same diamond, triangle, and square templates.

Peony patch. This was probably created in the spring when the pioneer women grew these beautiful flowers.

The background of this block is pieced, and then the stem and leaves are appliquéd on top:

1. Make the templates.

2. Cut a 12½ by 3½-inch rectangle of background fabric.

3. Mark and cut out the fabric pieces, adding on the ¼-inch seam allowances and lay out the block in front of you.

4. Start by picking up two diamonds and sewing them from dot to dot with the right sides together. Sew all six diamonds together to form the petals (see Figure a).

5. Sew on the triangles and squares in the correct positions. Be sure to sew from the widest part of the diamond to the tip of the points.

Don't Get Stuck!

Remember to always sew from the inside of the patch to the outer seam allowance. We want to make sure the squares and triangles will lay flat and all the dots line up.

6. Sew the background rectangle onto the bottom of the block.

7. Prepare the appliqué stem and leaves. Baste along the seam allowances. Turn the tip of the leaves down then baste all around, turning under the raw edges. Use a contrasting-color thread to baste (see Figure b).

Peony templates—the Peony block uses many of the same pattern pieces as the Eight Point Star.

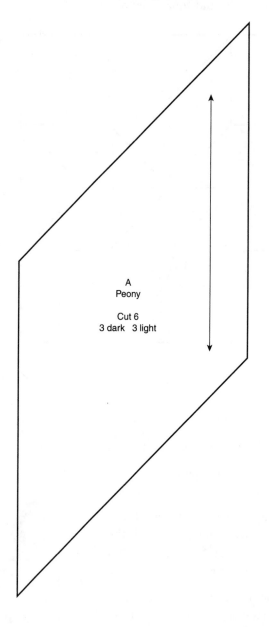

A
Peony

Cut 6
3 dark   3 light

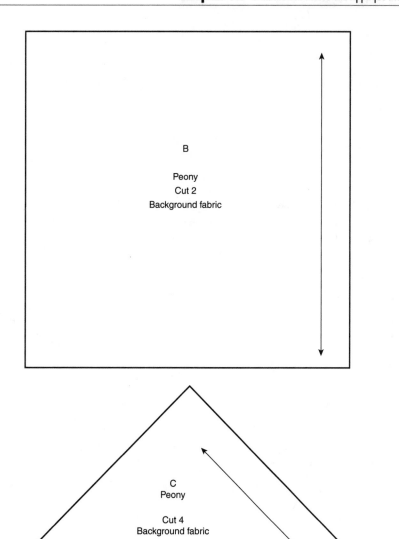

B

Peony
Cut 2
Background fabric

C
Peony

Cut 4
Background fabric

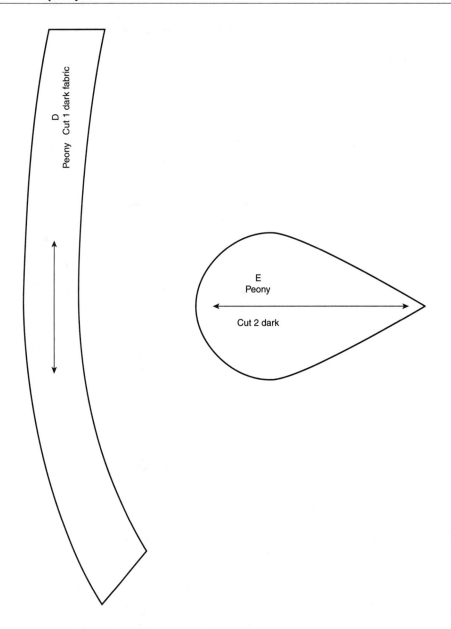

D

Peony Cut 1 dark fabric

E
Peony

Cut 2 dark

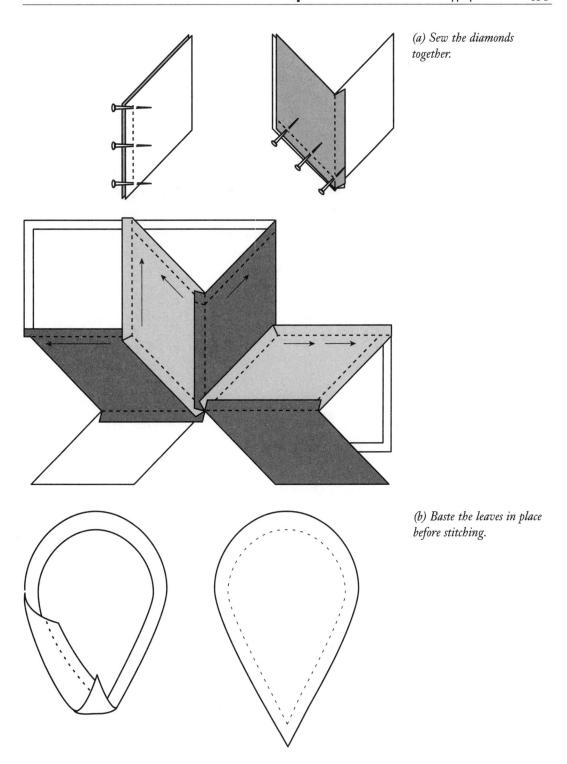

(a) Sew the diamonds together.

(b) Baste the leaves in place before stitching.

8. Appliqué the leaves and stems into place.

9. Remove all basting stitches, press, and you have your Peony.

These quilt blocks are getting us ready for traditional appliqué, where shaping is so important for a visual picture.

The Least You Need to Know

◆ Identifying the difference between patchwork and appliqué pieces will help you choose blocks equal to your ability.

◆ When you decide to appliqué, make sure you complete all the necessary steps to ensure the edges will not ravel.

◆ Baste on the seam line to stay stitch your appliqué design.

◆ Look at the fabric motif—if it has a point (the teardrop in the Honey Bee or leaves in the Peony or a heart), be sure you turn it under first, and then baste.

◆ Press using an up-and-down motion so that your appliqué fabric will not stretch.

12

Traditional Appliqué Block Patterns: Add a Layer to Your Quilt

In This Chapter

- ◆ Reviewing techniques of traditional appliqué
- ◆ Alternative methods of preparing fabric for appliqué
- ◆ Specialty stitches for decorating appliqué pieces
- ◆ Preparing traditional appliqué blocks

Traditional appliqué motifs are separate pieces of fabric that form pictorial designs when positioned in a set pattern. The cutout shapes of fabric need to have the edges turned under then sewn to the background or base fabric. The traditional appliqué differs from the combined pieced and appliqué blocks in that there is very little or no hand piecing in these patches.

This chapter reviews handy hints for creating appliqué, and you'll get directions for tackling some of the most popular traditional appliqué blocks. I'll show you some interesting and unusual methods to prepare appliqué pieces and also easier ways to finish fabric edges. Soon you will be "painting" your quilts with fabric designs and loving it.

Strange Ways to Check Your Frays

It's time for your traditional appliqué to take shape. Each fabric piece, cut from the templates, needs to get "finished off" to remove all the edges that may ravel or fray. Turning under the edges may be done as described in Chapter 11.

The fabric shapes must be exact so they will look like the design. As you are working with fabric pictures, you will be using your iron to press these pieces into shapes. As you press, you may have to manipulate the edges to get them to lay flat. Small indentations around the outside need to be turned under and pressed. But deep Vs (such as those on the outer edge of the center of the Hearts All Around) need to be clipped. Clipping means making one small cut into the seam allowance allowing that fabric to lie flat when turned under. Make a clip toward the dot at the bottom of the V.

> **Don't Get Stuck!**
>
> Be sure to clip the seam allowance to within a few threads from the dot. Do not cut all the way to the dot because the fabric may ravel and cause a hole in your quilt. Spray starching may alleviate stretching, or use a product called Fray Check to prevent raveling.

Press the seam allowance down by putting the tip of the iron right by the dot, spreading the seam. On concave curves, if the seams do not lie flat, clip the allowance a few times throughout the curve, and then press down. Don't let these patterns throw you a "curve."

Pressing indentations and curves.

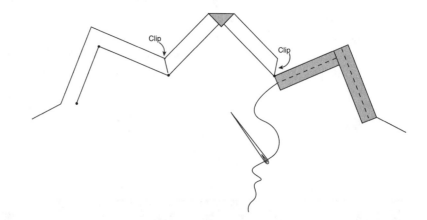

I've already described the traditional steps to prepare your fabric designs for appliqué in Chapter 11. Quilters have created several unique methods that are slightly different and that you may want to try. You may need some strange materials like spray starch, freezer paper, or even used dryer sheets in your quest to make your appliqué pictures. Check out each method and see which one you prefer.

Spray Starch Your Templates

In this method you are going to iron the template itself.

Prepare the template, then mark and cut out your fabric design. Cut out a second template made only of cardboard—you should not put sandpaper on the back because you don't want any glue on this pattern. Put your fabric wrong side up so you can see the markings. Spray a fine mist of starch over the seam allowances around the edge of the fabric. Match the cardboard template with the markings. Don't use steam, but a dry, hot iron. Carefully iron the seam allowances over the template, making a firm crease on the sewing line. Remove the cardboard template and you should have a perfect shape. Turn the fabric piece to the right side and press again. This forms the sharpest motif of all the following methods, but some quilters still prefer the other techniques.

Plastic Templates Only

This method of appliqué needs a plastic template, water-soluble glue, and masking tape. Sheets of plastic can be purchased in craft and art stores in squares the size of poster board.

Mark and cut out your fabric motif adding on ¼-inch seam allowances. Position the plastic template on the wrong side of the fabric motif. Using a water-soluble glue stick, spread glue around the outer edges of the plastic pattern. Turn the seam allowances onto the glued edge. Press with your fingers to hold the seam allowances down.

Turn the fabric motif with the template right side up and position it onto the block's background. Use masking tape on the right side of the block to hold the motif into place. You don't need pins! Turn to the wrong side of the block, and carefully fold the background under the motif. The plastic template will hold this fold rigid. Using the appliqué stitch or a *whipstitch*, sew the piece into place, stitching from the wrong side of the background. The stitches should catch the end of the background and the

Quilt Talk

A **whipstitch** is similar to the appliqué stitch. It holds two finished edges together with tiny straight stitches. The fabrics are folded back on each other and the needle is inserted at a right angle to the edge from the back fabric to the front.

motif, hitting the plastic template so the stitches should not go through to the front of the block.

Turn to the wrong side of the block, fold the fabric over the template, and take small stitches around the pattern through the fabric motif and background.

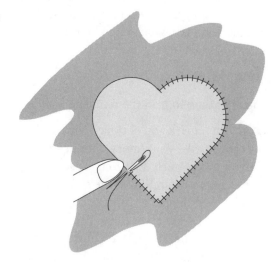

Now I know you're are thinking that the template is still inside, and you are right. We have to remove the plastic pattern. Turn the block over so the wrong side of the background fabric is facing up. With sharp small scissors, make a cut into the background fabric and trim it away to ¼ inch from the stitches. Pull out the template.

This technique makes a stabilized, perfectly shaped motif but is not for the faint of heart. Beginners are hesitant to cut and trim out that background, and you do have to be careful not to clip into the right side of the block.

Trim away the background to take out the plastic template.

Freezer Paper

You may think this is crazy, but you can use freezer paper from the supermarket to make appliquéing easier. This method is similar to the template method, but the background of the block is not trimmed out. Trace the templates onto the dull side of the freezer paper; do not add on any seam allowances. Cut the freezer paper out on the traced lines. Pin all the shapes shiny side down on the wrong side of your fabric. Press these onto the fabric using an iron set at a low temperature. The freezer paper will stick to the fabric. Now add on the ¼-inch seam allowances around the outside edge and cut around the shapes. Press, turning under the seam allowances, so that when folded the fabric sticks to the freezer paper. Pin the piece into position on the background of the block and start stitching the appliqué into place. When you are almost finished sewing the design, pull the freezer paper out through the small opening, and then complete appliquéing on the motif.

Iron freezer paper onto fabric, cut out around shapes, and press under the seam allowance.

Dryer Sheet Method

This is the technique that I like to use when preparing hearts, flowers, or any freestanding shape for appliqué, because the appliqué will turn out the perfect shape as long as you can sew accurately. It does require using the sewing machine to create small, stable stitches. It's great for recycling all those dryer sheets after they have been used and used and used so all the scented finish has been removed. That's when we are ready to use them in our quilts. Here's how.

Mark the wrong side of the fabric with the tem-plates. Cut out, adding ¼-inch seam allowances. Pin the right side of the fabric to a dryer sheet (see Figure a). Sew by machine on the marked seam line.

Clip and trim the seam allowances (see Figure b). Carefully pull the dryer sheet away from the fabric and put a small cut into the sheet.

Be careful when cutting the dryer sheet not to cut into the fabric.

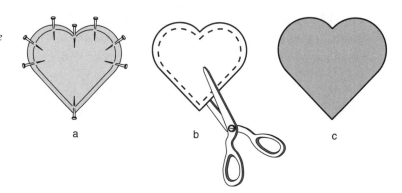

a   b   c

Pull the right side of the fabric through the dryer sheet cut, turning it inside out to form the fabric motif. Press out the design so that it is the correct shape. I sometimes use a pointer, a sewing tool, or an orange stick, which is a pointed stick used to push back your cuticles when manicuring your nails. Press.

Pin and baste the fabric motif into the correct position. Then appliqué. This gives a good stabilized base so that appliquéing is easy, and there is no chance of the edges raveling. The dryer sheet remains attached and is thin enough that quilting through it is a breeze.

Appliqué on the Bias

Chapter 5 discussed the bias grainline. Now it's time to use that bias. Small strips of fabric, cut on the bias, are used for stems of flowers. It is easier to appliqué *bias strips*, or fabric that is cut on the bias, because they curve and bend without puckering.

Measure and cut on the bias the amount designated for the stem. For most, cut the length of the stem 1 inch wide.

Quilt Talk

Bias strips are cut on the diagonal of the fabric. Find the finished selvage and fold it up on a perpendicular angle. The diagonal that is formed is the true bias.

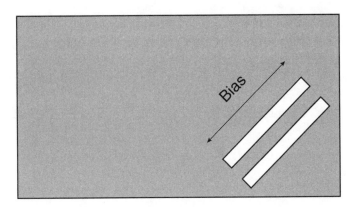

Cutting bias stems.

Fold the fabric in half all the way down the length, wrong sides together, forming a long tube, matching the raw edges. Sew by hand or machine ¼ inch down the long side with the raw edges. Shift the seam line so that it is in the middle of the tube. Press flat so that the seam doesn't show.

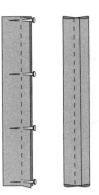

Sew down the long edge to make a tube and press.

Position the stem so the seam does not show, then pin and appliqué. This way makes appliquéing easy because the tube that is formed will not change size or ravel. Now you can draw your stem lines with bias and they will stretch whichever way you want.

Decorative Stitching for Appliqué

Sometimes when you appliqué, you can use decorative stitches to embellish your designs for a country look. I like the blanket stitch or the buttonhole stitch. They are similar, but the buttonhole stitches are closer together. When you use these stitches to hold the fabric design, the piece to be sewn on should be pinned and basted into position. It can also be held in place with a *fusible fabric* webbing like (Wonder Under or Stitch Witchery) inserted in between the fabric design and the background of the block. When the design is secure, use a decorative stitch to embellish the edge.

The blanket stitches worked from the left to the right with the edge of the fabric facing toward you. Bring your first stitch up from under the block background into the edge of the fabric design. Point the needle toward you and insert it about ¼ inch above the edge and over from the first stitch and into the fabric design. Be sure to keep the thread under your needle. Push the needle through the edge of the fabric design and the thread loop. Then take another stitch ¼ inch over, repeating the process.

The blanket stitch gives your appliqué a country look.

Put Your Techniques to Work

It's time for you to practice what I've preached. The blocks in this chapter exemplify pure traditional appliqué. Look through each block's directions and decide which finishing methods you want to use to turn under the edges of your fabric designs.

Hearts All Around

This patch has 12 hearts surrounding a "pointed" circle. The base of the hearts touch the points of the center. When preparing this patch for a Sampler quilt, it is a good foil for the rounded look of the Dresden Plate. By the time the block is completed, you will be an expert on folding under the points of the seam allowances and making hearts.

Hearts All Around: This block will steal your heart.

There are two templates, a pointed, circular center (template A), and a heart (template B). The 12 hearts can be cut in 2, 3, or 4 colors—whatever your heart's desire.

Several years ago one of my overachiever students made an entire quilt of Hearts All Around blocks within a month! Her husband had just passed away, and this quilt helped her work through her grief. My class was admiring her workmanship and I mentioned that her fabric looked unusual. She said that she used fabrics cut up from her husband's shirts. I said that it still looked like strange shirt fabrics. She finally admitted that she did make several hearts by cutting up boxer shorts! Recycling started with the pioneer women's frugality.

1. Prepare the templates and choose the fabrics.

2. Mark your fabrics and add on the ¼-inch seam allowances; then cut.

3. Cut out the background patch by marking a 12-inch square, then add half an inch all the way around. I like to make seam allowances slightly larger to accommodate all the handling and raveling that may occur. Be sure to mark the normal seam line so that you don't position the design so it is too spread out.

Quilting Bee

When choosing a fabric for a Hearts All Around quilt, pick a well-woven fabric that doesn't ravel or stretch for the center of the block. Manipulating all those points and Vs in the center would be a disaster with a flimsy fabric.

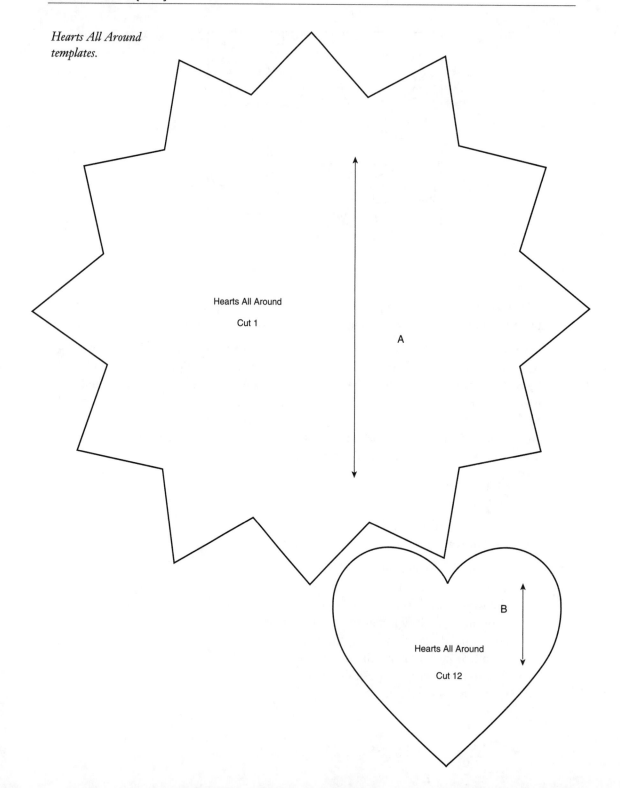

Hearts All Around templates.

Hearts All Around

Cut 1

A

B

Hearts All Around

Cut 12

4. Prepare the center template A. Turn under the tip of the point; then fold under the seam allowances. Mark the dots accurately and clip the seam allowances almost to the point of the V, as illustrated. Baste the seam allowances down as you go around the center.

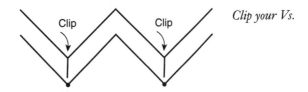

Clip your Vs.

5. Position the center piece in the middle of the background fabric. Pin and baste around the outside edge.

6. Appliqué around the outer edge of the center piece.

7. Prepare the hearts for appliqué in your favorite method explained in the beginning of this chapter.

8. Position the hearts so their tips just about touch the points of the center piece. Pin and baste down; then appliqué.

9. Remove the basting and press.

Tulip Block

Let's try to draw a picture with our fabrics. Tulips are a Pennsylvania Dutch or Amish motif. This block has four tulips with intersecting stems that make an X pattern on the background fabric.

Tulip block. Tulips symbolize love in quilts.

There are three templates: tulip base (template A), tulip petal (template B), and leaves (template C). We'll use bias strips to make the stems.

Each tulip can be made with two different colors, or you can have distinctive color combinations for each tulip. Don't worry if you don't have any green fabric in your color scheme. You may choose a fabric with a dark value for the stems and leaves. Get a green thumb, and grow tulips.

Quilting Bee

As you are appliquéing a block, the background fabric can ravel and stretch. It is always better to have more seam allowance and cut off the excess when the patch is complete, because you can't add on.

1. Prepare the templates, and choose the fabrics.

2. Mark, then add on ¼-inch seam allowances for traditional appliqué. Cut out the fabric designs.

3. Cut out the background fabric by marking a 12-inch square. Cut the seam allowances half an inch larger all the way around.

4. Fold the background square in half on the diagonals. Then fold it on the horizontal and vertical fold. Baste on these lines to help the placement of the stems.

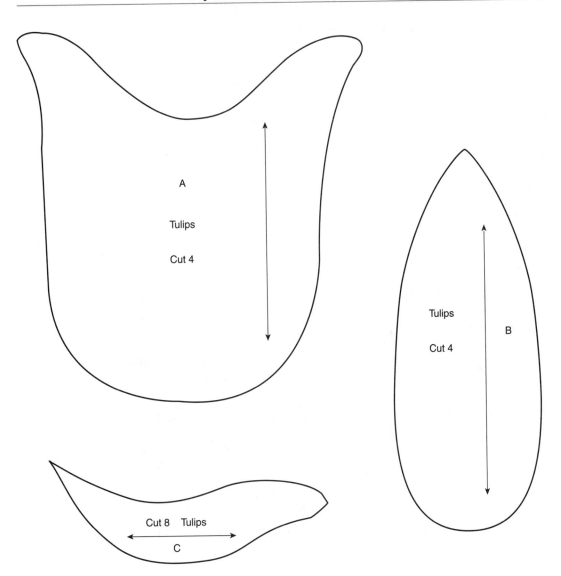

Tulip block templates.

Fold the background in half and baste on those lines.

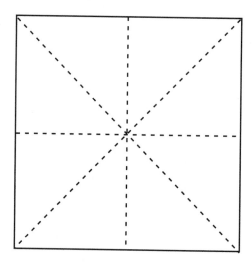

5. Make the stems. Cut two bias strips 1 inch by 6 inches. Fold them lengthwise, wrong sides together, and sew a ¼-inch seam down the long side forming a tube. See the beginning of the chapter for more details on stems.

6. Position and pin-baste the bias stems on the X diagonals. Baste and appliqué the stems to the block background (see Figure a).

(a) Appliqué stems into position.

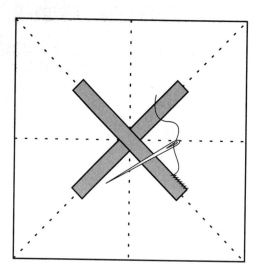

7. Prepare the tulip base (template A). Turn under the tips and baste under the seam allowances. Clip the curved edge and baste (see Figure b).

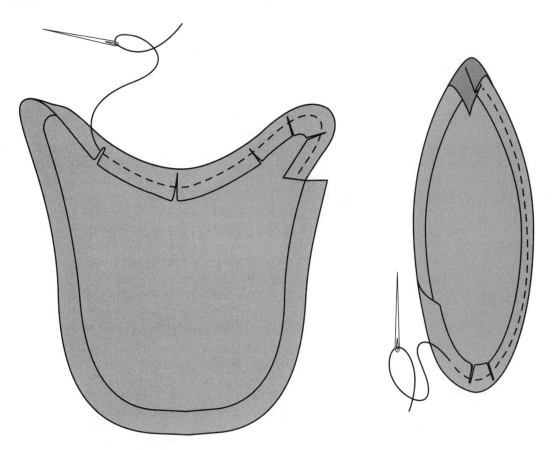

(b) Clip curves and turn under tips.

8. Place the tulip piece A into position at the end of the stems.

9. Prepare the leaves, template C, turning under tips first, then basting around the outside edge.

10. Put the leaves in position with their ends touching the stems. Pin and baste into place.

11. Appliqué around all the leaves and tulips.

12. Prepare the tulip petal B, turning under the seam allowances and basting around. Apply on top of the tulip base. Baste and appliqué to the tulip base A (see Figure c).

13. Remove all basting—and there is a lot of it!

14. Press.

(c) Place tulips on stems.

The Least You Need to Know

- Clipping the seam allowance close to a dot or seam line allows the seam to be pressed flat.

- Spray starch the appliqué designs and press the seam allowances under to make crisp creases.

- Press the seam allowance of an appliqué motif around the design's cardboard template or freezer paper.

- Strips made out of bias fabric can stretch and curve easily and are great for stems.

- Use basting lines to mark the diagonal, horizontal, and vertical lines of the background to aid in appliqué placement.

- If a portion of an appliqué motif is hidden under another piece, you don't have to finish that edge.

Chapter 13

Use Your Sewing Machine: Machine-Pieced Blocks

In This Chapter

- ◆ Getting your sewing machine ready for quilting
- ◆ Choosing and modifying patchwork patterns for the machine
- ◆ Hints on machine piecing
- ◆ Directions for machine piecing Log Cabin and Rail Fence blocks

To create machine-made quilts, you first have to really be proficient, and second, enjoy using the sewing machine. It is more difficult to handle piecing the blocks—you will need sound eye-hand, and even eye-foot, coordination. To make your life easier, choose a patch that lends itself to machine sewing, and modify the templates by including the ¼-inch seam allowances. Special techniques, like strip piecing and chaining, make machine piecing even faster. If you know how to sew and enjoy it, this chapter is for you.

Pressure but No Pain—Your Machine Tension

Knowing your sewing machine and its proper use is utmost in the piecing and quilting process. Be sure your machine is in good working order. Let's learn about parts of the sewing machine so we know the proper terminology. I hate to be talking about the feed dogs and have you think this book is about animals! Get out your owner's manual and compare the diagram of my machine to yours.

Compare this sewing machine to yours.

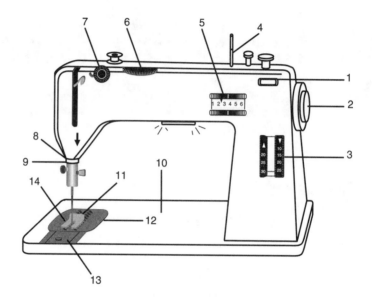

1. Power switch
2. Hand wheel
3. Stitch length regulator
4. Spool pin
5. Needle position
6. Stitch width regulator
7. Tension dial
8. Thread cutter
9. Pressor foot lifter
10. Bed
11. Presser foot
12. Throat plate
13. Slide plate
14. Feed dogs

Let's Start at the Top

Here are some important parts of the machine that you can easily see. I'll be talking about them in this chapter, so make sure you can identify them:

- **Power on-off switch.** Turns the machine on and off.

- **Hand wheel.** Raises or lowers the needle.

- **Stitch length regulator.** Changes the length of the stitch.

- **Stitch width regulator.** Determines the width of zigzag stitches.

- **Spool pin.** Holds the spool of thread on top of the machine.

- **Needle position.** Most new machines have this selection. Check to see if your needle is set on the left, center, or right. It can affect the size of your seam.

- **Tension dial and disc.** Control the top thread tension. Tension is the balance of the tightness of the top thread to the bottom bobbin thread. If the tension is unbalanced, the seam will pucker.

- **Thread cutter.** Cuts threads at the ends of the seams.

- **Presser foot lifter.** Lets you raise and lower the presser foot and is found at the back of the machine.

- **Presser foot.** Holds the fabric against the bed as the fabric is fed through the machine.

> **Quilting Bee**
>
> The width of the stitch will make the stitch zig and zag. A zero stitch width is a straight stitch; usually the larger the number, the wider the zigzag.

Under the Bed

The following important parts of your sewing machine are not easily seen but are just as important in accomplishing your sewing projects.

- **Bed.** Now is not the time to take a nap; the bed is the work surface at the base of the machine.

- **Throat plate.** Supports the fabric during sewing and has seam line guides for different widths.

- **Slide plate.** Opens for easy removal and replacement of the bobbin.

- **Feed dogs** (or feed system—I just liked the term because it helped jog my home economics students' memory). These teeth move the fabric under the presser foot.

- **Bobbin case.** Under the slide plate, it holds the bobbin, which contains the bottom thread of the stitch.

Now it's time to start sewing. When you sew the seam, put the right sides together and line up the side of the presser foot with the raw edge. Measure the width of the seam—usually the presser foot when lined up in this manner makes a ¼-inch seam—perfect for quilting. If aligning the presser foot along the raw edge does not produce a ¼-inch seam, then measure ¼ inch from the needle and place a narrow piece of masking tape on the throat plate for your guideline.

Guide your seam with the presser foot or masking tape.

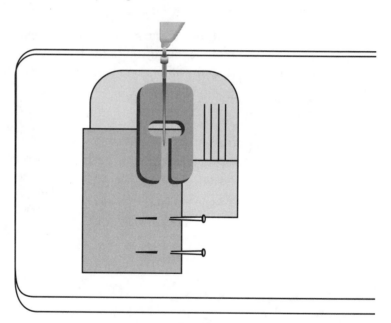

Now your seam should be perfect; let's look at the stitches.

Practice stitching two pieces of scrap fabric together to guarantee that the seam line is not *puckered* and has no *skipped stitches*.

Look in your sewing machine instruction manual to fix your stitches. When there is a problem, always check out whether you have threaded the machine correctly, and then remove and replace the bobbin to

Quilt Talk

A **puckered** seam looks almost gathered, with wrinkles under the stitches even when pressed. A seam with **skipped stitches** has missing stitches, giving the seam large stitches and low durability.

see if it is inserted properly. If there is still a problem, here are some hints to troubleshoot when your machine isn't up to the quilt experience.

If you have skipped stitches, check to see if your needle is dull, or if you are using the right thread.

When your seam line is puckered, you may have to change the tension by turning the tension regulator slightly, but read your manual. The tension is very important. You may even need a tune-up for your machine if you can't correct it.

When your stitches are in balance, it's time to sew!

Hints for Machine Piecing

My students complain that I make machine sewing look too easy. I always apologize to them, but it is easy if you pin accurately and work slowly and carefully. I don't think you should try machine piecing until you have done hand piecing. After you are familiar with the order of piecing and techniques, you can attempt it on the machine.

The first modification can be in changing your templates. As with hand piecing, you can use the typical template and add on the ¼-inch seam allowance when marking the fabric. Or to save time, you can make the template with the ¼-inch seam allowance already included. Because the presser foot measures the ¼ inch, you don't have to mark the seam line. There is a problem, however, because there are no dots to match up—so this method is not as accurate as hand piecing.

To sew basic seams by machine, put the right sides of the fabric together and pin at each end and at every few inches on the seam line. Insert your pin perpendicular to the seam line. For regular piecing, there is no need for backstitching. In most cases, the seam is strong enough. Start at one end, and with the presser foot aligned with the raw edges, sew to the other end. Machine piecing diamonds is a little tricky. When you align the pieces without dots, there is a tendency to pin them incorrectly. You must have a quarter inch of the tip of the diamond or triangle sticking out for the seams to line up.

Quilting Bee _____

Choose a thread that is 100 percent cotton or an all-purpose, cotton-wrapped polyester. Do not use 100 percent polyester (the type that is usually in the sale bins at craft stores) because it knots and breaks too easily.

Sometimes as you are pinning, you can have trouble getting seams to match. You may have been inaccurate in marking, so take out your template, redraw the seam lines, and mark the dots. Then repin and sew.

Look how the diamonds for the Virginia Star are aligned for sewing.

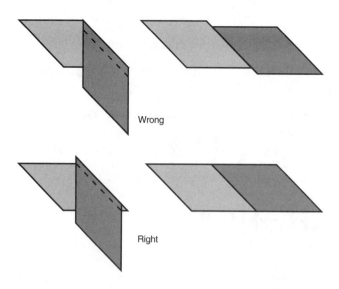

Wrong

Right

Another piecing problem for the sewing machine is inserting right-angled pieces. With this type of piecing, start sewing ¼ inch away from the end of the seam allowance, as if there was a dot. Move the hand wheel so that you can position the needle right into the seam, then release the presser foot. Sew from the inside of the angle to the outside. Look at the Eight Point Star. The diamonds are sewn together, and it is time to put in the squares and triangles. Position the block on the bed of the sewing machine, and make sure that the fabric is flat with no folds underneath. Sew slowly and carefully, pulling out pins as you sew.

In the Eight Point Star, for inserting right-angled pieces, pin and sew from the inside out.

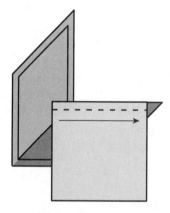

When machine sewing intersecting seams together, it is best to press as you go. This is different from hand piecing where you press when the patch is done. Think before you press. It is smart to butt the seams so that as the machine sews over them, the fabric of the top seam is pushed against the bottom seam and is held in place.

Pin into the seam of the intersecting seam lines. The seam allowance of the top should be ironed in one direction and the bottom pressed the opposite way. When you seam over these lines of stitching, the seam allowances will lay in opposite directions. Look how intersecting seams should be pressed for easy sewing.

The secret to accurate machine piecing is to pin and press carefully. Sew slowly and make sure that the pieces seamed together have no tucks or puckers. Take out your pins as you go.

Quilting Bee

When butting intersecting seams of two rows, the seams of the top and bottom rows are pressed in opposite directions. This yields less bulkiness than having both seams on top of one another.

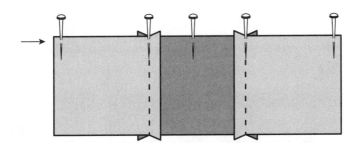

Press the seams that meet in opposite directions.

Quick Methods for Joining Blocks

Now for some quick method strategies. So many creative, smart quilters have developed these methods. Obviously they were in a hurry and needed to finish their quilt by a deadline, like most of us. Check out how to sew in chains and strips and try them out on the blocks in this chapter.

Chain Piecing

I'm for anything that saves time, and sewing fabric pieces in a production line makes sense. Chain piecing makes sewing several blocks at a time easy. I hate cutting threads and restarting seam lines, especially when half of the time I start the seam and the needle unthreads because I didn't have the needle at the highest point. It's so annoying to have to rethread the needle. With chain piecing, you sew the first two fabric pieces together, but do not cut the threads at the end of the seam line. Instead, you sew two or three stitches more, and then put the next set of fabric pieces by the presser foot and continue the same seam line. Do this for all the fabric pieces, forming a long string of pieces.

Chaining together a long string of fabric pieces.

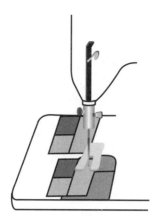

This technique is perfect to practice on the Log Cabin block because there are four units in one patch. You can string together four centers to template A, then cut the line of units apart. Position the first unit right sides together with template B and seam all four units. Cut them apart, and sew each template in a spiral manner until the unit is totally complete.

Chaining together the Log Cabin.

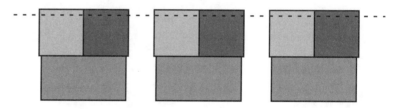

Quilting Bee

When strip piecing, cut the strips from selvage to selvage, making them approximately 42 inches in length. The strips of fabric can be cut with a rotary cutter in one quick roll, or carefully layer several fabrics, marking only the top fabric. Several strips can be cut at one time. You must have good scissors to give an accurate cut.

Strip Piecing

My favorite quick sewing method is strip piecing. I have made many different types of quilts with this procedure—sewing squares of the Trip Around the World, Boston Commons, Double Irish Chain, and even the diamonds of the Lone Star. When I teach this technique, I tell my students, "Trust me, it's like magic, it just works!" Blocks are analyzed and long strips of fabrics are sewn together in set patterns. There may be one, two, or three different units of strips. These units are then sliced apart and combined to make a row. Then different row units are pressed and sewn together to form the block. Many great books give specific instructions on this technique.

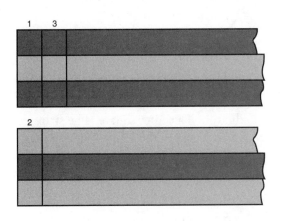

See how easy the center of the Double Nine Patch can be made if you strip piece?

Many great blocks use the strip-quilting method. You can practice on the Rail Fence with the patterns and directions in this chapter, and then you'll be ready to strip your quilts.

Scraps and Pieces

The Seminole Indians in Florida first developed the technique of strip quilting. The Indians were given sewing machines on their reservation at the beginning of the 1900s. They perfected the strip method and made long narrow rows of small, intricately pieced squares and triangles. These strips were not used in bed coverings but to adorn colorful clothing. Solid, bright-colored fabric was used. Quilters now use their procedure to make blocks.

Machine-Pieced Blocks

The patches in this chapter, Log Cabin and Rail Fence, can be sewn either by hand or machine. If you stitch by hand, cut and prepare the templates as discussed in Chapter 6. Mark and cut out the fabrics, and then hand stitch the pieces together following the block's directions.

Using the sewing machine for these blocks will be good practice for chain piecing or strip quilting. The patches will whet your appetite for these techniques without overwhelming you. But whether sewn by hand or machine, these blocks are great!

Quilting Bee

If you have a lot of scraps, each template for the Log Cabin block can be cut from a different fabric.

Log Cabin Block

The Log Cabin is one of the most popular patchwork quilts, and although it looks complicated, it's not. The combination of light and dark colors make this block versatile in its ability to look either sophisticated, modern, or country.

This patch is formed by strips (logs) that are built around a center square. The strips get longer as they spiral around the center. There are 36 pieces to the 12-inch square Log Cabin block. Five templates, a square for the middle (template A) and four rectangles (templates B, C, D, and the longest E), are used to make a 6-inch square unit.

Four of these units are put together as in a four-patch block. The choice of fabrics is extremely important so that the darks and lights create dramatic diagonal contrast. This half-light, half-dark combination can be turned to make many variations in your quilt.

My first machine quilt was a Quilt-As-You-Go Log Cabin. I made it for my parent's house in the Pocono Mountains of Pennsylvania. The house is now sold, but I have the quilt; it's more than a quarter of a century old and I still cherish it. Make your memories: Start with a block and follow the directions step by step, and then just keep going for a full quilt.

Don't Get Stuck!

To make the light and dark colors go on the diagonal, careful planning is important. My first attempt at the Log Cabin was a disaster. I didn't follow the cutting directions for the colors. The darkest and lightest colors are cut from template A. Then each spiraling-out template is cut from both a light and a dark color. Careful placement of the light and dark colors is essential to get the diagonal effect.

Log Cabin block—do you see the hearth and logs?

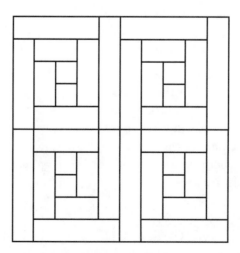

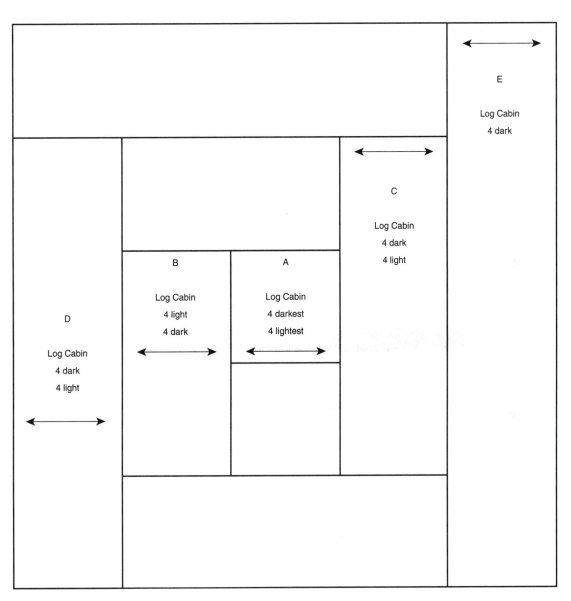

Log Cabin templates.

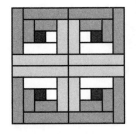 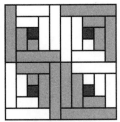 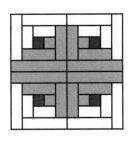

Look how you can turn the individual unit to change the design of the Log Cabin.

1. Choose colors so half of the square divided diagonally is composed of two light colors. The other diagonal half of the unit has three dark fabrics; the darkest one is the center square.

Study the position of the templates in the 6-inch square unit.

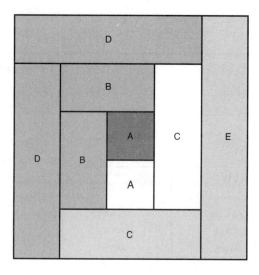

2. Make the templates and mark the fabric. Cut out the fabric pieces adding on ¼-inch seam allowances.

3. Lay out the design on the table in front of you, or use the chain-piecing method described in the beginning of the chapter.

4. Pin the right sides together of both A templates (darkest and lightest color fabrics).

5. Pin the right side of the lightest color of template B to the combined A's unit. Sew the seam down the left side. Sew all other three units in the block (see Figure a).

6. Pin the dark piece B to the top of the AB unit. Then sew and open the piece flat (see Figure b).

7. Pin the dark piece C to the side of the AB unit and sew (see Figure c).

Quilting Bee

When using the quick strip-piecing method, cut a fabric strip 1¼ inch from selvage to selvage. That amount already has the seam allowance added on and you just have to cut off the correct length, measuring the unit as you sew. Don't even mark.

Don't Get Stuck!

Before you sew the Log Cabin block, make sure you open up the pieces to see if they fit into the layout. The darkest A should be on the top, otherwise the colors will spiral in the wrong direction.

8. Pin the light piece C to the bottom of the ABC unit. Sew and open (see Figure d).

9. Pin the light piece D to the left side of the unit and sew (see Figure e).

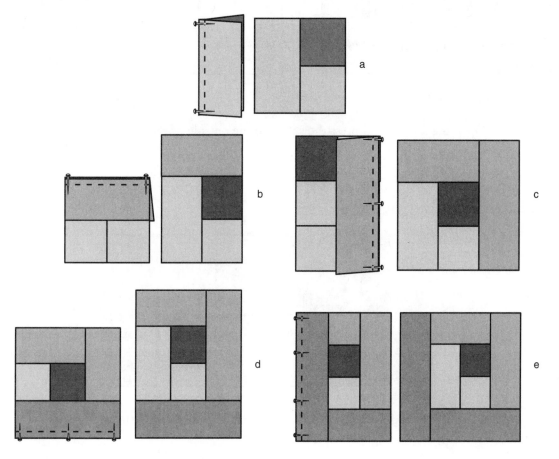

Sewing order of the Log Cabin: Follow Figures a through e.

10. Sew the dark piece D to the top of the unit (see Figure f).

11. Finally, pin and sew the dark piece E to the right side of the unit (see Figure g).

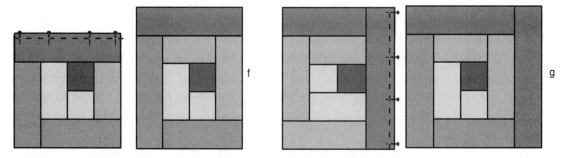

Sewing order of the Log Cabin: Follow Figures f and g.

12. Open the last log and press the seams to the outside of the unit.

13. Make the other three units, and decide on their position.

14. Sew two units together to form the top row. Then sew the bottom two units together.

The Log Cabin is assembled as a four patch, sewing the top to the bottom row.

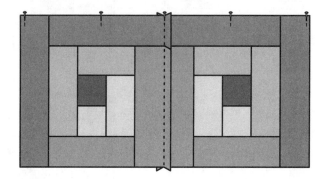

15. Pin the ends and the center seam together. Then stitch from the inside seam line out.

Scraps and Pieces

It is believed that the Log Cabin design started in the 1860s as a tribute to Abraham Lincoln, who was born in a log cabin. Traditionally, the center square was a red square that represented the home fires or the hearth of the cabin. It is not surprising that this patch was unpopular in the South during the period of the Civil War.

Rail Fence

The Rail Fence is a terrific and easy quilt block that uses the strip-piecing method. It is a nine patch in which each 4-inch square is divided into four 1-inch rectangles. There are 36 fabric pieces in all; if you are using the strip-piecing method, however, you need to cut only long strips. No separate cutting or marking is needed. There are four shades of fabric that make up each 4-inch square.

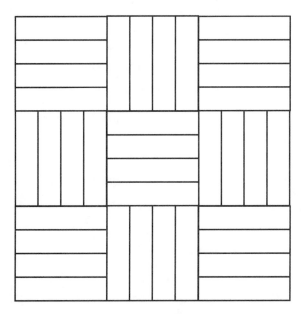

Rail Fence block. Don't the lines of this block remind you of the fences that line a farmer's field?

If you are assembling this by hand, then there is only one template. Cut out the 1-inch by 4-inch rectangle and make the template of cardboard and sandpaper.

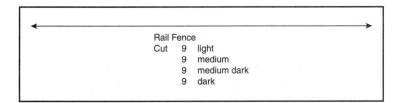

Rail Fence
Cut 9 light
9 medium
9 medium dark
9 dark

Rail Fence template.

Then mark and cut, adding on the ¼-inch seam allowances. Put four rectangles together to form a 4-inch square. Assemble as in a nine patch. For those that want to attempt the strip-piecing technique, here are the directions; but don't let your anxiety "fence you in":

Don't Get Stuck! _____

When strip piecing, use a see-through ruler with grids so that the line you are marking is perpendicular to the sewn lines. You do not want the strips to be running on an angle.

Quilting Bee _____

Cutting the Rail Fence strips into squares is the perfect use for your rotary cutter and clear-lipped ruler. You won't even have to mark—just line up your ruler at 4¼ inches and slice "à la pizza cutter."

1. Cut 1½-inch strips from selvage to selvage from four different fabrics.

2. Sew the four strips together lengthwise, with the lightest on top and the darkest on the bottom.

3. Press all the seams toward the darkest strip.

4. Cut off the left end to form a right angle. Then measure 4½ inches from the left and mark the sewn strip to form a square. Mark every 4½ inches. There should be nine 4½-inch squares.

5. Cut the strips into nine 4½-inch squares.

6. Lay out the blocks, rotating the colors.

7. Sew the blocks into rows. Press the seams of the top and bottom rows to the right, and the seams of the middle row to the left.

8. Pin the rows right sides together at each seam allowance. Sew the rows together.

9. Press.

Strips of Rail Fence sewn together with darkest strip on the bottom.

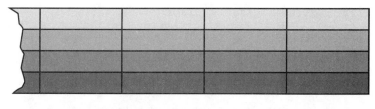

Strips of Rail Fence marked for cutting into squares.

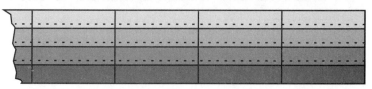

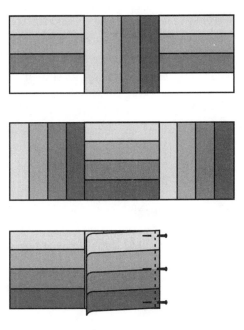

Squares of Rail Fence sewn into rows.

Let's Zig and Zag Your Appliqué Blocks

It is very durable and fast if you appliqué by sewing machine. The look is folksy and homemade, and perhaps this is the look you prefer. If you choose to machine appliqué, there are several modifications to consider before starting your appliqué patch.

I think one of the most important things to remember is to be sure to use a fabric that is sturdy and will not ravel. Use a material that is 50 to 100 percent cotton and is densely woven.

The thread for your machine should be a cotton-wrapped polyester or 100 percent mercerized cotton. You can use a thread color that blends into the appliqué motif to give it a softer, more polished look. Or if you choose a contrasting thread, your eye will be drawn to the zigzag stitch, which will give it a real country look. Be sure to have your bobbin thread the same color as your top thread.

Quilting Bee

Fabric always stretches on the bias; but if it stretches along the straight of grain, you will have trouble sewing with the zigzag stitch. On the other hand, do not use a fabric that is too thick, like broadcloth or poplin, because it will be too thick to quilt.

It's time to cut out your fabric designs and place them on your patch. There are two ways to do this. If you choose a fabric that doesn't ravel, such as felt, you don't even have to add on the seam allowances or turn them under. This is a real time-saver.

Don't Get Stuck!

Be sure to choose a fusible webbing such as Wonder-Under or Stitch Witchery and not a fusible interfacing. The webbing totally dissolves and glues your appliqué design to your background fabric. I've used these several times; but be careful, it is really difficult to quilt through this glue if you are planning to hand quilt.

The second way is similar to the traditional appliqué method, in which you mark and cut out your appliqué designs, adding on the seam allowances. Baste the seam allowances under and pin them into position.

Keeping these designs flat and in the correct place is really a challenge. I continuously baste the designs onto the background. Machines tend to drag the fabric out of place very easily. You can even use a fusible webbing or a glue stick to hold these designs down.

Cut the sheet of webbing the same size as your template.

Cut the fusible webbing and press it into place under the appliqué designs.

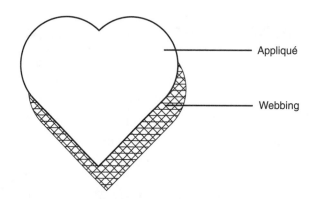

Appliqué

Webbing

Place the fusible webbing between your appliqué design and the background fabric. Then it's as easy as pressing to fuse these pieces into place. Now for the zig and the zag.

I've talked about the sewing machine and how to use the straight stitch to piece your blocks. Now it's time to learn how to use the other optional stitches on your machine. Experiment with your sewing machine, changing the stitch width regulator and the stitch length. Choose a zigzag satin stitch, which is so densely sewn that you will not see the fabric through it. The width of the stitch is your preference, but I find that a more narrow stitch width is easier to maneuver around your design. Allow the machine feed dog to push your fabric through—being sure not to pull the fabric or your stitches will be uneven. Be sure the stitches land exactly on the edge. If the stitches pucker, change the tension on your machine.

Position the zigzag stitching to land on the edge of the appliqué.

The Least You Need to Know

◆ Properly using and caring for your machine is important for perfect stitches.

◆ Use your presser foot or place a piece of masking tape on the throat plate of the sewing machine to mark the ¼ inch for seam allowances.

◆ When chain piecing a quilt with one block, you can sew all the patches together at the same time in a production line.

◆ Strip piecing means sewing long strips of fabrics together into several patterns that, when cut apart and resewn, form blocks.

◆ Position the zigzag stitches so that the stitches land on the edge of the appliqué design.

14

Setting It All Together

In This Chapter

- ◆ Positioning and balancing colors and designs
- ◆ How placement of blocks can change a quilt's look
- ◆ Piecing blocks into a quilt top
- ◆ Framing out the quilt top with borders
- ◆ Mitering corners

This chapter covers the proper technique for sewing together the quilt top and provides hints on pressing. Just like a painting, the quilt top needs the correct frame. Borders and how to assemble them are discussed. I'll also reveal the secret of mitering corners for the long sashing borders. Get ready to be demystified.

Solving the Quilt Puzzle

Before starting to lay out your blocks in the quilt top, you want to make sure the size of all the blocks is the same. All the blocks in this book should measure 12 inches square from seam line to seam line.

You would be surprised how uneven the blocks can get. How can this happen? I've found that fabrics with different qualities may stretch when handled or pressed during piecing. This is especially true of patches that have bias edges around their borders—for example, the triangles in the Eight Point Star. I have found that pieces of fabric can grow almost half an inch just by mishandling them. It also could be that you have not stitched exactly on the seam line. Being just $\frac{1}{16}$ of an inch off can grow to a $\frac{1}{2}$-inch mistake. So check your blocks and be sure to leave at least $\frac{1}{4}$-inch seam allowances all around.

When the size of your blocks is uniform, it's time to find their correct placement on the quilt top. As a beginner, you may have chosen to do a Sampler quilt to hone your skills. Sampler quilts are more of a challenge when it comes to getting your blocks to balance in color and pattern. This is one of my favorite times in quilt class because everyone has their say. We all stand around a table where the blocks are laid out and call out suggestions where to move them. It is really fun to mix and match block placement in your quilt. At the end, when everyone is satisfied, the quilt will be in perfect balance. Here are some hints on block placement.

- Try not to have blocks with the same basic design next to each other. For example, don't put an Ohio Star next to a Churn Dash—there is too much similarity in the nine patches.

- Spread accent or bright colors throughout the quilt. Do not have too many dark colors in one area or your eyes will look only at the dark part and not appreciate the whole quilt.

- If you have a problem block, one that may have a different background fabric or has a unique design, you may have to move it to the center or make a block that complements it. Unfortunately, your last choice is not to use the block.

- Blocks that are similar (like Hearts All Around and Dresden Plate) should be placed opposite each other in a quilt so they will balance.

Quilting Bee

If your block does not measure 12 inches from seam to seam, here is an easy way to make it right: Cut a 12-inch square out of cardboard; then turn the block to the wrong side, place the square on top, and redraw the lines as necessary.

Don't Get Stuck!

To check the size of your block, remember to measure from seam line to seam line, not from the raw edges of the block. People cut seam allowances inconsistently. Do not cut off any excess. You can cut away the large seam allowances after the blocks are sewn together.

Quilting Bee

I use the "squint method" to test balance. I put all the blocks in the designated order on my bed, step out of the room, then come in with my eyes squinted. First impressions make any unbalance obvious, and I can make changes.

If you choose not to use a patch, you can always use it later in a pillow project!

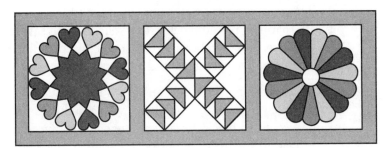

Look how you can balance your quilt with different designs.

Side-by-Side Blocks

In this type of layout, the patches are sewn to each other rather than framed with *lattices*, or *sashing*.

The interplay of shapes and colors of the blocks forms new designs and looks very contemporary. Appliqué blocks are perfect for this method, because there is one large uniform background that basically frames out each appliqué motif.

Quilt Talk

Lattices are strips of fabric that separate and frame out each individual block. These are also known as **sashing**.

See how new patterns are formed by the side-by-side design.

Alternate with Solid Blocks

This is an easy way to separate your quilt blocks, alternating a pieced block with a solid 12-inch square of fabric. Your patches are really emphasized by the simplicity that surrounds them.

One nice thing about this method is that you have to piece fewer blocks to complete a whole quilt. Instead of piecing 15 blocks for a twin-size quilt, you need to piece only 8—the other blocks are solid fabric. The solid blocks, however, do need to have an intricate design quilted on them, so it really isn't a time-saver in the long run.

See how the patches are set apart and are more dramatic when separated by solid blocks.

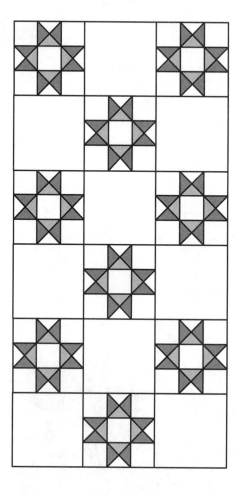

Lattice Alone

Sashing or lattice strips separate and frame the blocks in your quilt. Lattices can vary in size and complexity. Fabrics for the frame are chosen to complement your blocks, with a color taken from the color scheme, or you can use a neutral, solid-color muslin, or black. Proportionately, the lattices should be no larger than one third the size of the block (in this case, 4 inches).

You can insert a solid lattice by cutting a rectangle the length of the block plus seam allowances (12½ inches) by the width decided upon plus seam allowances (3½ inches).

The lattices are sewn to the sides of the patches as you sew the rows together. Then measure the finished width of the quilt row and add ½ inch for the seam allowances. The patches seem to be floating on the lattice fabric.

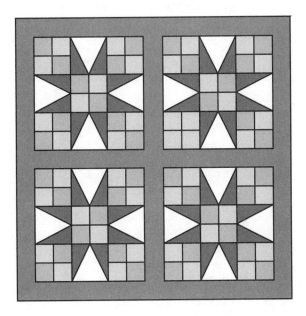

Notice how the solid lattice frames out the blocks.

If you want to add a little more interest, you can sew squares into the corner of each block. Many quilters use this technique to add the accent color from their blocks.

The lattices will all measure 12½ inches in length by the chosen width (3 inches) plus seam allowances (3½ inches). To measure the corner squares, take the width of the lattice and add on the seam allowances (3½-inch square). Be sure to measure and count correctly.

Lattice with corner squares.

When you become more experienced, you can try a complex lattice. The rectangle can be divided into three different color fabrics or have intricate piecing in each. Look at the following illustration of an advanced lattice.

Intricate lattices can be almost as time-consuming as making your block, but look at the results!

Use a Different Slant

For a slightly different twist, you can use any of the previous methods of setting the blocks but turn the blocks on the diagonal. Look at the following figure to see how the blocks can change just by rotating them.

This design can be confusing to a beginner. Notice the sides of the quilt—there are side triangles that square out the quilt. I have used either solid triangles of the background fabric or even cut quilt blocks in half on the diagonal—yes, I did say cut quilt blocks—to fill in the open side areas. The plan of alternating blocks is probably the best approach because the solid blocks are easier to insert for a beginner.

Put all your patches in a pleasing order and let's sew them together.

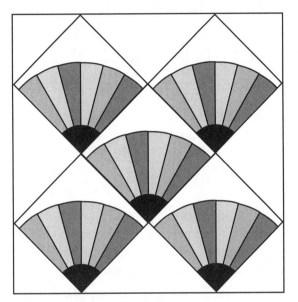

Quilt blocks set on the diagonal.

Joining It All Together

Consider your quilt top as one very large block. After you have decided the block placement, you need to analyze how to tackle sewing this together. Don't get overwhelmed—just divide the quilt face into rows, either horizontal or on the diagonal. You now have a plan of attack.

Each quilt is unique, so there are no set rules or instructions from now on. I can just tell you what to consider as you complete your quilt. Calculate how many and measure the size of framing lattices needed for your quilt. Mark and cut out lattices or blocks being certain to add on the seam allowances. The blocks are alternated with the lattices, then sewn together in a horizontal row. If you have chosen the solid lattice, then one length of fabric is added above and below the row (see the following figure). Then the next row of the quilt is pinned and sewn to the first row unit.

Sewing horizontal rows of a quilt and then adding either a solid lattice or a lattice with corner squares.

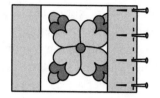

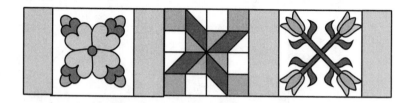

In this stage of quilt making, even if I have hand pieced my quilt, I usually resort to using the sewing machine. With all those long seam lines, the machine is such a time-saver. However, you must be confident in using the sewing machine, because there are so many seam lines to match up. Otherwise slow and steady hand stitching is more accurate.

When you want to create a lattice with corner squares, you use the same technique of alternating lattice and blocks across the rows. The difference comes in sewing the horizontal framing rows. You need to start with a square, sew it to the short end of a lattice, a square, and lattice all the way across the quilt.

Now it's time to sew these rows together. Sew the lattice row to the top of the block row. Do this for all block rows. Sew the lattices to the top of the blocks only.

Then sew all the row units together, pinning and sewing carefully, aligning all the intersecting seams. Soon you have sewn all these rows together, and before you know it, the quilt top is completed. Press all the horizontal seam allowances toward the lattices. Finally, turn the quilt top so the finished side is facing up and press the right side; then cut off all the threads—that in itself is an afternoon project! Are you ready for the last piecing step?

Sewing the lattices and corner squares. Before sewing, press all seam allowances in opposite directions.

It's Time to Cross the Borders

Can you imagine the *Mona Lisa* without a frame? Neither should your quilted work of art be without a border. A border can be as simple as a solid fabric, or a series of bands of colors chosen from your color scheme. Expert quilters even create intricately pieced or appliquéd borders to surround their quilts. It's all a matter of aesthetics. Balance, proportion, color, and the corner treatments are all variables you have to consider. You should think of borders as an essential part of the overall quilt design.

The corners of borders can be squared off, can have corner squares at the ends, or can even be *mitered*.

The first step is to decide on the fabric for the borders. I usually lay out my quilt top on a bed and fold pieces of fabrics from the quilt next to it. Then I use the "squint method" to see which fabric or combination of fabrics looks best.

Quilt Talk _____

To **miter** is to join together the corner of two perpendicular edges with a 45-degree-angle seam.

Measure the finished edges of your quilt and be sure each parallel side is the same size. If they are accurate in length, it's time to cut out your borders. For the side borders, measure from edge to edge, which is the length you need to cut.

If possible, avoid sewing seams—cut the border from a full length of fabric that runs down the straight of grain. If you don't have enough fabric, it is totally acceptable to use the crosswise grain and cut the border from selvage to selvage, creating one seam. Sew the side borders onto the quilt, open them out, and press the seam allowances toward the border.

(a) Simple, mitered, and expert borders.

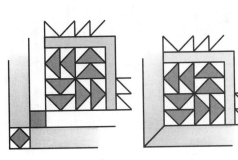
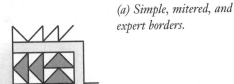

Now it's time to work on the top and bottom borders. Measure from the edge of the left border across the quilt to the edge of the right border. This is the measurement for both the top and bottom borders. Sew on these borders (see Figure a). If you decide on attaching more than one band of color, repeat the process, measuring and adding on the side borders, then the top and bottom borders.

Don't Get Stuck!

When measuring your quilt, start your measurement 2 or 3 inches in from the outer edge. The outer edge tends to stretch, causing your measurement to be incorrect.

If your corner design includes squares, measure only the top and bottom of the quilt top; do not include the borders. Then cut four squares the size of the width of the side border and add one square to each end of the top and bottom borders (see Figure b). Make sure to add seam allowances for the border and square pieces.

There are endless possibilities for border designs, so be creative and go into the borderline.

(a)

Measuring and sewing borders.

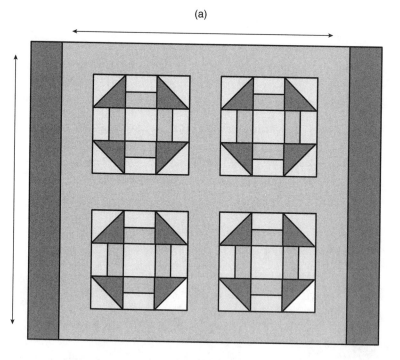

(b)

To Miter or Not to Miter

Mitering the corners of the border gives your quilt a smooth, professional look. This type of finish requires more fabric than the other borders, so if you are low on fabric, choose another method. When your border design calls for several bands of colors, cut all the fabrics the same size and sew them together into one unit, then proceed with the following directions. When making a mitered border it is essential to measure and sew accurately. These instructions will make mitering effortless.

1. **Measure and cut.** All border measurements are calculated by measuring the length of the quilt top then adding the width of both borders on each side of the quilt. If a quilt is 80 inches by 50 inches and the borders are 5 inches wide all around the perimeter, let's determine the measurements for the mitered border. The calculations would look like this:

   For the two side borders, add: 80 inches (quilt length) + 5 inches (top border width) + 5 inches (bottom border width) + 1 inch (fudge factor) = 91 inches by 5½ inches wide. (Remember to add on the seam allowance for the border width.) For the top and bottom borders, add 50 inches (quilt width) + 5 inches (left-side border width) + 5 inches (right-side border width) + 1 inch (fudge factor) = 61 inches by 5½ inches wide. I always add an inch "just in case"; you can always cut it off.

2. **Pin.** Pin the center point of the border's right sides together to the middle point of the quilt top. There should be an equal amount of fabric hanging off the ends. This really looks strange!

3. **Sew.** Start ¼ inch from the top edge of the quilt and backstitch. Then sew along the side edge of the quilt top on the marked ¼-inch seam line. Stop sewing ¼ inch from the end and backstitch (see Figure a). Sew all four borders, stopping at ¼ inch and backstitching. Try to get the stitches from both seams to meet at the same point (see Figure b).

4. **Miter.** Most of my students get to this point and then bring me their quilt, with these ends hanging off, and say "Help!" Here's how to finish. Turn to the wrong side of your quilt. Cut off excess fabrics. Take a gridded plastic ruler, one that has a 45-degree angle, and draw a line from the backstitch point diagonally to the corner of the border (see Figure c). Pin and check to see whether the border lays flat. If so, sew on the drawn lines. Cut the excess from the border leaving a ¼-inch seam allowance.

5. **Press.** Press seam allowances to the borders and the mitered seam open.

Whatever border method you have chosen, I know that your quilt top is beautiful and, more important, *it's finished!* Next stop—quilting!

Steps for sewing mitered borders.

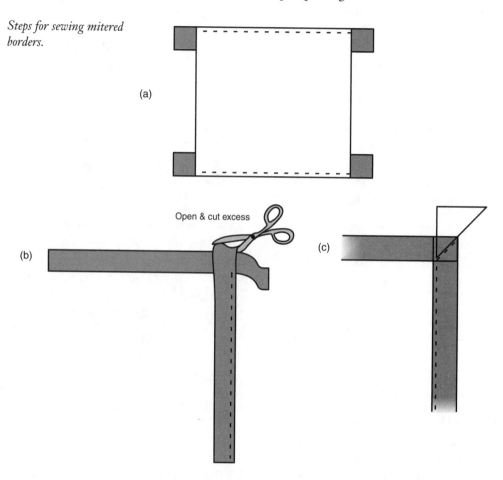

The Least You Need to Know

- ◆ If all of your patches are not 12 inches square, redraw the seam lines.
- ◆ Arrange your blocks so the colors and designs are evenly distributed around the quilt top.
- ◆ Set your quilt together by sewing horizontal rows of blocks and lattices.
- ◆ Borders frame your quilt and should complement its color and proportion.
- ◆ Mitered border corners are sewn together at a 45-degree angle.

15

The Three B's: Batting, Backing, and Basting

In This Chapter

- ◆ Pros and cons of different kinds of batting
- ◆ Choosing backing for quiltability
- ◆ How to assemble the quilt top
- ◆ Various methods of basting for a wrinkle-free quilt

Now is the time for all good quilters to unite your quilt! Your quilt top demonstrates your artistry and creativity—now let's add dimension.

Your quilt is ready to be assembled and it is very important to hold the three layers securely together. Basting is essential. There will be weeks, months, or sometimes years of handling your quilt while you stitch and put on the finish touches. You can use several methods of basting to secure a stable unit. You can choose which method best suits your needs. But get ready to baste, baste, baste.

Don't Go Batty—Know All the Types of Batting

A quilt has three layers: the quilt top, batting (or filling), and backing. The middle layer is usually a soft, puffy batting, which adds dimension to your quilt. The type of batting you choose will dramatically change the quilt's appearance and your ability to quilt. Let's consider different types of batting and find out their good and bad characteristics.

Quilt Talk

The **loft,** or thickness, of the batting can range from 1/8 inch to 2 inches.

Quilting Bee

Some people get allergic reactions when using polyester battings that have been bonded with a chemical, resin finish. If you are one of those people, be sure to buy heat-bonded polyester battings.

Polyester Batting

This is the most popular and easy to use of all the fillers. It comes already cut in a variety of sizes and packed in plastic bags. All you have to do is open the bag and unroll the batting. These manufactured battings come in different *lofts*, or thicknesses, and are bonded to prevent shifting when quilted.

The thicker the loft, the warmer the quilt. Each manufacturer has its own description of thickness: low loft, Fatt Batt, or Ultra-Loft, for instance. Ask to see samples to determine which thickness you prefer. Polyester battings are bonded by heat setting or a resin finish. Did you ever have a comforter that after you washed it, all the stuffing had moved around and formed uneven lumps? It would be really discouraging to have that happen after all the work you have done. So it is important to have battings that are bonded.

Polyester Batting on a Roll or Bolt

This type of batting is found in many fabric or craft stores. It is the same quality as the batting found in bags, but the advantage is you can feel the weight and loft. Then the sales person can unroll and cut off the exact amount you need. It is sometimes more expensive than the bagged batting though.

Cotton Batting

This type of batting works well in clothing and thin quilts. It is not as puffy as polyester batting, but is a more traditional thickness. Students who have used cotton batting have said cotton is very easy to quilt through, and your stitches can be very small. One disadvantage is that cotton shrinks—many brands of cotton batting need to be shrunk and some also need to have residual cotton oil washed out before use. Check to see if the cotton batting you are considering needs to be washed. (It is a messy project to wash this in a bathtub.) Some of the newer cotton battings are pre-washed, but please make sure. You do have to stitch your quilting lines closer together than with the polyester batting because it will shift in the quilt.

Other Fillings

The fillings discussed earlier are the most popular battings for quilts. Here are some unusual items that can be used for the inside layer. Cotton flannel sheets or wool blankets add warmth but not fluffiness. I've used a flannel sheet in a quilted tablecloth where I wanted a thin batting. It would be horrible to put down a wine glass on a puffy tablecloth and have the glass not sit right—dry cleaner, here we come. A flannel sheet, which feels cooler than polyester, can be used in quilts meant for summer use. Many times old quilts were used as a batting. Open up one quilt and find another!

> **Scraps and Pieces**
>
> Quilters, being very resourceful, have filled their quilts with many unusual items. I've heard of women who, during the pioneer days, used cotton right from the harvested boles or carded wool. Antique dealers can authenticate a quilt by holding it up to a light and seeing if any seeds are visible in the cotton filling. Many times frugal quilters who had nothing else for batting pieced together sacks that held cottonseed, flour, or fertilizer products. During the Depression, women also used newspapers, rags, old clothes, or even feathers—anything to add warmth to the quilt.

Backing: It's Not Always the Wrong Side

Is the backing the wrong side of the quilt? Not always. Many times quilters use an attractive fabric for the quilt back so they can use the quilt on its reverse side. Traditionally a single length of fabric, the backing can be solid, printed, or pieced. It was expensive for pioneer women to purchase a solid length, so many times they pieced together feed or flour sacks that were opened and cleaned.

Don't Get Stuck!

Don't use a percale bed sheet for backing—the thread count is much too dense for a needle to pierce it. You should not use a muslin sheet either. They may have a finish that makes them unquiltable.

One trait that a backing should have is "quiltability," or ease of quilting. A backing fabric should have a low thread count and should be loosely woven. Traditionally muslin was used because it was the easiest to sew and inexpensive. You may be tempted to use a bed sheet because of its size. Don't do it! One time I made an octagonal wall hanging and I thought that a bed sheet would eliminate the necessity of seaming it together. What a mistake! I suffered with blisters through the whole quilting process.

Since quilting has become so popular, manufacturers have started marketing muslin that is 80 to 90 inches wide, perfect for quilt backing. Muslin and all fabrics for the backing must be shrunk before use, as were your fabrics for the quilt top.

What Size Should the Backing and Batting Be?

The batting and backing should be slightly larger than your finished quilt top. For the batting, it is easy to get the correct size—just measure the finished top and purchase a bag with the size that corresponds to your measurements.

Don't worry if your batting is too small or if you want to use up leftover pieces— there is a way of joining them together. Be sure that all the battings are the same loft or thickness. Then cut out as many pieces as you need to form the correct size, 1 inch larger than your quilt top. But do not overlap the battings that need to be united (see Figure a).

Quilting Bee

Open up your bag of batting, unroll the batting carefully, and let it sit out for a few hours to relax the folds it accumulated from being in the bag.

Using a needle threaded and knotted with quilting thread, baste the battings together. I use what I call a Z stitch. Take a horizontal stitch on the right batting to the left batting, then move your needle down ½ inch, taking another stitch in the right to left batting (see Figure b).

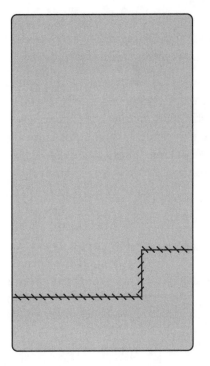

(a) Join batting pieces with a basting stitch.

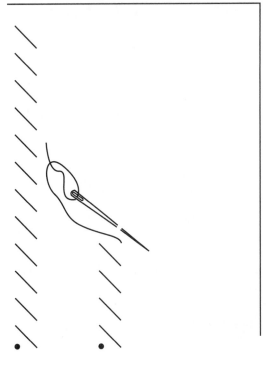

(b) Don't let these Z's put you to sleep—your quilt will be finished soon.

If you are making a bed quilt, it is probably necessary to seam the backing. You can do this in several ways, and the method you choose depends on your preferences and the size of the quilt. Look at the following figure to see three ways you can seam together the backing.

Determine how much fabric you need to buy. If you are making a small quilt, like a wall hanging or a crib quilt, measure the dimensions of the quilt top and add 2 inches all around the perimeter. If the quilt is large—a bed size, for example—you will need to piece the backing. There are several ways to seam the backing together. Traditionally, the most acceptable way is to seam three lengths of fabric, of equal widths, vertically down the backing. This is used especially when the quilt is wider than two lengths of fabric sewed together. I am more practical and don't mind piecing together fabric of unequal widths as long as the seams run parallel to the sides and are not crooked. Depending on the size of your quilt and the amount of fabric you have, you may even seam the backing horizontally.

> **Don't Get Stuck!**
>
> When basting battings together, don't overlap them or pull the stitches too tight because a lump will develop.

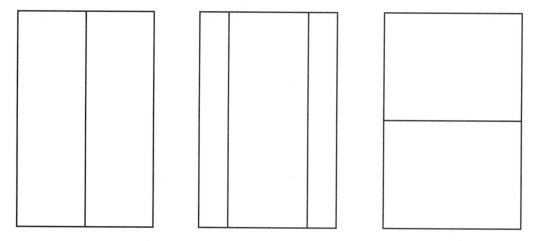

You can seam your backing vertically down the middle, vertically into three sections, or horizontally across the middle.

Whichever method you decide to use, measure the quilt top and compute how many lengths you need to purchase. Shrink the backing fabric and cut off the selvages. Remember that the selvage shrinks and puckers when washed, so remove it first. Sew together the seams and press. If you are sewing by machine, press the seams open. Press the whole backing. Now you are ready to layer your quilt.

Wrinkle-Free Basting for Your Quilt Layers

When each of the three layers is pieced, prepared, and cut to the correct size, you are ready to assemble your quilt. Remember, this is the last time you will be able to press the quilt top and the backing, so make them look perfect.

I use two different approaches to basting, depending on the size of the project. Find a large, flat working space (a dining room table, Ping-Pong table, or a hard floor) and, if possible, a friend to help you—an extra set of hands is a great time-saver.

Basting a Small Project

Follow these steps to baste a small project:

1. Put the backing fabric on the floor, wrong side up. It should be 2 inches larger all around the circumference of the quilt top.

2. Lift the batting carefully and put it over the backing fabric. (The batting is cut about 1 inch smaller than the backing and 1 inch larger than the quilt top.) Spread with your hands to smooth out the lumps.

3. Center the quilt face on top of the batting, right side up.

4. As you spread these layers, the fabric shifts. Cut off any excess of batting and backing: backing that is more than 2 inches all around quilt top; and batting 1 inch all the way around quilt top.

5. Pin through all three layers using extra-long quilting pins with very large heads.

6. Using a contrasting thread with a large knot, start stitching the Z stitch at the center of the quilt and baste parallel to the side of the quilt until you reach the bottom edge. Then start in the center and baste up. Each time start in the center of the quilt and baste vertically, horizontally, and then diagonally. The basting lines should look like a sunburst. If any slippage occurs, it may be necessary to baste more lines parallel to the sides.

Don't Get Stuck!

This literally is a don't-get-stuck! When pinning together your quilt layers, be sure you can see all of the pins so you can remove them after you stitch up your quilt. I made a quilt for my niece and her husband, and a pin must have gotten lost in the batting. They soon learned pins and waterbeds do not get along. Use pins with large heads or safety pins that won't wander into the quilt.

Baste a small project in a sunburst pattern.

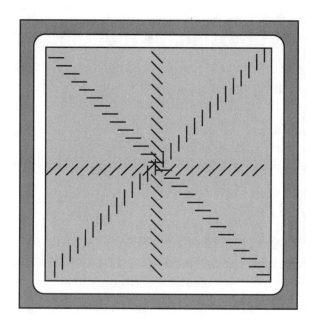

Basting Large Projects

Follow these steps to baste large projects:

1. Lay the backing on the floor, wrong side up. Hold the edges down with masking tape so the backing is stretched taut against the floor with no wrinkles.

2. Place the batting on top of the backing and then spread it smooth with your hands.

3. Center the quilt face, right side up, on top of backing and batting. Measure to see that the backing's seams are parallel to the sides of the quilt top.

4. Pin the layers together with extra-long quilting pins with large heads. Be sure to pin through all three layers.

5. Starting at the center of the quilt, run a line of basting stitches (Z stitches or running stitches) vertically and horizontally. On large projects, run the basting stitches every 4 to 6 inches parallel to the sides, forming a grid of basting.

> **Don't Get Stuck!**
>
> If you are laying out your backing on a rug, watch out for some problems. First, the masking tape will not stick to a rug, so the backing may be wrinkled. Second, you might baste through your quilt to the rug. I've done this and had to cut some of the basting stitches. You can purchase a 6-foot folding cardboard cutting board if there is no table or floor to use.

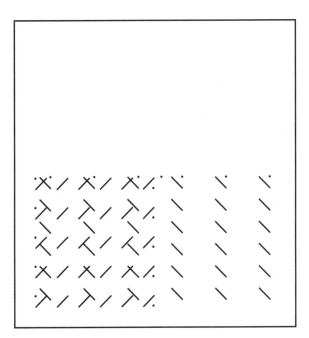

Baste large projects in a grid. Sew from the middle to the outsides.

If you can't tape the backing to the floor, you can use an alternative method. First, spread out the backing, wrong side up, and then put the batting on top. Baste the backing to the batting, be sure that there are no wrinkles in this unit. Then, start at the center, and run basting stitches on the unit, parallel to the sides. Check to see that the backing is smooth. Then center the quilt top, right side up, on the basted unit. Pin and baste the quilt top parallel to the top edge. Start basting in the center, and form a grid with perpendicular basting stitches on the front and back of the quilt.

If you don't want to hand baste your layers together, you can use safety pins. Quilting manufacturers have produced large nickel-plated safety pins that will not rust or tarnish on your quilt. Be careful: I once had a quilt that I was quilting at my leisure (in other words, very slowly), and when I removed the pins, they left holes in the fabric. Don't leave pins in for too long. The safety pins are great for basting projects that are machine quilted. Sometimes the presser foot may catch on the Z basting stitches, but safety pins will make machine quilting easier.

The Least You Need to Know

- Prepare batting by letting wrinkles unfold and piecing similar lofts together, if necessary.

- Cut the batting one inch larger than the perimeter of the quilt top.

◆ Backing must be shrunk with selvages cut off, and sewn into a length of fabric that is 2 inches larger, all around, than the quilt top.

◆ Basting holds together all three layers with either a Z stitch or running stitch in a contrasting-color thread.

◆ Small projects are basted in a sunburst design from the center out. Large projects are sewn in a 4- to 6-inch grid of basting stitches starting from the center and sewing horizontally and vertically.

Chapter 16

Quilting 101

In This Chapter

- How to mark quilt designs
- Steps to hand quilting
- Alternative methods of keeping a quilt together
- Hints on machine quilting

It's finally time to quilt! Your quilting stitches will add dimension to your quilt by adding shadows and subtle designs while enhancing the motifs of the printed fabric. Before taking your first stitch, you need to plan where those stitches will go. That decision will affect the overall look of your completed quilt. I suggest that beginners think fewer stitches—but don't skimp. Quilting can be tedious for novices. Consider this quilt as a learning experience and don't obsess over the size of the quilting stitches.

First decide on a quilting design and where to stitch. Then transfer your design to the quilt top. There is a dilemma ahead: You need to see your markings while quilting, but then not see the markings when you are finished. Today there are many modern quilting innovations—plastic stencils and wash-out pens, to name a few—that our quilting ancestors would be in heaven over. We'll discuss equipment to make marking your designs easy and worry free.

You will also learn how to bond your three layers into one quilt. I will give detailed instructions on how I was taught to hand quilt and then explain alternative methods of tying your quilt and quilting by machine. Each has advantages and disadvantages, so you can evaluate which is best for you. So relax, pull up a chair, and let's quilt.

Choosing Quilt Designs

With modern batting choices, where you quilt will be based on artistry, not necessity. When our ancestors used fillers such as cotton or wool batting, their lines of quilting had to be only 2 inches apart, otherwise the fillers would shift and lump. Because most of the batting manufactured today is bonded, it will not shift, allowing us to attach the layers every 6 to 8 inches apart.

The amount of quilting you do is up to you! You can make your designs simple or intricate. Let me suggest some ideas for quilting, ranging from the simplicity of outline quilting to the excessive echo quilting:

- ◆ **Traditional quilting.** The traditional method is to follow the outline of the block's design. Stitch ¼ inch from each seam line of your pieced or appliquéd patch. The amount of the ¼ inch is significant because it is just outside the pressed seam allowances.

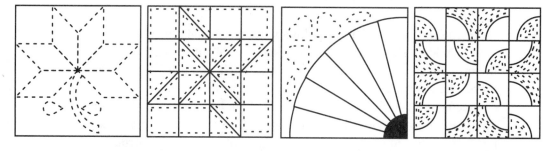

Four different ways to quilt your blocks, from left to right: stitch in the ditch, traditional, special design, or echo.

- ◆ **Stitch in the ditch.** Doesn't that sound strange? This is another process of quilting that follows the pieces of the block's design—only this time you stitch right into the seam. The shape of the entire design then becomes distinct. The stitches are almost invisible because the fabric on each side of the seam will puff up around the stitches.

◆ **Design quilting.** You can also embellish your quilt blocks with a set design. With the many *quilt stencils* available for purchase, you can simply trace onto your patch in the open spaces.

◆ **Echo design quilting.** Lines of stitching follow the outline of a block's basic design, then are repeated, like ripples in a pond, every ¾ inch. The concentric lines make waves of heavy quilting. This is a lot of work and not for beginners.

Quilt Talk

A **quilt stencil** is a plastic sheet that has grooves cut out in a specific design, sometimes hearts, flowers, or geometric shapes.

◆ **Overall design.** These lines of quilting ignore the block's pattern and use an overall design. You can quilt a grid of squares, diagonal lines, or a clamshell design.

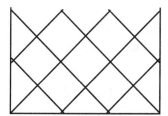 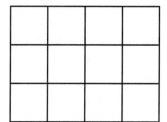 

Three overall designs. These diamond, square, or clamshell overall designs add patterning to your quilt.

For large solid spaces, I suggest using a stencil of a quilt design. You can make your own with plastic sheeting and an X-acto knife, but I don't recommend it for beginners. Manufactured stencils come in a wide variety of shapes and are relatively inexpensive.

If you are determined to design your own patterns for quilting, trace common shapes and mark them in a specific order. Draw and cut out a cardboard heart or diamond or use a glass to trace a cardboard circle to style your own designs.

Quilting Bee

Two instances when you should quilt less: Don't waste time on an intricate design if you are quilting on a highly patterned fabric. (The stitches will not show up.) And, if you want a thick, puffy quilt, use less stitching, because the quilting stitches compact the batting, making it flatter—good-bye, thick quilt.

Look at pictures of quilts to get ideas on quilting styles that you like. Use your imagination! Decide on how you want to quilt and let's transfer your mind's creations to your quilt.

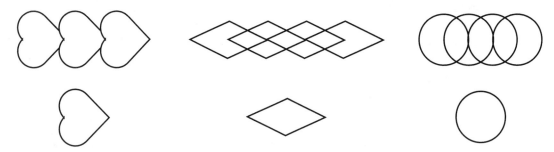

Cut out and trace shapes from cardboard to style your own designs.

Got an Idea? Mark Your Quilt!

Some quilters mark their quilt top before putting all the layers together. I prefer to mark after the quilt is assembled. My quilts are usually a work in progress, and I often change my mind as I go along.

You will need to purchase certain marking supplies. So let's examine the different methods of marking.

If you have chosen to stitch in the ditch, you won't need any special supplies because your seams are your sewing guides. When marking for traditional quilting, however, you have several marking options.

◆ **A number 2.5 or 3 pencil.** You'll get a fine, sharp line that won't smudge.

◆ **Wash-out markers.** You draw a line to mark the design and then, when you've completed quilting, wipe the line with a wet cloth and the marks dissolve. There are two popular brands of markers on the market: One is blue and needs water to remove it; the other is purple and evaporates on its own in a day or two—by magic, the lines disappear!

> **Quilting Bee**
>
> When marking your quilt, draw as light a line as possible that you can still see easily. Don't use a number 2 pencil—it's so soft that it may smear and make your fabric look dirty.

◆ **Masking tape.** This is my favorite option for marking a ¾-inch seam line. Buy masking tape that is ¾-inch wide, cut off the amount you need, and line it up to the seam you are following. Then lift and move it to another seam. You don't have to get involved with any drawing or worry about erasing.

- **Tailor's chalk.** These lines can be brushed off when you finish quilting. The chalk makes thicker lines as it dulls, and thin lines are better for accuracy. You can purchase powdered chalk that rolls onto the fabric and comes in a variety of colors for marking dark and light fabrics.

Don't Get Stuck!

Always test markers on your scrap fabrics first. Students have used regular markers by mistake, and then there was nothing they could do to get rid of the marks!

- **Soap slivers.** This is one way our ancestors marked their quilts. It is a useful technique even today, especially on dark fabrics where a pencil or marker line will not show. Save all those old soap pieces from your bathtub, but don't use deodorant soaps because they have extra chemicals.

One hint on using stencils: The grooves are cut out in the design so you can trace it with your marking tool (not masking tape). Notice that the design is not continuous, but that there is an inch every so often that is not cut. Many beginners stop at each end of the grooves and then start again, making a partial design. You are supposed to bridge these spaces with stitches. The manufacturer had to stop the groove or the stencil would fall apart!

Mark your designs, then get your needle, thread, and thimble. It's time to quilt!

Place the masking tape against the straight seam you are following. Then encircle your work with a hoop.

Be sure to bridge the gaps to have continuous lines.

Hand Quilting

Quilting is short, evenly spaced running stitches that are worked through all three layers of the quilt, adding strength and decorative textures. Let's proceed with putting our quilt layers together. I find hand quilting relaxing and enjoy quilting while my husband watches sports on TV. I feel as if I'm spending time with him while I accomplish something.

Hoop or Frame?

Hoops and frames are specialized tools that help you hand quilt. Besides your quilting thread, quilting needles (sizes 8 to 10), and your thimble, you need something to hold your quilt taut. It is very important to stretch the fabric slightly to eliminate tucks on the backing.

Quilt Talk

A **quilting frame** is a free-standing rectangle that holds a quilt, allowing several people to stitch a section, then roll the quilt to another section, quilting until the whole quilt is finished.

Quilting Frames

When most people think of quilting, they picture women sitting around a *quilting frame*. I unfortunately have never had the opportunity to work my quilts on one. There just isn't enough room in my house and frames can be costly. Legs or wooden sawhorses support a large rectangular frame. The quilting frame holds your project so you can use both hands to quilt. Beginners should probably not work on a frame, because it is stationary and it takes practice to sew in the various directions of your quilting designs.

This PVC quilting frame is found in the classroom of my favorite quilting store— Acme Fabrics. Groups can work on quilt projects together with a frame like this one.

Hoops

I prefer using a hoop because I like to have my projects portable. A hoop consists of two round, oval, or square shapes that fit over one another and hold the quilt tightly between the two pieces. More basting is needed when you use a hoop because you will be moving and handling the fabric as you change the hoop's positions. Hoops come in several styles. The traditional wooden hoops have two round or oval hoops that fit into one another. The top hoop has a large screw that allows the hoop to open larger to accommodate the thickness of the batting.

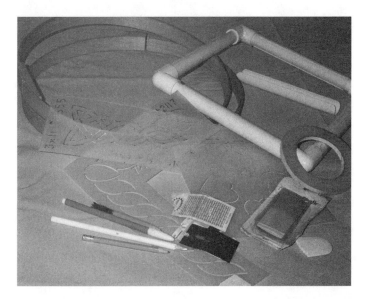

What's all the hoop-la? Here is the traditional hoop for quilting, along with other marking and quilting equipment.

I like using a round hoop rather than an oval one—it's easier to move in any direction. Make sure your hoop has a large screw so that you can open it to expand the hoop at least 1 inch!

A new type of hoop is made out of plastic PVC piping. One of my students found that the PVC stretched and didn't hold the quilt tightly. So I suggest you don't use this type of hoop on quilts that have extra loft or thickness.

Some quilters are able to quilt without a frame or hoop, but they increase the amount of basting. Also, continually check the back of the quilt for wrinkles or tucks. Choose the best tool for you and make your quilting experience great.

Rock Your Stitches

Gather all your quilting equipment, get comfortable, and let's quilt! Although quilting simply consists of running stitches, the trick is to catch all three layers in very small uniform stitches. Making small stitches is a matter of practice. My first quilting teacher said she didn't like her stitches sewn the first 20 minutes she quilted, so she always ripped them out! Remember, this is your first project and your stitches may be large. Never fear, practice makes perfect.

Take apart your hoop and place your project over the bottom part. Take the top hoop and unscrew it as large as possible. Position the top hoop over the bottom, trapping your quilt in between.

Give your quilt a face-lift—straighten your quilt to smooth out a wrinkle here and a tuck there.

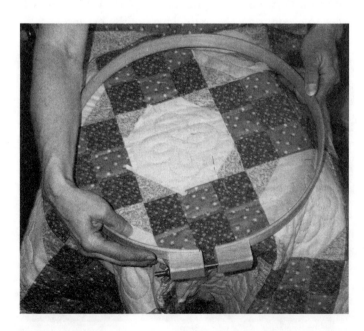

Tighten the screw so that the fabric is taut but not stretched out of shape. Turn the hoop over and check that you have no folds or tucks in the backing. Tug on the backing slightly to straighten it out.

It's time for your first stitch. Start with about 18 inches of quilt thread, and make the small knot that you have been using for piecing. Begin working at the center of your project and quilt toward the outside edges. Your hand with the needle is on the top of the hoop and your other hand is under the hoop, pushing up the needle and guiding where the stitches go. On the top side, put your needle about a ½ inch from where you want to start quilting. I call this no man's land. Push the needle through the batting, but don't let it go through to the backing. Then bring the needle up on the line that you want to stitch. Pull the thread through.

Don't Get Stuck!

When starting to quilt, be sure the needle does not go all the way through to the backing, but keep it parallel in the batting until it reaches the quilting line. Then bring the needle up.

Start in no man's land.

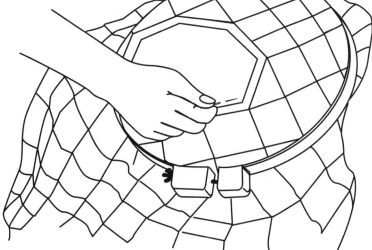

Now I know you are thinking about the knot that is on the top of the quilt. Tug on the thread and the little knot will pop into the batting and be hidden. On the marked quilting line, take a backstitch and then start your running stitches, going through all three layers to secure them.

Pop goes the knot into the batting.

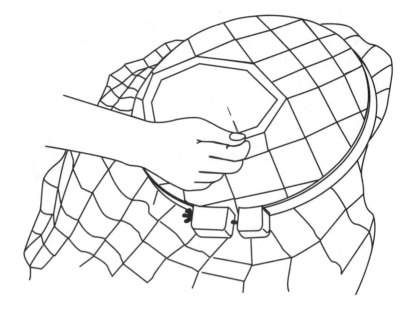

With your top hand, push the needle in perpendicular to the surface and, with your thumb, roll the needle to a 45-degree angle while your pointer finger holds down the fabric. Your stitches will be moving away from you. You will know you have gone through all three layers when the needle pricks your finger under the hoop. Ouch! Some people like to quilt toward themselves and use their pointer finger to push the needle and use their thumb to hold down the fabric. I usually alternate directions to give my fingers a rest.

Quilting Bee

You can use a leather thimble to protect the finger of your bottom hand, but I like to paint my finger with several coats of clear nail polish. It protects my finger but I can still feel the stitches. Don't apply nail polish if you have an open cut—that would hurt.

Pull the thread through and start another stitch, making sure the stitches are uniform in size. Eventually you will develop a rocking motion as you stitch. Move the needle down and then roll it up. Use both thumb and pointer finger to position the needle on the quilting line, then push with your pointer finger while the thumb holds the fabric down in front of the stitch. It may be more comfortable to push with your thumb and hold the fabric with your pointer finger. It's your choice.

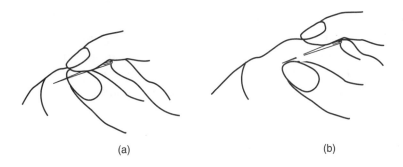

Rock your stitches.

(a)   (b)

Take only one stitch at a time, especially around curves. As you get better, you can take several stitches on your needle.

It's possible to move your line of quilting from one design to another by having the needle travel through the batting to get to another spot. When traveling, do not go all the way through to the backing. It's like taking one long stitch through the middle of the quilt.

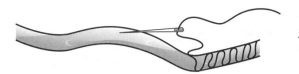

Pack your thread and let your needle travel through the batting.

Stabbing Is a No-No

Try not to *stab* your quilt by pushing the needle into the top and pulling it out underneath with your other hand. The stitches may look right on the top of the quilt, but the stitches on the underside may be uneven and crooked. Use this method only when stitching is so hard that normal quilting is impossible—for example, when many seam allowances intersect or the quilt is too stiff to put your needle through with a running stitch.

Quilt Talk

You are **stabbing** when you insert the needle into your quilt with your top hand and pull it out the bottom with your other hand under the hoop. Then, with your bottom hand, you push the needle from the bottom to the top. When you stab, you are use both hands to quilt your stitches.

Securing Your Stitching

Now you are at the point where there are only a few inches of thread left on your needle. What do you do to secure and knot off the line of quilting stitches? Through the years I have learned from my students several ways of finishing these quilting seams. The easiest way for beginners is this: Take a large stitch in the batting and then backstitch into the last two stitches of the seam. Bring the needle through the batting into no man's land and out the top of the quilt. Cut this thread so ¼ inch is showing. Insert the needle in the batting near the thread parallel to the top and move it back and forth catching the thread, making it disappear into the batting.

Don't be at the end of your rope—backstitch and make your thread disappear into the batting.

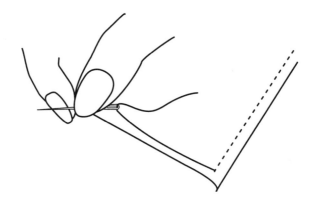

Tie Your Quilt into Knots

Sometimes you may want your quilt to be thick and fluffy. You may also be short on time. Because traditional quilting is time-consuming and does compact the batting, you may want an alternative. I have found the answer to both problems: Secure your layers with knots. Yarn or embroidery floss can be used to prevent your quilt from shifting. These quilts are called tied or tufted quilts.

Here are some pointers for tying your quilt:

1. Pin and baste together the quilt top, batting, and backing.

2. Thread the embroidery needle with floss or yarn in a color that blends or contrasts with your color scheme, depending on your taste.

☆ **Don't Get Stuck!**

When you tie your quilt, you must use a bonded batting so the batting won't shift.

3. Decide on the arrangement of the knots. You can choose an overall pattern (such as every five inches in a grid) or follow the block's designs.

4. Starting from the center of the quilt, take a ¼ inch stitch from the top to the bottom through all three layers and up to the top. Don't pull all the way through; instead, leave a 3-inch tail. Be sure you have caught all three layers.

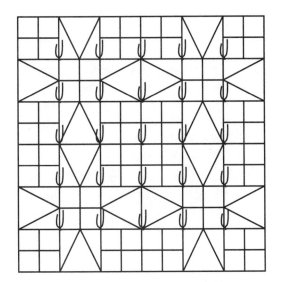
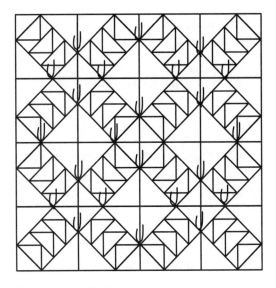

Where to tie or not to tie? Use an overall design or follow the design your blocks make.

5. With the ends, tie a square knot. Remember your scout lessons? Put the right end over the left end and under; then put the left end over the right end and under.

6. Pull the knot tight to secure it, and trim the ends to the desired length.

7. Repeat tying the knots in the designated design working to the outside edges.

Our quilting ancestors did not have all their covers quilted with complex designs. Many of their quilts were tied. For modern quilters, tying a quilt is great when you have to get a project done quickly; but make sure you use enough ties to hold your quilt together and that your knots are secure. Do get yourself tied up in knots!

Quilting Bee _____

When tying their quilts, some people like to leave a ½-inch tuft, whereas others leave longer ends and tie a bow.

Machine Quilting

Machine quilting calls for advanced knowledge of your sewing machine. It is a quick way to quilt but, unfortunately, several problems may develop when quilting. You may need to find solutions by tinkering with your machine. Here are some problems and, I hope, some useful solutions. Practice on a small square of your three layers to get your stitches perfect.

Problem	Solution
The presser foot may push the top fabric along, making the top stretch move and pucker.	Use a "walking foot" (a special attachment to the presser foot that has rollers to the fabric); drop the feed dogs so you can maneuver the quilt though the seam; or loosen the top tension slightly.
You may quilt in tucks on the backing.	Baste more closely or use a hoop.
The stitches may be uneven and tension three too loose.	Experiment with stitching through all layers. Your machine may not be up to quilting, or you may have to choose a thinner batting.
There is too much fabric and bulk when you stitch a large-size quilt.	Try to roll up each end and secure it with safety pins. As you finish quilting an area, unpin and reroll to another section.
The basting stitches get caught on the presser foot while you sew.	Sew smaller basting stitches on the quilt top, or if using a hoop, remove the basting inside the hoop area.

Thread, Bobbins, and Presser Feet

Use a straight or narrow zigzag stitch of 100 percent cotton or cotton-covered poly-ester thread. Choose a color that complements your color scheme. You can even choose a different color for the bobbin to give your quilt reversibility. Slide your quilt and the hoop under the needle. It can be difficult to accomplish this, and depending on your machine, you may have to remove the presser foot. Turn the hand wheel to lower the needle and start your first stitch. Hold on to the top thread, making the lower bobbin thread come up to the top of the quilt top. Be sure you lower the presser foot down. Don't forget because you would have nothing to move your quilt through the machine. Then sew on your marked lines. There is no need to back-stitch, but sew slowly and carefully. Clip threads at the end of quilting.

Support and Seams

Set up your workspace for your convenience. Keep the bulk of the quilt laying on a table behind your machine, so the weight of the quilt won't pull and cause puckers or uneven stitches. The best way for beginners to machine quilt is to use the stitch in the ditch method; remember that you sew right on the seam line following the block's pattern. The seams add strength to the quilt seam and the fabric won't shift as much. Please practice on a small project, like a pillow or crib quilt. Using your sewing machine can make your quilting quick, and if you are really interested, look for other books and resources that explain all this in detail.

The Least You Need to Know

- ◆ The three layers of the quilt must be held together with hand or machine quilting or knots.

- ◆ Quilting designs can follow the outline of your block's pattern, be an overall design, or be a specific design drawn from a quilting stencil.

- ◆ Mark your quilt with as light a marker as possible, but make sure you can still see the lines.

- ◆ Start quilting or tying from the center and work to the outside edge.

- ◆ Be experienced on handling your machine if you want to do machine quilting.

Chapter 17

Your Finished Quilt

In This Chapter

- ◆ Finishing the edges of your quilt
- ◆ Making your own bias binding
- ◆ Signing your quilt

Your quilt is beautiful! We're down to the last leg of the race. It's almost time to put it on your bed. I bet you can't wait to finish off those raveling edges with batting sticking out. There are several strategies for binding off the edges. Some methods use the quilt top border fabric, the backing, or a separate bias binding. Bindings can be purchased in a multitude of colors, or you can make them using a fabric from your color scheme.

Making your own bias tape can be confusing, but I'll show you the "molar" method that one of my first quilting teachers taught me. Follow the directions step by step and you won't get into a "bind."

Every artist signs his or her work of art, and you should, too. Whether with quilting thread, floss, or indelible ink pens, you can write your name, the date of completion, the name of the quilt, and perhaps the occasion for giving it as a gift. Let's get started—I know you can't wait to use your quilt!

Finally Get Rid of Those Frayed Edges

You are probably tired of getting everything, especially your rings, caught on the ragged outer edge of your quilt. As soon as I finish quilting—and celebrating—the *binding* that encloses those ragged edges comes soon after.

Quilt Talk _____

Binding is a strip of fabric, usually cut on the bias so it can stretch, that covers the outer edge of your quilt.

Quilting Bee _____

Some people like to cut the batting flush with the quilt top, but I like to leave an extra ½ inch to give the binding body and thickness.

Don't Get Stuck! _____

Binding your quilt with a border fabric or the backing is often looked down on because the methods do not produce a replaceable binding. As a quilt is used, the binding is usually the first part to get worn. If that happens, the quilt top will be damaged—sometimes irreparably.

There are four ways to bind the edge of your quilt, and each gives a different look. Each method has advantages and disadvantages. Read through this chapter and determine how you want to end your ends.

You must make some last-minute preparations before neatly finishing the ends. Take out all the basting threads. Cut off all errant threads throughout your quilt top. (I don't know where they all come from—they just appear.) Spread your layered quilt out and cut the excess batting to ½ inch all the way around the quilt top.

The backing will be cut off differently depending on the binding technique you use, so don't do anything until you decide how to bind the edge.

The first two methods I call the cheater's way, because they really are the easiest.

Turning the Border Fabric to the Back

This finish binds your edges so that the quilt border is the last color framing the outside of the quilt top. Cut the batting and backing fabric to 1 inch less than the border all around the quilt. Turn the border fabric under ½ inch, then fold about ½ inch of it around the quilt to the backing side. The back of the quilt will have ½ inch of the border fabric folded and sewn to it. Pin about 2 feet at a time of the border fabric folded to the backing. Use an appliqué stitch or a catch stitch. If you don't remember how to sew invisibly, check out Chapter 11.

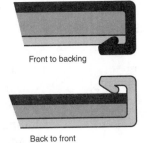

Front to backing

Back to front

You can fold the border from the front to the back or roll the backing to the front. Which way should you go?

Turning the Backing Fabric to the Front

This finish is very similar to finishing with a border fabric—it's just reversed. This time cut the batting about ½ inch larger than the quilt top. The backing should be an inch larger all the way around. Turn the backing fabric under ¼ inch so wrong sides are together. Then turn it over to the front, making sure the ¼-inch fold covers the edge. Pin so that the binding is even, about ½ inch, and sew with an invisible stitch. You have to be sure that the backing fabric coordinates with the quilt top because the binding forms a small frame on the front.

Attached Bias Binding

There are several steps to this method. Follow these step-by-step directions carefully:

1. Cut the batting and backing ½ inch larger than the quilt top. With a contrasting color, baste all around the outer raw edge of the quilt top at ¼ inch.

2. Purchase or make a bias binding. Open up one ¼-inch folded edge and place the right side of the binding to the quilt top with the raw edge facing the outer edge.

3. Pin into the ¼-inch fold, turning the short end of the binding under to finish it off.

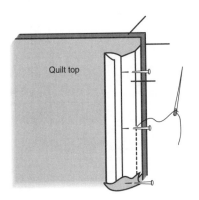

Quilt top

Doesn't this procedure look backward? Pin and align the raw edges of the quilt top to finish off the end.

Don't Get Stuck!

If you sew by machine, take care not to pull the bias binding—it has a tendency to stretch and pucker.

4. Stitch the bias binding to the quilt top in the ¼-inch fold, either by hand or machine.

5. Sew to within ¼ inch from the end of the seam, backstitch, stop the seam, and cut the threads. Now miter the corner. Make about a ½-inch pleat at the corner before turning. Pin the bias binding so that ½ inch is sticking up, and on the adjacent side put your needle where the other line of stitching ended and start sewing a new line of stitching.

Now this really looks wrong, but it's right. Pivot the binding and start stitching where the other line ended.

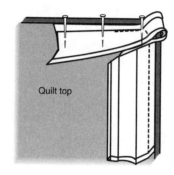

6. Stitch all around the perimeter of the quilt. Overlap the binding, ending where you began.

7. Fold the bias binding over the edge of the quilt and pin, making sure that the binding is turned evenly.

8. Sew with an invisible stitch until you get to the corner.

Be a magician and make your stitches in the binding disappear!

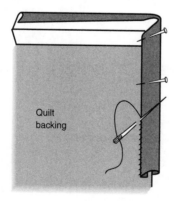

9. Now for the part of the binding that is sticking up—fold the right side of the binding up and then the top side down to form an accurate, mitered 45-degree angle.

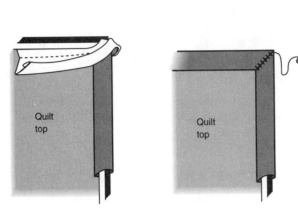

Fold under and miter the corner by turning the binding to the back and making a 45-degree angle at the corner.

10. Stitch to hold down the folded corner.

A bias binding adds a small border of color that can contrast with your quilt top, creating a frame.

Pillow Technique

One of my students uses this method regularly and it is very nice for baby quilts because you can insert lace into the edging. This finishing technique actually has to be done before the project is quilted. I do not recommend this method for beginners—it is very difficult to sew and manipulate the fabric. It is a problem to get the quilt to lay flat and not look bunchy. If you use this procedure for your next quilt, here are the instructions:

1. Cut the batting and the backing even with the quilt top.

2. Place the quilt top right sides together with the backing. Sew by machine all along the perimeter of the quilt leaving about 2 feet open to turn it right side out.

Quilting Bee

If you use the pillow technique, you can insert lace before you sew the backing. Place the tape end of the lace against the raw outer edges of your quilt. You can check out Chapter 18 to see how to insert lace, piping, and ruffles.

3. Pin the batting evenly all around the outside edge. Hand stitch this down on top of the same seam line. I know that the two steps seem repetitive, but it prevents the batting from stretching out of shape and getting caught on the presser foot as you sew.

4. Very carefully, reach your hand inside the quilt and turn it right side out.

5. Flatten and smooth out the three layers, pushing out the corners. Baste with a Z stitch in 6-inch grids.

6. Quilt.

The edges are finished and are inside the quilt.

Do Get Into a Bind

Quilters have found that a bias binding or bias tape is more durable than fabric cut on the straight of grain, and it can also bend to make finished rounded or mitered corners with 45-degree angles. Measure the perimeter of your quilt, adding about 5 inches for mitering the corners and finishing the ends. After you have that measurement, you can plan the amount you need to buy or make. If you can find a packaged binding in a color that coordinates with the quilt top, buy it! A great deal of time will be saved. The rectangular packages come in a variety of sizes and widths, but the best to purchase is a double-folded quilt binding.

Making Bias Strips

Bias strips can be cut from the diagonal of one of your fabrics used in your quilt. It is great being able to have a coordinating fabric frame your quilt. The strips can be 1½ inches wide for a regular tape size or 2½ inches wide if you want to double-fold your binding. Cut the strips as long as possible. Remember to draw the diagonal and measure the width of each strip. Cut the strips carefully, and don't stretch them. Pin right sides together at a right angle; it doesn't look right, but it works. Open the binding to check if you pinned it correctly. Sew a ½-inch seam, then press it open. Sew the ends together with a ½-inch seam allowance.

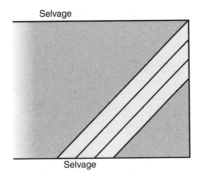

Angle your strips so they will stretch, and yes, I'm certain that's how to pin them.

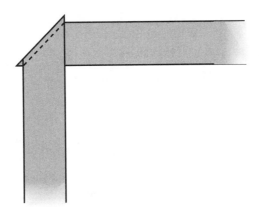

Molar Method of Making Bias

Another method of cutting the bias strips is faster and easier, especially if you are cutting large amounts of binding. I call it the molar method, but its true name is the continuous-roll technique. One 36-inch square of fabric will make approximately 15 yards of 1½-inch binding or 12 yards of 2½-inch binding. If you use the entire width of your fabric, 43 inches, you will make 22 yards of 1½-inch binding or 15 yards of 2½-inch binding. Isn't that amazing? The directions may seem puzzling, but I describe them here step by step:

1. Cut a square of fabric either 36 or 43 inches square, depending on how much binding you need.

2. Cut the square in half on the diagonal to form two triangles. If you want, pin a paper with letters to each of the sides so you can figure out which ones are sewn together. Follow Figure a. Side A is opposite side B, and side C is across from side D.

Cut apart the square into two triangles. (b) Pin and sew sides A and B to make a big tooth—hence the molar!

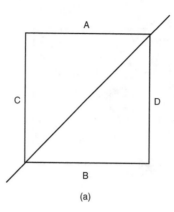

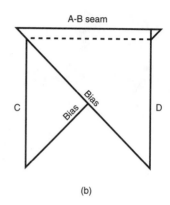

(a)

(b)

3. Sew sides' A and B right sides together to form the molar shape. Make a ½-inch seam down the A-B side (see Figure b).

4. Open up this tooth to form a parallelogram. Press open the seam.

Don't Get Stuck!

When sewing by the molar technique, be sure the seam is on the straight of grain and does not stretch. Pull the roots of the molar and be sure they *do* stretch. Look at Figure b. I can't tell you how many times my bias did not stretch because I didn't correctly sew the seams.

5. On the wrong side of your fabric, use a see-through ruler to draw lines parallel to the bias sides. If you are using the binding for a full-size quilt, the width should be between 2 to 2½ inches; for a smaller project, measure 1½ to 2 inches (see Figure c).

6. Carefully hold together sides C to D; they are the straight of grain and will not stretch. This may seem backward because the seams are going in opposite directions. You will form a tube or sleeve, but shift the right side down one bias line so the top left side has formed a tail sticking up (see Figure d). Pin to match the drawn lines.

(c) Draw parallel lines from side C to D.

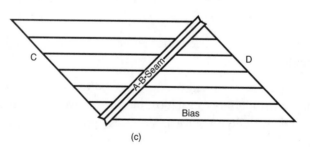

(c)

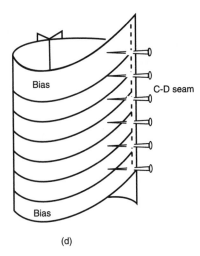

(d)

(d) Be the boss of your fabric—form a tube or sleeve with a tail off the top the size of the bias width.

7. Pin and sew a ½-inch seam and be certain there is a tail on each end. Press this seam open.

8. Begin cutting at the top tail on the drawn line and spiral around the tube in one long cut (see Figure e).

9. As I cut each yard of binding, I press it immediately and wrap it around a cardboard square. Can you imagine 20 yards of stretchy strips! It is so much easier to do a yard or two at a time. For a regular bias, press both sides under ¼ inch, then the entire strip in half down the center. When making a double bias, where the fabric is doubled, just fold the bias tape in half (see Figure f).

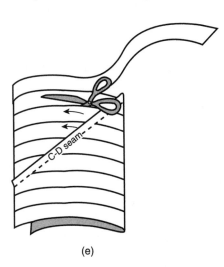

(e)

(e) This is one long cutting line. Just start at the top and cut in a spiral around and around and around.

(f) Don't get into a bind. Press as you go.

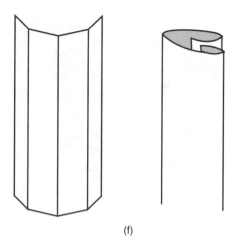

(f)

10. Sew together the bias tape right sides to the quilt top right sides, around the perimeter of your quilt. Fold over and whipstitch or use an appliqué stitch to secure.

I told you this method of making binding was tricky, but it is so efficient when making large amounts of binding that it's worth the effort.

Signing Your Quilt

Signing your quilt is the finishing touch to your quilting experience. Your work of art should be signed and dated. A running stitch of quilting thread signing your name can be sewn on the front or back of your quilt. If you want your name and date to stand out more, you can use embroidery floss and a decorative embroidery stitch.

Many of my students sign their quilts with labels placed on the back. One class assembled a wall hanging of different storybook characters for the children's room of a library. We signed the back of the quilt with all of our names on a label shaped like an open book.

Many terrific books deal with calligraphy and styling memorable labels. Wash and shrink the fabric you plan on using for the label. Practice writing with an indelible fine-point pen. Record your name, the date of completion, occasion for making the quilt, and who you are giving it to. Some quilts are like cards hallmarking events and including memorable quotations. Turn under ¼ inch all around the label. You can hand or machine embroider the edges and designs around your insignia.

Attach your label with an invisible stitch to the lower corner of the backing. Sign your quilt and shout to the world your quilt is complete!

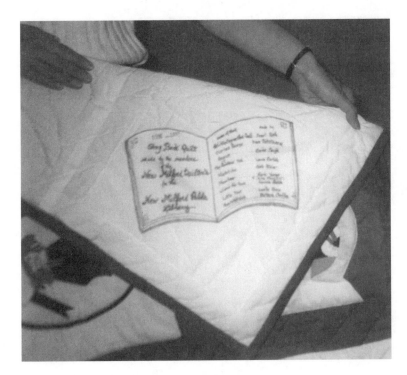

Hallmark events with your labels.

Scraps and Pieces

Those who collect quilts can date and follow a quilt's history with the information found from the signing. Many quilts were found with names signed on the front of special blocks. These were called Album quilts. Album quilts were often group projects that had each block signed by the designer. Blocks were even developed with a special space for signing your name. Our quilting ancestors took this signing seriously and developed special ink, quill pens, and patterned metal stencil plates. Calligraphy was practiced until their handwriting was perfected.

The Least You Need to Know

♦ Folding fabric over the quilt ends will enclose the raveling edges.

♦ Bias binding is the most durable technique for finishing ends, and it can be made in one continuous roll.

♦ Signing and dating your quilt is the final step to the completion of your quilt.

♦ When making a label, wash and shrink the fabric and use a permanent-ink pen.

Quilting Project: A Basic Pillow

In This Chapter

♦ Preparing a pillow from a quilt block

♦ How to insert lace, piping, or a ruffle onto the edges

♦ Methods of hanging a quilt

Small projects are a good beginning for novices. Not everyone is ready to make a bed-size quilt, but you may want to make a pillow or wall hanging. Display your creation so the world can see it. Hanging quilts on the wall is very popular in decorating today. From modern geometric shapes to countrified Sampler quilts, a quilted wall hanging can enhance your room. There are different styles and methods of hanging your quilt. Decide on the look you want to achieve. Your quilt can appear to be floating on the wall, or you can make a tab top with loops of fabric, adding to your quilt's decorative value. The choice is yours.

Remember when I said not to worry if you decided not to use one of your patches? Now is the time to use it in a pillow. Your pillow can be tailored with piping, or very feminine with lace or a ruffle. Stuffing your pillow and setting it on your couch or bed is very satisfying. Now it's time for you to learn how to make two small projects from start to finish.

Making a Pillow

Here are instructions for making a basic pillow. If you get really ambitious, I'll give you directions for embellishing your edges with a ruffle, lace, or *piping*.

Use a patch that coordinates with your quilt to make an ensemble.

1. Make the block of your choice, or use an extra one left over from your quilt. Add a border if you want to make your pillow larger than 12 inches. You can prepare a regular border and miter the corners. (Check out Chapter 14 for instructions on borders and mitering.)

2. Press your pillow top.

3. Add batting and a muslin backing. Baste together all three layers in sunburst lines.

4. Quilt decorative stitches in your chosen design, such as the stitch in the ditch, outline, overall, or echo designs. (Look at Chapter 16.)

5. Insert any decorative edging, piping, lace, or ruffle. Each insert is discussed later in this chapter.

6. Prepare the pillow back in a coordinating fabric. You can have one solid piece of fabric for the backing, a zippered backing, or a lapped backing held together with Velcro. I discuss how to prepare the backing later in this chapter.

7. To assemble the pillow, pin the layered pillow top to the pillow back, right sides together. Sew around the perimeter of the pillowcase at ¼ inch from the edge. If the backing is one solid piece of fabric, leave about 6 inches unsewn on the bottom seam so you can turn the pillowcase right side out. If the back is lapped with Velcro or a zipper, you can sew the seam all the way around.

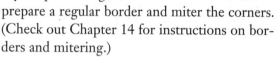

Quilt Talk

Piping is a tiny contrasting strip of bias fabric with a cord inside. This corded fabric is sewed into a seam, forming a decorative edge.

Quilting Bee

Use an inexpensive washed muslin for the backing of the pillow top. No one will ever see it because it will be inside the pillow.

Don't Get Stuck!

When a zipper is used on the backing of the pillow, leave the zipper open several inches before you sew the pillow backing and layered pillow top together. This way you can pull the pillowcase through the opening.

8. Reach into the open seam or zipper and pull the pillowcase through, turning it right side out.

9. Use a pillow form or pack your pillow until firm with polyester fiberfill. Push the stuffing into the corners with a ruler or pencil and then add more if needed.

Quilting Bee

Push out the pillow corners to form a crisp point. I use the eraser end of a pencil.

10. Fold the seam allowances over and invisibly stitch the opening at the bottom of the pillow if necessary.

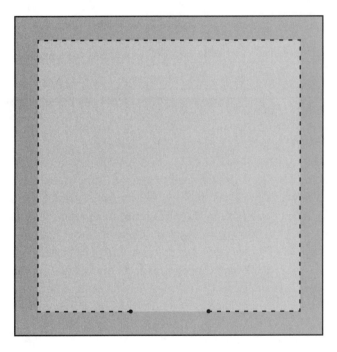

Place right sides together and then sew around, leaving open about 6 inches on one side.

Now learn how you can make our pillow even fancier.

Lace Insertions

Measure the perimeter of the pillow and add 4 more inches for finishing the corners and the ends. Purchase that amount of lace. Align the straight edge of the lace, right sides together, to the outside edge of the pillow top, with the ruffled edge facing in.

Start pinning in the middle of the bottom side of the pillow top. Make a ½-inch fold at each corner and pin the lace securely all around the pillow top. When you've reached where you started, angle both ends of the lace into the edge of the seam allowance. Sew lace all around the outside edge. Continue with step 6, in the "Making a Pillow" section to prepare the pillow backing.

This looks backward, but it's not. Sew all around the outside edge, angling the lace off the edges.

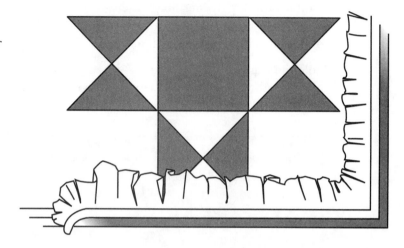

Inserting Piping

Sometimes you want to add a contrasting color but want a more tailored edge to finish your pillow. This is when you'd use piping. Measure the sides of the pillow and add about 2 inches more to the length. The round fabric cording can be purchased at fabric or craft stores in a variety of colors. The piping is applied in the same manner as lace, placing the piping's raw edge next to the pillow top's edges with the bulky cord facing to the center. Pin to the corner; then clip the tape up to the cord, allowing the tape to open. Turn the corner, continuing to pin up the next side. Sew along the piping's line of stitches. Use a *zipper foot* if you need to, securing the piping onto the pillow top.

Quilt Talk

The **zipper foot** is a presser foot that can slide to one side and is used to sew in zippers. But it can also let you sew very closely to the piping cord. Use it when sewing the piping to the pillow back.

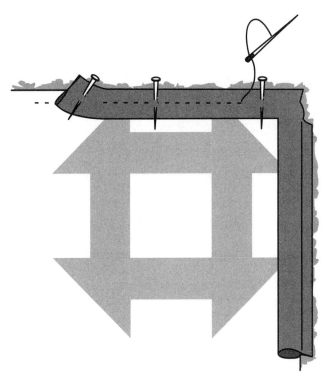

Clip into each corner to turn the piping around the pillow corner.

Applying a Ruffle

When you get really ambitious, you may want to add a ruffle to the edge of your pillow. This gets a little complicated, so I hope you are ready:

1. Cut the ruffle strips. Measure around the outside edge of the pillow, then double it to calculate the amount needed. If your pillow is 15 inches square, you need to cut a strip 120 inches. (15 + 15 + 15 + 15 = 60 × 2 = 120 inches.) Determine how wide you want your ruffle. Let's say 2 inches. Double that amount and add on ½ inch for the seam allowance. (2 + 2 + ½ = 4½ inches.) The ruffle should be cut 120 inches by 4½ inches. Cut the strips from selvage to selvage across the width of the fabric, usually 3 strips of 40 inches.

Quilting Bee

To make a ruffle, baste by machine at ¼ inch with the longest stitch. Sew another line of basting about ⅛ inch away from the raw edge. These two lines of basting are used to gather the ruffle. You sew two lines to ensure that, if one thread breaks, you still have one to work with (see Figure b).

2. Sew each short end together; then sew the final ends together to form a circular strip. Fold the ruffle in half, wrong sides together, so the strip is 2½ inches wide.

3. Divide the ruffle into four equal sections and insert four pins, one to mark each section. Baste with your sewing machine ¼ inch from the edge, stopping the seam at each pin, leaving an inch-long thread between each section (see Figure b).

4. Secure a pin at the middle of each side of the pillow top, aligning the raw edges together, the ruffle facing into the center (see Figure c). Match the pins on the ruffle to the pins in the center of the pillow top sides. Do not pin the pins into the corners, but center the sections in the middle of each side. This way it will work for any size pillow, square or rectangular.

Gather the ruffles.

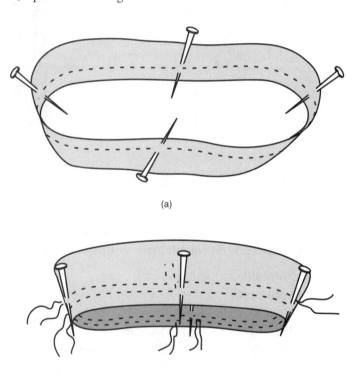

(a)

(b)

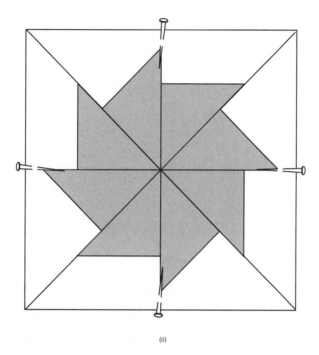

(c)

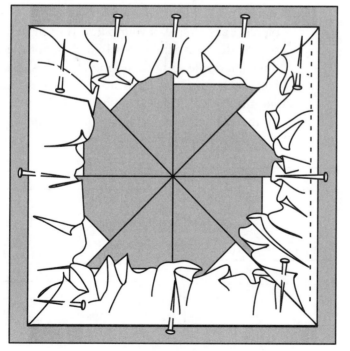

Don't get ruffled—pin the corners of the ruffle so the fabric won't shift.

5. Pull the ends of the threads between each section to gather the ruffle to fit the sides of the pillow. Pin the ruffle every few inches to secure it to the pillow top.

6. Baste the ruffle to the pillow top ¼ inch from the raw edges; then continue preparing the pillow back in step 6 of "Making a Pillow."

Finishing the Pillow Back

The pillow I gave you instructions for earlier is made with a solid square of fabric as the backing. But if you ever want to remove the pillowcase for cleaning, you will need to make a different kind of backing. In that case, divide the backing into two overlapping sections or two sections held together with a zipper. The zipper application is for experienced sewers only.

Quilting Bee

Occasionally pin the finished edge of the ruffle to the pillow top, around the corners especially. There is a tendency for the ruffle to shift and get caught in the seam when you sew the pillow backing to the pillow top.

Be sure the pillow backings are large enough. There should be enough of a lap so the backing doesn't pull open when the pillow is inside. Measure the size of your pillow, and add 1 inch to the horizontal size. However, you must add considerably more in the other direction: Calculate half the size of the pillow, and then add 4 inches for a fold. Cut two of these pieces. For example, if your pillow is 15 inches square, the horizontal size is 16 inches. For the other direction divide 15 by 2, making 7½ inches. Add 4 inches for a total of 11½ inches. Cut two backing sides 16 by 11½ inches. Fold down ¼ inch to finish off the edge; then press under 1 inch all the way across (see Figure a).

Fold ¼ inch under and then fold 1 more inch to finish the lap. Position by overlapping these edges.

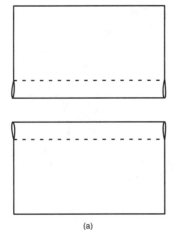

(a)

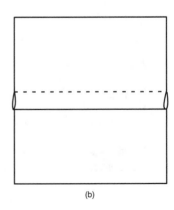

(b)

Overlap these folded edges so they are the same size as the pillow top (see Figure b). Baste both ends of the lapped pieces together to hold securely. Turn this lapped backing right side to the right side of the pillow top. Pin the pillow top and backing together and sew at ¼ inch all the way around the outside edges.

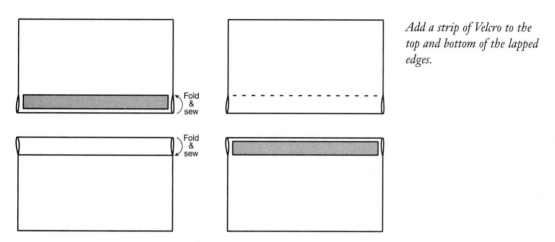

Add a strip of Velcro to the top and bottom of the lapped edges.

After you sew together the pieces, pull the right side of the pillowcase through the opening of the lap. Insert your pillow form and you have a pillow.

Some people who want a professional-looking pillow insert a zipper into the backing. Beware: This is not easy. Cut two pieces of backing fabric, half the size of the backing, and then add 1 inch to both pieces where the zipper will be attached.

The zipper should be about 2 inches shorter than the width of the pillow. Read the directions on the inside of the zipper package for how to prepare the zipper placket and then stitch the zipper into the seam. Turn the backing over and center it over the pillow top, right sides together. Sew all around the outside edge. Then turn the pillow right side out.

Don't Get Stuck!

Be sure the zipper is open when you sew the pillow backing to the pillow top so you can pull the pillowcase through the opening. I've made that mistake and then tried to open the zipper from the back. I finally had to rip out some of the bottom of the seam.

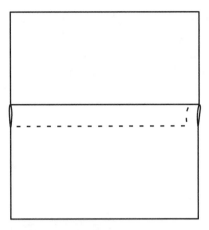

Zip into your pillow—calculate the size of each backing piece.

Quilts Are the New Artwork

Quilts can be found in museums and are recognized as an art form. We can hang quilts in our houses, too. Make your home a gallery to display your quilts. There are several lines of thought on ways to hang quilts. You can attach a sleeve or casing to the top of the backing and push a dowel, curtain rod, or furring strip through as a hanger. The quilt in this method appears to be floating on the wall, because the casing and rod are invisible on the front. On the other hand, you can make the style of hanging a decorative part of the quilt design. Loops or tabs are sewn to the top of the quilt and hung on a fancy rod. Let's decide which you want to make.

Hidden Sleeve Method

Measure the horizontal width of your quilt and subtract 2 inches from that amount. You want to have enough room at each end of the sleeve to have the rod hang on a nail. If your quilt is very wide, you may want to divide the sleeve in half, forming two pockets. Then you will be able to hang the rod on three nails, one at each end and then one in the middle. You don't want your rod to bow under the quilt's weight.

> **Quilting Bee**
>
> Do not sew with the tube stretched flat against the backing. Allow an excess on the top half of the tube to hang loose, making more room for the rod to slip into the sleeve.

Cut a strip 3 to 4 inches wide, depending on the size of the rod and the length of the horizontal measurement of the quilt. Finish each short end of the strip.

Then fold the length in half and sew a ¼-inch seam. Finger press the tube so that the seam runs down the center. Center this casing and pin it across the backing about ½ inch from the top of the quilt. Invisibly stitch the top of the casing, then sew the bottom length of the sleeve.

Put your sanded dowel or rod through the sleeve and hang your work of art.

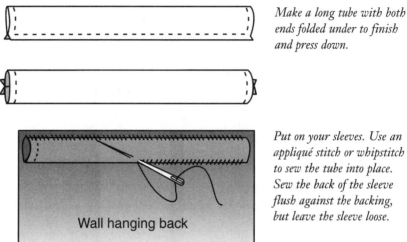

Make a long tube with both ends folded under to finish and press down.

Put on your sleeves. Use an appliqué stitch or whipstitch to sew the tube into place. Sew the back of the sleeve flush against the backing, but leave the sleeve loose.

Wall hanging back

Fabric Loops

This method has visible fabric loops to hold the rod. Read on to find out how to make those loops look so beautiful:

1. Decide on the width of the loops. I like about 2 inches. Double that amount and add ½ inch for seam allowances. I cut my strips 2 + 2 + ½ = 4½ inches wide, and from selvage to selvage for the length, making the strip 4½ by the fabric width.

2. Fold this strip in half lengthwise with right sides together.

3. Sew a ¼-inch seam down the length and press the seam down the center, forming a tube (see Figure a).

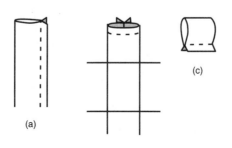

(a)

(b)

(c)

Don't get loopy! Sew and press the seam and then turn the tube right side out. Cut it into sections.

4. Cut the tube into sections, double the size you want for each loop, and then add a ½-inch seam allowance to determine the amount. If you want a 2-inch loop, cut the tube into 4½-inch sections (see Figure b).

5. Sew the ends of each section together to form a circular loop (see Figure c).

6. Evenly space and attach loops to the top of the backing and whipstitch or invisible stitch.

This quilt hanging looks like a banner that announces your quilt artistry. If your quilt bottom ripples, you may want to put a sleeve on the bottom of the backing so the rod will hold your quilt flush to the wall.

Sew loop to loop to loop to hang your quilt.

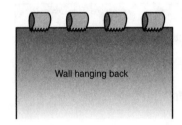

Wall hanging back

The Least You Need to Know

♦ A pillow top must be quilted with a batting and backing before the pillow back is attached.

♦ Lace, piping, and a ruffle are inserted after the pillow top is quilted but before the pillow back is attached.

♦ When cutting the pillow back for use with a zipper or lapped back, be sure to have more fabric to accommodate the finished edges and the overlapping fabric.

♦ You can hang quilts with a hidden sleeve or top loops, depending on the appearance you want.

Part 2

Embroidery

Although embroidery is a bit more difficult than some other forms of needlework, it's a great place to start. Whether it's getting up to speed on color choices, thread quality, or specific stitches and techniques, you'll learn the basics in this part. You'll also complete two projects, including a monogramming lesson.

Tools of the Trade

In This Chapter

- ◆ Choosing the perfect background
- ◆ Learning the basic types of needles and threads
- ◆ Keeping it all together with frames
- ◆ Starting with a beginner's kit

With your new design and color sense, and a feeling of what style will work for you, you are ready to get to work. But like any good craftsperson, you will need the right tools before you start stitching away. As a novice embroiderer, it's important to learn about needle size, appropriate fabrics, frames, and thread types, as well as the kinds of kits that are available. The beauty of embroidery is the harmony created with the pairing of canvas and threads, the correct gauge needles and stitches, and the design for the project at hand.

The Material World of Embroidery

Quite a range of background fabrics is available for any embroidery project. Actually, any fabric can be embroidered as long as it is firm enough to hold stitches, supple enough to allow a needle to pass through and wear-resistant enough to hold up during stitching. Most embroidery fabrics range from fine silks to thick wools. Solid fabrics are the norm, but printed and patterned fabrics can be used as a design guide, as you follow the print with your needle and thread.

Woven fabrics work well, too. A wide range of *evenweave* fabrics is available for counted-thread techniques, which rely on counting the threads of the fabric to achieve the pattern. The four types of natural fabrics most commonly used for embroidery are cottons, silks, linens, and wools.

A very popular embroidery cloth is 14-count Aida cloth. This versatile cotton fabric is available in a wide range of colors and is suitable for many types of threads and designs. Stitching is enjoyable because your needle and thread can be easily brought in and out of the fabric. Aida is woven in a design that looks like little squares, making it easy to place one stitch in each square and to count spaces. This fabric is also available with a colored grid to make stitch counting from a chart easier and is thus a good choice for beginners. The colored threads are removed when the stitching is done. You can readily find 14-count Aida cloth at stitchery shops and craft stores. Aida also comes in other thread counts, including 11 count for tired eyes and 18 count for more delicate effects.

Needlework 101

Evenweave is a type of fabric that has the same number of warp threads (the threads that go up and down) as it has weft threads (the ones that go side to side) per square inch. For example, an 18-count evenweave fabric has 18 threads to the inch, both vertically and horizontally.

Evenweave fabrics are a good choice for counted-thread techniques such as cross-stitch.

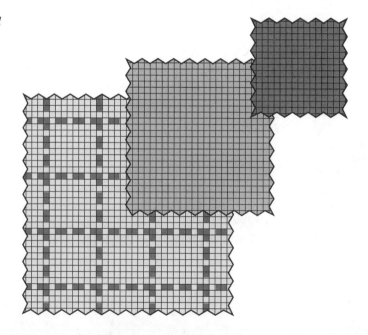

Nice Threads!

Threads come in an exciting range of colors and fibers. Some popular fibers used for threads are silks, cottons, linens, wools, metals, and synthetics. Particular weights and thickness of threads are suited for certain types of background fabrics. You can also experiment with other yarns, such as those made for knitting or crochet. Familiarize yourself with the following embroidery threads and examples of backgrounds that can be used with each:

♦ **Embroidery floss.** A loosely twisted six-strand cotton thread that is easily divided into single threads. Works well on linen or cotton fabrics.

♦ **Matte embroidery thread.** A thick, soft, tightly twisted thread. Works well on evenweave fabrics in linen and cotton.

♦ **Crewel yarn.** A fine two-*ply* wool or acrylic yarn. Works well on linen.

♦ **Flower thread.** A fine thread that cannot be divided and has a matte finish. Works well on tightly woven fabrics and cottons and linens.

♦ **Pearl cotton.** A strong, twisted thread that cannot be divided and has a high sheen. Works well on cottons, linens, and wools.

♦ **Persian yarn.** Loosely twisted three-strand wool or acrylic yarn that is easily divided. Works well on cottons, wools, and linens.

> **Needlework 101**
>
> **Ply** is a component of a strand of thread or yarn. Plies make up the strand, and strands make up the thread or yarn. For example, if you remove one strand from a six-strand floss and untwist the strand, you will see that the single strand is composed of two plies.

The best way to choose yarn, if it is not already prepackaged in a kit, is to assess the look that you want for your design and the type of fabric you are using. Fine threads will look neat on delicate fabrics, whereas woolly threads will be bulkier-looking and may require a rougher, heavier fabric. But sometimes the most creative looks come when you match rough with refined—you know, opposites attract ... silk thread on wool and wool thread on silk fabric. The most important thing to keep in mind when you buy your thread is its weight and thickness. If it's too heavy, it will distort the fabric that you are working on; too flimsy, and you will not be able to see your stitching. Experiment with different threads and fabrics, and you can come up with some clever combinations.

The Fine Points of Needles

Embroidery needles are made in a range of sizes, usually in categories classified by the type of work or fabric they are designed for. Fine-gauge needles, which are small and thin, are for finer cloths or grounds (the background fabric on which needlework is done), and larger-gauge needles are used for coarser grounds. A good rule of thumb to remember is that the finer the needle, the higher the number.

Usually the eye of the needle is long to make threading it easier. One exception is the needle used for metal work. The eye is round to hold the thread in place so that it will not slide within the eye. This protects the rest of the thread, outside the eye, from the abrasion of being pulled through the eye.

Types of needles: crewel, che-nille, tapestry, and beading.

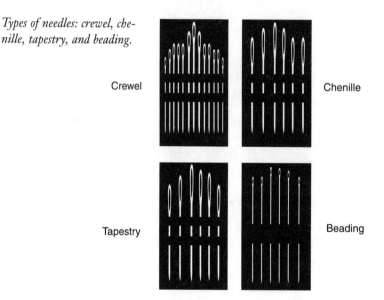

Crewel

Chenille

Tapestry

Beading

You may have already guessed that different types of embroidery work require differ-ent needles. Some of the most common embroidery needles include the following:

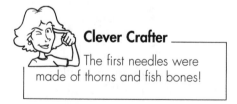

Clever Crafter

The first needles were made of thorns and fish bones!

◆ **Crewel or embroidery needle.** This is the most commonly used needle. It has a sharp point and large eye that is used for crewel work.

◆ **Chenille needle.** Similar to a crewel needle but with a thicker shaft. The chenille needle is good for heavy threads and coarse grounds.

- **Tapestry needle.** A thick-shafted, large-eyed needle with a round-pointed end; the tapestry (or yarn) needle works best for evenweave fabrics because it is designed to slip between the threads rather than to pierce them as a crewel needle does.

- **Beading needle.** A fine, long needle with a tiny eye used for sewing small beads.

Taut and Tidy Frames

Embroidery frames are used to hold the ground fabric taut so the embroiderer can concentrate on the task at hand. Small projects may not necessarily need a frame, but a frame helps to make the work easier to handle and quicker to stitch. It also helps to hold the fabric permanently taut and evenly stretched to ensure even stitches. Your work stays cleaner with a frame because it is handled less. Also, a frame on a stand allows your hands to be free to work the stitches. Two basic types of frames are round (hoop frame) and straight sided.

The *hoop frame* is most popular because it is portable, lightweight, and easy to mount. It can be made of wood, plastic, or metal, and it ranges in sizes from 5 to 10 inches in diameter. The frame is composed of two hoops that are placed one inside the other, stretching the fabric between them. The outer hoop has an opening in it and a screw to adjust the tension.

The *straight-sided frame* (also known as a stretcher frame) has a roller top and bottom and is usually used for larger wall hangings, but is suitable for all types of embroidery. A straight frame stretches the fabric very evenly and allows for a large part of the work to be visible (good for freehand design). Although more time is needed to mount a piece on a straight-sided frame, the piece is quickly moved into a new position as your stitching progresses. The latest Q-snap frames are made of PVC pipe. Not only are they inexpensive, available in many sizes, and a "snap" to use, but they also provide excellent tension and do not crease the fabric—which is the chief drawback of hoops. For many people, Q-snap frames have replaced roller frames because there is no tedious mounting process. They work well for small and medium-size projects.

Both types of frames are available as floor or lap stands, which allow both hands to be free. The hoop frame is easily portable, so I often carry this type when I am stitching small projects on the go. At home, I love my frames on stands for larger projects, such as a wall hanging. The stand is always set up, and I can work on it at different times throughout the day.

Types of frames: hoop, straight sided, hoop on stand, and straight sided on stand.

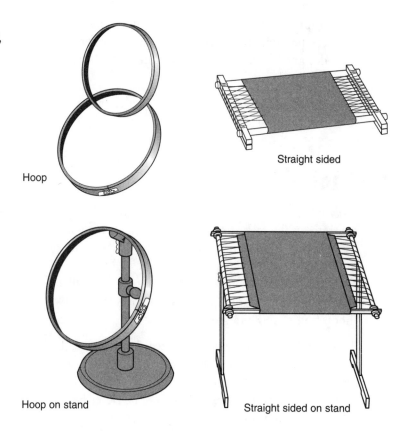

Hoop

Straight sided

Hoop on stand

Straight sided on stand

Little Extras Make a Big Difference

Good results in embroidery come from using good-quality implements. Along with the right needles and threads, fill your embroiderer's basket with the following:

Decorator's Do's and Don'ts

Don't be in the dark! Set up your embroidery stand in a well-lit area. It should be under direct lighting or at least a directed spotlight. Good lighting is essential for working embroidery. It protects your eyes and helps you to differentiate between different color tones of yarn and pattern.

◆ **Embroidery scissors.** Find a pair that is sharp, light, and pointed.

◆ **Dressmaker shears.** Use for cutting fabric.

◆ **Thimble.** Protect your fingertips. A good thimble should have well-defined indentations.

◆ **Pincushion.** Use it to corral pins and needles and protect them from rust.

◆ **Embroidery marker.** Try this for drawing designs on fabric.

◆ **Embroidery-transfer pencil.** Use for hot-iron transfer designs.

- **Needle threader.** Makes threading a needle easier.

- **Masking tape.** Use to bind edges of fabric to prevent raveling.

- **Dressmaker's carbon paper.** Use to transfer designs to fabric.

- **Magnifiers.** Use to aid in the magnification of the work at hand. Some are available in the form of eyeglasses or a stand, both allowing your hands to be free.

Kits: Packaged Goods

Most beginner needleworkers start with a kit. Embroidery kits are prepackaged and contain ground cloth, a needle, embroidery floss, and directions. Kits have predetermined designs and colors of yarn and come in all levels of difficulties, prices, and tastes. Some kits are designed by professional needlework designers, and these are usually more expensive and available at specialty needlework stores or through catalogues. Others are manufactured by commercial companies that cater to every taste and budget and are available in the craft section of local chain stores or at craft stores. Basic cross-stitch is probably the most popular because it is quick and easy to master. You will learn how to cross-stitch in Chapter 21.

The Least You Need to Know

- Any fabric can be embroidered as long as it is firm enough to hold stitches and supple enough to allow a needle to pass through.

- Particular weights and thicknesses of threads are suited for different ground cloths.

- Different needles are used for different types of embroidery and grounds.

- Embroidery frames hold your cloth taut and are available in hoop or straight style.

- Embroidery kits are a good option for a beginner needleworker.

Chapter 20

Technique Chic

In This Chapter

- ◆ Preparing tight and tidy frames
- ◆ Setting up your fabric and threads
- ◆ Improving your look with basic techniques and tips
- ◆ Getting the designs you want with enlarging, reducing, and transferring techniques

Needlework preparation is like starting your day with a good breakfast. Correctly preparing your project before you start will help you concentrate on your design, just as a nutritious breakfast starts your day off right. Now, grab a bowl full of fabric and thread, and let's get to work!

Consider Yourself Framed!

In Chapter 19, you learned about round (hoop) and straight-sided frames that can be used to hold your project in place while you work. Lightweight hoop frames are suitable for small pieces of fabric, and straight-sided frames are good choices for larger pieces. The hoop is fairly easy to mount. The straight-sided frame takes a little longer to put together because the fabric needs to be affixed to the frame. Both are available on floor or lap stands that allow you to keep both hands free.

Setting Up the Hoop Frame

Before placing the fabric in the hoop frame, loosen the tension screw on the outer hoop. Lay the fabric on the inner hoop with the section to be embroidered facing you. Always keep the fabric smooth. Place the outer hoop down on top of the inner hoop, keeping the fabric correctly positioned. Press gently and pull the fabric taut. Tighten the outer hoop screw to hold the fabric firmly in position, as shown in the next figure.

Fabric in a hoop frame should be drum-tight.

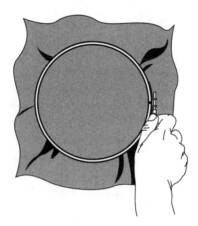

Mounting Odd Shapes

You may find yourself with pieces that are too small or irregularly shaped to fit into your frame. To embroider them, you'll need to baste these small or odd pieces to a larger piece of fabric. To baste, simply sew the smaller piece on top of the larger one, using large stitches. You can then mount the entire piece into a frame. When the piece is firmly in place, cut away the supporting fabric underneath the design, leaving your design ready for embroidering, as shown on the following page.

Mount the fabric in the usual way after you have basted the smaller fabric onto the larger piece.

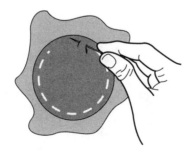

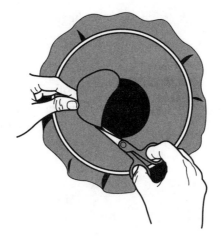

When cutting away your supporting fabric, take extra care to avoid nipping your design!

Binding the Frame

Sometimes fine embroidery fabrics such as silk or satin sag in the frame while you are working. To correct this, you need to bind the inner hoop with woven tape as shown in the following figure. Stitch the ends of the binding tape together. This also prevents your fabric from shifting in the frame.

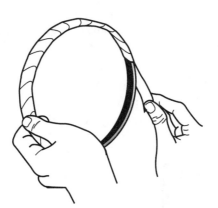

Be sure to fasten the ends of the woven tape with a few stitches while binding the frame.

Preparing the Straight-Sided Frame

Straight-sided frames are a little more complicated to mount and disassemble because the top and bottom of the fabric are sewn on the roller webbing and the sides need to be laced to the frame.

Clever Crafter

Old, unfinished needlework stretched on a large straight-sided frame can be hung as artwork on a wall in your home!

Before you begin, hem all the edges of your fabric or bind them with ¾-inch-wide cotton tape. Mark a center point on both the top and bottom edges. As pictured, match the center points of fabric with center points of rollers on the frame. Stitch the fabric to the roller webbing, starting from the center and working outward, as shown in the following figure.

Be sure to mark the center of the rollers and the top and bottom of the fabric when stitching the fabric to the roller webbing.

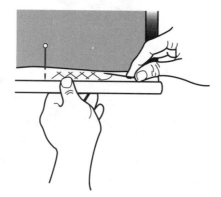

Slot the sides into the rollers and pull taut by adjusting screws or pegs. As shown in the following figure, lace the sides of the fabric to the sides of the frame with strong thread such as button thread (thread that is specifically used for sewing on buttons because of its strength). Lace sides loosely at first, but then tighten them alternately, getting an equal pull on both sides. Adjust the fabric at the top as well, and keep making adjustments until the fabric is evenly taut and secure with firm knots.

It is essential to get an even stretch across the entire surface of the fabric. Adjustment of the lacing and rollers may be necessary.

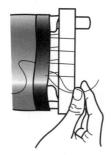

The Nitty-Gritty Basics

Now that you know how to prepare a frame, you're ready to prepare your fabric and threads and learn some basic techniques to start and finish your work.

Cutting and Binding

If you choose to use your own fabric and not a kit, cut your fabric 2 inches larger than the overall design. If you plan to frame your completed embroidery, add 4 inches to the overall pattern. For example, if your finished design is 6 inches by 6 inches and you want to frame it, cut your cloth 14 inches by 14 inches. Cut your fabric with care—use straight lines and try to follow the warp and weft threads of the fabric's weave.

Binding your embroidery fabric prevents the edges from fraying while you work, especially if your fabric is loosely woven. Three popular choices are to machine-zigzag the outer edge of your cloth, turn under the edges and hand sew in place, or tape the outer edge with masking tape. If your sewing machine has a serger (a feature that binds the edges of fabric with threads close together), you can serge the outer edges.

 A Stitch in Time

If you are stitching a large area in the same color, cut your threads or yarn to 18-inch lengths before you start. Fold the threads into half bundles, tie with a loop end, and use as needed.

Preparing the Threads

The working thread, which is the thread you are using, should be 18 inches or less. Any longer and the thread will become tangled, fray, or lose its sheen.

Embroidery floss, matte embroidery cotton, and Persian yarn are all loosely twisted threads. These can be separated into finer threads for use, but wait until you are actually ready to work before separating them. This will prevent them from getting tangled before use.

From Start to Finish

To secure a new working thread, turn your work to the backside and slide your threaded needle through the underside of the previous stitches. Allow enough thread to leave a tail that is easily worked, say a half inch to an inch. Bring your needle up onto the right side of the fabric, and continue with your design (see the following figure).

To secure your thread at the start of stitching, hold the end of the wrong side of the fabric and work stitches over the tail.

Starting a new thread in this manner ensures that there are no knots to cause a bumpy surface.

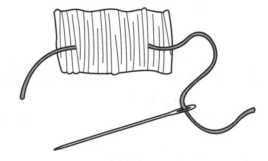

When you are ready to end your thread, again turn your work to the back, and slide the needle under 1½ inches of the worked stitches. Neatly cut the thread at the point where it emerges from the worked stitches (see the following figure).

When you are finished with a thread, be sure that you secure it on the wrong side of the fabric.

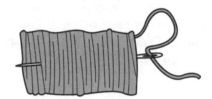

Knots in threads can show through your work. Don't make a knot when you are starting or finishing a length of thread. Either weave the end into the stitches on the back of your work or use a tiny backstitch. (See the "Flat Stitches" section in Chapter 21.)

Helpful Tips

Learning even the smallest tips and techniques used by the pros will help make your work look professional, too!

A Stitch in Time

When piercing your fabric with your needle, a stabbing motion works best. You'll make a clean hole in the fabric, eliminating any damage to the surface of the fabric. Be sure to pull thread slowly and carefully.

- Always use good light to avoid straining your eyes.

- Follow guidelines, the printed lines of the pattern on the cloth, carefully so they will not show in the finished design. Kits will usually have the printed design lines already on the cloth.

- Be sure to match your needle and thread in type and weight.

- Keep stitch tension even.

◆ Use a "stabbing motion" whenever possible for even tension when piercing the fabric.

◆ If your thread twists, let the needle fall freely and the thread will untwist itself.

◆ Choose shorter stitches if the item is to be handled or worn frequently. Shorter stitches hold up better, whereas longer stitches tend to snag and show wear more quickly.

Clever Crafter

Reuse plastic comforter covers with zippers to store your large embroidery projects!

Enlarging and Reducing Designs

The easiest way to enlarge a design is to use a photocopier that allows you to bring the design up to 200 percent. You can also take it to a professional copy store if you need it larger than that. A more time-consuming way to enlarge a design is the grid method, as shown in the following figure.

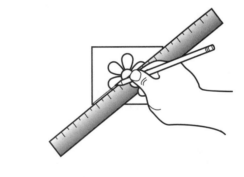

Step 1. With a pencil, trace your pattern on tracing paper. Then go over all of the lines with a black felt-tip marker. Draw a rectangle around the new tracing. Draw a diagonal line from the bottom-left corner to the top-right corner.

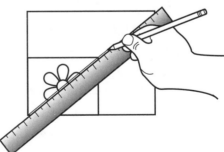

Step 2. Place your traced rectangle in the bottom-left corner of a sheet of paper ample enough for the size of your final design. Tape down the traced design, and extend your diagonal line from the tracing paper to across the larger paper.

Step 3. Remove the tracing paper, and complete the diagonal line on the paper where the tracing used to be. At the top of your design on the tracing that you have just removed, use a triangle to draw a horizontal line to cross diagonally. From the point of intersection, draw a vertical line down to the bottom edge.

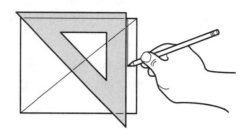

Step 4. Then draw equal-sized squares on the original tracing so that you have a grid. Draw the same number of squares onto the paper enlargement. Draw the lines of your design in each of the large squares on the paper, copying from the small squares on the tracing. Mark the points where the pattern lines intersect the grid, and join them together.

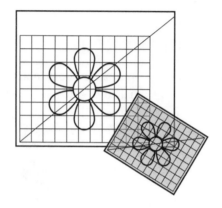

To reduce a design, making it smaller to fit your fabric, reverse the order of enlarging. Start with step 1, but place a small piece of paper on the tracing paper in the bottom-left corner rather than a large one. Continue on with steps 3 and 4.

Transferring a Design

If you choose not to use a kit, how will you transfer your design to your fabric? There are several ways. The method that you choose will depend on the texture of the fabric and the type of design.

Decorator's Do's and Don'ts

Don't be afraid of ornate patterns and intricate designs. If a pattern you adore is very detailed, try to simplify the outline for your design, and be sure to keep the scale in mind.

Freehand Embroidery

If you are already at ease with drawing and know some stitches, you can design a pattern as you stitch. If you do not feel comfortable with freehand stitching and you are artistically inclined, you can draw your pattern directly onto the fabric by using a pencil or embroidery marker, which is a water-soluble fine-tip marker. Color in areas if you need an entire picture in front of you.

Clever Crafter _____

Embroider your experiences in grid form. One square could be the state where you live; another could be your favorite hobby or the initials of your children or spouse, your dog Fluffy, etc.

Tracing With Dressmaker's Carbon

Dressmaker's carbon works well on smooth fabrics. Use dark dressmaker's carbon for light fabrics and light dressmaker's carbon for dark fabrics. That way, when you trace your pattern on the fabric, the outlines will show up better. Place the carbon between your drawing and the fabric with the drawing on top. Draw over the outlines. Remove the carbon, and your design is ready to go!

If the fabric is sheer enough and you are comfortable with tracing, you can trace directly onto your fabric. Always test the carbon paper on a sample fabric before you draw directly on your embroidery cloth. Test whether you can remove lines (in case you make a mistake) and that the cloth will take the carbon lines.

Hot Iron Transfer

Another way to transfer your design is to use a hot iron transfer. Begin by copying the design onto tracing paper. Turn the paper over, and trace the lines with an embroidery-transfer pencil. Place the paper with the marker-side down on your fabric, and pin together. With your iron on low heat, press over the pattern, applying pressure as you do so. Do not slide the iron back and forth because smudging may occur. Pull back a corner of the tracing paper to see whether the pattern has been transferred. If so, remove the pins and the tracing.

Do not remove the transfer paper unless you have checked to be sure that the design is visible on the fabric.

Clever Crafter
A fast way to transfer a design is to use a rubber stamp with your favorite motif. Stamp onto your fabric and you're ready to begin!

Basting Through Tissue Paper

Basting a pattern onto tissue paper is a good method for coarse fabrics that might not take to the carbon very well. Trace your design on the tissue paper. Pin the tissue paper to your fabric, and baste the pattern through the tissue onto the fabric. Gently remove the tissue, leaving stitches in place on the fabric. After completing your embroidery, pull out any visible basting stitches with a pair of tweezers.

It is a good idea to choose a thread color that contrasts with your fabric. Then, when you remove the basting threads, the stitches are easily visible.

Tracing-Paper Templates

Using tracing-paper templates is a good method if you are embroidering simple shapes. You will need heavyweight tracing paper or clear acetate (which can be reused). Draw your design onto the paper or acetate, and cut out each piece separately. Pin all shapes onto the fabric, and draw around them with your embroidery marker. If the fabric is coarse, baste around the templates instead. If repeating the design, repin the templates and redraw on next section.

The Least You Need to Know

♦ Frames help to keep your embroidery fabric taut to ensure even stitching. They also help to keep your project clean. Frames on stands allow both hands to be free.

♦ You can copy and embroider patterns that you admire by using various transfer techniques. By using the techniques of enlarging and reducing, you can suit any pattern to the size of your project.

Chapter 21

In Stitches

In This Chapter

- ◆ The basis of all sewing—the flat stitch
- ◆ The best-known embroidery stitch—the cross-stitch
- ◆ The versatile looped stitch
- ◆ The textured knotted stitch

There are hundreds of stitches to use in embroidery. You can probably live an entire lifetime without even coming close to learning them all. Don't panic! You won't need to know every type of stitch before attempting the craft. Needleworkers around the world use many of the same stitches, some indigenous to their region, but all are variations from the four basic "food" groups of embroidery: flat, crossed, looped, and knotted.

At First Stitch

As a novice embroiderer, it might seem a little nerve-racking to start a project that requires you to concentrate on everything at once: the design, the thread and fabric, the needle, the positioning of the fabric in the frame, and the stitching technique. Putting down that first stitch will be the toughest, but don't hesitate—pick up that needle and thread and get to work. And don't forget to enjoy your project!

The following needlework tips are sure to keep you in stitches:

◆ Always work in good light so you can see your stitching!

◆ Keep your thread tangle free by using a length of 18 inches or less as the working thread.

◆ Use blunt-tipped needles for cross-stitch and sharp-tipped needles for all other embroidery. The needle should be small enough to enter the fabric easily without leaving an obvious hole but large enough not to fall through to the back of the fabric.

Flat Stitches

Flat stitches consist of straight surface stitches worked in different lengths and directions. They are referred to as flat stitches because they are not raised up from the fabric and tend to lie "flat" on the fabric. Flat stitches are the easiest to learn and some of the oldest stitches known. Types of flat stitches that you will learn are running, double running, back, stem, encroaching, split, straight, satin, and seed.

Running Stitch

The running stitch is the simplest of all the stitches. It is used for making lines, for outlining, and as a foundation for other stitches. On its own, as shown in the following figure, the running stitch looks like a broken line. The running and double running stitch are reversible—they appear the same on the back and front of the fabric.

To work the running stitch, take several small, neat stitches at one time. This is a stitch that uses a sewing motion.

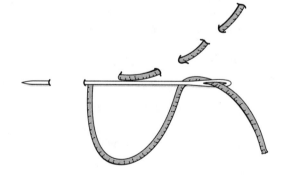

Double Running Stitch

The double running stitch is the leapfrog of all stitches, created by jumping under and over itself. First, work a row of running stitches. Then start at the beginning of your first row and work a second row in between the stitches you already laid down. You will be stitching in the same direction to fill in the gaps.

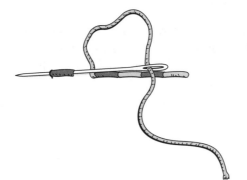

Use the same or a contrasting color for the second row of double running stitches.

Be sure to create a nice, even line by moving the thread in and out of the thread holes created by the first row of running stitches. Use the double running stitch for both outlines and fillings.

A Stitch in Time _____

The double running stitch is also known as the Roumanian stitch or Holbein stitch.

Backstitch

The backstitch is worked in a straight line like the running stitch. The difference between the two is that backstitches are worked end to end with no spaces left in between. To create the backstitch, first bring the needle to the front of the fabric at your starting point. Take a small backward stitch by placing the needle behind your starting point and bringing it down through the fabric and then up through the fabric in front of the starting point so there is space between your thread and the stitch you just made. Continue with the back and front pattern to create a neat line or outline.

Backstitches should be small and even, similar to machine stitching.

The backstitch, also known as the *point de sable* stitch, is more raised than the double running stitch.

Stem Stitch

The stem, or "crewel," stitch is a principal embroidery stitch used for outlines, lines, grounds, fillings, and shading.

To begin, bring the needle to the front side of the fabric at the starting point. Pull the needle through to the front of the fabric halfway between your starting point and your first stitch. Create another full stitch next to the first one, and continue working the stitches, raising the thread slightly above the previous stitch. Work from left to right, keeping the stitch length consistent. On a corner or tight curves, make your stem stitches a bit shorter to create a smooth-looking line. Stem stitches are great for flowing or curvy lines.

Stem stitches are slanted backstitches stitched side by side to look like rope.

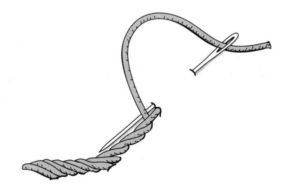

Straight Stitch

Straight stitches are single stitches spaced a little apart. Unlike running and double running stitches, straight stitches can vary in size. Bring your needle in and out of the fabric in single, spaced stitches.

Satin Stitch

Satin stitches are straight stitches that are worked side by side to completely fill an area. Start at the widest section of your design. Bring the needle from the back of the fabric through to the front, coming up at the base of the stitch. Then go back down at the top of the stitch. Keep the satin stitches close together as you progress toward the narrower sections of the design.

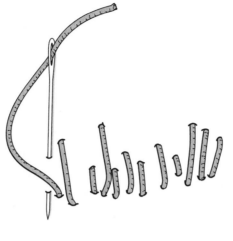

Straight stitches are best when created short and close together. They are good for filling patterns or depicting things like grass or landscape items.

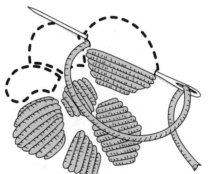

Although the satin stitch looks simple, its beauty lies in placing the stitches evenly and close together.

The satin stitch is used for outlining, filling, shaded effects, and geometric patterns. Try to keep your tension the same throughout so that the stitches lie smoothly, without looking too tight or too loose. Don't make the stitches too long. Long stitches can become loose and untidy.

Seed Stitch

Seed stitches are very small, uniform stitches—hence the name "seed"—that are used to fill in an area. The seed stitch gives a more raised surface than the running stitch.

Make two side-by-side backstitches into the same holes, leaving a space between the next pair of stitches. The two stitches together give a stronger effect than a single seed stitch.

The seed stitch can be used to give a dotted effect.

Encroaching Satin Stitch

The encroaching satin stitch is used for blending colors and providing soft tonal effects. I also like to use it to depict birds and animals.

For the first row, use the same technique as you would for the regular satin stitch described earlier. Work the second and subsequent rows so that the head of the new stitch lies between the bases of the stitches in the first row, as in the following figure.

Clever Crafter

When using the encroaching satin stitch, the tones can be changed in every row to produce a very subtle effect.

The encroaching satin stitch is used for blending colors and giving soft tonal effects.

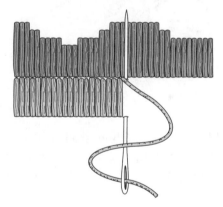

Cross-Stitches

The cross-stitch is the best-known, as well as one of the oldest and most popular, of all of the embroidery stitches. It's probably the stitch that you envision when thinking of embroidery. This stitch is quick and easy to master.

Basic Cross-Stitch

The basic cross-stitch is composed of two stitches, or "legs," that cross each other to form an X shape. The first stitch is a diagonal stitch to the right, and the second stitch is a diagonal stitch to the left that crosses on top of the first one.

Start by working one or more evenly spaced and separate slanted stitches in one direction. Cover each stitch with another stitch slanting in the opposite direction or work all the underneath stitches in one journey and then make a second return journey in the opposite direction, working all the top stitches. All stitches should cross in the same direction.

I love cross-stitched initials on hand towels. It is an easy project on which to begin learning this stitch.

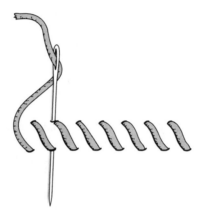

Your own designs are simple to prepare on graph paper by using different colored pencils to shade the areas that are to be cross-stitched.

Long-Armed Cross-Stitch

The long-armed cross-stitch is worked in long and short diagonal stitches whose subsequent crosses overlap. It has one "longer" stitch and one "shorter" stitch—unlike the basic cross-stitch, in which each stitch is the same length.

Bring your needle through the fabric at the stitching baseline and make a long cross-stitch (diagonal) at the desired height of your stitches. Bring the needle to the back of the fabric. Now you are ready to do the short arm. If you are doing freehand embroidery, measure, or simply eyeball, the horizontal distance from the beginning point of the stitch to the ending point. Bring out the needle at one half of this distance to the left and on top of the stitching line.

Note that if you are working on an evenweave fabric, simply count the number of fabric threads over which you have worked the long cross-stitch, divide by two, and bring up the needle at that halfway point to begin the short stitch.

Make a second diagonal cross-stitch back to the baseline, and insert the needle directly below the point where the needle was inserted on the top line. Bring the needle out directly below the point where it emerged on top of the line.

The long-armed stitch looks attractive on borders and makes a braided geometric pattern.

Use the long-armed cross stitch for fillings and borders.

Herringbone Stitch

The herringbone stitch is used for edgings and fillings, but it is also the foundation for many other stitches.

Bring your needle through your fabric on the baseline, and insert it on the top line a little to the right. Next, bring up the needle to the left of the top line and insert it on the baseline so that it crosses the top of the first stitch. This completes the first herringbone stitch.

The herringbone stitch is worked from left to right.

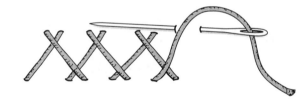

A Stitch in Time

The herringbone stitch is also known as the Russian stitch because of its age-old use in that country.

As you work the herringbone stitch, be sure to rest the thread above the needle and keep your stitches spaced evenly. Repeat the herringbone pattern as shown, spacing evenly so that the diagonals are parallel. Herringbone stitches make overlapping V patterns on the face of the fabric and parallel running stitches on the back of the fabric.

Basket Stitch

Like the long-armed cross-stitch, the basket stitch is worked from left to right. Make the first stitch by working a diagonal with your thread from the baseline to the top line, with the needle inserted vertically down through the design lines. Make the second stitch by taking a vertical stitch down toward the left and into the same holes as the two previous stitches.

The basket stitch is useful for fillings and edgings and produces a braided effect.

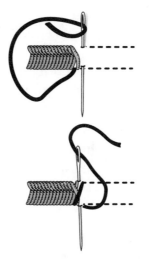

The basket stitch is similar to the long-armed stitch because it is worked with a forward and backward stitch.

Zigzag Stitch

The zigzag stitch is created—you guessed it—by making a zigzag pattern. This is done by alternating vertical stitches and diagonal long stitches to form a row.

Create a row of alternating diagonal and vertical stitches, working from left to right. On the return row, working right to left, take vertical stitches into the same holes as the previous vertical stitches and reverse the direction of the diagonal stitches so that they cross each other.

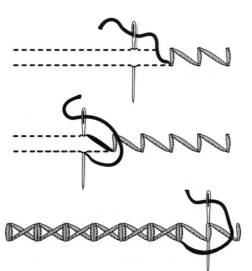

With consistent stitches and practice, the zigzag stitch forms an even geometric stitch for edging linens.

The zigzag stitch is used for edgings and fillings and for geometric lattice backgrounds.

Leaf Stitch

The leaf stitch is a light, open stitch that is ideal for filling in leaves. This stitch looks good when it is used in combination with an outline stitch that completes the leaf shape. It is also used for borders. The size of the stitch can be varied if need be.

Bring your needle up at left of center and insert it at the right of the leaf border. Now bring up your needle a little to right of center, as shown in the following figure. Insert your needle at the left of the leaf border, and bring it up at left of center below the stitch just formed. The leaf stitch is worked upward from side to side.

The leaf stitch is ideal for filling in leaves, as its name implies.

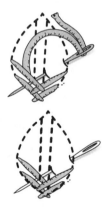

Looped Stitches

All looped stitches consist of loops that are held in place with small stitches. When used for outlining and for filling patterns, looped stitches create beautiful and interesting effects. Looped stitches are also used in blackwork and crewelwork. Both of these types of embroidery are discussed in more detail in Chapter 23.

Clever Crafter

The chain stitch is frequently seen in Chinese and Indian embroideries. It truly is one of the most versatile of all the embroidery stitches.

Chain Stitch

The chain stitch is the most important of all the looped stitches. It is a versatile stitch that can be worked with fine threads or thick yarns.

Bring your needle from the back of your fabric through to the front. Loop the thread and hold it down with your left thumb. Re-insert the needle where you first brought the needle through, and bring the needle tip out a short distance below this point. Keep the thread under the tip of the needle, and pull the needle through. Make the next stitch by inserting the needle into the hole from which it has just emerged.

The chain stitch is the basic stitch of the looped stitches.

Lazy Daisy

The lazy daisy stitch is also referred to as the detached chain stitch. It is commonly used to make leaf and flower shapes as well as for filling areas. It is worked similarly to the chain stitch except that each loop is fastened down with a small tiedown stitch.

Bring your needle out at the arrow indicated in the following figure and re-insert in the same hole, keeping the needle on top of the thread loop. Bring up the needle inside the loop, again keeping the needle on top of the thread. Finally, create the tiedown by bringing the needle over the loop and inserting it under the loop.

The lazy daisy stitch is similar to the chain stitch except that each loop is tacked down.

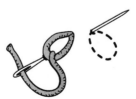

Blanket Stitch

The blanket stitch is universally known and sometimes referred to as the buttonhole stitch. It is perfect for edging hems and buttonholes. It is an important stitch for couching, laidwork, and cutwork (see Chapter 23).

The blanket stitch is perfect for edging blankets or linens.

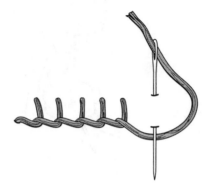

The blanket stitch is worked from left to right, bringing your thread out at the point for the looped edging. Insert the needle above and a little to the left of this point. Take a straight downward stitch, being sure that the thread is under the tip of the needle. Pull up on the stitch to make a square loop, and continue the same steps to form a continuous chain.

Checkered Chain Stitch

The checkered chain stitch is a fancier variation of the chain stitch. It is worked with two threads of contrasting colors. Work the stitch the same as the chain stitch, but keep the color of thread that is not in use above the point of the needle.

The checkered chain stitch is a fancier variation of the chain stitch.

Open Chain

The open chain, or ladder, stitch forms a pattern similar to that of a ladder. It is used for bandings and for filling motifs of graduating size with varying stitch widths.

Bring your needle through the fabric at the left guideline and then insert it at the right guideline. Bring the thread out again at the left guideline with the thread under the needle. A "ladder" pattern will appear.

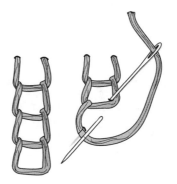

The open chain stitch forms a pattern similar to a ladder.

Feather Stitch

The feather stitch is similar to the blanket stitch, but the "arms" are angled. It is used for smocking (see Chapter 23), edgings, and borders. Bring your thread and needle from top to bottom. Using the following figure as a guide, bring your needle out at A, and hold the thread to the left. Insert the needle at B, and bring it out at C, taking care to keep the loop under the needle.

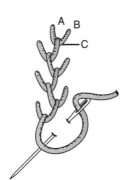

The feather stitch is similar to the blanket stitch.

Cretan Stitch

The Cretan stitch is a very decorative filling stitch also known as the long-armed feather. It can be worked to fit broad or narrow shapes simply by varying the stitch sizes.

Clever Crafter

The Cretan stitch takes its name from the island of Crete, where it has been used on clothing for hundreds of years.

Begin by bringing your needle through the middle at the left side of the guideline, with the needle pointing inward on the pattern and the thread under the tip of the needle.

Take a small stitch on the upper guideline, with the needle pointing inward toward the pattern and the thread under the needle. Repeat these steps until the shape is filled.

The Cretan stitch is a decorative filling stitch.

Knotted Stitches

Knotted stitches provide exciting textures for embroidered goods. They are formed by looping thread around a needle and then pulling the needle through the loops to form a knot or twist on the surface of the fabric.

A Stitch in Time

Practice a few knotted stitches on a scrap of fabric before starting on your embroidery. It takes practice to get the tension of the knots even.

French Knot

The French knot is commonly used to give a "sprinkling" effect, to denote dots, or to make a solid filling for motifs. French knots are very effective when massed together for abstract designs or landscapes. They also make a charming coat for a little sheep.

The French knot adds a dotted relief effect.

A Stitch in Time

Use a frame when making French knots so that both hands are free to secure the knot.

Bring your needle out at the point where you want the knot to be. Twist the needle two or three times around the thread. Turn the needle and insert it just above the point where the thread first emerged. Keeping the needle vertical, hold the working thread taut and pull the thread through to the back of the work with your left hand. For larger knots, use two or more strands of thread rather than more twists.

Coral Stitch

The coral stitch is a principal knotted stitch. It can be used for irregular lines, outlines, borders, and for some fillings.

Begin working from left to right. Bring your thread out, and hold it with your left thumb along the line to be worked. Take a small stitch under and over the working thread. A loop forms below the line. Pull the thread through the loop to form the knot. The knots can be spaced at various intervals.

The coral stitch is an important knotted stitch.

Bullion Stitch

The bullion stitch is a large, long knot that is used like the French knot but gives greater impact. A cluster of bullions makes a rosette. Bullions are particularly decorative when used with different color threads, and many Chinese types of embroidery employ this method.

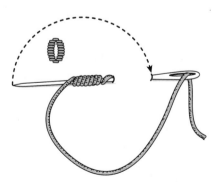

The bullion stitch adds great impact to your embroidery.

Clever Crafter

When making a knotted stitch, prevent the thread from tangling by holding down the loop of thread with your left thumb when you pull the needle through.

Make a backstitch that is the length you want the finished bullion knot to be. Then bring the needle halfway up at the point where it first emerged. Twist the thread around the needle as many times as needed to accommodate the size of the backstitch. Hold your left thumb on the coiled thread, and pull the needle through the wraps. If the wraps look uneven, gently stroke them with your needle. Then turn the needle back to where it was inserted and pull the thread through to the back of the fabric so that the bullion knot lies flat.

Scroll Stitch

The scroll stitch makes a beautiful flowing line that resembles little waves of water. It is also used for borders and banding.

The scroll stitch makes beautiful flowing lines.

Work the scroll stitch from left to right, bringing the needle out on your guideline. Loop the thread to the right and over the working thread, as shown in the figure. Pull through to form a knot. Be sure that you don't pull the thread too tightly.

Zigzag Stitch

The zigzag stitch is used for decorative bands and wide borders. It is worked exactly like the coral stitch, but from top to bottom and in zigzag fashion, as shown.

The zigzag stitch is used for decorative bands and borders.

Four-Legged Knot

The four-legged stitch looks like an upright cross with a knot in the center. It can be used for fillings or borders when used in a row.

Begin by taking a vertical stitch and bringing the needle out at the point where the center of the knot will be.

Lay the thread across the vertical stitch to form the first step of the knot. Pass the needle under the vertical stitch and then over the working thread. Pull through to create the knot. Now take the needle to the back to make the last leg of the cross.

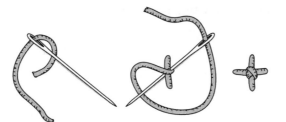

The four-legged knot resembles an upright cross with a knot in the middle.

Knotted Chain Stitch

The knotted chain stitch, also known as the link stitch, produces a very distinctive line and looks even more striking when a thick thread is used.

Take an upward diagonal stitch, and bring out the needle just below the point where it was inserted. Pass the needle between the stitch and the fabric, keeping the looped thread to the left. Now, loop the working thread under the tip of the needle and pull through to form the knot, ready to make the next stitch.

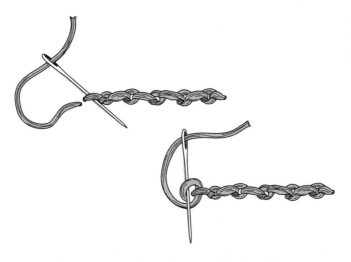

The knotted chain stitch works well with a thick thread.

The Least You Need to Know

◆ Embroidery stitches break down into four groups: flat, crossed, looped, and knotted.

◆ Flat stitches are the easiest stitches to work.

◆ Cross-stitch is one of the oldest and most popular embroidery techniques. It is easily mastered.

◆ Of all of the looped stitches, the chain stitch is the most decorative stitch, especially with color and texture changes.

◆ Knotted stitches produce exciting raised textures.

22

Embroidery Project:
The Art of Monogramming

In This Chapter

♦ Signing your work as an artist

♦ Relearning your ABCs with needle and thread

♦ Using chained, padded, and couched techniques for easy and attractive letters

♦ Creating the classic sampler

Needlework has a long tradition as a skill for creating "useful" things, such as pillows, coasters, hand towels, and those beloved tea cozies and toaster covers. This association with utilitarian, or even frivolous, items has caused many people to consider it as more of a craft than an art form. But needleworking *is* an art, and this means you are now an artist, even if you've never considered yourself one. As an artist, learn to "sign" your work, as all great artists do. Personalizing your creations with your initials or your own signature design will be a satisfying way to complete your work. And you'll leave your mark for generations to come!

Clever Crafter

Did you know that household linens of the aristocracy were originally embroidered with motifs of crowns and coronets to signify the rank of the owner? By the eighteenth century, however, these motifs had become traditional designs used to fill in awkward spaces.

Making It Your Own

As well as signing your work, you can use embroidered monograms, initials, and messages to add a personal touch to gifts, home accessories, and clothing. From a single letter stitched on a dishtowel to your favorite motto on a sampler, hand-embroidered lettering is a priceless form of needlework that can help create the most coveted possessions. Learning the techniques of padded satin stitch, braid work, and openwork will add variety to your letters, as well as apply your knowledge of the stitches you have learned in previous chapters.

The A to Z of Monograms

Early embroidered letters were used as a practical form of identification of household linens. The markings were usually somewhat hidden, placed on the upper-right corner of pillowcases, towels, and sheets. Today, monogrammed items are fashionable with the lettering front and center, in all sizes and in matching or contrasting thread.

A Stitch in Time

When stitching letters, try to use a frame. This will keep the stitches even and prevent the fabric from puckering.

Embroidered letters were also often used to stitch messages that revealed religious beliefs or had moral overtones. In the eighteenth and nineteenth centuries, young girls learned messages of morality along with the art of embroidery. Embroidered valentines and postcards were seen in the nineteenth century, as well as hearthside inscriptions such as "Home Sweet Home."

Know Your Alphabets

The following charts provide a cross-stitch alphabet, an alphabet for satin stitch, and a numerals list. You can work the cross-stitch alphabet directly from the chart, because each square equals one stitch. The satin stitch alphabet and the numerals chart need to be traced and transferred to your fabric. (See Chapter 20 to read up on transferring techniques.)

By stitching and practicing your numerals, you can date all of your embroideries with ease!

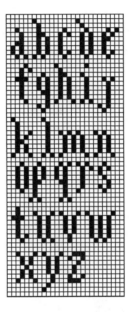

Don't be afraid of curvy letters. Practice a few on a scrap piece of fabric, and you will feel very confident about stitching curvy letters such as S and C.

The satin stitch gives letters a polished look.

Stitching Simple Letters and Monograms

For effective, clearly readable letter embroidery, the letters must be stitched with even stitches and defined lines. The next three figures show you letters worked in three different techniques and stitches: chain, cross, and satin stitch.

These stitches offer the quickest way to work letters that have already been marked on fabric. You can embellish the letters with other techniques (discussed further on in this chapter) or with a simple frame of stitching. For a classic look, leave the letters or monogram unadorned.

An easy stitch for free-form letters, the chain stitch can be effectively outlined with the stem stitch.

Cross-stitched letters are easily spaced by using the weave of the fabric as a grid pattern.

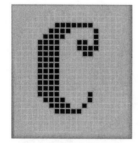

The satin stitch must be worked with even and smooth stitches. Practice one letter before embarking on an entire monogram.

Padding Your Lettering

Padding is a technique used to give emphasis, definition, and dimensionality to a motif. The padding slightly raises the stitching above the surface of the fabric. An easy way to pad a motif is to work running stitches within and around the motif, following its shape. I often suggest that you use the same color for the padding as you do for the satin stitch that you stitch over the padding.

Padded stitched lettering is often worked in the same color as the background fabric. For example, a white-on-white look could be a white linen sheet having a raised, or "padded," monogram in a white satin stitch. The effect of such a monochromatic combination is truly handsome!

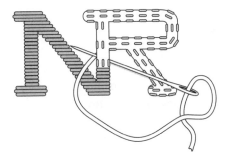

Work the outline of the letter in running stitches, and fill in with a satin stitch. See Chapter 21 for a refresher on the satin stitch.

Clever Crafter _____

Use the unique "negative" satin stitch for a clever visual effect on monograms and crests. It is the reverse of the padded satin stitch because you stitch in the negative areas around the letters and not the letters themselves. To begin, outline the background of the monogram and around the letter. Use the padded satin stitch to fill in the background. Your letters will become visible as you fill in the background.

Braid and Ribbon Lettering

Fine braiding or ribbon can make very effective lettering. The ribbon or braid is attached, or tied down, with small, closely spaced stitches using a technique called couching (see Chapter 23 for more). Press the short ends of the braid or ribbon to the wrong side of your fabric and tack in place with two or three

A Stitch in Time _____

When using braid or ribbon for lettering, try to use one continuous piece so that there are no breaks in the line of braid or ribbon.

small straight stitches. On narrow ribbon or braid, stitch down the middle, and on wider ribbon, stitch both edges to make the piece lie flat.

Patterned ribbon adds another visual dimension to the lettering.

Using Openwork

Openwork provides an interesting background for lettering, especially a satin-stitched letter. In this technique, stitches form an "open" pattern that creates a setting for the letter.

The openwork wave stitch is an example of how this technique can be used to fill in a background area. The wave pattern consists of a series of rows of vertical, evenly spaced stitches worked across the background of the letter area. Always embroider the letter first and then the background. It is easier to stitch the openwork around the letter as opposed to doing the letter over the background of openwork. The openwork forms an attractive latticelike effect that is easily accomplished by following the directions given next. Border the letter with a stem stitch to emphasize the letter and separate it from the background. (See Chapter 21 for more on the stem stitch.)

The background of openwork stitches nicely shows off the satin-stitched letter.

To begin, work a row of small, evenly spaced vertical stitches. Bring your needle out below and to the right of the last stitch and, working backward, make a row of V-like loops by passing your needle under the vertical stitches.

Continue to make the same V loops on the following rows by passing the needle under the pairs of stitch bases in the row above.

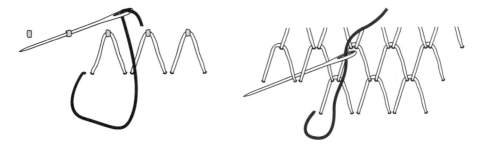

Openwork wave stitch: steps 1 and 2.

Clever Crafter

You can embellish your letters or monograms with stitched flowers, leaves, or other motifs pertinent to the letters. For example, if you embroider the word *violet* on your fabric, you may want to stitch purple flowers that resemble violets around the letters.

The Simplicity of Samplers

Today, *samplers* are typically very personalized items, used for display and gifts. Originally, however, samplers were used as a reference tool, a way to record—on fabric—the many different stitches that the needleworker might need, with many left unsigned. They stitched openwork patterns and worked in parallel bands on narrow strips of linen for embroidery on household linens. In the sixteenth century, the first stitch book was published, and this paved the way for the use of samplers for more decorative purposes.

The sixteenth and early seventeenth centuries are characterized by spot samplers (motifs done randomly), and the late seventeenth century by band samplers, bands of patterns worked on a long, narrow cloth. In fact, the seventeenth century is known as the golden age

Needlework 101

Sampler comes from the Latin word *exemplum*, meaning "an example to be followed."

of samplers because of the complicated techniques, sophisticated design, and luxury materials (pearls, jewels, silk, gold) used in these samplers. The early eighteenth century is associated with pictorial samplers, including pious verses and alphabets surrounded by a decorative border.

By the late eighteenth and nineteenth centuries, the sampler had become a technical exercise by which young girls learned moral values and the alphabet and numbers. Other types of schoolroom samplers taught geography (map samplers, although these were not very accurate), arithmetic (multiplication table samplers), and domestic skills (plain sewing and darning samplers). Although childhood samplers marked the decline of the sampler, their very unsophisticated nature and the childish mistakes make them the most charming and popular of antique samplers to collect. What we think of today as a typical sampler is actually the square pictorial style.

> **Clever Crafter** _____
>
> Some of the most cherished samplers are those that commemorate weddings. It is usually the bride's most treasured gift!

You can also buy inexpensive kits that have a variety of sampler designs. Re-create museum samplers by studying them. Or design your own and stitch a message that reveals your family's philosophy. Add the alphabet at the bottom, along with a line of numbers and maybe a stitched picture of your home at the top, with people on either side—you and your important others. Be sure to stitch your name and the date along with the place you live (city and state).

Although today we often see letters on samplers spaced evenly, I like to see quirky stitching where you may have run out of room and squeezed some letters together. This imperfect look, emulating the childish efforts of young stitchers 200 the stitcher years ago, adds tremendous character and panache.

The Least You Need to Know

- The alphabet can be worked in various embroidery stitches and used as part of a design.

- Monograms add a personal touch to household linens, clothing, and gifts, as well as provide identification for your work.

- Chain, padded satin, cross-stitch, and couching are different stitches and techniques for embroidering letters or monograms.

Chapter 23

Combining Stitches and Special Effects

In This Chapter

◆ Securing threads and filling in with couching and laidwork

◆ Adding pizzazz with smocking and beadwork

◆ Combining and creating stitches for special effects

Now that you have mastered the beginner basics, you are ready for the next level. This is the stage where embroidery becomes a little easier and more fun because you can now start experimenting with what you know. Learning more interesting stitches and how to combine stitches to create special effects will help advance your skill to master the craft!

Special Techniques

Couching, laidwork, and smocking are special techniques that will broaden your embroidery knowledge. Couching is a method of securing threads that have been laid on the fabric surface. Laidwork forms gridlike patterns, and smocking eliminates fullness and provides a decorative pattern.

Couching

Couching is an embroidery technique used to attach "laid threads" (threads that have been placed to lie flat on the fabric). The laid threads are secured with a separate strand of thread and small stitches taken at intervals. This method is often used to work fragile metal or gold threads. Such threads can be easily damaged if passed through fabric and so are nicely worked by laying them on the surface of the fabric. More than one thread can be laid together to create bold lines or outlines. Couching is also a good method to use for filling large areas of solid color.

Working from left to right, position the thread or threads on your fabric, using your thumb to hold them in place. Bring out the working couching thread from underneath the fabric, just below the laid thread. Secure the laid thread at regular intervals with a couching stitch, as shown in the following figure. Finish at the end of the line by taking both the couching thread and the laid thread to the back of the fabric.

Generally the laid threads are heavier than the couching thread, which is typically a finer weight.

If you want to continue couching, turn the loose laid thread to the right and stitch across the turn. Turn work upside down, and couch the second row of threads next to the first, placing stitches in between the stitches of the previous row.

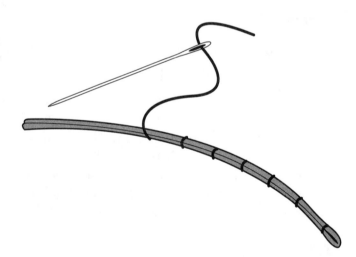

Laidwork

Laidwork is a version of couching and is usually used for covering large areas. It is a quick and very effective way of filling both backgrounds and motifs because you use long stitches in a grid fashion. These stitches are secured at the intersecting threads with a separate thread. Laidwork can be very decorative, forming a pattern of simple stripes, chevrons, swirls, or trellises. The easiest laidwork pattern produces a grid effect, as shown in the next figure.

1. Work horizontal stitches, evenly spaced, across the area to be filled.

2. Create the grid effect by laying vertical stitches across the horizontal threads in the same way.

3. Bring the couching thread from the back of the fabric through to the front at the top-left corner of the grid, and stitch the intersection of the vertical and horizontal threads with a small slanted stitch.

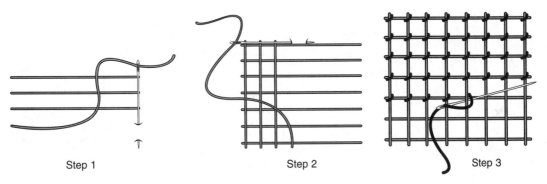

| Step 1 | Step 2 | Step 3 |

Steps for laidwork.

Smocking

Smocking reduces fullness in fabric with a very attractive gathered stitch pattern. It is a popular method used for shaping and decorating adult and young children's clothing. Baby items decorated in smocking become precious heirlooms.

Any type of fabric can be smocked as long as it is supple enough to be gathered. Checked or dot-patterned fabrics are popular because the checks or dots can be used as a guideline for gathering stitches.

Needlework 101

The word **smocking** comes from the old English word *smock*, meaning a "shift" or "chemise"—an article of clothing that is worn as a top.

Smocking is worked by gathering fabric into even-sized folds, called pleats, before the garment or piece is assembled. Be sure you start with fabric that is about three times the actual finished width of the garment or item so that you have enough fabric for the pleats.

Printed transfer papers are available in needlework shops and craft stores. These are transfer papers marked with equally spaced smocking dots that can be ironed on the face of the fabric to give you a guide for stitching. Another option is to check with quilt stores, fabric shops, and stitchery shops, because they sometimes offer pleating services.

When preparing your fabric for smocking, gather the back of the fabric in rows, picking up a small piece of fabric at each dot. There are several stitches to use for this technique (see the following sections), depending on the design you are trying to achieve. After you have worked all of your rows, tie the thread ends together in pairs.

If you are smocking a solid fabric, you need to mark some dots to use as a guide for gathering.

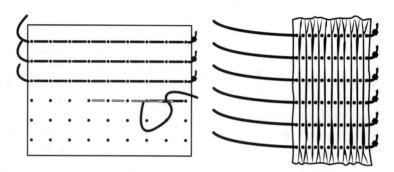

Smocking Stitches

A wide variety of smocking patterns can be formed from any of the basic stitches. For the purposes of this book, I've chosen stitches that are worked on the right side of the fabric, from left to right, so as not to confuse you. In England, some smocking is done from the backside of the fabric.

![Decorator's Do's and Don'ts icon]

Decorator's Do's and Don'ts

When using transfer papers, *do* be sure that each dot falls on the weave line of the fabric; if not, the fabric is likely to stretch and wrinkle.

Start in the upper-right corner for your first stitch. Be sure to hold the needle parallel to the gathering threads, and take the stitches at about one third of the depth of each pleat. A good trick is to leave the first gathered row free of stitches so that you can join one smocked panel to another. Simple attractive patterns can be achieved with one stitch, or intricate ones with a combination of stitches. Remember to keep the gaps between rows small and tight to prevent the pleats from puffing out.

Stem Stitch

With your gathered fabric, work a basic stem stitch (explained in Chapter 21) as the top row of smocking. To do this, bring the needle out to the left of the first pleat. Then take a stitch through the top of each fold, keeping the thread below the needle as you work.

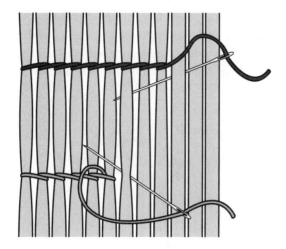

The stem stitch creates accordion-style pleats.

Cable Stitch

The cable stitch in smocking is worked with stem stitches that form a cable (your thread) that goes in and out of the folds of the fabric.

To start, bring the needle to the surface of your fabric through the first fold on the left. Insert the needle horizontally, and work stem stitches into each fold with the thread alternately above and then below the needle.

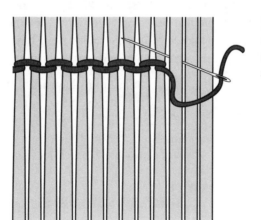

The smocking cable stitch creates more decorative folds than a plain smocking stem stitch.

Honeycomb Stitch

The honeycomb stitch is aptly named due to its honeycomb appearance. The honeycomb stitch is worked along two lines of gathering stitches.

Working from left to right, bring the needle out on the first line and make a backstitch to draw together the second and first folds. Then take a second stitch over the two folds, bringing the needle out at the lower line of gathering stitches and between the first and second fold. Make another backstitch to draw the third and second folds together. Return the needle to the first line again, only this time at the third fold. Draw the fourth and third folds together. Continue working in the same way, alternately up and down to the end of each row.

Honeycomb stitches form a smocking pattern that looks like the inside of a beehive.

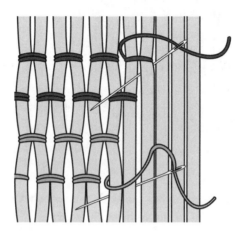

Beadwork

Beadwork is a form of embroidery that uses beads and sequins applied with a needle and thread and special techniques. Beads and sequins have been used throughout the ages to add richness and sparkle to textiles and clothing. They are the most effective way of transforming simple patterns into beautiful and exotic designs.

Beads and sequins have many fun applications. They can be used to create an entire picture, trim the hem of a skirt, highlight wall hangings and pillows, and add the finishing touch on a small project (such as two single beads for the eyes of an elephant).

Stitching With Beads

On the spot where you plan to place your bead, bring your needle out from the back of the fabric to the front and thread the bead. Use an ordinary sewing needle for beads with large holes, but use a special beading needle (obtainable at bead shops, craft stores, and stitching shops) for beads with small holes.

> **Decorator's Do's and Don'ts**
>
> Be sure your knots are secure and your backstitches are not forgotten when doing beadwork! Want to add pizzazz to a pillow or skirt hem by fringing the perimeter with beads? Thread the beads on a well-knotted thread for desired length and secure to hem or edging with a small backstitch. Repeat for each strand.

Use strong thread for items that will receive handling or use. Special beading thread and beading wire are available. Another idea is to make your own beading thread by waxing your thread with beeswax to strengthen it. Or you can stitch through each bead twice to add strength.

If the bead is round, insert the needle back through the same hole in the fabric. If the bead is a long cylindrical one (like a bugle bead), hold down the bead with your thumb and insert the needle close to the edge of the bead; pull the thread through to the back of the fabric. Repeat these steps to form a row of beads.

Applying Sequins

Sequins can be applied to fabric with invisible or visible stitching. You can decide whether you want the thread to be decorative for a contrasting effect, or hidden so that only the sequins show. Use sequins to border collars or cuffs, or scatter them on an embroidery to add sparkle.

To create invisible stitches, overlap the sequins and work a backstitch into the left side of the first set. To do this, place a single sequin on the fabric and take the needle through its eye (hole). Place another sequin on top of the first sequin—half covering it. Be sure the right edge covers the eye of the one before. Bring your needle back up at the left edge of the second sequin and into the eye, at the same time inserting the needle into the eye of the previous sequin.

The sequins are built up on one another, thus hiding the stitches.

To stitch on only one side of a sequin, bring the needle from the back of your fabric through to the front and then insert it through the eye of the sequin. Make a backstitch over the right side of the sequin. Bring your needle out to the left, ready to thread through the eye of a second sequin. Place the second sequin next to the previous one, edge to edge. Secure the rest of your sequins this way.

The thread becomes a decorative feature when stitches are worked on one side only.

Combining Stitches for Special Effects

After you've mastered some of the basic embroidery stitches from Chapter 21, try combining stitches to produce some unique effects with the most time-honored forms of embroidery. Some that we will discuss are crewelwork, stumpwork, whitework, and blackwork.

Needlework 101

Crewelwork derives its name from the crewel wool with which it is worked. (The word *crewel* comes from the Anglo-Saxon word *cleowen*, meaning "ball of thread.")

Crewelwork

Crewelwork is a traditional form of embroidery that combines outline stitches for borders and broad stitches for filling in shapes. These two types of stitches are used to form free-flowing motifs like trees and flowers. Traditional motifs have always been animals, birds, and naturalistic scenes. The basic shapes are stitched in an outline stitch and then filled in with broad stitches, such as the satin stitch, or textural ones, such as French knots.

Stumpwork

Stumpwork is a technique dating from the seventeenth century that makes embroidery three-dimensional. It is a combination of padded appliqué (cut-out shapes that are sewn on a fabric and stuffed with batting) and embroidery stitches such as the padded satin stitch, couching, and the various knotted stitches. In the elaborate stumpwork creations of the seventeenth century, fine wire was incorporated to provide shape and support (for example, to make a butterfly's wing raise up for flight).

To try some simple stumpwork, cut out a shape just a bit larger than the finished size and baste it to the fabric. If you use felt, it won't fray, making it a perfect choice. Leave a small section open, and stuff some batting into it to pad the shape. Sew the opening shut, and decorate the shape by bordering it with such stitches as the padded satin stitch, couching, or knotted stitches. Remove the basting stitches.

Whitework

Whitework is the name given to any white embroidery used on a white background. It is often seen on bed linens, blouses, handkerchiefs, and table linens.

You can create monochromatic contrasts by mixing a rough, no-sheen fabric, such as linen, with a shiny thread, such as high-sheen pearl cotton.

Blackwork

Blackwork is a very old form of embroidery that is traditionally worked with dark thread on a lighter, linen fabric, the usual combination being black thread on white fabric. Blackwork is based on a counted-thread technique, with patterns being stitched in backstitch, running stitch, and cross-stitch. Outline stitches, such as the chain stitch, stem stitch, and couching, are used to add a finishing touch to the patterns.

A Stitch in Time

Add even more contrast to whitework by using the cutwork method, a type of embroidery in which the ground fabric is cut away. Trace some small circles or other shapes onto your fabric. With pearl cotton thread, work a double outline around the shape, using a small running stitch. Then work a blanket (buttonhole) stitch (see Chapter 21), just wide enough to cover the running stitch. With small, sharp scissors, carefully cut away the interior fabric, revealing a hole shaped like your drawing. This leaves a very attractive lacy pattern.

Blackwork is traditionally worked with black thread on white linen.

Now that you have some ideas for experimenting, it's time to try some out. When you start creating your own combinations of stitches and techniques, there's no turning back—you'll probably never buy a kit again!

The Least You Need to Know

- ◆ Couching is an effective way to secure threads that cannot be drawn through the fabric.

- ◆ Laidwork is usually used to decoratively fill and cover large areas of your embroidery.

- ◆ Smocking is a way of reducing fullness in a fabric as well as decorating it.

- ◆ Beadwork is a very old embroidery method that adds sparkle and richness to a fabric.

- ◆ Combining different stitches results in very special effects, such as crewelwork, stumpwork, whitework, and blackwork.

24

Designing Your Own Embroidery

In This Chapter

- ◆ Preparing your own free-form designs by studying others
- ◆ Learning some design tips
- ◆ Picking up special techniques for pictorial embroidery

With your new knowledge of stitches and techniques, you are ready to explore some ideas for designing your own embroideries. Designing and crafting your own needlework is one of most fulfilling aspects of needlework. You can be proud to be the creator and the maker of a handmade item!

The Forming of Forms

What is an embroidery design? A simple, single leaf stitched on a pillowcase? A monogram on a hand towel? A lilac on a dinner napkin? All of these are considered embroideries. But wait—add smaller motifs to create an edging for the monogrammed hand towel, and *now* you have a design.

With the techniques that you learned in Chapter 20, you can actually enlarge a tiny, single motif and use it as the central pattern on a larger piece, such as a pillow or bath towel. If you repeat the single motif at regular intervals, the background fabric will be covered with a pretty, overall pattern and the motif will become the entire design. Bands of different colors and stitches can be used to make a design, and you can even alternate stripes of stitches with plain ground fabric. The sky is the limit with embroidery designs!

Decorator's Do's and Don'ts

Choose a subject that you love! You will have an incentive to complete your project. If you love dogs, then stitch an image of your pet. Don't stitch cats if they are of no interest—you'll never finish it.

If you are just beginning to learn embroidery, go easy. For an original design, start with an easy pattern that has a couple of stitches for the motif and maybe a third stitch for a special textured effect. Practice stitching part of your idea on a scrap piece of fabric before attempting the real thing. For more detailed designs, sketch them on a piece of paper or on your fabric so that you have a visual picture to follow. Experiment with different methods; soon you'll find the best fit for you.

Inspiration for Designs

Where can you find inspiration for your embroidery designs? Look out the window and take in what nature has to offer. A flower? A tree? An entire landscape? Go to a museum and review some paintings or photographs that appeal to you. The decorative arts section usually has antique textiles with embroidery that you could imitate or adapt as an embellishment. Not only will you find ideas for texture and design in these old embroideries, but you will also see classic combinations of colors, patterns, threads, stitches, and background fabric. Porcelain patterns are another source that can be copied and embroidered. Book illustrations and wallpapers may inspire you as well.

Clever Crafter

In ancient China, embroidery symbolized rank or circumstance. Wishes for the wearer were also stitched on clothing. Flowers and fruits were significant images on marriage garments. The lotus symbolized fruitfulness and purity, and the pomegranate represented hopes of fertility.

Every original embroidery design begins with an idea. An idea is sparked by your daily life and outside influences. Maybe you saw a piece of trim on your neighbor's drapery? What about the dress pattern you liked that was worn by the woman in a painting? Go through your closets. Look at the edgings on your clothes. The possibilities are endless!

Helpful Hints for Preparing Your Design

Deciding on the size of your design, type of fabric, and method of stitching will help you on your way with an overall design scheme for your embroidery.

Design Decisions

Go through your files and select designs that suit your project. You need to decide whether you can transfer them as is. These designs may not be the right size. You may need to enlarge or reduce them as you learned in Chapter 20.

Type of Fabric

The ground fabric you choose depends on the type of design, kind of stitches, and the threads you use, as discussed in Chapter 19. You might choose a printed fabric and then stitch the outlines of the motifs or embroider the motif itself. A solid even-weave fabric would be appropriate for cross-stitch embroidery. A light-colored background fabric could show off dark-colored threads but also display a subtle pattern with a similar color thread. Using opposite materials can be attractive, such as a rough burlap background with smooth silk thread. Use your imagination, and your design will be unique.

Outlines

Outlines really help to define the shape of designs. For a subtle outline, choose a thread color similar to the color of the shape being outlined. For emphasis, choose a contrasting thread color. Metallic threads might add just the spark that your design needs. Couching the outline of a design is another way to add emphasis (see Chapter 23). Use several rows of outlining to add even greater accent.

And don't forget the outlining doesn't have to be straight stitching! Chain stitches add a curvaceous edge to the pattern.

> **A Stitch in Time** _____
> Did you know that outlining a pattern can cover up any "less-than-perfect" worked edges?

Voiding

A unique way to design embroidery is to use the voiding method, in which the motif is left unstitched and instead the background is filled

> **Clever Crafter** _____
> Voiding is typically found in Greek and Assisi embroideries.

in. Start by outlining the motif. Then fill in the background around the motif, leaving the actual interior of the motif "undone." You could use a stem stitch for outlining the motif and a satin stitch for filling in the background.

Like outlining, couching also enhances the outlines of motifs and can be effectively combined with the voiding method.

Backgrounds

As you learned in the previous section on voiding, the background of a pattern or motif can be either left exposed or stitched in various ways. It's common to think of your background fabric as less significant because it's in the background. True, the ground fabric is the means used to create your embroidery, but it is also a big part of your design.

You can use your background fabric in other ways that will complement your design and create special effects. Try stitching geometric shapes at different intervals so as to "dot" the background and leave the spaces between the "dots" unworked. An overall pattern is achieved. You could also try couching the outlines of your motifs for extra emphasis of the exposed background.

> **Decorator's Do's and Don'ts**
>
> Don't be afraid to stitch a pattern using a thread that is similar in color to the background fabric and combining them with the voiding method. A linen background with a similar color thread is a stunning use of tone on tone. This will create texture, which is a visual delight.

Color and Thread Combos

It is amazing how so many embroideries can be "engineered" by combining different options for threads and stitches. Simply by changing the colors of the threads but using the same stitch, a pattern can take on a new look. Even with the same color thread and the same stitch, you can develop a new pattern by changing the direction of the stitch.

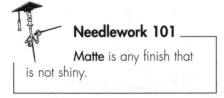

> **Needlework 101**
>
> **Matte** is any finish that is not shiny.

◆ **Same stitch, different threads.** Try using the same stitch on identical designs but introducing different types of threads to achieve a textural effect. The old saying "opposites attract" is a good philosophy to use in your embroidery! Highlight shiny threads with *matte* threads, and use wool threads to highlight glossy threads.

- **Same stitch, same thread.** Many embroideries are worked in the same stitch throughout and the same color of thread. The pattern is formed by the arrangement of the stitches. You will read in the next section on pictorial embroidery that the same thread and stitch can be used to form pictures. Shiny threads, such as silk worked in a satin stitch vertically and horizontally, will reflect light differently, thus creating a pattern with the change in color tones. Matte threads, such as wool, have less-dramatic changes but still create a pattern with different directions of stitches.

- **Same color, different stitches.** Different stitches used together form rich patterns, as can be seen in whitework and blackwork. A sampler done in one color throughout but with various embroidery stitches can be a beautiful way to use the "same color thread but different stitch" concept.

Different Color Effects

By using complementary colors, colors in the same family, you can create shading and illumination. For subtle accents, a slowly graduating effect is achieved by using several tones from dark to light. For a heathered look, thread your needle with various tones of the same color such as reds, pinks, and raspberries. Some threads come predyed in several different shades and tones that create an antiqued effect when stitched. The faded look is already built in!

Pictorial Embroidery

In pictorial embroidery, as the name suggests, pictures are formed with stitches. Animals and birds are easily depicted with threads and stitches that resemble fur and feathers. Human faces and skin are a little harder to portray, but nature—animals, water, trees, and the sky—can be easily embroidered by following these hints for choosing stitches:

- **Fur and hair.** For straight fur or hair, use the satin stitch in various lengths. For rigid fur, use fillings of a blanket stitch. For wooly fur or curly hair, use French knots. For wavy fur or hair, use the chain stitch.

- **Feathers.** Use satin stitches of various lengths and directions to follow the line of a feather.

Clever Crafter
Ancient Chinese embroideries often portrayed water in gold couched coils.

- **Sky and water.** For calming effects, use flat stitches. For storms, use swirling or circular stitch arrangements, such as the chain stitch, or couch partial circles to resemble water movement or cloud shapes.

◆ **Wind and rain.** For gusts of wind, suddenly change the direction of your stitches. For rain, use irregularly sized strokes of top stitching.

◆ **Landscapes.** To create a sense of distance, use long stitches in the background and shorter ones in foreground.

◆ **Faces.** Although faces are one of the harder items to stitch, try using the stem stitch in concentric circles. Start at the cheekbone and work outward in wider circles. Change the tones of your thread to add shading and dimension. The features can be added on top in fine detail. Split stitch and satin stitch are alternatives to try.

The Least You Need to Know

◆ Cultivate inspiration through exposure to museums, home décor books, magazines, clothing patterns, and various forms of needlework.

◆ Explore different combinations of thread color and stitch type. You will be amazed at the variety you can achieve.

◆ By combining different tones of the same color thread (monochromatic), you can create illumination and shading in your work.

◆ For pictorial embroidery, nature scenes and faces can be created by working standard stitches in new ways.

Chapter 25

The Embroiderer's Finishing Touch

In This Chapter

- Learning the art of blocking and mounting
- Framing it yourself or going to a pro
- Cleaning, caring, and storing embroideries

After you have decided how you'd like to finish your embroidery, you must prepare it. First you might need to straighten it a bit if it has become distorted during stitching. Although most pieces need only a light pressing, some embroideries need to be stretched and straightened by using a technique called blocking. And if you plan to hang your embroidery as wall décor, you need to mount and frame your piece. It's also good to learn about cleaning, care, and storage of old and new embroideries, because dust, dirt, and insects are the main enemies of embroidered textiles.

The Finishing Touches

After you have sewn your last stitch to complete your embroidery design, you still have a few steps to go before you can say you have actually "finished" your needle-work. You must prepare it for its intended use by getting it into shape if there was any distortion during stitching or preparing it for framing if you choose to hang it on a wall.

Blocking

Blocking is the process of straightening an embroidery that has become distorted during stitching and restoring it to its original shape. To do this, soak the embroidery in cold water (for a wet block), wrap it in a towel to remove excess moisture (don't wring it), and pin it to a board for straightening. Blocking also removes creases and gives a professional look to your piece.

Always be sure that your fabrics and threads are *colorfast* before you do any wet block-ing. Otherwise, the color could run and all your hard work might be ruined! Older embroideries are more prone to this. Most of today's fabrics are colorfast, but never take a chance! To test, press a wet cotton ball onto some of the threads to see if any dye is transferred to the cotton ball. If so, you will have to dry block your embroidery. To dry block, just pin your embroidery into shape and then add moisture (but not enough to cause running colors) by passing a steam iron over (not *on*) the embroidery.

Needlework 101

Colorfast refers to dyes in fabrics or threads that will not run when wet.

Follow these steps for colorfast fabrics and threads if your embroidery needs straighten-ing. Skip step 1 if embroidery is not colorfast:

1. Soak the embroidery in cold water. Roll in a clean towel to remove excess moisture.

2. Cover a soft board like a cork bulletin board with cotton or plastic. Pin your embroidery at each corner, keeping the pins on the outside of the stitching. Gently stretch the piece as you pin at 1-inch intervals, starting at center. Leave pinned until dry.

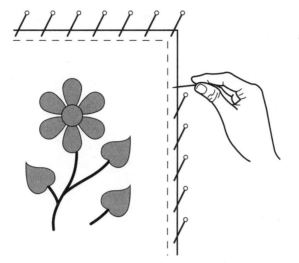

Be sure you leave the pins in place until your embroidery is completely dry.

Mounting

Mounting prepares your work for framing. You will need a piece of stiff cardboard or foamcore. The cardboard should be at least the size of the needlework, and preferably larger to allow for a margin to show beyond the design. When mounting, you need to fold the edges of your fabric to the back of the cardboard, so be sure that the cardboard is sturdy enough for this.

Decorator's Do's and Don'ts

A scorch mark is not part of the design! Never put an iron on the right side of your embroidery work. It may scorch the piece and flatten the stitches. Instead, place your piece right side down on a padded surface. Cover it with a cloth (damp or dry, depending on the fabric). Press very gently at the proper setting for your fabric type, lifting—not sliding—your iron as you progress from area to area.

Some designs may require a very small border of fabric, whereas others may need to have a significant amount of fabric showing. For example, a small monogram may be framed in a large-scale frame so that it stands out from the background fabric. An entire landscape may meet the edges of the frame without any border of background fabric showing at all. Critique each work separately.

To mount your embroidery, first fold the side edges of your fabric to the back side of the cardboard. Use a strong thread such as button thread to lace the edges back and forth as shown in the following figure. Adjust the lacing threads so that your work is stretched smoothly across the board. When you are satisfied with the look of the piece, pull the stitches to tighten them and secure the lacing thread with a few back-stitches.

Now fold back the top and bottom edges and lace in the same way. Your work is ready to be framed.

Pull the lacing threads firmly and evenly to ensure that your work is smoothly stretched and ready for framing.

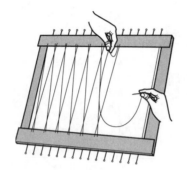

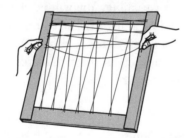

Framing

If you choose to frame your own needlework, after blocking and mounting it, you will need to find a frame that fits. You can add a mat to cover any gaps that might appear with a noncustom frame. Never trim your embroidery until you have selected the proper-size cardboard to mount and frame.

Take both your mounted piece and the measurements when you buy a frame. Hold your piece up to several different types of frames so that you can get an idea of the finished look. You may find the perfect frame, but it may come with a mat that needs to be resized to accommodate your work. No problem. Use an X-acto knife and a ruler (wait until you get home, of course!) to trim the inside area of your mat board.

Decorator's Do's and Don'ts _____

Don't be ordinary! And don't use unattractive plastic frames that might be included in your kit. Mix traditional embroideries with contemporary frames like a piece of plain glass (that actually has no frame!) and clips that holds the glass and work together. Use a weathered wooden frame for a fancy crewelwork done in white wool on white linen.

Selecting a frame that is ready-made or using one you already have is the most inexpensive way to frame your embroidery. However, if you are nervous about doing the framing yourself, you may want to get an estimate from a professional framer.

Professional Framers

A custom framer is the easiest way to have your work framed, but also the most expensive. However, you have the advantage of being able to select from a cajillion different types and styles of frames, as well as mat colors and types. Another advantage of professional framing is that the framer will back the piece with a protective cover and attach the correct gauge wire for hanging. A piece of glass or Plexiglas will protect the front side as well as show off your hard work.

Your professional framer will also know about conservation framing, which is a method of framing that does not harm the textile. Some cardboards, mats, and wood frames contain acids that, over time, actually eat away the fabric and thread fibers. Always specify acid-free materials.

Another caveat—whether you frame a piece yourself or have it framed, be sure that the glass does not sit directly on the embroidery. A mat ensures some space between the embroidery and the glass and eliminates the trapping of moisture.

Check out several framers in your area, and ask other needleworkers whom they use before committing to a particular shop. Costs for framing will vary drastically, as will the level of service and professionalism.

Getting It on the Wall

Displaying and hanging your work on walls can be a daunting decorating task. To help you, I've gathered the following "Lucky 7" guidelines for hanging and grouping pictures that have different sizes, styles, and mats. These guidelines will help your pictures get the attention they deserve and produce the best effect for your room:

1. Unify a mismatched collection of prints by using the same mat and frame for each.

2. Group pictures together instead of scattering them around the room.

3. Hang several small, identical frames close together to make one large "picture" over a sofa.

4. For symmetrical arrangements, hang similar sizes and frames either vertically or horizontally.

5. For asymmetrical arrangements, place the largest picture to one side and arrange the smaller ones together on the other side to balance out the display.

6. Don't hang pictures too high or too low! Consider the proportions of the picture and the wall surface area as well as the surrounding furniture.

7. To make walls look wider and longer, arrange pictures horizontally. To make walls look higher, arrange pictures vertically.

> **Decorator's Do's and Don'ts**
>
> Don't hang your embroideries in direct sunlight! The sun can be very damaging to some textiles, causing fading and weakening of fibers. Do consider placement on a wall or on furniture that is away from windows.

In the Wash

All embroideries will need to be cleaned because dust and dirt are the true enemies of any textile. Even though you might think that your piece is absolutely clean because you see no visible spots or stains, you still need to clean it. Oil stains from your hands and dust from the environment are invisible now, but will be apparent years later, especially on cotton pieces. By removing the oil and dust, you help to ensure a long life for your beautiful piece. Of course, if your embroidery is old and valuable, you should not clean it at home; take it to a dry cleaning specialist instead.

> **Decorator's Do's and Don'ts**
>
> Never use a stiff brush to clean your embroideries. You will damage the stitches!

Before washing any embroidery, don't forget the colorfast test mentioned earlier. Press a wet ball of cotton to threads to see whether any dye runs into it. (Reds and purples are particularly susceptible to running.) If you see color on the cotton ball, do not wash the embroidery.

Place some pure soap flakes or mild detergent for delicate fabrics in your sink or in a bucket, and wash the piece gently by hand without rubbing. Orvus is a concentrated biodegradable quilt "soap," available in quilt stores, with no phosphorus—and no soap in it. It is perfect for delicate embroideries. Rinse your embroideries several times in lukewarm water until the water is clear. For the last rinse, use cold water. Use distilled water for the last rinse if you have iron in your water; otherwise, rust stains will show up years later.

If your embroidery has specific stains that may need special treatment, check the following list before attempting to clean them.

Some pieces may not be washable. They may need spot-cleaning instead of being immersed in water. Here are some alternatives to washing:

- **Vacuum.** Clean embroideries with a vacuum if they are dusty. Use the nozzle attachment. Often it is recommended that you place a soft nylon screen over the stitching (test a section so the screen will not snag any stitches) and then move the nozzle back and forth over the screen to protect the stitching.

- **Dry clean.** Large and valuable embroideries such as wall hangings, upholstered pieces, those with a lot of raised work, or pieces having bad stains should be dry cleaned and not washed. Of course, those items that do not pass the colorfast test will also need to be dry cleaned to prevent the dye in the threads or fabric from running. Be sure to choose a reputable cleaner.

- **Sable paintbrush method.** Embroidery having stitching that is "raised" from the cloth is delicate, as is embroidery having metal threads, such as gold or silver. Use a sable paintbrush to very gently stroke in and out of crevices that may have collected dust or dirt.

A Stitch in Time

Do your embroidered napkins or tablecloths have candle wax on them? If the wax is still soft, harden it with an ice cube then, gently scrape away the wax with a dull knife. Be careful not to damage any of the stitches. Then, lay the embroidery face down between two sheets of blotting paper. Press a warm iron over the surface of the paper, letting the wax soak into the paper. If the candles were colored and left a stain, try dipping a sponge in alcohol and blotting up the color, but only after the wax has been removed.

Keep Away, Moths!

Take care when storing your embroideries. Bugs, moths, and mildew can cause irreversible damage to textiles. Moths love wool and will make holes in improperly stored fabrics. And of course, moisture causes mildew, which turns fabrics black with rot.

When your embroideries are not in use, store them wrapped in acid-free paper and in a dark place off the floor. Lay them flat to avoid creases that form after time. If a piece cannot be laid flat, roll it in acid-free tissue paper. Most people like plastic bags for storing things, but plastic bags are not recommended for permanent storage because the plastic gives off a gas harmful to textiles, plus moisture could get in the bag and bring on the mildew. However, you can mitigate the effects by punching some small holes in the plastic or by sealing the bag loosely. My friend Diane uses clean, old pillowcases to store her needlework. Check periodically for moths and mildew. It is also a good idea to clean your embroideries every once in a while.

A Stitch in Time

Don't pass by unfinished embroideries at yard sales! They are some of my best finds and only a few dollars. They usually come with appropriate thread to finish them. If they need cleaning, refer to the cleaning tips in this chapter.

The Least You Need to Know

◆ Make the planning and stitching of your needlework projects efficient and easy by keeping an embroidery basket or bag handy for all your needles, threads, and fabrics, plus the basic tools needed to finish your work.

◆ Learning the art of mounting and blocking will help you finish your embroideries with a professional look.

◆ Selecting frames for your finished work requires a good sense of design and scale. Hanging embroideries in different groupings and mixing with other art can heighten the impact of your work.

◆ Cleaning, caring for, and storing your embroideries properly will preserve your work for generations.

Chapter 26

Embroidery Project: An ABCs Sampler

In This Chapter

- Stitching your ABCs—a sampler
- Preparation is the best way to start any project
- Use graphs to design your own samplers

This chapter guides you step by step as you create a sampler, from the materials needed to get started to advice on finishing your sampler, with plenty of helpful hints along the way. You will embroider the alphabet and numbers and a couple of stars! Nothing is quite as comforting as a charming sampler framed as wall décor to be treasured for generations to come.

Small, Simple, and Sweet: A Sampler

The sampler is a perfect choice for a first embroidery project, because you can get acquainted with your materials as well as learn the ins and outs of stitching letters and numbers. This practice comes in handy when you want to sign and date your pieces. Let's start with a very simple sampler that showcases the alphabet in uppercase as well as lowercase and the numbers 1 through 10, with some star motifs for variety.

Getting Acquainted with the Materials

A good way to begin a new craft is to collect all the necessary materials and then try them out ... see how the thread works with the needle and fabric. Here is the list of materials that you need to stitch the small sampler project. You can purchase them at your local stitchery shop or at a large chain store.

- 12-inch by 12-inch 14-count Aida cloth in ivory
- DMC Six Stranded Embroidery Cotton (347), dark salmon
- No. 26 tapestry needle
- Embroidery hoop, 9 inch
- Pencil
- Ruler
- Cotton thread for basting (different color than DMC 347)
- Embroidery scissors, 3 or 4 inch

The Fabric

For your sampler, you will be using Aida cloth, a sturdy cotton fabric woven in such a way that small squares are formed, producing a gridlike effect. One cross-stitch is placed in each square, and a tiny hole at each corner makes it clear where the needle comes up and goes down. Because this particular size of Aida cloth is woven so that there are 14 holes, or squares, per inch, it is called 14-count Aida.

Clever Crafter

The earliest surviving dated sampler was stitched by Jane Bostocke in 1598, and it now resides in the Victoria and Albert Museum in London.

The Needle

The needle for this project is a tapestry needle rather than a sharp-tipped needle. Because of its blunt tip, the tapestry needle will slip through the holes in the Aida fabric without piercing it, as a sharp-tipped needle would. You'll use a size 26 in this project.

The Thread

The thread used for this cross-stitch project is DMC Six Stranded Embroidery Floss, a high-quality mercerized cotton floss. If you look at the cut end of the floss, you can clearly see the six separate strands that are gently twisted to create the floss. To cross-stitch on 14-count Aida cloth, you will work with only two of the six strands. Pull a length of thread from the skein (pull from the label end) and separate out, or "strip," the two strands. This produces a fuller-looking stitch because the stripped strands lie side by side when recombined.

Helpful Tools

A hoop will help keep your sampler fabric taut and clean. Use your pencil to mark the arrow for the center points on the chart. Use the basting thread to mark the center vertical and horizontal points of the fabric. If these tools are always kept in your embroidery basket, it makes your projects so much easier to start and complete.

Reading the Chart

The chart is illustrated on graph paper using a symbol to guide you. This sampler is done in one color for ease and style. Each symbol—a small cross—represents a stitch on the chart. Each square on the chart represents one square on the fabric. The symbols on the chart show where the stitches go and also represent the color to be used for the stitch. By embroidering cross-stitches in the corresponding squares of the Aida cloth, you will be able to make your sampler come to life! Be sure to mark the vertical and horizontal midpoints with an arrow so that you can find the center of the chart.

The Stitch

Use the cross-stitch on this sampler. Refer to the diagram and instructions in Chapter 21 for help on how to work the basic cross-stitch. It is one of the easiest to master.

Preparing Your Thread

Follow these steps to prepare your thread:

1. Cut the embroidery floss into lengths of approximately 18 inches. This is an easy length to work with.

2. Pull the thread from the label end of the skein; it pulls easier from that end. Keep holding on to the label end of the thread, and cut off the desired length.

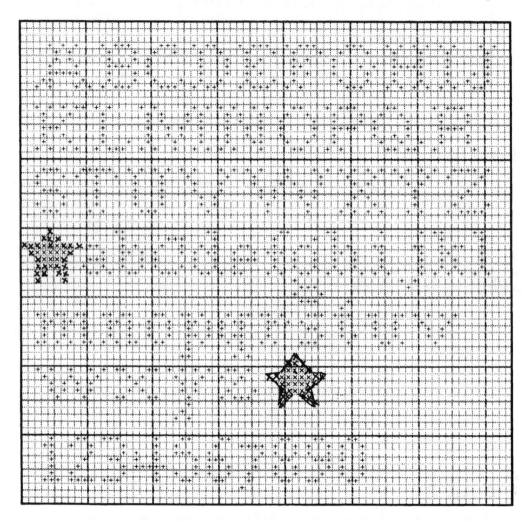

3. Hold that end in your right hand, near the top of the thread. With your left hand, tap the top several times. The strands will fluff out and separate (sometimes called "blooming"). Now you can easily select a strand to pull. Pull a single strand straight up with your left hand while firmly holding the remainder of the length with your right.

4. After the strand has been pulled out, give the length in your right hand a shake. The remaining strands will fall smoothly back in place. If the strands bunch up instead of falling free, you are holding the wrong end. Simply turn the length of thread upside down and tap again.

5. Continue to pull out as many strands
   as you need, one by one. Recombine
   the appropriate number (two for this
   sampler).

6. Note that the end you tapped is also the
   end you thread into the needle. Orienting
   the thread this way keeps the thread from
   snarling as you pull it through the fabric.
   This method is almost foolproof.

Decorator's Do's and Don'ts

Never knot your thread!
Leave a 1-inch tail of thread at
the back of the fabric. Hold the
tail with your finger and make
your stitches so that they cover
the tail on the back. The stitches
will anchor the tail.

Thread your needle with the two strands of floss.

Preparing Your Fabric

To prepare your fabric, follow these steps:

1. Turn under and sew, serge, or zigzag the edges of the fabric to prevent fraying.

2. Find the center of your fabric by folding the fabric in half, and in half again, and
   creasing lightly.

3. Baste along both fold lines—where the two lines cross is the center reference
   point. These lines will guide you when following the chart.

4. After each stitching session, be sure to remove the embroidery hoop. If left in
   place, it eventually leaves a permanent crease (it actually breaks the fibers) on
   the fabric. Refer to Chapter 19 to refresh your memory on how to use the hoop.

Ready, Set, Stitch

Now, it's time to stitch:

1. Thread your needle with two strands of thread.

2. Find the center point of the chart. Start your cross-stitch (see Chapter 21 to
   review) at the top-left corner of the chart.

3. Measure the inches from the top-left corner and from the left edge of the fabric
   to where the finished design will be centered.

4. Count over to the first stitch to begin. Use your chart as your guide—remember
   that each symbol on the graph represents one cross-stitch on your fabric.

5. Count your stitches frequently to eliminate the chances of making a mistake.

If the floss becomes tightly twisted while embroidering, drop the needle and let it hang. The floss will untwist by itself. Tightly twisted floss appears thin and will not cover the fabric.

Framing

When you have completed the sampler, frame it so that you can show the world your first stab at embroidery! Refer to Chapter 25 for blocking and mounting your sampler. The finished size of this sampler should be 9 by 9 inches. An antique frame will give your work instant age and heritage. A sleek frame, such as a piece of glass with clips, will show off the edges of the sampler, a combination of traditional and modern.

Clever Crafter

To give an instant aged appearance to your sampler, dip the fabric in a coffee or tea solution. To a quart of boiling water, add 6 teaspoons of instant coffee or tea leaves. Bring to a boil and remove from heat. Dip your sampler in cold water and then in the hot solution for 1 minute. Place on an absorbent cloth and iron by placing a clean cloth on top of your stitching. Always be sure your materials are colorfast!

Decorator's Do's and Don'ts

Don't jump too far from one area to another. Threads that run across the back of the embroidery, especially dark colors, will show through on the front. Finish one area; then start again.

Grids to Make Your Own

After you complete this sampler, you may want to design your own sampler, or perhaps you have a different type of design in mind that you just can't wait to start stitching. Strike out on your own and use the graph paper provided in this chapter to sketch your own patterns and designs. Feel free to photocopy these sheets if you need more paper.

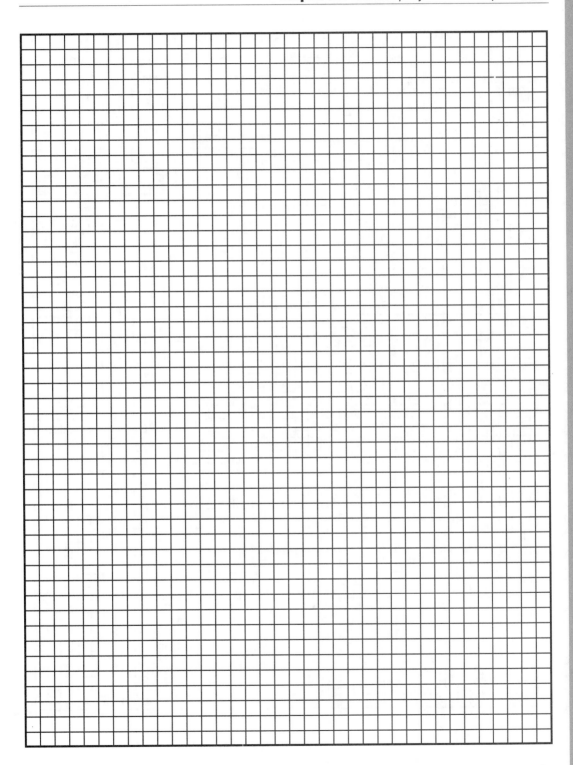

The Least You Need to Know

- Small projects are a good beginning for novices.

- A good way to start a new craft is to get a feel for your materials ... how the thread works with the needle and fabric.

- Preparing your threads and fabric before starting makes a project easier.

- Graph paper is great for drawing your own designs.

Part 3

Needlepoint

Throughout this part, you will gather ideas about the many possibilities for needlepoint, including where to find inspiration for your own designs and what you can create. You'll learn many of the stitches used in needlepoint, the tools necessary for each craft, projects that you can start with, and finishing techniques to give your piece a professional look.

Chapter 27

Needlepoint Tools of the Trade

In This Chapter

- ◆ Learning the right size and type of canvases
- ◆ Knowing your needlepoint needles and the weights of yarns
- ◆ Using kits: a beginner's salvation

Needlepoint is sometimes known as "tapestry," because items stitched with the basic needlepoint stitches (tent, diagonal, and straight) have a woven look that resembles a tapestry wall hanging. Compared with the embroidery stitches that you learned earlier, needlepoint stitches are very easy to learn.

In addition to canvas, needlepoint essentials include needles and yarn, which all must be carefully matched to work together. A frame, as well as other small tools, can make needlepoint easier. Color-coordinated kits with all these items prepackaged may be the simplest way to start.

Your Canvas

As in painting, needlepoint uses a "canvas" to work on. Unlike painting, however, the needlepoint canvas is not made from canvas at all. Most needlepoint canvases are made from cotton or linen. They are *mesh* fabrics with criss-crossing fibers that form a grid. The open spaces allow the needle and yarn to pass through to form the needlepoint work.

> ### Needlework 101
>
> **Mesh** is any fabric of open texture having a netlike quality.

You can purchase canvas by the yard, depending on the size of your design/project. It comes in basic colors of antique brown, white, and cream, which are suitable for most applications; as well as a variety of specialty colors, such as black, sage, peach, and pale blue.

Besides having a choice of color, you have a choice of mesh size. The mesh size, or gauge, is determined by the number of threads per inch. The higher the number, the finer the canvas, and vice versa—the lower the number, the coarser the canvas. For example, very detailed work may require a fine-gauge canvas of 22 threads per inch, whereas a rug will require thick rug canvas with a gauge of 3 threads per inch. A common gauge used in needlepoint is 10, which you now know means 10 threads per inch.

Mono Canvas

Mono canvas is sold in the largest range of gauges. It consists of single threads that form a grid. When you learn about needlepoint stitches in Chapter 29, you will find out that mono canvas is not suitable for working half- and cross-stitches.

Mono canvas comes in the widest range of gauges.

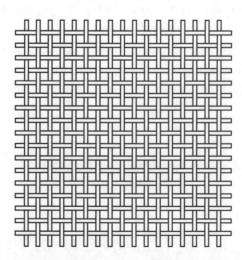

Double or Penelope Canvas

The double, or "Penelope," canvas is made with pairs of horizontal and vertical threads. You can work your stitches over each pair or split them for smaller stitches when you need more detail. This is sometimes referred to as "pricking the ground."

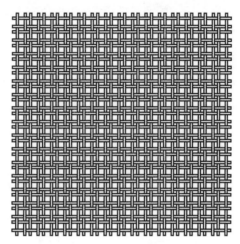

In double, or Penelope, canvas, the threads can be split for smaller stitches or can be worked in pairs.

Interlock and Rug Canvases

Other types of canvases are interlock and rug, used for wall hangings and rugs. Interlock canvas is made of pairs of twisted vertical threads that intersect single horizontal threads. This weave makes interlock less likely to distort or fray.

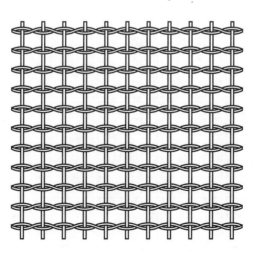

Interlock canvas is less likely to distort during stitching.

Rug canvas is a sturdy canvas used for needlepoint and rug-making. It is formed by two lengthwise threads twisted around each other and a pair of crosswise threads. The threads cannot be separated. Rug canvas comes in three to five gauges and is used primarily for rugs.

Rug canvas has interlocking construction to give it shape.

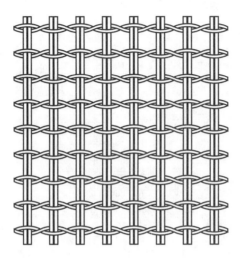

Plastic and Paper Canvas

Plastic canvas is a molded, rather than woven, canvas-looking material that comes in precut sheets with a medium gauge. It is typically used for place mats, cards, and craft decorations such as ornaments. Plastic canvas has a stiff feel and is not recommended for fine needlework.

Plastic and paper canvas is used for "crafty" items like place mats, cards, and deco-rations.

Fourteen-count perforated paper, available in ecru, brown, and other colors (sometimes gold, silver, and red) is a stiff, heavy paper that has been coated for durability. It is suitable for both needlepoint and cross-stitch decorations and cards.

To the Point: Needles

Tapestry needles are specifically used for needlepoint. They have blunt ends to protect the thread and canvas from being split during stitching. Their large eyes make it easy to thread heavier weights of yarn. They are available in various sizes ranging from 28, the smallest, to 13, the largest. The smaller sizes are primarily used in cross-stitch, and the larger ones in needlepoint, with size 24 being used for both. A size 18 needle is suitable for 10- and 12-mesh canvas. Be sure you select a size that fits the mesh holes of your canvas without distorting them.

A Stitch in Time

It is very important to choose the right needle. The needle and yarn should pass easily through the canvas. A kit will include the correct-size yarn and needle, or a specialty shop owner can advise you.

Yarn

Three types of wool yarn are manufactured for needlepoint: crewel, tapestry, and Persian. They are colorfast, durable, and available in many beautiful shades. Other yarns tailored for more specific types of projects include rug wool, crochet, embroidery cottons, silk floss, and metallic threads.

Crewel is the finest of the wool needlepoint yarns, a little finer than Persian yarn. It can be worked in a single strand on a very fine mesh canvas, or two, three, or four strands can be combined for coarser work.

Persian wool is made up of three easily divided strands. These strands can be separated to suit the gauge of your canvas.

Tapestry wool is a single-strand yarn, a bit finer than three strands of Persian wool. It is usually used with medium-gauge canvas.

Decorator's Do's and Don'ts

If you work with dark-color yarns, don't choose a white canvas. Select brown canvas so that any gaps in your stitching won't be noticeable and spoil your design.

Rug wool is a very thick, long-lasting, single-strand yarn.

All four types of yarn are available in a man-made fiber—acrylic—which is less expensive and easier to wash but not as handsome for heirloom projects.

Crochet or embroidery cottons, silks, and metal threads can be used alone or in conjunction with other threads for outlining or accents.

Yarns pictured from top to bottom are crewel, tapestry, and Persian.

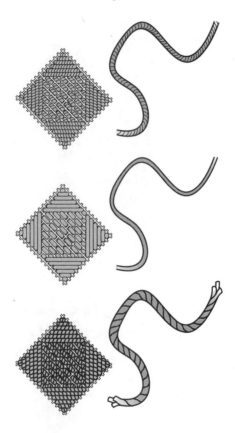

Frames

Although frames aren't absolutely necessary for working a needlepoint design, they are helpful for keeping the canvas stretched evenly and for preventing distortion. If the frame is supported by a stand, then both of your hands can be free. The flat, straight-sided frame works best for canvas. An adjustable straight frame on a stand is best for large pieces of canvas. Refresh your memory by reading the section on frames in Chapter 19.

The Little Extras

Good results in needlework come from using good-quality implements. Along with the right needles and threads, fill your needlepoint bag or basket with the following:

◆ **Embroidery scissors.** Find a pair that is sharp, light, pointed, and small (3 to 4 inches long). Blunt-tipped scissors, like those sold for children, aren't suitable.

◆ **Dressmaker shears.** These are best for cutting fabric. If you use them to cut canvas, be aware that over time they will become dull from the rough canvas threads.

◆ **Felt-tip marker.** Markers are great for drawing designs on fabric. Stock up on waterproof-type markers only, in lots of colors.

◆ **Masking tape.** Use tape to bind the edges of the canvas to prevent raveling and to keep the edges from snagging your yarn.

◆ **Dressmaker's carbon paper.** Use it to transfer designs to canvas.

◆ **Acrylic paints.** These paints are good for painting designs or for changing a color on a preprinted design.

◆ **Paintbrush.** If you decide to paint your own canvases, you will need to invest in an acrylic paintbrush.

Needlepoint ... Ready to Go

Just as in the fashion world of ready-to-wear clothing, there is ready-to-do needlepoint in the needlework world. It is the quickest way to get going on a project, with the canvas already preprinted with a design and materials specified or prepackaged. Read on to see the possibilities and best choice for you.

Kits

Needlepoint kits are great for the beginner because they already have the right needle, the proper amount and weight of yarn in the specified colors, and the correct gauge of canvas. What could be easier? The design is usually printed on the canvas or in chart form included in the kit. The chart will be a graph, like the graph in the last chapter, in which each square represents a stitch.

Hand-Painted Designs

Canvases having hand-painted designs are another option. These may be one-of-a-kind or limited-production designs. You select and buy your own yarn to match the colors of the paint, although some canvases come with the matching colored yarn. A specialty shop owner can recommend the proper yarn and amounts of each color.

Charts

Charted designs have squares that represent a stitch. The squares are marked with colored inks or with symbols, defined in a key at the side of the chart. The charts are printed on paper, and the canvas is blank. By measuring and counting meshes and using the color chart on the paper as a guide, you can begin stitching. Each square on the paper represents a color and type of stitch.

Tramméd Canvas

Some canvases come with long, horizontal stitches, called *tramé*, which run across the design. Diagonal stitches are then worked over the horizontal stitches to add thickness and strength to the canvas. Pieces that will get a lot of wear, like seat or footstool covers, are often tramméd.

The Least You Need to Know

- ◆ Needlepoint requires only a few tools and is easy to pick up.
- ◆ Needlepoint canvases come in many different gauges that require the appropriate-sized needle and weight of yarn.
- ◆ Tapestry needles are required for needlepoint because of their blunt ends and large eyes.
- ◆ Yarns come in many different colors and weights. Be sure to choose the right yarn that will work best with your needle and canvas.
- ◆ Kits are the easiest way to begin doing needlepoint.

28

Needlepoint Tips and Tricks

In This Chapter

- ◆ Preparing your canvas for handling
- ◆ Stitching at the beginning and end
- ◆ Learning pointers on thread
- ◆ Tackling techniques for transferring needlepoint designs

Before you grab that canvas, needle, and thread for your first stab at needlepoint, you'll want to read some of the techniques in this chapter that will make needlepoint easier, neater, and fun! Although needlepoint is a breeze to pick up, you'll find that by learning some stitching tips and the basics of handling the canvas, starting your design, and finishing off your work, your project will be that much easier and satisfying.

Fragile ... Handle with Care!

Older canvas materials tended to fray easily. Although today's canvases don't fray nearly as much, it is still a good idea to place masking tape neatly around the edges, especially if you will be handling the project for a length of time (usually the case with large canvases or those you carry around a lot). Taping will keep the edges of your canvas neat and clean.

If your canvas is very large, try rolling it up to the section you are working on and securing it with clothespins to make it less cumbersome to work with. Be sure to roll upward with the design on the inside.

Before blocking your needlepoint projects, be sure to make a paper template of the original size and shape of your canvas so that when you do reshape it you will have a guide to go by. As you learned in embroidery (Chapter 25), you will need to block your finished needlepoint to return it to its original shape. An easy way to view the original size (for small designs) is to photocopy it at full size.

Take a Stab at Stitches

There are two methods of stitching in needlepoint: the stabbing method and the sewing method. The stabbing method requires two movements to make a stitch and is easier to use with a frame. The sewing method requires one movement. Either method may be used for handheld needlepoint. See which one works for you!

The stabbing method requires two movements for each stitch. Insert the needle into your canvas from the back side through to the right side of the canvas at the point where stitch is to be formed. Then pull the needle and yarn through to the back side of the canvas.

Decorator's Do's and Don'ts

Don't use yarn that's too thin! Use a proper thickness that will cover your canvas and prevent the mesh from showing. A good way to test which yarn is right for your project is to stitch a sample section. If the yarn is too thin, add another strand or two until the mesh is covered. If it's difficult to pull the thread through the canvas or if the canvas seems to ripple, decrease the number of strands.

The stabbing method.

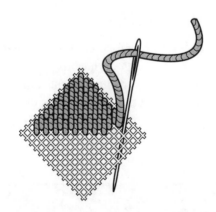

The sewing method requires one motion: The needle is inserted into the canvas from the right side of your canvas and brought out at the point where the next stitch is to be formed. Pull the thread through to the front.

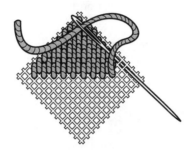

The sewing method.

Thread Tech

The following tips about threads and yarns will help you keep frustrations at bay and your needlepoint looking its best.

Points to remember:

◆ If the thread begins to twist or tangle, let it drop down from the canvas and unwind before you continue.

◆ Begin with a working thread of 18 inches to prevent fraying as you work it through the canvas.

◆ Do not start and end new threads at the same point. The thickness of the threads will cause a bumpy ridge that will be visible from the right side of your work.

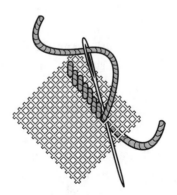

Leave at least an inch of thread at the back. Work a few stitches over it to secure it, then cut off any excess.

♦ Never start a new thread with a knot. This will form bumps in your work.

♦ Wool yarn has a right and wrong end. The right end must thread the needle. Run your thumb and forefinger downward along the length of the yarn. If it feels smooth, you have the right end.

Bring the needle through to the back of your work. Weave the thread through the back side of the canvas through the last 6 to 8 stitches, then cut off the excess.

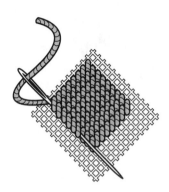

Transferring Techniques

As you learn some of the basic techniques with your needle, canvas, and threads, you may be thinking of some patterns that you would like to borrow and turn into a needlepoint. You can transfer a pattern or your drawing with one of the following methods.

Decorator's Do's and Don'ts

Don't use plain carbon paper for transferring your designs. Regular carbon will ruin your fabric. Use dressmaker's carbon only.

A Stitch in Time

It's a good idea to buy only waterproof markers for your "tool kit." That way, when you block your needlepoint, you'll be sure that the marker colors won't run.

Using Dressmaker's Carbon

The dressmaker's carbon paper method is ideal if you are using a fine-gauge canvas. With tracing paper, copy the original pattern or drawing. Then place a sheet of dressmaker's carbon between the tracing and the canvas and retrace the outline. The pattern will show up on the canvas.

The Homemade Light Box Trick

To transfer a picture or pattern that you already have, try using a homemade light box. This method is actually simple to do, and the transfer is easy. Place a sheet of glass between two chairs (or use a glass tabletop), and put a lamp with high wattage underneath it. Now place the drawing or pattern on top of the glass and the canvas on top of the drawing. The light will pass through both pieces so you can easily follow the outline of the drawing. You can also simply hold your pattern up to a window for a similar effect.

Use a fine felt-tip waterproof pen to mark the design on the canvas. Referring to the original pattern as a guide, mark the colors you will use for the needlepoint stitches on the canvas. Use acrylic paints or felt-tip markers to color in the design.

Transferring With Markers and Paints

If you are creating a design from scratch, first make a rough sketch of it on paper. Don't re-create it on your canvas just yet. Practice a few sketches—don't skip this step unless you're a solid artist. Later, when you actually transfer your design to canvas, you'll be glad you tried it out on paper first!

When you're happy with your practice run, draw your design in full scale and color it in with markers. Draw a square (or rectangle) outline around the outer edges of the pattern. Divide the design into even quarters by drawing one horizontal and one vertical line intersecting at the center point. This will be useful for transferring your design with paints as well as for charting your design.

Cut your canvas with a 3-inch border all around. Mark the top of the canvas with a fine waterproof felt-tip marker. Draw lines on the canvas dividing the canvas into even quarters. Place the canvas over the drawing, and match up the center lines that you just drew. Tape down the corners of the canvas, and draw the outer edges of the design onto the canvas with a waterproof felt-tip pen.

Remove the tape from the corners, and lift the canvas from the design. You can now paint the design with colors, using your original drawing design as a guide. Let the canvas completely dry before starting your needlepoint.

A Stitch in Time _____

If you feel nervous about painting your canvas, try some trial runs on blank canvases so you can get used to the feel of the paints.

Decorator's Do's and Don'ts

Oil paints have an odor and take a long time to dry. Use acrylic paints instead of oil paints to paint your canvas.

Charting a Design

Charting a design on graph paper will allow you to work out the design on canvas with accurate details. Mark the center point of the graph paper and, referring to your original sketch, use the center points to chart your design on the graph paper. On the graph paper, mark each square of the design in the appropriate color until your design is charted. Remember that each square represents one stitch, and each stitch is worked over one intersection of the canvas.

Decorator's Do's and Don'ts

Don't assume that your graph paper is the same scale as your canvas. For example, your charted or graphed flower that is 6 inches tall on the graph paper may be much smaller on the canvas. To determine the finished design size, count the number of squares on the graph (length and width) and divide by the gauge of the canvas. Stitch a sample of a part of your pattern to assess the scale.

The Least You Need to Know

- Handle canvases with care! Bind the edges with masking tape to prevent fraying.

- There are two methods of stitching: the sewing and the stabbing method. Both are fine for handheld canvases, but the stabbing method is better for framed canvases.

- By using the correct techniques for starting and ending your thread or yarn, you avoid getting ridges and bumps in your work.

- There are several ways to transfer your favorite pattern to your needlepoint canvas: using dressmaker's carbon, a light box, paints and markers, or graph paper.

29

Just Point and Stitch

In This Chapter

- ◆ Getting the hang of needlepoint by learning tent and other diagonal stitches
- ◆ Trying out the basic and not-so-basic crossed and straight stitches
- ◆ Fancying up your designs with star and loop stitches

With the right tools and some basic techniques, you can move ahead and learn all the many needlepoint stitches that will make your designs come alive with texture and personality. In needlepoint, simply by changing directions with some stitches and combining others, your designs can take on fabulous looks.

Keep in mind one of the biggest rules in needlepoint: Never work stitches over more than 10 canvas threads. The loops of long stitches are liable to snag. All of the needlepoint stitches in this chapter are worked on either mono or double canvas.

Tent

Tent stitches are small diagonal stitches worked in the same direction over one *intersection* of canvas. There are three variations: the half-cross-stitch, the continental stitch, and the basketweave stitch. The half-cross-stitch is the easiest to execute and uses the least amount of yarn. It is also the least durable. It cannot be used on mono canvas because the stitches tend to slip.

Needlework 101

Intersection in needle-point refers to the point at which a horizontal and a vertical canvas thread meet.

Both the half-cross-stitch and continental stitch tend to distort the canvas, so using a frame is a good idea if you are working a large area. The basketweave stitch does not distort the canvas. However, it uses more yarn than the half-cross-stitch and continental stitch.

Half-Cross-Stitch

The half-cross-stitch is worked in horizontal rows from left to right. To begin, bring the needle through to the front of the canvas. Now take it diagonally up to the right and over one horizontal thread, pulling through to the back, as shown in the next figure. Bring your needle up again, ready to make the next stitch.

The half-cross-stitch is a popular needlepoint stitch used for fillings, backgrounds, and outlines.

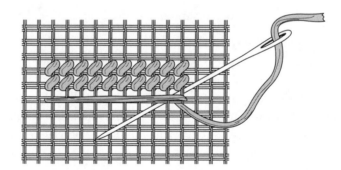

When you complete the first row, turn your canvas upside down to start the next row in the same manner. Repeat by bringing your needle up and taking it down at the first intersection to the right.

Continental Stitch

The continental stitch is worked in rows from right to left, just the opposite of the half-cross-stitch.

To start, bring the needle through to the front of the canvas and take it diagonally up and over one canvas intersection to the right. Then take the needle diagonally under one intersection to the left. At the end of the row, turn your canvas upside down for the return row.

The continental stitch can be used on single canvas.

Basketweave Stitch

The basketweave stitch resembles the weave of a basket on the back side of the canvas. This stitch is excellent for upholstery pieces that receive wear, such as seat covers and piano bench covers, because the large amount of yarn on the back side protects the canvas.

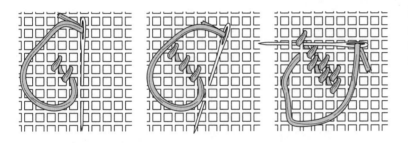

Basketweave is the perfect stitch to work over large areas because it won't distort the canvas.

For this stitch, you will work up and down the canvas in a diagonal pattern. First, take a stitch up to the right over one intersection and insert your needle down under two horizontal canvas threads.

Diagonal

The tent stitch is a diagonal stitch formed over one canvas mesh and produces an even texture applicable to any type of needlepoint design. The following diagonal stitches are formed over two canvas meshes and are stitched in a slanted direction over the canvas threads. The diagonal stitches described in this section—Gobelin, condensed Scottish, checker, and Byzantine—form various patterns, such as checkerboard, zigzag, and stripes, all of which are further emphasized by combining different colors of yarn.

Gobelin Stitch

No, *Gobelin* is not a stitch that was invented by a famous goblin. Rather, the Gobelin stitch (note the different spelling from a gremlinlike creature) was born in a famous Paris tapestry factory of the same name and is a larger version of *petit point* (called *gros point*).

For the Gobelin stitch, you need to work on single canvas only, because *the stitches tend to slip.* This stitch is worked from left to right and alternately from right to left.

The Gobelin stitch is a larger version of petit point.

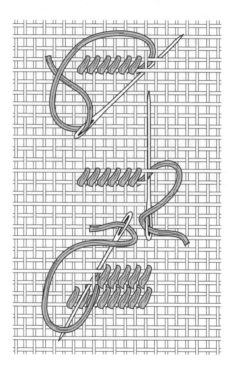

![Needlework 101]
Needlework 101

Petit point, meaning "small stitch," is the French term for tent stitch. **Gros point,** meaning "large point" in French, is another name for the **Gobelin** stitch. It is a larger version of the tent stitch.

Bring your needle through to the front of the canvas, and insert it two horizontal canvas threads up and one vertical canvas thread to the right. The needle is now at the back of the canvas. Bring the needle to the front, two horizontal threads down and one vertical stitch to the left of the stitch just taken.

In the next row, work new stitches one stitch length below your previous row. Create these stitches in the same slanting direction.

Encroaching Gobelin

The encroaching Gobelin stitch is a form of the Gobelin, but the stitches are longer. Work it the same way as the Gobelin stitch, except take each stitch over four (or five) canvas threads, slanting over one vertical thread. On the next rows, overlap the tops of the stitches by one thread.

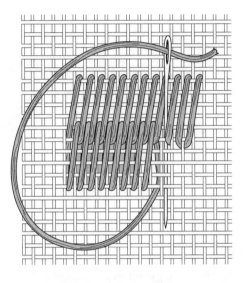

The encroaching Gobelin is a perfect choice for filling large areas and giving shaded effects.

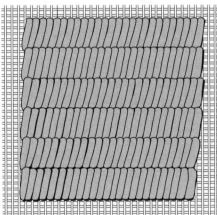

Working Graduated Diagonal Stitches

Graduated diagonal stitches are formed by using different lengths of diagonal stitches, and patterns happen!

The square in the following figure is worked over a graduating number of intersections in the canvas. It is worked in a group of seven stitches over 1, 2, 3, 4, 3, 2, and 1 intersections.

Various patterns can be formed by combining different lengths of diagonal stitches.

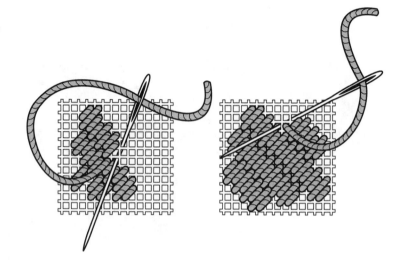

Condensed Scottish Stitch

The condensed Scottish stitch is a group of four diagonal stitches worked over 2, 3, 4, and 3 canvas intersections. It is always worked diagonally. Work the graduated stitches in diagonal rows starting at the top right. The basic unit of the pattern is a group of the four diagonal stitches that are worked over 2, 3, 4, and 3 canvas intersections. Repeat the same stitch sequence for the next row, placing the shortest stitch next to the longest stitch of the previous row.

Checker Stitch

Another of the slanted variety, the checker stitch is worked in graduated diagonal stitches over four horizontal and four vertical canvas threads.

Begin at the top left. In the first row, fill each square with seven diagonal stitches worked over 1, 2, 3, 4, 3, 2, and 1 intersections. (For the stitch pattern, refer to the preceding figure.)

In the second row, you'll create the "checker" effect by using tent stitches. Work 16 tent stitches (half-cross, continental, or any of your choosing) into each new square. These new squares fit neatly into the previous row's squares.

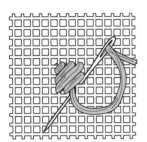 

If worked in different colors, the condensed Scottish stitch forms a striped pattern.

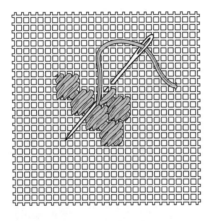

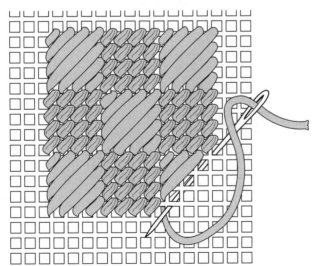

The checker stitch for—what else?—a checkerboard effect.

Byzantine Stitch

The zigzag-style rows of the Byzantine stitch are worked diagonally from top to bottom, then in reverse from bottom to top. Work each stitch over two canvas intersections. Start forming your zigzags by making three diagonal stitches across the canvas horizontally and then three diagonal stitches either up or down the canvas (depending on the direction of your design).

The second set of stitches fits neatly into the preceding row, like a puzzle.

The Byzantine stitch is a quick stitch for filling in large areas with a zigzag pattern.

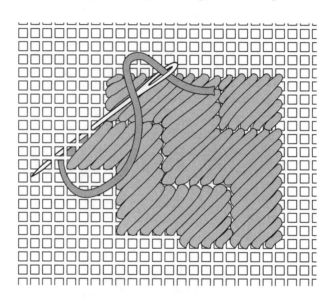

Crossed

The basic cross-stitch is worked on double, or Penelope, canvas only, but other types of cross-stitches can be worked on mono canvas. The basic cross-stitch can be worked horizontally or diagonally on double canvas. The stitches can go over one or more intersections, depending on the gauge of the canvas. Keep all the top stitches of the crosses lying in the same direction for a neat finish.

Basic Horizontal Cross-Stitch

The horizontal cross-stitch is worked just as it sounds—horizontally. Every row is worked from left to right.

For your first stitch, bring the needle out through the canvas, up to the left, and over two canvas intersections. Insert the needle, bringing it out under two horizontal canvas threads.

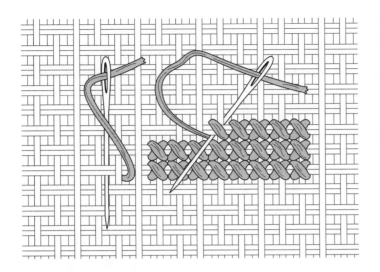

Work horizontal cross-stitches from left to right.

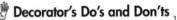

Cross this stitch with a diagonal backstitch over the same intersection, but slant it in the opposite direction. Bring the needle out, ready to make the next cross-stitch.

Diagonal Cross-Stitch

The diagonal cross-stitch is similar to the horizontal cross-stitch. Starting from the bottom left, make your first stitch just like you did in the horizontal method.

⃠ ✋ Decorator's Do's and Don'ts

Don't pull too tightly on your diagonal stitches! They tend to distort the canvas more than any other stitch. Do try to use a frame to prevent warping.

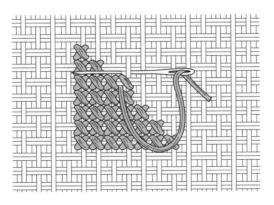

Work the diagonal cross-stitch from bottom left.

Oblong Cross-Stitch

The oblong cross-stitch is worked from right to left and then left to right. Bring out the needle on the front side, and take a stitch up to the left over four horizontal and two vertical canvas threads. Insert the needle, and take a stitch under four horizontal threads. Repeat this until the end of the row.

At the end of the first row, work your way back, crossing with stitches worked in the opposite direction. At the end of the row, bring the needle out four threads down, ready to start the first stitch of the next new row.

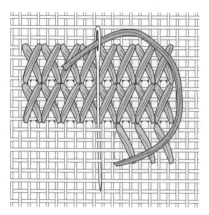
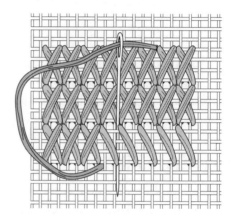

The oblong cross-stitch resembles a series of elongated X's.

Rice Stitch

The rice stitch is really a two-step stitch. Bring out the needle at the top left. Stitching horizontally, work a row of large cross-stitches over four canvas intersections.

Now, on the return, take a backstitch at right angles and over the center of each cross-stitch. Each one of the backstitches covers two canvas intersections. Essentially, you are crossing the "legs" of each larger cross-stitch with a smaller stitch. Work each new row into the base of the stitches from the previous row.

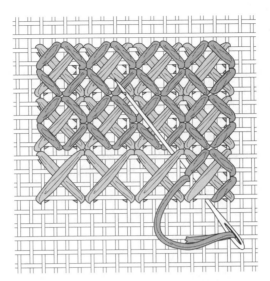

The rice stitch has a doubling X effect.

Straight

Straight stitches are easy and quick to stitch. Although not very unique, they can be more interesting if you combine different lengths. Straight stitches are usually worked on single canvas, but you can use double. The following stitches are worked in horizontal rows.

Upright Gobelin Stitch

The rows of the upright Gobelin are first worked left to right and then right to left. Bring your needle out *to the front of your canvas,* and insert it up over two horizontal threads and down to the right. Underneath the fabric, move the needle over one vertical and two horizontal threads. Bring your needle out, and start the next stitch the same way. In the next and succeeding rows, work the tops of the stitches into the bases of the previous row.

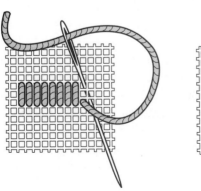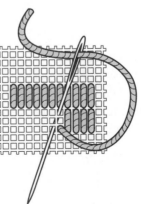

The upright Gobelin produces a hard-wearing stitch that has a ridged surface.

Gobelin Filling Stitch

Work the first row of the Gobelin filling stitch in the same fashion as the upright Gobelin stitch. For the filling stitch, however, work each stitch over six horizontal threads and space them two vertical canvas threads apart. The rows overlap to produce a basketweave effect. This is a good stitch to use just as the name implies—for filling in areas.

For the next and succeeding rows, work the stitches between the stitches of the previous row. The base of each row should be three horizontal threads below the base of the previous stitches.

The Gobelin filling stitch produces a basketweave effect.

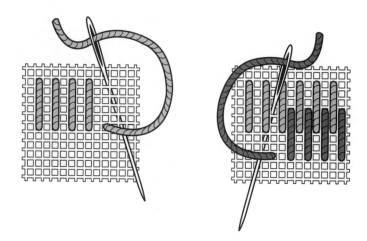

Random Long Stitch

Work the random long stitch the same as the upright Gobelin stitch, but vary the length of the stitches by working them randomly over 1, 2, 3, or 4 horizontal threads. Use this stitch to quickly fill in large areas.

Long and Short Stitch

The long and short stitch combines one row of long stitches with two rows of shorter stitches. It is quick and easy to work. Make four stitches, moving up one canvas thread for each stitch and covering four horizontal threads with each stitch. Now work three stitches, moving down *to the right* one thread for each. Continue the same steps, and a zigzag will begin to form.

Work the next two rows in the same manner, but take smaller stitches worked over two threads. Continue working one row of the long stitches, alternating with two rows of the short stitches.

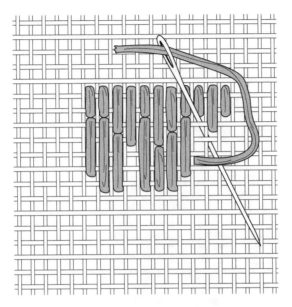

The random long stitch quickly fills large areas.

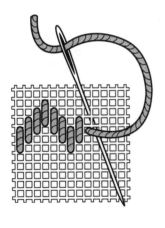
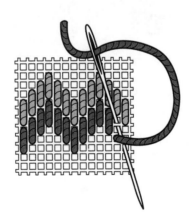

The long and short stitch creates a tweedlike effect.

Star

Star stitches are composite stitches made from straight, diagonal, and crossed stitches. They are large stitches that form starlike shapes. They can be framed with other stitches emphasizing a geometric shape. Be sure to use a mono canvas and thick yarn so that the mesh is covered. A very popular star stitch is the large Algerian eye stitch.

Large Algerian Eye Stitch

For the large Algerian eye stitch, you must first form a large square "star." To do this, work 16 stitches clockwise from the same hole, taking your yarn over four canvas threads or canvas intersections at the corners of the square star that is formed, leaving two canvas threads unworked between each stitch at the outer part of the stitches.

The large Algerian eye stitch resembles little boxes with starlike patterns.

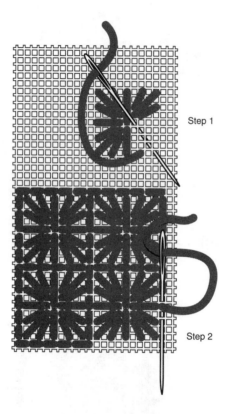

Step 1

Step 2

Frame your square stars with backstitches that are worked over two canvas threads.

Looped

Looped stitches are knotted loops that add unusual texture to a canvas. Some looped stitches can be cut to form a shaggy *pile* like a rug. Others remain loopy.

Velvet Stitch

The velvet stitch is made in the same way that velvet fabric is woven. Its loops are cut to create a pile. Work this stitch on double, or Penelope, canvas or any rug canvas.

Bring the needle through to the front of the canvas at the bottom-left corner and, by working left to right, take a diagonal backstitch over two canvas intersections up to the right.

Bring the needle up to the right again, and insert it in the same place where the needle first came up to start the backstitch. Hold down the thread with your finger and make a loop; take the needle down to the right at the top of the backstitch. Bring the needle out two horizontal threads down.

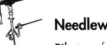

Needlework 101

Pile is a furry surface formed on fabrics by short raised loops of yarn that are sometimes sheared.

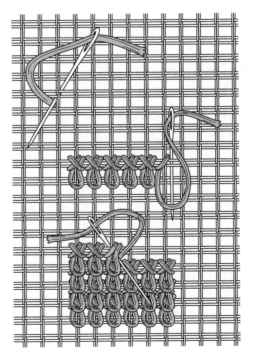

The velvet stitch is worked in loops that are cut to form a pile.

A Stitch in Time _____

When you form loops, slip a knitting needle (or crotchet hook, pencil, etc.) into the loop to size it. This will help you create more uniform loops.

Continue to hold down the loop with your finger while you take a diagonal backstitch up to the left and over two canvas intersections.

Repeat these steps to the end of the row. For the next row and the ones to follow, keep stitching above the previous row. When you have completed your work, cut the loops to form a pile and trim to desired length.

The Least You Need to Know

♦ Tent stitches are small diagonal stitches worked in the same direction over one intersection of canvas.

♦ Diagonal stitches are worked so that they are stitched in a slanted direction over the canvas threads.

♦ Crossed stitches are formed by either diagonal or straight stitches crossing over each other.

♦ Straight stitches are easy and quickly stitched. They can be interesting if you combine different lengths.

♦ Star stitches are composite stitches made from straight, diagonal, and crossed stitches.

♦ Looped stitches are knotted loops that add unusual texture to a canvas.

30

Bargello Design

In This Chapter

- ◆ Choosing your colors for Bargello design
- ◆ Creating the ups and downs of basic Bargello stitches
- ◆ Making your own designs

Bargello design is a very popular traditional needlepoint work, often referred to as "flamestitch" or "Florentine." Its stitches are straight, graduating, and upright and form zigzag-patterned rows. By changing the size and spacing of the stitches, the zigzags can be smoothed into curves or sharpened into peaks. Whether you're looking to recreate a good old Charlie Brown zigzag look or a more advanced fish scale motif, this is an excellent technique to use.

Take a stab at Bargello and see what the fuss is all about!

Bargello Basics

Bargello patterns are worked horizontally across the canvas. To get nice, even rows and to achieve the zigzag design, you need to create a guideline.

Because the first line of stitching is worked from the center of the canvas out to both the left and right edges, create your guideline at the center.

Find the center point by dividing your canvas into quarters with a felt-tip marker. This forms the beginning of your design. Work your rows from left to right and right to left, above and below the center point, until your canvas is filled.

Bargello stitches are sometimes quite long, so the tail of the thread must be firmly secured. A backstitch can firmly hold the beginning or ending threads.

Fundamental Zigzag

The zigzag stitch is the easiest one to learn and is the basis for all types of Bargello stitches. Start with a "4-2" zigzag pattern, which means that the stitch length is 4 horizontal threads, and that the step up, or down, for the next stitch is 2 horizontal threads.

Needlework 101

Step is the term for the number of crosswise canvas threads between the bases of neighboring stitches.

To begin, bring your needle out at the center point (where the felt-tip marker lines on your canvas intersect). Take your needle up four horizontal threads, and insert it to the back of the canvas. Then, to make the *step*, bring out the needle two horizontal threads below the top of the last stitch and one vertical thread to the right.

Repeat those first steps three times going *up* the canvas. On the third stitch, bring your needle out six horizontal threads below the top of your last stitch.

The easiest way to learn Bargello is to start with the basic zigzag.

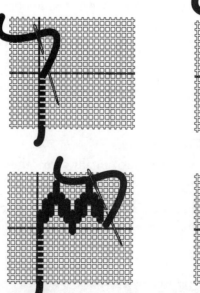

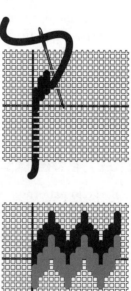

Work the next three stitches *down* the canvas to form the first upside-down V of the zigzag pattern. Repeat all these steps, alternating three stitches up and three stitches down the canvas.

Work your next color into the base of the first zigzag row.

A Stitch in Time

You can use a 22-inch-long working thread in Bargello work because the thread slides through the canvas easily.

Adding Curves

You can adjust the basic zigzag to form a curvy pattern. At the top and base of each zigzag peak, work two or more stitches the same length as the preceding stitch. More than two stitches will create an elongated curve, and just two stitches will create a more peaked curve.

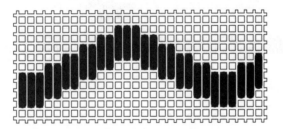

Practice a few continuous curves before starting a large Bargello project. They are easy to master, but they do require some thought!

Catching Waves

To create a wavy Bargello pattern, apply the curvy technique, but elongate the curves by adding more stitches at the zigzag peak.

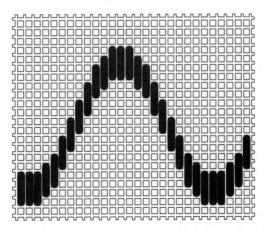

In Bargello, the more stitches you use to form the peak, the longer the wave.

The wave technique is different from creating curves because you are adding stitches at the end of your zigzags and not piling them above the peaks.

Fish Scales

For a fish scale–looking row, use the same method as you did for the curves but, at the base, leave only one stitch to form a peak. This will form the scales. Use this to form a somewhat soft scalloped pattern for a change from hard peaks in the zigzag patterns.

Keep the tops of the peaks curvy and the bases pointed to form a Bargello scalloped effect, like that of fish scales.

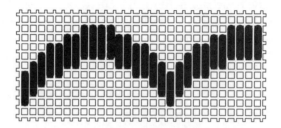

Two-Way Bargello

In two-way Bargello, the pattern is reversed in the second row to form a mirror image.

The first row that you stitch is the beginning of the pattern. Work the first row like the basic zigzag stitch shown in the first section of this chapter. Turn your canvas upside down and then stitch another row of basic zigzags to form a mirror image of the first row.

Because the second row will be created in reverse, you will have empty spaces in between the two rows. Fill the empty spots with upright stitches in a different color of yarn. Using upright stitches will offset the look of the two-way Bargello pattern so that you don't lose the effect you were going for in the first place!

A Stitch in Time

You can achieve attractive and contrasting patterns by combining curves and steep peaks. Vary the shades of your yarn colors to add the illusion of depth to your pattern.

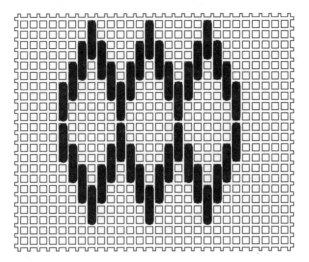

To form the mirror image of two-way Bargello, the bases of the rows must meet.

Four-Way Bargello

The four-way Bargello stitch is perfect for square designs like bags or pillows. As in all Bargello, the central stitch starts the pattern and continues out to the edges. When you do this in four-way Bargello, you'll form one large motif.

Cut your canvas into a square. Mark two diagonal lines, from corner to corner, with a felt-tip marker. Make four stitches in the center like a cross, as shown in the following figure.

Clever Crafter _____

Hold a mirror up to your new design. The reverse image will help you to see a new pattern to repeat.

Continue the pattern in this manner, stitching each quarter of the canvas in an identical way.

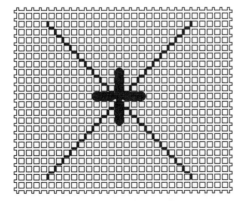

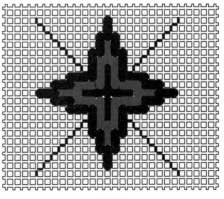

The four-way Bargello forms a unique pattern that is perfect for a pillow or bag design.

Effects of Color

All Bargello work is stitched in rows of different colors. A three-color pattern, using colors from the same family, forms a monochromatic tone. For example, pale blue, medium blue, and dark blue will create a calm, soft look. Using three very different colors such as red, green, and blue will have quite the opposite effect—bolder, more jarring to the eye, and a more distinctive pattern.

Combining harmonious colors (colors that are next to each other on the color wheel) is another method. A combination of blue, blue-violet, and violet illustrates a harmony of colors.

You can even use primary colors for wonderful possibilities. If the intensity of the pure hues is too strong for you, substitute gold for yellow, claret for red, and navy for blue. The primaries will take on a whole new feeling! Another triangle of colors, the secondaries of violet, orange, and green, might work for you as well. Complementary colors are pairings that are opposite each other on the color wheel, such as red/green, orange/blue, and yellow-green/red-violet.

The Least You Need to Know

◆ Bargello design is a very popular traditional needlepoint technique often referred to as "flamestitch" or "Florentine" work.

◆ Bargello patterns are worked horizontally across the canvas.

◆ The basic zigzag is the easiest Bargello stitch to learn.

◆ All Bargello work is stitched in rows of different colors.

Chapter 31

Designing Your Own Needlepoint

In This Chapter

- ◆ Finding inspirations for needlepoint
- ◆ Creating different types of samplers
- ◆ Trying your hand at freehand design
- ◆ Transferring large designs onto canvas sections

Designing your own needlepoint is so much fun because there are so many subjects, stitches, colors, and techniques to choose from. Adding a twist to borrowed ideas or creating your own designs is the most rewarding part of needlepoint. Embellish plain designs with decorative stitches or interesting colors of yarn. You can use part of a larger design on a very small piece, thus creating quite a dramatic effect. Or go all out and create your own patterns from scratch! An original design will show off your personal style.

Inspirations for Needlepoint Ideas

Designing your own needlepoint allows you to stitch your favorite subjects, like your children, your home, your pet turtle Sparky, or anything else that is special to you. Still having trouble deciding on something? What about re-creating a favorite picture? How about stitching some letters or a personal message on canvas?

Items in your home, like bouquets of flowers, china patterns, and wall-covering designs, provide ideas for colors and shapes to sketch. When you start noticing patterns in everything, there will be no stopping you!

You can needlepoint many items. Some projects to consider for your designs include the following:

- Pillows
- Picture frames
- Brick covers for doorstops
- Gift boxes
- Handbags
- Slippers
- Bookmarks

- Holiday ornaments
- Holiday cards
- Dollhouse rugs
- Bell pulls
- Footstool covers
- Chair covers
- Samplers

These ideas are just the beginning of how you can use needlepoint to convey your personal style.

Sampling Samplers

As in embroidery, needlepoint samplers show off different stitches. Needlepoint samplers are stitched with straight, looped, crossed, diagonal, and star stitches, or a combination. Fabulous patterns can also be achieved with just one type of stitch!

Use a variety of colors in your sampler, and it becomes a beautiful work of art. Traditionally, samplers were worked to show the various types of stitches, but pictorials were done as well. A combination of different colors and various stitches can make a great design. This is where your imagination and personal style can shine with clever expression. Embellish your sampler by stitching a message or your name with the date of your work. Use classic colors and not the latest trends, which will fade in popularity and make your work look dated. A glow-in-the-dark kitten might be cute now, but you might be quite tired of it next month!

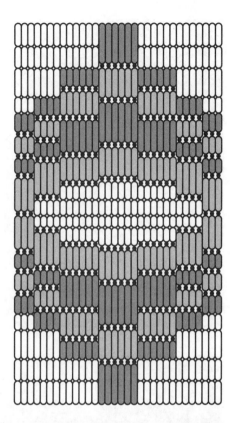

Straight stitches can make very interesting patterns.

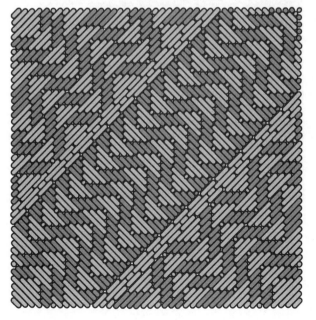

Diagonal stitches and different colors form blocks of diagonal stripes.

Crossed stitches and colors combine to make a diagonal motif.

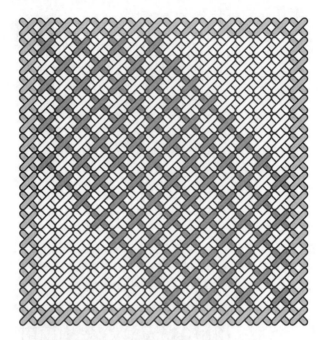

This intricate-looking sampler is composed of framed star stitches that give the effect of stars within a box.

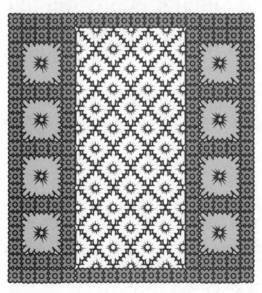

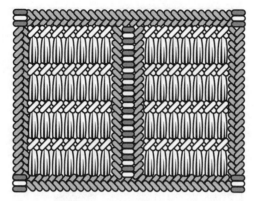

Cut loops turn into tassels on this sampler.

Freehand Design

What do you do if you have a blank canvas? You could try some freehand work by drawing directly onto your canvas or stitching your own design without any guides. Both require a little courage and practice. But after you have tried a few and had successful outcomes, you'll find that stitching your own design is almost as easy as stitching a prepainted canvas. You will be making a one-of-a-kind design, and that alone is worth your effort!

Drawing Directly on Canvas

Drawing your idea on paper will give you a better sense of how the final design will look on canvas. Don't panic if drawing is not your bag—you don't need to be Monet to sketch a design. Keep trying out sketches until you're happy before moving on to a canvas. Even if your first design from a sketch isn't your best work, don't give up! As in anything, the more you do it, the better you'll be.

Be sure that your sketched pattern fits the size of your canvas and the intended size of your project. You might have trouble fitting a 24-inch-tall bouquet on a 12-inch-square piece of canvas. If you are sketching a different size than your model, you will need to sketch your items to scale.

After drawing your initial sketches, draw your design on canvas to the scale that you will stitch it in. Keep the outline of your drawing bold and distinct. Color in as much of your design as you want with colored pencils to get an even better sense of how your design will look. After outlining and coloring in, draw vertical and horizontal lines to quarter the canvas so you can be ready to chart it on graph paper (as you learned in Chapter 28) or paint your design directly on the canvas.

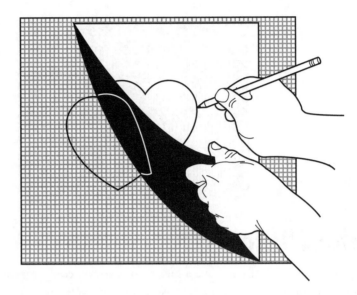

Drawing or painting on canvas can be a quick and easy way to start your needlepoint design.

To paint on the canvas without guidelines, imagine you are creating an actual painting. Again, create clear outlines and fill in each part with paint colors that correspond to the yarn colors you will use. Acrylic paints will dry faster than thinned oil paints and will smell much better. Use white nylon brushes that are stiff so that they work well on the roughness of the canvas. Small brushes are better because large ones will cause the paints to bleed. Let the canvas dry thoroughly after painting before you pick it up again. Any movement during drying will distort the design.

Stitching Directly on Canvas

Creating a design on your canvas with stitches alone can be nerve-racking for some and liberating for others. You'll only know which category you fit into when you try it!

Designing your own pattern on canvas allows you to be totally free in your choices of stitches and colors. Be sure to have a clear image in mind before you begin, and stitch according to that. A geometric design is easier to figure because of its up-and-down and side-to-side stitching as opposed to a very curvy design, but both can be done with ease after you get the hang of it.

It might be helpful to stitch some outlines or guidelines before you fill in the entire design. This will give you a better idea of how each part of the design relates in scale to the other parts. You will also be able to tell whether you like the way the design has transferred from your head onto the canvas.

After you have some stitching guidelines in place, the next step is to stitch just the outline of your design. If you are happy with that, you can fill in the rest of the design and then stitch the background. For example, if you design a motif of a flower, do the outline of the petals and the stem first. If you are satisfied with them, go ahead and fill in the petals using different directions of stitching, and finally stitch a patterned or solid background.

Decorator's Do's and Don'ts

Don't fill in any part of your background until you've stitched all of the design! This will give you more flexibility in case you need to alter anything, because you will not have to contend with an already-stitched background.

Supersize It!

Ever wonder how large-scale designs like oversized wall tapestries or needlepoint rugs are hand-stitched? They are worked in sections because the canvas isn't big enough to accommodate the design.

To create a large-scale design, cut your canvas into sections of equal size, remembering to leave a border for sewing the sections together after you have finished. Careful transferring of the design to the canvas is critical for a well-put-together pattern.

To section your design, first draw your pattern on paper or chart it on graph paper. Divide it into equal-sized sections that are labeled *A, B, C, D.* Cut the canvas sections, and mark the sections to correspond to the sections of the drawing. Transfer the drawings onto the canvas, and you are ready to begin. If you have drawn on graph paper, then transferring will not be necessary—you can read from the graph and begin stitching. When the work is completed, each section must be blocked and joined together (see Chapter 33) in the correct sequence to create the design you are after.

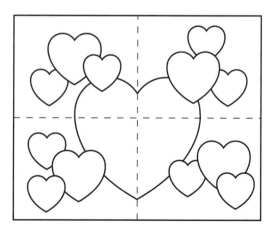

Draw your pattern on paper, and divide it into equal sections.

An example of transferring a large design onto canvas, along with a border allowance.

The Least You Need to Know

- ◆ Creating your own designs is a rewarding part of needlepoint.

- ◆ Samplers can show off any of the straight, diagonal, crossed, looped, or starred stitches. They can also be embellished with personal messages or initials and dates.

- ◆ Freehand designs can be tricky but are well worth the effort.

- ◆ Large-scale designs need to be worked in sections because your canvas may not be big enough to accommodate your design.

Adding Your Own Flair

In This Chapter

- ◆ Moving backgrounds forward
- ◆ Getting a feel for texture
- ◆ Sprucing up borders

Now that you have entered the world of design, you can learn how to add pizzazz to store-bought patterns and your own needlepoint designs. You can embellish plain backgrounds with a variety of techniques; emphasize textures with color, yarns, or beads; and frame a central motif with a stitched border.

Backgrounds

Many needlepoint designs concentrate on a central motif, like a bouquet of flowers, and pair it with a solid background. If the background is good sized, it can be a bit dull to keep stitching in the same color or in the same pattern. Keep your designs alive by jazzing up your backgrounds. Even though you might think the background is "just the background," anything you do to spruce it up will help your overall design.

Not-So-Plain Jane

You can enhance "plain" backgrounds or backgrounds of the same color by changing the stitches. For most stitchers, the tent stitch or the cross-stitch is the stitch of choice for backgrounds, but that doesn't have to be *your* choice. The same goes for kits. You don't have to use the stitch specified in the kit, though you do have to keep in mind the amount of yarn available in the kit for the background. Try using more interesting stitches such as the upright Gobelin, the long and short stitch, or the Byzantine.

Blended Tones

Needlepoint backgrounds can be subtly changed by stitching blended shades of similar colors. The main design is still the focal point, but the background has a shaded effect. Some yarns and threads are available already shaded, which makes this technique easy. If you want blended tones in the background and you don't have pre-blended yarn, you can combine strands of different colored yarns to create different combinations.

To make your own shaded yarn, select three or four similar tones of thread or yarn.

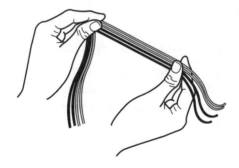

Untwist each of the different colors of yarn or threads and then recombine the different tones to make a new one.

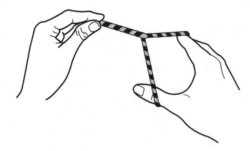

Marbled Backgrounds

Marbled effects are very beautiful, but they are a little more difficult to work. Try using yarn colors of very pale blues, grays, tans, and whites; a little yellow; and subtle blended tones of each for different irregular horizontal patterns. Work sections in the individual colors in different-sized wavy rows. This will create a subtle irregular pattern similar to that of marble. Further enhance your work by using wool threads and highlighting areas with silk threads.

Patterned Backgrounds

Patterned backgrounds can be equally as visual as the foreground motif. They are incorporated as part of the overall design. Florals, geometrics, stripes, checks, and Bargello patterns can all be tastefully incorporated to ensure that the main motif is still the main attraction.

Try to coordinate the colors of the main motif with the background pattern for harmony in the overall design. For example, if the main motif is a sunflower in yellows, browns, and greens, needlepoint the background in a solid brown with a dotlike pattern (created from a few stitches) in yellow. Or consider sharply contrasting the colors for a more pronounced motif.

Unworked Backgrounds

Another idea is to use fabric instead of canvas for your design. That way, you don't need to work the background—the fabric becomes the pattern.

A good fabric to use is an evenweave linen. The threads of the linen become your canvas and are distinct and easy to stitch. Also try patterned fabric—the type you can find in a sewing department for dress- or curtain-making. You can use the pattern lines as guidelines when you stitch.

Both linen and patterned fabric will instantly become the background design, with no stitching involved! By using fabric, your main needlepoint design becomes the focus, and it's a quick way to get a patterned background!

Shading Techniques

The shading technique is quite simple to do. You have to decide which method you want to use for the particular look of your needlepoint. Preshaded threads give a random shaded effect and, depending on the stitch used, you can create a shaded and textured look. For example, create a field of hay by using preshaded gold and rows of the encroaching Gobelin stitch to simulate the hay texture. The sky can be simulated by using shaded yarns in pale blues, grays, and white and a condensed Scottish stitch.

You can achieve antique-looking shading by using subtle colors that you combine yourself. These yarns produce an uneven shading, which is typical of antique or old and faded needlework pieces.

Creating Texture

To create textures with your needlepoint, use different combinations of canvas, threads/yarn, and stitching. Using just one stitch in different directions makes a pattern of texture. Combining more than one stitch will also create a textured look. If you are working with red yarn only, try working a design that includes a sampling of the stitches that we have covered in earlier chapters. You will see how the different stitches create patterns by using the same color yarn. Your color and thread choice can further emphasize the texture.

Imitating textures in pictorial work, like a shingled roof or a lace curtain, requires attention to stitch selection and thread to create both the look and the "feel" in your needlepoint.

Direction of Stitches

The stitch direction will emphasize the way an object is put together. For example, you can create bales of hay or a grassy field by using straight or diagonal stitches.

Changing Tone

Color variations and shading will affect texture. To create the subtly changing colors in a sunset, try using harmonious colors of red: pinks, reds, and oranges.

Raised Effects

You can dramatically change the surface of your needlepoint by using raised stitches for *relief* effects.

Needlework 101

Relief is the projection of a figure or part of the ground. In needlepoint, any figure that is raised above the surface of the needlepoint is considered a "relief."

Raised stitches form relief effects on their own. Other relief effects can be made by tramming your stitches. Tramméd pieces can be purchased and come complete with yarn in the correct amounts and colors for completing the piece. Half-cross-stitch is worked over these long stitches, thus creating the padding. If you want to tram your own piece, bring the needle with yarn through the canvas from the right-hand side between the double threads on one row. Carry it across the top of the double mesh and insert at the point where the color changes. Then work half-cross-stitches over the "laid" threads to create a double thickness.

Relief effects are easily created with the velvet stitch. The velvet stitch can be left looped for a fuzzy look or cut for a pile look. For a flower pattern, you can combine a cross-stitch for the stem and center of the flower and an uncut velvet stitch for the petals. The possibilities are endless!

Touching Up Borders

Borders act like a frame to your piece and can be solid, patterned, square, oval, round—you name it. Some may be integral parts of the design or just the edging that surrounds the main design or pictorial. Choose a border as you would a picture frame—bold and wide if you want it to be very noticeable and part of the overall design, or narrow and discreet for just an edging to finish off the look.

Border Effects

Just by changing the width of your border, you change the whole design. A 4-inch border and a 1-inch border have dramatically different effects. A wide border becomes a significant part of the overall design, whereas a narrow border allows the motif to have a stronger presence.

And of course, color plays a role in the effect of the border. You probably have had a similar experience when choosing a frame for a piece of artwork. Do you choose a darker or a lighter frame? You asked yourself which one would show off the artwork the best. Do the same with your needlepoint.

A light- or dark-colored frame can take away from, or call attention to, your main design. Consider these qualities when selecting the type of border for your needlepoint.

Shaped Borders

Stitched borders run the gambit. There are the traditional circles, ovals, and squares, as well as window shapes like *Palladian* or rectangular ones with panes (yes, panes stitched right in the design).

Needlework 101

Palladian is an architectural term that refers to the style of window that is straight on three sides and arched at the top.

Borders can also be the shape of the design, say a heart, a boat, a vase, or even a star or diamond. More traditional borders, like rectangles or squares, can be stitched in one color or in geometrics like checks, stripes, diagonal lines, or diamond motifs. Floral motifs worked at intervals make a pretty border and enliven a design.

Corners

If you choose to stitch designs in the borders at regular intervals, be sure to consider the corners. You will want to "engineer" your pattern so that the proper number of stitches comes together at the right points. You may want to chart your corner pattern on graph paper before you begin stitching.

Often the corners are a solid color or a single motif like a rose or some type of flower. This way, the sides are easily stitched in a pattern, and you don't have to worry about making your border pattern work in the corners.

Overflowing Borders

When the main design flows into the border or the border is an integral part of the design, the border is considered overflowing. The stitches of the main motif become harmonious with the pattern.

An example would be a bouquet of flowers in which the leaves are stitched to appear as if they're falling into the border. You can also reverse that concept, stitching the pattern of the border into the motif.

The Least You Need to Know

- ◆ Needlepoint backgrounds don't have to be plain; they can be enhanced with fabric, shading, patterns, and beads.

- ◆ Needlepoint can take on a variety of textures with different combinations of canvas, threads/yarn, and stitches.

- ◆ Borders act like a frame for your designs. They can be solid, patterned, square, oval, round, or shapes of the design themselves, like a heart, diamond, vase, or star.

Chapter

33

Finishing Your Needlepoint

In This Chapter

- ◆ Finishing your work with the right tools and with blocking and joining techniques
- ◆ Mounting and framing your work
- ◆ Cleaning and repairing needlepoint

Now that you've created a beautiful needlepoint project, and the hard part of designing, stitching, and fretting is over, it's time to finish the job. Like embroidery, your needlepoint will have become distorted while working on it, so you'll need to use the blocking method to get it back into shape. If you are joining the design to something else or want to frame your work, there are tips and tricks to learn that apply only to needlepoint.

Necessary Tools

Finishing your needlepoint requires you to add a few extra tools to your toolbox: A small tape measure, a hammer, and tacks are items you will need to help you get your needlepoint in shape if any distortion occurred during stitching. You will also need a board that is soft enough to allow tacks to go through it (such as chipboard) and a piece of plastic. You are now ready to "block" your needlepoint. (Do you recall from Part 2 what blocking means?) Read on to learn how to apply this technique to needlepoint.

The First Step: Blocking

Blocking, as you learned in embroidery, is a process that stretches your canvas back into its original shape, erasing any distortion that may have occurred during stitching.

This is where your paper or cardboard template of the canvas—the one that you created before you started stitching—comes in handy. Needlepoint is blocked with the stitches face down, unless there are looped stitches that would be crushed during the process. Keep these needlepoints face up and dampen them from the back before tacking them down. Apply a spray lightly to looped stitched items.

Follow these easy steps to block your needlepoint:

1. Place the needlepoint face down on a soft board with your original canvas template underneath and a piece of plastic between the template and needlepoint. Tape down the corners.

2. Spray the canvas with distilled water or moisten with a sponge.

3. At the center top of the canvas, hammer a tack through the unworked mesh of the canvas (the unworked border). Continue tacking in intervals about 1 inch apart around the needlepoint. Stretch the needlepoint into shape using more spray if necessary, and align with the original template.

4. Adjust the tacks and stretching until the original shape is achieved.

5. Leave the canvas tacked in place until it is completely dry. It may take days for the needlepoint to dry.

6. For badly distorted pieces, restretch if the piece still looks "off" or seems to partially return to its preblocked state. You may need to resort to hiring a professional to save your piece if your results are not satisfactory.

> **A Stitch in Time**
>
> Always check your needlepoint before starting the blocking process to be sure that there are no stitches missing from the needlepoint. You can do this easily by holding the work up to the light. If you see light, there is a missing stitch.

Joining Needlework Pieces

Sewing sections of needlepoint together is a process called joining. Each piece needs to be blocked separately and then "joined" together with a needle and either buttonhole thread or matching yarn.

To join two pieces, first trim both canvas edges to about half an inch. Fold the half-inch edges to the wrong side of the fabric.

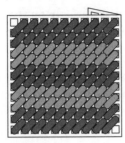 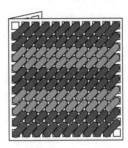

Do not stitch through the turned-back canvas, because this would cause an unnecessary ridge.

With right sides together, lay the pieces edge to edge, matching the pattern row by row. Pin and baste together if this will help you keep the pattern straight. Remove the pins before you begin sewing the pieces together on the front side.

Bring the needle up through the first hole of the left-hand piece and insert it down through the first hole of the adjacent piece. Be sure that you secure the tail of the thread in stitching. Then come up in the second hole of the left piece and down into the second hole of the adjacent piece. Continue until the two edges are stitched together. The edges butt against each other, and the seam is relatively invisible if the same color thread is used.

If you are joining a piece of fabric to the back of your needlepoint to make a pillow, a sewing machine is fine to use to sew around the joined pieces.

Clever Crafter

Don't always think that the seams shouldn't show! The seams that join sections of needlepoint can be invisible, but, by using contrasting yarns, they can also be a decorative addition to your work.

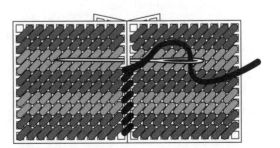

Sometimes, by leaving the joining stitches loose and tightening them every five or six laces, it is easier to see what you are doing.

Mounting Techniques

Before you frame your work, you need to mount it on a board to keep it taut and firmly in place. One method is to mount the piece directly onto a board by using the same process you learned in Chapter 25. Refer to the section on mounting in Chapter 25 if this is the method that you choose.

Another way is to mount your work on a stretcher. This is the quickest and easiest way to mount your work. A stretcher is a wooden frame over which your needlepoint is stretched and tacked down.

Keeping the needlepoint taut on the stretcher will give the framed piece a more professional look.

1. First, lay the needlepoint face down and place the stretcher on the back of the needlepoint as if you were going to gift wrap a present. Fold the unworked areas to the back.

2. Insert a tack in the middle of each side, being sure your needlepoint is positioned correctly with threads at right angles.

3. Tack all around the sides from the center points to the corners, adjusting so that needlepoint is evenly stretched.

4. Miter the unworked corners by folding one corner at a time in toward the piece (it will look like a triangle) and then folding in the two unworked side pieces so that they meet and neatly cover the corner. Hold this in place with a tack or a hand-sewn tack.

5. Hammer the tacks in firmly.

Framing Your Work

Framing your needlepoint will give it a permanent resting place, protect it from dust and dirt, and show off your beautiful work to its best advantage.

If you are going to frame it yourself and are using a piece of glass, be sure that the glass does not touch the needlepoint—it will flatten the stitches. Place small strips of wood between the glass and the needlepoint to create space. If you choose to have your work professionally done, your framer will know to do this.

Some needlepoint pieces look great in a frame without glass, but the only drawback is that dirt and dust collect on these pieces. If you choose this method, periodic cleaning is critical to preserving your work.

Hanging Your Needlepoint

Framing isn't your only option for needlepoint. It can also be hung as wall décor. After you have lined the back of the needlepoint, you can choose from several methods for hanging.

A Stitch in Time

You can also hang your needlepoint as a wall tapestry. These pieces need to be lined to maintain the shape of the needlepoint. The lining should be a fabric that is lighter in weight than the needlepoint to allow the work to hang properly. Too heavy a fabric will distort the work. Always prewash fabric so that when you clean your needlepoint, the lining won't shrink.

One way is to attach a strip of wood the same size as the width of your piece to the top of your needlepoint. To do this, first nail a piece of *Velcro* to the wooden strip, using upholstery tacks. Then sew the matching piece of Velcro to the top of the lined needlework. Screw the wood strip to the wall, and attach the needlework at the top by matching up the Velcro pieces.

Needlework 101

Velcro is a soft pliable fabric with tiny hooks on the surface that attach to a matching piece with looped fabric that clings to the hooks.

Another way is to use curtain hooks and screws to hang your work. Hand-stitch curtain hooks to the back of your lined needlepoint at even intervals, and attach the hooks to screw eyes that have been inserted into the wall at the same intervals as the curtain hooks.

A curtain rod is another choice for hanging your piece. Hand-sew a strip of lining to the top of the lined needlepoint to form a sleeve. Slip a curtain rod through the sleeve, and hang it on the wall with decorative cord.

Instead of a sleeve, you can also sew tabs to slip over the curtain rod. First measure how many tabs you will need for the rod and how long and wide the tabs will be.

Decorator's Do's and Don'ts

Do take care when placing your framed work. Don't hang it near heat, in direct sunlight, or in areas of great dampness.

To create the tabs, cut and sew small pieces of same-sized material to form individual pockets that will hold the rod. You will be folding these tabs lengthwise and widthwise to eliminate raw edges, so be sure you double all measurements. Hem across the width of each tab, and sew the tabs at intervals onto your lining and slip a rod through the tabs. Attach a cord to each end of the rod and hang on the wall.

Decorator's Do's and Don'ts

Correctly storing a piece of needlework is just as important as knowing how to display a piece! If you cannot lay it flat, roll it up. Always roll it between acid-free tissue paper and away from sunlight and dust.

Clean but Don't Scrub!

Needlework made of wool can be kept clean fairly easily. Vacuum dust away with a small upholstery attachment. If the threads are silk, dry clean your piece. If the yarns are colorfast, you may be able to hand-wash your needlework.

Follow these easy steps for hand washing:

1. Use the cotton ball method (see Chapter 25) to check whether the threads are colorfast.

2. Make a paper template of the original size of the needlepoint.

3. Fill a container that will accommodate the size of your work with soapy water (use a soapless quilt "soap"), and immerse the needlepoint. If your needlepoint is wool, use cold water to avoid shrinkage. Or roll in a damp towel instead of immersion. If you are worried about shrinkage, have your needlepoint professionally dry-cleaned.

4. Let the needlepoint soak and then press gently. Drain and rinse the needlepoint in clean water until the rinse water is clear.

5. Lay the needlepoint flat with the right side up, and blot up excess water with a clean, dry sponge.

6. Reblock the piece, using the instructions given earlier in this chapter.

Decorator's Do's and Don'ts

Do not use a metal bowl to clean your needlework in! Sometimes metal can react negatively with colors, which could ruin your design.

A Stitch in Time

Treat stained needlepoints as you would your fine clothing. Check a cleaning guide on how to remove different types of spot stains. If needleworks are very badly stained, ask a professional cleaner how to save the work.

The Least You Need to Know

◆ Blocking is a process that returns your canvas to its original shape and eliminates any distortion that may have occurred during stitching.

◆ With the joining method, you can hand-sew sections of needlepoint together.

◆ Before you can frame your work, you need to mount it on a board to keep it taut and firmly in place.

◆ Framing your needlepoint lengthens its life by protecting it from dust and dirt and turns your work into framed art that you can admire daily!

◆ Cleaning your needlework is critical for preserving your hard work.

Chapter 34

Needlepoint Project: A Dollhouse Rug

In This Chapter

- ◆ Start small—making a dollhouse rug
- ◆ Preparation is the best way to start any project

As a novice, it's good to begin with small projects. You may not be ready to make a 9-foot by 12-foot needlepoint rug, but a dollhouse rug is a fine place to start. If you or your child don't have a dollhouse, consider giving the rug away as a gift to a niece or grandchild or to someone you know who is a dollhouse hobbyist.

This chapter guides you step by step, from the materials needed to get started to advice on finishing the project, with plenty of helpful hints along the way.

All the information that you learned in the earlier chapters on needlepoint will be refreshed by the act of doing and stitching with your own two hands. Clear instructions will make your first needlepoint project fun and easy!

Making a Dollhouse Rug

A dollhouse rug is a perfect choice for your first needlepoint piece. It is a small, simple project that you can begin and finish with ease. This project will ready you for other projects like pillows and wall décor.

The color key for your rug is made up of symbols that match the symbols on the rug chart.

Key to Colors			
O	Salmon	?	Gold
+	Red	^	Bright blue
/	Yellow	X	Pale blue

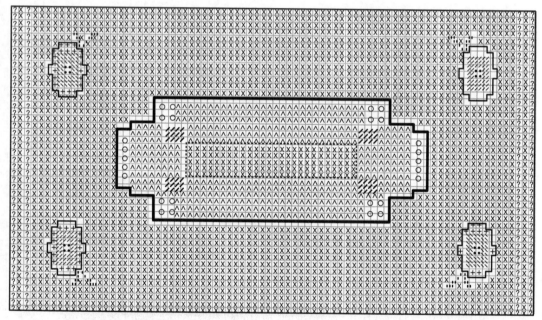

A dollhouse rug to stitch.

Getting Acquainted with the Materials

Start your project by getting a feel for your materials. How the yarn is threaded through the eye of the needle, how the yarn and needle work through the canvas, and how you hold your canvas—these are all new concepts until you start and get used to the materials and stitches.

You need the following materials:

- 12-count double (Penelope) canvas cut 10 inches by 6 inches
- Number 18 tapestry needle
- Wool tapestry yarn in six colors (check key), one skein each color, except two of pale blue
- Piece of blue felt to cover the back, cut approximately 8 inches by 4 inches
- Blue cotton thread
- Masking tape

Clever Crafter

Chart your monogram on a rug, or if you needlepoint one for a friend, chart your friend's monogram. There is nothing more treasured than a personalized gift.

The Canvas

For your miniature rug, you'll need double canvas (12 threads per inch). This mesh is made of pairs of threads, and you will work your stitches over the pairs. Be sure to tape the canvas edges with masking tape to prevent fraying. Your rug will be approximately 7½ inches in length and 3½ inches in width when finished.

Decorator's Do's and Don'ts

Don't start and end your threads in the same place! The extra thickness will form an unsightly ridge.

The Needle

You will be using a tapestry (blunt-tipped) needle, because your stitches will be placed in the holes in the canvas and you will not need to pierce the canvas threads with a sharp needle. A number 18 tapestry needle has a large round eye for easy threading and will comfortably fit through the mesh holes without distorting the canvas.

The Yarn

For this rug, the type of yarn and colors will help create the final look. The colors are specified in the materials list, and so is the type of yarn. You will use wool tapestry yarn, which is a single-strand yarn. It is slightly finer than three strands of Persian yarn. Feel free to experiment with other colors.

Cut the yarn into 18-inch lengths to prevent it from fraying while you are pulling it through the canvas mesh holes.

If the yarn becomes twisted while you are needle pointing, drop the needle and let it hang. The yarn will untwist by itself. Don't try to stitch with twisted yarn; it will appear thin and will not cover the fabric.

The Chart

The chart is illustrated on graph paper in the previous figure, using symbols to guide you with the correct color yarn. Each symbol also represents a stitch on the chart. As you stitch in the corresponding holes on the canvas, your rug will start to take shape.

The Stitch

Use the tent stitch on the entire rug. (Refer to Chapter 29 to refresh your memory on this basic stitch.) It is worked in a small diagonal, always slanting in the same direction. You will become familiar with the needle, canvas, and yarn all working together.

Ready to Start

Before you begin stitching, keep in mind the following tips:

- ◆ Begin stitching from the center of the design and work outward.
- ◆ Use one strand of tapestry yarn in the designated color that is listed on the key.
- ◆ Secure the tail of the yarn with beginning stitches and end the tail with the last stitches.
- ◆ Use the tent stitch to cover one intersection of the canvas threads that correspond to the symbol on the chart.
- ◆ Count your stitches frequently to eliminate the chances of making a mistake.

Finishing

When you have stitched the design, including the background, your rug is almost finished. If any distortion occurred, you will need to block your rug before attaching the felt backing. (Refer to Chapter 33 for a refresher.) If very little distortion occurred, steam the back of the rug with an iron and leave it to dry thoroughly. Trim the canvas edges to half an inch. Turn these back onto the wrong side, miter the corners, and lightly steam with an iron; wait for them to dry in place.

Trace the final measurement of the rug, and cut a piece of felt just slightly smaller than the pattern. Using the blue cotton thread, sew the felt onto the back of the rug with a simple slip stitch around the edges, attaching the felt and the canvas edges.

The slip stitch should be invisible on the felt and rug. Pick up a thread or two of the canvas mesh on the back side of the folded edges and then run the needle through the underside of the felt, just catching a small piece. Continue to catch the inside fold of the mesh and the underside of the felt first on one side, then the other.

Voilà! You have completed your first needlework.

Where to Go from Here?

Now that you have finished your rug, you have a good sense of the time that it takes to complete a canvas of this size. You also have a feel for the tension of the yarn, stitches, and canvas. The more needlepoint you do, the better you will become at it.

If you have a dollhouse, you can immediately give your rug a home. If not, you may want to give it as a gift. Or you may want to use the graph paper, make your own designs, and try to sell these little creations! Whatever you choose to do, you have created a fine piece of needlework, and you can be proud to have completed a hand-stitched piece all on your own!

The Least You Need to Know

- Small projects are a good start for novice needle pointers. A dollhouse rug is a perfect choice.
- Getting a feel for your materials is a good place to start for your first needlework. Understanding how the needle, yarn, and canvas work together is key.
- Preparing your materials ahead of time is a step toward a successful needlepoint project.

Part 4

Knitting

In this part, you'll find a step-by-step approach to mastering basic knitting. You'll learn how simple it can be to master a few basic stitches. And as you add more skills to your repertoire, you'll get a chance to try those skills on real pieces that you'll use again and again. This part includes the basics on yarn, reading a pattern, and fixing problems.

Chapter 35

Choose Your Poison: A Yarn Primer

In This Chapter

- ◆ Put up your yarn: Common packaging
- ◆ The right thickness for the right job
- ◆ Selecting a fiber
- ◆ Gleaning valuable information from yarn labels
- ◆ Determining how much yarn to buy
- ◆ Choosing yarns that fit into your budget

All you need to knit or crochet is a needle and some string or yarn. That's it. This chapter helps you wade through the mind-boggling number of yarn choices available and helps you determine exactly what type of yarn meets your needs for different projects.

Put Up Your Yarn: Common Yarn Packaging

Walk into a crafts store and you'll be overwhelmed with the vast array of yarn and thread choices available for knitting and crocheting. Most of what you'll see, however, is packaged—or "put up"—in one of four common ways.

Here's a short explanation of each type of packaging:

♦ **Ball.** A ball is exactly what you would expect. Yarn is wound into a ball-like shape, and often the yarn can be pulled from the center of the ball. Cotton crochet thread is almost always packaged in balls.

♦ **Skein.** A skein is a clever machine-wound bundle of yarn that enables you to pull the yarn from the center. Most synthetic-fiber yarn and many commercial wool or cotton yarns are packaged in skeins.

♦ **Hank.** A hank is a big circle of yarn twisted in to a neater package. To knit or crochet a hank of yarn, you have to untwist the yarn and wind it into a ball. Remember all those Ma and Pa Kettle movies in which a man sat on the porch holding yarn across his forearms while a woman wound it into a ball? That yarn came from a hank. If you don't have a friend available to hold the yarn, you can always drape the big circle over your knees, over the back of a chair, or over a doorknob.

♦ **Cone.** Cones are commercial put-ups of yarn that often come in 1-pound or greater quantities. Purchasing cones of yarn—if you have a good source—is an excellent option. The yarn is often sold by the pound cheaper than comparable amounts in a skein, hank, or ball, and you rarely have to deal with running out of yarn—and having to start up using another skein when you run out of yarn—midway through a project.

Pointers

Often lace crocheting and knitting are accomplished using thread, a finer, tighter, cotton yarn. Throughout this part, I'll refer to both yarn and thread as "yarn."

Yarn Spinning

Some artists specializing in knitting or crocheting have made their reputations by the unusual "yarn" they choose to manipulate into loops. One example is Katherine Cobey, a Maine-based artist who gained renown for knitting a wedding gown from strips of white garbage bags.

Watching Your Weight: Choosing the Right Thickness for the Right Job

Yarns are categorized according to weight or thickness. Weighted from very fine to bulky, different thicknesses are suitable for different jobs. This section will help you sort out your options.

Threads

Cotton thread is generally used for crochet projects, although many knitting projects also call for this material. The thread varies from gossamer to bulky weight. Thread differs from yarn mainly in its structure. Thread is twisted much more tightly than yarn and, consequently, has less give than yarn. As a result, cotton thread is an exceptional choice for doilies, placemats, bedspreads, lace edgings, and other projects that require a piece to tautly keep its shape and firmness.

Cotton threads are sized according to numbers. The higher the number, the finer the thread. Numbers start with size 3 and go up to 100. The most common weight is bedspread weight, which is generally a 10-weight size.

Some manufacturers give their cotton thread names instead of numbers, but the label of the product usually describes the type of projects that are suitable for that particular weight.

Yarn Spinning

When crochet appeared in Middle Europe—Italy, France, Belgium, and England—it was considered a lace-making art. Italy referred to this art as "Orvieto lace."

Yarns

Although many people choose to work with cotton thread, the overwhelming majority of knitters and crocheters choose yarn. The most often-used size is worsted weight, but this is certainly not the only choice available.

Yarn is sized according to weight, or the thickness of a single strand. The range goes from fingering weight to bulky. The classifications listed here start with the thinnest and go up to the thickest:

Here's a rundown of available yarn choices:

 ◆ **Fingering weight or baby weight.** This thin yarn is well-suited to sweaters with intricate color patterns (such as traditional Fair Isle sweaters), lightweight gloves, airy shawls, baby clothes, and fine-weight socks.

- **Sport weight.** Another popular weight of yarn, this is about twice as thick as fingering weight. Use it for gloves, socks, baby clothes, lightweight sweaters, and shawls.

- **Double-knitting (DK) weight.** This yarn is a smidge thicker than sport weight and a mite thinner than worsted weight. You can use it for any purpose listed for either of these two other yarns.

Yarn Spinning

As part of the restoration of the eighteenth-century Warner House in Portsmouth, New Hampshire, 47 volunteers knit an elaborate bedspread to mimic one that had been in the house during the nineteenth century. Using tiny needles and miles of cotton thread, the volunteers knit 1,024 squares, which were then pieced together. The project was started in January 1996 and completed in June 1997.

- **Worsted weight.** The most popular thickness of yarn, this weight can be used for nearly any project: mittens, socks, sweaters, afghans—you name it!

- **Chunky weight.** A hefty yarn perfect for hunting sweaters, thick woolen socks, jackets, and afghans.

- **Bulky weight.** The thickest available yarn, bulky is wonderfully warm and thick. Use it for heavy sweaters, jackets, coats, afghans, and pillow covers. Because you can progress incredibly quickly when working with bulky-weight yarn, it's perfect for making impressive last-minute gifts.

Some available yarn thicknesses: double-knitting weight, sport weight, worsted weight, and chunky weight.

Selecting a Fiber

Buying yarn is like buying clothes. Some of us like fluffy fabrics that ooze glamour; others of us find the fibers make us sneeze. Some of us won't go near anything synthetic; others like the easy care acrylics and nylons provide.

- **Wool yarns.** Wool continues to be the most popular choice of knitters and crocheters. Perhaps because it was one of the first materials formed into garments, perhaps because it can create garments that look beautiful for decades, or perhaps because it feels good to work with and keeps its wearer warm. Wool is a wonderful choice for any autumn or winter garment. Afghans are beautiful from wool, but unless made with a *superwash* variety, can be a bear to clean.

- **Cotton yarns.** Ah, the comfort of cotton. Cotton yarn feels good to work with, wears well, and washes up in the washing machine. On the downside, cotton stretches out of shape more easily than wool, often fades with washing, and has less "tug" on needles than wool, so stitches can get dropped off the needle when knitting.

- **Synthetic yarns.** Synthetics aren't what they used to be. Many are beautiful, affordable, vibrant, and attractive—and they require little care and don't attract pests. Synthetic yarns such as acrylic are exceptional for afghans and baby clothes—items that are difficult or very inconvenient to wash by hand. On the other hand, some synthetics pill and can look cheap. As a rule of thumb—if you're making an heirloom, use wool. If you're making a good, solid item to last for a few years, go with synthetics.

Needle Talk _____

Superwash wool is wool specially treated to be machine washed and dried without incident. Superwash is a wonderful choice for knitting baby clothes: You get the warmth and comfort of wool without troubling a new mother with time-consuming fabric care.

Pointers _____

If you're a fairly inexperienced knitter working with cotton, use wooden needles. The needles hold onto slick cotton yarn more easily than metal ones do.

- **Longhaired yarns.** If you've seen an Ed Wood movie, you're familiar with angora and its cousin, mohair. Both are beautiful yarns that feature long "hairs" to make the knitted or crocheted item fuzzy. Generally speaking, mohair is priced around the same as wool; angora is upward of three times the price of wool. If you're new to knitting and crocheting, save the longhaired yarn for later; the yarns don't let you clearly see stitches you're forming, which can cause a lot of frustration.

- **Novelty yarns.** Fun, funky yarns—made of both natural and synthetic fibers—are created each year. Some examples are metallic threads, chubby bouclé, and soft chenille. In fact, any fiber—from ribbon to raffia—can be knit or crocheted. Have fun using novelty yarns, but keep in mind how an item is going to be used. If you want to make something that will need frequent laundering, choose a fiber that will allow you this option.

Needle Talk

Dye-lot is an indicator of the time the yarn was dyed. Different dye lots—even in the same color yarn—have slight variations in tone. Always check the dye lot (which appears right below the color name and number) and be sure you purchase enough skeins or hanks of yarn in the same dye lot to complete your project.

Digging for Clues: Learning to Read Yarn Labels

The label on a package of yarn contains innumerable clues to the yarn's make-up. Familiarize yourself with the information that appears on a yarn label. Everything you want to know is there, from fiber content to *dye-lot* number. Take a look at the following list and yarn label. When it comes time to purchase your yarn you will know just what to look for.

The yarn label speaks volumes about the yarn you're going to purchase.

Let's walk through what each of these items on a yarn label means:

- **Color name/number.** The color name and/or number is the name the company has given this color. An example might be: 063067 Sunset Gold.

- **Dye-lot number.** The dye-lot number indicates exactly in which dye this yarn was colored. Just as you'll get slight color and tone variations if you use different dye lots when wallpapering your house, you'll get slight but noticeable color variations if you knit or crochet an item using several different dye lots of the same color. Some synthetic yarn doesn't have a dye lot; this information is usually indicated—in bold letters—on the front of the yarn.

♦ **Manufacturer's name.** This is the name of the company that made the yarn. For example, Classic Elite or Patons.

♦ **Brand name.** The brand name is the name the company assigned this line of yarn. Some examples are La Gran (by Classic Elite) and Chunky (by Patons).

♦ **Fiber content.** You guessed it—this is the place where you'll learn what the yarn is made from. Examples are 100 percent alpaca and 75 percent cotton/ 25 percent ramie.

♦ **Yarn size or ply.** This is where you'll learn whether the yarn is a fingering weight, worsted weight, or bulky.

Pointers _____

Find some yarn in your grandma's workbasket, and you're not sure whether it's wool or synthetic? Try this simple test: Use a match to light the end of the yarn. If it melts together, it's synthetic. If it burns and flakes off, it's wool.

♦ **Put-up weight.** The put-up weight is the actual weight of the skein. In many cases, the yardage is a better indicator of how much yarn the skein contains and how much you'll need to finish a project.

♦ **Yarn length in yards/meters.** The yarn length is a more accurate indicator than weight of how much yarn the skein contains. Because yards of different fibers weigh differing amounts (cotton, for example, is generally heavier than wool), when you're substituting yarn you'll want to pay special attention to yardage.

♦ **Suggested gauge.** You'll learn more about gauge in the next chapter. For now, just know that these small pictures depict what the yarn manufacturer believes will be the gauge (stitches required to make an inch) if you use the size knitting needle or crochet hook shown on the label.

♦ **Care instructions.** Here's where you get to the meat of the matter—how to care for the yarn. Let's walk through the four symbols you see in the previous figure. The first symbol shows that you may wash the wool in 40° Celsius/104° Fahrenheit water; if the symbol had had an X through it, you could not wash it in water. The second symbol indicates that you may wash the wool in a washing machine. The third symbol indicates that you may not bleach the yarn; if this symbol didn't contain an X, you could bleach. The final symbol shows that the garment may be dry cleaned using any dry-cleaning solu- tion; if the symbol had an X through it, it could not be dry cleaned.

Pointers _____

Always read the yarn label and follow the manufacturer's advice before you wash or dry clean your finished product. Your time and effort is going into your project, you want the results to last.

How Much to Buy?

Most patterns you use tell you the type of yarn suggested (or used for the model) and the number of ounces or number of yards necessary to complete the project. If you use the yarn suggested in the pattern, always buy at least the number of skeins indicated. To be safe, buy one extra. You generally can exchange the extra for other store merchandise or use it for other projects. Nothing's worse than running out of yarn and being unable to get the last bit you need.

In many cases, you'll find that you want to substitute in a different yarn; consequently, you'll need to know how much of the substitute yarn to purchase. Here's how to determine how much yarn you need:

1. If the indicated yarn includes yardage per skein, multiply the number of yards in each ball by the number of skeins required. For example, if each skein contains 100 yards and the pattern requires you to have 9 skeins, you'll need 900 yards. (100 yards per skein times 9 skeins = 900 yards.)

Pointers _____

If a pattern includes only the weight (number of ounces) of the yarn but not the yardage, call a local yarn shop and explain that you need the yardage of a specific skein of yarn. Generally, these shops have published resources they can use to track yardage.

2. Find the yardage of each skein of the yarn you want to substitute and divide the number of total yards you need by the number of yards in each skein. For example, if the yarn you're substituting contains 150 yards per skein, you'll need 6 skeins. (900 yards needed divided by 150 yards per skein = 6 skeins.)

Pointers _____

If you have true budgetary concerns, buy thin yarn. Four ounces of fingering-weight wool can keep you happily knitting for weeks. If price is no object and you love seeing fast results, buy thicker yarn.

Spinning Yarn into Gold

All right, let's get down to reality here. There's all this talk of beautiful angora yarns, captivating, heirloom-creating wools, and fine bleached cotton thread glamorous enough to make a vintage-looking bedspread. No doubt one thought is going through your head: What's all this going to cost me?

Keep in mind that price does not always indicate quality. Often solid wool is relatively inexpensive and space-dyed acrylic that pills in the first washing is prohibitively costly. As a rule of thumb, start with a medium-price wool or cotton in a color and weight you love.

Pointers

Most large chain craft stores such as Michael's and Hobby Lobby will have some wool and cotton at workable prices. Two examples are Sugar 'n Cream cotton, which is generally no more than $1.75 per 2½-ounce skein, and Lion Brand undyed Fisherman's Wool, which is no more than $8.99 per 8-ounce skein.

If you have no idea where to start, walk into a local yarn shop, tell the salesperson you are a beginning knitter and want to spend no more than $10 total for a couple skeins of wool or cotton, and see what happens. If the salesperson is rude and dismissive, don't darken her doors again.

Here are some ideas for keeping prices down while you are learning to knit or crochet:

♦ **Buy cones of yarn.** This sounds like a crazy notion—buying in bulk when you're learning a craft—but it's almost always the cheapest way to buy high-quality natural fibers. Two great sources for cones of yarn can be found on the Internet at Webs Wool (www.yarn.com) and School Products at (www.schoolproducts.com). Webs Wool ranges from $8.95 to $23.95 per pound; School Products sells wool at $20 per pound.

♦ **Look for close-outs.** Like clothing stores, yarn stores need to clear out last-year's colors to make room for this-year's merchandise. Often, you'll find savings of more than 50 percent off the original price by simply frequenting stores fairly often.

♦ **Check out thrift stores.** Amazingly, some of the best yarn deals around are found in thrift stores. Some knitters have reported finding bags of mohair and wool for less than $2.

♦ **Put out the word.** If you have friends who knit or crochet, they'll probably be thrilled to provide you with some of their leftover skeins from long-ago completed projects.

The Least You Need to Know

- ◆ Yarn options are limitless and exciting; no matter what thickness, fiber, color, or texture you desire, it's available.

- ◆ The label on yarn provides invaluable information about the yarn you are purchasing, including care information.

- ◆ Always check the dye lot and make sure you're purchasing all skeins of yarn from a single dye lot.

- ◆ Knowing the number of yards of yarn required to finish a project is often much more accurate than knowing the number of ounces.

- ◆ Knitting and crocheting does not have to break the bank; cost-conscious yarn options are available.

Chapter 36

Don't Skip This Chapter! Checking Your Gauge

In This Chapter

- ◆ What is gauge?
- ◆ When to be concerned with gauge
- ◆ Swatching patterns to determine gauge
- ◆ Fixing incorrect gauge

What comes to mind when you think of *gauge?* A measure of tire pressure? Pounds per pressure when canning summer tomatoes? The name of the toddler in *Pet Sematary* who killed Fred Gwynne, TV's lovable Herman Munster? It's all these things, but gauge is also the most important concept you will learn in knitting and crocheting.

What Is Gauge?

Gauge when knitting or crocheting follows the same concept as gauges used in other practices; it is a measurement of how big or small each of your stitches will be, based on several factors:

- The stitch

- How tightly or loosely you knit or crochet

- The yarn

- The size of the knitting needles or crochet hook

In addition, your mood can sometimes affect gauge. As you become more accustomed to knitting and crocheting, you might find that the stitches you knit an evening after you've been stuck in a traffic jam for 90 minutes are tighter than those you make while sipping a martini at Martha's Vineyard. Unless you have tumultuous, mood swings, the difference between your relaxed knitting and your tense knitting won't be significant enough to worry you.

Can I See Gauge in Action?

Let's start by looking for *gauge* differences in knitted items. Are you wearing a T-shirt? Take a look at it. Notice the tiny adjoining loops that make up the fabric? You're looking at a very tight gauge. Now look at a sweater. If it's a bulky hand knit, you'll notice that it still contains loops—just like the T-shirt—but the loops are much larger. This is a much looser gauge. Both items are knitted, but the size of the stitches varies significantly.

Likewise, look at a crocheted doily. Notice a difference in the loop sizes between the doily and the afghan on the back of your couch?

Needle Talk _____

Gauge is the number of stitches you need to complete a specified length of knitted fabric. Gauge is typically measured by the inch, such as 5 stitches per inch or 7 stitches per inch.

Think about it. If you're using thick needles and thick yarn, it stands to reason that you'll get chunkier stitches.

The following illustration shows two knitted pieces. Both pieces are 20 stitches wide and 15 deep, but one is knit on size 2 needles using baby-weight yarn, whereas the other is knit on size 11 needles using chunky-weight yarn. You don't need your sleuthing hat to see the obvious differences between these two samples.

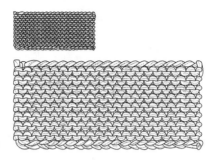

Knitting the same number of stitches using different-size needles and different thickness of yarn.

How Does Gauge Affect Me?

Suppose that you want to make a beautiful oversized sweater that should be about 44 inches around when complete. You'll need to make sure that the gauge and the number of stitches you work with match the size of sweater you want to make. Generally speaking, knitwear designers use the following formula when creating patterns:

Stitches per inch (gauge) × number of inches = number of stitches

How Do Patterns Specify Gauge?

Most patterns specify knitting gauge. It might be called something else, such as "stitch measurement" or "tension," but the information is the same. This gauge tells you the number of stitches you make to complete a specified amount of knitted fabric. If your gauge when knitting or crocheting matches the gauge given in the pattern, the item you're making will be the same size as the one indicated in the pattern. If your gauge is off, the finished item will also be off.

Suppose, for example, that a pattern shows the following:

Gauge: 20 stitches equal 4 inches (10 centimeters)

This means the pattern assumes that when you knit or crochet, every 20 stitches you complete will be 4 inches wide in the fabric. If you divide the 20 stitches by 4 (the number of inches), you see that every inch will be 5 stitches:

20 stitches (number of stitches) ÷ 4 (number of inches) = 5 stitches per inch

This is a gauge of 5 stitches per inch.

What Happens If My Gauge Doesn't Match the Pattern?

So what happens if you decide to pooh-pooh gauge? Let's do a little math.

Say you're making a sweater that is to be 44 inches around when finished. That means the front and back each will be 22 inches across (plus a seam, if you have one, but never mind that for now). The pattern specifies that the gauge should be 5 stitches to the inch (20 stitches per 4 inches), and that you should cast on 110 stitches.

Here's why the designer chose 110 stitches:

22 (completed inches) × 5 (stitches per inch) = 110

But what if you work a bit tighter than the pattern specifies? Not much tighter, mind you, but say you knit or crochet about 6 stitches per inch. Now you've got to divide that 110 stitches by 6 and you get a lot fewer inches:

110 (total stitches) ÷ 6 (number of stitches per inch) = 18⅓ inches (completed inches)

If both the front and back of the sweater are 18⅓ inches wide rather than 22 inches, you're going to end up with a 36- to 37-inch, fanny-hugging sweater.

What if you work a bit looser than the pattern specifies? Not a lot looser, but let's say your actual gauge is 4 stitches per inch rather than the specified 5 stitches per inch. Here's that math again:

110 (total stitches) ÷ 4 (number of stitches per inch) = 27½ (completed inches)

If both the front and back of the sweater are 27½ inches wide rather than 22 inches, your sweater will be a whopping 55 inches around.

As you'll learn later in this chapter, diverting disaster can be as easy as changing the size of needle or hook you use.

Is Gauge Ever Unimportant?

Some projects don't have to be so precise, and you can be a bit cavalier with gauge. All the patterns in this book, except the knitted cap, don't require you to be militant about gauge. These items, if they're a little bigger or a little smaller than the specified size, will still be completely useful and legitimate. (All the patterns include a gauge, but they also indicate when gauge isn't so important.) In many cases if your gauge is close, you're fine. For example, if you're making any of these items, you don't really need to worry too much about gauge:

- Afghans
- Pillows made with stuffing not pillow forms
- Washcloths and dishcloths
- Hot pads
- Scarves
- Placemats
- Unfitted shawls

Checking Your Gauge

Checking your gauge, then, is an essential step when you're knitting or crocheting any item that is size sensitive. Imagine a pair of socks three times as wide as your ankles.

To check gauge, you have to knit or crochet a sample, called a *swatch*, and measure that sample. To measure your swatch, you can use either a good old-fashioned measuring tape or a commercial *gauge counter.*

Needle Talk _____

A **swatch** is a sample you knit or crochet to determine whether your gauge is where it should be. **Gauge counters** are valuable tools for measuring gauge. You lay the counter over your knitting or crocheting and count the number of stitches that appear in the window.

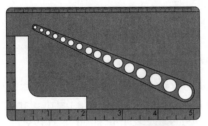

Two tools for measuring swatches: A gauge counter and a measuring tape.

Measuring Gauge When Knitting

To measure gauge when knitting, knit the specified number of inches and rows, and measure them. If the pattern specifies a particular type of stitch to measure (such as, "20 stitches per 4 inches over moss stitch"), knit your swatch using that stitch. Otherwise, use the stockinette stitch: Knit one row, purl one row.

Do you have more stitches per inch than the pattern specifies? Try a larger needle size. Do you have fewer stitches per inch than the pattern requires? Try a smaller needle size. Continue moving up or down one needle size until your swatches match the gauge indicated in the pattern.

Unless you're using a yarn that isn't compatible for what you're trying, the gauge will come out correctly after you fiddle a bit with different needle sizes. If you're trying to use a chunky hand-spun yarn on a pattern that features fine baby yarn, however, you're probably barking up the wrong tree. Even drastically changing needle sizes can't work those kind of miracles.

Check knitting gauge using either a measuring tape or gauge counter.

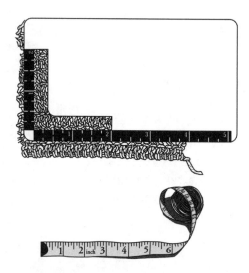

Measuring Gauge When Crocheting

To measure gauge when crocheting, crochet the specified number of inches and rows, and measure them. If the pattern specifies a particular type of stitch to measure (such as, "15 stitches per 4 inches over triple shell"), knit your swatch using that stitch. Otherwise, use single crochet.

Do you have more stitches per inch than the pattern specifies? Try a larger hook. Do you have fewer stitches per inch than the pattern requires? Try a smaller hook. Continue moving up or down one hook size until your swatches match the gauge indicated in the pattern.

The Height's Okay, but the Weight's a Bit Hefty

In some cases, you'll be able to get either the width (20 stitches equals 4 inches) or height (24 rows equal 4 inches) correct, but both won't cooperate at the same time. Suppose, for instance, that 20 stitches equals 4 inches, but 24 rows equals 3¾ inches.

In most cases, you must get the width right. Look through the rest of the pattern. Does it tell you to knit or crochet in inches rather than rows, like this:

> Continue knitting until sleeve cap equals 5 inches.

If so, just be sure that the width is correct, and you should be fine with the rows. You may, however, need additional yarn—to compensate for the additional rows—to finish the project.

Extra Helps: Searching for Gauge Clues

If the yarn is a teensy bit off from the gauge specified in your pattern, you can usually fiddle with needle sizes to get the gauge you need. If the yarn label specifies that the gauge is 18 stitches to 4 inches and you need 16 stitches to 4 inches, for example, you can probably use bigger-size needles and get the correct gauge. If the yarn specifies 20 stitches to 4 inches and you need 12 stitches to 4 inches, however, pick another yarn.

Switching from Swatching

When you're first learning to knit or crochet, fiddling with swatches can be tiresome enough to make you want to give up the hobby. Initially you won't be a speedy stitcher, so creating a 4-inch square of fabric that you won't use for anything can be heartbreaking. Make up a few dishcloths and a scarf instead. When you feel comfortable with the process and feel a little quicker and more ready to tackle a bigger project, then dig out a project that will require size to be accurate. As an added bonus, as you get more comfortable knitting and crocheting, your personal gauge will become more regular and predictable.

A Final Exhortation

If this all seems like too much work, think of the time it'll take you to knit an item using the wrong gauge, rip out the item, and knit it again. Or think of how heartbreaking it would be to see an ill-fitting item you've tenderly knitted for a loved one stuffed at the bottom of a drawer because you didn't check gauge. Checking the gauge is worth every second you spend knitting up swatches. If you just aren't into gauge, stick to knitting items in which gauge isn't important.

Is Gauge Nothing but a Boil on My Neck?

Absolutely not. Although making swatches and checking for gauge in patterns might seem like a big pain, knowing the gauge can be incredibly important when you want to break away from a pattern and forge your own path.

Even if all knitters and crocheters were equal and if, provided you used the needle or hook size and yarn type specified, you could be guaranteed that the gauge would be correct and match the pattern precisely, you still want to know how to check gauge. Why?

◆ Suppose you come across a beautiful vintage pattern you want to try, but the yarn is no longer available. By using gauge you can determine another yarn to use that will produce the same-size results.

- What if you find a pattern you love but for which the yarn specified is, in your opinion, frightfully ugly or prohibitively expensive? By understanding gauge, you easily can substitute in another yarn. You just need to be sure that the new yarn works up to the gauge in the pattern.

- What if you have a gorgeous yarn in your stash that you want to try on a pattern you've found? Stitch up a swatch and see whether the yarn can be used in that pattern.

What Do I Do with All These Little Squares?

Although swatches help you determine gauge, they can also serve several other purposes. After you work up a swatch, you can throw it in the washer and dryer to test for shrinkage. You can rub on it a bit to see whether it has a tendency to pill (little fiber balls appear, a result of static electricity from fiction binding fibers to each other). You can also pin it to some clothes you're wearing and walk around in it all day, to see how it wears.

If you're feeling ambitious and you're one of those people who saves everything because you can't stand being wasteful, you can save all your swatches and later sew them into a crazy-quilt afghan. If you don't have quite enough swatches for a whole afghan, you can make placemats or pillow covers.

The Least You Need to Know

- The stitch, yarn type, and needle size determine gauge, as does how loosely or tightly you knit.

- Not all items require gauge to be correct; afghans, pillows, and scarves are safe items to make when you don't feel like dinking with gauge.

- To determine gauge, work a swatch of fabric and measure to determine whether the stitches you make per inch match the number specified in the pattern.

- To change gauge, change the needle or hook size: higher for a looser gauge, smaller for a tighter gauge.

- Always test gauge when making a sweater or other fitted item; you'll save yourself lots of time in the end.

- Use the needle or hook sizes indicated in patterns as a guide, but determine the size you should use by working a swatch and measuring gauge.

Chapter 37

An Overview of Knitting Tools

In This Chapter

- ◆ Knitting Needles 101
- ◆ Wading through the needle-sizing muddle
- ◆ Other accessories that add to your stitching enjoyment

As you begin to explore knitting, the mind-blowing number of accessories might confuse you: cable needles, stitch markers, yarn bras? This chapter explains the most common and basic knitting tools—those that make your knitting more enjoyable, more productive, and more beautiful.

Knitting Needles

Knitting needles are one of only two items necessary for successful knitting—the other item is yarn. Walk into any knitting store, however, and you can easily be overwhelmed and intimidated by the number of options. This section helps you sort out the tangle of needle options.

Straight or Circular?

Knitting needles come in two varieties: straight and circular.

Likewise, straight needles come in two varieties: single pointed and double pointed. Single-pointed needles have a point at one end and a nub or knob at the other; the point is what you knit from, and the nub is what keeps stitches from falling off the needle. These needles are sold in pairs and are used for flat knitting, such as scarves. Many sweaters, as well, are knitted in pieces using single-pointed needles. Most cartoon characters you see knitting are using single-pointed needles with nubs. As you'll learn in the next chapter, however, these characters' form is all wrong.

Single-pointed needles are used for knitting flat pieces such as scarves.

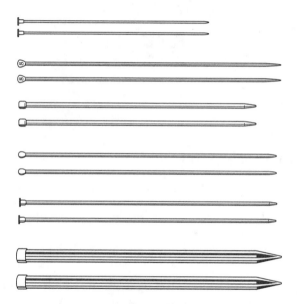

Double-pointed straight needles, as you might guess, have points at both ends. Consequently, you can knit from both ends. As you'll learn in Chapter 44, you generally use these needles to make tubular, seamless items such as socks or mittens. Double-pointed straight needles are sold in sets of four or five needles.

Double-pointed straight needles let you work tubular items like socks and mittens.

Circular needles create tubes in much the same way as do double-pointed straight needles. Unlike double-pointed needles, however, circular needles enable you to work on one needle only, knitting in a continuous circle. Circular needles have two short single-pointed knitting needles on each end attached by a flexible cord. Circular knitting needles come in sizes ranging from 12 inches (for socks and mittens) to 36 inches (for the largest sweaters imaginable).

Pointers

In some cases, if a flat piece such as an afghan has more stitches than will fit on a pair of single-pointed needles, you might use a circular needle to knit back and forth—rather than in a circle—to accommodate all the stitches. In addition, the flexibility of a circular needle means that your work can lay in your lap; you don't have to support its full heft as you would with straight needles.

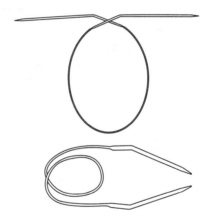

Circular knitting needles enable you to knit in a circle.

Is That American or English?

Knitting needles come in different sizes, and these sizes affect the size of the finished stitch. Easy enough. But going by nothing but a number can get a little tricky because knitting needles can be sized using three different systems: U.S., English/U.K., and Continental Rim systems. The following chart shows the needle equivalents for these three systems.

CHART OF INTERNATIONAL NEEDLE EQUIVALENTS														
U.S. System	0	1	2	3	4	5	6	7	8	9	10	10 1/2	11	13	15
English/U.K. System	13	12	11	10	9	8	7	6	5	4	3	2	1	00	000
Continental Rim System	2 1/4	2 1/2	3	3 1/4	3 1/2	4	4 1/2	5	5 1/2	6	6 1/2	7	7 1/2	8 1/2	9

Trekking Through the Material World

The materials from which knitting needles are made vary considerably. Don't be surprised if you find needles made of the following:

- Plastic
- Aluminum
- Teflon
- Wood

- Bamboo
- Bone
- Ivory (although this is extremely rare)

Generally, most needles are made from wood, bamboo, or aluminum. If you don't already have needles and need to buy some, start with a wood or bamboo set. Stitches slide around more on aluminum needles, which can be disconcerting for new knitters. Also, aluminum conducts heat and cold. If you're knitting by a fire, your needles might get hot and uncomfortable to the touch. If you're sitting on the porch on a brisk autumn day, the needles could get cold and uncomfortable to the touch. Wood and bamboo stay at a fairly standard temperature.

Snarls

Always check patterns carefully to determine which sizing systems were used. Sometimes this involves a little creative sleuthing. If a pattern book was originally printed in England, for example, it very well might use English/U.K. sizing; if it was printed in America, it probably uses U.S. sizing. Often patterns will provide both U.S. and English/U.K. sizing. The patterns in this book are all sized using the U.S. system.

Yarn Spinning

The day he was beheaded in 1649, King Charles (Charles Stuart) wore a shirt made by a master knitter. Today, the shirt is on display at the London Museum.

Accessories Make the Job Easier

There's a gadget for just about anything you can imagine—and some things you can't. The mail-order business has made a fortune selling Ginsu knife sharpeners, turkey-jerky-dehydrating machines, bloomin'-onion devices, and a million other accessories. As you might guess, knitting hasn't escaped this phenomena. Some accessories add little to your knitting experience, but the ones mentioned in this section will prove invaluable as you gain experience.

Measuring Tools

A good tape measure and gauge counter help you immeasurably (no pun intended) as you begin knitting. You can use both to check knitting gauge, as you learned in Chapter 36. In addition, you can use the tape measure for a million other knitting tasks: measuring the length of a sock from cuff to heel; taking the true waist size of your best friend, to whom you promised a sweater; and so on.

Although you can wait to purchase most of the accessories in this section, go out at lunch and buy yourself a good tape measure. You'll be using it almost immediately.

> **Snarls**
>
> A rough point on the end of your needle will snag your yarn when you insert the needle into your stitch. It is very important to have a smooth, sharp—but not deadly—point to stitch properly and comfortably.

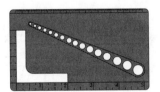

Various measuring tools.

Stitch Holders

Stitch holders are exactly what the name implies: a place to hold stitches that you aren't currently using but will need again. Shaped like big safety pins, stitch holders come in a variety of lengths. In a pinch, if you only need to hold on to a couple of stitches, you can use a safety pin.

> **Needle Talk**
>
> **Stitch holders** are safety pin–shaped accessories that hold knitting stitches you aren't currently using but will use later.

A variety of stitch holders in different sizes.

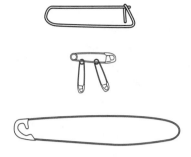

Stitch Markers

Stitch markers are the knitting equivalent of a looped string around your finger: They remind you of important steps in your knitting. These little plastic or metal discs slide onto your needle and cue you to changes in the knitted fabric. You might use them to remind you of which stitch on the row you need to start a cable pattern, or where you need to decrease a stitch.

> **Needle Talk** _____
>
> **Stitch markers** are little discs that slide onto your knitting needle and cue you at the point when it's time to do something to the knitted fabric.

Stitch markers are available in a variety of shapes; because you need one large enough to slip from needle to needle but not so large as to be obtrusive, you might ultimately need to purchase some in different sizes. In a pinch, you can use a loop of contrasting yarn, a safety pin, or a paper clip as a stitch marker.

Stitch markers help you remember important steps in your knitting.

> **Needle Talk** _____
>
> **Cable needles** are small double-pointed needles made expressly for creating patterned cables, such as those on Aran sweaters.

Cable Needles

Look at an Aran-knit sweater and you'll probably be perplexed by the different patterns twisting and swirling up and through the garment. These details are courtesy of *cable needles*, small, double-pointed needles that hold stitches and help you "move" stitches across a knitting piece.

The most common shapes are straight, straight with a bend in the middle, and U-shaped. The last two are especially handy as the stitches do not slide off the cable needle. Like regular needles, cable needles are available in a variety of sizes. In a pinch, you can use a regular double-pointed needle or a crochet hook as a cable needle, but these can be more cumbersome and cause you to drop stitches.

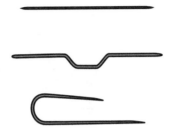

Cable needles enable you to make richly patterned designs.

Bobbins

Bobbins are helpful accessories to have on hand when you're working in multiple colors. These little gems are made of plastic and are easy to find in yarn shops. Bobbins look similar to bread-bag tabs, only larger. To use a bobbin, wrap yarn around it and knit from the bobbin, rather than from a ball of yarn. You can then unwind only what you need for the next few stitches, and you won't have to negotiate cumbersome amounts of yarn.

 Needle Talk _____

Bobbins are plastic tabs that hold small amounts of yarn. They are invaluable when working on pieces that have many color changes.

Bobbins help you keep your work from becoming a tangled mess.

Crochet Hooks

"Wait!" you say, "This is the section on knitting." True, but you'll still find yourself thankful for a crochet hook. A crochet hook helps you pick up dropped stitches (which you will learn about in Chapter 48); it enables you to add finishing crochet to the edge of knitted items; it allows you to join seams using a crochet stitch; it lets you attach fringe. You should have at least a few sizes of crochet hooks in your knitting basket. I suggest a steel hook size 0 and an aluminum hook size G.

Snarls

If you want to avoid real snarls or making your own "cat's cradle" when working in multicolors, take the time to wind small amounts of yarn around bobbins. If you use large skeins or balls of yarn, you'll find that in a short period of time you have to stop working and start the task of unsnarling.

A crochet hook might become your favorite knitting companion.

Needles and Pins

These little helps are irreplaceable when it comes time to finishing your work. You'll use straight pins to block your pieces and hold seams together as you sew or crochet them into place. You'll use yarn needles, which are special needles with dull points and large eyes, to tuck in yarn ends and sew together seams.

The Least You Need to Know

◆ Different varieties of knitting needles enable you to knit either flat or tubular pieces.

◆ Knitting needles come in three varieties—the U.S., English/U.K., and Continental Rim systems—and each uses a different sizing scheme.

◆ A couple of additional accessories such as cable needles and pins will make your life much easier.

38

Building the Foundation: Casting On Stitches

In This Chapter

♦ The thumb and cable cast-on methods

♦ Determining tail length

♦ The single method cast-on for left-handed knitters

When you're *casting on* stitches, you're making that first row of loops. This chapter walks you through various cast-on methods, each of which serves a particular purpose in knitting. In addition, a special section helps those who are left-handed make sense of the process.

Casting What?

Suppose you want to build a greenhouse in your backyard. Do you start with the roof? The walls? No. You start by laying a solid foundation for your building. The same is true with knitting. Before you can begin

Needle Talk

Casting on is creating the foundation row of stitches from which you will knit. Casting on is tying a slip knot, attaching the knot to your needle, and adding stitches. The cast-on row is often referred to as **bottom selvage** in instructions.

Needle Talk

The **tail** is the amount of yarn between the end of the yarn and where something—such as tying a slip knot—occurs. The length of the tail you leave (before tying the slip knot to cast on) differs based on the cast-on method you choose.

knitting, you need a foundation row of stitches from which to knit. You create this row, also called the *bottom selvage*, by *casting on* stitches.

In this chapter, you'll learn three methods for casting on. Two methods involve casting on by winding zyarn around your thumb: the single method and the double method. The third method, called the cable cast-on, actually uses a form of knitting to place the stitches on the needle.

Setting the Stage

You have to cast on before you knit, and to begin casting on, you have to tie a slip knot. This slip knot is how you attach yarn to the needle.

Depending on the method of casting on you choose, you will have either a long or short *tail* of yarn before you tie the slip knot. But we'll get to that soon enough. For now, tie the slip knot about 20 inches from the end of the yarn.

The following figures illustrate a tidy three-step method for tying a slip knot.

Loop the yarn around your left index finger.

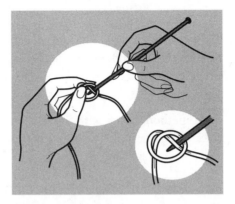

Slip the yarn from your finger and hold the loop between your thumb and index finger.

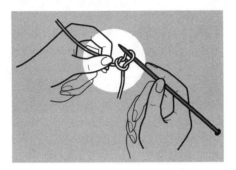

Use the needle, held in your right hand, to draw the loop up and tighten around the needle.

Pointers

If you cast on your stitches too tightly, you'll end with a pinched bottom edge on your finished piece. After you practice knitting a bit, check to see whether the bottom selvage is much tighter and less elastic than the knitted stitches. If so, you'll need to cast on more loosely. To help you make a looser foundation row, cast on stitches using a needle two sizes bigger than the size from which you will be knitting. If the pattern calls for a size 6 needle, for example, use a size 8 needle to cast on.

After the knot is on the needle, you can gently tug at both ends of the yarn to lightly tighten the knot. Don't pull too tightly, however. You want the slip knot to be loose enough to move freely on your needle. The loop made from the slip knot is counted as the first stitch on your needle.

The Single Life

The single method is the most direct way of casting on. This method is especially easy to follow, making it ideal for beginners. Young children also pick up this cast on well. The single method creates a fairly elastic selvage, so it's perfect for sweaters, jackets, and hats: items for which you want some "give" at the bottom.

To cast on using the single method, begin with the slip knot on your needle. With your right hand, grip the needle that holds the slip knot as you would a wooden spoon. Then follow the steps in these figures.

In your left hand, wrap the yarn that is coming from the skein around your thumb from front to back. Close your left fingers over the yarn in your palm to keep it in place.

Insert your right-hand needle upward through the strand of yarn facing you at the base of your left thumb.

Slip the loop off your thumb onto your needle. Gently pull down on the long strand to tighten the yarn.

Beautiful! You've just cast on your first stitch. You now have two stitches on the needle; the slip knot counts as your first stitch.

Continue this procedure as many times as you want. Try to keep all the stitches uniform by gently pulling down the long strand of yarn after you make each loop. Initially, your stitches will look fairly uneven: Some will be tight and pinched while others will be gaudy and loose. It takes time to get the tension even in all the stitches, and you won't get it right the first time out of the gate.

Snarls

Be sure when using both the single method and cable cast-on that you are using the yarn feeding from the skein, not the tail of yarn, to cast on stitches.

Doubles, Anyone?

As you would expect, the double method involves doubles—not thumbs, but two ends of yarn. Your thumb is still a big player here, but you will be adding a few fingers to expedite the procedure. Like the single method, the double method creates a fairly elastic selvage, so it's perfect for sweaters, jackets, and hats.

Start with the same slip knot you used for the single method. This time, however, the length of the yarn tail before you tie the slip knot is important; you use the tail to help cast on stitches.

Pointers

The easiest way to determine where to tie the slip knot is to figure 1 inch of yarn for each stitch you will be casting on. Add an extra 4 inches so that after you finish casting on, you'll still have a little tail; you'll weave in this tail after you finish knitting. If you want to cast on 20 stitches, start your slip knot 24 inches from the end of the yarn: 20 inches (20 stitches) + 4 inches (tail) = 24 inches

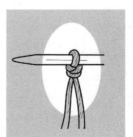

Make a slip knot far enough from the end of the yarn to accommodate 1 inch per stitch you'll cast on, plus 4 inches.

Grasp the shorter end of yarn with your left hand as you did for the single method; wrap it around your thumb and secure it against your palm. Now wrap the yarn from the skein over your right index finger and hold the yarn against your right palm.

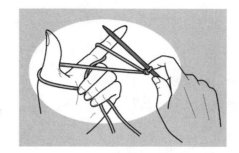

Insert your needle upward at the base of your left thumb, as you did for the single method. Bring the yarn from your index finger over the point of the needle from the back to the front.

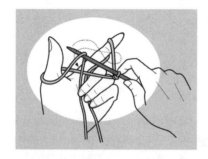

With the yarn over the needle, pull the needle through the loop made by your thumb so that the new loop you created is on the needle.

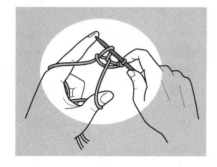

Pointers

Sometimes a pattern calls for adding more stitches to the edge of a piece—maybe to create a geometrically shaped sweater. In these cases, use the cable cast-on to add the necessary stitches.

Now gently pull the short end of the yarn to tighten the stitch on the needle. Nice work. You have just completed a double cast-on. You now have two stitches on the needle; the slip knot counts as your first stitch.

Go ahead and practice a few more stitches. If you run out of your yarn tail, just pull out the stitches, tie another slip knot, and start again. Initially, the tension on your stitches is going to vary quite a bit. Just keep practicing and soon the stitches will be fairly even.

The Able Cable

The last method of casting on is the cable cast-on. This method requires two needles—you'll actually be knitting your stitches onto the needle. The cable cast-on creates a fairly firm selvage, so it works best for items that need a straight, firm edge, such as scarves and afghans. To begin, tie a slip knot, leaving about a 4-inch tail. Then follow the steps in these figures.

Insert the tip of your right-hand needle into the slip knot on your left needle, from front to back, under the left-hand needle.

With your right hand, bring the yarn under and then over the point of the right-hand needle; you now have a loop on the right needle.

Use the right-hand needle to slide the new loop onto the left-hand needle. You now have two loops on the left-hand needle.

Insert the right-hand needle between the two stitches on your left-hand needle.

Again loop the yarn around the point of the right-hand needle as you did before. Be sure that you insert the right-hand needle between stitch loops *on the left-hand needle, rather than* through *the loops.*

The Single Method Cast-On with Your Left Hand

Casting on for left-handed knitters starts with a slip knot—just like it does for right-handed knitters. Because slip knots know no boundaries, what works for the right hand works for the left hand.

To start, make a slip knot, leaving about a 4-inch tail. You're now ready to cast on a stitch. With your left hand, grip the needle that holds the slip knot as you would hold a wooden spoon. Then follow the steps in these figures.

Grasp the shorter end of yarn with your right hand and wrap it around your thumb from front to back. Then wrap the yarn from the skein over your left index finger and hold both yarn ends with your right palm.

Now insert your needle upward at the base of your right thumb into the loop around your thumb.

Slip the loop off your thumb onto your needle. Gently pull on the long strand to tighten your stitch.

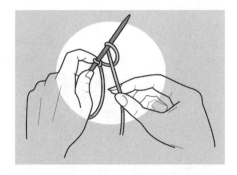

Cast on some more stitches, trying to keep them even. Initially, your stitches are going to vary somewhat: some tight, some loose. Just keep practicing. After a bit, your stitches will even up and you'll feel more comfortable with casting on.

The Least You Need to Know

- ◆ Casting on means building a foundation of stitches from which you'll knit.

- ◆ You can cast on one needle, or you can cast on using two needles in a modified knitting style.

- ◆ It takes practice to get stitches even.

39

The Big Three: Knitting, Purling, and Binding Off

In This Chapter

- ◆ Common knit abbreviations
- ◆ Mastering the noble knit stitch
- ◆ Playing with purling
- ◆ Binding off and bringing your work to a graceful close
- ◆ Left-handed knitting
- ◆ Garter stitch and stockinette stitch

In this chapter, you're going to learn to knit. Really knit. By the time you finish the chapter, you'll be able to casually let drop at cocktail parties, "Why yes, I do love Glenlivet. And I knit, as well." You'll have something to do with your hands the next rainy Saturday afternoon you spend watching a Joan Crawford moviethon. You'll be a knitter.

You'll also know how to purl and bind off stitches. With these three skills, and the cast-on methods you learned in the previous chapter, you'll have everything you need to begin making exquisite pieces.

Common Knitting and Purling Abbreviations

The following universal abbreviations will come in handy as you work through the stitches in this chapter.

Abbreviation ...	What It Means ...
bo	Bind off
k	Knit
p	Purl
rev st st	Reverse stockinette stitch
rs	Right side
st st	Stockinette stitch
ws	Wrong side

Same Stitch, Different Look: Knitting and Purling

As you've learned, knitting is a way of creating fabric using interlocking loops. Knitting and its best buddy purling, which you'll learn about in this chapter, are two complementary ways to join those loops and create more. You knit or purl in rows, using the stitches you cast on the needle.

Here's where things get interesting: Knitting and purling are really the *same* stitch. The only difference lies in whether you pull the end of the loop toward you or move it away from you. A knitted stitch, from the back, looks like a purled stitch; a purled stitch from the back looks like a knitted stitch.

This means that if you purl every row, you'll ultimately end up with the same-looking fabric as if you knit every row. This concept might sound confusing, but as you begin watching what your hands are doing, you'll understand how knitting and purling interact to create interesting patterns and effects.

Knitting 101

It's time. You're going to knit. If you plan to knit along with these instructions, cast on about 20 stitches. This is a nice number because it's not so many as to be daunting, but it's enough to see what you're creating.

Getting a Grip

Comfortable knitting begins with properly positioning the yarn and the needles. Follow these instructions.

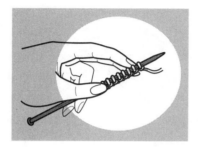

With your left hand, grip the needle with the cast-on stitches, lightly holding the first stitch on the needle with your index finger near the point end of the needle.

In your right hand, hold the second needle as you would a pencil.

Place the long end of the yarn over your first finger, under your second, over your third, and under your fourth.

You will want to practice holding your needles with the yarn. When you actually start to work, you will find that you will probably make adjustments as you go, so that everything feels comfortable.

Taking the Plunge

You are now ready to make your first knit stitch. To begin, move your hands closer together. Now follow these steps.

Insert the tip of the right-hand needle, front to back, into the first stitch on the left-hand needle—under the left needle.

Rest the right-hand needle on top of your left forefinger. The yarn is at the right of your work in your right hand. With your right hand, bring the yarn under and then over the point of the right-hand needle.

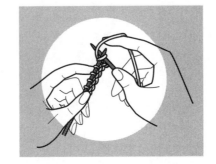

With the help of your left forefinger, slide the point of the right-hand needle back toward you. Using the right-hand needle point, catch the loop made by the yarn over the needle.

Pull the stitch off the left-hand needle. You now have a stitch on the right-hand needle.

You have just knitted your first stitch. The process might seem awkward. In fact, the first stitch on the row always feels a bit awkward—even after you're an experienced knitter. Try another stitch. The process gets easier as you move across the row. In addition, you'll soon find that your right thumb instinctively moves in to steady the new stitch.

Yarn Spinning

Many years ago, when children were routinely taught to knit, a wonderful phrase was taught to make the process easier. Try chanting it; it will help you remember the steps: "In, over, through, and off."

Turning Your Work

At some point, you'll run out of stitches on the left needle and you'll have a fresh new row of stitches on your right-hand needle. You are now ready to turn your work so you can knit the second row.

As you turn your work, you will at the same time transfer the needle with the stitches from your right hand to your left hand. You will be looking at the back of the stitches you previously knitted. In this case, because you knit the stitches and the ends of the loops were pointed away from you when you worked the row, they will now be pointed toward you when you turn the stitches; this accounts for the row's bumpy appearance.

Pointers

Needles are referred to as either right or left, when in actuality they are neither. When the needle is in your right hand it is the "right needle." The same holds true if it should be in your left hand as it would be called your "left needle."

You are now starting over with the empty needle in your right hand and the yarn being held using the technique you learned in the section "Getting a Grip," earlier in this chapter.

When your yarn is in place, repeat the steps for knitting you learned in the section "Taking the Plunge." You're knitting!

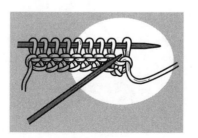

Knitting into a knit stitch on the second row.

Purls of Wisdom

It's time to learn the yin to knitting's yang: the purl stitch. *Purling* is knitting in reverse: You pull the end of the loop toward you so that the end of the loop faces you. Consequently, the row you're working will have a bumpy texture.

There are two major differences between a knit and a purl stitch. The first is the position of your yarn while you work the stitch. In knitting, the yarn is kept or held to the back of the work. In purling, the yarn is kept or held to the front of the work.

The second difference between the two stitches is where you insert the needle. In knitting, you insert the needle front to back. In purling, you insert it back to front.

> **Needle Talk** _____
>
> **Purling** means forming rows of interconnecting loops in which the ends of the loops face toward you as you work.

To make your first purl stitch use the same yarn and needle positioning you learned in the section "Getting a Grip." If you plan to purl along with these instructions, cast on about 20 stitches. Bring the yarn forward in front of your right-hand needle. From the right side, insert the tip of the right-hand needle into the front of the first stitch.

Using your right index finger, wrap the yarn around the right-hand needle counterclockwise.

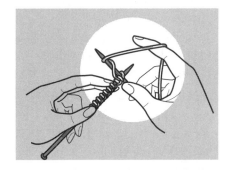

Keeping the new loop on the right-hand needle, slide the point of the right needle backward, down and out. Keep the new loop on your right-hand needle, allowing the original stitch to slide off the left-hand needle.

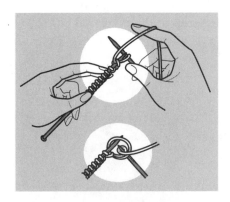

You have just completed your first purl stitch. If you are purling across the row, turn your work when you get to the end of the row, then purl across the next row. Do you notice that this piece worked in all purl stitches looks like the one you worked in all knit stitches?

Bringing It to a Close

Just as you had to work a special row to get ready to knit, you have to work a special row to finish your knitted pieces. This row is made by following a procedure called *binding off*. Binding off actually creates a final row of knitted fabric, so, as you might expect, you bind off differently when you are knitting than when you are purling.

Needle Talk

Binding off is the process in which you "lock up" all active stitches on the needle so that they can't unravel. You bind off stitches when you're finished with a piece or want to shape an area—such as an armhole in a sweater.

Snarls

Always hold your yarn loosely when binding off. Otherwise, you'll end up with a knitted piece that ends looking pinched and unpleasant. If you find you are an uptight binder-offer, bind off using needles that are one or two sizes larger than the size you used to knit the piece.

To begin binding off in knitting, loosely knit the first 2 stitches in the row; you now have 2 stitches on the right needle. Then follow these steps.

From the left side of the stitch, insert the point of your left-hand needle into the first stitch on your right-hand needle.

Using the left-hand needle, lift the stitch from the right needle. Bring the stitch up and over the second stitch and off the point of the right-hand needle.

You had two stitches on the needle and you looped one over the other to end up with only one stitch. If you ever made potholders as a kid using those looms with colored nylon loops, you've bound off stitches before, just in a different context.

Here's how to continue binding off across the row:

1. Knit the next stitch on your left needle onto your right-hand needle. You again have two stitches on your right-hand needle.

2. Following the preceding illustrations, use your left-hand needle to lift the first stitch on the right-hand needle over the second stitch.

3. Repeat steps 1 and 2 until you have bound off all but one stitch.

4. Cut the end of your yarn at least 3 inches from the needle; pull the yarn end through the last remaining stitch and pull tightly.

You have just secured the last stitch. Your knitted piece now can't unravel.

Pointers _____

In pattern instructions you will often read, "bind off in pattern." This means that you should bind off in whatever stitch you would use to continue the established pattern. If the row you are working on has both knit and purl stitches, you knit "off" the knits, and purl "off" the purls.

Binding Off in Purling

Binding off on a row you would otherwise purl is almost exactly like binding off on a row you would otherwise knit. Follow the same procedure you learned in the preceding section with one difference: Purl the stitches rather than knit them. When you have bound off all but one stitch, cut your yarn, leave a tail, and pull the end of the yarn through your last stitch.

Left-Handed Knitting

Left-handed knitting is like right-handed knitting: easy as pie, after you understand the concept. The procedures in this section are specifically geared toward those steps that differ from right-handed knitting. Therefore, it's important that you read all the instructions at the beginning of this chapter before you start.

Your Starting Position

Comfortable knitting begins with properly positioning the yarn and the needles. Follow these instructions.

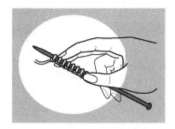

With your right hand, grip the needle that contains the cast-on stitches, lightly holding the first stitch on the needle with your index finger near the point end of the needle.

In your left hand, hold the second needle as you would a pencil.

Place the long end of the yarn over your first finger, under your second, over your third, and under your fourth.

How's it feel? This is the position you'll use to begin knitting.

The Knit Stitch

You're sitting there, holding the needle, the yarn twisted around your fingers at the ready. Now what? You're ready to knit your first stitch! Here's how.

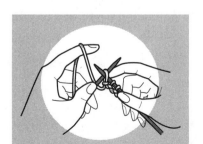

Insert the tip of your left-hand needle, into the first stitch on your right-hand needle, under the right needle.

Rest the right-hand needle on top of your left forefinger. The yarn is at the left of your work in your left hand. Using your left hand, bring the yarn under and then over the point of the left-hand needle.

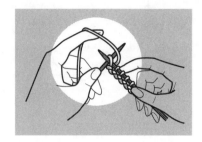

With the help of your right forefinger, slide the point of the left-hand needle back toward you. Using the left-hand needle point, catch the loop made by the yarn over the needle.

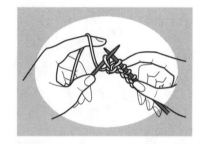

Pull the stitch off the right-hand needle so that it now rests on the left-hand needle. You now have a stitch on the left-hand needle.

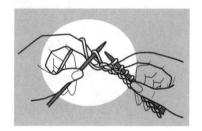

Pointers

When you are ready to bind off, follow the instructions earlier in this chapter for binding off.

You just produced your first knit stitch! The process might seem awkward—the first stitch on the row always feels a bit awkward, even after you're an experienced knitter. Try another stitch. The process gets easier as you move across the row. In addition, you'll soon find that your right thumb instinctively moves in to steady the new stitch.

> ☝ **Pointers** _____
>
> If you need clarification on how to do a procedure left-handed, hold a mirror next to the right-handed illustrations so that you can see the image reversed. The reversed image will give you the necessary information you need to work left-handed. If you're lucky enough to have a friend who's a right-handed knitter, sit facing him and mirror his steps.

The Purl Stitch

The purl stitch is almost the same as the knit stitch. Starting as you did with the knit stitch, follow these steps.

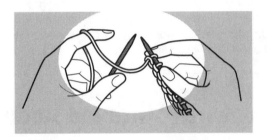

Bring the yarn forward in front of your left-hand needle.

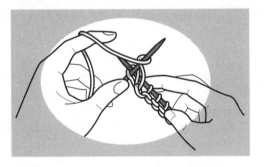

From the left side, insert the left-hand needle point into the back of the first stitch on the right-hand needle. The left needle is in front of the right needle. Using your left index finger, wrap the yarn around the left-hand needle clockwise.

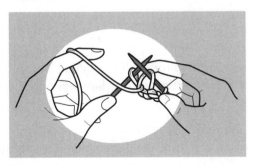

Keeping the new loop on the left-hand needle, slide the point of the left needle backward, down and out. Keep the new loop on your left-hand needle, allowing the original stitch to slide off the right-hand needle.

Pointers

When you are ready to bind off, follow the instructions given earlier in this chapter for binding off. You need to purl two stitches, and then use your left needle to pull the first stitch you purled over the second stitch you purled. Then purl one more stitch and pull the first stitch over the second. Continue this way across the row.

That's it! You're a knitter! And a left-handed knitter, to boot!

Snarls

Fit to be tied? It can happen. If you are a left-handed knitter and reading directions for right-handed knitting; remember that you *must* substitute the words *right* for *left*, and *left* for *right*. To avoid confusion as you work, use two different colors to highlight the words *right* and *left* in your patterns.

The Fabulous Two: Garter Stitch and Stockinette Stitch

At this point, you know how to knit and how to purl. Let's talk about the two most basic and common of all knitted patterns: *garter stitch* and *stockinette stitch*.

Needle Talk

Garter stitch is a common pattern that is created by knitting every row; it has a fairly bumpy surface. **Stockinette stitch** is another common pattern; it is created by alternating one row of knitting with one row of purling. Stockinette stitch creates a fabric that is smooth on one side and bumpy on the other.

Garter Stitch

You create garter stitch by knitting (or purling—but no one does) every row. If you made practice swatches in the knitting and purling sections of this chapter, you have swatches of garter stitch.

Garter stitch is a firm, attractive pattern that is bumpy on both sides of the fabric. If you look closer, however, you'll see the garter stitch actually alternates a smooth row with a bumpy row, but the smooth rows are hard to see. Ridges, or two rows of knitting, are the bumpy rows you see on both sides of garter-stitch fabric.

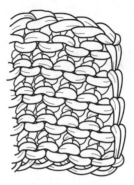

Knitting every row creates garter stitch.

Stockinette Stitch

Stockinette stitch (abbreviated st st) is the stitch that really defines knitting. You're already intimately familiar with this stitch, even if you don't know it. Stockinette stitch is made by alternating one row of knitting with one row of purling. The result is a fabric that is smooth on one side (the knit side or *right side*) and bumpy on the other (the purl side or *wrong side*). The bumpy side is known as reverse stockinette stitch.

> **Needle Talk** _____
>
> The **right side** (abbreviated rs) of knitted fabric is the side that will be showing, such as the outside of a sweater. The **wrong side** (abbreviated ws) is the side that faces inward.

Almost everything you own that is knitted is made of stockinette stitch: T-shirts, jersey sheets, many sweaters, sweatshirts, and so on. Next time you put on a T-shirt, take a look at how it's made. You'll notice that the side facing out is smooth, whereas the inside is comprised of tiny bumps. You're looking at stockinette stitch at work.

> **Pointers** _____
>
> The knit stitch is slightly thinner and shorter than the purl stitch. This means that the edges of pieces knit in stockinette stitch—where one side is all knit stitches and one side is all purl stitches—curl toward the knit side. Some designers use this natural curling tendency to make sweaters with rolled collars or hats with rolled brims. To anchor stockinette stitch and keep it from curling, you need to edge stockinette stitch pieces either with garter stitch or with a stitch that contains knitting and purling in the same row. Many sweaters feature ribbing to keep edges from rolling.

The knit side of stockinette stitch.

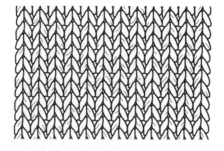

Reverse stockinette stitch.

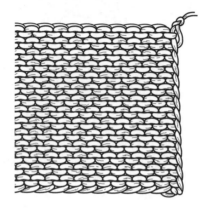

Pointers _____

When you work in stockinette stitch, you knit the first row and purl the second row. You keep repeating these two rows until you have worked as many rows as you want. If you get confused as to what row you are on, look at your stitches and work them as they appear. If the smooth side is facing you, then you knit. If the bumpy side is facing you, then you purl.

The Least You Need to Know

♦ The knit and purl stitches are really the same stitch, but the method used to create them is different.

♦ Stockinette stitch is created by alternating knit and purl rows. Garter stitch is created by knitting every row.

♦ Binding off is a way to lock up your stitches when you finish a piece.

Chapter 40

Special Stitches Using Knitting and Purling

In This Chapter

- ◆ Common pattern abbreviations
- ◆ Stitch patterns that combine the knit and purl stitches
- ◆ Using a cable needle to add a new twist to your knitting

Knitting and purling open the door to all types of special stitches, from simple ribbing at the bottom of a sweater to intricate cabling running up and down an Aran-knit afghan.

In this chapter, you'll learn several variations on the knit and purl stitches—how to make interesting patterns by alternating these two stitches.

Then you'll learn one of the most exciting concepts in knitting: using a cable needle to create patterns by knitting stitches out of order.

Common Stitching Abbreviations

The following universal abbreviations will come in handy when you're working with pattern stitches.

Abbreviation	What It Means
c2b	Cable 2 back
c4b	Cable 4 back
c2f	Cable 2 front
c4f	Cable 4 front
cn	Cable needle
k	Knit
p	Purl
rs	Right side
ws	Wrong side

Simple Patterns That Use the Basic Stitches

In the preceding chapter, you learned the garter stitch and stockinette stitch. Both these stitches are made by changing how you arrange rows of knitting and purling. Now you're going to learn some more stitches that you make by arranging stitches within a single row. Most of these patterns will look familiar. They're commonly used in knitted items.

Pointers

When you work knit and purl stitches on the same row, pay very special attention to the position of the yarn before you start the next stitch. You'll need to move the yarn into position to get ready for the next stitch. Remember: Yarn in back for knitting, yarn in front for purling.

Seed Stitch

Seed stitch is a wonderful basic pattern that dresses up plain sweaters or jackets. In addition, because the pattern you create has the same texture on both sides, you can use seed stitch to make beautiful wool scarves or wonderful cotton washcloths.

This pattern, when completed, resembles little seeds scattered across the knit fabric.

> **Pointers**
>
> A *stitch multiple* is the number of stitches necessary to complete a pattern stitch. A pattern of knit 2, purl 2 requires 4 stitches, so it would have a stitch multiple of 4. Often a stitch multiple includes an extra stitch or two at the beginning or end of a row of patterned stitches. For example, a stitch multiple of "4 plus 2" means you can start by casting on a number divisible by 4, plus an extra 2 stitches. For this example, you could use 14:
>
> 4 (stitch multiple) × 3 (number of times you want to repeat the stitch) + 2 = 14
>
> This means you can work the pattern three times, plus have the extra two stitches required.

The seed stitch pattern.

Stitch multiple: 2.

Row 1 (right side): Knit 1, purl 1. Repeat this pattern across the row.

Row 2 (wrong side): Purl 1, knit 1. Repeat this pattern across the row.

Repeat **Rows 1** and **2** for pattern.

Keep working these two rows as long as you like. Because you are alternating knit and purl stitches, the fabric you create has an even texture all over.

Ribbing

Ribbing is a stitch made by combining knit and purl stitches to form an elastic fabric. This fabric can stretch and then return to its original shape. Ribbing often begins and ends sweater projects, as well as hats, mittens, and socks.

Ribbing uses the same knit 1, purl 1 combination you just used in the seed stitch. Unlike seed stitch, however, you align the knit and purl rows so that you create a vertical texture rather than an overall pattern.

The edges of pieces knit in stockinette stitch roll toward the knit side. This happens because the knit stitches are *slightly* thinner and shorter than the purl stitches, so the piece rolls toward the knit side. To prevent the rolling, pieces knit in stockinette stitch must be edged at the bottom with either garter stitch or a pattern that contains some knitting and purling on every row. This is why you often see sweaters edged in ribbing. The ribbing, being snug and elastic, both keeps the sweater edges from rolling and provides snug, wind-cheating openings.

In this section, you'll learn two variations on the basic rib.

Knit 1, purl 1 ribbing.

Stitch multiple: 2 plus 1.

Row 1 (right side): Knit 1. Purl 1, knit 1; repeat these last two stitches across the row.

Row 2 (wrong side): Purl 1. Knit 1, purl 1; Repeat these last two stitches across the row.

Repeat **Rows 1** and **2** for pattern.

Keep working these two rows as long as you like. The fabric you create looks a lot like the bottom of your favorite sweater. When you grow weary of ribbing, try alternating knit and purl rows to get an idea of how a sweater is created.

The elasticity of ribbing is determined by how far apart you place the knit and purl stitches. The farther apart, the less "give" in the ribbing. You're now going to try a ribbing with a little less give: knit 2, purl 2 ribbing. This creates ribs that are—as you might expect—twice as wide as knit 1, purl 1 ribbing.

Pointers _____

When working in rib, you work your stitches as they appear. In other words, if you're about to work into a smooth stitch in which the loop end is facing away from you, you knit this stitch. If you are about to work into a bumpy stitch in which the loop end faces toward you, you purl this stitch. In ribbing, the knit stitches are prominent and the purl stitches recede between the knit stitches.

Knit 2, purl 2 ribbing.

Stitch multiple: 4 plus 2.

Row 1 (right side): Knit 2. Purl 2, knit 2; repeat these last four stitches across the row.

Row 2 (wrong side): Purl 2. Knit 2, purl 2; Repeat these last four stitches across the row.

Repeat **Rows 1** and **2** for pattern.

Keep working these two rows as long as you like. The ribs are thicker than in the knit 1, purl 1 ribbing, but the fabric you create is still very elastic.

Checkers, Anyone?

In ribbing, you work your patterns vertically. When you make the checkerboard pattern, however, you form blocks or squares rather than vertical lines. The checkerboard pattern makes a visually interesting pattern that looks the same on the front and back of the fabric. This pattern is great for dishcloths, washcloths, afghans, and scarves. In fact, if you want to see a variation of this pattern in action, try the checkerboard scarf pattern in Chapter 41.

You begin working this pattern the same way you work knit 1, purl 2 ribbing. After several rows, however, you alternate the placement of the pattern.

The versatile checkerboard pattern.

Stitch multiple: 4 plus 2.

Row 1 (right side): Knit 2. Purl 2, knit 2; repeat these last four stitches across the row.

Row 2 (wrong side): Purl 2. Knit 2, purl 2; repeat these last four stitches across the row.

Row 3: Repeat **Row 1**.

Row 4: Repeat **Row 1**.

Row 5: Repeat **Row 2**.

Row 6: Repeat **Row 1**.

Repeat **Rows 1–6** for pattern.

Keep repeating these six rows until you grow tired of working the checkerboard pattern. Notice how this pattern lies flat, whereas in ribbing the knit and purl columns are much more distinct. This is much of the fun in trying new stitches—depending on how you arrange the knit and purl stitches, you can come up with many different and compelling effects.

Cable Knitting

Cable knitting has a reputation for being complex and advanced. Whereas some very intricate patterns are a challenge even for experienced knitters, the basic *cable* stitch is easy and rewarding. The pattern uses a combination of knit and purl stitches, which are then physically rearranged ("crossed over") on the fabric. The process you'll learn here is the basis of many specialized types of knitting, including the intricate Aran sweaters from Ireland.

To produce a cable, you need one piece of specialized equipment: a cable needle. If you don't have a cable needle, you can use either a double-pointed needle or a crochet hook, but the process will be a bit more awkward.

Although the strategy you're going to learn here can be applied to knitting any stitches out of order and creating eye-popping effects of texture, we'll just be making a very simple cable. This type of cable is worked in stockinette stitch, with the knitted stitches on the right side of the fabric being cabled. For the cables to stand out, plan on at least two purl stitches on either side of your *cable panel*.

Needle Talk

Cables are specialized knitting patterns created by physically moving stitches and knitting them out of their original order. In the cable's simplest form, the first half of a group of stitches is placed on "hold" while the second half is worked. The stitches on hold are then worked, creating a spiral effect. The **cable panel** is the stockinette stitch column on which the cable is worked.

Cable 4 Back (c4b)

The first of the two basic cables is a cable 4 back (c4b). This stitch makes a cable that twists to the right. In the next section, you'll learn to make a cable 4 front (c4f), which produces a cable that twists to the left.

The following instructions might seem cumbersome. Don't get discouraged reading them: It takes longer to explain cables then it does to make them.

Stitch multiple: 6 plus 2.

Row 1 (right side): Purl 2. Knit 4, purl 2; repeat the last six stitches across the row. (The four stitches you just knit are the cable panel.)

Row 2 (wrong side): Knit 2. Purl 4, knit 2; repeat the last six stitches across the row.

Row 3: Repeat **Row 1.**

Row 4: Repeat **Row 2.**

Row 5: Purl 2. Now complete these steps that follow to make your first cable. This is called a cable 4 back, abbreviated c4b.

Slip the next two stitches onto a cable needle and hold the cable needle in the back of your work.

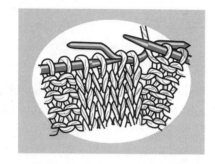

Knit the next two stitches from the left-hand needle.

Now knit the two stitches from your cable needle.

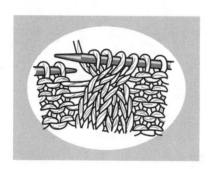

To finish Row 5, purl 2. Continue across the row, making the cable and purling 2, to the end of the row.

Row 6: Repeat **Row 2.**

Very easy, isn't it? And can you see how using a cable needle can enable you to move stitches all over your knitted fabric, cabling up and down and across? This technique is a great one for you to casually pull out in the company of people you want to impress: Your mastery of not two but three needles will have everyone impressed with your knitting prowess.

Cable 4 Front (c4f)

The cable 4 front (c4f) stitch is almost identical to the cable 4 back, with two exceptions: You hold the stitches on the cable needle in front of your work, and the stitch produces a pattern that twists to the left.

Stitch multiple: 6 plus 2.

Row 1 (right side): Purl 2. Knit 4, purl 2; repeat the last six stitches across the row. (The four stitches you knit are the cable panel.)

Row 2 (wrong side): Knit 2. Purl 4, knit 2; repeat these last six stitches across the row.

Row 3: Repeat **Row 1.**

Row 4: Repeat **Row 2.**

Row 5: Purl 2. Now complete the following steps to make the cable. This is called a cable 4 front, abbreviated c4f.

Slip the next two stitches onto a cable needle and hold the cable needle in the front of your work.

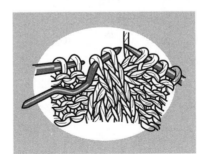

Knit the next two stitches from the left-hand needle.

Now knit the two stitches from the cable needle.

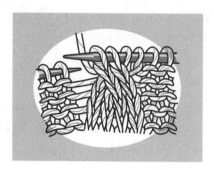

To finish **Row 5,** purl 2. Continue across the row, making the cable and purling 2, to the end of the row.

Row 6: Repeat **Row 2.**

Pointers

When working cables, you have to allow enough rows between your cable twist so that you can work the twist and keep the cable in a spiral. The greater the number of stitches in the cable panel, the more rows you need between cable twists. Pattern instructions will tell you how often to work the twist.

The Least You Need to Know

- You can make numerous stitch patterns by strategically placing knit and purl stitches on a row.

- How stitches are placed determines their final appearance: whether flat like the checkerboard pattern or alternately raised and recessed like ribbing.

- Ribbing generally edges the bottom, neck, and cuffs of sweaters because it provides an elastic edge and makes the sweater cozier.

- You make cables by using a cable needle to change the order you knit stitches.

Chapter 41

Knitting Project: Whip Up a Neck-Loving Scarf

In This Chapter

- ◆ The supplies you need to get started
- ◆ How to make a scarf that is functional, attractive, and lets you practice knitting
- ◆ Additional variations and ideas with your basic pattern

It's inevitable. Every new knitter has to make a scarf. Think about it: They're rectangular—or for new knitters—relatively square—meaning no shaping. They're useful. Gauge is relatively unimportant. They make great gifts for significant others who are proud of your newfound skills. They let you play with saucy novelty yarns without worrying about shaping a garment.

This scarf is a bit special because you won't be creating the classic garter stitch scarf most knitters begin with. Instead, you'll make a fun checkerboard-patterned scarf that hides mistakes well, but looks like it came from a more advanced knitter. Let's get started on your scarf!

What Do I Need?

These scarves are fabulous because you can make an infinite number of variations by changing the yarn, needle size, or—in some cases—the number of stitches that you cast on. You'll learn more about the variations at the end of this chapter.

Snarls

After you have a little more experience knitting, you might want to try this pattern in a fun mohair. Because the long hairs of mohair don't enable you to see stitches clearly—something crucial for new knitters—you'll save yourself a lot of frustration by steering clear of mohair your first time out.

Pointers

Many knitters find that yarn slips less on wood needles than on aluminum ones. If you're buying new needles especially for this project, consider buying wood.

To make a basic scarf about 6 inches wide by about 60 inches long, you need only three supplies:

- About 7 or 8 ounces (250 to 300 yards) of any bulky yarn. Choose any yarn that is attractive, that feels nice, and that will knit up to somewhere around 4 stitches to the inch.

- Straight, single-pointed needles in size 8, 9, or 10. The smaller the needle, the narrower the scarf will be, but any of these sizes is fine.

- A yarn needle for weaving in the ends at the beginning and end of the project.

How Do I Make It?

This scarf uses a checkerboard design, which is also called a basketweave design. You make even squares of stockinette stitch and reverse stockinette stitch. The process is simple, but the results are impressive.

You can make different sizes of checkerboards. Here is a two-stitch-wide design; your scarf has a four-stitch-wide design.

Start by casting on 24 stitches. You can actually cast on a greater or lesser number of stitches, so long as that number is divisible by 8. For this first outing, however, go ahead and cast on 24 stitches; this will give you a scarf that is approximately 6 inches wide.

Rows 1 through 4: Follow this pattern across the entire row: Knit 4, purl 4. Because you have cast on 24 stitches, you'll actually do the following:

> Knit 4, purl 4, knit 4, purl 4, knit 4, purl 4

Rows 5 through 8: Follow this pattern across the entire row: Purl 4, knit 4. Because you have cast on 24 stitches, you'll actually do the following:

> Purl 4, knit 4, purl 4, knit 4, purl 4, knit 4

You'll start to see a checkerboard pattern emerging on the scarf. Because you're working with a thick yarn, that pattern emerges fairly quickly.

At some point you will need to add on a new skein of yarn. When you see you're running low, finish the current row using the first skein. Then begin knitting the next row with the second skein. A couple stitches into the row, you can loosely tie (don't knot!) the two ends together. When you finish the project, you'll use a yarn needle to weave the ends into the finished scarf.

Next-to-last row: When the scarf is as long as you want it, finish up the next full block of checks (knit either a Row 4 or a Row 8).

Final Row: Bind off the 24 stitches on the needle.

To finish: Use a yarn needle to work the yarn ends into the scarf so that they don't show.

Snarls

If your counting gets off slightly, you might forget to change patterns every four rows and end up with a couple checks that are slightly taller than the other checks. Don't sweat it. This pattern is very forgiving; no one but you will know about the difference in check height.

Pointers

To help you keep track of count, you can tick rows on a sheet of paper. When you get to four ticks, you know it's time to change the pattern: from beginning the row with knit 4 to beginning with purl 4, or vice versa.

Variations on a Theme

Want to get adventuresome? Try these modifications:

◆ If you're not feeling up to knitting and purling, just knit every row. You'll create a beautiful, homey, nubby scarf of all garter stitch. Rustic wool looks great in garter stitch.

◆ If you want to make this scarf more luxurious, try working it in a chenille yarn. Harlequin chenille is a beautiful, multicolored yarn that works up wonderfully in this pattern on a size 8 needle. You'll definitely want to use wooden needles if you use a chenille yarn: Chenille slides all over metal needles like a car on a rainy highway.

◆ Knit with two strands of yarn together to create a beautiful blended color. You might, for example, find two gorgeous sport-weight yarns—one in purple, one in blue—and combine them for a knockout glamorous result.

◆ If terms such as "sport weight" and "chunky" have you feeling faint, turn to Chapter 35 for a quick refresher course on available yarn thicknesses.

◆ For a little added pizzazz, turn to Chapter 51 and follow the directions for adding fringe.

◆ Try knitting with a *variegated yarn* to create color blasts without worrying yourself with changing colors.

◆ After you make the scarf in bulky yarn, try it with smaller needles (say, size 5 or 6) and a worsted-weight yarn. Cast on more stitches, in multiples of 8. For example, you might cast on 40 stitches instead of 24. The scarf worked in a smaller yarn on smaller needles has a greater number of checks, giving it a different-looking texture.

The Least You Need to Know

◆ You don't have to be a knitting expert to make a professional-looking, wearable scarf.

◆ With this basic pattern you have a world of knitting opportunities open to you simply by changing the yarn, the needle size, or the number of stitches you cast on.

◆ You can track the rows you're on by ticking the row count on a piece of paper.

42

What Goes Up Must Come Down: Increasing and Decreasing

In This Chapter

♦ Understanding common increase and decrease abbreviations

♦ Adding stitches … intentionally

♦ Discreetly decreasing stitches

♦ Using increase and decrease stitches decoratively

In this chapter, you'll learn the basic procedures for increasing and decreasing stitches. In addition, however, you'll also learn how to use increasing and decreasing stitches to create interesting patterns in your knitting.

Common Increase/Decrease Abbreviations

The following abbreviations are commonly used to indicate increasing and decreasing stitches.

Abbreviation	What It Means
dec	Decrease
inc	Increase
k2Tog	Knit 2 together
m1	Make 1
psso	Pass slipped stitch over
sl	Slip
ssk	Slip slip knit
yo	Yarn over

The following sections explain what all this chicken scratch means.

When Too Much Isn't Enough: Increasing

You'll often find yourself increasing the number of stitches: as you shape a sleeve from the wrist up, for example, or as you make the thumb gusset on a mitten. This section covers three common types of increases: yarn over, bar increases, and make 1.

Yarn Over (yo)

Yarn over is the simplest way to increase, and it creates a lacy "hole" in the fabric. Obviously, you only want to use a yarn-over increase if you *want* a lacy hole in the fabric.

To yarn over when knitting, get ready to knit the next stitch, but don't insert the right-hand needle into the loop on the left-hand needle. Wrap the yarn over the needle. The needle now has an extra loop on it.

Yarn-over increases are accomplished by wrapping the yarn over the needle, creating an extra stitch and a lacy hole.

Continue knitting the row as usual. On the next row, when you knit into the extra loop, the hole will appear. To make a yarn over by purling, wrap the yarn from the front of the needle to the back, under the needle, and back to the front. Then continue purling.

Bar Increase

A bar increase is literally a "bar" of yarn where you increase stitches. The bar increase is fairly unnoticeable and creates no decorative hole, making it perfect for increasing when you want to discreetly add stitches without calling attention to the increases.

Here's how to make a bar increase when knitting:

Pointers

The bar increase is the default increase. In other words, if a pattern indicates that you should increase stitches, but it doesn't indicate which stitch to use, you can safely use the bar increase.

1. Prepare to knit a stitch. Insert the right-hand needle into the *front* of the first loop on the left-hand needle, pull the new stitch through the old stitch, but don't yet slide the stitch off the left-hand needle.

   If you're knitting left-handed, reverse the left and right needle designations.

Beginning a bar increase by knitting into the front of a stitch.

2. Now insert the point of the right-hand needle into the *back* of the first stitch on the left-hand needle and complete another knit stitch.

Knitting into the back of the same stitch.

3. Now slide the stitch off the left-hand needle. You'll have two stitches on the right-hand needle for the one stitch you had on the left-hand needle.

If you need to increase a stitch while purling a row, simply purl into the back and front of the stitch.

Make 1 (m1)

Make 1 is the trickiest of the increase stitches, but also the most versatile. This stitch creates a nearly invisible increase if done one way, or a decorative hole if done another way. The idea behind m1 is that you are *making* a stitch from the knitted fabric where one didn't exist. Here's all you need to do:

1. Find the horizontal line of yarn between the stitch on the left needle and the stitch on the right.

Finding the horizontal line between the stitches on the right-hand and left-hand needles.

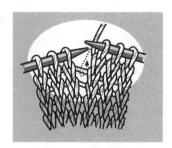

2. Insert the tip of the right-hand needle into this line; then pull the line onto the left-hand needle, making an extra stitch on that needle.

Pulling the horizontal line onto the left needle.

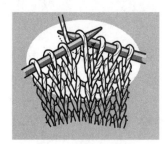

3. If you want to create a decorative hole, knit into the *front* of this new stitch and slide the stitch off the left-hand needle onto the right-hand needle.

If you want no hole, knit into the *back* of this new stitch and slide the stitch off the left-hand needle onto the right-hand needle.

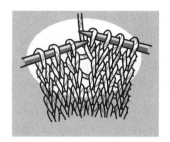

Completing the increase.

Losing the Girth: Decreasing

So what if you need to get rid of stitches rather than add them? This section covers three common types of decreases: knit 2 together (k2Tog); slip slip knit (ssk); and slip, knit, pass slipped stitch over (sl, k, psso).

> **Pointers**
>
> Knit 2 together is the default decrease. In other words, if a pattern indicates that you should decrease stitches, but it doesn't indicate which stitch to use, you can safely use knit 2 together.

Knit 2 Together (k2Tog)

Knit 2 together is the simplest and most common way to decrease stitches. As the name implies, you are knitting two stitches together. This stitch causes a decrease that leans to the right.

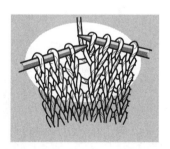

Knitting two stitches together.

To decrease this way while purling, purl two stitches together.

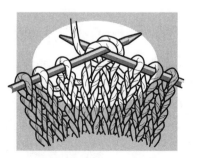

Purling two stitches together.

Slip Slip Knit (ssk)

Slip slip knit is exactly what it sounds like. You slip, you slip, and then you knit. The trick involves what you slip and how you knit. This stitch causes a decrease that leans to the left. Here's how you do it:

1. Insert the right-hand needle into the first loop on the left-hand needle, as if you were going to knit; slip the stitch onto the right-hand needle. Do the same thing with the next stitch on the needle. You now have two stitches that haven't been knitted on the right-hand needle.

Slipping a stitch.

2. Now insert the left-hand needle through both loops on the right-hand needle.

3. Bring the yarn around and knit the stitch, keeping the new stitch on the right-hand needle.

Knitting the two slipped stitches from the right-hand needle.

Slip, Knit, Pass Slipped Stitch Over (sl, k, psso)

As with slip slip knit, this decrease makes a stitch that slants to the left. Here's how you do it:

1. Insert the right-hand needle into the first loop on the left-hand needle, as if you were going to knit; slip the stitch onto the right-hand needle.

Slipping a stitch.

2. Knit the next stitch.

3. Now insert the left-hand needle into slipped stitch.

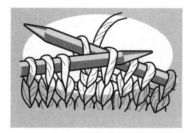

Inserting the needle into the slipped stitch.

4. Using the needle, bring the slipped stitch over the knitted stitch.

Passing the slipped stitch over the knitted stitch.

5. Pull the slipped stitch off the right-hand needle, and then release the stitch.

When Increasing and Decreasing Doesn't Do Either

You might have noticed that several of the stitches not only add or subtract stitches on the needle, they also slightly change the look of the knitted fabric. Suppose, then, that on a row you increase and decrease the same number of stitches but place those increases and decreases strategically to create a specific pattern. Do you know what you'd get? Lace.

Look at this illustration. This simple gull-wing lace is a repeat of seven stitches. To create the pattern, the knitter increased and decreased the same number of stitches in each row by using techniques you learned in this chapter: yarn over (yo), knit 2 together (k2Tog), and slip slip knit (ssk).

Gull-wing lace created by using increase and decrease stitches.

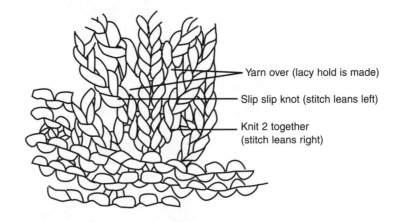

Yarn over (lacy hold is made)

Slip slip knot (stitch leans left)

Knit 2 together (stitch leans right)

Pointers _____

To try the gull-wing pattern yourself, cast on any number of stitches that is divisible by 7 (such as 14, 21, or 28). The pattern is seven stitches long, and you repeat this pattern across the row. **Row 1:** k1, k2Tog, yo, k1, yo, ssk, k1. **Row 2:** Purl. **Row 3:** k2Tog, yo, k3, yo, ssk. **Row 4:** Purl.

The Least You Need to Know

- ◆ With a few simple techniques, you can shape your knitting using increasing and decreasing stitches.

- ◆ You can strategically use increasing and decreasing stitches to create a pattern within knitted fabric rather than to shape the fabric.

Chapter 43

Knitting Project: Making a Cotton Dishcloth

In This Chapter

♦ The supplies you need to get started

♦ How to make a smashing dishcloth

♦ Additional variations and ideas with your basic pattern

Did you read the title of this chapter and snort, "Dishcloths? Who wants to make dishcloths?" Not so fast. These cloths are addicting. Pretty soon you'll find yourself scoping Sunday sale papers, looking for specials on cotton yarn. You'll find you stop using the dishwasher so that you can wear out cloths quicker, necessitating the production of more. You'll begin stringing together the cloths to make attractive ensembles to wear Saturday nights on the town.

The dishcloth you're about to make has a host of advantages: It allows you to finish a project quickly; it lets you practice basic knitting as well as increasing and decreasing; it's infinitely usable and practical; it makes a great gift; and, if the yarn is bought on sale, it costs about 50 cents to produce. In addition, its construction is interesting: Rather than knitting from top to bottom in a square, you knit from one corner to the other. Are you intrigued? Let's go!

What Do I Need?

You need very little to make these dishcloths. I give you needle suggestions, but *needle size and gauge aren't tremendously important*. If a dishcloth is a little bigger or smaller than you planned, big deal.

To make a cloth that's about 7 inches square, you need these supplies:

♦ About 1¼ ounces (60 yards) of bulky cotton yarn. Two popular brands of bulky cotton are Sugar 'n Cream and Bernat Handicrafter. Both of these brands go on sale periodically at craft superstores. One solid-colored 2½ skein of Sugar 'n Cream provides enough yarn for two dishcloths.

Pointers

Most yarns in solid colors come in slightly larger skeins than ombre or variegated yarn. For example, solid-color Sugar 'n Cream cotton is sold in 2½- ounce skeins, but variegated Sugar 'n Cream is sold in 2- ounce skeins.

♦ Straight, single-pointed needles in size 6, 7, 8, 9, or 10. Being a particularly vigorous dish-washer, I prefer size 6 needles because the resulting dishcloths are fairly firm and tight and wear longer, but any size in this range will do. Why not split the difference and use a size 8 needle? If you're buying new needles for this project, buy wood; cotton can be a tiny bit slick, and it slides less on wooden needles than on aluminum ones.

♦ A yarn needle for weaving in the ends at the beginning and end of the project.

How Do I Make It?

Start by casting on four stitches. (How in the world will you make a large dishcloth with only four stitches? Stick with me; it works.)

Row 1: Knit across. This row might be a little tricky to knit because the stitches feel very big and very loose. Don't worry about it.

Row 2: Knit two stitches. In the next stitch, knit into the front and then the back of the stitch (one bar increase made). Knit the last stitch on the row.

Row 3: Knit two stitches. Yarn over (one increase made). Knit to the end of the row.

Repeat **Row 3** until you have 46 stitches on the needle. You have a triangle at this point, and the long edge of the triangle is on your needle.

Next row: Knit one stitch, knit together the next two stitches (one decrease made), yarn over (one increase made), knit two stitches together (one decrease made), knit to the end of the row.

Repeat this last row until five stitches remain on the needle.

Next row: Knit two stitches, knit the next two stitches together (one decrease made), knit the last stitch.

Last row: Bind off the four stitches on the needle.

To finish: Use a yarn needle to work the yarn ends into the dishcloth so that they don't show.

Weaving in the ends is the last step; now your dishcloth is finished!

Pointers

Here's how the pattern would look abbreviated. Soon you'll be able to read patterns like this:

co 4. k 1 row. In next row, k2, inc in next st, k1. In next row, k2, yo, k to end of row; repeat this row until 46 sts are on needle. Next row, k1, k2Tog, yo, k2Tog, k to end of row. Repeat this row until 5 stitches remain. k2, k2Tog, k1. Bind off 4 sts.

Variations on a Theme

Want to get adventuresome? Try some of these variations:

◆ Increase the number of stitches—say to about 55—and create a fabulous face-cloth. If you're really ambitious, turn to Chapter 50 and make a crochet chain of about eight stitches; fold the chain in half and sew it on a corner of the facecloth to make a hanging loop.

Pointers

Hungry to try more? Check out www.keyway.net/crafts/ Facecloth.htm on the Internet. You'll find patterns for several dozen cloths—many with pictures showing how the finished cloth will look—all using the same inexpensive cotton yarn.

◆ Knit up batches of these dishcloths; they make great TV-watching fare once you get down the concept. Combine three or more brightly colored dishcloths in a basket with a bottle of hand lotion and some kitchen soap. Voilà! You have an instant, thoughtful, and inexpensive housewarming gift.

◆ Try new pattern stitches by making cotton swatches that can then be used as dishcloths.

The Least You Need to Know

◆ You can knit a stunning, usable piece with your limited knitting experience!

◆ Dishcloths and facecloths make savvy, usable homemade gifts.

◆ You can play with different patterns to create unique dishcloths without investing lots of time or money.

Chapter 44

Knitting in the Round

In This Chapter

- ◆ Common in-the-round abbreviations
- ◆ The advantages of knitting in the round
- ◆ Joining with a circular needle
- ◆ Using double-pointed needles

In this chapter, you'll learn the benefits of knitting in the round. You'll also learn how to use the correct tools—double-pointed needles and circular needles—to do so.

Common in-the-Round Abbreviations

The following universal abbreviations will come in handy when you're working in the round.

Abbreviation	What It Means
dpn	Double-pointed needle
pm	Place marker
rnd	Round

Why Go 'Round and 'Round?

Knitting in the round has many advantages you don't get with flat knitting. So many, in fact, that some knitters all but refuse to work pieces flat. Although I won't go so far as to ban you from using straight needles, knitting in the round does have these benefits:

♦ **You get to use the knit stitch more.** Most pieces are made of stockinette stitch (knit one row, purl one row), or some variation, and most knitters find they enjoy making the knit stitch more than they enjoy making the purl stitch. Unfortunately, knitting flat stockinette stitch pieces requires half your stitches to be purled. When you knit in the round, however, you are knitting one long, continuous row. Consequently, you never need to purl unless you're making a pattern in the knitted fabric.

♦ **Finishing on some pieces is often minimal.** Suppose you're making a sweater. If you knit the pieces flat, you'll eventually need to sew up at least six seams: two arm seams, two joining seams of arms and body, and the left and right body seams. Now look at a sweater knit in the round. You need to sew up two tiny seams only; the rest of your time is spent knitting.

Knitting in the round often lets you spend more time knitting than sewing.

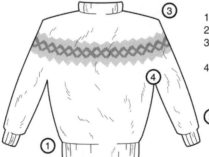

1. Body is knit in a tube.
2. Sleeves are knit tubes.
3. Sleeves and body are joined on one circular needle and yoke is knit.
4. Small seams at underarms joining body and sleeves are sewn.

♦ **You can see how a piece will fit.** Unlike straight needles, circular needles are flexible. As you're working, you can try on a pullover sweater knit in the round to see if it fits. Working pieces flat, you have guess at sizing.

♦ **Some pieces are simply better constructed when made in seamless tubes.** Socks, mittens, and the necks on turtlenecks are more ideally made tubes without seams to either irritate the wearer or break the flow of the knitted fabric.

Knitting on a Circular Needle

For new knitters, working on a circular needle is a much easier way to knit in the round than working with a set of four or five double-pointed needles. You only have one needle to navigate, and you never have to worry about stitches looking consistent, as you sometimes must when knitting on double-pointed needles.

Pointers

When knitting on a circular needle, you must be conscientious of needle length. When you knit on straight needles, you can use the part of the needle you need (such as using 14-inch needles to knit a 7-inch wide scarf). When knitting tubes on circular needles, the needle must be the same size or slightly smaller than the item you're knitting. If it's much smaller, you could have trouble keeping stitches on the needle. If it's much larger, you'll stretch your fabric. When knitting on circular needles, you may need to change to needles of different lengths—or even double-pointed needles—as you increase or decrease.

To knit on a circular needle, follow these steps:

1. Cast on the number of stitches required by the pattern. Slide a stitch marker onto the left-hand end of the needle. This marker indicates the start of every new row.

2. Lay the circular needle on a flat surface and make sure that the cast-on stitches are all facing inward—toward the middle of the circle. Check very carefully to make sure that the cast-on row is straight and that none of the stitches are twisted around the needle.

   The tail of the yarn should be on the left side, and the yarn coming from the skein should be on the right. If you're knitting left-handed, reverse these instructions.

Make sure that the stitches aren't twisted before you begin knitting.

3. Carefully pick up the needle. Slip the stitch marker from the left-hand side of the needle to the right-hand side. You're now ready to begin knitting.

4. Knit the first stitch from the left-hand side of the needle to the right-hand side. You've now joined the circle. Knit around the circle.

Beginning to knit in the round.

5. When you finish the first round and come to the stitch marker, slide it from the left to the right tip and keep knitting.

You can also use circular needles to knit flat pieces. Often when you're knitting extremely large pieces, you'll need the extra needle real estate that a 29-inch circular needle can provide. To knit flat pieces on a circular needle, pretend that the two ends of the circular needle are two single-pointed straight needles. Turn your work as you normally would, and work from one side of the needle to the other.

Snarls _____

In flat knitting, if you twist stitches around the needle, they'll right themselves when you knit the first row. In circular knitting, if you twist stitches around the needle, they'll remain twisted and you'll eventually have to rip them out and start again.

Knitting on Double-Pointed Needles

You may never need to knit on double-pointed needles. Circular needles now come in sizes so small you can knit socks on them. For some knitters, however, these needles can be hard to use—your hands may feel like they're all over each other in the middle of a tiny tube of fabric. You also need to learn to use double-pointed needles because you will need to use them if you are beginning or ending a circle of fabric. For example, if you're knitting a cap, you'll need to use double-pointed needles for the very top where the tube of fabric closes over the top of your head.

Here's how to use double-pointed needles:

1. Cast on all the stitches onto one needle. If you are making a piece small enough so that all the stitches fit onto one double-pointed needle, go ahead and use one. Otherwise, you can cast onto a straight, single-pointed needle.

2. Now determine how many needles you'll be using. You can knit using either a set of four or a set of five needles. If you use a set of four, you'll have stitches on three needles and keep one needle free. If you use a set of five, you'll have stitches on four needles and keep one needle free. Unless you can't hold all the stitches on three needles, I suggest you only work with four needles.

3. Now mentally divide the number of stitches by the number of needles holding stitches. For example, if you cast on 60 stitches and are using a set of 4 needles in which 3 needles will be active, you know that you need to have 20 stitches on each needle:

    60 (total stitches) ÷ 3 (number of active needles) = 20 (stitches on each needle)

4. Evenly divide the stitches onto the number of active needles.

5. Lay the needles on a flat surface in a triangular shape. If you're using a set of five needles, with four active, lay the needles in a diamond shape. The top of the triangle or diamond should be the two needles that are not yet joined by stitches; this is where you'll begin knitting.

    The tail of the yarn should be on the left side, and the yarn coming from the skein should be on the right. If you're knitting left-handed, reverse these instructions.

6. Make sure that the cast-on stitches are all facing inward—toward the middle of the triangle or diamond. Check very carefully to make sure that the cast-on row is straight and that none of the stitches are twisted around the needle.

Getting ready to begin knitting on double-pointed needles.

7. Using the free needle, knit the first stitch from the left side of the triangle. As you knit, pull the yarn fairly tightly; the first stitch joining double-pointed needles is sloppy unless you tug the yarn. You have now joined the circle of knitting.

Knitting the first stitch to join the round.

8. Continue knitting from the stitches on the left needle to the spare needle on the right. When you finish knitting all the stitches on that needle, you'll be holding an empty needle in your left hand.

9. Transfer the spare needle to your right hand and knit all the stitches from the next needle.

10. Keep on knitting each needle's stitches onto the spare needle, knitting round and round. Take special care to knit the first and last stitch of each needle tightly; otherwise, you could end up with a visible "seam" running up the fabric where the needles join.

Pointers

If you're not careful, you can get a stretched-looking line running up the fabric where the needles join. To prevent this problem, knit all the stitches on each needle plus one of the stitches on the next needle onto the spare needle. You then won't have a consistent spot where the needles join, so you won't have a line running up the fabric. If you do this, slip a stitch marker onto the spot where the row begins, just as you would if working on a circular needle.

The tail coming from where the needles were first joined shows you where each row starts (so that you can keep track), but you might want to stick a safety pin at this spot so that you can quickly see where the row begins. Keep moving the safety pin up as the knitted fabric grows.

The Least You Need to Know

- ◆ Knitting in the round lets you create tubes or flat circles of fabric.

- ◆ You must use the correct length needle when knitting in the round on a circular needle.

- ◆ When knitting on double-pointed needles, you need to knit the first and last stitch of each needle tightly to prevent a seam from running up the fabric.

Chapter 45

Making Your Knitting Colorful

In This Chapter

- ◆ Common colorwork abbreviations
- ◆ Striping rows
- ◆ The basics of Fair Isle knitting
- ◆ Working separate blocks of color using Intarsia knitting
- ◆ Creating a little knitting deception through duplicate stitch

Knitting and color have gone through many trends over the years—from the argyle-knitting craze of the 1950s to the color-splashed pieces that fiber artist *Kaffe Fassett* introduced in the 1980s. Although working in color is rewarding and often breathtaking, for many knitters it is one of the biggest hurdles to conquer.

Needle Talk _____

Kaffe Fassett (pronounced to rhyme with "safe asset") revolutionized the world of knitting with his colorful, fun, and sometimes outrageous patterns and by working swatches into afgans. Unlike designers who preceded him and used color conservatively, Mr. Fassett used sweater fabric in much the same way a painter uses a canvas. The result was a welcome jolt to the knitting world. Check out his patterns in the now-classic *Glorious Knits* and his website www.kaffefassett.com.

This chapter covers four ways to add color: three knitting techniques and one embroidery embellishment. We'll work through the knitting techniques in what I believe to be the easiest-to-hardest order. You can work your way through each of these methods, getting your feet wet with one technique before moving on to another.

Common Color Abbreviations

The following universal abbreviations will come in handy when you're working in color.

Abbreviation	What It Means
alt	Alternate
cc	Contrasting color
col	Color
mc	Main color
rs	Right side
ws	Wrong side

On Your Mark, Get Set, Stripe ...

The simplest means of adding color is striping. As you might guess, striping involves changing colors either at the end of a row when flat knitting or at the end of a round when knitting in the round.

To add a stripe, stop knitting with the first color and begin knitting with the second color. A few stitches into the second color, go back and loosely tie the two yarn ends together.

A couple extra pointers about striping:

♦ If you are working stripes of no more than six rows of one color, you don't need to cut the yarn. Instead, you can let the yarn end run from one stripe to another on the back of the fabric.

♦ If you are striping an item such as a scarf or afghan in which both sides will show, do cut the yarn and weave it invisibly into the knitted fabric. Loops of yarn between stripes will show and look messy.

Fair Isle Knitting

Traditional *Fair Isle knitting* is worked with two colors per row. At any time, you are using only one of those colors, so the other color is carried, or *stranded*, across the back of the piece. For this reason, if you look on the inside of a traditional Fair Isle piece, you'll see that strands of yarn run horizontally across the fabric on the wrong side.

Although Fair Isle patterns feature a burst of many shades of color, they are always created keeping two rules in mind:

♦ Each row uses only two colors, although these two colors can change every few rows.

♦ Each color in a row is used at least every five stitches. This guideline keeps the stranded yarn in the back of the piece from becoming unwieldy.

Needle Talk _____

Fair Isle knitting is a form of knitting in which two colors are used per row, and the color not in use is carried or stranded along the wrong side of the piece. **Stranding** means carrying the yarn not currently used for a stitch along the back of a piece, ready to be used. You should not strand yarn for more than five stitches at a time, and you should take care to ensure that the stranded yarn isn't left so tight that it puckers the front of the piece.

Stranding Yarn from the Right Side

Fair Isle patterns are worked in stockinette stitch, with the knit side being the right side. You keep the stranded yarn on the purl or wrong side. To work a Fair Isle pattern on the right or knit side of your piece, follow these steps:

1. Knit with the first color until you are ready to work with the second color.

2. Let go of the strand of the first color and pick up the strand of the second color.

Snarls

If you will be stranding yarn for more than five stitches, you need to use the twist method to prevent yarn from forming large loops—that can snag—on the wrong side of your piece. For details, see the section "Doing the Twist the Fair Isle Way" later in this chapter.

3. Now knit the next stitch in the second color. Be careful not to pull up the stranded yarn so tightly that the front of the piece puckers; let the stranded yarn rest easily in the back of the piece.

4. When you are finished knitting with the second color and are ready to knit again with the first, gently pull the first color across to the needle point and knit with it. Be careful not to pull up the stranded yarn so tightly that the front of the piece puckers; let it rest easily in the back of the piece.

Changing yarn colors from the first color to the second color.

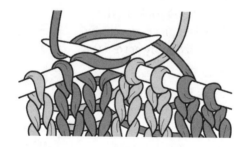

Changing yarn colors from the second color back to the first color.

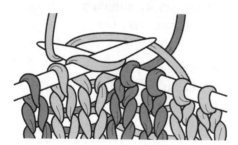

A couple things to keep in mind when using this method:

◆ Consistently keep one color of yarn stranded above the other. In the figures in this section, notice that the second color is always stranded above the first. Let the colors lay easily in place behind the sweater; don't twist them in the back of the piece.

◆ I can't say it enough … don't pull up the strands so tightly in the back that they pucker the front of the sweater. Let them lay gently on the wrong side of the sweater so that the design can lay flat.

Yarn Spinning

Color knitting is frequently associated with Fair Isle knitting. Legend has it that this form of knitting was brought to the Fair Isles by the shipwrecked sailors of the Spanish Armada in 1588.

Stranding Yarn from the Wrong Side

You purl in Fair Isle almost the same way that you knit. The only difference is that when you're purling, you're facing the stranded yarn. Here's what you do:

1. Purl with the first color until you are ready to work with the second color.

2. Let go of the strand of the first color and pick up the strand of the second color.

3. Now purl the next stitch in the second color. Be careful not to pull up the stranded yarn so tightly that the front of the piece puckers; let the stranded yarn rest easily.

Changing yarn colors from the first color to the second color.

4. When you are finished purling with the second color and ready to purl again with the first, gently pull the first color across to the needle point and purl with it. Be careful not to pull up the stranded yarn so tightly that the front of the piece puckers; let it rest easily in the back of the piece.

As with knitting in Fair Isle, be sure that you don't pull up the yarn too tightly, and be sure that you consistently strand one yarn above the other. In the illustrations in this section, the second color is consistently stranded above the first color.

Changing yarn colors from the second color back to the first color.

Doing the Twist the Fair Isle Way

Suppose you need to strand the yarn for more than five stitches? What then? Unless you take a little extra precaution to catch the yarn, you'll end up with cumbersome stranded loops that can catch and pull.

Needle Talk _____

Twisting is a method of anchoring yarn being carried in the back of your work for more than five stitches.

That extra precaution is called *twisting*. This method is similar to stranding; the only difference, however, is that the yarn is anchored every three or four stitches by twisting it around the working yarn.

To twist yarn, you literally twist the color you are not using with the color you are using. What you are doing, in essence, is catching the yarn in the back of the piece so that it can be carried more gracefully.

Twisting yarn on the right side.

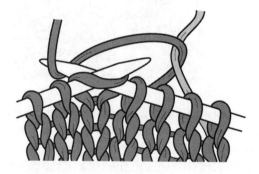

Twisting yarn on the wrong side.

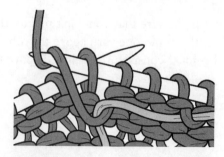

Intarsia Knitting

In Intarsia knitting, the yarn is not carried across the back of the work. Instead, a separate ball of yarn—or bobbin of yarn—is used for each block of color in the knitting. Intarsia is the most challenging type of color knitting, but it also produces some of the most spectacular results.

If you will be working with bobbins—which I recommend—wind yarn around the bobbin. Use one bobbin for each block of color. The bobbins can then hang freely from the back of your work, and as you need to use a color, you can unwind the amount that you need.

Snarls

The only time when twisting yarn can create a problem is if you are carrying a dark color behind a light color. In such cases, the twisted yarn can end up slightly showing through on the right side at the place the twist was made. The result is a fabric that doesn't have completely clean, crisp color changes.

When it comes time to change yarn colors, on the wrong side of the piece, twist the new color around the old. If you skip this step, you'll have holes in the fabric where the colors change.

Let's start by learning to work Intarsia on the wrong or purl side. You'll begin by having a separate ball of yarn or bobbin for each color block you'll be making. Then follow these steps:

1. Purl with the first color until you are ready to work with the second color.

2. Let go of the strand of the first color. Pick up the strand of the second color.

3. Wrap the strand of the second color around the strand of the first color.

4. Now purl using the second color.

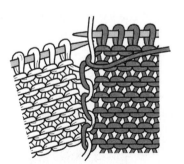

To prevent a hole in the fabric, wrap yarn strands before beginning a new color block.

When knitting in *Intarsia,* you use the same method. The only difference is that you wrap the yarn at the *back* of your work before continuing knitting in a new color.

Duplicate Stitch

Duplicate stitch is an easy way to add color to your knitwear. A duplicate stitch is exactly what it sounds like: a duplicate of a knitting stitch. You use this stitch to embroider, rather than knit, color patterns into your knitting.

Like Fair Isle and Intarsia, instructions for duplicate stitch are written in color charts; these charts are very much like needlepoint charts. Instead of seeing every square on the pattern as a spot on a canvas, however, view it as a knit stitch you embroider over.

To add duplicate stitch to a finished piece of knitting, follow these steps. If you are working a row of duplicate stitches, you will be working from right to left:

1. Determine where on your knitting you will begin the new pattern. Then thread a yarn needle with a contrasting yarn about 20 inches long.

2. With the right side of the work facing you, insert the yarn needle, back to front, into the base of the stitch you will be stitching over. Leave a 3-inch yarn tail in the back of your work.

3. Insert the yarn needle across the back of the stitch being worked, inserting it into the upper-right corner and pulling it out at the upper-left corner.

4. Now insert the needle, front to back, into the base of the stitch, where you began the *dup*licate stitch. You now have a stitch that appears to have been knit in a different color.

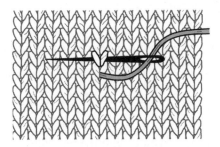

Working a duplicate stitch.

If you will be working the stitch to the left of the one you just knit, insert the needle tip, back to front, into the base of the stitch to the left.

To work duplicate stitch vertically, work the first stitch as you did for the horizontal row. When you are ready to work the second stitch, however, bring the tip of the needle up through the base of the stitch directly above the stitch that you just worked.

When you finish with the duplicate stitch embellishment, weave the ends of the yarn invisibly into the back of the knitted fabric.

Creating a vertical line of duplicate stitch.

The Least You Need to Know

- ◆ Color knitting often seems intimidating; it is actually very easy.

- ◆ If you are knitting five or fewer rows in a stripe, you don't need to cut the yarn.

- ◆ If you are going to strand more than five stitches, you need to twist the yarn on the wrong side.

- ◆ Intarsia knitting enables you to knit discrete blocks of color.

- ◆ You can use duplicate stitch to embroider color patterns on completed knitting pieces.

Chapter 46

Knitting Project: Knit Up a Hat in the Round

In This Chapter

- ◆ The supplies you need to get started
- ◆ Instructions for making a colorful hat that lets you practice working in the round, changing colors, and decreasing
- ◆ Additional variations and ideas with your basic pattern

The idea of knitting in the round can be intimidating. Reading about a concept and actually doing it are, of course, two different things. Here's a project to get you over the hump. This hat is functional, warm, stylish, and versatile. In addition, while knitting it you can try your hand at working in the round and changing colors, and you'll learn about working different numbers of stitches to accommodate for different sizes.

What Do I Need?

Because the basic hat has three colors, you can choose colors you love, mixing and matching with abandon. Spend an hour or two in a knit shop and put together as many variations as you like until you find one you adore.

> **Snarls**
>
> Unlike the two previous items you've made, gauge is important with this hat. Be sure to check your gauge or you could end up with a hat so large you resemble Mushmouth from *Fat Albert and the Cosby Kids* or so small it won't fit your schnauzer.

To make the basic hat in either an adult medium (about 18 inches around, plus some give when stretched) or an adult large (about 20 inches around, plus some give when stretched), you need the following supplies:

♦ Three different colors of bulky yarn:

About 3 ounces (100 yards) of a main color (mc)

About 1 ounce (35 yards) of a contrasting color (A)

About 1 ounce (35 yards) of a second contrasting color (B)

For this sample, I used a teal (main color), black (contrasting color A), and heather gray (contrasting color B). For maximum contrast, you want the mc to be a medium color, A to be a dark color, and B to be a light color.

♦ One set of double-pointed needles in size 8, 9, or 10, and, optionally, one 16-inch circular needle the same size. I say "about" because you will need to check gauge and make sure that your gauge matches the chapter instructions. Try the size 9 needle first; if your gauge shows too many stitches to the inch, try a size 10. If the size 9 shows too few stitches to the inch, try a size 8.

♦ About 10 stitch markers.

♦ A yarn needle for weaving in the ends at the beginning and end of the project.

> **Snarls**
>
> Double-pointed needles can sometimes be hard to navigate, especially the first time you use them, so I suggest that you instead try to find a 16-inch circular needle. If you opt for the circular needle, you will need to switch to double-pointed needles after you begin decreasing stitches—at whatever point continuing to use the circular needle heavily stretches the fabric. If you do get only double-pointed needles, look for wood, which has a less slick surface than aluminum.

How Do I Make It

The brim of this hat rolls naturally because it is knit in stockinette stitch; this means that by knitting every stitch, you can create a distinctive design element. (Can you guess how roll-neck sweaters are made? Exactly. You work the neck in stockinette stitch.)

To begin this pattern, swatch the yarn with size 9 needles. If you measure your gauge and find that it's at 4 stitches to the inch, you're ready to begin. If you end up with a different gauge, you'll need to try a different-size set of needles until the gauge matches four stitches to the inch.

Because this pattern shows directions for two different sizes (adult medium and adult large), you might want to read through the pattern and circle the numbers that apply to the size you make. You'll then be able to clearly see which directions to follow.

Gauge: Four stitches to the inch; be sure to check your gauge.

After you have the right gauge, use the main color (mc) to cast on 72 stitches for an adult medium hat or 80 stitches for an adult large hat. If you are using double-pointed needles, divide these stitches evenly across the needles. (Remember to keep one needle free to work the stitches.)

Place a stitch marker right before the first stitch you are about to knit. Now join the round, being very careful not to twist the stitches.

Snarls

When you're knitting with a set of double-pointed needles (as opposed to one circular needle), you can very easily accidentally pick up "extra" stitches at the end of the needle. Watch your first several rounds carefully and count the number of stitches on each needle as you finish with each needle.

Follow these steps to knit the hat:

1. Knit 2½ inches in the main color for a medium hat or 3 inches for a large hat.

2. Change to color A and knit two rounds.

3. Change to color B and knit six rounds.

4. Change back to color A and knit two more rounds.

5. Change to mc and continue knitting. For the medium-size hat, knit until you have 6½ inches total from the beginning row. For the large-size hat, knit until you have 7 inches total from the beginning row.

6. Now you begin decreasing. To do so, knit six stitches, knit two stitches together, and slide a marker onto the needle.

   Complete this step 9 times total for the medium hat or 10 times total for the large hat. If you're making the medium hat, you now have 64 stitches on the needle(s); if you're making the large hat, you now have 72 stitches on the needle(s).

7. Knit one round.

8. Knit to two stitches before the first marker, knit two stitches together. Slide the marker to the right-hand needle.

   If you're making the medium hat, complete this step a total of 9 times, or 10 times for a large hat.

9. Repeat Steps 7 and 8 until you have only two stitches between each marker.

   If you are using a circular needle, at some point the stitches will begin to stretch to accommodate the needle. At that point, you need to switch to using double-pointed needles.

   If you're making the medium hat, you now have 18 stitches total on the needle(s); if you're making the large hat, you have 20 stitches total on the needle(s).

10. Knit one round.

11. Knit two stitches together. Repeat this step across the row, simultaneously removing the stitch markers from the needle. (They no longer serve any purpose.)

    If you're making the medium hat, you now have 9 stitches on the needle(s), or 10 stitches for a large hat.

12. If you're making the medium hat, knit one; then knit two stitches together four times. You now have five stitches on the needle.

    If you're making the large hat, knit two stitches together five times. You now have five stitches on the needle.

13. Break off the yarn, thread a yarn needle, and run the needle through the stitches remaining on your knitting needles. Draw up this yarn so that you close the hole in the top of the hat.

To finish, use a yarn needle to weave all yarn ends into the fabric of the inside of the hat.

Variations on a Theme

Want to stray from the beaten path? Try some of these modifications:

◆ Make a cuffed edge rather than a rolled one. To do this, work the first 2½ inches in knit 2, purl 2 ribbing. Then purl one row to make a turning point; when you wear the hat, you'll fold the cuff up at this point. Then continue knitting. Because the cuff obscures the original stripe, why not knit the ribbed cuff in one color and the rest of the hat in another?

◆ Add a pom-pom to the top, using all three colors from the hat.

◆ Make the hat for a baby. To do so, use double-knitting-weight yarn. You'll need 1½ ounces main color, ½ ounce contrasting color A, and 1 ounce contrasting color B. Use size 5 needles (or the size necessary to get a gauge of 5 stitches to the inch); if you are beginning on a circular needle, use a 16-inch needle. Cast on 72 stitches for a 6-month-old size and 80 stitches for about a 1-year-old size. When you've knit 2 inches, add the stripe. Begin decreasing at 4 inches for a small size and 4¼ inches for a larger size. Shape in exactly the same way as the adult size.

The Least You Need to Know

◆ Changing needle size and yarn thickness, you can change some adult-size items into baby sizes.

◆ When making items such as clothing, carefully checking gauge is very important.

47

Talking the Talk: Reading a Knit Pattern

In This Chapter

- ◆ Deciphering common knit abbreviations
- ◆ Working with the language of repeats
- ◆ Reading charts rather than words
- ◆ Cracking the sizing code

Open a book of knitting patterns, and your memories might take you back to childhood games where you drew treasure maps written in a secret code known only by your best friends—k1, p2, sl st, k2Tog, psso. Does this tell you how to make a sweater or where to find the chest of gold?

Because longhand knitting patterns would be cumbersome to write and inefficient to read, a standard pattern-writing abbreviated language was devised. This language enables you to work through and understand patterns more quickly, and to carry a pattern for a complex Aran sweater on a single sheet of paper rather than in a novel-sized book. Like your secret backyard language, however, unless you know the code, you can't read the pattern.

After you finish reading this chapter, you'll be able to decipher abbreviations, repeats, and even wordless patterns.

Common Knit Abbreviations

Most common knit terms have a universal abbreviation. In almost every pattern you read, these abbreviations allow complex patterns to be written quickly and cleanly. As you'll find when you begin knitting more frequently, this abbreviation system actually makes patterns less cumbersome to read and follow.

Abbreviation	Full Name
alt	Alternate
approx	Approximately
beg	Begin(ing)
bet	Between
bo	Bind off
cc	Contrasting color
c4b	cable 4 back
c4f	cable 4 front
col	Color
cont	Continue(ing)
dbl	Double
dec	Decrease(ing)
dpn	Double pointed
fin	Finished
foll	Following
g or gr	Gram(s)
in(s)	Inch(es)
inc	Increase(ing)
k	Knit
k2Tog	Knit 2 together
kbl	Knit through back of loop
kwise	Knitwise
lp(s)	Loop(s)
mc	Main color

Abbreviation	Full Name
med	Medium
mm	Millimeter
m1	Make 1
mult	Multiple
opp	Opposite
oz	Ounces
p	Purl
p2Tog	Purl two together
pat(s)	Pattern(s)
pm	Place marker
p tbl	Purl through back of loop
psso	Pass slip stitch over
pwise	Purlwise
rem	Remaining
rep	Repeat
rev st st	Reverse stockinette stitch
rib	Ribbing
rnd(s)	Round(s)
rs	Right side
sc	Single crochet
sk	Skip
sl	Slip
sl st	Slip stitch
sp(s)	Space(s)
ssk	Slip slip knit
st(s)	Stitch(es)
st st	Stockinette stitch
tbl	Through back of loop
tog	Together
ws	Wrong side
wyib	With yarn in back
wyif	With yarn in front

continues

continued

Abbreviation	Full Name
yb	Yarn back
yf	Yarn forward
yo	Yarn over
ytb	Yarn to back
ytf	Yarn to front

And Asterisks for All!

When you first glance at a knit pattern, you'll initially adjust your glasses and get ready to write an angry letter to the publisher. With so many weird symbols, it looks like a computer program gone awry.

Amazingly, these patterns are created using standardized symbols written in conjunction with the knit abbreviations. The system *does* make sense. If you need help, refer to the list of knit abbreviations.

The Asterisk Makes Its Mark

Asterisks play a crucial role in knit patterns. They indicate the start of a section that you will repeat.

When you see any of these asterisk combinations, it means "repeat from":

   *

   **

   ***

In other words, You need to repeat the instructions following the *, **, or *** as many times as given. You would first work the information given once. Then you would repeat that information as many times as specified.

Here's an example:

   *k2Tog, yo. Repeat from * to end of row.

This pattern is telling you to knit two stitches together and then do a yarn over. You then repeat these two procedures all the way across the rest of the row.

Parenthetical Considerations

Parentheses work in much the same way as asterisks. When you see the following, it means "work what is in the parentheses as many times as given":

( )

Here's an example:

(p2, kb1, p1) 3 times

This means that you should purl two, knit to the back of the loop in the next stitch, and purl one a total of three times.

Plus a Couple Extra Knit Stitches ...

Plus signs indicate that you should repeat something between the plus signs. When you see the following, it means "work the instructions between the plus signs and repeat as many times as specified":

+ to +

Here's an example:

+p1, k2Tog, p1+. Repeat + to + 5 more times.

This means you would purl one, knit two together, and purl one; you would then repeat this sequence five more times.

Pointers

Reading PatternSpeak becomes easier when you really start to work from a pattern. If you're initially confused about what the instructions are saying, write them out in longhand and work through them step-by-step. This method might take a little extra time, but it will help you get used to reading patterns. In addition, it might save you the time and heartbreak of ripping out and redoing your work.

Charting the Patterns

Recently, patterns have been written more in charted symbols than in written words. These symbols show either changes in the stitching, such as changing from knitting to purling or adding a cable, or they show changes in color. This strategy has several advantages:

♦ Charted patterns enable you to easily see where you are in a pattern and help ensure that you are on the right track. With a visual pattern, you can somewhat compare the pattern with your knitted fabric. If the two match, you're okay. If not, you might need to look at the pattern again.

Pointers

As a help when reading charted patterns, place a Post-it note on the pattern so that it aligns with the bottom of the row you're currently working. Each time you finish a row, move the paper up one row on the chart. If the phone rings and you get into a long conversation, you'll be able to come back to your knitting without spending 15 minutes figuring out which row you were on.

♦ Charted patterns generally contain fewer printed errors. No one's perfect, and knitted patterns *can* contain typos and other errors. Just as you can verify your work against the pattern, so can the author. If written instructions are incorrect, the mistakes can sometimes go unnoticed. Patterns can all too easily be printed with typos such as "k3" rather than "k2." In the middle of a complex series of instructions, this seemingly simple mistake can cause even the most stoic knitter to break down. It's much harder, however, to print a chart incorrectly; if the pattern in the printed chart doesn't resemble what it's supposed to resemble, the author can generally see immediately that something is amiss.

♦ After you get the hang of it, charted patterns are easy to follow—for many people, easier than written patterns.

Take a look at this pattern for a 10-stitch cable pattern. To read the pattern, work the odd rows from right to left and the even rows from left to right.

For this pattern, start the first row in the lower-right corner, and follow **Row 1** from right to left, **Row 2** from left to right, and so on. If you are a left-handed knitter, reverse this: Read odd rows from left to right and even rows from right to left.

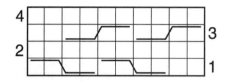

Charted patterns often make working in complex patterns easier.

KEY

☐ Knit on the right side, purl on the wrong side.

Slip first 2 stitches to cable needle and hold in back of work. Knit 2. Knit 2 from cable needle.

Slip first 2 stitches to cable needle and hold in front of work. Knit 2. Knit 2 from cable needle.

Here's how the pattern would look if written out:

> **Row 1:** K2, c4f twice.
>
> **Row 2:** P across.
>
> **Row 3:** C4b twice, k2.
>
> **Row 4:** P across.

Can you seen how looking at the chart might give you a better idea of where your stitches will fall?

Snarls

This parenthetical annotation system is wonderful for writing lots of instructions compactly, but it can be hazardous if you're not paying close attention. To avoid accidentally following the wrong sizing instructions, before you start knitting, go through the pattern and circle the instructions for the size that you will be knitting. You can then easily see the numbers you need to follow.

Calling All Sizes

Knitting patterns have one more unique attribute that you need to understand. Because sweater patterns are made to be adaptable to both your petite little sister and your oversized Uncle Fred, they are written with the variations for each size included. These variations are typically included in parentheses.

A pattern, for example, might begin like this:

To fit chest size 34" (36", 38", 40", 42")

This means that the entire pattern is written using this same parenthetical annotation for larger sizes. If you are making the 36-inch size, then, for any shaping or patterning instructions you will always follow the first number in the parentheses. For example, as you're shaping the armhole, you might see the following:

bo 6 (8, 9, 10, 12) st at beg of next row.

You would then bind off eight stitches—the first number in the parentheses. Follow this same system throughout the pattern.

The Least You Need to Know

♦ Universal abbreviations mean that patterns can be read and written more quickly and effectively.

♦ Asterisks, parentheses, and plus signs are used to indicate repeats in a pattern.

♦ Charted patterns enable you to verify your stitches by comparing the knitted fabric with the chart.

♦ Patterns often come with various sizes written into the pattern; you follow the number that aligns with the size you want to make.

48

Correcting Common Knitting Gaffes

In This Chapter

- ◆ Stopping mistakes before they happen
- ◆ Turning twisted stitches
- ◆ Catching dropped stitches
- ◆ Correcting sloppy stitches
- ◆ Letting 'er rip

We all make mistakes. Even in knitting, one of the most relaxing and enjoyable of pursuits, mistakes occur that can dampen your enthusiasm for the craft.

Fortunately, most knitting *faux pas* are minor and easily correctable. This chapter walks you through the best ways to prevent and correct the most common mistakes, and helps you determine when to forget correcting and just start over.

As you learn any new craft, you need to feel comfortable and in control. Don't be afraid to make or to correct mistakes.

Taking the Bull by the Horns: Preventing Mistakes

Some the most common knitting errors are due to not watching what you're doing. As you become adept at knitting, you won't even have to look at your knitting to know something's gone awry. Instead, your hands will know what to feel for as you're flying across each row, and they'll stop you when something's amiss.

When you're first learning to knit, however, you have to be much more conscious of what your hands are doing. You can usually avoid the two common mistakes—dropped stitches and adding stitches—if you watch your hands as you knit.

In addition, count the stitches after every completed row. Sure, this exercise seems tedious, but you'll immediately know whether you lost or added a stitch. You can then look over the row, one stitch at a time. Check to see whether a stitch has been dropped from the needle or whether the needle contains a loop of yarn that isn't part of a stitch.

Needle Talk _____

Twisted stitches are stitches twisted on your needle. Because the knitted loops are twisted, the stitches are tighter than correctly knit stitches and don't open when stretched.

Turning Twisted Stitches

In knitting, *twisted stitches* are exactly what the name says: stitches that get twisted on your needle. You generally get twisted stitches one of two ways: by knitting into the front, rather than the back, of the needle, or by incorrectly unraveling stitches (which you'll learn about later in this chapter).

To correct twisted stitches, use the point of the needle that the stitch isn't on to slide the stitch off the needle. Untwist it, and place it back on the needle.

Pointers _____

If you feel fairly comfortable with knitting, you can correct twisted stitches by the way you insert your needle while you are working. To correct a stitch, knit or purl through the back loop on a twisted stitch.

Untwisting a twisted stitch.

Catching Dropped Stitches

Probably the most common mistake in knitting is losing a stitch. You start out with 20 stitches on your needle and after a period of time, you find you have only 19.

Being an optimist, you might shrug and decide to just add back a couple stitches and be on your way. Trouble is, a *dropped stitch* has a tendency to run. Think of what pantyhose do when they get a small hole; your knitted items will do the same. Now think how wonderful it would be if you could close up the pantyhose hole before it ran. When you're knitting, you can.

Needle Talk _____

Dropped stitches are stitches that accidentally slide off the needle during knitting. If left unfixed, dropped stitches can run down through the knitted fabric.

Using Needles to Pick Up a Dropped Knit Stitch

Suppose you're working in stockinette stitch (knit 1 row, purl 1 row) and notice you have a dropped stitch in the row below. What now? Fortunately, you can use your knitting needles to salvage the stitch before it runs farther down the knitted piece. Here's all you do:

1. From the front (right side) of your work, knit across the row to the position of the dropped stitch.

Yarn Spinning _____

Some patterns call for you to drop stitches intentionally. First, you knit an entire piece. On the last row, you drop specific stitches—maybe every tenth stitch. The result is a lacelike pattern running vertically through the piece.

Locate the dropped stitch and knit to it.

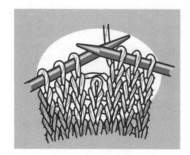

2. Insert the right-hand needle, from front to back, into both the loop of the dropped stitch and the horizontal strand of yarn in the row above the dropped stitch. Make sure that the strand is positioned left of the stitch on the needle.

Insert the needle into the dropped stitch and the line of yarn above the stitch.

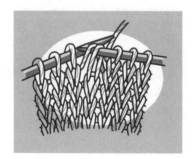

3. Insert the left-hand needle, back to front, into the loop of the dropped stitch. Then lift the loop over the strand of yarn on the needle. This action is just like binding off a stitch. Now the corrected stitch is on the right-hand needle.

Pass the dropped stitch over the horizontal bar of yarn.

4. Slip the corrected stitch from the right-hand needle to the left-hand needle.

Move the stitch to the left-hand needle and keep on knitting.

Knit away. The dropped stitch is now history.

Using Needles to Pick Up a Dropped Purl Stitch

Picking up a purl stitch is a lot like picking up a knit stitch; you just need to reverse a few things. Here's how:

1. Purl across the row to the position of the dropped stitch.

Locate the dropped stitch and purl to it.

2. Insert the right-hand needle, from front to back, into both the loop of the dropped stitch and the horizontal strand of yarn in the row above the dropped stitch. Make sure that the strand is positioned left of the stitch on the needle.

*Insert the needle into the
dropped stitch and the line of
yarn above the stitch.*

3. Insert the left-hand needle, from back to front, into the loop of the dropped
   stitch. Then lift the loop over the strand of yarn on the needle. This action
   is just like binding off a stitch. Now the corrected stitch is on the right-hand
   needle.

*Pass the dropped stitch over
the horizontal bar of yarn.*

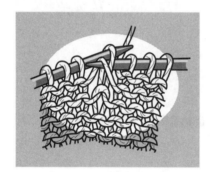

4. Slip the corrected stitch from the right-hand needle to the left-hand needle.

*Move the stitch to the left-
hand needle and keep on
purlin'.*

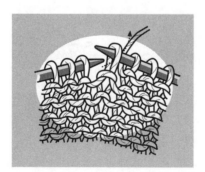

That's all there is to it.

How to Become a Major Pick-Up Artist

At times, a dropped stitch goes unnoticed for several rows before you discover that you have a problem. When you notice the mistake, attach a safety pin just under the dropped stitch so that you can identify the area.

Although you can use a knitting needle and laboriously follow the stitch-saving steps in the previous sections, you'll find the work goes much faster with a crochet hook.

To pick up the stitches, insert the crochet hook, front to back, into the dropped stitch. Now use the hook to catch the horizontal line of yarn above the dropped stitch, and pull this yarn through the stitch. Continue working the stitch up the "ladder" of yarn until you get to the end.

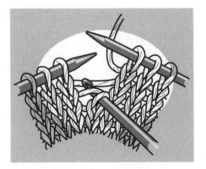

Using a crochet hook to work a dropped stitch up the "ladder."

To pick up stitches when purling, follow the same steps as for knitting, but insert the hook back to front.

To pick up a dropped stitch when working garter stitch (knit every row), alternate the knitting and purling instructions. Make sure that you use the knitting technique when the row is smooth and the purling technique when the row is bumpy.

Using a crochet hook to fix a dropped stitch on a garter stitch piece.

Showing Sloppy Stitches Who's Boss

At some point, you're going to stop knitting, hold up your piece admirably, and notice a hole in the middle. You've checked; it's not a dropped stitch. It's just a much larger (shall we dare say sloppier) stitch than the others in the piece. What to do?

Grab your spare knitting needle and gently poke into the stitches surrounding the larger stitch. You're trying to slightly stretch those stitches to take up yarn and even out all the stitches. After a minute or so of adjusting the surrounding stitches, you'll never know the larger stitch was there.

When All Else Fails: Let 'Er Rip!

Some mistakes are just too time-consuming or too impossible to fix. Suppose, for example, that you're working a cable and find one row where you forgot to work the pattern. If you can live with it, do. If you determine that you'll always feel inferior when you look at the product, get ready to learn the fine art of unraveling.

Snarls

If you don't insert an unraveled stitch onto the needle correctly, you'll wind up with a twisted stitch. Be sure that when you place an unraveled stitch on the left-hand needle, the part of the loop in front of the needle leans toward the right.

Taking Out Just a Few Stitches

If the area you need to unravel to is one row or fewer of stitches, you'll want to pull the stitches out one stitch at a time.

To unravel stitches one at a time, follow these steps:

1. Slide the first stitch off the right-hand needle.

2. Gently tug the yarn that "feeds" into your knitting to unravel the stitch.

3. Place the remaining stitch onto the left-hand needle. Be sure to insert the needle into the middle of the loop.

Unraveling knit stitches one by one.

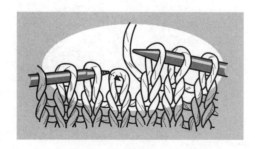

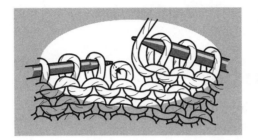

Unraveling purl stitches one by one.

Going Wild!

Let's say that the mistake isn't three stitches down the needle, but three inches down the knitted fabric. Heartbreaking as undoing work can be, you're about to be introduced to the most cathartic move in knitting: *ripping out* stitches.

To unravel several rows of stitches, first use a safety pin to mark the offending row. Then slide the knitting off the needles and pull the yarn with wild abandon.

When you get down to one row above the problem row, slow down. Use the procedure in the preceding section to, one by one, unravel the stitches and place them back on the needle.

Wind the unraveled thread back on your ball, take a deep breath, and proceed.

Extra, Extra!

Another common knitting gaffe is to end up with too many stitches on a row. If you find one row a bit hefty, look carefully at your work to identify the problem. Then mark the trouble spot with a safety pin. Chances are, you grabbed an extra loop of yarn and didn't notice the problem until you had knit several rows.

To correct the mistake, unravel your work to the problem stitch. Unravel that stitch. Count

Snarls

To avoid an extra stitch at the beginning of a row, make sure your yarn is at the *back* of your work when you start a knit row and in the *front* of your work when you start a purl row.

Needle Talk

Ripping out means unraveling or pulling out stitches. You rip out when you find that you don't like the look or size of the knitted fabric, or when you find a mistake that you need to undo.

Yarn Spinning

The members of the electronic KnitList on the Internet have their own words for ripping out stitches (www.knitlist.com). *Tink* refers to taking out stitches one at a time; *tink* is *knit* backward. *Frog* refers to ripping out large batches of knitting; they claim that "rip it! rip it!" sounds like "ribbit! ribbit!"

the stitches to make sure the number is correct. Go grab a cup of tea, and come back to your knitting.

The Least You Need to Know

♦ Mistakes don't have to frighten you away from knitting—many are either avoidable or easily fixable.

♦ You can use a crochet hook to catch stitches that you dropped several rows back.

♦ You can disguise a too-big stitch by evening out the stitches around it.

♦ Unraveling great loads of knitting can be terribly cathartic.

Part 5

Crocheting

This part will teach you the basics of crocheting, including the slight differences among the tools, the stitches and factors involved with color, and shaping. Patterns can be a bit difficult with this style, so this part shows you the ins and outs, ensuring you understand the complexities. By the end, you'll be creating your own afghan like a pro.

Chapter 49

An Overview of Crochet Tools

In This Chapter

- ◆ Understanding the anatomy of a crochet hook
- ◆ Unscrambling the various needle sizes
- ◆ Additional accessories to enhance your crocheting

Crocheting requires two basic supplies: yarn and a crochet hook. You learned about your yarn options in Chapter 35; now it's time to learn about crochet hooks. This chapter also covers some of the other available tools that can make your crocheting easier.

Crochet Hooks

Crochet hooks come in sizes so small that you can only feel the point with your fingertip and so large they look as though they could double as boat anchors. As you'd expect, they also come in every size in between.

For every yarn on the market, there is a *suggested* hook size to use with it. Despite the suggestions, however, you won't find a scientific formula for combining hook size and yarn weight. Because each individual project is designed with a specific look in mind, you might find yourself crocheting cotton thread with a large needle or working worsted-weight cotton with a small one. In addition, crocheters differ in how tightly or loosely they crochet, which makes it even more difficult to come up with a set formula.

✋ **Pointers**

The most important concept you can learn in your hook-size selection is gauge: How many stitches you need to crochet to make an inch. Gauge varies based on the type of yarn you select, the size of hook you use, and how tightly or loosely you crochet. If you're feeling woozy by all this talk, flip back to Chapter 35 for a refresher on gauge.

The humble crochet hook is actually made up of four distinct parts.

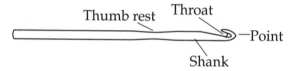

Parts of a Crochet Hook

Before I go into crochet hook sizes, let's take a look at what a crochet hook really looks like and what each part is named.

Each part of the hook has a unique function:

◆ **The point** goes into the stitch on the crocheted fabric.

◆ **The throat** catches the yarn. The throat needs to be large enough to accommodate the yarn being used.

🧵 **Yarn Spinning**

During the mid-nineteenth century, the noble ladies of England had time on their hands and an interest in finding a hobby. They turned to crochet. As you might expect, the craft experienced a surge in popularity at this time.

◆ **The shank** holds the loops with which you're working. The shank is really what determines the size of your stitches.

◆ **The thumb rest** is just that—a place to rest your thumb so that you can rotate the hook with ease while working.

These four simple parts have been designed for comfort and to help speed your work.

Reverting to Type: Crochet Hook Sizes and Types

Crochet hooks come in different sizes—and different materials. The material used to make the hook corresponds with the hook's size.

Steel hooks are the smallest: Some are so fine you might mistake them for darning needles. Next in size are aluminum and plastic hooks. In addition, some wooden hooks are available in larger sizes. The average length of a crochet hook is about 6 inches.

Here's where things get tricky. Crochet hooks are sized according to three different systems: U.S., English, and Continental systems. Each system uses a different numbering or lettering system to indicate size. As a result, a new crocheter not familiar with the differences in these three types can become puzzled fairly quickly.

To simplify it all, earmark this page. You'll want to refer often to the charts that follow.

U.S.	1	2	3	4	5	6	7	8	9	10	11	12	13	14
English	3/0	2/0	1/0	1	1 1/2	2	2 1/2	3	4	5	5 1/2	6	6 1/2	7
Continental Rim	3	2.5		2		1.75	1.5	1.25	1	0.75		0.6		

Sizing chart for steel crochet hooks.

U.S.	1/B	2/C	3/D	4/E	5/F	6/G	8/H	9/I	10/J	10 1/2 /K
English	12	11	10	9	8	7	6	5	4	2
Continental Rim	2 1/2	3		3 1/2	4	4 1/2	5	5 1/2	6	7

Sizing chart for aluminum and plastic crochet hooks.

Although crochet hook sizing and the wide variety of hook options might seem intimidating, it can also work to your advantage. If you buy a larger size hook and experience some difficulties with the hook and the yarn, try the same size in another material. For example, you might find you prefer wood to aluminum. In addition, try a hook with a differently shaped point—perhaps one that's more round than sharply angled. With some practice, you'll find the type of hook you prefer, and you'll use this type for all your projects.

Afghan Hooks

One type of specialized crochet—called *Afghan or Tunisian crochet*—requires you to hold many stitches on the hook simultaneously. Obviously, if the average length of a crochet hook is 6 inches, you'd run out of room quickly on a regular crochet hook. As you might expect, specialized tools were created to make a crocheter's life easier.

> **Needle Talk**
>
> **Afghan (Tunisian) crochet** is a special type of crochet that requires the crocheter to hold many stitches on the crochet hook. Special Afghan hooks that look like a cross between a crochet hook and a knitting needle are available for this purpose.

Afghan hooks are much longer than regular crochet hooks; they come in three lengths: 9 inch, 14 inch, and 20 inch. In addition, the hooks have a cap or knob on the opposite end from the hook; this knob serves the same purpose as the knob at the end of a knitting needle: It keeps stitches from falling off the end.

Now you can even find Afghan hooks that have a long flexible cord on one end. These cords hold many stitches, and the flexibility of the cord means that your work can more easily rest in your lap.

Flexible Afghan hooks make Afghan crochet even easier.

Measuring Tools

The most important accessory is a good tape measure or a gauge counter. As you learned in Chapter 36, accurate gauge is often crucial in crocheting, and good measuring tools are crucial to accurate gauge. In addition, you'll use the tape measure for a million different measuring tasks: cutting fringe, counting a number of inches on a sweater front before shaping for armholes, verifying the size of the crocheted placemats, and so on.

Bobbins

Bobbins are helpful accessories to have on hand when you're working in multiple colors. These little gems are made of plastic and are easy to find in yarn shops. Bobbins look similar to bread-bag tabs, only larger. To use a bobbin, wrap yarn around it and crochet from the bobbin, rather than from a ball of yarn. You can then unwind only what you need for the next few stitches, and you won't have to negotiate cumbersome amounts of yarn.

If you're feeling ambitious, you can make your own bobbins out of cardboard. Just follow the shape of the illustration of any of the following bobbins

> **Needle Talk** _____
>
> **Bobbins** are plastic tabs that hold small amounts of yarn. They are invaluable when working on pieces that have many color changes.

Bobbins enable you to work in multiple colors without creating a tangled mess of yarn.

Stitch Markers

Stitch markers are also handy. When you work certain patterns, you need to keep track of information such as where to increase or when to repeat a particular stitch pattern. To use stitch markers, you affix them to the crocheted fabric. If you don't want to purchase another accessory, just use a safety pin.

> **Needle Talk** _____
>
> **Stitch markers** are little rings of plastic you use to mark a specific spot in a piece.

Stitch markers.

Finishing Accessories

To finish your pieces, you'll need some needles and pins—at least one needle and a few pins.

You'll use the pins to hold your work together for sewing seams and for blocking pieces. (In a pinch, you can also use straight pins as stitch markers, but I don't recommend it; inadvertently finding a pinpoint is jolting.)

Yarn needles, which have dull rather than sharp points, enable you to weave in yarn ends and sew together seams. These needles come in varying sizes to accommodate different thicknesses of yarn.

The Least You Need to Know

♦ Crochet hooks come in three varieties—U.S., English, and Continental styles—and each uses a different sizing scheme.

♦ Crochet hooks are made from different products (wood, aluminum, steel, and plastic) and with differing point shapes. You can experiment to find the shape and material you like best.

♦ A couple of accessories such as bobbins and yarn needles will enhance your crocheting.

50

Getting Started: Basic Crochet Stitches

In This Chapter

- ◆ Getting ready to start hooking
- ◆ First things first: making a foundation chain
- ◆ Practicing the basic stitches
- ◆ Left-handed crochet principles

The step-by-step, hand-by-hand illustrations in the pages that follow will make it easy to learn how to crochet. By the time you finish this chapter, with crochet hook comfortably in hand, you'll be able to make a slip knot and a chain, work slip stitches, and perform stitches with ease.

Common Basic Crochet Abbreviations

The following abbreviations are commonly used in *crochet* patterns.

Abbreviation	What It Means
ch st	Chain stitch
dc	Double crochet
hdc	Half-double crochet
sc	Single crochet
sl st	Slip stitch
trc	Triple crochet
yo	Yarn over

The following sections explain the meaning of all this mumbo jumbo.

Basic Training

Like all needlecrafts, crochet begins with getting a proper grip on your tools. There are two easy ways to hold a crochet hook. Try them and decide which feels best for you.

You can hold the hook one of two ways. Either position and lightly grip your hook in your hand as you would hold a pencil, or hold the hook how you would grip a spoon when stirring something thick.

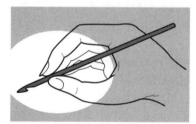 

Slip Knot in the Making

With the crochet hook comfortably in your hand you're ready to begin working with the yarn. First, make a slip knot and attach the yarn to your hook. Here's a simple three-step way to tie the slip knot.

Loop the yarn around your left index finger.

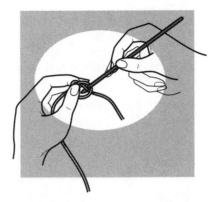

Slip the yarn from your finger and hold the loop between your thumb and index finger.

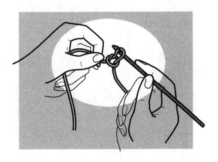

Use the crochet hook, held in your right hand, to draw the loop up and around the hook.

Finally, gently pull each of the ends in opposite directions. This tightens the knot and makes it smaller. It's that simple!

The Whole Yarn in Your Hands

The techniques in this section enable you to control how the yarn is "fed" into your work. Take the yarn with your left hand. With the palm of your left hand facing up, thread the yarn through your fingers.

Practice holding the yarn so that it can flow through your fingers. Moving your index finger up and down lets you increase or decrease the tautness of the yarn. You'll begin to find a rhythm as you start to work, and soon the movement will feel very natural. To get ready to crochet, follow these instructions.

Needle Talk

A **slip knot** is a knot that slips easily along the cord around which it is tied. Also called a "running knot," it is the most widely used knot for making a noose—but stick to using it for crocheting!

Grasp the yarn between your ring and little finger, 4 inches or so from the hook.

Draw the yarn toward you—from your little and ring fingers—threaded over your middle finger and leading under your index finger.

Adjust the yarn so that it lays firmly but not tightly around your fingers.

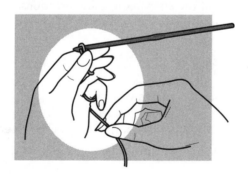

One more fundamental before I move on: catching the yarn. This movement, catching the yarn with your hook, is called a yarn over, abbreviated yo. The hook is under the yarn, the yarn is over the hook. Your index finger comes into play here, because each time you catch the hook, you guide the yarn by moving your index finger up and down.

To do a yarn over, pass the hook under and over the yarn from back to front.

Pointers

Here's an alternative if you're having trouble "wrapping" the yarn around all your fingers: Instead of wrapping the yarn, let it flow behind your index finger, in front of your middle and ring fingers, and back behind your little finger.

The Base of All Crochet: The Foundation Chain

Needle Talk

The **foundation chain** is a chain-stitched row that stands as the base of your crocheting—the foundation from which a piece is built.

If you were constructing a building, you would need to start with a solid foundation. Crocheting is no different. The start is comprised of a *foundation chain*. It is this base that holds your stitches and all succeeding rows. The next section shows you how to build a foundation chain.

Making the Chain

Now make another chain stitch, and then another, and another. As you work, keep moving your thumb up and hold the yarn right below your hook. This movement becomes second nature as you practice.

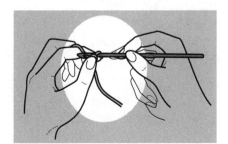

To start a chain, grasp the short end of the yarn, right below the slip knot.

With your crochet hook, catch the yarn that's between your thumb and index finger by going under the yarn. Then pull the hook through the slip loop on your hook. You just made your first chain stitch.

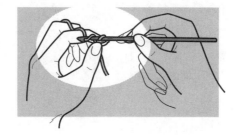

Making a row of chain stitches.

Now chain on. The more you practice making *chain stitches*, the more natural the movement will become for you.

Heads or Tails?

It's important to recognize the chain's front from its back. Always count your chain stitches on the front. You start and add to your foundation row on the front or right side of the chain.

Crochet instructions always tell you how many chains to make and where to start your work on the foundation chain.

Count chains from the front of the chain. Begin counting with the first complete stitch above the slip knot.

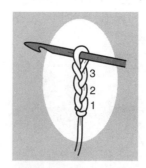

The chain's back has small bumpy loops.

Pointers

Counting chains means the same thing as counting chain stitches. For example, if you see the instruction "count 20 chains," you do not have to make 20 individual foundation chains. Instead, you make one foundation chain of 20 stitches.

Turning Chains

Obviously, at some point you have to quit making your foundation chain and actually add rows above it. To prepare to begin a new row, you make *turning chains*.

When you come to the end of a row, you need to work a certain number of chain stitches to bring your work to the height of the next row. This height is determined by the kind of stitch you will be using on that row: The taller the stitch, the greater the number of extra chains you have to make.

Needle Talk

Turning chains are extra chain stitches you make at the end of each row to accommodate for the height of the stitch of the next row.

Different stitches are different heights, and turning chains enables you to accommodate for the stitch height.

The following chart shows the number of turning chains needed to accommodate for different crochet stitches. Granted, you haven't yet learned most of these stitches. Just bear with me; you'll need this information very soon!

Stitch Name	Turn Chains Needed
Slip stitch	1
Single crochet	1
Half-double crochet	2
Double crochet	3
Triple crochet	4

Using the information on this chart, suppose you are making a foundation row of 20 stitches and will be double crocheting the next row. You would then need to chain 23 stitches:

> 20 stitches (foundation row) + 3 stitches (turning chains to accommodate for double crochet) = 23 stitches

Now you ready to begin the basic stitches.

Snarls

If you forget to make turning chains at the end of a row, you will find yourself in a real pickle. The ends of your work will squash down because there won't be room for the row of stitches. To fix the problem, carefully unravel your work back to the end of the proceeding row and make the turning chains.

Basic Stitches

The stitches in this section are the basis for almost every crochet technique—no matter how fancy. As you follow along, why not make an example of every stitch you learn? You'll want to refer back to these samples later.

If you plan to make samples, use the same weight yarn and the same hook for each. I suggest a size G hook and worsted-weight yarn because both are a nice medium size—not too small as to be hard to handle, and not so large as to be cumbersome.

Slip Stitch (sl st)

The *slip stitch* is the smallest of all the crochet stitches. It is used mainly for joining (such as a ring or seams) and moving across existing stitches without obscuring them. It's also an ideal stitch to use as a finish because it makes a nice firm edge.

Making a slip stitch is easy. The only difference between making a slip stitch and a chain stitch is that you are now working off a foundation chain or off other stitches. Because you already know how to do a chain stitch, you know how to make a slip stitch.

To make a slip stitch, insert your hook, front to back, under the two top loops of a chain or stitch. Yarn over, and in one motion pull through the chain or stitch and the loop on your hook. One loop remains on the hook.

Needle Talk _____

A **slip stitch** is much like a chain stitch except that you are creating the stitch by working it from a foundation chain or other stitches. The slip stitch is abbreviated in instructions as sl st.

Many circular items such as doilies and tablecloths begin with the foundation chain joined in a ring. The slip stitch is what is used to join the ring.

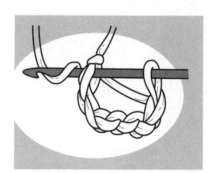

To use a slip stitch to join a ring, insert your hook under the two top loops of the first foundation chain, and then yarn over.

Pull the hook through the chain and the loop on the hook. One loop remains on the hook, and you have now completed a slip stitch and made a ring.

Single Crochet (sc)

Single crochet is truly the "basic" of all the crochet stitches. You will use it over and over when you start to make projects. To make single crochet stitch, begin with a foundation chain. Make sure that the front side of the chain is facing you, then follow these steps.

Count to the second chain from the hook. Insert the hook, front to back, under the two top loops of the foundation chain.

You now have two loops on your hook: the original loop, and the "loop" made from the two strands of yarn you went under. Yarn over, pulling through the "loop" of two strands.

You again have two loops on your hook.

Yarn over again and pull through both loops on your hook. You now have one loop left on your needle and have just made your first single crochet!

If you're following along making a sample, go ahead and finish out your row in single crochet. When you get to the end of the foundation chain, make one turn chain to accommodate the height of the single crochet. Now, with the hook in your work, turn your work so that the reverse side is facing you.

The second row in single crochet might seem different from the first because you will be working into the first row's single crochet stitches rather than into a foundation chain. Actually, the procedure is exactly the same: You insert the crochet hook, front to back, into the two loops at the top of the crocheted stitch, and then you complete the stitch.

Continue practicing your single-crochet stitches until you feel comfortable with the concept.

Half-Double Crochet (hdc)

The *half-double crochet* stitch is slightly taller than the single crochet. The single crochet requires one turning chain; the half-double requires two turning chains. This stitch is the first of the basic stitches that requires a yarn over *before* you insert the hook.

Needle Talk

Single crochet is the most basic of crochet stitches and is abbreviated sc. To complete a single crochet stitch, insert the hook through a chain (or stitch); yarn over, pull the loop through the chain (or stitch), yarn over again, and pull through both loops on the hook. **Half-double crochet** is a cross between a single crochet stitch and a double crochet stitch and is abbreviated hdc. To complete a half-double crochet stitch, begin with a yarn over, insert the hook into a stitch, yarn over and pull through the stitch, do another yarn over, and pull through the three loops on your hook.

To make a half-double crochet stitch, begin with a foundation chain. With the front side of the foundation chain facing you, yarn over the hook.

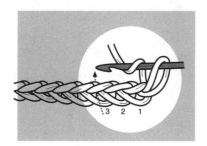

Insert the hook, front to back, under the two top loops of the third chain from the hook. Yarn over and pull the yarn through to draw up a loop.

There are now three loops on your hook. Yarn over and pull through all three loops.

If you're following along making a sample, go ahead and finish out your row in half-double crochet. When you get to the end of the foundation chain, make two turn chains to accommodate the height of the half-double crochet. Now, with the hook in your work, turn your work so that the reverse side is facing you.

Double Crochet (dc)

Double crochet is one of the most called-for stitches in patterns. As with the half-double crochet stitch, you start with a yarn over before you insert the hook. Because the double crochet has one more yarn over than does the half-double crochet, it's taller than the half-double crochet stitch.

> **Needle Talk**
>
> **Double crochet** is a versatile stitch and is abbreviated dc. To make the double crochet stitch, begin with a yarn over, then insert the hook into a stitch, yarn over and pull through the loop, yarn over and pull through two loops, yarn over and pull through the remaining loops.

Double crochet has one significant difference over the stitches you've already learned. When you begin a row, you need to count the turning chain as the first double crochet stitch.

To make a double crochet stitch, begin with a foundation chain. With the front side of the foundation chain facing you, yarn over the hook, then follow these steps.

Insert the hook, front to back, under the top two loops of the fourth chain from the hook.

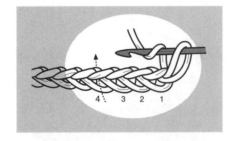

Pull through the loop. You have three loops on your hook. Yarn over again.

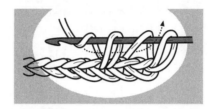

Pull through the two loops closest to the hook's point. Two loops remain on the hook.

Yarn over once more, and pull through the two remaining loops.

You now have a single loop remaining on the hook.

You just completed a double-crochet stitch. If you're following along making a sample, go ahead and finish out your row in double-crochet stitches. Remember that you'll actually complete one fewer double-crochet stitches than the row contains stitches because the turn chains count as the first double-crochet stitch.

When you get to the end of the foundation chain, make three turn chains to accommodate the height of the double-crochet stitches. Now, with the hook in your work, turn your work so that the reverse side is facing you.

Triple Crochet (trc)

The *triple-crochet* stitch, the last of the basic stitches, is also the tallest. This stitch starts with two yarn overs before you insert the hook. Working this stitch is similar to working double crochet; you just need to work one more yarn over. Also, double-crochet stitches equals three turn chains, whereas triple-crochet stitches equals four. As with double-crochet stitches, the first chain or turning chain counts as the first stitch.

To make a triple-crochet stitch, begin with a foundation chain. With the front side of the foundation chain facing you, yarn over the hook twice then follow these steps.

Insert the hook, front to back, under the top two loops of the fifth chain from the hook. Pull through the loop. You now have four loops on the hook.

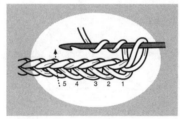

Yarn over and pull through the first two loops closest to the point of the hook; then yarn over again and pull through the next two loops closest to the point of the hook.

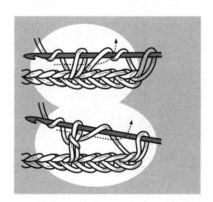

Two loops remain on the hook. Yarn over one last time and pull through both loops.

One loop remains on your hook.

You've just made a triple-crochet stitch. If you're following along, making a sample, go ahead and finish out your row in triple-crochet stitches. Remember that you'll actually complete one fewer triple-crochet stitch than the row contains stitches because the turn chains count as the first triple-crochet stitch.

When you get to the end of the foundation chain, make four turn chains to accommodate the height of the triple-crochet stitch. Now, with the hook in your work, turn your work so that the reverse side is facing you.

Left-Handed Crochet

Before you begin this section, read the instructions and tips in the section "Basic Training," earlier in this chapter. All the information in that section is identical whether you're crocheting with your right or left hand.

The following sections illustrate a couple techniques specifically for left-handers: how to hold the yarn, how to make a chain stitch, and how to single-crochet stitch.

Left-Handed Basics

The beginning procedures in crochet, such as how to hold the hook and yarn, are the same for left-handed people as they are for right-handed people. Of course, you'll be doing the major work with your left, rather than right hand. The first thing you need to know is how to hold your hook. It's very simple; you have been doing it ever since you first held a pencil.

You hold the hook one of two ways. Either position and lightly grip your hook in your hand as you would hold a pencil, or hold the hook as you would grip a spoon when stirring something thick.

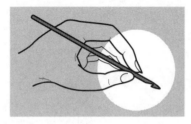

Next you need to get the yarn onto the hook. The instructions for making a slip knot don't differ whether you're right- or left-handed. Refer to the section "Slip Knot in the Making," earlier in this chapter, for directions on how to make a slip knot.

You have the slip knot on your hook and you're ready to get down to the business of holding your yarn. Follow these steps.

With your right palm facing up, approximately 4 inches or so from your hook, grasp the yarn between your third and little fingers.

Draw the yarn toward you; thread the yarn over your middle finger, leading under your index finger.

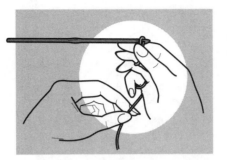

Adjust the yarn so that it lies firmly but not tightly around your fingers.

Initially, this configuration may feel a little strange. Practice holding a hook and yarn; soon this will become second nature.

Get Ready to Make Your First Chain

As you have already read in this chapter, the foundation chain is the base of all crochet. The following illustrations show you how to make a chain.

With yarn in hand and on the hook, use your thumb and middle finger to grab the slip knot right below the hook.

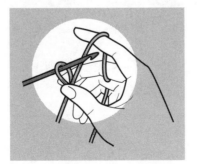

Now use the crochet hook to catch the yarn between your thumb and finger.

Pull the loop through the first loop on your hook.

![Snarls icon]

Snarls _____

Because this section only details those concepts that are different for south-paws, you could get very confused reading only the left-handed information and skipping over the material at the beginning of the chapter. If you haven't done so yet, go back and read the basic information at the start of the chapter.

Left-Handed Single Crochet (sc)

To try out the single crochet, I suggest a size G needle and worsted-weight yarn; both are a good medium weight with which to start practicing. To make single-crochet stitch, begin with a foundation chain. Make sure that the front side of the chain is facing you, then follow these steps.

Count to the second chain from the hook. Insert the hook, front to back, under the top two loops of the foundation chain.

Yarn over and pull the loop through the foundation chain.

You now have two loops on your hook, yarn over again and pull through both loops on the hook. One loop remains.

If you're following along making a sample, go ahead and finish out your row in single crochet. When you get to the end of the foundation chain, make one turn chain to accommodate the height of the single crochet. Now, with the hook in your work, turn your work so that the reverse side is facing you.

The second row in single crochet might seem different from the first because you will be working into the first row's single-crochet stitches. Actually, the procedure is exactly the same: You insert the crochet hook, front to back, into the two loops at the top of the crocheted stitch, and then finish the stitch.

The Least You Need to Know

- ◆ Hold your hook and yarn so that it's comfortable for you.
- ◆ Foundation chains are the basis on which you build your crochet fabric.
- ◆ A yarn over (yo) is the most basic of all crochet fundamentals.
- ◆ Each stitch is abbreviated a specific way; when you know those abbreviations, you can read crochet patterns.

Chapter **51**

Crocheting Project: A Cozy Afghan

In This Chapter

- The supplies you need to get started
- How to crochet an impressive afghan in almost no time
- Additional variations and ideas with your basic pattern

This project has a lot to recommend it: It's fast, made relatively inexpensively, looks great, offers multiple color-combination possibilities, and is as thick as the dickens. In addition, as with all the patterns in this book, you can dink with the basic structure and look and never make the same afghan twice.

What Do I Need?

To make an afghan that's about 60 inches long (plus fringe) by 40 inches wide, you need these supplies:

- About 72 ounces (about 4,700 yards) of worsted-weight yarn. Because of the heft of this afghan, acrylic is really your best bet; it'll machine wash and dry easily and emerge softer and fluffier than ever.

If you buy 4-ounce acrylic skeins, you'll need 18 skeins. You crochet this afghan by combining three different strands of yarn into one strand, so you might want to choose nine skeins in one color and nine in another; or you might want to choose six skeins in three different colors. Or you might want to choose all the skeins in one color.

♦ A size Q crochet hook. This size is enormous, halfway resembling a garden spade. You can find this size hook at craft or super-department stores (such as Wal-Mart or Meijer). You'll not only use the hook to crochet the afghan; when you finish, you'll also use it to attach fringe around two of the edges.

Pointers

Acrylic yarn often doesn't have a dye lot. Generally, if this is the case, a banner will run across the bottom of the front label touting, "No dye lot."

♦ A yarn needle for weaving in the yarn ends.

♦ A yardstick, ruler, or other straight surface for measuring the fringe.

How Do I Make It?

With the 3 strands of yarn together, start by making a chain of 76 stitches. Turn.

First row: In second chain from needle, single crochet. Single crochet across the row. At end of the row, make one turn chain and turn.

Remaining rows: Repeat the first row a total of 70 times, or until afghan is as long as you want. Secure the last loop.

You combine three strands of yarn into one to make this chunky afghan.

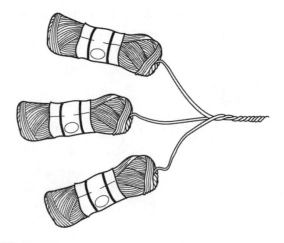

If you complete 70 rows, you'll have an afghan that is approximately 60 inches long and 40 inches high.

Now use the yarn needle to weave in all the ends. Next you're going to add fringe to the two shorter sides of the afghan. Here's how to add fringe:

1. Cut pieces of yarn that are about 12 inches long. This makes about 5½-inch fringe. If you want longer or shorter fringe, cut a different size. You need about 150 pieces of cut yarn, give or take about 20. I'd cut 150 pieces, and then cut more on an as-needed basis as you're finishing up the fringe.

2. Take four strands of the cut yarn in your hand, and line them up (to even out the ends).

3. Fold the four strands in half.

4. Using the crochet hook, insert the hook from the top to the bottom of the afghan. Grab the folded yarn with the crochet hook and pull it partway through the afghan.

5. Pull the ends of the fringe through the loop.

6. Continue adding fringe at intervals of about every 2 inches—more frequently if you want a fringier afghan.

7. Lay the afghan out on the floor and "comb" the fringe straight with your fingers. Using a pair of scissors, even up straggly ends.

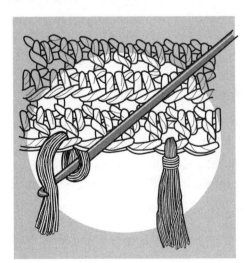

Fringe finishes the afghan.

Pointers _____

Here's how this pattern would look abbreviated. Soon you'll be able to read patterns like this:

Ch 77. Turn. Sc in 2nd st from needle. Continue for 70 rows. Attach fringe at 2" intervals on short ends.

Pointers _____

Lion Brand makes a wonderful wool-blend yarn called Wool-Ease. Comprised of 80 percent acrylic and 20 percent wool, the yarn has the depth of wool and the easy care of acrylic. To receive a Lion Brand catalog, call 1-800-258-YARN (9276).

Variations on a Theme

The beauty of this afghan is that, although it's easy, it's also infinitely flexible. Try some of these other options:

♦ For a lacier look, crochet with only two strands of yarn rather than three. Your gauge is nearly the same, but the stitches are a bit lighter.

♦ Try mixing two colors on the afghan: two strands of one color and one strand of the other. Then make the fringe solely out of the second color.

♦ If you're ready for a challenge, work stripes on the afghan: about 10 rows of each color. You can then make the fringe coordinate with the stripes.

♦ Make an afghan in the colors of your favorite sports-lover's favorite team. This would be a pretty kickin' piece in, say, classic Dodgers white and blue.

♦ Fashion a memorable baby shower gift by making this afghan using two strands of baby-weight yarn and a size H crochet hook.

The Least You Need to Know

♦ By doubling or tripling yarn and using a large crochet hook, you can finish a large project in a relatively short amount of time.

♦ Acrylic yarn often is the best choice when making heavy pieces that would be difficult to care for if they couldn't be machine washed and dried.

♦ Use a crochet hook to attach fringe.

♦ The afghan in this chapter is adaptable to any color combination, yarn texture, or size.

Shaping Your Work

In This Chapter

- ◆ Adding and subtracting stitches
- ◆ Big changes happen depending on the way you insert your hook
- ◆ Working with circles and squares
- ◆ The Granny Square makes a cameo

Now you're ready to learn some more advanced crochet techniques. In this chapter, you'll learn to add and subtract stitches (called increasing and decreasing). As a bonus, you'll learn to break a few rules while stitching, playing with where you insert the hook and gallantly crocheting around in circles, rather than back and forth in rows.

Common Shaping Abbreviations

The following abbreviations are commonly used to indicate shaping in crochet.

Abbreviation	What It Means
1 sc dec	Single-crochet decrease
inc	Increase
dec 1 dc	Double-crochet decrease
fpdc	Front-post double crochet
bpdc	Back-post double crochet

Upping the Ante

All is not even in crochet. A little increasing adds interest. To *increase*, no matter what the stitch, you work two stitches in the same spot.

Needle Talk

In crochet, when you work more then one stitch into an already existing stitch you have made an **increase**. An increase is abbreviated in crochet instructions as inc.

To try increasing, begin with a foundation chain. Make sure that the front side of the chain is facing you. Work one or more rows of single crochet, chain 1 and turn.

At the beginning of the next row, increase one single crochet by working two single crochets into the first stitch. At the end of the row also work an increase. You now have two more single crochets on the row than you started with.

Increasing two stitches: one at the beginning and one at the end of the row.

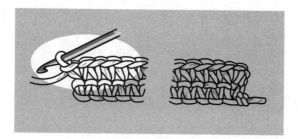

Less Is More—Sometimes

The buddy of increasing stitches is—you guessed it—decreasing stitches. Like increasing, decreasing enables you to shape the look of what you're crocheting. To complete a decrease, you have to start with two partially worked stitches. Sound complicated? It's not.

Singles, Anyone? Decreasing in Single Crochet

To obtain a *single-crochet decrease*, you partially complete two stitches, and then merge them together. Here's how.

Needle Talk

A single-crochet decrease subtracts one stitch by combining two single crochets. It is abbreviated 1 sc dec.

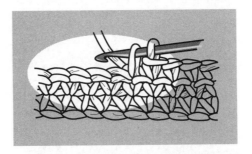

At the place where you want to decrease, insert the hook into the top two loops of the next stitch, yarn over, and pull through a loop. Don't finish the stitch!

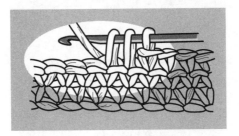

Insert the hook into the next stitch, yarn over, and pull through a loop. You now have three loops on your hook.

Yarn over one more time. This time, pull through all three loops on your hook.

Decreasing in Double Crochet

You make a *double-crochet decrease* in a very similar way as you create a single-crochet decrease. Here's all you need to do.

Needle Talk

A double-crochet decrease subtracts one stitch by combining two double-crochet stitches. It is abbreviated dec 1 dc.

At the place where you want to decrease, work a double crochet down to two loops on your hook.

Yarn over, insert the hook into the top two loops of the next stitch, and work that stitch down until you have three loops on the hook.

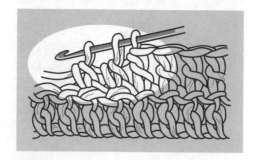

Yarn over one more time and pull through all three loops.

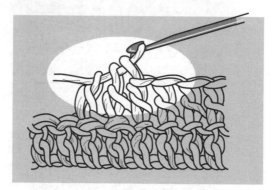

You have just completed your first decrease in double crochet.

Decreasing in Triple Crochet

You work a triple-crochet decrease the same way you work the double-crochet decrease. The only difference is that you begin each triple crochet with two yarn overs; consequently, you have to complete one more step to get down to two loops.

As with a double-crochet decrease, when you have three loops on the hook, work a final yarn over and pull the yarn through all three loops.

New Threads

Now it's time to break a few rules and give your work a different look. Slight changes in how you crochet can have a huge impact on the look of your pieces.

Working Under One Loop

Every sample you've done so far has had you inserting your hook under the two top loops of a stitch. Often, however, crochet instructions direct you to insert your hook under only one loop of a stitch. You can then insert the hook under the back loop only or under the front loop only. Each of these procedures forms a ridge that gives your finished fabric a different appearance from inserting under both loops.

To try inserting the hook into only one loop, start with a small swatch of single crochet. Working across the row and inserting the hook into the back loop only makes a front ridge all the way across the row. If you're working along on a swatch, turn your work and crochet another row working in the back loops only.

Pointers _____

When you work in the back loop only of a stitch, you form a ridge on the front of your work. When you work in the front loop only, you form a ridge on the back of your work.

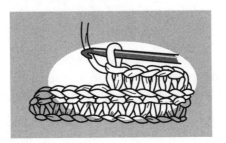

Insert your hook in the back loop only.

You can use the same concept to insert your hook into the front loop only of each stitch, which causes a ridge to appear on the back.

Working Around the Post of a Stitch

Another interesting technique also involves how you insert the hook. You have gone from working under two loops to working only under one loop. Now you won't work through *any* loops. Instead, you'll work using a stitch in the row below. This is called working around the post of a stitch. This procedure works best with double-crochet or triple-crochet stitches.

You can work around the post of a previous stitch in one of two ways: around the front of a post or around the back of a post.

If you want to try this new stitch, make a small swatch of about 20 stitches of double crochet.

To work a front-post double crochet, yarn over. Then insert the hook by going behind *the post of the stitch in the row below.*

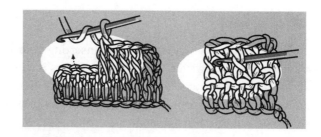

Complete the double crochet as you normally would.

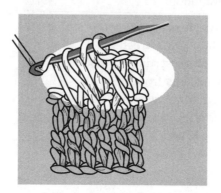

The *front-post double crochet* stitch is three-dimensional. If you're working on a swatch, work across the row by alternating one stitch of regular double crochet with one stitch of front-post double crochet. You'll see the difference in these stitches.

The *back-post double crochet* stitch is similar to the front-post double crochet. The only difference is that you're inserting your hook into the back of the post of the row below.

Needle Talk

A **front-post double crochet** is a special stitch that involves working into the front of the post of a crochet stitch on the row below. It is abbreviated fpdc. A **back-post double crochet** is a special stitch that involves working into the back of the post of a crochet stitch on the row. It is abbreviated as *bpdc*.

If you want to try this new stitch, make a small swatch of about 20 stitches of double crochet. If you're working on a swatch, work across the row by alternating one stitch of regular double crochet with one stitch of back-post double crochet.

Pointers _____

To create the look of knitted ribbing, work two front-post double-crochet stitches stitches followed by two regular double-crochet stitches. Continue to alternate these

---

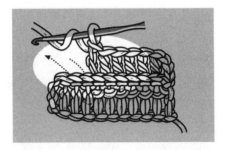

To work a back-post double crochet, yarn over. Then insert the hook by going in front of the post of the stitch in the row below.

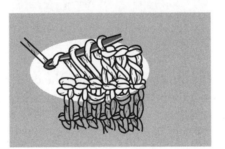

Complete the double crochet as you normally would.

Crocheting Around in Circles and Squares

All is not straight in crochet. Working in circles and squares (called *motifs*) is one of the most interesting concepts you can learn.

You can make an endless number of projects—from home décor to fashion—by working squares and circles around a central point. To create this "central point," you use a slip stitch to join a small chain; the result is a ring.

Needle Talk _____

Motifs, in crochet, are pieces worked around a central point rather than back and forth. Doilies and Granny Squares are two examples of motifs.

How to Work Around and Around

To begin working around rather than back and forth, follow these steps:

1. Make a foundation chain of about four stitches. This number might vary slightly based on the project you're making, but four stitches is a good average.

2. With the right side of the chain facing you, insert your hook into the first chain, going under the two top loops. You're going to slip stitch the two ends of the loop together.

3. Yarn over the hook, draw through both the first chain and the loop on your hook. You've just completed the closing slip stitch.

Using slip stitch to turn a foundation chain into a ring.

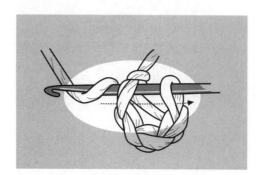

After you form the ring, you work stitches into the center *over* the chain loop. The stitches are worked as they would be on a flat foundation chain; the only difference is you'll be working in rounds.

Want to see this in action? Here's how to work single-crochet stitches into the center ring:

1. Insert your crochet hook, front to back, into the center of the ring.

2. Work a single-crochet stitch into the ring over the chain loop.

3. Add seven more single-crochet stitches into the ring, working around the ring as you go. The ring now holds a total of eight single-crochet stitches.

Making a single crochet in the ring.

4. Now close your round with a slip stitch. Insert the hook under the top two loops of the first single-crochet stitch. Yarn over; draw through both loops on your hook. You have just completed **Round 1.**

When working in rounds, mark the last stitch in each round with a small safety pin. Move the pin up on each round so you will know when you have come to the end of that round.

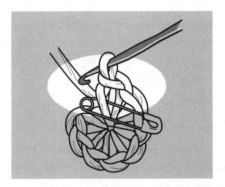

Mark the beginning of rounds with a safety pin.

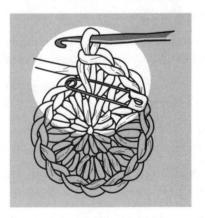

Move up the pin with each row.

Making the Circle Behave

As you might guess, if you keep the number of stitches in the round constant, you'll make more of a tube than a flat circle. With the second and all succeeding rounds, then, you must increase stitches steadily. Here is a helpful guide:

Round 1: Given number of stitches.

Round 2: Double given number of stitches.

Round 3: Increase one stitch in every other stitch.

Round 4: Increase one stitch in every third stitch.

Round 5: Increase one stitch in every fourth stitch.

Can you see a pattern? Continue this increase pattern on each succeeding round.

Working Rounds in Double and Triple Crochet

When you work in rounds with double- or triple-crochet stitches, you have to bring your work up to the height of the stitch you will be creating. To do so, make the number of chains equal to the height of the stitch. These chains always count as the first stitch on the round. Close the round after working your stitches by slip stitching in the top chain, going under the two top loops.

Grannies Have More Fun

The Granny Square is the most famous of all motifs. Who hasn't snuggled up under a Granny Square afghan? At the very least, we've all delighted in the variety of colors that can go on forever and be adapted to any home décor. And here's the best part: It's one of the easiest crochet projects you can undertake.

Here's how to make a fabulous Granny Square—the foundation for all types of creative projects. This Granny Square is made of double-crochet stitches:

1. Make a center ring by making a foundation chain of six stitches and joining the stitches with a slip stitch.

2. Bring your work up to double-crochet stitch height by chaining three stitches. These stitches are the first stitch of the next round.

3. Now work two double-crochet stitches in the ring by inserting your needle into the center of the chain space.

4. Chain three stitches; these stitches make up your first corner space.

5. Work three more double-crochet stitches into the ring and chain three stitches for the next corner space.

6. Repeat step 5 two more times.

7. Close the square by slip stitching into the top of the first chain three you made at the beginning of the row.

8. Slip stitch into the top of next two double-crochet stitches; slip stitch into the corner space. Chain three.

Closing the first round of a Granny Square.

9. In the same corner space, make two double-crochet stitches; then chain three for a new corner.

10. Complete three double-crochet stitches in the same corner space. You just made the first corner of **Round 2.** Chain one.

11. In the next corner space, work three double-crochet stitches, chain three, and work three double-crochet stitches. You've now completed the next corner. Chain one.

12. Continue in this manner for the next two corner spaces.

Working around the corners of a Granny Square.

13. To close the round, slip stitch on top of the first chain three as you did in **Round 1.** This completes **Round 2. Round 3** starts out the same as **Round 2.**

14. Slip stitch into the top of next two double-crochet stitches; slip stitch into the corner space.

15. Chain three; in the same corner space make two double-crochet stitches, chain three for a new corner, and make three double-crochet stitches all in the same space. This is the first corner of **Round 3.**

16. Chain one. Skip the next three double-crochet stitches, and complete three double crochets in the next space from the previous row; this space appears between two clusters of double-crochet stitches.

Completing the first corner
of Round 3.

17. In the next corner, complete three double-crochet stitches, chain three, and complete three double-crochet stitches.

18. Continue working corners, working double-crochet stitches into spaces between corners, and using slip stitches to close up rounds.

You can make them any size you want, use fine or bulky yarn, and change color between rows.

Pointers

You might get so charged up about Granny Squares that you decide to tackle an afghan. If so, as you finish each square, stack that square on top of the other completed squares. Each square in the stack should be the same size as the others. Uniform square size is very important because when it comes time to put the squares together, if the squares aren't the same size and shape, you're going to end up with one funky afghan.

The Least You Need to Know

♦ Increasing is as easy as working two stitches in the same stitch.

♦ Decreasing is working two stitches together as one.

♦ How you insert your hook into a stitch before you work changes the look of the new stitch.

♦ Working circles or squares is simply a matter of working around rather than back and forth. The only difference between circles and squares is the addition of corners.

53

Chameleon Moves: Becoming a Colorful Crocheter

In This Chapter

◆ Adding festive stripes

◆ Hiding in ends while you change colors

◆ Fun with bobbins

Up to this point you've worked in one color. Some of the most beautiful pieces are often made with only one color. But what if you're ready for a little more pizzazz? Changing colors is easy by working in stripes or color groups.

Adding a New Color at the End of a Row

To get striping you only need a crochet hook, two colors of yarn, and your creativity. Here's how to stripe:

1. Make a foundation chain and work one row in single crochet. Work across the second row but stop right before the last stitch on the row.

2. Insert your hook into the stitch, yarn over, and pull up a loop. You have two loops on your hook.

3. With the new yarn color, make a loop 4 inches long; using the hook, pull the loop through your stitch to close the single crochet (*closing a stitch*). A single loop, of the second color, remains on your hook.

4. Work the necessary number of turning chains and turn your work. You are now starting the row with your new color.

5. Trim the first color yarn, leaving about 4 inches from its end. You'll have to use a yarn needle to weave in these ends later. In the meantime, keep striping!

Preparing to change colors.

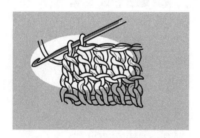

Starting to crochet with a second color.

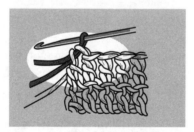

Your Secret Mission: Hiding Ends in Color Blocks

To work in color blocks—changing colors mid-row—do some planning ahead. About three stitches before the actual color change occurs you can work the yarn end into your crocheting and save yourself some end-weaving time later. Here's what you need to do:

1. Make a foundation chain of about 20 stitches and single crochet a couple rows.

2. In the third row, single crochet eight stitches. Make a color change in the eleventh stitch.

3. Add a second color by laying the new color on top of the second row of stitches.

Placing the new color of yarn over the current color.

4. Work two single-crochet stitches, simultaneously working over the yarn end laying on top of the stitches.

5. Now work one more single-crochet stitch until you have two loops on the hook.

6. Pick up the second yarn strand. With a yarn over, pull the new color through the two loops.

7. Close your stitch with the new color and finish the swatch.

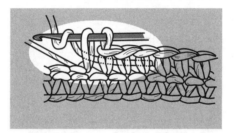

Closing the stitch with the new color.

You just completed a color block. To complete another, single crochet to three stitches before the stitch for which you want to change color, and follow these steps again.

Crocheting with Bobbins

Carrying yarn within stitches is clever, but if you carry more than one strand of yarn, the fabric will become stiff and heavy. Does this mean you're restricted to using two colors only? No, you can crochet with as many colors simultaneously as you want; you just have to work with small spools or bobbins.

To use bobbins, you wind small amounts of colored yarn around each bobbin. You then crochet yarn from the bobbin as necessary. As long as you use a color every five or six stitches, you don't need to cut ends and weave them into the crocheted fabric. Instead, you can let yarn run across the back or wrong side of the piece, behind the stitches rather than worked into them.

Needle Talk _____

The **main color** is the predominant color in a multicolor piece; it is abbreviated mc. The contrasting color(s) is an accent color used in a piece; it is abbreviated cc. You may have more than one contrasting color.

Here's an example? You'll need three yarns: a *main color* (mc), a second color (A), and a third color (B). Wind small amounts of A and B on separate bobbins; these bobbins will hang freely from the work—unobtrusive but ready for you when you need them. Here are the steps:

1. Make a foundation row of 20 stitches.

2. With the main color, work two rows even in single crochet.

3. On the next row, work two single crochets with the main color, closing the second stitch with color A.

4. Work two single crochets with A, closing the second stitch with the main color.

5. Now work two single crochets, closing the second stitch with color B.

You now have an colorful row of crochet. To work longer with bobbins, try making this design; you've already worked the first three rows. To read the pattern, read odd rows left to right and even rows right to left.

Try working a fun pattern using bobbins and multiple colors of yarn.

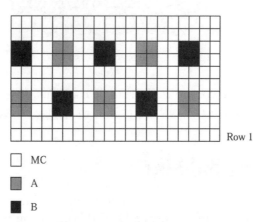

Row 1

☐ MC

▨ A

■ B

The Least You Need to Know

♦ To change colors, always close the current stitch with the new color.

♦ You can carry the ends of new stitches in your crocheting and save yourself from having to weave them in later.

♦ Bobbins enable you to work with many different colors simultaneously.

54

Cracking the Code: Reading Crochet Patterns

In This Chapter

◆ Deciphering common crochet abbreviations

◆ Understanding repeats

◆ Dealing with wordless patterns

◆ Determining which set of directions to follow

Because some crochet designs would require reams and reams of paper to write out fully, a universal shorthand was devised for documenting patterns. In this chapter, you'll learn about common abbreviations, how to read a chart, and what all those asterisks mean.

Common Crochet Abbreviations

Most common crochet terms have a universal abbreviation. In almost every pattern you read, including many of the stitch patterns in Chapter 55, these abbreviations allow complex patterns to be written quickly and cleanly. As you'll find when you begin crocheting more frequently, this abbreviation system actually makes patterns less cumbersome to read and follow.

Abbreviation	Full Name
blk	Block
blo	Back loop only
cc	Contrasting color
ch st	Chain stitch
ch	Chain
cont	Continue(ing)
dc	Double crochet
dec	Decrease(ing)
hdc	Half-double crochet
inc	Increase(ing)
lp(s)	Loop(s)
mc	Main color
oz	Ounces
pat(s)	Pattern(s)
pc st	Popcorn stitch
rem	Remaining
rep	Repeat
rnd(s)	Round(s)
rs	Right side
sc	Single crochet
sl st	Slip stitch
slip	Slip
sp(s)	Space(s)
trc	Triple crochet
tog	Together
tr	Triple
ws	Wrong side
yo	Yarn over

Is This an Asterisk Before Me?

It's hard to believe, but patterns are written with standardized terms. By the time you finish this section when you see parentheses () and an asterisk *, you'll know just what to do. The system *does* make sense. If you need help, refer to the list of crochet abbreviations.

Acing the Asterisks

Asterisks play a crucial role in crochet patterns. They indicate the start of a section that you will repeat. When you see any of these asterisk combinations, it means "repeat from":

*

**

***

In other words, You need to repeat the instructions following the *, **, or *** as many times as given. You would first work the information given once. Then you would repeat that information as many times as specified.

Here's an example:

*Sc in first st. Repeat from * 5 more times.

This pattern tells you to single crochet in the next stitch, and then repeat this step (the step following the asterisk) five more times.

Practicing with Parentheses

Parentheses work in much the same way as asterisks. When you see this it means "work what is in the parentheses as many times as given":

( )

Here's an example:

(sc, dc, sc) 3 times.

This means that you should single crochet, double crochet, and single crochet a total of three times.

Primed for the Pluses

Plus signs indicate that you should repeat something between the plus signs. When you see this, it means "work the instructions between the plus signs and repeat as many times as specified":

+ to +

Here's an example:

+sc, dc, sc in next st+. Repeat + to + 5 more times.

This means you would single crochet, double crochet, and single crochet into the next stitch, and then repeat this action five more times.

Pointers _____

Reading PatternSpeak becomes easier when you really start to work from a pattern. If you're initially confused about what the instructions are saying, write them out in longhand and work through them step-by-step. This method might take a little extra time, but it will help you get used to reading patterns. In addition, it might save you the time and heartbreak of ripping out and redoing your work.

The Sounds of Silence: Patterns Without Words

Have you ever thumbed through pattern booklets where all the instructions are given in symbols? These symbols actually look like the stitches they represent. In fact, when you see an entire pattern worked out in symbols, it really looks very much like the completed project.

Reading symbols is an acquired skill. In fact, writing and reading in symbols isn't really any faster than writing and reading in crochet shorthand; this method simply makes the information international without requiring a language translation.

The following figure shows a list of the basic stitches you might run across in symbol patterns.

Playing the Sizing Game

Often, crochet patterns for clothing are written to fit different-size people, and the patterns have to accommodate for the sizing differences. Variations in sizes are typically included in parentheses.

A pattern, for example, might begin like this:

> To fit chest size 34" (36", 38", 40", 42")

This means that the entire pattern is written using this same parenthetical annotation for larger sizes. If you are making the 36-inch size, then, for any shaping or patterning instructions you will always follow the first number in the parentheses. For example, as you begin the pattern, you might see the following:

> Ch 80 (90, 100, 110, 120)

If you were making the 36-inch size, you would make a foundation chain of 90—the first number in the parentheses. Follow this same system throughout the pattern.

The Least You Need to Know

- ◆ Universal abbreviations mean that patterns can be read and written more quickly and effectively.

- ◆ Asterisks, parentheses, and plus signs are used to indicate repeats in a pattern.

- ◆ Some patterns are written completely in symbols to make them universal without translation.

- ◆ If a pattern contains instructions for multiple sizes, go through and highlight all the instructions you'll be using for your size before you begin the project.

Specialty Stitches and Patterns

In This Chapter

◆ Filet crochet, spaces, and blocks

◆ Afghan crochet holds more stitches than meet the eye

◆ Putting your stitch skills into patterns

◆ Crocheted motifs add depth and beauty to your work

This chapter deals with some specialized crochet stitches and techniques; delicate and lacy filet crochet, functional and cuddly Afghan crochet, and a host of specialty stitches you can make by rearranging the basic stitches you've already learned.

This chapter uses a lot of the pattern-reading skills you learned in the previous chapter. If you get stuck reading some of these wacky symbols, flip back to Chapter 54 for help.

We're Not Talking Fish Here

One of the most popular uses for crochet over the years has been *filet crochet*. Filet crochet is a unique art that creates images by filling in blocks over a background mesh of crochet. Filet crochet is basic, fast, and enjoyable.

Filet in Spaces and Blocks—Oh, My!

Filet crochet is made up of two elements: background mesh and filled blocks. Mesh can be put together in a number of different ways. Think of mesh as double- or triple-crochet stitches separated by chains to form little squares or spaces. These spaces are the background on which blocks of crochet are worked to form illustrations or patterns. You can work two spaces together as one, thus creating a double space. You can also work a lacet over a double space to form a lacier look. The following table defines the different stitches and steps in filet crochet.

Filet Crochet Terms

Term	Definition
mesh	The filet background.
space	The element formed by chains separating double-crochet stitches in the mesh.
double space	Two spaces worked as one.
block	A space filled in with double-crochet stitches.
double block	Two spaces filled in with double-crochet stitches.
lacet	Two chains, one single crochet and two chains worked over a double space.

Spinning the Web: Creating Your First Mesh Piece

Are you eager to make a sample of filet crochet? This section shows you how to create mesh by combining double crochet with chains. You can apply the concepts you learn in this section to any other filet crochet projects.

If you'll be following along, creating a swatch with the instructions, you'll need yarn and a crochet hook. A good medium-size combination is worsted-weight yarn with a size H crochet hook, but you can use any yarn weight and hook size you choose.

Follow these steps to make your first mesh piece:

1. Make a foundation chain of 23 stitches.

2. Work a double-crochet stitch in the eighth chain from the hook to make the first space. Do you know why you left the first seven chains alone and double crocheted in the eighth chain from the hook? Look at this math:

   ◆ Two chains form the bottom of the first space.

   ◆ Three chains count as the first double crochet on **Row 1** (the right side of the first space).

   ◆ Two chains form the top of the first space.

   ◆ Seven chains total, leaving the eighth chain to create the first space.

Double crochet in the eighth chain from the hook to create the first space.

3. To continue the row, follow this pattern:

   *Chain two, skip the next two chains, double crochet in the next chain (one space made), repeat from * four more times (total of six spaces have been made). Chain five, turn.

   On the second row, the chain five will count as the first double crochet plus chain-two space.

A row of spaces is made by working a double crochet, chain-two pattern across the row.

4. Double crochet into the second double crochet on the row. You've now made a second space over the first space in the row.

5. To complete the row, follow this pattern:

   *Chain two, one double crochet in next double crochet (space over space made), repeat from * three more times. Work last double crochet in fifth chain of initial chain seven (final space made). Chain five.

6. Repeat steps 4 and 5 for four more rows, working the last double crochet on each row in the third chain of turning chain five.

   You now have completed six rows of mesh.

7. On the next row, work a beginning space over space, as you have done on the last five rows. Then make a double space as follows:

   Chain five, skip the next double crochet, double crochet in the next double crochet.

   You've now made a double space: the chain five counts as two chains, one double crochet, and two chains.

8. Chain five again, work another double space. End the row by working a single space over the last space. Chain five.

9. Start the next row by working a space over a space: Double crochet into the second double crochet, as you have done on the other rows.

10. Now chain two, skip two chains, double crochet into the next chain, chain two, skip the next two chains, and double crochet into the next chain.

    You have now completed two spaces over a double space.

11. Repeat this procedure over the next double space. End the row working a space over a space.

It's very exciting to see how you can combine the basic steps you learned earlier—chaining and double crocheting—to create a new type of piece.

Filling in the Dots

To form a pattern on a mesh background, just create blocks of double crochet rather than spaces. In other words, rather than following this pattern to form a space:

Chain two, one double crochet in next double crochet.

You would follow this pattern:

Three double crochet.

Filling in the blocks.

Forming a Lacet

Up to this point, you've only worked single and double-square blocks. You can also form a lacet, which has a lacier look, by following these steps:

1. At the end of the last double crochet, chain three, skip the next two double crochets, single crochet into the next double crochet, chain three, skip two double crochets, double crochet in the next double crochet.

Forming a lacet by single crocheting rather than double crocheting.

2. On the next row, work a double space over the lacet.

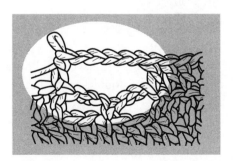

The row following a lacet.

Increasing and Decreasing in Filet Crochet

When you increase and decrease in filet crochet, you can do so a block or space at a time. The pattern you're following always tells you when and how to increase or decrease, so after you have down the basic concepts, you're on your way.

To increase a space and a block at the *beginning* of a row follow these two simple procedures:

♦ **To increase a block at the beginning of a row, chain five at the end of your last row.** On the next row, double crochet into the fourth chain from the hook and each of the next two chains. Double crochet into the next double-crochet stitch. You've now made a block increase.

♦ **To increase a space at the beginning of a row, chain five at the end of your last row.** On the next row, double crochet into the first double-crochet stitch. You've now made a space increase.

A simple block increase at the beginning of a row.

A simple space increase at the beginning of a row.

To increase a block at the *end* of a row, you have to follow a specific procedure. In essence, you are making a chain and a double-crochet stitch at the same time. Let's give it a try:

1. Work across the row to the last double crochet.

2. Working in the base of last double crochet, work another double crochet as follows: yarn over, pull through one loop (this step forms the base chain), complete the double-crochet stitch.

3. When you have completed the stitch, repeat this process in the base of this stitch two more times. You have now completed a block increase.

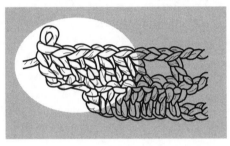

A block increase at the beginning of a row.

To decrease in filet crochet, just leave your blocks and spaces unworked either at the beginning or end of a row. Let's take a look:

♦ **To decrease at the beginning of a row, slip stitch over the required double crochets or chains.** Then chain the number required to complete the block or space.

Decreasing at the beginning of a row.

♦ **To decrease at the end of the row, stop working on the row at the point in which you want to decrease.** Turn and start working on the next row.

Decreasing at the end of a row.

Reading a Filet Crochet Chart

Filet crochet patterns are written as charts. Often, a pattern begins with instructions in words, but after a certain point, refers you to the chart for the remaining instructions. As you might expect, the dark areas indicate blocks and the white areas indicate spaces.

To read the chart, begin on **Row 1** and read from left to right. Read all odd-numbered rows from left to right and all even-numbered rows from right to left. If you are left-handed, read the odd-numbered rows from right to left and the even-numbered rows from left to right.

To find your place easily while you're reading the chart, you might affix a Post-it note under the row you're currently working on. You can then move up the Post-it note one row as you complete each row.

A filet crochet chart showing how to work the pattern.

Afghan (Tunisian) Crochet

When you hear "Afghan crochet," you might think of the item that is made: a cozy Granny Square number, for example. Actually, *Afghan (Tunisian) crochet* is a specific stitch that is very different from the stitches you have learned so far. It produces a thicker fabric, has a nice weight, and resembles knitting both in the execution and in the finished look.

Several things separate Afghan crochet from the other types of crochet you've learned so far. Afghan crochet requires a unique Afghan hook (named after the stitch, of course). The hook is much longer than a regular crochet hook and resembles a mix between a single-pointed knitting needle and a crochet hook. This special hook is necessary because, unlike the crochet stitches you've learned so far, you keep all your stitches on the hook, just

> **Needle Talk**
>
> Afghan (Tunisian) crochet is a special variation of crochet in which the stitches are held on the crochet hook. Special hooks are manufactured for this type of crochet.

like you would in knitting. The final difference between Afghan crochet and traditional crochet is that you don't turn your work. Instead, you work two rows to make one row of stitches.

This section walks you through the procedure of Afghan crochet. If you want to follow along by creating your own swatch, I recommend that you use a straight rather than flexible hook. The flexible Afghan hook is a little harder to handle initially than is the straight hook, so it's best used after you have mastered the technique.

Hooked on Afghans: Practice Makes Perfect

To start a piece in Afghan crochet, you begin with a foundation chain as you would in any other type of crochet. If you're swatching along with these instructions, cast on a foundation chain of about 20 chains. Now, here's where the magic begins:

1. In the second chain from the hook, insert the hook, front to back, under the two top loops.

2. Draw up a loop, leave the loop on your hook, and draw up another loop in the next chain (the third chain from the hook).

Drawing up loops to begin Afghan crochet.

3. Continue across the row, drawing up a loop in each chain, leaving them all on your hook.

Completing a row of loops.

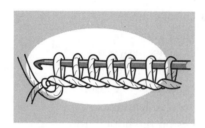

4. When you get to the end, count your loops. You should have the same number of loops as you had chains.

   Unlike the crochet techniques you've learned so far, the first loop on your hook counted as the first stitch.

5. Now you're going to complete the first row. Yarn over and draw through one loop.

Beginning to work back across the first row.

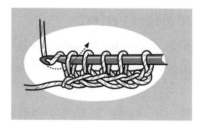

6. Yarn over and draw through two loops. You'll notice that the number of stitches on the hook is decreasing.

7. Work across the row as in step 6 until only one stitch remains on the hook. The last loop left on your hook always counts as your first stitch on the next row.

A completed row in Afghan crochet.

Now get ready for **Row 2.** This row also takes two procedures to complete:

1. Insert the hook horizontally through the front vertical bar (formed from the previous row) and draw up a loop.

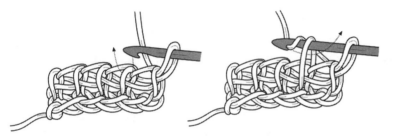

*Beginning **Row 2** by working through the vertical bars formed from the previous row.*

2. Repeat this across in each vertical bar until you reach the last vertical bar.

3. Go through the last vertical bar to the back (through both vertical loops). These steps gives the piece a firm edge.

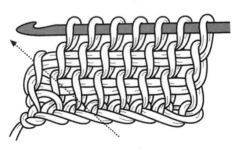

*Finishing the first half of **Row 2**.*

4. When you get to the end, count your loops. You should have the same number of loops as you had chains in your foundation chain.

Pointers

To increase in Afghan stitch, insert your hook into the horizontal chain stitch between two vertical bars. To decrease in Afghan stitch, insert the hook through the two front vertical bars at the same time, and then draw up one loop.

5. The second half of this row is worked the same way as the second half of the first row. To complete this row, follow steps 5 through 7 in the previous instructions.

You repeat the second row (both halves) to form the pattern.

This nice sturdy stitch makes for cozy afghans and is also great for making some gorgeous outerwear, such as jackets and heavy scarves.

A Stitch in Time

It's time to put all your knowledge to work and practice pattern stitches. The patterns that follow are representative of the kind you'll find in crochet instructions.

Keeping It Simple

This section contains several simple but attractive designs you can practice and integrate into your own crocheted designs.

The instructions that follow indicate the number of chains required and give you stitch multiples to make up the pattern.

Start with the following three easy patterns.

Pointers

A stitch multiple is the number of stitches necessary to complete a pattern stitch. A pattern of dc, ch2, dc requires four stitches, so it would have a stitch multiple of four. Often a stitch multiple includes an extra stitch or two at the beginning or end of a row of patterned stitches. For example, a stitch multiple of "4 plus 2" means you can start from a foundation chain of any number divisible by four, plus an extra two stitches. For this example, you could use 14:

4 (stitch multiple) × 3 (number of times you want to repeat the stitch) + 2 = 14

This means you can work the pattern three times, plus have the extra two stitches required.

Pattern 1.

Stitch multiple: Any length plus 1.

Row 1: Sc in second ch from hook, and each ch across. Ch 1 turn.

Row 2: Working in front loop only, sc in first sc and each sc across.

Row 3: Sc in first sc, and each sc across.

Repeat **Rows 2** and **3** for pattern.

You can also do this pattern with a half-double and a double-crochet stitch.

Pattern 2.

Stitch multiple: 2 plus 1.

Row 1: Sc in 2nd ch from hook, *dc in next ch, sc in next ch; rep from * across. Ch 1 turn.

Row 2: Sc in first dc of row below, *dc in next sc of row below, sc in next dc of row below; rep from * across. Ch 1 turn. Repeat **Row 2** for pattern.

Pattern 3.

Stitch multiple: 2 plus 2.

Row 1: Sc in 2nd ch from hook, *ch 1, skip 1 ch, sc in next ch; rep from * across. Ch 1 turn.

Row 2: *Sc in ch-1 space, ch 1; rep from * across, end with sc in top of turning ch. Ch 1 turn. Rep **Row 2** for pattern.

Cluster Stitches

Cluster stitches are groups of stitches that give the appearance of a single stitch. There are three distinct ways to form these stitches, even though the results appear quite similar. The three types of cluster stitches covered here are the popcorn stitch, the bobble stitch, and the puff stitch.

Needle Talk

Cluster stitches are groups of crocheted stitches that give the appearance of a single stitch.

Popcorn stitch. The popcorn stitch is a group of completed stitches worked in the same place and then closed together with a slip stitch. In crochet patterns, popcorn stitch is abbreviated pc st.

To begin a popcorn stitch, make a foundation chain. If you want to follow along, make a foundation chain at least 20 chains long, and then follow these steps.

In the eighth chain from the hook, work five double-crochet stitches. When they are completed, slide the hook from the loop currently on it.

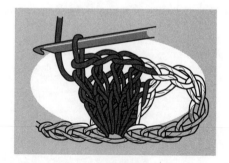

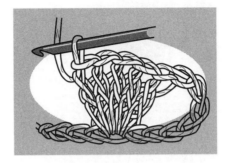

Insert the hook into the top of the first double-crochet stitch, going behind the stitches and pulling through the dropped loop.

To secure the popcorn stitch, chain one.

Bobble stitch. The bobble stitch differs from popcorn stitch in that it is made of double crochets that are not fully completed. These stitches are then closed to give the appearance of a single stitch.

To begin a bobble stitch, make a foundation chain. If you want to follow along, make a foundation chain at least 20 chains long, and then follow these steps.

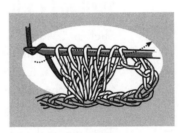

In the eighth chain from the hook, work a double-crochet stitch until one loop remains on the hook. Repeat this same procedure four more times.

Yarn over and draw through all the loops on the hook.

Secure the bobble with a chain stitch.

Puff stitch. The puff stitch is similar to a bobble stitch because it too is made up of incomplete stitches that are then closed to appear as a single stitch.

To begin a puff stitch, make a foundation chain. If you want to follow along, make a foundation chain at least 20 chains long, and then follow these steps.

In the eighth chain from the hook, work a hdc, *yo, insert the hook, and pull up a loop. Repeat from * two more times. There are now seven loops on the hook. Yo and draw through all the loops on the hook.

Close the puff stitch with a chain one.

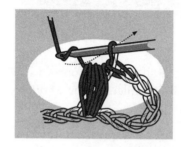

Shell and V Stitches

Shell and V stitches are also cluster stitches, but these multiples of stitches are worked into a single chain or stitch. Use at least a double-crochet stitch to make these stitches; the effect of the shell is lost with short stitches such as single-crochet or half-double crochet.

To begin, make a foundation chain. If you want to follow along, make a foundation chain at least 20 chains long.

In the eighth chain from the hook, work five complete double crochets.

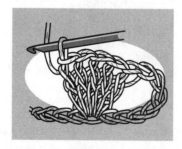

Variety Is the Spice of Crochet

Crochet is of course much more than just making "fabric." It's also about motifs. You've already been introduced to your first, the Granny Square. Let's go further back into crochet's past and work on one historically famous motif.

Irish Roses

Who hasn't seen wonderful examples of this incredible work, either in museums or as reproductions? Seemingly endless variations of Irish Crochet Rose motifs have been created and preserved over the years.

Instructions for Irish Crochet usually call for very fine thread. For ease in learning this technique, however, try your first Irish Rose using worsted-weight yarn and a size G crochet hook. You will be able to more easily see what to do.

An eight-petal Irish Rose.

As with all motifs, begin by forming a center ring. Ch 8, join to form the ring.

Here's how to make an Irish rose:

> **Round 1:** Ch 1,12 sc in ring. Join in first sc. **Round 2:** Ch 5, *skip 1 sc, sc in next sc, ch 4, rep from * 5 more times, sl st in first ch of ch 5. **Round 3:** In each ch loop, 1 sc, 1 hdc, 3 dc, 1 hdc, and 1 sc. **Round 4:** *Insert hook behind bar of next sc formed in Row 2, work 1 sc, ch 5, rep from * 5 more times. Join in first sc. **Round 5:** In each ch loop, 1 sc, 1 hdc, 5 dc, 1 hdc, and 1 sc. **Round 6:** *Insert hook behind bar of next sc formed in Row 4, 1 sc, ch 6, rep from * 5 more times. Join in first sc. **Round 7:** In each ch loop, 1 sc, 1 hdc, 7 dc, 1 hdc, 1 sc. Join behind bar of next sc in Round 6. Fasten off.

If you want to make a rose with more rounds, just continue adding in this same sequence.

Leaves for the Irish Rose

Every rose should be enhanced with a leaf or two. Here's how to make them:

Row 1: Ch 16, sc in 2nd ch from hook, and each ch across – 15 sc. Ch 3, working along bottom edge of foundation ch, sc in each ch across – 15 sc. Ch 3, working in back loops only from now on, sc in next 14 sc. Ch 3, turn. **Row 2:** Skip first sc, sc in each next 13 sc, 3 sc in ch-3 loop, sc in next 13 sc. Ch 3, turn. **Row 3:** Skip first sc, sc in each next 13 sc. Ch 3, skip 1 sc, sc in next 13 sc. Ch 3, turn. **Rows 4 and 5:** Rep Rows 2 and 3, working 12 sc. Fasten off.

You can increase the leaf's size by continuing the established sequence.

A leaf to complete your Irish Rose.

The Least You Need to Know

- ◆ Filet crochet is as easy as putting blocks and spaces together.
- ◆ Afghan crochet breaks two rules: the tool you use and how you count stitches.
- ◆ Pattern stitches combine the basic crochet stitches in new ways.
- ◆ Shaped motifs add dimension to your work.

Crocheting Project: Set a Stunning Table with Woven Placemats

In This Chapter

- The supplies you need to get started
- Instructions for stitching a plaid placemat following filet crochet techniques
- Learning a little weaving and a new way to make fringe
- Additional ideas about yarn variations

In this chapter, you'll use the procedure you learned to make filet crochet mesh and work it into an entirely different type of project. You'll also get to practice a bit more with colorwork and learn to use a neat crochet bonus: simple weaving. The result is a unique plaid placemat that will look great in your house or make a welcome gift.

What Do I Need?

The placemat is crocheted in two colors: a main color and a contrasting color. You can select two colors that are fairly close in tone, creating a subtle plaid, or two highly contrasting colors such as black and white.

To make a placemat that is approximately 20 inches wide and 14 inches tall, you need these supplies:

- Two different colors of worsted-weight yarn:

  About 3 ounces (200 yards) of a main color (mc)

  About 2 ounces (130 yards) of a contrasting color (cc)

  Acrylic washes up well, but wool makes beautiful rustic placemats. Depending on how heavily these will be used, choose either a natural or synthetic fiber.

- A size H crochet hook.

- A ruler or yardstick.

- A yarn needle for weaving in the ends at the beginning and end of the project, and for weaving the contrasting horizontal threads through the placemat.

How Do I Make It?

This placemat looks much more complex than it is because you don't actually create the plaid look all at the same time. Instead, you first crochet the mat, creating stripes as you work. Then you weave stripes into the mat in the opposite direction of the crocheted stripes. The result is a very simple-to-execute plaid.

Gauge isn't so important in this pattern, but if you use a gauge counter, you'll find that one double crochet, one space, one double crochet, and one space make up about an inch.

Follow these steps to crochet the placemat:

1. Beginning with the main color, make a foundation chain of 55 stitches.

2. Double crochet in the fifth chain from the hook. Chain one, double crochet in the second chain from the hook. Continue these two stitches all the way across a row.

Pointers

Does your first row look familiar? You are following the same pattern you used to create the filet crochet mesh in Chapter 55. Instead of filling in the blocks with double-crochet stitches, however, you'll ultimately fill these mesh blocks by weaving yarn in the opposite direction from the direction you're crocheting.

3. At the end of the row, chain four. Double crochet into the first double crochet on the preceding row.

4. Chain one, double crochet into the next double crochet on the preceding row. Continue these two stitches across the entire row.

5. Follow steps 3 and 4 a total of three more times. Don't close the final stitch using the main color; you will be switching colors. You now have five rows of mesh in the main color.

6. Change to the contrasting color and work two rows of mesh.

7. Change back to the main color and work five more rows of mesh.

8. Follow steps 6 and 7 a total of five times. You now have crocheting 40 rows of mesh.

9. Pull through the final loop. Weave in all the yarn ends.

10. Now use your ruler to cut lengths of yarn 60 inches long. Total, you'll need 20 lengths of the main color and 6 lengths of the contrasting color.

11. Thread the yarn needle with one of these lengths of the main color. Bring the needle to the very center of the yarn; you now have the needle threaded with a 30-inch double thickness of yarn.

12. Starting at one of the shorter sides of the placemat, insert the needle down through the first mesh hole, up through the next one, down through the next one, and so on all the way across the row. At the end of the row, snip the yarn where the needle is to free the needle.

Snarls

Be sure to weave in each strand of yarn in the opposite direction from the strand preceding it. If, for example, the strand preceding began with inserting the needle down through the hole, begin the next one by inserting the needle up through the hole.

You have now woven the first length of yarn across the mat. Stretch the mat slightly, making sure that the yarn being woven in isn't puckering the fabric. Adjust the ends of yarn coming from both sides of the mat so that they're basically even; you'll be trimming these soon.

13. Thread the needle with a second length of the main color and weave this through, beginning by inserting the needle up, then down, then up, then down, all the way across the row.

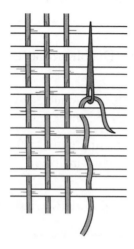

Weave the yarn strands through the fabric to create the plaid look.

14. Continue weaving the yarn. Total, you will work the following:

    5 lengths of the main color
    2 lengths of the contrasting color
    5 lengths of the main color
    2 lengths of the contrasting color
    5 lengths of the main color
    2 lengths of the contrasting color
    5 lengths of the main color

15. Now, working across one side, gather two strands of yarn from the first length of yarn and one from the second, and tie these together into a slip knot. The knot should rest against the fabric of the placemat, with the ends hanging down to create the fringe.

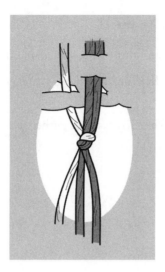

Secure the yarn and create fringe by tying three strands together, in a slip knot, across opposite sides of the mat.

16. Follow step 15, tying the second strand of yarn from the second length with the two strands from the third.

17. Continue across the row, tying three strands together at a time.

18. Tie the fringe on the other side of the mat.

To finish: Trim the fringe ends to even them out.

Variations on a Theme

These placemats are a lot of fun to make; they're simple but look impressive when you're finished. Here are some additional thoughts about making your mats unique:

♦ Choose four bright colors and make a set of four placemats, alternating which color is the main color and which is the contrasting. The result will be a Fiestaware-type set in which the mats belong together but aren't completely homogenous.

♦ To give the placemats extra interest, use a novelty yarn for the contrasting color.

♦ For a different look, crochet the mat using one color, and weave across all strands using a second color.

The Least You Need to Know

◆ You can use techniques you've learned and apply them in new and exciting ways.

◆ Crochet is very flexible and allows you to embellish it using different techniques such as weaving.

◆ You can make fringe by tying together woven strands, rather than adding a new tuft of yarn.

57

Finishing Your Work

In This Chapter

- ◆ Common finishing abbreviations
- ◆ The stellar selvage stitch
- ◆ Working through your seaming options
- ◆ Blocking to make your piece shape up
- ◆ A couple decorative crochet edges to add a fun touch

Many knitters and crocheters skimp on the finishing touches. Don't. The extra time you spend making your pieces look truly professional will be worth the effort. In this chapter, you'll learn how to professionally seam and block a piece. You'll also learn about some simple edgings that are fun to work and attractive to look at. So let's get started!

Common Abbreviations

The following universal abbreviations will come in handy when you're finishing your work.

Abbreviation	What It Means
fin	Finished
in(s)	Inch(es)
kwise	Knit-wise
pc	Picot crochet
pwise	Purl-wise
rem	Remaining
rs	Right side
sc	Single crochet
sl	Slip
sl st	Slip stitch
ws	Wrong side

You can actually add a finishing touch to your work *as* you knit by working a selvage stitch. These stitches produce a noncurling edge that provides a clean basis for sewing seams or adding neck ribbing. In fact, some pattern directions—such as those for shawls, scarves, and afghans—instruct you to work the first stitch of each row in a selvage stitch.

Pointers

A slip stitch is a stitch that is moved from needle to the other without being worked. When a pattern instructs you to "slip a stitch knit-wise" or "slip a stitch purl-wise," insert the needle into the stitch as though you were going to knit or purl the stitch. Now, just slip that stitch, un-worked, off the left needle and onto the right needle.

Here's how you make the simple chain-edge selvage on a stockinette stitched piece:

Row 1 (right side): Slip the first stitch knit-wise; work across the row; knit the last stitch in the row.

Row 2 (wrong side): Slip the first stitch purl-wise; work across the row; purl the last stitch in the row.

Work these two rows through the entire piece. You'll end up with clean, noncurling edges composed of chainlike stitches.

Another useful selvage stitch is the slipped garter edge. This stitch is decorative, making it ideal for edges that can stand alone. Here's how:

On every row, slip the first stitch knit-wise and knit the last stitch.

See? This selvage is very easy—and easy to remember because you do the same thing on each row.

Sewing Up the Seams

Imagine a world-class chef assembling the makings of a wonderful meal: imported truffles, free-range chicken breasts, spices found only in the tiny herb shop on Fifth Avenue. The chef carefully simmers the meal, sets out the Spode, meticulously tastes and retastes the sauce. All the love he has for food is poured into these preparations.

And then, moments before he is to serve a culinary delight never before experienced, he runs out of patience, turns up the stovetop, and boils every smidgen of flavor from the meal until he ends with something the worst chain restaurant wouldn't dream of serving.

Have I made my point? All the work and time you put into knitting and crocheting pieces means that those pieces deserve your care and attention at the end of the project—when it comes time to piece them together. If you're feeling impatient, go work on something else for a while. Never give your finishing work short shrift.

This section covers the many methods available for joining pieces. Complete this step carefully and thoughtfully, and don't be afraid to pull out the seams and rework them if they look uneven.

To piece together your work, you need a yarn needle and, depending on the method you choose, a crochet hook. You also need some straight pins to hold the seams while you're joining them.

Pointers _____

To assemble pieces, lie them on a flat surface and gently stretch them so that they match through the seam. Pin the beginning and end of the seam. Now align the pieces at the center of the seam, and pin this area. Continue matching and pinning until the seam is completely pinned—with pins approximately 1 inch to 2 inches apart. If you are seaming a piece in which the front and back have a matching stitch pattern—such as a cable-knit sweater—match these patterns carefully. Also be sure to pin the *right* sides together so that the seam is on the inside.

Backstitching

Backstitching is a means of hand sewing your pieces together. As you might guess, you need a yarn needle to backstitch. Backstitching provides a fairly elastic, flexible seam that is also sturdy. For this reason, it's great for curved edges and delicate pieces.

To backstitch, use the same yarn you used to knit or crochet the piece. Insert the needle into the beginning of the seam, about a half-stitch in from the side selvage. Now insert the needle about two stitches down the seam from the original position. Count back one stitch and reinsert the needle. Count forward two stitches and reinsert the needle. Count back two stitches and reinsert the needle. Continue in this method all the way down the seam.

When you backstitch, be sure that the stitches are close enough together to prevent the seam from gaping or leaving holes that can pull open. If you can see holes in the seam, you've probably created stitches that are too large and you will need to pull out and redo the seam.

Backstitching a knitted piece.

Backstitching a crocheted piece.

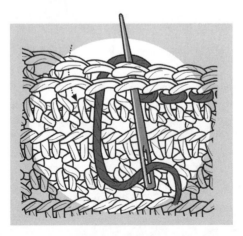

Pointers

You determine the size of yarn needle you need by the weight of the yarn with which you're sewing. You need to be able to thread the yarn through the eye of the needle. Because you'll no doubt be working with different weights of yarn in your knitting and crocheting career, next time you feel like treating yourself, why not pick up some yarn needles in different sizes?

Overcast or Whipstitching Together

Overcast or whipstitching, also worked with a yarn needle, is a great way to join squares or strips together. Just as its name implies, you are "whipping" your pieces together. This produces an effect inside the seam that looks a lot like the vests cowboys wear in western movies.

To whipstitch, insert your needle, back to front, working over the last stitch only on each piece. Repeat this process, being careful not to pull the yarn too tight.

Pointers

You can create some interesting and decorative effects by whipstitching in a color that contrasts the pieces you're sewing. In these cases, the whipstitching is to be on the outside, so you need to pin the *wrong* sides of the pieces together.

Whipstitching a knitted piece.

Whipstitching a crocheted piece.

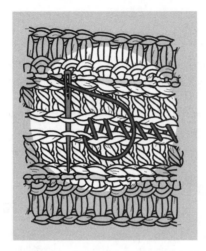

You can create a decorative effect by whipping together the two front loops of the pattern stitch.

Slip Stitching Together

Put down the yarn needle. This next seaming technique requires a crochet hook. Slip stitching a seam together creates a very firm, even edge that works well for straight seams. If you make a mistake, you can easily remove the seam pulling back the *slip stitches*. Because this seaming method can produce a fairly inflexible seam, it's not great for curved areas such as armholes.

To slip stitch a seam, attach the yarn to the two outer loops of your pattern stitch. Now slip stitch in every stitch of the seam. (If you need a little extra slip-stitch help, turn to Chapter 50.)

Check your seam often to be sure that it's not puckering. If the fabric is being pulled into the seam, rip out the seam and slip stitch more loosely; the seam needs to lie flat. A slip-stitched seam can get bulky if you're not careful. To cut down on extra bulk, only stitch through one loop of every stitch, rather than both loops.

Slip stitching a seam on a knitted piece.

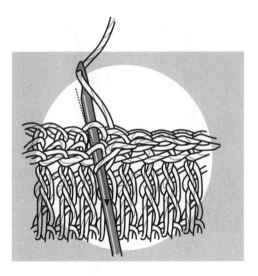

Slip stitching a seam on a crocheted piece.

Weaving Together Seams and Ends

Weaving together is the most inconspicuous of all methods of joining. In weaving, you are butting the two pieces together rather than sewing a seam from the selvage. As a result, the piece has no visible seams.

You weave on the *right* side of your work using a yarn needle. Be careful to match the rows when you put your pieces together. To weave, you'll need a yarn needle and the same yarn you used on the project.

With the two pieces laying flat and the right sides facing up, insert the needle into the first half of the stitch on the left-hand side. Pass the needle from the front to the back on the right-hand corresponding stitch; you now come back up on the right-hand side. Continue this process all the way up the seam.

The seam should remain flat. If you notice it puckering, pull out the stitches and rework the seam with a looser hand.

Weaving a seam on a knitted piece.

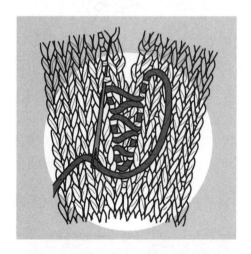

Weaving a seam on a crocheted piece.

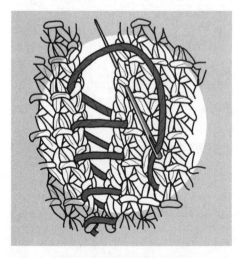

For Knitters Only: Grafting

Knitters have one final option not open to crocheters: *grafting*. Also called the *kitchener stitch*, this clever little stitch enables you to, essentially, create a knitted row using a yarn needle. You can then join together active stitches, provided the two pieces you're joining have the same number of active stitches.

Needle Talk

Grafting or **kitchener stitch** is a means of joining two active rows of knitting so that the join resembles a row of knitted stitches.

You can use grafting to create a nearly invisible seam at the shoulders of sweaters, the ends of socks, and the tips of mittens.

This stitch is a little tricky initially. Just follow the instructions to the letter and you'll be fine:

1. Cut the active yarn (the yarn currently feeding from the end of your work) with a tail about 1½ inches long for every stitch you'll be grafting. Thread this yarn through a yarn needle.

2. With the two rows of stitches to be joined, align the wrong sides of the stitches together.

Insert the yarn needle, as if to knit, through the first stitch on the front needle. Slip this stitch off the knitting needle.

Insert the yarn needle, as if to purl, through the next stitch on the needle in front. Leave this stitch on the knitting needle.

Insert the yarn needle, as if to purl, through the first stitch on the back needle. Slip this stitch off the knitting needle.

3. Insert the yarn needle, as if to knit, through the next stitch on the back needle. Leave this stitch on the knitting needle.

4. Repeat these steps—beginning with step 2, working through the illustrations, and ending with step 3—until you have only one stitch remaining. Draw the yarn through this stitch and secure it on the wrong side.

Grafting creates a seam that resembles a knitted row.

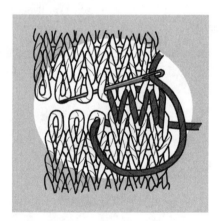

Final Call: Weaving In Yarn Tails

By the time you finish a piece, you'll find you have lots of small yarn tails that need attention. To hide them, you weave in the ends. Begin with a yarn needle or a small crochet hook. Now use the needle or hook to work the ends into the wrong side of the fabric. Using the needle, pull the yarn through, making sure that it doesn't show from the right side. Then, using sharp scissors, snip the ends of the yarn, taking special care not to cut through the fabric.

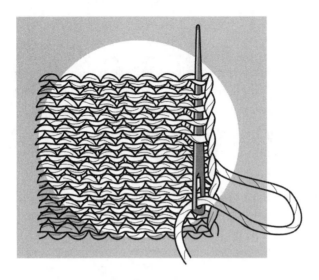

Using a yarn needle to weave in yarn tails on a knitted piece.

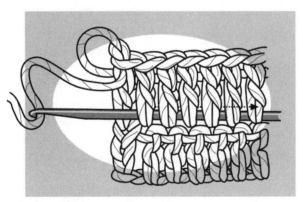

Using a crochet hook to weave in yarn tails on a crocheted piece.

Blocking

After you finish seaming a piece, you might look at it and be mildly disappointed. It's not that the seams don't lie flat. They do. It's just that, somehow, the piece seems a little wobbly. A little out of shape. Here's where *blocking* comes in.

Blocking is one of the easiest-to-execute and most often neglected steps in knitting and crocheting. I admit I always skipped this step. "Too complex!" I exclaimed. Nonsense. Blocking is very easy and rewarding. It's also somewhat addicting once you see what a metamorphosis your piece undergoes during this final step.

Needle Talk

Blocking means wetting a piece and working it into its final shape.

Wet Blocking

To start, first prepare a surface on which you'll leave the item to dry. Your bed is a good choice. Or a spot on the floor that will get little foot traffic. Get almost every towel you have in the house; you'll need lots. Lay down a couple thicknesses of towels on the area; the towel area should be slightly larger than the item you're blocking.

Begin by filling the sink with lukewarm water. If the temperature is significantly different from the room temperature, you could scare some fibers into reacting crazily: shrinking or felting or pilling.

Gently submerge the knitted or crocheted item into the water. If the piece is made of wool, you might have to gently work it up and down to wet it; wool has natural water-repellent properties.

Pointers _____

Blocking is an integral step for shaping fitted pieces such as sweaters and socks. It's also wonderful for shaping wool blankets and pillow tops. If, however, you're making an acrylic or machine-washable and -dryable cotton afghan, blanket, or pillow top, don't bother blocking. Throw the item in the washer and dryer. It'll actually come out fluffier and cozier than if you blocked it.

When the item is wetted down, let the water out of the sink, and very gently press down on the item to squeeze out some excess water.

Lay down a couple towels next to the sink, lay the item on these, and roll up the towels. Gently press down on the towels to get rid of excess water. The towels might now be soaked. You might need to lay down another set of towels and repeat the rolling and squeezing process.

Now lay out the item on the prepared surface. Get out your measuring tape and use it to determine how wide and long the piece should be. Gently stretch the piece into this size. Match up all the seams. Run your hands gently over the piece to smooth it flat; you are essentially "ironing" the piece with your hands. Wait a while.

Come back in about an hour and, if necessary, place dry towels under the piece. Keep doing this until the piece is dry. It'll be wonderfully shaped, with flat seams, ready to use.

Dry Blocking (The Pinning Method)

The pinning method requires a lot more pins and a lot less water than the wet-blocking method.

To begin, you need to prepare a surface. You'll be pinning the finished piece to this surface and then wetting down the piece. If the piece is small, you can fold two towels in half and stack them on top of each other (to create a surface four towels thick). If the piece is larger, you'll need to wrap a towel over a piece of board, such as plywood.

After you've prepared the surface, pin the piece to the surface using the measurements given in the pattern for the finished piece. For example, if a sweater should be 23 inches long from the shoulder to the bottom, measure and pin it at 23 inches long.

Measure and pin the length of the piece. Then measure and pin the width. Then measure and pin rounded or irregular areas such as the neckline. Finally, pin any edges that are rolling.

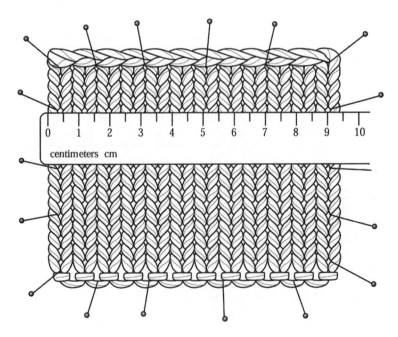

Measure and pin a piece to prepare it for blocking.

Now either spritz the piece gently with water, or lay wet towels on it. Then wait a while. When the water dries, unpin the piece. The seams will be flat and the piece will be in its finished shape.

A Final Bonus: Crocheted Edges

Crocheted edgings can add a special touch to knitted or crocheted items. Let's play around with a couple; you'll want to keep these little gems in your bag of tricks to pull out when you need to add a special zing to a piece. Edgings are usually started on the right side, and you can generally plan on working one edge stitch into each stitch of the knitted or crocheted piece.

Slip-Stitch Edging

Slip-stitch edging is an easy stitch that leaves an attractive, firm edge. You can use this edging as an accent in a different color from the main piece, or as a finishing edge in the same color as the main piece. To work this edging, follow the same procedure you learned in Chapter 50 for slip stitching.

> **Pointers**
>
> Keep your work flat when you are adding edging. Otherwise, the piece will pucker into the edging, ruining the effect. To ensure flatness, you might even want to work the edging with the piece resting on a table rather than in your lap. If you are working around corners, work three stitches into each corner so that the corners will remain firm squares.

Reverse single crochet adds a braidlike edge to your pieces.

If you've read Chapters 50 and 55, you're very familiar with working a single crochet stitch. Now try working a *reverse single crochet stitch* edging. Instead of working from right to left, you'll be working from left to right.

Reverse single crochet gives you the look of a braided edge. This step can be a little rough initially; practice for a bit to get all your stitches even.

Here are easy instructions for working reverse single crochet:

1. Attach your yarn to a stitch on the left side of your work and pull up a loop.

2. Moving from left to right, insert your hook into the next stitch and again pull up a loop. Yarn over the hook to complete the single crochet.

3. Continue steps 1 and 2 to complete the edge.

Needle Talk _____

Working a single crochet left to right across a row of stitches makes a **reverse single crochet stitch.**

To create a slip-stitched edge, insert your crochet hook into the top of a stitch and pull up a loop.

When you come to corners, complete as many reverse stitches as are necessary to keep the corners sharp and flat. Three reverse single crochets to each corner is a good rule of thumb.

Picot Edging

Picot is another very distinctive edging. It offers a lacy look that is wonderful for finishing baby projects and doilies, and it makes a great alternative to fringe on a shawl.

Picots, formed with three, four, or five chains can be made on top of most stitches. Here's how to make a three-chain picot edge formed with single crochet; to work a four- or five-chain picot, simply make four or five chains in the first step:

Needle Talk _____

Picot means peak in French. Picot edging is a decorative stitch that features little points of crochet.

1. With the right side of the work facing you, attach the yarn, work three single crochets, and then chain three.

2. Repeat step 1 across the edge.

The Least You Need to Know

♦ Using selvage stitch while knitting can prepare edges to be seamed.

♦ Take your time when finishing your piece; a bad finishing job can negate all your hard knitting and crocheting work.

♦ Blocking pieces shapes them up and gives them a professional look.

♦ You can add decorative crocheted edges to either knitted or crocheted pieces.

Part 6

Sewing

Everyone who sews knows it's not easy. But this part provides you with all the techniques needed for the most basic repairs—from hems to zippers to buttons. After you learn the basic techniques, you can be sure your home is as well accessorized as your wardrobe, adorned with curtains and pillows that reflect your flair.

Chapter 58

Man vs. Machine

In This Chapter

- ♦ Grappling with your machine's gizmos
- ♦ Guiding the thread and bobbins without any snags
- ♦ Deciphering stitch selection and length
- ♦ Demystifying thread tension
- ♦ Handling hand stitching and repairs

"Let your fingers do the walking" may sound like a good idea when you need a phone number, but when you need to do some serious home sewing, give your fingers a rest and let your machine take over. Your sewing machine (and serger) can work wonders, saving your delicate digits from the wear and tear of hand sewing. The machine is, indeed, mightier than the needle-wielding hand.

Machines have become so simple, easy, and stress-free that you can use them for most of your sewing needs. But they're not robots—you have to understand how they operate. That's why it's crucial that you get acquainted with every knob, button, wheel, and gizmo so that you can take full advantage of your machine, whether it's a 1940s metal model with a treadle or a brand new computerized wizard fresh from the factory. If you've been too intimidated to turn on your machine, this chapter will encourage you to take it out of the box (or the basement) and get your motor going, gizmos all in place and accounted for, so that you can ride down sewing easy street.

As much as I love using my machine for almost everything—a two-second bartack or a two-week evening gown—there are times when hand stitching is the only way to fly. Hand stitching (which involves threading a needle, tying the knot, and working the needle and thread through the fabric) is useful for hemming, sewing on buttons, detail work, and a lot of repairs. If you're a needle novice and think you're all thumbs, this chapter will introduce you to your inner seamstress, from threading a needle to taking your first stitch. And, most important, it tells you when to ditch hand stitching in favor of the machine and when good old-fashioned elbow grease is the only answer.

Machine Make-Up: Know Your Working Parts

When you first used a computer, you were probably like me—completely cowed by all the seemingly incomprehensible bells and whistles. Now you probably can't imagine life without your computer. Well, sitting down at your sewing machine for the first time is usually a similar experience, but let me assure you that practice will change your sewing machine from an alien creature into a creature comfort.

All machines are different, and therefore, need to be used, threaded, and serviced differently. Even with all the advances made in machines, which are now computerized, some things remain the same—the basic inner workings never change. To illustrate all the knobs and working parts (see the following figure), I've picked a midlevel electronic model that does almost everything you need to make a couture creation. You don't want to get tangled up before you've even turned on your machine!

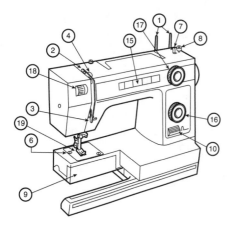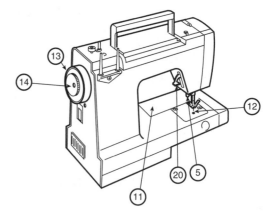

Sewing machine.

1. **Spool or thread spindle.** This is where your spool is placed, so that it unravels with ease.

2. **Thread guide.** Usually a metal loop that keeps your thread in line before it enters the tension mechanism or take-up lever.

3. **Thread spring guide.** The spring has some give so that the pull of the movement doesn't snap your thread.

4. **Thread take-up lever.** As your machine turns, the thread take-up lever moves up and down, precisely synchronizing the movement and the amount of thread needed for stitching.

5. **Needle and needle clamp screw.** This holds your needle in place, unscrewing so that you can remove it.

6. **Throat or needle plate.** This is the metal plate that fits over the bobbin case and feed dogs (more on those later). The needle slips in and out of the hole in this plate, which must be in alignment so that you don't break your needles.

7. **Bobbin winder spindle.** This is where you place the bobbin to wind it.

8. **Bobbin winder stop.** You press the bobbin against this to wind it. It will usually "pop" and stop automatically when the bobbin is fully wound.

9. **Bobbin case.** The bobbin snaps into its own case, which in turn snaps into place under the needle.

10. **Reverse button.** A quick press on this button switches your machine into reverse. This backstitching secures the beginning and end of your stitching so that your seams don't come undone.

Stitch in Your Side

If you ever thread your machine wrong, you'll find out—fast—that if you bypass the thread take-up lever, you'll end up with a snarled mess. Don't worry, though; threading your machine will soon become second nature. Before it does, however, you want to check every contact point, especially the take-up lever, so that you don't end up frustrated.

Sew Far, Sew Good

Check your throat plate for some guidelines—seam guidelines, that is. Most plates have notched lines at $\frac{1}{4}$-inch increments to gauge your seam allowance. Just like the center and side lines on a road, these will steer you through many a hem and a difficult curve, keeping you on the straight and narrow without any fender benders.

11. **Free arm.** This is a great convenience; by removing a portion of the body of the machine, you expose the free arm, which is the narrow strip that holds the needle and bobbin works so that you can sew circles around things (pants cuffs, sleeves, small clothing, and so on).

12. **Feed dogs (or feed teeth).** The metal teeth that move your fabric forward or backward as your machine stitches are called feed dogs. You can usually adjust the feed dogs. I keep them in the highest, or most "up" position almost all the time unless I'm working with especially thick and piled fabric; in that case, I move them down a bit so that my fabric doesn't move too slowly through the machine.

13. **Handwheel.** In the olden days, before motors, this wheel was controlled by a rubber band conveyer belt that turned the wheel and drove the motion of the machine. Now that it's electric, it moves with great speed, but you can always move the handwheel (or balance wheel or flywheel as it's sometimes called) by hand.

14. **Stop motion or clutch wheel.** This stops the machine from stitching while still allowing the wheel to move. It's used only when winding the bobbin.

Noteworthy Notions

I always noticed my seamstress grandmother moving the handwheel around whenever she started or stopped the machine. She knew what she was doing—it's great to grease the wheels when you're just starting to stitch by turning the wheel slightly, and then letting the motor take over. Ditto for stopping. The top and bottom threads can often get caught up when you finish; let them loose with a little jiggle of the handwheel and you'll be set free, a flywheel fly girl.

15. **Stitch selector.** Old machines just stitched a straight line. Now you can touch a key pad for computerized monograms and preprogrammed stitch witchery. Check the manual for everything your machine has to offer.

16. **Stitch-length selector.** This selector determines how long your stitches are. This is a complicated choice, ruled by a few factors that we'll sort out later in the chapter.

17. **Stitch-width selector.** How wide do you wanna go? This selector is especially important when you are zigzagging.

18. **Tension selector.** Thread tension is crucial! We'll take the knots out of tension selection later in this chapter.

19. **Presser foot.** This foot holds your fabric in place, guiding it through the stitching process so that it doesn't fly right off the table and into your face. Unlike you, your machine has more than one kind of foot; special presser feet are slipped in place for different uses. The most common type is a zipper foot, which makes inserting a zipper a snap. We'll cover some other feet if you keep on walking—oops, I mean reading.

20. **Presser foot lever.** This raises and lowers the foot so that you can change it and move fabric in and out.

The Long and Winding Thread Road

You've decided to take the sewing plunge. You sit down at your machine, plug it in, and turn it on. If you're in luck, the light goes on, and you think you're ready to roll, right? Wrong! You've got a few hurdles to clear before you're stitching away. The first obstacle any sewer faces when sitting down at the machine is how to thread it. Sounds simple, doesn't it? This is where your machine's instructions come in handy. But what if your Aunt Tillie's machine came complete with a cache of thread from the 1920s, but no booklet? Following are a few threading do's and don'ts to take the mystery out of machine threading:

◆ Always raise the thread take-up lever to its highest point by turning the hand-wheel. You need to do this in order to thread the machine and to change or insert the needle.

Sew Far, Sew Good _____

Sewing machine makers are pretty crafty—it took me a while to figure out that most thread guides aren't completely circular loops that need to be threaded. They usually have openings or slits so that you just slip the thread into place instead of laboriously threading the loop. Take a good, hard look at your machine and see where you can save seconds while threading … they add up!

◆ After you've matched your needle to your sewing needs, you need to put the needle in. Drop the presser foot lever, and then loosen the needle clamp screw. Grab your needle and take a good look at it—there's a flat edge and a notched edge; the flat edge should face the machine, regardless of whether your machine needle faces front or side. After inserting it, tighten the clamp.

◆ Place the thread on the spindle. This is the usual machine thread course: Slip it through the thread guide, through the plates that control the tension, around the thread spring guide, into the take-up lever hole, and through lower thread guides until you reach your needle. Thread from front to back or from right to left, depending on your needle placement.

Bob-Bob-Bobbin Along

Stitches are formed by the intersecting looping of the top thread and the bobbin thread. *Bobbins* are plastic or metal minispools that you wind your thread around and pop into place under your needle. Winding a bobbin is a breeze. Just follow the instructions for your machine, and keep the following key bobbin tips in mind:

Sew You Were Saying ...

A **bobbin** is a plastic or metal spool that holds thread; it's inserted in the bobbin case, usually under the machine, where it loops with the needle thread to create the stitches.

Noteworthy Notions

Keep bobbins from becoming the bane of your existence. Wind up a storm of black, white, and "invisible" thread bobbins and keep 'em in your spool pool at all times. You'll be ready for any quick fix at a moment's notice.

◆ Always loosen the stop motion or clutch wheel before bobbin winding. The same motor that drives the needle turns the bobbin, and you don't want to do both at once. To prevent this, loosen the clutch wheel; this will stop the needle from working up and down while you're winding the bobbin.

◆ Wind at top speed. It's scary at first, but you'll get used to high-speed driving, and you'll sure save time.

◆ When putting the bobbin back in its case, make sure the thread moves in the correct direction. The following illustration shows the most common way to wind.

◆ Make sure you hear the telltale "snap" when you insert the bobbin into its case. That way, you know it's really nestled, snug enough to withstand machine tugs.

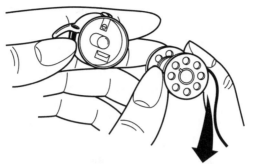

Common thread placement in a bobbin.

Bobbin Thread Direction

Tense About Tension?

If you have a computerized sewing machine that calibrates tension for you, you can skip ahead to the next section. But if you're like me, you may have tension anxiety! Since sewing involves two threads—the top and the bobbin—that loop together to form knots or stitches, the threads must have the same resistance to "pull" them when they reach the fabric or else they'll be out of whack. Ideally, the knot that forms the stitches should be balanced in the center of the fabric, rather than lying on the top or bottom of it. When the tension goes haywire, it will be obvious because the stitches will become loopy, snarled, and uneven.

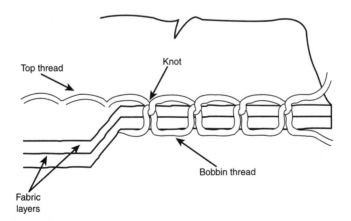

Perfect thread tension.

Top thread

Knot

Bobbin thread

Fabric layers

But not to worry! Both the top and bobbin threads can be adjusted. The bobbin's the easy one; it's controlled by a small screw on your bobbin case—go ahead, take it out and look at it right now and you'll see what I mean. You increase the tension by turning the screw to the right, and loosen by turning it to the left. But be careful! Turn in very small increments—no more than one quarter of an inch. Even the smallest turn of the screw will affect the tension dramatically. Usually, after it's set to a tension that works, you won't have to change it again for some time.

The top tension is more important, more variable, and—of course—more complicated. As the thread moves from the spool, it enters two plates that are tightened or loosened to control the tension. Depending on your machine, you can alter the top tension by turning a knob or screw, or by pushing a button. However, it's important that you know that just setting the tension at a certain number won't necessarily guarantee success; there are a lot of other variables. Fabric weight, stitch length, and the feed dogs and how they connect to the fabric all affect top thread tension.

> **Sew Far, Sew Good**
>
> There's an easy rule for telling whether it's the top or the bobbin thread that's off: If the problem is on the underside of the fabric, you need to fix the top thread tension; if you see loopy or "off" stitches on the top of the fabric, you know that the bobbin needs some work.

Without getting an advanced degree in tension—which I already thought I had as a New Yorker—the only real rule is experimentation and practice, with your machine and with different fabrics.

The Long and Short of It: Stitch Length

All those buttons on your machine actually make a difference, especially in stitch length. Stitch length is usually measured in millimeters per inch, ranging from 0 to 4, where 2.5 is the standard for medium-weight, firm fabric. Some machines may use stitches per inch, called spi.

Stitch in Your Side

Leftover fabric scraps are perfect for testing tension. Too many sewers start stitching on their 100 percent cashmere, only to get it tangled up with tension trouble. Test first on a sample scrap of the fabrics you'll be using so you can take care of the fine-tuning.

This is when your feed dogs come into play, so now is the time to explain their importance. The feed dogs are the metal teeth on your machine plate that move the fabric as the machine stitches. They rise and move a certain length, which is determined by your stitch length setting. Even if you never change your setting, however, different fabrics will move at different speeds. Thick, heavy, and rough fabrics move slower than thin and slippery ones.

The slower the fabric moves, the smaller the stitch—no matter what your setting is. So set it accordingly. As a general rule, sheers, organzas, and silks need shorter settings (from 1.5 to 2 mm), whereas thicker fabrics need longer settings (from 2.5 to 3 mm).

I like to follow this rule of thumb: Any time you do a stitch that shows, such as top-stitching, shorten your stitch length a tad. In general, tighter stitching looks tidier.

These Feet Were Made for Sewing

Don't let presser foot pressure get you down; learn how to change your feet with ease to suit your many sewing needs. You'll find that the all-purpose presser foot is in place most of the time when sewing; but when you need another foot, you really need it. For example, the zipper foot is a sewing life-saver, not only for zipper application, but also for cording and other bulky sewing projects. Here's a walk down presser foot lane:

- **All-purpose foot or zigzag foot.** Made of durable metal, this is the work shoe equivalent of the presser foot world. This foot has a 4 to 9 mm opening that can accommodate the sideways movement of your machine's zigzag stitch.

All-purpose or zigzag foot.

- **Zipper foot.** The zipper foot is exposed on one side so that a zipper, cording, or other bulky material can move with ease. Some zipper feet slide back and forth to accommodate a right or left application.

Zipper foot.

◆ **Blindhem foot.** Check out Chapter 63 for instructions on how to use this handy-dandy foot.

Blindhem foot.

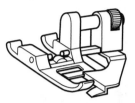

◆ **Buttonhole foot.** This foot enables you to sew perfect, symmetrical button-holes with identical stitching. The foot moves to and fro in a sliding tray that attaches to the machine.

Buttonhole foot.

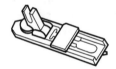

◆ **Narrow-rolled hem foot.** This foot has a special cone that feeds and folds the fabric to create a narrow hem. It comes in different widths for different size hems, so pick the one that is appropriate for your project.

Narrow-rolled hem foot.

◆ **Straightstitch/jeans foot.** This foot has a small opening for the needle to fit into instead of the wider hole of the zigzag foot. Use this with slippery-slidey fabrics that may get pulled into the feed dogs and with stiffer fabrics that need to be held in place. Make sure you set your machine on a straight stitch; if you have a zigzag or decorative stitch, the needle will hit the throat plate and snap. Use this foot with a compatible throat plate.

Straightstitch/jeans foot.

◆ **Button foot.** This foot holds a button in place so that it can be zigzag-stitched in place. If your machine comes with a tailor tack foot, that will also work well for sewing on buttons.

Button foot.

◆ **Serger feet.** Just as your traditional sewing machine has a variety of detachable feet, so does your serger. Check out what's available for your machine.

Sleight of Hand: Hand Stitching

No matter how much we're a product of the machine era, there's no escaping hand stitching. Whether you're faced with stitching a quick hem, fastening a button that's gone astray, or creating a fringed finish to a scarf, you need to know how to put the old standards—thread, needle, and your nimble hands—to work.

Needle-Threading Knowledge

I know you're out there—the kind of person who takes out your travel sewing kit (the one you took from the last hotel you stayed in), makes a few frantic stabs threading the needle, spits on the end of the thread a few more times in an attempt to get it right, and then just gives up, right? First the concentration, followed by the frustration, and then the decision of whether to spend the bucks and take your favorite shirt, which is a little frayed around the edges, to the tailor, or toss it into the trash heap. Believe it or not, you can master this relatively easy fix, and then move on to more advanced hand stitching tricks.

Sew Far, Sew Good

Cut your hand-stitching time in half by doubling up on your thread. Thread the needle, pull the strands to an equal length, and tie the ends together. Use this technique for heavy-duty stitching or buttonholes.

Noteworthy Notions

Having trouble with raggedy ends when threading? Try this trick: Cut your thread on an angle rather than straight across. Keep clipping until you have a clean sweep. If all else fails, wet the ends with God's gift to sewers: your saliva.

First, take a deep breath. Enter a Zenlike sewing state. You are a thread master. Choose your needle carefully. Unravel the thread from the spool about 18 inches, cutting it with sharp scissors. Then, thread the needle, leaving the shorter strand hanging a few inches. Knot the longer strand according to the following illustration. Now you're ready to take the plunge.

Tying a knot for hand stitching.

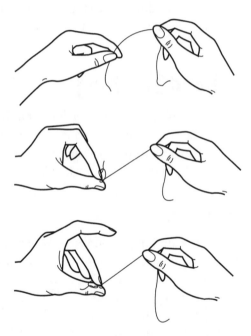

Simple Stitch Magic

The only time you ever need to make clothing completely by hand, without the benefit of a machine, is if you become a couture designer or a bespoke tailor, employing the Saville Row school of hand tailoring. Needless to say, very few people feel the urge to spend so many hours sewing by hand—and for good reason. Machine stitching produces even, neat, strong stitches, the kind that keep a pair of pants on and going strong. But there are times when hand sewn is the way to go. Following are some of the cases in which your hand needle is necessary:

◆ **Button fastening.** Buttons with a shank (rather than "sew through" with holes) must be sewn by hand. See Chapter 61 for the surest ways to secure buttons.

◆ **Hemming.** When you want a blind hem discreetly stitched into place with nary a telltale stitch, blindhemming by hand is the way to go. Chapter 63 gives you the details.

◆ **Astray seams.** A neat slipstitch will fix even hard-to-reach seams that have started to unravel.

Sew Far, Sew Good

Keep your fingers nimble with a thimble. Used on the second or middle finger of your sewing hand, a thimble pushes the needle through the fabric without poking a hole in your finger. Thimbles have come a long way from the simple metal caps of the past. Check out the new, snug varieties at your notion store—they fit almost as well as a Band Aid, and prevent the need for one after sewing! I like the leather sleeves that have a small metal coin for easy pushing; you'll have to find what works for you.

◆ **Attaching lining.** If you need to line a garment, you can't machine stitch it all into place because it will show on the outside of the garment. Instead, get out your needles and settle in for some hand stitching.

◆ **Closure.** Whenever you need to turn something (such as a pillow) inside out and stitch it closed, hand stitching will do the trick.

◆ **Finishing touches.** For tacking down facing, stitching on snaps, keeping a flap in place, and other last-minute details; when you're so close to finishing, you won't even mind doing some handwork.

◆ **Hand basting.** For a quick, easy, temporary way to hold some fabric together, nothing beats basting. You can even be as messy as you want because you'll take the stitches out later on.

Hand-Stitching How-To

Now that you know when to hand stitch, it's time to learn how. Here are the basics: Move from right to left; take small stitches; don't pull too tight (your fabric will pucker); and—the most important rule of all—don't lose your patience. Overeager stitching is the root of many a sewing disaster. To get started, check out the following list of stitches:

♦ **Running stitch.** This is the most basic of hand stitches. Take a few very small (from 1/16 inch up to 1/8 inch long) stitches in a straight line.

Running stitch.

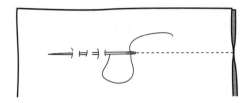

♦ **Backstitch.** The strongest hand stitch, this is as close as you can get to machine stitching using your hands. After making a stitch, back up halfway through your stitch and do another stitch (see the following figure). Bear in mind that the bottom stitches will be twice as long as the top stitches.

Backstitch.

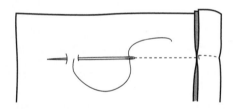

♦ **Slipstitch.** This stitch is perfect for those places you don't want a lot of stitching to show—hems, pockets, and so on. Follow the illustration, taking a tiny piece—just a few strands—from the bottom fabric, and taking a small stitch in the top fabric.

Slipstitch.

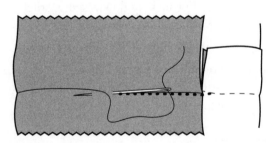

♦ **Blindhem stitch.** Check out Chapter 60 for the scoop on how to stitch without a smidge of it showing.

Blindhem stitch.

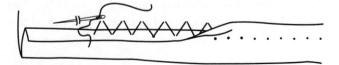

Tying the Knot

When you've reached the end of your hand-sewing rope and stitched your last stitch, how do you finish things up and not leave any threads hanging? You can simply do a couple of short stitches in place, or you can tie a knot. A knot is formed by making a loop and drawing the thread through the loop twice. Then pull it taut. Then, simply snip the thread and be on your merry way.

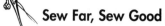

Sew Far, Sew Good

When you know that hand sewing is on the agenda, make yourself comfortable. Settle into an easy chair, put on some of your favorite music, and switch on the best light you've got. Make it a treat rather than a chore, and you'll come back for more.

Darn It!

The other use for hand sewing is to repair those holey messes—worn-out socks, done-in dungarees, and damaged workout wear, among other things. The first rule in repairing is take it to a pro if it's a prized possession. For example, my cashmere wrap met with a moth one summer. Rather than running the needle and thread through it, crisscrossing around, I took it to a professional weaver who treated it with the care it deserves. Know your garment—and your limitations.

On the Mend

If you need to mend a hole, the easiest way to repair it is to crisscross stitch through it, creating a meshwork effect with your stitches. If the hole is too large for that, you'll have to patch it in some way. A small hole can be treated with an interfacing patch, a type of temporary Band Aid that can stay you for a while. Always trim stray threads, making the material as flat as possible. Trim a piece of interfacing that is of a similar or lighter weight than your fabric, making sure that the interfacing patch overlaps on the edges. Secure the interfacing in place with a zigzag stitch.

Dodging with a Dart

I once spent hours toiling over a tailored shirt only to make a tiny tear right in the center of the back. Rather than scrap the whole shebang, I decided to add a new detail: a dart. If your tear is small, you may want to correct it with this quick fix. Make a tuck in the fabric, tapering it to a disappearing point equally on each side. Sew the dart. (See Chapter 59 for some dart pointers.) If you want to add to the

Noteworthy Notions

Rather than spending time sewing up a ripped running outfit, why not use an iron-on patch? It might not be the most elegant solution, but it takes only as long as it takes to heat your iron, and it saves that workout wear from the rag recycling bin.

illusion, make a matching dart on the other side of the garment, wherever it may be. In this way, you can make your errors your design strengths!

Sewing machines are a great invention, a keenly calibrated machine that works wonders. Spend some time with your machine and get to know it; soon sewing will be second nature. You'll be gratified to see how quickly your machine's mechanisms become your friend, with the thread, tension, and bobbins all falling neatly into place. But remember, your machine never replaces certain hand-stitching and sewing tasks.

The Least You Need to Know

- Follow this simple rule for feet (presser feet, that is): Always have zigzag and zipper presser feet available.

- Follow this simple rule for stitch length: It's usually measured in millimeters per inch from 0 to 4, with 2.5 mm being the average stitch length used. The standard stitch length is 2.5 mm.

- Follow this simple rule for correct tension: If the loops on the underside of the fabric are off, it's the top tension; if the loops on top of the fabric aren't right, you need to adjust the bobbin tension.

- Follow this simple rule for hand stitching: Take it slow and easy and never pull too tight.

Chapter 59

Ready, Set, Prep!

In This Chapter

- ◆ Give some thought to the grainline
- ◆ Build up blocking skills
- ◆ Pointers on pattern preparation
- ◆ The right marks, from pattern to fabric
- ◆ Tips on cutting quickly

A friend of mine is a carpenter, and creates stunning handmade furniture and shelving. I first heard the phrase "measure twice, cut once" from him, and have learned that it applies to so many tasks in life, but especially to sewing. Just like wood cutting and crafting, fabric blocking, layout, measuring, and cutting are essential to creating a fantastic finished product.

This is a step that I used to skimp on in my rush to get to the machine to do what I considered the "real work." And it's one of the reasons that so many of my early projects—like that basic wrap skirt or those horrendous kitchen curtains that I made for my first apartment—didn't work out. It's simple: Improperly blocked and cut fabric will never come together properly. And it's simple to ensure that you'll never have that problem again.

Preparing fabric for sewing is one of the great time and energy savers. You solve so many potential problems in these early stages, and pave the way for simple stitching and effortless fabric ease. Here's how to do it.

The Straight and Narrow: Finding the Grainline

Fabric has a mind of its own, and you have to understand its mind to work on it. Its "brain" is its *grainline*, the direction of the fibers that are woven into the fabric. Any finished project, whether it's a complicated suit or a nice, breezy curtain, will never hang correctly unless you locate the grainline and lay out the pattern along the lines. Pants will bulge, dresses will sag, and table linens will be askew if they're cut improperly. All of which is to say that if you don't pay attention to the fabric, your effort will all be for naught.

> **Sew You Were Saying …**
>
> **Grainline** is the direction of the weave of fabric.

Here's a basic course in understanding the grainline, and locating it so that your cutting and blocking is a breeze:

- **Selvage.** These are the two finished side edges of the fabric. The manufacturer tightly weaves together the edges, often printing a brand name or fabric make-up on the selvage edge.

- **Lengthwise grain.** Also known as the warp, this runs parallel to the selvage and is the all-important grainline. It's the strongest grainline and has the least amount of stretch.

- **Crosswise grain.** Also known as the weft, this runs from selvage to selvage and has more give than the lengthwise grain.

- **Bias.** This is the line that runs diagonally across the fabric. The true bias is always at a 45-degree angle to the crosswise and lengthwise grains and is the fabric's stretchiest point.

> **Stitch in Your Side**
>
> Knits are looped rather than woven, so you can never find their shifty grainline. But don't sweat it! Just try to align the fabric as straight as possible, draw a line across, and cut!

If I've lost you, the best thing to do is to buy a few yards of muslin, which is a medium weight woven fabric often used by beginners and fashion students because the grain is easily spotted, and the fabric is inexpensive. For these reasons, muslin is also used to make test garments, perfecting them before making the final garment with expensive fabrics.

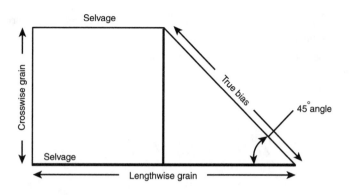

The grainlines.

The Rip Method

Grab a few yards of muslin and see if you can find the grain. Locate the two selvage lines and the crosswise grain that runs between them. Snip with your scissors into the selvage about an inch, and then rip it! That's right—rip it, don't cut it! It will rip exactly on the crosswise grainline, freeing you from using tape measures, grid patterns, and other measuring tools.

After ripping, place the fabric on a corner of the table and see how it lays. If the fabric aligns with the right angle of a table, the fabric is properly *blocked*. (That is, the grains are running straight.) If not, you need to block it yourself by pulling with both hands in the opposite direction; that is, if the fabric leans to the left, you need to pull on the right bias line, and vice versa. Now that the fabric is blocked you can press and cut it!

The rip method of finding the grain only works on fabric that is "rippable." Here's a short list of fabrics that will rip:

   ◆ Cottons

   ◆ Light linens

   ◆ Some silks (be careful!)

   ◆ Very lightweight wools

Sew Far, Sew Good _____

   Block fabric by locating the crosswise and lengthwise grains. They need to be aligned so that they run at an exact right-angle to each other. Check by lining them up at the edge of a table (or use a T-square), pulling at either end to straighten, and align them before laying out and cutting the fabric.

The Thread Method

Fabrics that have a raised surface, like corduroy, seersucker, velvet, and dupioni silks and other, heavier fabrics, must be cut along the grainline rather than ripped. Again, don't look for the grain by measuring; that will only lead to inaccuracy and error. Instead, snip with your scissors through the selvage and into the fabric. Pick a thread and pull it across the length of the fabric, puckering the fabric in a straight line. Now, you can cut across that line.

Straightening the grainline.

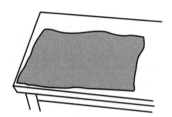

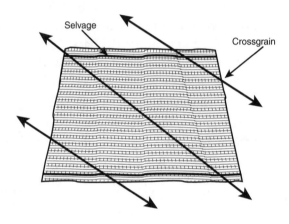

Using the thread method to locate the grainline.

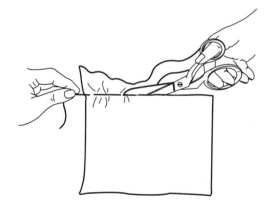

If you can't find the grainline by using either the rip or thread method (some fabrics just don't lend themselves to either approach), here's a last resort: Use a T-square to measure a right angle. Just place the short end of the square along the selvage and square across a straight line, making sure that the fabric is blocked properly. It's more accurate than measuring, and certainly quicker!

Stitch in Your Side

When buying fabric, check to see whether it's been treated with a permanent finish that will affect the way the fabric hangs. The giveaways are the terms *permanent press, stain-resistant, water-repellent,* and *bonded.* The resins used to treat these fabrics often make them not only permanent press, but permanently off-grain (that is to say that they will never hang right, not a good thing!). Do the table test before you buy: If you can't make the edge line up to the right angles of the cutting table, it will never line up to anything!

The Lowdown on Layout

When you understand and have completed the preliminaries—pretreating, locating the grainline, and blocking—go on to laying out and cutting up. I always do the cutting for a project ahead of time rather than cutting and sewing on the same day. This way I'm fresh when I start sewing.

Pattern Puzzles

After you get some sewing experience under your belt, the instructions that accompany these commercial patterns become less and less important. My sewing teacher never uses the pattern instructions. She just looks at the finished drawing, and imagines the garment as a puzzle with all different pieces that need to be fit together perfectly. She also advised me that you don't need to follow the layout religiously; you can often find better ways to fit the pattern pieces on your fabric piece. Just be sure to lay out all the pieces before cutting anything so that you're sure they fit, and always buy enough fabric!

Sew Far, Sew Good

If you're using a commercially prepared pattern to sew a garment, cut the pattern pieces roughly. Don't obsess and cut neatly around the edge. You have to cut the pieces again when they're placed on the fabric, so save the persnickety snipping for when it really counts!

Noteworthy Notions

Whenever you can, double up on cutting. Cut lining and interfacing at the same time that you cut the fabric. Put the thinnest, slipperiest fabrics on the top and the heaviest on the bottom.

Pressing Pattern Patter

This was a real shocker to me when I learned it: You must press all your tissue pattern pieces before cutting your fabric! Don't worry, the tissue can withstand the highest heat on your iron. It will make your cutting so much easier, and the heat creates static electricity that creates a bit of a bond between your fabric and tissue.

Weighty Measures

When I first started sewing, I laboriously pinned everything in sight, both during the cutting process and while sewing. Now, there's hardly a pin in sight unless I'm working on a tricky task like a sleeve. Even beginners should stay away from pins while cutting—really!

Use weights instead of pins, placed at the corners of the pattern pieces and along long stretches. Why? It's faster to put a few weights down than to struggle with pinning different fabrics to pattern pieces and interfacing. Plus, you'll completely avoid the risk of pin holes in the more delicate fabrics. (Sometimes, no matter how good the pin is, you'll still get a mark.) My favorite weights are curtain weights, the kind that are sewn into the bottom of drapes to make sure they hang properly. They're perfect for cutting fabric, because they're small, heavy, easy to store, and cheap. My whole sewing class started using them when I whipped them out while cutting, and they never went back to using soup cans! You can also use commercial sewing weights—look for the brand Weight Mates.

> **Noteworthy Notions**
>
> When cutting a slippery fabric like silk, use some of the tissue that you would use for gift wrapping as an anchor. Lay the tissue down first, pin the silk on top, and then place your pattern on top of the silk. Cut through all the layers and you'll have a much more accurate set of fabric pieces!

> **Stitch in Your Side**
>
> If you're marking up your fabric with chalk or a water or air-soluble marker, test it first! You don't want it to show up on the finished garment. And be careful when snipping the fabric—deep snips translate into holes!

Marking Up

Marks—notches, clips, placement lines, dart lines, and so on—are essential when you're putting together your material and making anything from a Roman shade to a shirt. The smart sewer knows that you don't have to transfer every single mark, but a few are indispensable to sewing anything that falls into place properly. Mark up your fabric while you cut—I mean, really, who wants to stop a sewing streak just to find out where that darned dart should go?

Many books and courses recommend that you transfer markings with tailor's tacks, a thread loop that is loosely sewn through the fabric and pattern pieces. When the pattern tissue is removed, the tacks remain in the fabric. I personally find tailor's tacks laborious and try to avoid them. Why sew before you sew? I transfer marks with a number of different tools, relying mostly on chalk and air- and water-soluble markers, making sure they're removable.

Here's a quick drill for transferring markings: If you have a small dot or line (for example, the tip of a dart, which is usually marked with a circle), take a pin and tear a small hole in the tissue pattern. Use a marker of your choice (I like tailor's chalk) to make a small dot on the fabric without moving the tissue pattern. I use this method for almost all of my markings. Just be sure that you don't tear too large a hole or line in the tissue piece. If you do, try tape. For a really big tear, you can always transfer the damaged tissue pattern to a new piece of paper. Try brown wrapping paper, or, if you want to look like a pro, pick up gridded pattern paper from a notions store.

Here's a brief description of the types of marks you should keep an eye out for while you're prepping and cutting your fabric:

- **Notches.** These are indicated on your pattern and are used to match fabric pieces together accurately. Rather than cutting a V outward (as they're drawn on the pattern), snip notches about ¼ of an inch into the seam allowance. Single notches always indicate the front of a garment, whereas double notches indicate the back.

- **Darts.** Instead of drawing all the lines of a dart on your fabric, snip the ends into the *seam allowance* of the fabric, and mark the point with a pencil, or water- or air-soluble fabric marker. If you do this first, it will be super-easy to pin the dart into place without any further marking!

- **Center points.** This is the midpoint or center of a piece of a garment, such as a collar or sleeve. Even if these points aren't marked on your pattern, snip into the seam allowance at the centers of your

Stitch in Your Side

V snips just won't cut it when marking fabric for serging. The serger will trim the *seam allowance*, snipping away your markings. Rather, make a mark exactly on the seam line so that you can see it when the serger blade cuts way the excess fabric.

Sew You Were Saying ...

The **seam allowance** is the amount of fabric added to your pattern to allow for stitching and trimming. Or, a little less technically, it's the space between where you've cut the fabric and where you stitch it. Almost all commercial patterns use a ⅝-inch seam allowance, but you can vary it according to your sewing needs.

pieces—for example, the garment's front, back, collar, and sleeve center—and anywhere else that the center line is crucial for lining and matching pattern pieces. If the pattern does mark the center with a circle, dot, or other indication, it is much easier to do the snip in a snap than to laboriously transfer the markings.

♦ **Buttonhole lines.** I never transfer buttonhole markings; I always wait until I get to the sewing stage before deciding on the buttonhole placement. It's rare that I don't alter the clothing in some way, and any alteration will change the button placement pretty dramatically.

Sew Far, Sew Good

When cutting the pattern pieces, take care not to lift the scissors from the table—keep the bottom blade fixed, gliding the top blade carefully. Don't use a choppy, sawing motion, and never cut all the way to the tip of the scissors—stop and move on before you get to the end.

♦ **Circles, triangles, and dots.** You will often see these markings on many pattern pieces. Transfer these placement lines judiciously. A lot of them just aren't necessary. For example, the dots that are usually placed on a sleeve cap to indicate where you should start your ease stitch can be left out as long as you snipped your notches. Use the snips as a place to begin and end your ease stitch.

♦ **Zipper placement.** Zippers are marked on patterns with a cross-hatched line that ends in a circle. No need to transfer all the marks—just mark the end point (the bottom of the zipper).

The Least You Need to Know

♦ The first step in preparing fabric is locating the grainline, the direction of the threads that are woven into the fabric.

♦ Block the fabric so that the crosswise and lengthwise grains are at right angles, meaning that the fabric hangs straight, not askew.

♦ Lay out the pattern pieces on the blocked fabric, following the grainline direction.

♦ Transfer the markings with the pattern pieces in place.

♦ Cut the pieces, taking care not to lift the scissors from the table.

60

The Ace of Baste: Seams

In This Chapter

- ◆ Prep your fabric pieces
- ◆ Master simple stitches
- ◆ Conquer seam finishes
- ◆ Drive around curves
- ◆ Rip the ragged results

It's time for me to take you on a ride through the basics of stitching, from towing the line—the straight line—to the hitches and how to fix them so that you can master finished seams—the ultimate driving test of any home sewer. After we've finished that, you'll be ready for the open road!

Before You Take Your First Stitch

Before you take your first stitch, you need to get a few things straight. The first order of the day is thread tension. After threading your machine and inserting your bobbin, you need to test your tension on a swatch of the exact fabric and fabric thickness that you'll be using. The two threads that loop together to form your stitches must fall almost exactly in the center of the fabric to stitch properly.

After you've taken the tension stress test and passed, you can move on to stitch length. The standard stitch measurement is in millimeters per inch, and is usually scaled on the machine from 0 to 4, with 2.5 being the average stitch length. Set stitch length at 0 mm to stitch in place; set it at 4 mm for a long basting stitch.

Seam Allowances

You thought you were through with allowances, didn't you? Not quite! A seam allowance is the amount of fabric added to your pattern to allow for stitching and trimming. Or, a little less technically, it's the space between where you've cut the fabric and where you stitch it.

Almost all commercial patterns use a ⅝-inch seam allowance, which is pretty big. They like to give you space for alterations and errors. Whenever I make something without a pattern—like pillows and curtains—or use my own patterns that I've made over the years, I always use a ½-inch seam allowance. It's a nice easy number, both to measure and to remember. Most machines have markings on the *throat plate*—the metal plate that surrounds your needle hole—at ⅛-inch intervals so that you can guide the fabric accordingly.

Sew You Were Saying ...

The **throat plate** is a metal plate on your sewing machine that surrounds your needle hole. It is below the needle mechanism and covers the bobbin mechanism. There are often different, detachable throat plates to accommodate different stitches. This is because the needle movement may swing wider from side to side in a zigzag manner, necessitating a larger or different hole in the plate. Check your machine's manual for the details.

Prepare Your Pieces

Any time you sew, you're stitching two or more pieces of fabric together. The pieces must be aligned properly—whether it's just two pieces of straight fabric or a rounded sleeve and armhole section or even the complicated pin-tucked bodice of a dress—before you can sew them. Experienced sewers can manipulate the fabric with their hands, and have the ability to work with just the feel of the fabric. Beginning sewers have to work a little harder. Always align the fabric pieces, matching any notches, symbols, or other sewing guidelines before sitting down at your machine. Make sure to pin around curves, fitted areas or seams, particularly on slippery fabric, or anywhere you think you need guidance.

After practicing with pinning, learn to sew straight seams without any pins at all. Let your hands be the pins, guiding the fabric pieces. If you want, start slow—pin the middle and ends only. In general, save the pinning for more serious tasks, like sleeve caps.

Noteworthy Notions

When people ask how I get my seams so straight, I tell them I cheat! I used a magnetic seam guide when I first started sewing. It sticks to the machine and forms a little shelf that you press your fabric against as you sew. If you don't want to buy anything, put some masking tape on your machine to mark your seam allowance.

Ready, Set, Straight Stitch!

All systems are go! Here's what to keep in mind to make perfect straight stitches, the most common seam in sewing:

◆ **Thread placement.** Pull the threads out a few inches and slide them behind the presser foot before starting, but keep the top thread going between the "toes" of the presser foot. You'll end up with two tails of thread in the back of your machine.

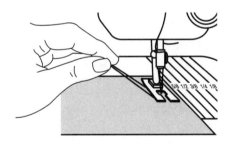

Pulling the thread tails before sewing.

◆ **Fabric placement.** Now put the fabric in the "start" position: Align the right, raw edges of the fabric, place them on the throat plate with the desired seam allowance, and leave the rest of the fabric hanging off to the left. Drop the presser foot and lower the needle into the fabric with a manual turn of the handwheel.

◆ **Hand guidance.** My teacher always says that sewing is like driving. Your hands guide the fabric, steering like you would a car. Let your hands gently move the fabric as it's fed into the machine—don't push it, though, the feed dogs will take care of that—and certainly don't pull it from the back. Get used to working with different weights of fabrics and how they move.

♦ **Beginning and ending.** How do you secure the thread at the start and finish of a seam? Never, ever, tie a knot by hand! Instead, as you begin a seam, stitch a few stitches forward, then a few back, and you're set. The backstitch, as it's called, will hold. Another method is to set your stitch length at 0, sew a few stitches in place, and your seam will stay put. Some machines have a bartack setting on the machine that will do this for you.

Sew Far, Sew Good

When you start your first stitches, does your fabric sometimes get pushed down into the needle hole, dragging down your sewing? Try putting a separate swatch of fabric underneath your real fabric so that the two overlap slightly. Start sewing on the swatch and continue into your real fabric, and the problem will go away!

If the seam you've just sewn will cross another seam line, don't waste any time with backstitching; the intersecting seam will take care of finishing it for you.

And again, practice, practice, practice! Practice is all you need to make the straight stitch second nature. Pick up some small pieces or remnants of different fabrics to practice stitching so that when you get to the real thing, your instincts will take over.

Stitch List

Here's an easy reference guide to the most used, simple, straight stitches:

♦ **Topstitch.** Stitch about ¼ inch from the seam or edge. This stitch can secure a seam, design element, or may just serve as a decorative touch.

♦ **Edgestitch.** Use this to keep finished edges flat, strengthen seams, attach pockets, or for a more polished look. Stitch about ⅛ inch from the finished edge or seam. Used particularly on pockets, collars, jacket, shirt fronts and edges, and so on.

♦ **Backstitch.** To begin and end seams, just do a few stitches in reverse. Most machines have a button or tab for switching directions in a flash. I used to stitch back and forth quite a bit, thinking that was the only way the seam would hold. Well, all I did was add stitching bulk and mess. Remember, you only need to backstitch one or two stitches to secure the seams, so don't overdo it.

◆ **Basting.** This a temporary stitch to hold fabric in place while constructing your project. It's important to baste any time the sewing gets tough or you're unsure about the results, either because of your skill level or because you want to test drive before adding a more permanent stitch. The basting stitch, which uses the longest machine stitch length (4 mm on most machines), or a long hand basting stitch, is removed later, when the pieces have been permanently stitched in place. The long stitch makes it easier to cut and remove. If you can, use your weakest thread—cotton, rather than polyester—because you actually want it to break easily.

Stitch in Your Side

Now's the time to clip your thread—be very careful to just snip the stragglers, not the fabric itself!—that'll be left hanging at the start and end of any seam. Go ahead and clip the thread right next to the edge of the fabric.

Sew Far, Sew Good

Want to take basting out in seconds? Use a contrasting color—like red if you're making white curtains—and it'll be clear that the red gets the ripper!

◆ **Staystitch.** Curved areas, like collars, necklines, and certain seams, have a tendency to stretch when stitched, so you need to "stay" the fabric with a staystitch. Straight stitch ⅛ inch from the edge inside the seam allowance. This stitch is not a seam; it doesn't sew together two pieces of fabric. Rather, it grounds one piece, providing a template so that the fabric stays put instead of stretching. I used to skip this step, thinking it was unnecessary because it wasn't a construction element. Well, when the front edge of my cashmere vest drooped, I saw the error of my ways. Follow your pattern instructions, and staystitch where needed. A good rule is that any fabric stitched along the bias (whether the true bias or not), has a tendency to stretch. Curb it with a staystitch.

Fancy Finishings

The first step—the straight seam—is under control. Now you need to take charge of finishing the raw edges of the seam, making its appearance as fantastic as its utility. And not just because it looks a lot better. Almost all fabrics, especially woven and knitted materials, will unravel, some an enormous amount, some not so much. But time and repeated washings usually bring straggly threads unless they're tamed with the proper finish. No one wants to look inside a pair of pants to see thread chaos. If you're planning on lining your garment, don't worry about seam finishes. The lining will cover a lot of sewing messes. Here are a few options, from the simple to the fancy:

- **Pinking.** If you're using tightly woven fabrics that are pretty stable—silks, cotton, canvas, and the like—get out your pinking shears and trim the edges of your seams. This nice serrated set of shears keeps fraying in check within seconds. Don't use this on material that unravels easily, like knits, stretchy fabrics and linens, because it just won't make a dent in the disarray.

Pinking seam finish.

Seam

Pinked edges

- **Pinking and stitching.** If you need to crank up the hold volume on a pinked edge, sew a straight stitch on the inside of your seam edge and pink as close to it as you can without clipping into it.

Pinked and stitched seam finish.

- **Zigzag.** If your machine has a zigzag stitch, use it! After sewing your straight seam, sew a line of zigzag stitching on the raw edge, stitching the zig in the fabric and letting the zag come right up to or fall off the raw edge. You're done!

Zigzag seam finish.

- **Baby hem.** This finishing, which has a silly but accurate name, takes a little more time, but is worth it for a fine finish. It is essentially a double-turned hem on each side of the seam. You should only use this on seam that has ½- to ⅝-inch allowance or more, but no less.

1. Turn in from ⅛ inch to ¼ inch of your raw seam edge and press in place.

2. Turn again another ⅛ inch to ¼ inch and press in place.

3. Now stitch this baby hem in place, using the presser foot as a seam guide.

4. You need to baby hem both sides of the seam allowance, and then press open so the seam lays flat.

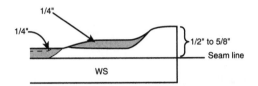

Baby hem seam finish.

◆ **Bias bound.** This is by far the most time-consuming finishing we'll cover, to be used when a fabulous interior look is more important than anything else. Bias-bound seams are particularly useful on an unlined coat or jacket. They're a sleek solution to bulky fabric, like coating, which can't be baby hemmed or French seamed, for example, because of the thickness of the fabric. The bias-bound finish is made with a strip of bias tape or bias material which is sewn around the raw edges of the seam.

You can make your own bias strip out of the fabric you're using, or you can do it the extremely easy way: Buy bias tape in a finished width of ½ inch in a color that matches or complements your fabric. The bias tape has a preformed fold and turns under so that it's ready to go: no folding, measuring, or prestitching on your part.

1. Both seam allowances need to be bound separately, so start with one side.

2. Enclose the raw edge of the seam allowance in the bias tape, butting the edges of the bottom and top against the seam.

3. Pin into place.

4. Topstitch the bias tape into place, sandwiching the seam allowance into the bias tape, sewing all three layers at once.

5. Sew the next side. Now you're beautifully bound!

No matter what seam finish you use, always trim the excess from ¼ inch to ⅛ inch. No one likes bulky layers, so grade them, or trim one ¼ inch and the other ⅛ inch, when two layers lie against each other. You'll see the smooth difference it'll make!

> **Noteworthy Notions**
>
> If you need to make bias tape from your fabric, try a Bias Tape Maker, a handy little metal gizmo that makes perfect single-fold bias tape from fabric strips. To go the extra style mile on a bias-bound finish for the inside of a beautiful jacket, use a piece of satin fabric rather than the jacket fabric or bias tape. It adds an incredible sheen, and is worth the minimal investment.

Serging Ahead

A quick aside: A serger will finish seams with an overcast stitch, creating neatly encased seams that are cut and finished at the same time. If you're sewing a lot for utility, you should definitely get a serger and cut your seam finishing time to zero.

Beyond the Straight Seam

Variety is not only the spice of life, it's a sewing staple. Although the straight seam is your all-purpose choice, other options out there may better complement your fabric and garment. As you become comfortable with different fabrics and how they work, you'll notice that certain seams need extra care because they're bulky, are more visible, or need a splash of dash.

Experimentation in seams, as in all things, is the key to success. Even though almost all commercial patterns call for straight seams, bear in mind that you can use your creativity and know-how to improve on the pattern. Here's a sampling of my most-used seams, just a few of many!

> **Stitch in Your Side**
>
> Make sure to trim enough of the seam allowance when sewing a French seam. Otherwise, those little straggles will show through on the finished seam. Yuk! Also, don't forget to leave enough seam allowance to start. This seam works beautifully with the commercial ⅝-inch seam allowance.

French Seams

This is my favorite seam of all time. It totally encases the raw edges, adding a couture look to even the simplest of outfits. It's a great all-purpose seam when you want the inside of anything to look sleek and stylish. It definitely takes more care, including sewing two seam lines and extra pressing, but it's the ultimate in fancy finishings. The one place it really must be used is on sheer fabrics such as thin silks, organza, and chiffon. These see-through fabrics can be a dead giveaway of an extremely sloppy seam. Don't be scared off, though! French seams can actually become an integral part of your sewing regimen.

1. Match the right sides of your fabric together (that is, the finished sides of the fabric, not the inside or what's known as the "wrong side").

2. Sew a ⅜-inch seam.

3. Trim a close ⅛ inch.

4. Press the fabric flat with the seam allowance on either side.

5. Fold over the seam with the wrong sides out, encasing the raw edge, press again with the right sides together.

6. Sew a ¼-inch seam, press to one side. Voilà!

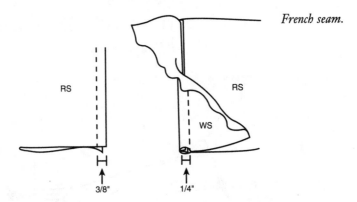

French seam.

Mock French Seams

Don't use this stitch on anything too heavy—it'll create too much bulk. But for light- to medium- weight fabric seams—ooh la la!

1. Sew a straight ⅝-inch seam with the wrong sides together. Don't press open.

2. Turn over each edge ¼ inch toward the seam, press in place.

3. Edgestitch the pressed edges together. Press to one side.

Noteworthy Notions

Want to add a little extra *je ne sais quoi* to a French seam? After finishing and pressing the seam to one side, edgestitch the free edge down so that it lays flat on the fabric. This finish is used in men's tailored shirts to make them look like a million bucks (or at least a few hundred!).

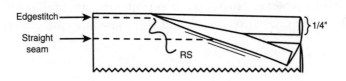

Mock French seam.

Noteworthy Notions

Why not try a reverse flat-fell seam; that is, put the right sides of your fabric together and stitch on the outside of your project? You can even use a contrast thread color to add to the decorative mix.

Flat-Fell Seams

This is a slightly breezier seam to sew than the French seam, with a slightly different look. Use it for heavy fabrics to reduce bulk while still adding style:

1. Sew a ⅝-inch seam on the wrong side of the fabric.

2. Trim one seam allowance to ⅛ to ¼ inch.

3. Turn the other seam allowance under ¼ inch, press into place.

4. Place over trimmed edge, press, and edgestitch into place.

Flat-fell seam.

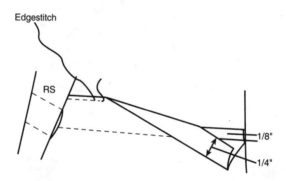

Seems Like It Will Never Fit? On to Curved Seams

The great thing about fabric is that it rolls with the punches. It moves with your groove, around necks, waists, shoulders—all your curved areas. How do these two-dimensional pieces of fabric do it? Sometimes it seems like a mystery, especially when you're stitching together two pieces of fabric that look like they'll never come together. Two good examples are collars and princess seams, which are seams that curve around waists and hips.

When two pieces of fabric fit together to form a curved area, there is one inner curve piece and one outer curve. For example, a princess seam is often used to curve along the waistline and hips of a jacket or blouse, creating contouring that follows the human shape. If you lay the two pattern pieces and corresponding fabric down flat, it looks like they could never fit. Follow these guidelines and you'll be able to create hourglass garments in no time:

1. Staystitch the curved edges right inside the seam allowance.

2. Clip the inner curved edge to the staystitching, making sure not to cut into the stitches. Cut small wedges into the outer curved edge at regular intervals.

3. Place the outer curved edge over the inner curved edge, matching your notches and pinning into place. (This is one time you really need to pin at the key places!)

4. Stitch the seam, carefully guiding the fabric around the curve.

5. Proper pressing is very important for a curved or princess seam. The seam should be pressed over a tailor's ham, with the seam opened. Clip notches where necessary to allow the seam to lay flat.

Sew Far, Sew Good

If you're sewing two curves together, use the inner curve as the anchor fabric, pinning the outer curve to it. The inner curve should be on the bottom, against the presser feet, which is a more stable position. The outer curve will shift more while you guide it, giving you greater mobility.

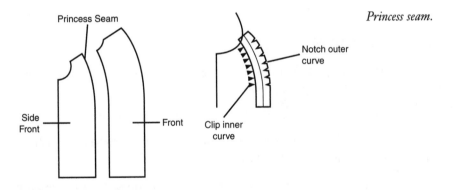

Princess Seam

Side Front

Front

Notch outer curve

Clip inner curve

Princess seam.

Unseemly Seams: How to Rip Them Up

No chapter on sewing seams would be complete without telling you how to un-complete your seams. The familiar lament "As ye sew, so shall ye rip" will become second nature to you. No matter your level of expertise, you'll find yourself making mistakes and ripping out seams—a laborious process, but well worth it to make something that looks just so. My teacher is very fond of saying that if you leave a mistake in and just blithely sew on, your eye will always go straight to the mistake, ruining your experience as well as your sewing project.

Get used to your seam ripper. Find a way that's comfortable for you to hold the seam ripper and the fabric. Rip a few stitches at a time. Never, ever, try to rip straight through the entire seam in one fell swoop. Remove the threads after you've ripped the stitches. If necessary, use tweezers to pull out the threads rather than leaving them in when you restitch.

You have just learned to take your first stitching steps, and you're already off and running. Sure, there are plenty of other specialty seams and seam finishes, but the basic stitches and seams that we've covered allow you the opportunity to make almost any garment or home furnishing, from a simple pillow to a fancy jacket.

Using a seam ripper.

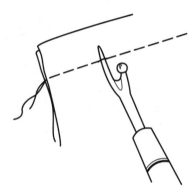

The Least You Need to Know

- Check your thread tension and stitch length, and prep your pieces, pinning where necessary and aligning properly.

- If you're crossing another seam, there's no need to backstitch.

- Before stitching, decide on your seam finish; make sure the seam finish is appropriate for the look and feel of the fabric.

- Before moving on, make sure your seam is straight and sewn properly; if not, rip it out rather than compounding the problem.

Chapter 61

Buttons in a Snap

In This Chapter

- ◆ Hand-sewing hints: the simple button
- ◆ Make way for wiggle room: the shank
- ◆ Buttons-a-go-go: machine stitching
- ◆ Button boundaries: placement
- ◆ Bungleproof buttonholes: machine magic

You can conquer buttons and buttonholes with relative ease as long as you know how to get around the holey messes. Plenty of little hints make hand sewing buttons not only simpler, but also stronger, so that you don't waste time resewing. Although I'm an advocate of machine stitching whenever possible, there are times when your button pops off on a trip, or just as you're about to run out to a business lunch, or two seconds before you walk down the aisle. Hand sewing can't be beat when you're beating the clock and are far away from a set-up sewing machine. A little button know-how goes a long way during these moments of button stress. But hand sewing is just the tip of the needle.

Noteworthy Notions

If one button out of four on your jacket has gone astray, instead of painstakingly trying to match the missing button, why not pick completely new buttons? They can update or change the look of a jacket, making it seem new for a fraction of the cost.

Even the cheaper machines can stitch a button on in no time. There are also everyday uses for your button skills—it really helps to know the ABCs of button application so that you can apply your skill at any given moment. We're going to tackle hand sewing first, and then move on to machine stitching, finally working our way up to creating, placing, and perfecting buttonholes, the yin to the button's yang. With a few fundamentals and fun facts, you'll be able to make buttonholes with a Zenlike calm. So put aside your safety pins and masking tape, because now you can be all buttoned up without losing your cool.

Getting Your Buttons Straight

There are two basic types of buttons: sew-through and shank. There are other, more exotic types, but these two are your all-purpose standards. Sew-throughs have two or, more commonly, four holes and lie flat.

Button varieties: Sew-Through and Shank.

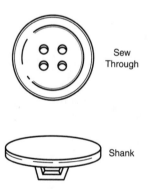

Sew Through

Shank

Shank buttons do not have holes and lift the button from the surface of the garment, making them especially useful on heavy clothes that give the buttons a workout, like overcoats. Both types of buttons, however, need at least a little space that gives them a lift, allowing for some give so that the button unbuttons and buttons easily: This space is called a shank as well, causing a little button confusion. Don't confuse your shanks. I'll let you know how you can get a sew-through button to have a shank, making it look like it's sewn on by a pro.

Buttoned Up: Hand Stitching

Although this is the most common sewing fix-it, it also seems to be the most dreaded. So many of us become all thumbs when it comes to buttons. It doesn't have to be that way. The simple rules for hand stitching on buttons will hold you (and keep your buttons on) for the long haul. First, we'll run through sew-through buttons, and move on to the shank button, covering all you'll ever need to stay buttoned up.

Sew-Through Made Sew Easy

Sew-through buttons are the most commonly used button type; they often lie flat and have two or four holes for stitching right through the button to the fabric.

- Use a sharp needle (say, a size 6 or an embroidery needle if you're using thick thread).

- Use heavy-duty, monofilament ("invisible"), or buttonhole twist thread for optimal strength for outerwear or jackets that get a lot of wear. All-purpose 100 percent polyester thread works on the majority of buttons that don't get too much wear and tear. Avoid cotton thread because of its tendency to snap under stress.

- Half your sewing time by quadrupling the thread. That is, fold the thread in half, pushing the center fold through the needle eye, fold in half again, and knot the end.

- Backstitch once over the button placement, and then sew on the button. Stitch only twice through each hole set (so you sew twice for a two-hole button and four times for a four-hole).

- If need be (and usually, you need to), create a shank, or a "lift" between the fabric and the button for ease of use. Simply place a toothpick, thick needle, or even a wooden matchstick across the button between the holes. Make five or so stitches over the toothpick and through the holes. After going through the hole the last time, toss the toothpick. Take the thread under the button and wrap it around the bottom

Noteworthy Notions

For button-stitching dazzle, use silk buttonhole twist. The beautiful sheen can't be beat. But bear one important thing in mind: Silk has a tendency to be slippery, so make sure you secure the ends with two knots rather than just one. Also, because buttonhole twist is thicker, there's no need to double or quadruple the thread when stitching; a single thread does the trick.

stitches about five times, completely encasing the stitches in a neat coil of thread.

◆ Tie off the button by making a small knot on the right side or by making a bunch of very tight stitches in place under the button.

Creating a shank with a toothpick.

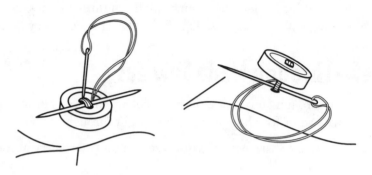

Frank Shank Advice

Hand sewing on a shank button is even easier. Simply anchor the thread with a back-stitch, stitch twice through the shank if your thread is quadrupled (four times if it's doubled), and secure the button with a few small stitches or a tiny knot.

Security Measures: Button Anchors

Some buttons need some extra strength, especially on overcoats, sportswear, outer-wear, or children's clothing. An anchor, whether it's a button or fabric, placed on the inside of the garment does the trick. I realized how important this is after my fiancé's leather buttons on his hipster suede jacket popped off for the last time. The interior button anchor has stayed the course.

Sew Far, Sew Good

Because thread is twisted, both in its construction and around a spool, it gets as coiled as your old-fashioned telephone cord. Just like you, it needs to unwind to sew well. To cut down on thread snags, pull the thread off of the spool with one hand, let-ting it unravel over a finger from your other hand. Pull out as much as you think you'll need, and let it dangle and unwind before stitching.

- Use a flat button that's a bit smaller than the outside button. Often, a clear button is the best choice because it's unobtrusive, blending into the background.

- Follow the same steps for a sew-through button, but place the smaller button on the inside of the garment, directly behind the fashion button, aligning the holes, sewing straight through from one side to another.

Machine Button Magic

Nothing beats the speed and strength of machine-sewn buttons. Mastering this technique frees your thimble-ridden hands to do so many other things, and shaves minutes off your sewing projects. For example, I'm a fan of throw pillows with button closures on the back, but I used to balk at this extra effort before I learned the minute method of machine stitching. It's the fastest, so take the plunge:

- You need a machine with a zigzag stitch and a button presser foot (a tailor tack foot also works wonders, with the bar aiding in creating the shank).

- It's crucial that you secure the button in place so it doesn't slip-slide away while sewing. You can do this with Scotch Magic tape, some Sobo glue, or a dab of a glue stick under the button.

- Drop the feed dogs, lower the presser foot, set the stitch length at 0, and set the stitch width that matches the holes in your button.

- Stitch about six times. Put the stitch width at 0 and stitch a couple of times in one hole to tie it off.

Take off the tape, and ta-da!—a perfect machine-sewn button!

Sew Far, Sew Good

For lighter-weight fabrics such as silk, where you need some extra button oomph, instead of using a button anchor, use a small piece of the garment fabric or a square of interfacing, sewing through the layers and securing on the back.

Sew Far, Sew Good

To check that you have the right stitch width that matches the holes in your buttons, put aside your pedal and use your handwheel, giving it a good manual turn, making sure the needle drops right into the holes. This prevents broken needles and nicked buttons from the needle jamming into the button rather than the hole.

Bungleproof Buttonholes

Machine-stitched buttonholes are God's gift to sewers. Back before the home machine revolution, buttonholes were tailored with laborious hand stitching or even more laboriously bound (a couture technique that binds the hole in fabric, not stitches). Nowadays, even the simplest of home machines can handle buttonholes, and with a little practice, this erstwhile impossible task will take no time.

Button Boundaries: Placement

Ever try on a shirt and find that it just doesn't hang properly? The bust gaps, the V-neck is too long, or maybe there's just too much space in between the buttons, showing a little more skin than you're willing to show on one of your shy days? Sometimes the problem is in the cut, but lots of times, simply rearranging the button placement can mean the difference between a bust button flying off at just the wrong moment, exposing your new bra, and a spectacular entrance in a smooth-fitting blouse. The key is proper placement of the buttons, which is actually dictated by where you put the buttonholes.

Commercial patterns come with buttonhole placement guides so that you can mark your fabric. But almost no one I know is made like the tissue-paper person it's patterned on, so there's no way the pattern can tell you where the buttons should go. If you're short-waisted, long-waisted, voluptuous, thick-in-the-middle, barrel-chested, or thin-as-a-rail, you need to put the buttons where they'll do the work they're supposed to, which is to keep your clothes on, laying smooth, pucker-free, and without any stress lines. So chuck the buttonhole pattern, and follow these steps to make your buttonholes:

◆ **Up or down.** There are two kinds of buttonholes: horizontal and vertical. Horizontal ones are used more often on places where buttons are used more often, as well as on women's clothes, where curvy bodies create stress (and I'm not talking about PMS). Vertical ones show up on menswear, cuffs, in smaller areas, and wherever you want a clean, straight line. The nice thing is that you can decide what works for you and your garment.

◆ **Starting point.** Vertical buttons should
be placed on the center front of a garment. Horizontal buttons should begin
⅛ inch from the center front toward the
edge of the garment. What does this mean
in plain English? I boil it down to this:
You should usually start a buttonhole ⅜ to
½ inch from the edge of the garment.
Period. But play around with your garment while it lies flat and pin it in place.
Try it on. See for yourself.

◆ **First buttonhole.** The first buttonhole
needs to be placed at the bustline for a
woman's shirt or at the widest point of
the chest for a guy's duds. After locating
the starting point, place each button 2
to 3 inches apart, dividing as equally as
you can so they are at regular intervals.

◆ **Marking up.** After you've decided
where they go, you need to mark buttonholes on the front of your fabric. You can
do this a couple of ways: Use a water- or
air-soluble marker (which you tested first),
or—my favorite—place a piece of Scotch
tape directly above the buttonhole, marking with a pencil or pen the end points.

Stitch in Your Side

Instead of becoming an
expert in snap-front jackets
because you're afraid of your
fancy-schmancy buttonhole settings, take time to learn your
machine's capabilities. Whether
you have a computerized
machine that calculates the buttonholes and memorizes them, or
just a standard buttonholer, know
your machine. Embrace your
inner buttonholer.

Sew Far, Sew Good

Button placement starts with
the buttonhole, not the button.
That's why I recommend that you
mark and make the buttonholes
first, and then sew on the buttons.

Buttonhole placement.

◆ **Buttonhole length.** How long do you make the buttonhole? Use this rule: Measure the diameter of the button (which is very important if it's rounded or domed button), calculate the thickness, and then add ⅛ inch for some give. This allows a longer length for thicker buttons and a shorter length for flat ones.

Still befuddled about buttonhole length? Try this easy test: Wrap a piece of string, strip of fabric, or even a ribbon around the button and mark where it meets. Divide this in half and add ⅛ inch. It's foolproof.

Marking buttonhole placement with Scotch tape.

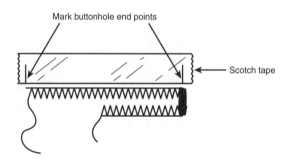

Determining buttonhole length.

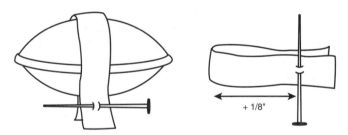

Taking the Buttonhole Plunge

I'm sure you've been told to look before you leap, and buttons are no different! Here are some things to keep an eye on before you get in over your head:

◆ **Needle news.** Use a fresh, sharp needle. You need these stitches to cut right through, with no snags or pulls. Use a needle that works perfectly with your fabric: a Universal for everyday fabrics, a ballpoint for stretchy stuff, and so on.

◆ **Stitch standards.** This is a crucial buttonhole point. A buttonhole is formed by a zigzag stitch that goes up one end, crosses the breach, and then goes down the other end, finally connecting the two lines, or beads, as they're called in the trade. The zigzag stitches have to be just right; if they're too tight and packed in, they'll cause the fabric to pull and pucker. If they're too loose, the stitching has a tendency to unravel after the buttonhole is cut, defeating the purpose of binding the fabric. How do you find this middle ground? Start by setting the stitch length at .5 mm. See how tightly packed it is and how it looks. Trust your eye; does it look like your pro buttonholes, or a really lame version? Adjust, adapt, alter.

♦ **Tension truths.** You actually want your buttonhole tension to be a little "off." That is, you want the knot to form on the bottom of the fabric, rather than in the middle or on the top. You can do this by loosening the top tension slightly and/or tightening your bobbin tension slightly. But ever so slightly ….

♦ **Directional direction.** You should start sewing the buttonhole on the left bead going toward your fabric edge. Stitch the left bead first. Stop at your end point. Set your stitch length at 0. Stitch five stitches that span the bottom of the buttonhole. Now you're ready for the right bead. This one has a tendency to look a little different because it's moving backward. Don't be alarmed; just adjust the stitch length a little if necessary and make sure to pull the fabric taut.

Sew Far, Sew Good

Always sew the lower buttonholes first. If you make a mistake at the bottom of a shirt or skirt, not too many people will notice. That bottom button wears an invisible sign that says, "If you can see any mistakes on this, you're too close."

Sew You Were Saying …

A **buttonhole bead** is the row of stitching on each side of the buttonhole that encases the fabric in zigzag stitches, preventing raveling when you cut the hole.

Noteworthy Notions

Does your fabric fail when you try to stitch a buttonhole? Don't want to add too much stiffness? Try one of these stabilizers: A liquid stabilizer, such as Perfect Sew, is applied to the fabric. After it dries, stitch the buttonhole and remove the stabilizer with water. A tear-away stabilizer like Stitch-n-Tear is applied and the remainder ripped. Avalon Soluble stabilizer washes away with water. All that's left is what's under the buttonhole stitches.

- **Reinforcement rules.** Buttonholes are almost always made somewhere where there's some reinforcement: a snappy (and stiff) cuff, a blouse front with facing and/or interfacing, etc. If you find that your fabric can't support the buttonhole, add some light interfacing or a stabilizer.

- **Now you're ready to test!** You know the basics, now test the buttonhole on your exact fabric; that is, if you have fabric with interfacing and facing, use that, test it, and see how it works. If you have problems, solve them on your test fabric rather than on your project.

- **Buttonhole bravery.** Go for it—buttonhole on your project. Conquer brave new button worlds.

Cutting In: Cutting Buttonholes

Your buttonholes are stitched, set, and ready to cut. Here's how to keep them intact:

- Use small scissors, a seam ripper, or a straight razor to open the buttonhole. To ensure that you don't clip over the end line, place your fingers on each end before clipping or place a pin on the end stitching—buttonhole insurance at no cost.

  Try this groovy trick that I use almost every time I cut buttonholes. Fold them in half lengthwise, and then snip the middle with your scissors. No special tools needed, just a careful and steady hand.

Cutting a buttonhole.

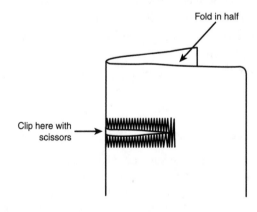

Fold in half

Clip here with
scissors

- Use a little seam sealant, like Fray Check, on the center of the buttonhole before cutting it. If it goes on too heavy, use a toothpick to apply it.

- Cut away and throw all caution to the wind.

> **Noteworthy Notions**
>
> Buy yourself a special chisel-shaped blade with a handle that just cuts buttonholes. You'll need to use it on a wooden cutting board or a cutting mat, but you'll never have to worry about snipping off the end of your hard-earned buttonhole labor again.

Stitch in Your Side

When it comes to buttonholes, do not wing it! Be sure you take the time to test your technique on a practice piece of fabric. You don't want to have spent 20 hours on a tailored jacket, only to ruin it with one off-kilter buttonhole right on the center front. Why, oh why, didn't you test?

Braving buttons has made you a stronger sewer. Hand stitching was just the start; now you know how to get some closure on all those jackets and tailored shirts that you've been avoiding. And now you see there was nothing real to fear: Buttonholes open a whole new world of garments and home furnishings that will leave you thirsting for more challenges.

The Least You Need to Know

- Don't ever hand stitch buttons like crazy, zigzagging around the holes of sew-through buttons, pulling the thread too tight, creating button mayhem. A few neat and well tied-off stitches do the trick.

- When hand stitching a common sew-through button on to a garment, create a shank, or "lift," between the fabric and the button by stitching over a toothpick or matchstick.

- Vertical buttons should be placed directly on the center front line. Horizontal buttons should be placed ⅛ inch from the center toward the edge.

- Accurate marking, correct tension, proper length and width of the stitches, and how tightly packed your stitches are will determine buttonhole success.

Chapter 62

Win One for the Zipper

In This Chapter

- Zipper preliminaries: length and type
- Zipper zones: inserting a centered zipper
- Advanced zipper course: the lapped and invisible zipper
- Zipper fix-its

Into each life, a few zipper mishaps must fall. Whether it's a torn zipper, nasty broken teeth, or a rotten pull, zippers have a tendency to give out long before your garment. But you can actually zip through zippers, from simple repairs to setting in an invisible zipper that barely shows except for the telltale pull.

Sure, sewing in a zipper can be scary, and often strikes fear into the heart of many a sewer. For some reason, zippers get a bad rap for being a difficult and dreary repair destined for failure. This needn't be the case; tailors know only a few more secrets than your average sewer, and I'm going to let you in on them. Soon, your zipper fear will disappear!

First, I'll show you how to insert a zipper so you understand zipper basics. Then we'll conquer invisible zippers, a nifty couture trick that's actually easier than inserting a regular zipper. And finally, you're ready for zipper renovation—replacing a broken zipper and putting in a spanking new one.

Your tailor may not thank you for mastering this expensive little repair, but you'll be pleased to know that zippers usually cost between $1 and $2, less than a cappuccino at your local café.

From A to Z(ippers)

Zippers, like everything else, have changed over the years. Go to a flea market or used-clothing store—you'll find metal zippers in even the most delicate of garments, including your Aunt Tillie's old wedding dress. Now, plastic, nylon, or polyester is the favored zipper material except when used with heavy fabrics, outdoor wear, or crafts such as denim, patio cushions, and so on, where metal is still *de rigueur*.

There are a few terms you need to know to be able to talk about zippers, so check out the following figure.

Zipper terminology.

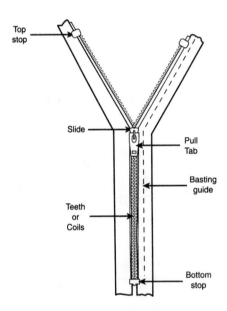

But what's the difference between metal and plastic? Metal zippers have teeth; plastic ones have coils. Metals come in limited colors (steel being the top choice), whereas plastics come in a huge variety of colors, so you should be able to find one that matches or complements even your wildest creations.

There are several kinds of zippers: standard zippers, invisible zippers, and separating zippers. I'll dive into the difference between standard and invisible zippers later in the chapter. Separating zippers do just that—split into two separate pieces. They're used on the front of jackets and with some craft items that need to open entirely.

The Long and Short of It: Zipper Length

Zippers are made in many lengths, usually from 7 inches on up. I used to check my pattern or my project to buy a zipper in the exact length needed. Believe it or not, this is actually a big mistake! Always buy zippers that are longer than the project calls for. That way, you can make the zipper any length you want with nary a care; it's a snap to custom-shorten any zipper from either the top or bottom, creating your own stops.

The other reason it's wise to insert a longer zipper (always use a minimum of 1 inch longer) is so the pull extends past the fabric when you're stitching it in place. By doing this, you can be sure that the bulky pull doesn't get in the way of the stitching, creating any unsightly skips or crooked stitching that will show on your garment. The zipper then conforms to your garment or project, instead of the other way around. Here's how to shorten a zipper:

1. To shorten a zipper from the bottom, figure out the length of the zipper you need. Stitch back and forth five times over that length (yup, right over the zipper coils) and backstitch to hold it. Cut ¼ inch below the stitching, and it'll stop a running train (or at least a zipper pull). Don't try this on a metal zipper, though; it will snap the needle.

2. To shorten a zipper from the top—my favorite and easiest way of dealing with the top stop—place the zipper so that it extends a couple of inches above the fabric. Close the zipper. That is, pull the zipper pull up so that it's above the fabric. Sew in the zipper, pull the pull down, stitch across the top of each side, creating a stitched stop for the top of the zipper. Now you're ready to roll.

> **Sew Far, Sew Good**
>
> Why is shortening the zipper from the top the tops in sewing ease? This way, you don't have to sew around the pull, a difficult and bumpy ride that creates the most common zipper stitching complications. And who needs that?

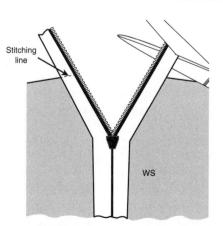

Shortening a zipper from the top.

Stitching line

WS

Zipper Zones: Centered, Lapped, Invisible

All zippers are not made alike. There are two distinct types of zippers you can purchase, and you need to decide ahead of time which zipper will work with your project before you start stitching (not only the zipper, but also the project's seams).

The standard zipper is sewn into a seam. The zipper coils are somewhat visible (depending on how it's inserted) and there is topstitching around the zipper that shows on the outside of the garment or project. A centered zipper is the easiest insertion: the zipper is aligned with the seam and stitched into place. Because the coils can be seen, it's a good idea to try to match the zipper color to the fabric.

A lapped zipper has a flap on one side that covers the zipper to a large extent. The invisible zipper is an entirely different beast. It's constructed differently and has a neat little pull. Use this kind of zipper when you want to tuck the zipper inside the seam, making it look exactly like a seam to the untrained eye. The only telltale sign is the pull.

Staying Centered: The Centered Zipper

The easiest way to insert a zipper is to put it in a seam. Whether on a back seam or a side seam, it's simple to drop in a zipper, which also makes it possible to remove your pants without doing the Watusi!

Stitch in Your Side

This may seem like an obvious caution, but always check to see if the zipper pull is positioned out before inserting it. Have you ever tried to unzip your pants from the inside when you're wearing them? It's not pretty, and neither is removing the zipper and starting over.

There are two kinds of seam zippers: centered and lapped, with centered zippers being the easiest and most common. I use this method all the time, and you will, too!

First you've got to mark the zipper placement on the fabric. Commercial patterns always indicate the zipper with the markings in the following figure. But you don't have to transfer all the markings; when you cut your fabric, just mark with either a snip into the seam allowance, a chalk mark, or a disappearing marker where the end point of the zipper is (usually shown on the pattern with a circle). Now you'll be ready when you get to the zipper zone.

Zipper pattern marking.

After you've marked the zipper placement, the next place to go is your foot—your zipper foot, that is. You need to replace the regular sewing machine foot with the zipper foot, which is thinner and sits on one side of the needle so that it can ride right next to the zipper teeth. Sometimes the zipper foot is made to swing from left to right so that you can position it properly around both sides of your zipper. When that's in place, follow these steps:

1. Stitch the seam that will include the zipper. When you reach the exact point that's the bottom of the zipper (you did mark the placement, didn't you?), stop and bartack or backstitch to secure the stitching.

2. When you reach the point where the zipper begins and you've backstitched, keep sewing the seam exactly as you would normally, but switch to a basting stitch. In practical terms, this means that you should change to your longest machine stitch and sew to the top of the seam.

3. Press the seam open from the wrong side.

4. Close, or zip up, the zipper and center it on the wrong side of the seam. Make sure that the pull is facing out. Place the bottom stop at the exact bottom point that you've indicated (or create a new stop with stitching).

Noteworthy Notions

Run out of basting tape? Or don't want to run out and get some? Instead, use some good ol' regular household tape (the Scotch Magic brand does just fine), placing it on the sides of the zipper and removing it later.

Sew Far, Sew Good

Want your zipper stitching to be smooth and flat? Always stitch across the bottom of the zipper first and then stitch from bottom to top on both sides. It'll produce a pucker-free zipper zone.

5. You're going to have to stitch the zipper exactly into place so that it's perfectly centered. How do you do that? Definitely not with hand basting! There are a few tricks to keep a zipper from slipping and sliding when you're stitching. My favorite is ⅛-inch basting tape, a double-sided sticky tape backed with paper. Place it on the edges of the zipper, peel away the paper, and position the zipper where you want it to stick.

6. Now that the zipper is stuck, turn over the garment to the right side so that you can sew the zipper in place. This is where you need the stitching to be straight and perfect. Remember, topstitching shows. But how do you indicate the stitching lines on the right side of your project? Easy: Position ½-inch transparent tape exactly centered on the seam. Use it as a stitching guide and stitch around it. Some people like to baste, others like to use water- or air-soluble markers, but I've found that tape is the easiest method of all—just tape on, stitch, and yank off, revealing perfect stitching results each time.

7. If the zipper is too long, pull the zipper pull down and snip off the excess zipper sticking out on each side. Stitch back and forth right across the top of both sides to keep the zipper pull from pulling right off. Warning: Always pull the zipper pull down before cutting and stitching!

Sew Far, Sew Good

If you have to do a lot of altering, and your skirts or pants need taking in or letting out, place the zipper in the back seam rather than the side. Then your clothes can fluctuate with your ever-changing sizes without serious zipper alteration altercations.

Scotch tape, basting tape, or Sobo glue can come in handy when getting a zipper to stay put, but it can sure gum up the works of your machine needle. Never sew over this sticky stuff, or you'll ruin your needle and maybe even get goo caught in the bobbin mechanism.

One last little tip if you've been having some problems: If your zipper doesn't glide smoothly, buy a little bit of paraffin wax from the hardware store. Rub it across both sides of the zipper teeth and it'll slide with the greatest of ease.

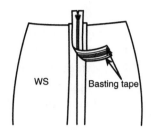

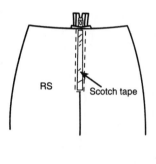

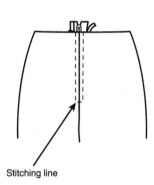

Sewing the centered zipper.

Lapping It Up: The Lapped Zipper

Sometimes you need to shake things up a bit. So, instead of a centered zipper, you might want to try a lapped zipper. The term "lapped" comes from age-old construction speak: A lap joint is one where two boards or metal parts are pieced together with the edges overlapping slightly so the surface stays flat. It works just as well for fabric: The zipper is hidden under a flap that falls on one side of the seam and is stitched into place, leaving only one stitching line showing on one side of the seam (when you're wearing it). This differs from a centered zipper, which always has an equal amount of fabric on each side and a double row of stitching.

1. Repeat step 1 for inserting the centered zipper, stitching and securing the stitches where the zipper will begin. Rather than baste all the way up to the top, turn and press the right side ½ inch, then turn and press the left side ⅝ inch. The left side will create the flap that laps.

Noteworthy Notions

If you're making pants out of Day-Glo fabric from the 1970s and can't quite find psychedelic pink among your zipper choices, try changing your centered zipper to a lapped zipper. You won't see the zipper teeth and their color at all, and you can paint the pull with nail polish or craft paint.

2. You can open or close your zipper to do the next few steps. Most patterns say open; I say closure is best because it prevents puckers from forming when the zipper is closed later. Put the basting tape on the right edge of the zipper, sticking it in place. Switch to a zipper foot. On the right side of the garment, stitch from bottom to top as close as you can to the zipper teeth. You won't need a stitching guide because the seam will be open and you can see where you're going.

Sewing the lapped zipper.

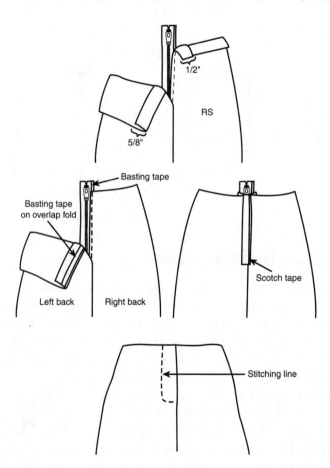

1/2"

RS

5/8"

Basting tape

Basting tape on overlap fold

Scotch tape

Left back   Right back

Stitching line

![] **Sew Far, Sew Good** _____

Keep the machine needle down whenever you shift your fabric to start stitching in a new direction. For example, when you stitch across the bottom of the zipper, and then shift to go up one side, make sure to position your needle at the corner, put it down into the fabric, and then shift. Remember when your teacher said "Pencils down!?" Now think of it as "Needles down!"

3. Put basting tape on the edge of the left side, then press into place over the right side where you've already stitched. Make sure the zipper is stuck. Here's where you need some stitching guidance. Position ½-inch transparent tape on the right side of the fabric along the edge of the overlap. Stitch carefully around your tape, starting at the bottom, shifting, and then taking a turn up until you reach the top of the seam.

4. Take off the tape, trim and finish the top of the zipper if it's too long, and be on your merry way.

On the Fly: The Fly-Front Zipper

The only traditional zipper that's not sewn on a seam is the fly-front zipper, a tailoring technique that you'll find on men's and women's trousers. I find that some jobs just aren't worth the investment, like remodeling your kitchen yourself, making puff pastry for a dinner party of 30, or rewiring your son's sound system for his garage band. I think fly-front zippers fit into this category if you're a beginning sewer. If you're determined to make tailored pants, take them to your tailor when you get to the fly front or save it for when your skill level increases.

The Amazing Disappearing Zipper: The Invisible Zipper

You're putting together a wedding dress; it's a simple white number with a beautiful V-neck. Perhaps you're making a complicated blouse with lots of top details. Or you want to make an envelope bag out of a fabulous vintage fabric. Where and how do you insert the zipper? The answer, with a resounding shout, is the invisible zipper! The reason it's called "invisible" is because there's no topstitching, no way to see the zipper coils, no nothing on the right side of the fabric until you get to the pull, the only telltale sign that it isn't just a seam.

The invisible zipper is sewn on the right side of the fabric, very close to the coils. When you pull the zipper closed, it turns the coils to the inside, pulling the fabric over them, closing it for a neat seamlike look. This may sound complicated, but it's actually easier than inserting a regular zipper because there's no outer stitching.

Invisible zippers are inserted in a completely different way than other zippers. You can use a conventional zipper foot to insert an invisible zipper, but you'll find that it's much easier if you have a zipper roller foot. This neat little hinged foot has a couple of grooves on the bottom that glide over the zipper coils and roll with all the invisible zipper punches and fabric bunches.

Here's how to make your zippers disappear:

1. Unlike other zippers that are inserted into an already-sewn seam, you sew in an invisible zipper first, and then sew the rest of the seam around the zipper. Start with the zipper and build from there.

2. Press the zipper on the wrong side so that the coils stand up straight, making it possible for them to fit into the presser foot groove. Avoid pressing the coils—they melt! This isn't one of those steps that makes something look nice; it's actually important to the construction process.

Sew Far, Sew Good

Whenever you wash or dry clean your clothes, remember to pull your zipper up. It'll prevent zipper tooth decay and coil spoilage.

3. Open up the zipper. Position it, right side to right side of fabric, with the zipper teeth at the $\frac{5}{8}$-inch seam allowance.

4. Starting at the top, stitch down the length of the zipper side right next to the coils. This is crucial! For it to be truly invisible, you must sew as close to the coils as you can. Stitch as far as you can. There will be a few stitches that you can't sew because of the zipper stop. No worry. Go as far as you can and stop.

Pressing the invisible zipper.

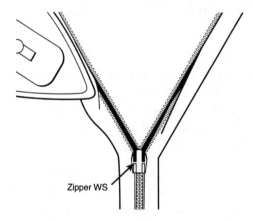

Zipper WS

Stitching the invisible zipper.

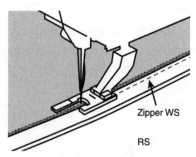

Zipper WS

RS

5. Close the zipper and pin the other, unsewn side to the top, making sure everything lays nice and flat, without any bulges. Open the zipper and sew the remaining side, again, as close as possible to the coils.

6. With your zipper perfectly in place, you can now sew the seam. Now you need to replace the regular zipper foot. Slip it on so that you can stitch the seam as close as possible to the zipper. Close the zipper, place the fabric right sides together, backstitch or bartack, and then sew with the same ⅝-inch allowance until you've cleared the zipper by a few inches or so. Then switch to the standard presser foot and sew on down the line.

Each zipper is easy to insert; after you've played around with the different types and know how to handle them, you can decide for yourself the best zipper and placement, creating the right look while making it easy to zip in and out of any garment.

Good as New: Replacing a Zipper

Now that you know how to put in a zipper, you can certainly take a broken one out and put a new one in. Removing the offending broken zipper takes a sharp seam ripper and some patience.

After you've gotten the zipper loose and removed all the straggly threads, make sure you mark the placement along the same lines. Baste the seam all the way to the top, and simply follow the directions for inserting the type of zipper—centered or lapped—you just took out. If you're removing an invisible zipper, take out several inches of the seam as well as the zipper so that you can resew it properly.

Every time a once-zipper-cowed sewer turns the tables on zippers and realizes how easy it is to insert, replace, and fix them, she's shocked at how silly it was to be scared of them in the first place!

> **Noteworthy Notions**
> If you've just ripped out a zipper and can't catch all those stray leftover threads, try tweezers. It's easier and less painful than plucking your eyebrows.

The Least You Need to Know

◆ Always buy zippers that are at least 1 to 2 inches longer than the finished zipper length. You can create your own zipper stops on both the top and bottom, tailoring the zipper to you and your garment, rather than the other way around.

◆ When inserting a centered zipper, the topstitching lines are all important. These lines show on the outside, and need to be fair and square. Use a Scotch tape guide for easy sewing.

◆ When topstitching will ruin the look of a project, use an invisible zipper. Remember this important rule: When inserting a standard zipper, sew the seam first, and then insert the zipper. When applying an invisible zipper, sew in the zipper first, and then sew the rest of the seam.

◆ Now there's no need to take zipper repairs to your local tailor. Get out your seam ripper, remove the zipper, and replace it, employing basting tape for the proper zipper positioning.

Chapter 63

The Bottom Line: Hems

In This Chapter

◆ Handling hand hemming

◆ Easing through ease

◆ Motoring through machine hemming

◆ Seeing through blindhem stitching

◆ Tacking like a tailor

I hate to hem. Or at least, I used to. Hemming is either the last touch on something that you've been making (meaning that you want to cut corners, rushing through it just to get it done), or the last-minute fix on that fantastic new dress you bought that would be perfect for tonight's party, but just happens to be too long.

What you need is a way to cut corners that doesn't create curvy hems, a way to finish off a project, whether it's a set of table linens or a ball gown, so that you actually do finish it, instead of putting if off because of the dreaded hem. Or worse yet, send it to the tailor because you can't cross the finish line.

To get you to go the distance, I'll give you some general guidelines for different hem finishes. Then we'll get into the specifics for specific projects—pants, skirts, sleeves, linens—just about anything sewn. And finally, we'll end with hemming tailored pants, one of the most common sewing repairs. Why make your tailor any richer and yourself any poorer? You can learn to hem faster than you can say "no cuffs, please."

Hemming Can Be Your Friend

Hems are essentially a way of finishing the raw edge of anything sewn. Usually, a hem is at the bottom of pants, skirts, shirts, jackets, and sleeves. But you also need to hem curtains, table linens, tablecloths, pillowcases, and so on. The rule is that if it doesn't have an enclosed seam, it needs a hem. Period. So there's no way of getting around hemming.

Hem success depends on a few things. The most important is picking the right way to finish your project, whether it's simply turning it a few times and hand stitching it into place, or using a more complicated finish that's better suited to your suit. The other biggie is measuring properly. You need to mark and measure the garment or project carefully, making sure the lines are straight. After marking the finished hem length, you can choose the type of hem from the different hem options.

Brass Tailor's Tacks: Measuring

When measuring for a hem, especially on skirts, pants, and dresses, it's important to keep the following in mind:

- ◆ Always try on the garment the same way that you will wear it; that is, if you plan on wearing high heels, a snazzy belt, and stockings with a swingy dress, put them on when measuring the hem.

- ◆ Be sure that the waistline of the garment sits properly—don't pull your trousers up to your rib cage and then measure the hem.

- ◆ Stand naturally. Don't slouch. Take your hands off of your hips and let them fall. Face front.

- ◆ Ideally, someone else should measure while you stand absolutely still. Have your helper use a wooden or metal yardstick and move around you while you stand still, just like the tailor does. Mark with chalk and then pin.

- ◆ Try on the garment while pinned. Make sure it hangs properly all the way around. Correct any dips or curves.

Stitch in Your Side

If you need to hem a garment that's cut along the bias, make sure you hang it on a hanger overnight (or at least 24 hours) before measuring and hemming. Any garment constructed along the bias will stretch as it hangs, sometimes in unpredictable ways. Why try to see into the future? Let gravity take its course, and then take over.

The Hand Is Mightier Than the Machine

Ugh! I can't stand sewing anything by hand, whether it's hems or buttons. But sometimes you can't avoid hemming by hand, especially if you have a machine that's incapable of a blindhem stitch (more on that later in this chapter). So let's get the dirty work over first.

Hand hemming has its benefits. When you don't want the hem to show at all on the right side of your fabric, hand hemming is the best. You catch only a tiny thread from the front of the garment, creating a couture look to even the simplest of outfits.

The best time to use this is on the bottom of skirts and other garments when you want a clean look, one without stitching lines, bulk, or added details. This hem goes by a few names: tailor's blindhem stitch, designer hem stitch, or just blindstitch. Here's how to hem the way fine tailors do:

1. Use a sharp needle—and when I say sharp, I don't just mean honed. This is actually a needle classification. Choose the smallest size that you're comfortable using that works with your fabric. (Sizes 7 through 10 are used on most medium- to lightweight fabrics.) Thread the needle (single thread, not double) with a knot at the end.

2. Decide on the edge finish. (See later in this chapter and Chapter 60 for more on seam finishes if you need some guidance.) Turn the hem up the width you've decided is appropriate. Press into place.

3. Fold back the hem slightly. Working from right to left, catch just one or two threads from the front of the fabric, sewing short stitches. Make sure they're evenly spaced. Patience, please.

4. Every eight or so stitches, tie a knot in the hem, finishing the entire hem with a double knot. This prevents complete and total hem breakdown when you're out on a

Sew Far, Sew Good

Use long-staple polyester thread for hemming. It's stronger and lasts longer. Save cotton for more decorative uses. For a really sturdy hem hold, turn to the mono-filament "invisible" thread.

date. If you get your umbrella caught in your hem, only a tiny portion of it will droop, rather than the whole thing.

Hand hemming a blindstitch.

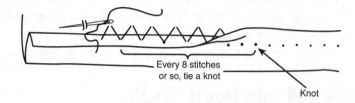

Every 8 stitches or so, tie a knot

Knot

For blindstitch hemming success, don't pull the stitches too tight or leave them too slack. Too tight means that you'll see puckers on the outside; too loose means they'll droop. Find the balance that works for you and your garment, and stick with it.

Noteworthy Notions

If you have trouble threading a needle, try these two tricks:

1. Use a needle threader. Loop the thread though the wire of the threader, pull it through the eye of your needle, and you're good to go.

2. Use a calyx-eyed needle. This has a teensy opening at the top of the eye of the needle so that you can just pull the thread down into the eye (instead of aiming for a miniscule target to shoot through!). This is perfect for people who hate needle threading (and who have a hard time seeing the tiny hole).

Ease-y Does It

Ease means a few things in sewing parlance. First, it applies to any time you need to fit a longer section of fabric to a shorter one. This almost always happens with a set-in sleeve, the cap of which needs to be eased to fit into the armhole, or a long hem where the folded fabric needs to be eased to fit the garment fabric. The extra fullness of the hem fabric fold needs to be carefully eased as you stitch so that you're not left, at the end of the hem, with a bulky bunch of fabric with nowhere to go. The top (folded) fabric also needs to be eased because the bottom (garment) fabric moves through the machine at a faster speed due to the feed dog pressure.

How to handle the bulk? Easy! Always pin the key points of a hem to be sure the hem fold lines up with the fabric—place one pin at each side seam to be sure. When stitching, carefully push the top piece of fabric with your fingertips toward the needle, feeding it at a slightly faster rate than it would naturally feed.

If you still have excess bulk, you can ease the fabric with a machine basting stitch.

Set your machine at its longest stitch length (usually 4 mm), edgestitch ¼ inch from the edge of the fabric, leaving a thread tail. Pull the thread, gathering the material slightly. Fold over the hem, pin at the key places, and distribute the ease throughout the hem with your fingertips. Stitch the hem into place.

Motoring Through Hems

Machine-stitched hems are by far my favorite, and definitely the faster and easier option. Motoring through hems provides an even, unmatched appearance, and can save hours when you're working on large amounts of fabric, such as curtains and bedspreads.

There are a number of different hemming stitches to master, starting with the simplest turned and stitched hems to the more complicated double-needle and fused hems.

Turned and Stitched Hems

This is the easiest way to sew a hem. You simply turn the fabric over the desired amount and sew a straight stitch, or an edgestitch along the edge of the turn. Use this on fabric that doesn't slip or stretch a lot. That means that silky, satiny fabrics are out, as are knits, Lycras, etc.

Sew Far, Sew Good

Here's an all-important tip for sewing a clean, straight, turned, and stitched hem. Decide on the finished length of your garment; mark it with tailor's chalk or a disappearing marker. Sew a straight stitch along the marked line. Use this stitching line as a stabilizer and guide so that you can turn the fabric cleanly. Make sure that the stitch line is just inside the hem so you can't see it from the outside.

Baby Steps: The Baby Hem

A baby hem is a turned and stitched hem with each fold a scant ⅛ to ¼ inch. These tiny turns create a small, neat, and even hem on the sleeves and bottom edge of blouses, home projects, and children's and baby (naturally) clothes. I use a baby hem to finish seam allowances on many a tidy tailored garment.

Machine Blindhem Stitch

This accomplishes exactly the same hem that you did with the blindstitch, but you hum along at a much speedier pace with the aid of your trusty sewing machine. You need a machine that has a blindhem foot, which usually comes with your machine. To accomplish this stitch, your machine must be able to zigzag stitch; if it can, it can blindhem stitch:

1. Attach the blindhem foot to your machine according to the instructions. Set the stitch length to 1 to 2 mm. (You may need to fiddle with this.) Release the upper tension a bit.

2. Press the hem in place. Fold the hem according to the following figure so that there is a ¼-inch overhang between the folded hem and the front of the fabric.

Folding fabric for a blindhem stitch.

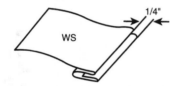

3. Place the fabric with the fold resting on the shelf of the blindhem foot and the ¼-inch overhang moving along the feed dogs of your machine. Here's how it works: As the machine stitches, it zigzags every fourth or so stitch, so that the zigzag catches only one or two threads from the front of the fabric, while the rest of the hem is sewn with straight stitches. Stitch slowly and carefully, making sure that the stitches catch the edge of the fold.

Stitching the blindhem stitch.

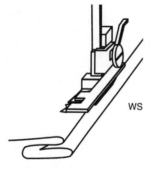

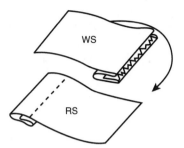

The finished blindhem stitch.

Rolling Along: The Narrow-Rolled Hem

This is perfect for anything that needs a very narrow hem that's evenly rolled and stitched. Sleeves, napkin edges, handkerchiefs, wide bias skirts—they'll look all the better with a rolled hem, especially if you're using lightweight fabric.

It's so frustrating trying to turn a tiny bit of fabric over, press it in place, and stitch it perfectly. But your machine will take care of it with a narrow-rolled hem foot (which attaches to most machines, even the older ones). They even come in different sizes, depending on the width you need the hem to be. The wider the funnel on the foot, the wider the hem, so be sure to use the right size.

The general rule is that the lighter and more sheer the fabric, the smaller the groove and the hem; the heavier the fabric, the wider the groove. But don't use this type of hem on heavy fabric—it just doesn't work because bulky or stiff fabric won't roll. Ditto for very sheer or lightweight fabrics—they don't feed properly into the funnel and can't roll right.

1. Attach the narrow-rolled hem foot. Set the machine for a straight stitch at a length of about 2.5 mm.

2. Place the fabric under the presser foot and stitch a few straight stitches in place. Create a thread tail by pulling on the nee-

Sew Far, Sew Good

If you're using a lightweight fabric that needs some extra help in rolling while narrow-rolled hemming, you may want to try some spray starch. The shot of starch will sometimes give the fabric what it needs to feed. Just don't try this on silks—they will be damaged by starch.

Stitch in Your Side

When rolling along with the narrow-rolled hem, don't be a control freak! Let the foot do all the walking for you. Instead of feeding the foot with an already rolled piece of fabric, let the foot turn the fabric while you pull from the back (and back off from the front).

dle and bobbin threads. The tails will be used as a guide to feed the rolled fabric into the curled foot.

3. Gently pull the thread tails so that the fabric moves into the funnel of the foot, folding over into a hem. Stitch.

The narrow-rolled hem.

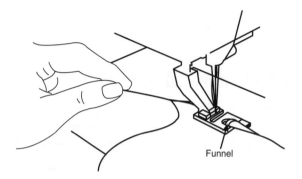

Funnel

Double the Fun: Double-Needle Hemming

This is one of those really smart inventions that make life easier for the sewer. A double row of stitches looks fantastic, hems like a dream, and lasts a long time. Wouldn't it be great if your machine could do this for you?

Well, if your machine has the capability for a zigzag stitch, it can double-hem with a double needle. These needles have one prong that fits into the sewing machine, with two needles that are attached to the prong. Each needle is threaded separately to sew an absolutely picture-perfect row of double stitching. The top of this double row of stitching is a straight stitch, whereas the bottom is a zigzag stitch that crosses between the two rows.

Sew Far, Sew Good

Got some stretchy stuff that needs hemming? Double-needle hemming will fit the bill—because of the zigzag bottom stitch, this hem allows for some give and take, retaining the stretch. Perfect when you don't want a hem to pull out when pulled!

These needles come in different sizes—the size indicates the width between the needles—translating into the width between the stitch lines. Use the ones made by Schmetz—by far the best, in my humble opinion—and try a 4.0/100 size for most hemming. The first number (4.0) is the width between the needles in millimeters, and the second number (100) is the needle size.

You'll need to thread the needles from two different thread sources. If you have a double spindle on your machine, great; if not, you can still double stitch:

Wind an extra bobbin with the thread you're using, and place it on the spindle first, and then place the spool on top of the bobbin.

To make sure that the threads move evenly through the machine, put each thread on one side of the tension discs, and then continue to the needles, threading them separately.

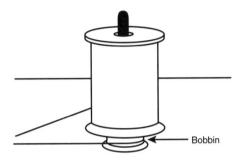

Place the thread spool on top of a bobbin to create two thread sources for double-needle stitching.

— Bobbin

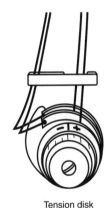

Double threading the tension discs.

Tension disk

1. Turn up the hem the desired amount and press into place.

2. Set the machine for a straight stitch. Set the stitch length at about 3 mm.

3. Topstitch the hem on the right side of the fabric, leaving about ½ to ¾ inch from the turned edge (depending on how you would like it to look).

You can multiply the multiple stitching fun by using a triple-needle stitch, creating three rows of even stitches.

Sew Far, Sew Good

When double-needle hemming, use the throat plate markings or a magnetic guide to help you keep your stitching on the straight and narrow. This is one hem that you really want to keep perfectly straight!

Double stitching a hem.

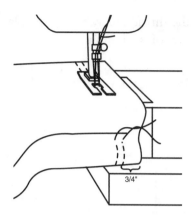

Fusing: The Lazy Alternative to Hand and Machine Sewing

If you really hate hemming, and hand and machine stitching has got you down, you can actually eliminate sewing (almost) entirely from hems. Just cut a strip of fusible webbing, which has adhesive on both sides, place it at the edge of the hem, and simply press it into place. Minimal sewing, minimal hassle! Use this for work clothes, shorts, casual skirts, children's clothes—anything where looks take a second place to speed and utility. Here's how to do it:

1. Decide on the hem width, then cut your fusible webbing ¼-inch thinner than the width of the hem.

2. Align the webbing with the hem, placing it ¼ inch from the edge of the fabric.

3. Fold the ¼-inch edge over, and then fold the hem in place. Fuse by using a damp press cloth. Using some elbow grease (pressure,that is), press with a steam iron for 10 lo-o-ong seconds.

Noteworthy Notions

A fusible webbing is the way to go for fast hems. There are two main types: a double-adhesive webbing such as Stitch Witchery, which has resin on both sides and works with a range of fabric weights, and a paper-backed webbing such as Wonder-Under and Heat'n'Bond, which can be used with more heavy-duty fabrics. Just peel off the paper and press.

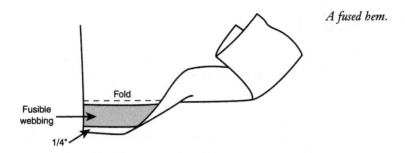

A fused hem.

Want to avoid any fusing problems when fusing hems? Instead of turning the edge ¼ inch, zigzag stitch (or serge) the interfacing to the fabric before turning the hem! You'll have finished the edge and prevented any sticky problems when pressing the fusible webbing.

The Finish Line: Hem Finishes

Just like finishing seams, you need to finish the edge of a hem so that it looks neat and tidy. When you're sitting at a dinner table and your red wrap-around skirt flips back, you don't want to turn red just because your hem is a mess! Hem finishes are very similar to seam finishes, with just a few extra touches:

♦ **Pinking.** Just cut the edge with your pinking shears! Use with fabrics that don't have a tendency to ravel.

♦ **Pink and stitch.** One more stitch, but still a simple finish.

♦ **Zigzag stitch.** Run a tight zigzag stitch along the hem edge, and it's secure.

♦ **Bias bound (or Hong Kong) finish.** Just like finishing a seam.

♦ **Turn or double turn.** This is just a quick turn (or double turn) so that the raw edge is enclosed within fabric and won't fray or unravel.

♦ **Serge.** If you have a serger, go for the neat, finished serged edge.

Stitch in Your Side

For a quick fix, always use bias tape for bias-bound hems, not bias-cut fabric! Bias tape comes prepackaged and ready to sew.

How Much to Hem?

Decisions, decisions! How do you decide how much hem allowance you should have? It really depends on the type of garment or project that you're working on, the fabric's personality, and the way you'd like the finished project to look. Here are a few guidelines:

- ◆ **Tailored pants: 2 to 2½ inches.** Men's trousers are usually pinked and hand sewn with a blindhem stitch, whereas women's trousers often have a more finished edge.

- ◆ **Straight skirt: 2 to 3 inches.** You can use any number of finishes for this item, from a hand stitch to a blindhem to a simple turn!

- ◆ **A-line skirt: 1 to 2 inches.** The best method for finishing this type of garment is just a double turn with an edge stitch or blindstitch (by hand or machine).

- ◆ **Extremely full skirt or round tablecloth: ¼-inch narrow-rolled hem.** This hem is great on table linens!

- ◆ **Sleeves: ¼ to 1 inch.** You can use a double-turned baby hem or a narrow-rolled hem here.

> **Sew Far, Sew Good**
>
> I love to reduce bulk wherever possible so seams and hems lie flat. The simplest way to do this is to trim the seam allowance between ¼ and ⅛ inch before turning up any kind of hem.

Tailored Pants

Tailors around the world are cleaning up on this relatively simple sewing fix. Whether you need to shorten men's tailored pants, or pick up a bit of your Capri pants to take advantage of the latest style, follow these simple steps.

> **Sew You Were Saying …**
>
> A **break** in trousers is exactly that—a break in the center crease or line of the pants leg, a small fold a few inches above the hem.

How Long Will You Go?

Decide on your pants' length. The rule is, the narrower the pant, the shorter they should be. Full pants usually touch the top of your shoe, while narrow pants often hit your ankle, or even slightly above.

Men's business trousers either fall at the top of the shoe or are slightly longer, giving them what's called a break. A *break* is a slight fold of about ¼ inch that shows when you're standing straight, but isn't visible when walking. This is, of course, a matter of taste, and what your mirror tells you looks good!

Making It Work

After you've figured out the length, it's time to mark with tailor's chalk and pin into place. When you're sure about the hem position, trim off the excess fabric and finish the edge. Men's trousers are usually pinked and hand sewn with a blindhem stitch, whereas women's trousers often have a more finished edge.

If you want to trim men's trousers like a pro, add a tip—a slight slope—from the front to the back of the hem. After marking the front of your trousers, mark the back ¼ inch longer. Draw a straight line between the front and back measurements, and then fold along this sloping line, blind stitching into place.

> **Noteworthy Notions**
>
> Next time you're shopping for notions, pick up a Dritz Ezy-Hem. This is a metal gauge that has a curved side and a straight side, each with markings to make the hem turnover easy to see, mark, and sew.

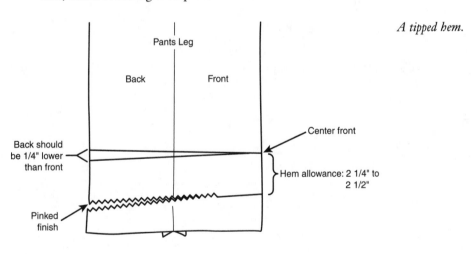

A tipped hem.

Finishing Up

We made it through hemming, and barely broke a sweat the whole time. These basic skills have the legs to carry you through many a droopy hem, curvy drapery, and overlong pants legs. Whether you're hand sewing or machine motoring, you can apply hemming hints to many aspects of your sewing repertoire. Now you won't be afraid to look down and see what you see!

The Least You Need to Know

◆ One of the most common and easiest ways of hemming is a hand-sewn blind-stitch hem. After turning the hem and pressing into place, stitch by catching just a few threads from the garment fabric and sewing to the hem fold, knotting every eight or so stitches.

◆ One of the most common and easiest ways of machine hemming is the double-turned hem. Simply fold twice and edgestitch. For some extra dash, especially with stretchy fabric, try a double-needle hem.

◆ Here are the most common hem widths: regular skirt or dress—2 inches to 3 inches; very wide skirt or tablecloth—¼-inch narrow-rolled or double-turned hem; tailored pants—2 inches to 2½ inches; sleeves: ¼-inch to 1-inch narrow-rolled or baby hem.

◆ Here are the most common hemming errors to look out for: mistaken measuring (keep your arms down and stand up straight!), uneven turning and pressing, wrong hem and edge finish, ease problems.

Chapter 64

Pressing Matters: Ironing Out the Wrinkles

In This Chapter

- Pressing as you sew
- Getting to the point of pressing: seams, darts, collars, and sleeves
- Foolproof fusing
- Fusible interfacing foibles and how to fix them

Pressing as you go is one of the unbendable rules of sewing. Pressing can actually change the shape of what you've sewn for the better (or sometimes worse if you're not careful): It can flatten seamlines, add curve to a collar, wrap a dart around a buxom shirt, flatten a popping pocket, and straighten edges and points. Pressing has power, and the more powerful your steam iron, the more power you've got at your disposal. This chapter tells you how to use your iron wisely, on both fabric and fusible interfacing.

The Pressing Points

I'm not being highfalutin' when I use the term *pressing;* there really is a difference between pressing and ironing, and pressing is preferable for sewing. The image of a person dragging a heavy iron over fabric is what ironing is all about—broad strokes sliding across the surface in a laborious, back-breaking way. This kind of motion and weight can distort fabric, stretching it, ruining the time you spent getting it into shape.

In pressing, you lift the iron and place it down, overlapping it across the fabric until you've covered the whole surface. This way, you won't make waves where you want smooth fabric. When pressing properly, you actually "set" the fabric, storing it's shape. It's very important that you press at each stage of the sewing process.

Steamed Seams

You must always press a seam before you cross it with another seam. If you don't, the next seam you sew could come out askew. Here's the best way to press a perfect seam every time:

Stitch in Your Side

Don't place the entire surface of the iron down when first pressing open a seam—use the tip; this prevents the seam line from being imprinted on the right side of the fabric. Save using the entire sole of the iron for when you're pressing the right side of the fabric, or when you're pressing broad expanses of fabric with no seam or other details.

Sew Far, Sew Good

Buy an iron with an iron guard that protects your fabric, often eliminating the need for a press cloth. I swear by my Rowenta Titan soleplate, which distributes heat evenly, prevents pressing shine, and cleans in a breeze.

1. Press the seam closed to ensure there aren't any sewing puckers or pulls. This "sets" the stitches.

2. Open the seam and press it on the wrong side over a seam roll, using the point of the iron and some steam if the fabric calls for it.

3. Go the extra iron mile: While the seam is warm, press down firmly with a clapper on it. The cool wood of the clapper will draw the heat out of the seam, "setting" it into shape. (On fabrics where a crisp finish isn't as important, you can skip the clapper stage. But if you have hard-to-press fabric or want a tailored look, a clapper can't be beat.)

4. Turn it over, and press on the right side of the fabric. Use a press cloth if necessary.

Darts

Darts are used to make curves that fit your body, so pressing them flat defeats their purpose. You need to press darts over a contoured surface that matches the dart's curve, and be careful with the point so that it doesn't pop (that is, stick out), an ugly detail that pressing can cure or create. Here's how:

1. Press the dart flat along the stitching line from the wide end until you're about ½ inch from the point.

2. Place the dart over a tailor's ham, finding a curve that matches that of the dart. Fold the dart to the side that it will face, ideally placing a piece of paper strip under the dart so that its imprint doesn't show on the right side. Use steam and a light touch.

Sew Far, Sew Good

Here's a quick rule of thumb for pressing darts: Vertical darts are pressed toward the center of a garment—front or back—and horizontal darts are pressed down.

3. Turn the dart over to the right side, positioning it over the tailor's ham, and press from the wide part down to the point, easing the point into the garment so that it practically disappears. Use a press cloth if necessary.

Sleeve Arms and Pants Legs

Here's where your big sausage seam roll does the trick. Just place it inside the circular fabric part and press, using the tip to press the seam, and the sole to press the rest. (If you haven't added a seam roll to your supplies, try a rolled-up magazine covered with a piece of muslin tied at the ends. Ensure that it's packed tight so you don't press puckers from the roll into the fabric.)

Set-In Sleeve

This is a pressing problem only if you don't have the right tools:

1. After setting in a sleeve, press the seam toward the sleeve (away from the garment). Don't ever press sleeve seams open!

2. Place the sleeve cap over a tailor's ham, steaming so that the rounded shape of the cap is retained. Nobody wants a sleeve that falls flat, and pressing prevents sloppy sleeves.

Enclosed Seams

Collars, turned edges, cuffs, and other areas all need special care:

1. Always press the seam flat first. If it's a seam on a collar or a tight surface, press over a point presser; if it's a curved surface, use a tailor's ham.

2. Turn and press on the right side of the fabric, being sure the seam is rolled toward the back so it doesn't show. Use a clapper for a finished look and a crisp crease.

Hot Stuff: Pressing Tips

Here are some things to keep in mind when you've got an iron in your hand:

♦ **The light touch.** Too much pressure can cause shine and overpressing. There's no need to press (despite the term "pressing") at all; just let the weight of the iron do it for you. Not only is it effortless, it's effective. The only exceptions are fusing interfacing or using a clapper, both of which require pressure.

♦ **Cooling.** After cloth is pressed, don't move it until it has cooled. While still warm, movement puts all those crinkles back, and you'll have to go back to the ironing board. It pays to press ahead and hang your warm garment like you would any other clothing article.

♦ **Pressing as basting.** Basting, in my opinion, is a drag. Whenever I can, I press hems, edges, and so on in place rather than pinning or basting—pressing power in action.

Sew Far, Sew Good

Always test the heat of the iron on the fabric before pressing it, either with a leftover scrap or with an invisible part of the garment. Use this quick heat guide: low for silk, rayon, nylon, and polyester; medium for blends, light wool, and light cotton; and high for heavier wool, cotton, and linen.

♦ **Pins.** Never press over pins, which can leave a permanent mark. (Also, plastic ballpoint pins can actually melt on to your fabric.)

♦ **Markings.** Take care to remove any markings, whether they're made with chalk or markers. Heat has a tendency to cook the marks into the fabric, making them impossible to ever get off. The same applies to stains. Never iron over a stain if you want clean clothes.

♦ **Zippers.** Never press on zipper coils—they melt! Also, stay away from hooks and eyes and other plastic pieces. Who wants plastic goo on a garment?

Full Course in Pressing: Fabrics

Certain fabrics need special steam and heat treatment. Don't take a frivolous attitude with these fabrics ... or else pressing meltdown may ensue:

◆ **Napped fabrics.** Any fabric with a pile, such as velvet, corduroy, velour, and fake fur is a real pressing challenge. Never press napped fabric on its right side, which crushes the nap. If creases exist, dampen them with a little white vinegar. Raise the nap with either a clothes brush or soft toothbrush. Steam lightly on the wrong side of the fabric.

You can also press over another piece of the fabric. Place the fabric, right side to right side, pressing lightly over the wrong side with a press cloth. This helps preserve the nap. For some serious pressing for velvets and other napped fabrics, try a *needleboard*.

◆ **Leather.** Press leather on the wrong side with a warm, dry iron (never hot, never with steam). If there is a crinkle on the front of the fabric that just won't go away, try pressing on the right side using paper as a press cloth. Be careful— if you touch the iron to the right side of the leather, it could leave a lasting impression.

◆ **Wool.** Wool should always be pressed with a press cloth.

◆ **Beaded fabrics.** Never use an iron or steam on sequined or beaded fabric— beads can melt, lose their shine, or curl. Finger press instead, or try the old travel trick—hang in the bathroom while you're taking a long, hot shower.

Sew You Were Saying ...

A **needleboard** is a bed of nylon bristles that preserves the nap of heavily piled fabrics while pressing. Place the fabric face down on the bed so the fur, velvet, and the like fall in between the "needles," maintaining their fluffy appearance.

Noteworthy Notions

Overstressed because you overpressed? Rather than leave that telltale shine, try this: Make a solution of 1 to 2 teaspoons of white vinegar to 1 cup of water. Dampen a cloth with the solution and carefully wipe the shiny surface. Then press lightly with a press cloth. Don't forget to test first to see whether the vinegar causes any discoloration of the fabric.

Pressing Interfacing So It Stays Put

The other major use of steam heat is fusing interfacing. Now it's time to get out your iron, test the fusible on your fabric, and learn how to make it stick for good.

A common sewing theme is the importance of testing. Nowhere is this more crucial than on interfacing. If you remember to think of fabric as an interactive material, changing with its environment, you'll begin to understand it better. Every fabric and interfacing combination reacts differently with heat, moisture, and pressure, taking on new characteristics. Here's how to find a perfect match.

Testing Tips

I've said it before, and I'll say it again before we're through: Always test first! It is crucial to test new techniques and fabrics before applying them to a serious (and costly) project:

1. Cut a strip of the fabric you'll be using, about 6 by 12 inches.

2. Cut 3-inch squares of different interfacing swatches of varying weights, pinking one side. Turn under one edge to use it as a pull tab later.

3. Fuse interfacing with your iron on the wool setting. (Skip ahead to the "Foolproof Fusing" section later in this chapter to see the instructions for this.)

4. Give the pull tab a good hard yank. Does the interfacing hold? If not, it's a reject right away. Does the interfacing fuse cleanly to the fabric?

Sew Far, Sew Good

Preshrink interfacing as soon as you buy it. Make a beeline to your bathroom, and follow these directions: Soak the interfacing in warm (not hot!) water until thoroughly wet, drain, carefully wring it out, wrap it in a towel to dry further, and hang dry. And remember—don't iron!

Are there any bubbles on the surface of the fabric or any shiny dots on the fabric (called "strike through")? If so, it's not the right interfacing choice. If the interfacing holds properly, fold the fabric over, roll it around in your hands, and let it drape. Which interfacing matches your fabric and adds the right amount of oomph? If the line of the interfacing shows, it's too much oomph—the interfacing is too heavy. After you've made your choice, fuse on.

Testing fusible interfacing.

Musing on Fusings

Almost every sewing book I've ever read says "Follow the manufacturer's instructions for fusing interfacing." I have rarely seen any instructions because interfacing is sold from large bolts with out any instructions. Left basically in the dark, you can follow general guidelines and do what I do—stumble around until I find the right heat, pressure, and time so that the fusing holds. If playing with all these variables doesn't produce a solid connection, give your fusible the boot and start over.

Foolproof Fusing

Here are some tricks and tips to make your fusing experience a faultless one:

1. Press the fabric first. You can't fuse to a flaky surface. The heat of the iron also "primes" the fabric, readying it for fusing.

2. Position the interfacing on the fabric, face down, that is, resin down. (Just so you know, that's the shiny side.) Hold the interfacing up to the light. Don't confuse sides! Also, be sure there are no foreign objects, such as hairs, scraps of fabric, or loose threads, in between the interfacing and fabric. These will fuse forever into the garment and can show through. Be thorough.

Sew Far, Sew Good

Because you cut your fabric and interfacing at the same time, fuse right away! I do it at least a day before I get to my machine, hang it up, and start sewing fresh.

3. With the iron on the wool setting, press lightly in a few areas, starting in the center, just to set the interfacing in the right place. Now you're ready for the serious pressure pressing.

4. Using a dampened press cloth, press firmly in one place for 10 seconds minimum (better yet, 15 seconds). No fast counting allowed. If you're one of those types, get a clock with a big fat second hand. Or count sheep very slowly. The point is, don't be impatient.

5. Press with both hands. Pretend that this is your workout gym. This is the only time where pressure is really important when pressing. Do this repeatedly, overlapping until you've covered the entire surface of the interfacing.

6. Let it cool before moving. Even more than fabric, interfacing retains whatever shape it takes when warm.

7. Turn it over and press on the right side, using a press cloth. Don't skip this extra step—it's important for creating a lasting bond.

Fusing Foibles

No matter how careful you are, there always seems to be some fusion confusion. Here's the hit list of horrors:

◆ **Fabric bubbling.** This is the most common and troubling fusing problem. Sometimes the reason for fabric bubbling is because the interfacing shrunk. The solution is preshrinking. The other more likely reason is that not enough pressure was applied when fusing—some areas stuck and others didn't—creating the bubbling effect. Time to break a sweat and apply a firmer hand.

◆ **Interfacing bubbling.** This is often caused by a too-hot iron. Take the temperature down a few notches and try again. It could also be that the fabric has shrunk, so you need to preshrink the interfacing.

◆ **Strike through.** This is the appearance of unsightly dots that show on the fabric. Its cause may be an iron that's too hot or interfacing that's too heavy for the fabric.

Take the weight and heat down a few notches and test again. When all else fails, try another interfacing.

♦ **Position problems.** If you position the interfacing incorrectly or just plain make a mistake and want to remove it, go right ahead. You should press the interfacing again to warm the resin and then remove it. You can never reuse interfacing, so don't even try. You can remove it, however, so get a new piece and do it again.

The Least You Need to Know

♦ Always set each sewn area with heat and steam before moving on to the rest of the garment.

♦ Always press a seam before you cross another one. Press the seam closed first to set the stitches. If appropriate, press the seam open. Then press with a press cloth on the right side of the fabric.

♦ Fusible interfacing requires the right combination of the following to hold for the long haul: the right weight and type of interfacing, and the right pressure, steam, moisture, and heat.

♦ Always test before using fusible interfacing. Test different types of interfacing and see what works best.

Chapter 65

Tissue Issues: Understanding Commercial Patterns

In This Chapter

- ◆ Conquering the pattern catalogue
- ◆ Picking a pattern like a pro
- ◆ Sizing up the right pattern size
- ◆ Deciphering pattern details
- ◆ Allaying layout fears
- ◆ Tackling tissue pattern symbols

Commercial patterns speak a foreign language, one that you have to decipher and understand before you can take advantage of everything they have to offer. You enter that world through the pattern catalogues; flip through them to find fashions and home-sewing projects that you want to make. You have to know what their secret code is telling you, and how to read it before moving on to the pattern envelope and its contents, the pattern instructions, and actual tissue pattern pieces.

Flipping Through Catalogues at a Fast Clip

The catalogue—a book listing the currently available patterns—is your first key to what's going on when it comes to patterns. The big names—Vogue, McCall's, Simplicity, Burda, and so on—all have their own catalogues that are divided into sections by clothing and project category.

You can find pattern catalogues at stores that sell notions or, more often, at fabric stores, but check ahead to see which brands are available. Each brand uses what's called a *sloper*, or the master pattern for each garment. This means that there is a basic bodice sloper, a basic skirt sloper, etc., that is altered to form different designs. The sloper contributes to the slight differences in the brands and how they fit. These differences are further complicated by different sizing, markings, and instructions.

> **Sew You Were Saying ...**
>
> A **sloper** is the master pattern that a company uses for each garment part—bodice, pant, skirt, etc. Although each company uses their own sloper, the basic design is almost the same. Each unique sloper does contribute to differences in sizing and fitting, so it pays to become acquainted with each company's quirks.

It's So You!

When deciding on a pattern, pick a style that flatters you, that you know will look good because it's tried and true. It's a drag spending hours making something that you know will never look good on you, no matter how carefully crafted it is. If you look better in a V-neck rather than a scoop neck, if an A-line skirt just doesn't suit you, or if you know that a three-button jacket is more flattering, be sure you base your pattern decision on these criteria.

Keep a Level Head

> **Noteworthy Notions**
>
> Most companies have a basic fitting pattern that you can construct out of muslin, helping you determine how to alter their patterns to fit you exactly. The muslin is marked up and fitted properly, and then the alterations and markings are transferred to each individual pattern. This is worth the minimal time and cash investment.

Always choose something within your skill level, which is indicated in the catalogue and on the envelope. Beginners should start easy, building on their skills. It's no fun being frustrated when you simply can't conquer a detail that's above your nimble thimble level. Patterns are often ranked from "very easy" to "advanced."

Sizing Up

After choosing a style, you need to pick the proper size. The pattern envelope contains a wealth of information on sizing and body measurements. The common measurements included are bust, hips, waist, width at lower edge (across the hem of the jacket, shirt, dress, skirt, etc.), the finished back length or side lengths, and the pants width.

Always choose the pattern based on the measurements, not the sizing. Patterns are not sized the way ready-to-wear clothes are. The sizes are almost always smaller because they haven't been changed to reflect the way American bodies have changed over the years—they are still based on the measurements. Don't worry if you're a size 14 according to the pattern when you're normally a size 10. Measurements don't lie, and it doesn't matter what size the pattern is labeled.

Stitch in Your Side

If you buy the wrong size and need to alter it, remember that you can't simply add or subtract the same amount all around the pattern. For example, if you need to go up one size, the shoulder measurement simply will not change as much as the waist size. Rather than run pell-mell into alteration, try it in muslin first and mark up the changes.

Keep in mind these guidelines when choosing a size:

◆ **Top or jacket.** For a top, select the size according to the bust or chest measurement. You can make adjustments to the waist much easier than to the bustline, especially on a jacket.

◆ **Pants or skirt.** The hipline, rather than the waistline, is the key measurement. Again, it's much easier to alter the waist by taking it in or letting it out instead of changing the hip construction.

◆ **Between sizes.** If you fall between sizes on these measurements, you should usually choose the larger size rather than the smaller.

Figuring Fabric

When you've chosen a size, you can select the amount of fabric needed. The fabric chart is multisized for different fabric widths (35", 45", 54", 60", for example), so take note before you ask for a piece to be cut for you.

Some fabric must be laid out in one direction because it has a raised surface called a "nap" that lays in that direction. Fabrics with a nap include velvet, pane velvet, some corduroy, and fake fur. You must take this into account when deciding on the yardage.

Napped fabrics almost always use more fabric because the pieces must be laid out in one direction. This is indicated on the pattern envelope as the "with nap" yardage. If you have any doubt, buy the "with nap" yardage so you're not caught with too little fabric.

Sew Far, Sew Good

A lot of patterns provide a range of sizes in one pattern envelope, which is really helpful if you're a different top and bottom size; you can mix and match. If you're using a pattern with only one size and your top and bottom are lopsided, use this rule when choosing the pattern size: Follow your top (shoulder, bust, chest) measurements, rather than the bottom (waist, hips). This is because it's much easier to alter the bottom garment than the top—trust me.

Ditto for plaids and stripes—because the layout of these fabrics takes into account a repeating design, you'll often need more fabric. First, however, be sure your pattern envelope doesn't say that the pattern is unsuitable for stripes or plaids. This is not just a cautionary device—it really means that the pattern simply will not work with a repeating design. If you can use a plaid or stripe, allow for matching the pieces with an extra half-yard or yard, depending on how wide the repeat is. For a very wide repeat, buy at least an extra yard.

Don't Sway from What They Say

Pay attention to the fabric recommendations, which are always listed in the pattern instructions. If the catalogue says the pattern works only with double-knit or two-way stretch, believe it. Don't try to dress up a stiff linen in a garment made for a drapey silk—it won't work. If the catalogue says avoid stripes or prints, do it. If it suggests a crepe or chambray, and you're lost about which is which, ask for some help from the fabric sales staff. They're usually amazingly helpful and knowledgeable, and well worth consulting.

Pushing the Envelope

All the patterns in a catalogue are numbered to help you locate the pattern envelope. The contents of the envelope are the sewing instructions and the actual tissue pattern pieces. The front of the envelope displays the drawings or photos of the finished project. The back of the envelope has more information about the project and what you need to complete it. Among the details included are ...

 ◆ Description of the garment, including any design details, such as welt pockets, princess seams, set-in sleeve, etc., that help you decide on the time investment and skill level needed.

 ◆ Drawings of the front and back view of the garment, showing seam lines, particular details, and construction lines.

 ◆ A quick list of all the notions that are required, such as buttons, snaps, elastic, seam binding, cording, zippers, etc.

 ◆ Finished garment measurements.

 ◆ Fabric recommendations.

 ◆ Fabric yardages, interfacing yardages, and lining yardages.

Piecing Together Patterns

Decisions have been made, fabric has been purchased. Now's the time to open the envelope, hunker down, and get cracking. You're faced with two elements: the instruction sheet and the actual pattern pieces.

Deconstructing Instructions

What do all these symbols mean? An entire page of the instructions can be devoted to line drawings of the pattern pieces and the pattern, interfacing, and lining layouts. If you've never worked with them before, at first glance they can look like an engineering manual.

Don't be cowed. Start with the pattern pieces. Every pattern piece is numbered. Because most patterns have multiple garments, pay attention to the labeling on each actual piece and the list of which pieces are needed for each garment.

Cut out your project's pieces, leaving the others still attached to the tissue so that you can fold them back up and return them to your pattern envelope (or better yet, a larger bag). Cut loosely, without precision; the time to be precise is when you're cutting the fabric, so there's no need to waste time on pattern perfection.

Before laying out the pattern pieces and cutting your fabric, read through the step-by-step instructions carefully. Remember, there isn't just one way of skinning a fake-fur jacket. There are other ways of attacking a garment, and soon, you'll rely less and less on the instructions and more and more on your instincts and skills.

Following are the usual symbols and markings that point you in the right pattern direction:

♦ **Fabric key.** This helps you identify the fabric, both in the layout chart and the actual instructions, so you can determine the right side, wrong side, lining, and interfacing by their shading. For example, on the layout chart, the right side of the pattern is often white, the wrong side is dotted, and the fabric is black. But this changes with each company, so check your charts.

Sew Far, Sew Good

Don't forget to press (that is, iron) the tissue pattern pieces before laying them out on the fabric. Crinkly pattern pieces create inaccurate garments. Also, the static electricity created when ironing will actually help the tissue stick to the fabric, giving you a hand during the cutting process.

♦ **Layout charts.** These are maps that guide you on how to lay out your pattern on the fabric for cutting. You need to take care of where the selvage line, grainline, and folds are. In addition to the fabric layout, interfacing and lining layouts are provided.

♦ **Folding instructions.** Most fabric is folded selvage to selvage when cutting it out. Some layouts, however, suggest different folds for optimal use of the fabric. If a pattern piece is positioned on the fold, extending past it, it means that it should be cut on a single layer of fabric rather than a folded double layer.

A sample fabric key.

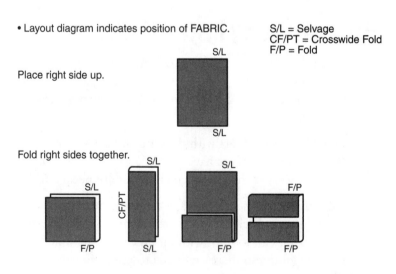

• Layout diagram indicates position of FABRIC.

S/L = Selvage
CF/PT = Crosswide Fold
F/P = Fold

Place right side up.

Fold right sides together.

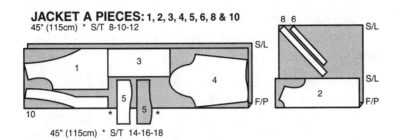

JACKET A PIECES: 1, 2, 3, 4, 5, 6, 8 & 10
45" (115cm) * S/T 8-10-12

45" (115cm) * S/T 14-16-18

Sample layout chart.

- **Star symbol.** This indicates special instructions involving the layout that can be found in the opening charts.

- **Term definitions.** If a special stitch is used, such as an easestitch or staystitch, the pattern will define it for you (but not very well, so don't rely too heavily on these definitions).

Sew Far, Sew Good

Many companies swear they give you the best way of laying out your pattern so you don't waste money on extra fabric. But this isn't always the case; you can certainly play around with the layout to find what suits you and your fabric best.

Getting the Pattern Pieces to Fall into Place

The tissue pieces have their own markings and symbols that are crucial when speaking pattern dialect. Take the time to learn them once, and just like riding a bike, you'll remember them forever.

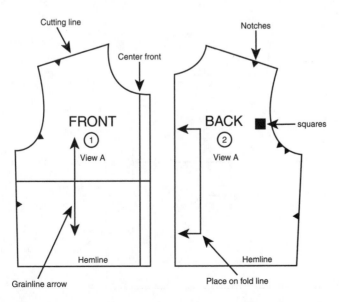

Sample pattern markings.

- **Cutting line.** This is the outside border of the pattern piece. On a single-size garment, it's a solid line. On a multisize garment, it'll be different for each size (for example, a broken line for size medium).

- **Grainline arrow.** Each piece has a grainline arrow that indicates how the pattern piece should be placed on the fabric. This is indicated with a solid line with directional arrows on it. This is crucial! If you don't place the grainline on the straight and narrow, your garment will never hang properly. The way to find the exact grainline placement is to measure the distance from one end of the grainline arrow to the selvage. Match the other end to the exact same measurement, and you're golden.

Stitch in Your Side

When you see a pattern piece with a grainline running diagonally (rather than straight up and down) through it, don't be distressed. This is a piece that should be cut on the bias. Just position the piece so that the straight line on the tissue piece aligns with the grainline, and you're set.

- **Notches.** These are indicated with small triangles that point out from the garment cutting line. They indicate where pieces of fabric are joined. It is the industry standard to place one notch in the front piece of a garment, two in the back, and three at other places. Never cut the triangles out as indicated—it's a total waste of time. Instead, make small snips with your scissors about ¼ inch into the garment's seam allowance. Never cut any deeper—you'll snip into the seam allowance or weaken it with a too-wide snip.

Aligning the grainline with the selvage.

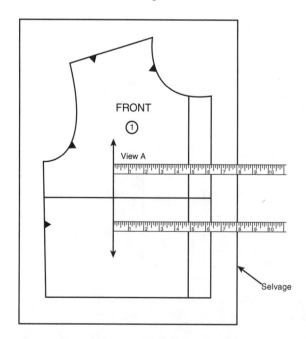

◆ **Position indicators.** The bust apex, the center front, the waistline, and more are all indicated on the pattern for your convenience.

◆ **Fold line.** If a piece of fabric is to be placed on a fold (making it twice the size of the pattern piece, an exact double on the other side), it's marked with a double-ended arrow that points to the fold and says "place on fold." It may take a few cutting disasters before you figure out how to prevent fold foibles. The standard fold pieces are the backs of shirts, jackets, or dresses, collars, and interfacing.

◆ **Circles, squares, and triangles.** There are a variety of placement symbols that are marked on the pattern, not all of which are completely necessary. Reading through the instructions ahead of time will help you decide which ones you need to transfer.

◆ **Zipper placement.** Zippers are indicated with a zigzag line and a circle at the end.

◆ **Hemline.** This is a line that shows the finished length of the garment. You can use this to lengthen or shorten the hem.

◆ **Adjustment lines.** This is where you may lengthen or shorten a garment without affecting its overall shape and fit. This is especially important on an arm or skirt where the shape and drape will be changed by simply raising or lowering the hemline.

Sew Far, Sew Good

Although the pattern always indicates the button placement, I like to wait until my garment is completely constructed before deciding on button placement. Buttons need to close a garment around you and your unique body. Wait until you're done and position the buttons where they should be on your body. Use this guideline: If it's a blouse or jacket that needs some real closure, always put one button exactly on the bust apex, building the other buttons around it.

◆ **Darts.** These are triangular broken lines that meet at a circle.

◆ **Buttonhole markings.** These are indicated either on the pattern pieces or on a separate buttonhole guide.

Noteworthy Notions _____

When you've learned the basics of putting together a home-sewn garment, get rid of your pattern instructions. Follow these simple steps and your garment will fall into place in the proper order, making it easy to fit as you sew:

1. Prepare darts, tucks, and pleats.
2. Sew style lines, except for side and shoulder seams.
3. Interface.
4. Prepare pockets.
5. Insert zippers.
6. Sew shoulder seams.
7. Close up side seams and inseams.
8. Prepare collar.
9. Prepare sleeves.
10. Attach collar.
11. Attach facings.
12. Set in sleeves.
13. For dresses, attach skirt to bodice.
14. For skirts or pants, attach waistband.
15. Hem.
16. Sew on buttons.
17. Sew any finishings.

The Least You Need to Know

♦ Don't ignore your own body type in favor of a trendy fashion when choosing a pattern.

♦ Follow the fabric suggestions, the notion needs, yardage, and size measurements that are listed on the pattern envelope.

♦ Press both your fabric and tissue pieces; locate the grainline of the fabric and lay it out accordingly; follow the "with nap" layout for piled fabrics; and pay attention to any special instructions, such as cutting on the fold.

♦ Don't forget to transfer all the key marking, clips, notches, and doohickeys (well, maybe not the doohickeys) from the pattern pieces to the garment fabric.

66

Sewing Project: Curtains and Shades

In This Chapter

- ◆ Widen your window style horizons
- ◆ Measure up curtain fabric
- ◆ Cook up some café curtains
- ◆ Hold your heading tape high
- ◆ Batten down Roman shades

Some of my earliest sewing forays were into window dressing. As a New Yorker, I'm surrounded by the Manhattan skyline—stunning views of high rises and skyscrapers. Although I love seeing out, I certainly don't want anyone to see in.

I've watched *Rear Window* a few too many times, so curtains are a necessity. I made a simple set for my first out-of-college apartment—just plain old-fashioned cotton panels hanging from a fabric casing—and have graduated to a fantastic set of lined, wrap-around vintage cotton curtains with a triple-pleat gather. They really set the tone for my whole bedroom, and so should your window treatments.

One Step at a Time: Getting Started

All of this can come to you at a minimal cost, both of time and money. I figured this out when I went to Manhattan's Lower East Side, famous for its fabric bargains and low-cost custom-made curtains. After finding a not-so-bargain-basement fabric that I thought I could live with, the estimates for making curtains for my bay window actually ran into the thousands of dollars!

> **Noteworthy Notions**
>
> In the market for some fabric accents for your home? Shop regularly with no particular goal in mind. Pop into fabric stores, scout the sales, and clip announcements of vintage auctions. You never know when the fabric that's the perfect companion to your unique nubby knit couch will show up.

This is when and where I took control; because I'd already covered the basics of plain old hemming and straight stitching, curtain creations were simply a matter of mastering measuring and hanging. We're going to learn the easy way to window dressing, starting with choosing the right look, measuring for fit, and hanging techniques. Before you actually buy the fabric, you need to measure properly. This is a three-step process: decide on the position of the curtain; decide on the hanging method (tracks or poles); and decide whether there will be a heading tape. Then, and only then, can you determine the fabric amount. After calculating fabric amounts, we'll glide through some of the most versatile, simple, and elegant window treatments, from breezy sheer sheaths to the Roman shade.

Homespun Fabric Choices

What kind of fabric you choose to decorate your windows is just as important as the style of window decoration. Flip through some decorating magazines and you'll see how a pair of heavy velvet curtains add weight, gravity, and richness to a room; a gauzy, free-flowing sheath can connote an airy, light, fantasy world; a tailored crisp cotton duck can mean clean lines and clarity; a heavy raw-silk swag in a rich burgundy can carry you away to the Far East.

Here are some important cues that will help guide your choice:

♦ **Weight.** The weight of the fabric should complement your home furnishings. If you have a house full of playful and colorful Ikea stuff, choose accordingly. If you favor Biedermeier and bulky antiques, your fabric needs to be made of sterner stuff. My apartment has streamlined 1950s furniture, so I chose a vintage cotton with a subtle print for my curtains.

◆ **Fabric color/print.** A splashy print can make a statement; a subdued solid hue can accent the furnishings rather than the window. Where's the focal point and where do you want your eye to be drawn? You can decide if you want the color of the curtains to either match, complement, or contrast with the walls and furnishings. Put together a set of paint chips and fabric swatches from your room, tuck them in your backpack, and you'll always be ready to mix or match possible fabric choices.

◆ **Light.** How much light do you want to let into your life? Light worshippers need to keep the coverage to a minimum, relying on lightweight sheers—cotton, linen, batiste, voile, organdy, and so on. If the song "Here Comes the Sun" makes you cringe, you want heavier, darker fabrics.

Noteworthy Notions

I love light, but not when I'm sleeping. Even if I'm catching 40 winks in the middle of the day, total darkness is required for some real shut-eye. This is easy to accomplish with some black-out lining, which is what is used on hotel room curtains. It's cheap (about $4 a yard), hangs well, protects your curtain fabric from dirt, and certainly keeps light from creeping into any bedroom. Buy it at any drapery store.

◆ **Window size and shape.** Got a tiny window? Hang the curtain outside of its border to make it look bigger. A shortie? Hang the curtains to the floor to lengthen the look. Wrap-around or bay windows need no size enhancement, so curtains can fit inside. Size is often an illusion; think about how tall Tom Cruise really is.

Stitch in Your Side

Remember those loud plaid pants that your Uncle Al wore? The ones that gave you a headache? Remember them when using a print on your windows. If you're using a large repeating pattern, is the window large enough to display the entire repeat (repeatedly!)? Is the print so loud it shouts down everything else in the room, including you and your Pucci print dress? Prints should go with your décor, not compete with it.

◆ **Use.** Are you the type who likes to get up in the morning and fling the curtains wide open? Or do you like stationary embellishments, elegantly draped swags that only serve a decorative purpose? Or because you occasionally vacuum while wearing your favorite teddy, do you favor shades that go up or down with a quick pull? Decide what your needs are, and the curtain design will fall into place.

♦ **Practicality.** If the exhaust of your local Chinese restaurant is aimed straight at your window, your curtains will be covered with chop suey slime and fried dumpling detritus—use washable fabrics only. Does the window face a cold front coming off of Lake Michigan? Use heavy, warm fabrics to keep the warmth in and the cold air out.

Sew Far, Sew Good

Decorators usually show fabrics in books filled with minuscule swatches. How could anyone make an educated choice with so little to go on? Instead, go the extra yard—buy a yard of fabric and live with it for awhile. Hang it up. Look at it in different lights. Pretend it's surrounded by people at a party. Does it live up to your lifestyle?

Noteworthy Notions

If you want to keep your curtains on track, buy quality tracks. Most are made from lightweight plastic, so be sure they can support the weight of the curtains. Also check that the gliders or runners move with the greatest of ease so that your curtains don't get all hung up.

Hangin' In There: Poles and Tracks

Now comes more drape decisions: what to hang your curtains on. The possibilities are endless, and you can let your creativity run rampant, but there are two traditional choices: poles and tracks.

♦ Poles are ideal for curtains that won't move much—café curtains, swags, and tunnel pocket curtains—all of which are meant to stay put or just be pulled back with a tie. Poles have become pretty sophisticated affairs over the years, a decorative element in their own right. A warm wood, a steely chrome, a sleek copper with fancy fillips—all make a room with a specific view, so decide on the right role for your pole.

♦ Tracks, on the other hand, are for quick-gliding drapes, slippin' and slidin' along, easy openin' and closin'. There are many varieties of tracks—invisible, visible, cording and overlap, and double valance—so scope out your local home decorator depot for the look you want and follow the kit instructions. Tracks are often cut to order, so it's important to measure the curtain space properly.

Before deciding on the kind of track or pole you use, ask yourself these three key questions:

1. Where will the poles be attached: inside the window sill; outside the window; around a curved corner; or on the ceiling?

2. Will they support the weight of the curtains?

3. Are they visible? If so, make sure the look of the pole or track matches your room or it is covered.

Hang 'Em High: Pole Placement

Pole and track placement is determined by the construction of the window and the look that you want the curtains to achieve. When you assess your curtain situation, take a good hard look at the windows and where they are. The most common pole placement is on the wall above the window. Is there space for the pole? Can the pole be attached or does the wall's construction make it difficult? If you get the thumb's up for this placement, you need to decide on the length of the pole. It has to extend far enough past the window for the curtains to fall neatly to the side. For sheers and lightweight curtains, you need a side clearance of at least 6 to 10 inches. Heavier and fuller fabrics need upward of 10 inches.

You can also attach the poles or tracks to the ceiling above the window. This is especially useful if the top of the window is very close to the ceiling. Make sure to buy poles that attach on the top rather than the sides for this placement.

If you have a recessed window, you can attach the pole to the window casing, the top of the window, or with a wooden batten.

Another option is a pole or a track with overlap arms and what is called "returns" on the side. This track gives the curtains room to blow in the breeze, extending out from the window with ease.

Ahead of the Game: Curtain Headings

If you've got a head on your shoulders (and what sewer doesn't?), you'll want to get a handle on heading tapes, a quick and easy way to tailor your curtains with pleats and gathers.

Stitch in Your Side

Always look before you sew! Check and see where the hook holes are, and make sure they're facing out. Sewing the tape on to the wrong side is a real gathering gaffe.

Heading tapes are ready-made strips of stiff fabric that you attach along the top border of curtains. They either have drawstrings to form even gathering or pockets for hooks that create different pleats (such as triple pleats or box pleats) without any complicated stitching on your part.

Sew Far, Sew Good

Make sure you position the tape correctly; if you have two curtains that meet, make sure the pleats start an equal amount into each curtain so they're evenly spaced.

They're a total pleasure to use, and can create a complex and tailored look by simply stitching into place; the pleats or gathers form automatically with either a quick pull of the drawstring or the addition of hooks to the headers. Because the fabric doesn't lie in a flat sheet, you will have to calculate the amount of extra fullness needed to create the folds. Following are the most common gathering tapes and the fabric fullness required.

Groovy Gathers: Standard Gathering Tape

Standard gathering tape is a relatively thin (usually 1 to 2 inches) tape that creates even, soft gathers. You will need 1½ to 2 times the track length of fabric fullness.

Noteworthy Notions

If you're attaching heading tape to slightly flimsy fabric, add some stiffness with a strip of interfacing. Your heading will stand at attention, doing away with droop.

Three Times as Nice: Triple-Pleat Tape

When you want to pull out all the stops and create formal, tailored curtains, nothing beats a triple-pleat tape. It's a deep, stiff tape with slots at the bottom for triple-pronged hooks that slip into the pockets, gathering the curtains into perfectly placed pleats with spacing in between. The fabric fullness required is two times the track length.

Picture-Perfect Pleats: Pencil-Pleat Tape

This tape creates thin, even pleats that are gathered together with cording. The fabric fullness required is 2¼ to 2½ times the track length.

Drop-Dead Gorgeous: Measuring the Drop

You've figured out the hard stuff—hanging, headings, and even fabric—now comes time for the hard math. Before cutting the fabric, get out your tape measure instead of your calculator. You need to measure up by first figuring the *drop*. This is the length of the finished curtain from where it will hang (whether on a pole or track) to the bottom. The length of the curtains, or the drop depends on the window style. Follow these guidelines:

- ◆ **Sill length.** Drapes should end ⅝ inch to 1 inch above a sill for clearance.

- ◆ **Below the sill.** Usually ends 2 to 4 inches below the window itself, depending on what's underneath the sill and the look you want.

Sew You Were Saying ...

The **drop** is the measurement of the finished curtains from where they will hang to their length.

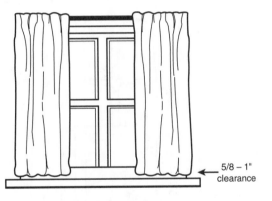

Sill-length curtains.

5/8 – 1"
clearance

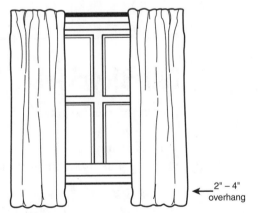

Below-the-sill curtains.

2" – 4"
overhang

- ◆ **Recessed curtains.** Recessed curtains are used with a recessed window—that is, a window that's set into the wall rather than flush with the wall. Because the window has its own set-in area, the curtains need to fit inside as well. Give a ⅝-inch to 1-inch clearance.

Recessed curtains.

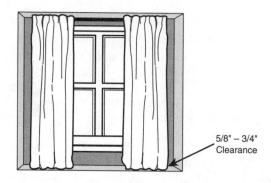

5/8" – 3/4"
Clearance

◆ **Floor length.** For the curtains to hang flat, leave a 1-inch floor clearance.

Floor-length curtains.

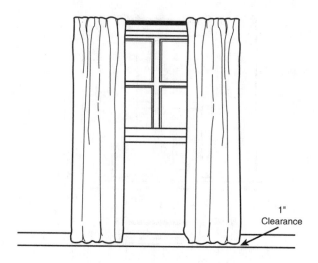

1"
Clearance

Noteworthy Notions

Going for the glam look, or a bit of drama? Instead of ending your floor-length curtains right below the floor, let them pool in a plush "puddle." Add anywhere from 2 to 10 inches to your drop length for a classic puddle. I personally love that word so much I want almost all my curtains to puddle, but I guess that's not practical.

Full-Blown Fabric Measuring

Curtains strike fear into the hardiest sewing hearts because of the amount of fabric involved. What if a miscalculation in width costs you not only an arm and a leg, but also many feet of fabric?

Expensive mistakes can be avoided with some handy calculating rules. They may look complicated, but after you dig in and start doing the math, you'll be whipping up café curtains in your spare time. Just remember this hard and fast rule: Measure for fabric only after you've decided on the fabric, attached the poles or tracks, and figured out the style of curtain, including the heading. Then, and only then, are you ready to whip out your tape measure.

Figuring fabric length:

1. Measure the drop from where the curtain hangs to the finished length.

2. Decide on the casing/heading. Determine the top hem. For most curtains, a 3-inch top hem will suffice.

3. Determine the bottom hem. This amount is usually 3 to 6 inches.

4. Add up the total length of fabric needed.

Sew Far, Sew Good

Now that sewing has inched its way into your life, your plastic tape measure always seems to be on hand. But for curtain measuring, only your steel or wooden tape measure will do for long-distance accuracy.

Figuring fabric width:

1. Determine the finished width. Measure the rod only where the curtain will hang (not any additional decorative elements). Be sure to measure the returns if you have them.

2. Multiply the width by the fullness amount.

3. Add the side hems. A standard hem, which you may alter, is a double-turned 1-inch hem, or 4 inches total for one panel. This is the total width.

Sew Far, Sew Good

It may seem like a money-waster, but always add more when estimating curtain fabric. No one likes to be left with the shades up, exposing one's lack of fabric savvy, by buying too little. That's the real waste of money.

Figuring fabric yardage:

1. Divide the total width of the finished fabric by the width of your fabric (be it 54 inches, 60 inches, etc.). This amount is the number of fabric widths that you need.

2. Multiply this number by the fabric length from above.

3. Divide this number by 36. This is the total number of yards needed to complete your curtains.

Sheer Magic

There's nothing better than a beautiful sheer curtain blowing in the wind, letting light in while adding an aura of decorative flair. Sheer curtains look best hanging on a rod with a simple casing rather than a fancy or complicated construction. And the real beauty is the bucks you'll save; these will cost a fraction of cookie-cutter curtains and come in just the color and size you want. Here's how to calculate the fabric measurements:

- ◆ **Bottom hem.** A double-turned 1-inch hem (2 inches total).

- ◆ **Side hems.** A double-turned ½-inch hem on each side for each panel (1 inch total per panel).

- ◆ **Top hem and casing.** Measure the rod width by wrapping a ribbon around the rod; mark and measure. Add 3 inches (½ inch for the hem turn and 2½ inches for some give) to the rod width for the total top hem.

- ◆ **Panels.** If you need to sew panels of fabric together, this is where your beautifully bound French seam comes in handy. Add ⅝ inch for each side of a panel you plan on using.

- ◆ **Fabric fullness.** Multiply the rod length by 2 to 2½ times to achieve a full rather than flimsy look for sheer curtains.

Length: Add the drop length plus the rod width plus 3 inches plus 2 inches.

Drop length: ___ + casing width: ___ + top hem (3 inches) + bottom hem (2 inches) = ___.

Width: Rod length multiplied 2 to 2½ times, plus hems of 1 inch for each side, plus ⅝ inch for each panel side that will be sewn together.

Rod length: ___ × 2 (or 2½) + hems (2 inches + ⅝ inch for each panel side that will be sewn together) = ___.

Now that you have your fabric measured, it's curtains time! Follow these simple steps for sewing sheer curtains:

1. Sew together each panel that you need to connect. Use French seams with a ⅝-inch seam allowance.

2. Double turn a ½-inch hem on each side.

3. Double turn 1 inch for the bottom hem.

4. Make the casing. Turn under ½ inch, press, and stitch into place. Turn over the rod width plus 2½ inches and stitch into place.

5. Press. Slip your rod into place, hang those bad boys, and watch them blowing in the wind with great satisfaction.

The Café Way

Unlined is the way to go when you want good looks fast. Imagine you're in an Italian bistro, and the cotton curtains are wafting in and out of the window along with the smell of coffee and biscotti.

They're hung on strips (or loops) of fabric, and their simplicity seduces you. Okay, maybe it's the wine and the gorgeous brunette. Either way, café curtains set the scene, and you can carry them into your kitchen with or without the brunette and biscotti.

Café curtains have very little gather, so they're great when you don't want to spend a lot of money on a lot of fabric.

- **Bottom hem.** A double-turned 2-inch hem (4 inches total).

- **Side hems.** A double-turned ½-inch hem (2 inches total).

- **Top hem.** A double-turned 2-inch hem (4 inches total).

- **Panels.** An additional ⅝-inch seam for each panel that needs to be joined together. Use a French seam if the fabric is sheer.

- **Fabric fullness.** The rod width plus 4 to 10 inches, depending on the fabric and the amount of fullness you would like.

    Width: Rod length plus 4 inches plus 1¼ inches plus ⅝ inch for each panel

    Length: Drop length plus 8 inches

Here I provide instructions for creating café curtains with fabric loops. These curtains don't require fussy finishings; they're hung on simple loops of fabric. The general rule is that one loop is sewn flush to each end, and then they're spaced evenly about 4 to 6 inches apart.

1. Follow Steps 1 through 4 for making sheer curtains.

2. Cut a strip of fabric 5 inches wide and long enough to make the number of loops you need. Their length is a matter of taste, depending on how low you wanna go. To the finished length of the strips, add 2 inches for stitching on to

the curtain. Multiply the loop length times the number of loops and you've got the total length of the strip.

3. Fold the strip in half with the right sides together and edgestitch ¼ inch along one side.

4. Cut the loop lengths. Stitch across one end at ⅝ inch, trimming to ¼ inch and grading the corners. Turn inside out and press.

5. Position the strips in place. Put one strip on each end and evenly position the rest of the strips in between, spacing them about 4 to 5 inches apart.

6. Place each loop on the wrong side of the curtain with the unfinished edge about 1 inch down from the top edge and baste into place. Bring the finished edge over the raw edge and topstitch into place, making a neat square. Keep going until you've completed all the loops.

7. Hang 'em and wallow in your craftiness.

Romancing Roman Shades

Whereas curtains can really draw you in, shades are an easy alternative, adding simple style with less effort and fabric. They're particularly fun and functional in a kitchen or bathroom, or wherever you want clean lines and a quick draw (up and down, that is).

When it's up, light has easy access; when it's down, the view is blocked in a neat way. And all you have to do is pull the cord.

There are a bunch of different shade types, from the simple, flat kind that zip up and down a roller, to balloon shades that have inverted pleats and a puffy look. But the most versatile are Roman shades.

These shades hang flat when closed, and pull up in horizontal folds, drawing up into neat sections when opened. It's best to line them for wash-'n-window-wear ease and a more finished look.

Whereas living room or bedroom curtains are often stately or staid, kitchen shades can really push the style envelope. They're great for fun and funky remnants that add spice and color to a kitchen. The Roman shade in my kitchen is made out of a 1950s linen that's a map of California, hand painted in glorious yellow, white, and red Technicolor. Who cares if it says that Mt. Whitney is the highest point in the United States?

It's the attitude, not the accuracy, that counts.

> **Noteworthy Notions**
>
> If one width of fabric won't do it and you have to use connecting panels, make sure you use an entire panel in the center with the cut panels on the side. But here's the tricky part where you should go that extra distance: Match the lining panel seams to the curtain seams. Why? Light often slips through a seam, and you don't want too many showy lines.

Batten Down the Hatches

Roman shades are attached to the top of the window by a batten, a small plank of wood that stabilizes the curtain, allowing for clearance for smooth shade sailing. The standard batten size is 1 inch wide by 2 inches deep by the length of the window. Buy a batten at any lumber or well-stocked hardware store (they will cut it to order), and attach it to the wall or window casing with metal L brackets.

Need to know how long your batten will be? Decide where your shade will be positioned with these two quick tips:

 ◆ If it'll hang in a recessed window, make it 1 inch shorter than the recess with the batten flush to the top of the recess. This ensures side clearance.

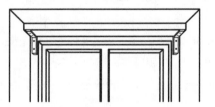

Recessed Roman shade batten.

Recessed batten

 ◆ Got a window that's flush with the wall? The batten should go on the wall above the window, extending 2 inches on each side. This ensures side coverage.

Roman shade batten.

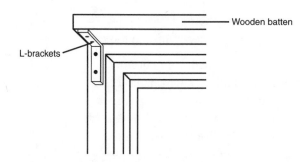

Shady Business: Measuring

Shed some light on your shade measurements with these tips:

- ◆ Calculate the width by measuring the batten and adding a side hem allowance of 2 inches (1 inch for each side).

- ◆ Calculate the length by measuring from the top of the batten to the sill. For a recessed shade, subtract 1 inch for clearance. For an outside-the-window shade, add 4 inches, plus 2 inches for the top and bottom hem (1 inch for each). You now have the length and the width.

- ◆ Here's where your shade math can get shaky, so pay attention. The lining is longer than the shade fabric. This is because the folds of the shade are formed with rods that are inserted in pockets in the lining that pleat when pulled with a cord.

- ◆ To calculate the rod pockets, get out your sketch pad and make a panel plan. Draw the finished curtain length. Make a horizontal line 4 inches up from the bottom. Divide the rest of the curtain into sections of about 12 inches, adjusting for the amount of fabric you have.

- ◆ For each line you make, you need to create a pocket that the rod will slip into. Add an extra 2½ inches for each rod. (This accounts for a rod or dowel of about ½ inch wide, which you can pick up at the hardware store.)

- ◆ Add top and bottom hems of 1 inch each (a double-turned ½-inch hem).

- ◆ Add it all up, and get stitching!

If you're feeling out of kilter and askew, drop the Roman shade sewing and wait until you're on track. These shades need absolutely straight lines for the rod casing so that they don't dip and droop; one rotten rod ruins the whole bunch. A shake of the wrists, a head-clearing stretch, with maybe a quick samba around the living room, and you should be ready for steady rolling.

Easy Hardware Rules: How to Hang Your Shade

Set aside your sewing machine and get out your toolkit for this part of the job. Anyone is handy enough to hang a shade without calling in a pro or getting out the power tools. Put these items on your shopping list: Velcro strip, three screw-in hooks and eyes, drapery cording.

1. The easiest way to attach the top of the curtain to the batten is with Velcro tape. Just cut the tape the same length as the batten and stick the tape on both the batten and top of the curtain. If need be, sew the Velcro to the curtain fabric for a secure hold.

2. The shades will draw up with a cord that's attached to plastic rings that are sewn onto each pocket. Position the rings 2 inches from each side and in the center. (Add additional rows if you have an extra-wide shade.) Sew 'em on with heavy-duty thread.

3. Screw a hook and eye into the batten directly above each row. Place one additional hook and eye 1 inch from one side of the batten.

4. Get out your curtain cording. (This special cording is available at drapery stores.) Tie one strand to the bottom plastic ring and thread it through each ring, then through the hook and eye, and over to the side hook and eye. Tie another cord to each bottom ring, threading it through the plastic rings and hook and eyes.

5. Cut the cords the same length, making sure they're long enough to wrap around a cleat or a hook when the shade is pulled up and long enough to hang freely when the shade is down.

Noteworthy Notions

To conceal a wooden batten, why not add a fabric flourish? Using a staple gun, get a grip on your fabric with the satisfying "kachung" of the gun. Or, for an even easier way, slap on a fresh coat of paint.

Roman shade hardware.

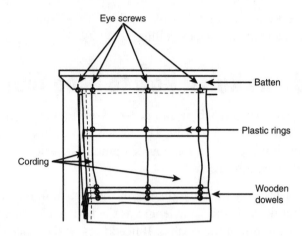

The Least You Need to Know

◆ When choosing a curtain style and fabric, keep these factors in mind: weight, fabric color/print, window shape and size, amount of light, practicality, and use.

◆ Poles are best for curtains that stay put or swag; tracks are useful for curtains that are opened and closed regularly.

◆ Before deciding on the fabric amount, make these decisions first: curtain placement, position of the poles or tracks, casing or heading style, and fabric fullness. Now you're ready to measure.

◆ Accurate measuring is crucial for curtains. It starts with getting the grainline straight. It's also important to calculate the fabric amount correctly.

Chapter 67

Sewing Project: Dressing Up the Home with Pillows and More

In This Chapter

- ◆ Pillow talk: the European sham
- ◆ Divine duvet covers
- ◆ The well-dressed table: tablecloths and linens
- ◆ It's raining shower curtains

A striking duvet cover, a couple of overstuffed pillows with a glam European sham, or a crisp linen tablecloth with matching napkins can turn the barest of homes into a plush and princely place, full of comfort. It's amazing the way a splash of fabric can transform any room, inviting you to sink into a cushioned seat, lie back against a pillow, and take a load off.

And all this can be accomplished without a load of trouble. Home decorating details are costly additions when you have to go out and lay down the cash for them. Just taking a stroll around a department store and doing a quick inventory of some new home additions will confirm your worst monetary fears—fancy-schmancy pillows can easily cost $50 and up, with tasseled and tied beauties running into the hundreds. Ditto for linens and bedclothes. Not so when they're home sewn!

Do-it-yourself decorating with fabric is the simplest of all sewing tasks; you already have all the skills you need. With a few cut-and-dry measuring, cutting, and stitching shortcuts, you'll be throwing together throw pillows in no time, putting your personal stamp on your most personal place—your home.

Pillow Talk

My brother once asked me, "What is it about chicks and pillows?" Well, we love 'em. And so do many of the male persuasion, mostly because they add color, richness, and a plush look with so little effort.

With the addition of a few nice pillows, a couch can go from drab to dramatic; side chairs can change from staid to stately; and a bedroom can become a full-fledged boudoir. Pillows use small amounts of fabric, and are the ideal use for remnants, flea-market finds, and leftover pieces from your major sewing projects.

If you can't afford a raw-silk bed cover, you can certainly cover your simple bed with silk throw pillows, creating the illusion of luxury—without the cost.

When you're looking around for pillow forms, you'll come across loose polyester fiberfill stuffing that's sold in bulk. Avoid it. It may seem like a cheap alternative, but no matter how you stuff a pillow with it, it never seems to hold the right shape, and turns out to be a lumpy mashed-potato pillow rather than a taut, neatly encased looker. Unfortunately, this is one time that you get what you pay for. Here's the low-down on pillow stuffings, from goose down right on through the price line:

   ◆ **Down.** The most luxurious pillow stuffing, down, is made of cleaned, de-quilled goose or duck feathers. It's available loose from specialty stores or in premade plain pillows of varying sizes.

   ◆ **Polyurethane foam.** You can find foam in sheets of ½ inch to 5 inches in precut sizes or cut from bulk pieces. The quality and density of foam varies—try to buy the most dense that you can find. (This is one of the few times that dense is a good thing!) Bear in mind that foam has hard, sharp corners and edges so the shape has to suit the use. For example, foam is great for seat cushions, not as great for bedding pillows.

◆ **Polyester forms.** The best all-purpose pillow filler. You can find polyester forms in all shapes and sizes.

◆ **Polyester fiberfill.** Loose polyester stuffing that's wadded into a pillow form. As I said, steer clear of this if you want a pillow that retains its shape after repeated pillow fights.

European Sham Glamour

A simple pillow is a welcome addition to any home, but a European sham—a pillow with a fabric border—really makes a statement and calls attention to itself. With a little extra effort, you'll have a real decorator's touch:

1. Cut the fabric with the following measurements:

   Pillow front: The length is the pillow length plus 5 inches; the width is pillow width plus 5 inches.

   Pillow back: The length is the pillow length plus 10 inches; the width is the pillow width plus 5 inches.

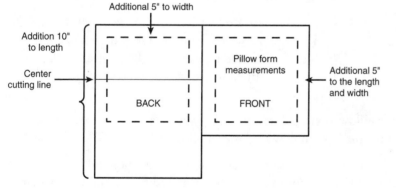

Marking and creating a European sham.

2. Fold the pillow back piece in half lengthwise and cut across the foldline. These two pieces will create the back opening and overlap.

3. Double turn a ½-inch hem on the edges of the overlap. Press and edgestitch.

4. Align the front piece and the two back pieces, right side to right side. Pin in place.

5. Stitch a ½-inch seam around the entire pillow. Trim the seam allowance and corners. Turn right side out.

6. Mark a 2-inch border around the pillow with chalk or a marker. Topstitch. Stuff it—the pillow, that is.

Making a simple overlap on the back of the pillow is the easiest way to create an opening. If you want a finished look, nothing beats buttons. I love to add vintage buttons to my pillows for that one-of-a-kind look.

Because the pillow instructions give you enough room for buttonholes on your overlap, simply mark and create the buttonholes before sewing the front and back pillow pieces together—the buttons come last. Usually, two will suffice, but you might need three for an extra-big pillow. Be sure to position them evenly along the back opening.

Another closure that can be completed with ease is Velcro tape, which is inserted in the back openings. Just position the tape on the edge of each back opening, stitching around the tape to secure it in place.

When measuring your pillow, don't pull too tight, or you'll be sorry later when you have to huff and puff to stuff your pillow into the case.

Pillows can complement your fabric decor or add a contrasting color and look, depending on the effect you want. For example, the oversized European pillows that anchor my bed are the reverse side of my curtains, with seafoam green dominating the curtains and the reverse, white, ruling the pillows. You want just enough variety for depth, and just enough unity to tie it all together.

Making the Case for Pillowcases

Let's face it: Most pillowcases are pretty drab affairs, cotton-poly blends without much goin' on. And the really nice ones—all-cotton, sateen, or linen—are pretty pricey. So you'll want to seek out great medium-weight cottons that feel nice against your skin; ditto for silks or linen.

Pillowcases are a breeze because they can be made out of one piece of fabric that's simply folded and stitched. Here's how to do it:

1. Cut the fabric with the following measurements: The width is the width of the pillow plus 1¼ inches; the length is twice the length of the pillow plus 9 inches.

2. Hem the edge of the pillow opening by double turning ½ inch and edgestitching.

3. Turn each edge 3 inches. Topstitch into place.

4. Fold the fabric in half lengthwise. Sew French seams on each side (not the pillow opening, obviously). Turn the pillowcase right side out, place a downy white pillow in it, and sigh with satisfaction.

> **Stitch in Your Side**
>
> Keep your head when choosing pillowcase fabric! A creamy silk may be sexy, but does it need to be dry cleaned? Think how often you'll be marching back and forth to your local cleaners. Or that elegant linen—do you really want to iron your pillowcases? That's a requirement for a heavy linen. Closely woven cottons are always a good bet for a good night's sleep.

The Well-Made Bed

If you're like me, you might own a menial bed: Mine's a platform made out of not-so-nice pine. But who would ever know? The 1940s dupioni silk duvet and the flood of pillows would cover even a cot in luxe finery. It makes you want to jump right in, which is exactly what a bed should say to you.

> **Noteworthy Notions**
>
> This is where your flea-market savvy really pays off. Old linens that are still in good shape can be cut down to create beautiful pillowcases—nothing beats the weight and feel of vintage linens, especially if they're worn in without being worn, threadbare, or yellowed.

How to Do an A-Okay Duvet

The fastest and easiest way to dress up a bed is with a duvet cover. Even more than a bedspread, a duvet is a luxurious blanket, which you can blanket in a luxe fabric to add allure and attitude. Furthermore, a duvet covers a multitude of sins, including an unmade bed; just toss a duvet over a bed with a quick snap of the wrist, and you're set. No tucking, no Army corners—what could be simpler?

A duvet cover is essentially a big rectangular bag that I like to fasten together with buttons, snaps, or Velcro. And even though you're working with a lot of fabric, the sewing is relatively simple:

1. Cut the fabric according to the following measurements: The width is the width of the duvet plus 1¼ inches; the length is the length of the duvet plus 3⅛ inches. You will need to cut two matching panels.

2. Make the top hem and border first. Turn the top edge over ½ inch, and press. Create a double-turned 1-inch border. Topstitch into place. Sew the same on the other top edge.

3. Align the two pieces. Sew a French seam on the bottom and sides of the duvet using a ⅝-inch seam allowance.

4. Edgestitch 12 inches from each side of the top of the duvet cover. The center opening is where you'll insert the duvet. You can go wild with whatever closure you desire. If you use buttons, place them at regular intervals in the opening, sewing the buttonholes first and then stitching on the buttons. Snap tale or Velcro also works well, especially with kids' covers that need more frequent trips to the laundry room. Better pick a closure that rips or snaps in a sec.

Noteworthy Notions

Although I'm partial to a clean look and favor buttons or Velcro as a duvet fastener, a lot of people prefer ties. If you like this fancy fastener, just cut strips of fabric that are about 6 inches by 3 inches. Fold the strips in half lengthwise, and stitch across the top and down one side with a ½-inch seam allowance, leaving one end unstitched. Trim, and turn inside out. Turn the cover inside out, turn the edges, and top-stitch. Stitch about 1 inch into the duvet cover in a rectangular fashion, positioning one tie on each end and spacing them about 4 inches apart. That's the way to tie one on with style!

The Well-Dressed Table

Wouldn't it be nice if dining room tables were disposable? It's my fantasy that, after a dinner party (especially one where your three nephews and their best friends have a food fight on your teak masterpiece), a new table shows up on your front doorstep. But life doesn't work that way. This is why we have tablecloths.

Besides protecting your favorite table, tablecloths add style and a stately presence to your parties, tying together your decor with a small detail. Choose the fabric carefully—if you live with a couple of messy kids, you may want to use stain-resistant, permanent-press fabric for easy care. Stay away from loud prints that need to be matched. Remember—home sewing is supposed to simplify your life.

Before you decide on the fabric amount, you need to decide how low you want to go. Or, put another way, how close to the floor you'd like the tablecloth to reach. You calculate this by determining the amount of the "drop." The drop is the length from the edge of the table to the floor. Take into account a couple of factors when determining drop: the overall proportions of the table and room; how much leg room you'd like to give your guests; the look of the table; if you have anything to hide (an unsightly card table, for example); and the cost of the fabric. Decide on your drop before dropping a bundle on pricey fabric!

The Angle on Rectangular Tablecloths

Faced with a rectangular shape to cover? Have no fear!

1. Cut the fabric according to the following measurements: The length is the length of the tabletop plus twice the drop plus 2 inches; the width is the width of the tabletop plus twice the drop plus 2 inches.

2. Double turn a 1-inch hem, press, and edgestitch. Now your table is Pouilly-Fuisse-proof!

Noteworthy Notions

To finish off your tablecloth with a flourish, add some crochet cotton cording around the edge in a complementary color. Lay it over your hem stitching line, on the right side of the fabric, and zigzag stitch it in place. To double your flourish fun, add the cording to your matching napkins as well.

All-Around Easy Round Tablecloths

Round tablecloths are perfect for hiding imperfections. A round tablecloth will turn anything into an elegant side or dining table, whether it's a cardboard table or a slab of glass on top of an old step stool:

1. Cut the fabric according to the following measurements: the diameter of the table plus twice the drop length plus ½ to 1 inch all around. Cut the fabric in a square.

2. Fold the fabric in half and then in half again. Pin in place. Draw an arc from corner to corner by measuring at regular intervals and marking. Cut through all four layers.

3. Sew a narrow-rolled hem. Snap your circular tablecloth into place. Add flowers, crystal, wine, and a few guests. You've got a party!

Round tablecloth template.

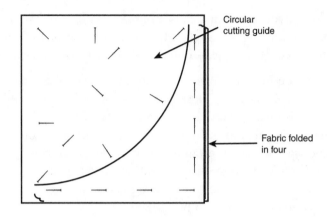

Circular cutting guide

Fabric folded in four

Lapping-Up Napkins

Sure, you can buy a stack of 100 paper napkins at your grocery store for a handful of pennies, but wouldn't you rather dab the corners of your mouth with some clean cotton napkins, the kind that are simple to sew and easy to wash—and that also cost pennies? Here's how:

> ### Sew Far, Sew Good
>
> Instead of those vinyl place-mats you've been using for years, why not make some new ones out of some stiff fabric (or some fabric that's stiffened up with a double layer with an interfacing in the middle). A common size is 16 inches by 14 inches—finish the edges by binding it in the napkin fabric and your table is as color-coordinated as your closet.

1. I'm a fan of a real laptop napkin, the kind that covers your lap in the event of a real spill. They look and feel luxurious, and save your suit better than those little pocket-square-size napkins. The standard sizes are 14- and 17-inches square. I personally like a bigger napkin that really does a lap justice, and often opt for a 20- to 24-inch square.

2. This is where your narrow-rolled hem comes into play (see Chapter 63). If you don't have a narrow-rolled hem attachment, double turn ¼ inch to finish off the napkins.

Be sure to use the appropriate fabric for napkins—a crisp cotton, linen, or a cotton blend. Don't use anything too heavy, or the napkins will be too uncomfortable; anything silky or too light won't hold the shape.

It's Raining Shower Curtains

Shower curtains do more to create atmosphere than any other bathroom accouterment. This means you can change the mood of your most-used room lickety-split by whipping up a new curtain. If you're having a mood indigo, confine your blue period to your bathroom, swaddling your shower in moony blue. I have a bathroom bathed in luminescent silvery gray, which makes every morning a treat. Treat yourself and your family by taking the following steps:

1. Cut the fabric according to the following measurements. The width is the width of the shower rod plus 4 inches. The length is the measurement from the shower curtain rings to at least 6 inches below the sill of the tub plus 10 inches.

2. Double turn a 1-inch side hem on each side, press, and stitch.

3. Double turn a 3-inch hem along the top and stitch; double turn a 2-inch hem along the bottom and stitch.

4. A standard shower curtain uses 12 shower curtain rings. Therefore, you need to make 12 buttonholes, positioning the first two ½ inch in from the sides. Now measure in between the two side buttonholes and divide by 10. This is where each buttonhole will be placed.

5. Mark each buttonhole. Place them ½ inch from the top of the curtain, making them ½ inch long.

6. Hang your curtain, along with a waterproof liner, and revel in your ingenuity.

Sew Far, Sew Good

Shower curtain fabric doesn't need to be waterproof, but it does need to have the right H_2O stuff to withstand the water treatment. This is not the time or place for 100 percent silk or pane velvet. Save your silks for scarves, and stick to bathroom friendly fabrics.

Noteworthy Notions

Create a couture commode—match your shower curtains to your towels. For example, you can use a fantastic fuschia terry, piping everything in white cotton for contrast. Move over, Mario Buatta.

The Least You Need to Know

- ◆ Pillows are a great way to create luxury without a huge time and money investment.

- ◆ The narrow-rolled hem really helps on the home front. Use it for napkin and tablecloth finishes that you can fly through.

- ◆ Napkins are a neat way to use leftover pieces of fabric, especially beautiful cottons and linens that you've used for garments or other home accents.

- ◆ Need a new look in your bathroom? Create a shower curtain. Use fabric that wears well with water. Measure properly, sew the side and top seams, and secure to the rings with buttonholes.

Chapter 68

Sewing Project: Crafty Gift Giving

In This Chapter

- ◆ Whip up an apron for a food lover
- ◆ Wrap up an evening stole for a socialite
- ◆ Stitch up a pocket square for a dandy
- ◆ Cheer up a kid with a hand puppet

Nothing says you care more than a home-sewn gift. Sure, anyone can go out and drop a bundle on a fine crystal decanter from a department store, a fancy French wine, or a glittery gold bauble. Now, I'm not knocking any of these beautiful store-bought presents; you can't beat them for last-minute occasions or quick pick-me-ups. But when you want to show that special family member or friend that you think they're not exchangeable (unlike the crystal decanter), give something you've made with your own two hands.

Noteworthy Notions

When I found a remnant of psychedelic pane velvet in my sewing box, I knew exactly what to do with it. I sat down at my machine and made a pair of pajamas for a groovy girlfriend whose taste is decidedly 1960s redux. She loves padding around her apartment in her out-of-this-world print, pretending she's been transported to Austin Powers's boudoir. Personalized gifts mean so much more than an off-the-rack purchase, so let your creativity and generosity run rampant!

Cooking Up Something Special: The Chef's Apron

Know someone who loves to cook? Instead of heading to your local department store for a special skillet or expensive kitchen gadget, how about making an apron? You can whip one up in about an hour, and you don't need any extra notions.

Sew Far, Sew Good

Does your favorite chef have a penchant for plaid? Make a gorgeous green and red Glen-plaid apron, put it into a steel mixing bowl along with some Scottish shortbread, and wrap it all in red transparent paper, using leftover fabric to make a matching bow. It's a wrap!

Stitch in Your Side

Don't be left with a too-tiny apron ... make sure you preshrink the apron fabric, especially if you're using 100 percent cotton. It pays to shrink cotton two or three times so you're not stuck with an itsy-bitsy apron.

The Raw Materials

The only thing you need to make an apron is one yard of fabric (at least 35 inches wide). When choosing your fabric, bear in mind that it's going to have to endure a lot of wear and tear. Between tomato-sauce splatters and greasy hand swipes, the fabric needs to be durable enough to withstand kitchen duty and regular washings. I prefer heavyweight cotton, poplin, canvas, or duck. You may want to use fabric that's treated so that it's stain-resistant, making it extra kitchen-proof.

The Works

1. Fold the fabric in half along the grainline.

2. Using a fabric marker and your tape measure, mark the apron measurements, as in the following illustration.

3. Measure and cut the ties. The two strips that fasten the waist are 1½ inches by 26 inches, and the neck strip is 1½ inches by 24 inches.

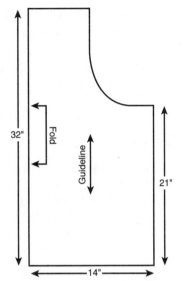

Easy apron measurements.

4. Sew the ties. Fold ¼ inch on each side of the strips, press into place, and then fold in half and press in place. Stitch close to the edge. There's no need to hem the ends of the waist strips—just tie them in a knot at the end and trim. If they start to unravel, use a drop of seam sealant such as Fray Check.

5. Hem the top of the apron by double turning ½ inch and stitching.

6. Hem the straight sides by double turning ½ inch and stitching.

7. Double turn a ½-inch hem on the sloping side of the apron (equivalent to the armhole if it were a shirt). Before stitching, pin the neck loop into place (making sure it's not twisted!), and the waist ties. Stitch, securing the ties.

Noteworthy Notions

A home-grown apron is a great his and hers gift that can be shared by both sexes. Just remember to match the fabric for the use—if your recipient *du jour* is a big barbecue fan, make sure you use seriously heavy fabric; if your cook is into delicate desserts, bear that in mind when choosing the fabric weight and appearance.

Fit to Be Tied: Scarves

Scarves are the all-time, all-purpose, tried and true crowd-pleasing gifts. They're a perfect use for stray pieces of fabric, they're quick and easy to make, and they can be as simple or as elaborate as you want. The possibilities with scarves are endless—get your creative juices going by checking out the scarves at your favorite store. You can take the basic, oblong scarf and dress it up with any number of notions: Put a tassel on each corner, sew rickrack along the top and bottom, or make a patchwork quilt scarf out of swatches.

Stitch in Your Side

If you go for a two-toned look—a scarf made of two different fabrics—try to pick fabrics that are about the same weight. The sewing gets tricky when you match a plush velvet with a sheer silk, with one fabric feeding through the machine at a much different pace than the other. If you don't pin everything carefully in place, checking your progress as you go, you'll end up with unequal pieces of fabric and a cockeyed scarf. Better to avoid that trap altogether and stick to similar fabrics.

The Raw Materials

You can concoct a scarf out of almost anything: beautiful cottons, luxe satins, gauzy silks, nubby wools, summer-weight wools, plush synthetics—the sky's the limit. First, you need to figure out your scarf mood; if you want a warm and fuzzy scarf, go for heavy wools. If you'd like a lean and sophisticated style, try an elegant white satin or silk jacquard.

When you've decided on the mood, you can match the look and weight of the fabric to the use: Long, flowing scarves are mostly decorative, an accent to an outfit; short, squat scarves are great for warmth and utility. Following are some common scarf measurements. These are the finished measurements, so be sure to add 1 inch all around for the seam allowance.

- **Stylish outdoor scarf.** 10 inches by 42 inches
- **Longer outdoor scarf.** 18 inches by 52 inches
- **Flowy accent scarf.** 12 inches by 75 inches
- **Wrap scarf.** 50 inches by 75 inches

The Works

There are two simple ways to make a scarf. The first is to cut a piece of fabric, fold it in half lengthwise, stitching around the open ends to create the scarf. The second—and, in my opinion, preferable—way is to cut two pieces of fabric, sandwiching them together and stitching around the edges to create the scarf. We'll stick to this method because I like the way these scarves hang and look. They also provide you with the opportunity to have two different pieces of fabric, making the scarf two-toned, reversible, and just plain snazzier. Just follow these steps:

1. Measure and cut two pieces of fabric according to the type of scarf you're creating. Make sure both pieces are cut along the same grainline, which should be parallel to the long side of the scarf.

2. Pin the pieces, right side together. Stitch around the edges with a ½-inch seam allowance, leaving a space open to turn the scarf right side out. The space you leave depends on the weight and amount of fabric. If you have a very large wrap scarf made of heavy wool, leave about 5 inches open. If you're making a small silk scarf, you only need to leave about 1½ inch. Trim the seam allowance.

3. Turn right side out, and then press.

4. Slipstitch the opening by hand, hiding the stitches inside the seam of the scarf.

Noteworthy Notions

You can add some extra oomph to this scarf with four tassels, one on each corner, stitched into place when you're done; or, you might add a row of tasseling on each end. Just sandwich the tasseling between the layers when you're pinning the sides together, stitching the seams and tasseling into place in one fell swoop. When you turn the scarf right side out, the tasseling will appear.

It's a Wrap: A Festive Wrap

If you want a more dramatic look (and who doesn't?), you can create a wrap that drapes elegantly over the bare shoulders of the holiday reveler. I love making this wrap, both as a gift and for myself because it's so cost-effective and attractive. You get a huge fashion bang for the bucks you've invested in the fabric, and the sewing time is short.

Wraps can completely change any look, creating a Cinderella-like transformation to even the simplest black sheath. I particularly favor lacy and luxe fabrics for this (red satin, off-white lace, and so on), but you can use a standard wool if you want a more traditional look.

> ### Noteworthy Notions
>
> My best wrap, the one that gets the most "oohs" and "ahs," is made out of one of my favorite fabrics—Ultrasuede. This 1970s fabric is perfect for a wrap because it needs no hemming (you just cut the edges), and there is no raveling or mess. Ultrasuede is also the ultimate in carefree maintenance—just hand wash and drip dry. No dry cleaning allowed. I knew I had a winner when someone rushed up to me with my lavender Ultrasuede wrap and asked if Halston designed it!

The Raw Materials

You'll need a piece of fabric that measures 43 inches by 94 inches, which you can piece together or cut in one fell swoop if the fabric you have is large enough (always the easiest and cleanest option).

The Works

This is the easy part: Double turn a ½-inch hem on all sides. You've made an elegant and easy evening wrap, one that's fit for the queen for the night.

In the Bag: Evening Clutch or Coin Purse

A simple fabric evening clutch is a wardrobe staple; a black velvet number works with almost any outfit, a richly embroidered brocade makes a statement, and a metallic quicksilver is an eye catcher. Why spend a lot of money on something so simple and easy to make? The same goes for an even tinier purse for coins and cosmetics.

> ### Sew Far, Sew Good
>
> Ever take a good look at most cosmetic bags? Most of them need their own cosmetic cover-up because of unsightly plastic, ungainly canvas, and bad construction. There's no need to be embarrassed by your minibag when it comes out of your handbag. The new vinyls and waterproof materials are perfect for toting your lipsticks, and they're simple to sew.

The Raw Materials

For an evening clutch, you need two pieces of fabric that measure 6 inches by 8 inches; for a coin bag, you need two pieces that are 5 inches by 8 inches. You also need a zipper that measures 7 inches. (I suggest using an invisible zipper in a matching or complementary color.)

The Works

1. Measure and cut two pieces of fabric.

2. The best zipper to use with this bag is an invisible zipper. This means that you will stitch the zipper into place first, and then stitch the rest of the bag. See Chapter 62 for easy instructions.

3. After inserting the zipper, align the pieces right side to right side and stitch around the remaining three sides, allowing for a ½-inch seam allowance. Trim the seam allowance, turn the bag right side out, and you're ready to roll.

Noteworthy Notions

This is a great little bag for a piece of fantastic beaded fabric. Beaded fabric requires a little bit of special sewing care. Here are some pointers: Remove the beads from the seams so you don't stitch over them; use a zipper foot; don't steam beads—they curl and wilt.

The Stockings That Dreams Are Made of: Christmas Stockings

I never owned a store-bought Christmas stocking as a child. My seamstress grandmother made new ones every year, transforming this relatively mundane holiday tradition into its own special event. My favorite was a stocking in the shape of a pink princess puppet, complete with a shiny tiara and a bejeweled bodice.

After you've created the basic stocking shape, go for the decorative gusto, from gluing on some glitter to making an animal shape to embroidering a few decorative fillips. Check out your local trimmings store and grab whatever sparks your imagination.

The Raw Materials

You can use any fabric you want to make a stocking—from crafty felt to rich cashmere—depending on whose stocking you're stuffing. The same goes for the notions: Be as creative as you like when adding decorations.

The Works

1. Enlarge the illustrated stocking pieces to the desired size (see the following figure). Mark and cut two pieces of the stocking and cuff, and one piece of the strip, which becomes the hanging loop.

2. Pin the right sides of the stocking together and stitch with a ¼-inch seam allowance, leaving the top open. Turn the stocking right side out.

3. Fold the hanging loop in half lengthwise (with the right sides together) and stitch along one side, leaving the ends open.

Simple stocking form.

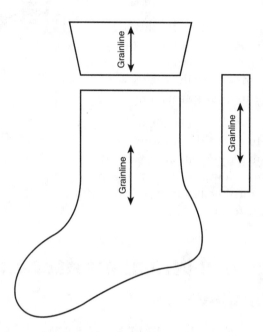

4. Pin the cuff pieces with the right sides facing each other and stitch on each side with ¼-inch seam allowance. To attach the cuff to the stocking, tuck it inside the stocking so that its edge aligns with the top of the stocking. Make sure the side seams face each other, not the stocking. Stitch along the edge. Pull out the cuff and roll it down.

5. Turn the loop right side out and attach it to the inside of the stocking with a quick hand or machine stitch.

The Least You Need to Know

◆ Plan ahead for special events and fit stitching into your life so that you can present your new godchild with a homemade romper. It'll go over big.

◆ Scarves are a fantastic gift—simple to sew and great to give. You can use all sorts of leftover fabric, from the most luxe to the simplest cotton and dress it up in any number of ways.

◆ Making kid-oriented crafts is an opportunity to have some fun with your young friends.

Glossary

acid-free tissue paper   A tissue paper made without the chemicals that would destroy the fabric fibers.

afghan crochet   A special type of crochet that requires the crocheter to hold many stitches on the crochet hook. Special afghan hooks that look like a cross between a crochet hook and a knitting needle are available for this purpose. Also called *Tunisian crochet*.

Album quilts   Friendship quilts assembled from individual blocks, each executed and signed by a different person, and presented to a friend or public figure on a special occasion.

Amish quilts   Quilts made by members of the Amish or Mennonite communities. The quilts are characterized by solid dark and bright colors with intricate, beautiful hand-quilting designs.

apex   The point of the bust. It's also the very tip of a dart (whether a bustline dart or not).

appliqué   A small piece of fabric, cut into a shape, that is placed on a background fabric and stitched down with small, almost invisible, stitches, usually by hand.

baby hem   A seam finish or hem in which the fabric is double turned a tiny amount (⅛ inch to ¼ inch maximum) and stitched.

back-post double crochet (bpdc)   A special crochet stitch that involves working into the back of the post of a crochet stitch on the row.

backing   The back, or bottom layer, of the quilt.

backstitch   1. A stitch taken backward from the direction you are sewing to reinforce the beginning and end of each seam. 2. Just like backing up a car, this is when you stitch in reverse. Your sewing machine has a button, knob, or switch that activates the reverse. Backstitching a couple of stitches will secure the beginning and end of your stitch lines so they don't come undone.

backstitching   A hand-sewing method of joining seams. In a backstitch, stitching front and then back reinforces each stitch. This stitch provides a sturdy but elastic seam.

Bargello   A classic needlepoint stitch that results in wavy or chevron-type patterns resembling flames.

bartack   A few stitches back and forth that secure your stitch lines. Some machines have a bartack setting.

baste   Temporarily pin together, or sew together with long stitches, one or more pieces of fabric or two or more layers.

basting tape   Double-sided sticky tape that holds fabric in place temporarily without the hassle of stitching. Great for zipper placement.

batting   The middle or filling layer placed between the quilt top and backing. It adds warmth and dimension to the quilt.

beading needle   A fine needle with a sharp tip that is used for beadwork.

bias   This is the line that runs diagonally across fabric. The true bias is always at a 45° angle to the crosswise and lengthwise grains, and is the fabric's stretchiest point.

bias tape   Prepackaged, commercially sold tape that is used to bind seams or hems. The tape comes in different sizes and colors, so buy accordingly.

bias-bound seam   Also known as a *Hong Kong seam*, this is a seam finish in which you bind the raw edges of the seam in a bias-cut strip of fabric.

binding   A long strip of fabric, usually bias, that finishes the raw edges of a quilt.

binding off   The process in which you "lock up" all active stitches on the needle so that they can't unravel. You bind off stitches when you're finished with a piece or want to shape an area—such as an armhole in a sweater.

blackwork   A counted thread embroidery in which repetitive patterns are used to fill design areas. Traditionally black silk thread was worked on linen. Today many colors are used.

blindhem   A hem in which the stitches don't show on the right side of the fabric. You can accomplish this by hand or by machine with a special presser foot attachment.

blindhem stitch   Machine stitching, using a blindhem presser foot, that creates a blindhem with the use of straight and zigzag stitches.

block   A complete design unit that makes up a quilt. It can be a square that has many shapes pieced or appliquéd into the unit.

blocking   A process for straightening a misshapen needlework piece by realigning the threads of the ground fabric, to eliminate the distortion that occurred during stitching.

bobbin   A plastic or metal spool that holds thread; it's inserted in the bobbin case, usually under the machine where it loops with the needle thread to create the stitches.

bolt   A large roll of cloth or fabric of a specific width.

border   A long continuous piece of fabric, or series of bands of colors, that frames the outside edge of the quilt top. Borders can be as simple as solid strips of fabric or very intricate geometric patterns or appliqués.

bottom selvage   The cast-on row in knitting.

buttonhole bead   One side of buttonhole stitches.

buttonhole chisel   A small tool with a sharp metal blade (usually ½-inch wide) used to cut a buttonhole open in one fell swoop. You need to use the chisel with either a self-repairing mat or a wooden block.

cable needles   Small double-pointed needles made expressly for creating patterned cables, such as those on Aran sweaters.

cable panel   The stockinette stitch column on which a cable is worked.

cables   Specialized knitting patterns created by physically moving stitches and knitting them out of their original order.

calico   A 100 percent cotton fabric used for quilting. The word originally meant a process of printing small floral designs using a roller.

canvas   Mesh fabric with criss-crossing fibers that form a grid; used to stitch needlepoint.

casting on   The process of creating the foundation row of stitches from which you will knit.

chain stitch (ch st)   A crochet stitch made by catching the yarn with the crochet hook and drawing the yarn through the loop on the hook.

clapper   A pressing tool that's a flat wooden block used to create serious creases. After using an iron, pressing with the clapper flattens that area while drawing the heat out of it, "setting" it in place.

clipping   Cutting into the seam allowance so the fabric lays flat.

closing a stitch   The step in crochet in which a stitch is finished and only one loop remains on the crochet hook. When changing colors, you always close the last stitch of the current color with the new color.

cluster stitches   Groups of crocheted stitches that give the appearance of a single stitch.

colorfast   A descriptive term referring to dyed fabrics or threads that will not run when wet.

complementary colors   The colors found across from each other on the color wheel. An example of complementary colors is red and green.

Continental knitting   A type of knitting in which you "catch" the yarn using the needle; you don't use your hand to drape or throw the yarn over the needle.

contrasting color (cc)   An accent color used in a piece. You may have more than one contrasting color.

couching   An embroidery technique by which a lighter-weight thread and small stitches are used to attach a heavier thread that has been laid flat on the surface of a ground fabric. Traditionally used to apply fragile metallic threads to a design.

Crazy quilts   Quilts that became popular around the time of the American Centennial and were made from random sizes and shapes of fabric (usually silks and velvets) with intricate embroidery to decorate the surface.

crewel needle   Sharp pointed, medium-length needles with large eyes for easy threading.

crewelwork   A traditional form of embroidery, typically employing wool thread and linen twill fabric, flowing designs, and stylized naturalistic motifs executed with various stitches.

crochet   A French word meaning "hook." The craft of crochet involves using a hook to join loops of yarn into a fabric.

cross-stitch   A popular embroidery stitch where all the stitches are formed by two "crossing arms."

crosswise grain   This is the fabric line that runs from selvage to selvage, perpendicular to the lengthwise grain. It's also known as the *weft* and always has more give or stretch than the lengthwise grain.

cutwork   A form of openwork embroidery where outlined designs are stitched with a buttonhole stitch and the middle is cutaway.

dart   A tapered tuck sewn into a garment to create contouring. Usually V shaped, the tuck narrows to the apex or the tip, and is most often placed at a bustline or waistline.

decrease (dec)   Subtracting the number of active stitches in your work.

dominant color   The main color of a quilt.

double crochet (dc)   A versatile, tall crochet stitch. To make the double-crochet stitch, begin with a yarn over; insert the hook into a stitch; yarn over and pull through loop; yarn over and pull through 2 loops; yarn over, and pull through the remaining loops.

double-crochet decrease (dec 1 dc)   A crochet stitch that subtracts one stitch by combining two double crochets.

double needle   A double-pronged needle that's joined in one shank for use with your machine. It creates a double row of evenly spaced stitches on the top while the bottom zigzags between the rows. Perfect for hemming, decorative topstitching, and working with stretchy fabrics.

dressmaker's carbon paper   A type of coated paper used to transfer designs to fabric.

dropped stitches   Stitches that accidentally came off the needle during knitting. If left unfixed, dropped stitches can run down through the knitted fabric.

duplicate stitch   A needlework technique in which you embroider over knit stitches. The result is a color pattern that appears to be knit in, but is actually embroidered.

dye lot   An indicator of the time the yarn was dyed. Different dye lots—even in the same color yarn—have slight variations in tone if they are dyed at different times.

ease   This means a few things in sewing terminology. First, it applies to any time you need to fit a longer section of fabric to a shorter one. This almost always happens with a set-in sleeve, the cap of which needs to be eased to fit into the armhole, or a long hem where the top or folded fabric needs to be eased to fit the bottom fabric. Second, it's the difference between your body's measurement and the garment measurement, or the allowance the garment gives you to move.

echo quilting   Quilting stitches that follow the outline of the blocks' basic design and are then repeated, like ripples, every ¼ inch in concentric lines.

edgestitch   Stitching that's placed a maximum of ⅛ inch from a turned edge, whether a hem or a fabric detail like a pocket.

elastic thread   Finely wound elastic that's used in place of regular thread.

embroidery   A form of needlework that embellishes clothing or fabric with stitching.

European sham   A pillow cover with a flat border of about 2 inches around the edges.

evenweave   A woven fabric that has the same number of vertical threads as horizontal threads.

Fair Isle knitting   A form of knitting in which two colors are used per row, and the color not in use is carried or stranded along the wrong side of the piece.

fat quarter   A ¼ yard of fabric cut 18 inches by 22 inches.

feed dogs   The teeth on the throat plate of your sewing machine that rise and fall back and forth, gripping the fabric and moving it as you stitch.

filet crochet   A type of crochet in which a pattern is created in the crocheting by arranging blocks and spaces.

flat stitches   Embroidery stitches that lie flat on the surface of a fabric.

flat-fell seam   A seam finish in which you stitch the right sides of the fabric together, trim one seam allowance and turn the other under, topstitching it into place, creating a double row of neat stitching and an encased seam. Good for reducing bulk in your seam finish.

floss   An embroidery thread composed of six loosely twisted strands that are easily separated into single threads.

foundation chain   A chain-stitched row that stands as the base of all crocheting—the foundation from which a piece is built.

free arm   The "arm" of your sewing machine is usually created by removing a detachable casing, exposing a narrow section that supports the needle and bobbin mechanisms. This enables you to sew tight circular areas like sleeves and cuffs without straining.

French seam   A completely encased seam that adds a finished, couture look to your home-sewn seams. The seam is sewn on the right side of the fabric, turned, pressed, trimmed, and encased, after which the wrong side is sewn. Imperative for see-through fabrics so the raw edges don't show.

front-post double crochet (fpdc)   A special crochet stitch that involves working into the front of the post of a crochet stitch on the row below.

fusible interfacing   Interfacing that is backed with a heat-activated resin that bonds with the fabric when ironed and steamed properly.

garter stitch   A common pattern created by knitting every row; it has a fairly bumpy surface.

gauge   The number of stitches you need to complete to finish a specified length of knitted or crocheted fabric. Gauge is typically measured by the inch.

gauge counter A tool for measuring gauge. To use one, lay the counter over your knitting or crocheting and count the number of stitches that appear in the window.

grafting A means of joining two active rows of knitting so that the join resembles a row of knitted stitches. Also called *Kitchener stitch*.

grain The direction that the threads are woven in a fabric. The lengthwise grain runs the length of the fabric and parallel to the selvage. Crosswise grain is the direction that runs at a right angle to the lengthwise grain.

grainline The direction of the weave of fabric.

ground fabric The background fabric of which needlework is done.

half-double crochet (hdc) A cross between a single crochet stitch and a double-crochet stitch. To complete a half-double crochet stitch, begin with a yarn over; insert the hook into a stitch; yarn over and pull through the stitch; do another yarn over; and pull through the three loops on your hook.

Hawaiian quilts Quilts made up of one piece of fabric folded and cut into a large overall design of leaves or flowers and then appliquéd onto a background fabric.

heading tape Ready-made strips of stiff fabric that you attach along the top border of curtains. They either have drawstrings to form even gathering, or pockets for hooks that create different pleats (such as triple pleats, pencil pleats, or box pleats) without any complicated stitching on your part.

Hong Kong finish Another name for a *bias-bound seam*.

hoop A round, portable, and lightweight frame used in needlework to keep the ground fabric taut during stitching.

hue The gradation or variety of a color, usually with a name further describing the color, such as navy blue or magenta.

increase (inc) Adding more stitches to your work.

intarsia A type of color knitting in which each block of color is knit from a separate ball or bobbin of yarn.

interfacing A layer of fabric that adds shape, stability, durability, and control to garments. It's usually used on the edges of clothes—armholes, necklines, or the edges of jackets and blouses—and on special details, such as collars, cuffs, and pockets, so they maintain their crisp look. The two basic kinds of interfacing are fusible (iron-on) and sew-on.

intersection A needlepoint term that refers to the intersecting points in the canvas grid.

invisible thread   A sturdy, clear plastic thread.

ironing press   A fantastic pressing tool for pressing large areas at once. This machine looks almost like a Xerox machine cover with a handle; pull down, placing the fabric on the bed, and the press provides about 100 pounds of pressure with almost no effort on your part. Great for fusing interfacing.

joining   A process in which two sections of needlepoint canvas are sewn together.

Kitchener stitch   *See* grafting.

knitting (k)   Forming rows of interconnecting loops in which the ends of the loops face away from you as you work.

lacet   A special type of mesh in filet crochet that is made by using a single crochet rather than a double or triple crochet. A lacet creates a soft, slightly rounded space.

Lap quilt   A small quilt usually under 60 inches square and put together with six or nine blocks.

lattice   A strip of fabric that separates and frames each block in a quilt. It can also be called sashing.

lengthwise grain   Running parallel to the selvage, this is the all-important grain-line. When commercial patterns indicate the grainline, they're referring to the lengthwise grain. It's the strongest and has the least amount of stretch. Also known as the *warp*.

loft   The thickness or puffiness of a quilt batting.

Log Cabin   A quilt pattern in which a block has a series of strips placed around a central square, which is usually red. One diagonal half of each block is colored with light fabrics, and the other diagonal half with dark fabrics.

Lone Star   Also called the Star of Bethlehem, which became popular in the 1820s. This quilt pattern is composed of many small fabric diamonds assembled into eight larger diamonds that form a star.

long-staple polyester thread   The best polyester thread that differs from all-purpose polyester in that it uses longer thread filaments (from 5 to 6½ inches) so that it's stronger and shinier.

magnetic seam guide   A small magnetic "shelf" that sticks to your machine throat plate, providing a stitching guideline to keep your seams straight.

main color (mc)   The predominant color in a multicolor piece.

matte   A finish that is not shiny.

Medallion quilt   A quilt assembled around one large central motif, with one or more borders to finish out the quilt.

mesh   The background of filet crochet; mesh is made up of double- or triple-crochet stitches separated by a chain or chains.

metal sewing gauge   A 6-inch metal ruler with a sliding plastic marker; an essential tool.

miter   To join two pieces of fabric so that the ends meet at a right angle with a diagonal seam.

mock French seam   A seam finish in which you turn the raw edges of the seam and sandwich them together, stitching the edges.

monogram   In embroidery, a decorative rendering of a person's initials that is stitched on fabric.

motifs   Pieces worked around a central point rather than back and forth. Doilies and granny squares are two examples of motifs.

mounting   The process of preparing to frame your work by securing it to a supporting board before attaching the actual frame.

muslin   An off-white woven cotton fabric.

nap   A quality of fabric that has its fibers brushed in one direction causing a different coloration. Velvet is an example. Patterns of any fabric with a one-way design can also be considered to have a nap.

narrow-rolled hem   Another name for a *rolled hem*.

needleboard   A bed of nylon bristles that preserves the nap of heavily piled fabrics while pressing. Place the fabric face down on the bed and the fur, velvet, and the like fall in between the "needles," maintaining their fluffy appearance.

needlepoint   A form of embroidery where canvas mesh fabric is stitched with yarn.

notions   A loose term that applies to all the parts of a sewing project besides the fabric, from thread to pins to needles to interfacing.

openwork   A type of embroidery where the stitches pull the fabric threads together creating open, lacelike patterns.

patchwork   A term that refers to the process of piecing or appliquéing various fabric shapes together.

pearle cotton   A strong twisted nondivisible thread with a high sheen.

Persian yarn   Loosely twisted three-strand wool or acrylic yarn that is easily divisible.

picot   A French word meaning *peak*.

piecing   Cutting out fabric shapes and sewing them together, two pieces at a time, with small running stitches to form a larger unit, usually a block.

pile   A furry-looking effect achieved by using various looped stitches on a ground fabric. The loops are sometimes sheared to resemble the pile of a rug.

pinking shears   Shears with serrated blades that cut a toothy, zigzag edge. Often used to prevent raw edges from unraveling or for a decorative finish.

piping   A tiny contrasting strip of bias fabric with a cord inside. This corded fabric is inserted into a seam, forming a decorative edge.

placket   A V-shaped opening or slit in a garment, usually at the sleeve or neckline. The most common placket is in a menswear-style sleeve that allows it to slip over the wrist and attach with a cuff.

point turner   A small utensil with a pointy edge that allows you to turn fine points—as in collars, cuffs, and pockets—fully so that you get that very last, tiny bit of fabric turned and pointed to perfection. The most common ones are made of bamboo or wood.

press cloth   A thin piece of fabric, often see-through, that's placed between your iron and your fabric to protect the fabric from damage or shine. It's a necessity for certain fabrics and for fusing interfacing.

presser foot   A sewing machine attachment that exerts pressure on the fabric, holding it in place while stitching. Presser feet are detachable, and there are many specialty presser feet, the most common of which are the standard foot that accompanies your machine and the zipper foot.

pressing mitt   A padded, double-sided mitt that slips over your hand while pressing, protecting your hand from heat.

purling (p)   Forming rows of interconnecting loops in which the ends of the loops face away from you as you work.

quilt stencil   A plastic sheet with grooves cut out in a specific design, for use in marking a quilt design on a quilt top.

quilt top   The completed patchwork design used as the right side or face of a quilt. It is the top layer of a quilt.

quilter's quarter   A plastic rod (¾ inch × ¾ inch × 8 inches) used to mark the ¾-inch seam line for quilting or cutting.

quilting   The process of securing all three layers of a quilt together with small running stitches.

quilting frame   A free-standing rectangle on legs that holds a quilt, allowing several people to stitch a section, then roll the quilt to another section until the whole quilt is finished.

reverse single crochet stitch (rscs)   An edging stitch made by working a single crochet left to right, rather than right to left, across a row of stitches.

ribbing   A stitch made by combining knit and purl stitches to form an elastic fabric. Ribbing often begins and ends sweater projects, as well as hats, mittens, and socks.

ridges   The bumps you see on both sides of garter-stitch fabric. Each ridge represents two rows of knitting.

right side (rs)   The side that will be showing on a knitted or crocheted item, such as the outside of a sweater.

ripping out   Unraveling or pulling out stitches. You rip out when you find that you don't like the look or size of the knitted fabric, or when you find a mistake that you need to undo.

rolled hem   This is a tiny, evenly rolled hem that's created with a special narrow-rolled hem presser foot. The fabric is fed into the funnel of the presser foot, turned, and then stitched.

rotary cutter   Essentially an Exacto knife that's shaped like a pizza wheel. As you roll it along, it accurately cuts fabric without lifting the cutter from the cutting surface. It must be used with a self-repairing mat—and yes, these little innovations actually repair themselves by "healing" the cut marks after you're done!

sampler   Originally, a piece of linen on which the embroiderer tried out and recorded various motifs and stitches for later use as a reference. In the eighteenth and nineteenth centuries, samplers became popular methods for teaching children their alphabet and numbers. Modern samplers typically still incorporate the alphabet while often commemorating a special occasion such as a birth, wedding, anniversary, or friendship.

sampler quilt   A quilt that combines blocks of different types of patterns, making it a perfect quilt for beginners to learn both piecing and appliqué techniques.

sashing   Another name for lattice, or the strips that frame each block.

satin stitch   A flat, straight, basic embroidery stitch. Satin stitches are placed close together, side by side, and are characterized by an equal amount of thread covering the front and the back of the fabric.

scissors   As opposed to shears, scissors are shorter and have the same size finger loops. Use them for cutting patterns, stray threads, etc., but not for cutting fabric.

seam allowance   This is the amount of fabric added to your pattern to allow for stitching and trimming. Or, a little less technically, it's the space between where you've cut the fabric and where you stitch it. Almost all commercial patterns use a ⅝-inch seam allowance, but you can vary it according to your sewing needs.

seam ripper   Basically a tool with a 2- to 4-inch handle and two prongs—a crescent-shaped blade and a shorter blunt edge—that's used to safely rip out the threads from a seam. If you're using it, you've made a mistake, which happens a lot.

seam sealant   A clear resin that's used to prevent edges from fraying. It's especially useful on buttonholes.

selvage (or selvedge)   The two parallel finished edges of fabric that do not ravel and are more closely woven than the rest of the fabric. They run in the same direction as the lengthwise grain.

serger   This is a machine that stitches the seams, cuts the excess fabric, and finishes the seams with an overcast stitch all at once. As a supplement to your traditional sewing machine, it's great for creating a finished, professional look.

set-in sleeve   The most common tailored sleeve in which the sleeve is slightly bigger than the armhole, meaning it must be eased or "set-in" to fit and hang properly. The other types of sleeves are raglan and kimono, both of which require no easing techniques.

setting the top   Arranging the completed blocks, lattices, and borders to form a quilt top. The process is also known as *setting together*.

shade   A hue that has been blended with black or a darker color. Cranberry is a shade of red.

shank   When referring to a button, this means the ringlike projection on the back that's sewn on to the garment. You can create a shank, or a raised area behind the button, out of a column of thread. A shank can also mean the top of the needle where it attaches to your sewing machine.

shears   Your most important sewing tools. These are special scissors that are longer than 6 inches and have a larger upper finger loop for cutting ease.

single crochet (sc) The most basic of crochet stitches. To complete a single crochet stitch, insert the hook through a chain (or stitch); yarn over; pull the loop through the chain (or stitch); yarn over again; and pull through both loops on the hook.

single crochet decrease (1 sc dec) A crochet stitch that subtracts one stitch by combining two single crochets.

sleeve roll A sausage-shaped hard cushion that's perfect for pressing sleeves and other circular or curved areas of a garment.

slip knot A knot that slips easily along the cord around which it is tied. Also called a *running knot.*

slip stitch (sl st) In crochet, a stitch much like a chain stitch except that you create the stitch by working it from a foundation chain or other stitches. In knitting, a stitch that is moved from one needle to the other without being worked.

slip stitch seaming Joining two pieces of work together with yarn and a crochet hook. This technique produces a strong, tight join that works well on flat seams.

sloper The master pattern that a commercial design company uses.

smocking An embroidery technique that reduces fullness in a fabric with very attractive gathered stitches.

stabbing A stitching technique for quilting using both hands in which you insert the needle into your quilt, pull it out the bottom with your other hand under the hoop, then push it up from the bottom to the top. The stitches are uneven and crooked on the underside.

stabilizer A temporary sheet of material that's applied to fabric when stitching to provide support and stiffness. There are three varieties: tear-away, water-soluble, and heat-soluble.

stash The inevitable squirreling away of pounds and pounds of yarn a knitter or crocheter doesn't immediately need but might use later.

staystitch A row of stitching for curved areas like collars, necklines, and seams that have a tendency to stretch when stitched. Before stitching your seam, you first "stay" the fabric with a staystitch just inside the permanent stitching line (usually about half an inch).

stitch holders Safety pin–shaped accessories that hold knitting stitches you aren't currently using but will use later.

stitch in the ditch   A stitching technique that allows you to stitch in the seam well formed by joining garment pieces (collars, cuffs, waistband, and so on) so that the stitching doesn't show on the front of the garment.

stitch markers   Little discs that slide onto your knitting needle or crocheted fabric. Markers cue you at the point when it's time to do something to the fabric, such as increase stitches or begin a new pattern.

stockinette stitch (st st)   A common pattern created by alternating one row of knitting with one row of purling. Stockinette stitch creates a fabric that is smooth on one side and bumpy on the other.

stranding   Carrying the yarn not currently used for a stitch along the back of a piece, ready to be used.

strip piecing   A method of creating quilts by taking long strips of fabric and sewing them together in a set sequence. This newly combined material is then cut apart and resewn to form a part of a quilt. A good example is a Rail Fence quilt pattern.

stumpwork   A seventeenth-century technique that makes embroidery three-dimensional by combining padded appliqué and embroidery stitches. Sometimes a fine wire is used to provide the underlying support and to give shape.

superwash wool   Specially treated wool that can be safely machine washed.

swatch   A sample you knit or crochet to determine whether your gauge is where it should be.

tail   The extra yarn left after you do something in knitting or crocheting, such as casting on a stitch or changing colors.

tailor's chalk   Chalk used for marking hems, transferring pattern markings, and indicating stitching lines. Make sure you buy real chalk, rather than chalk/wax combinations, which can melt into the fabric.

tailor's ham   This is a thick, heavy, ham-shaped cushion that's used for pressing open seams, especially in curved areas like darts, sleeve caps, collars, and waistbands.

tapestry needle   Blunt-tipped needles used for thread counting embroidery and needlepoint.

tapestry   A heavy, decoratively woven fabric with a pictorial design, traditionally used as a wall hanging.

template   A pattern shape of a quilt design made of plastic or cardboard and used to trace shapes for appliqué or piecing. Some templates include the seam allowances, whereas others, like the ones in this book, do not.

tension   The resistance or "pull" between the top and bobbin threads that creates even knots or stitches that lie in between the fabric pieces. Proper tension is essential for flawless stitching.

tent   A basic needlepoint stitch that is worked on the diagonal and in the same direction over one intersection of canvas.

throat plate   The metal plate on your sewing machine that surrounds your needle hole. It's usually marked with lines at graduated $\frac{1}{8}$-inch settings to gauge your seam allowances.

tint   A hue that is blended with light or white colors. Pink is a tint of red.

topstitch   Straight stitching sewn about $\frac{1}{4}$ inch from the seam or finished edge. Can be a decorative finish or utilitarian.

tramé   A technique used on needlepoint canvas in which horizontal stitches are run across each part of the design to add thickness and strength to the canvas. The tramming is done before the canvas is retailed, and the stitcher then completes it by working needlepoint stitches over the tramming.

triple crochet (trc)   A tall crochet stitch. To make this stitch, yarn over the hook twice; insert the hook into a stitch; yarn over and pull through yarn over again and pull through the first two loops (the two closest to the point); yarn over again and pull through the next two loops; yarn over one last time and pull through the remaining two loops.

Tunisian crochet   *See* afghan crochet.

turning chains   Extra chain stitches made at the end of each row to accommodate for the height of the stitch of the next row.

twin needle   Another name for a *double needle*.

twisted stitches   Stitches twisted on your needle. Because the knitted loops are twisted, the stitches are tighter than correctly knit stitches and don't open when stretched.

twisting   A method of anchoring yarn being carried in the back of your work for more than five stitches.

universal point needle   The most common needle size for use with most fabrics.

value   The lightness or darkness of a color—either tints or shades.

variegated yarn   Yarn dyed with many varying colors—blending from, say, yellow to green to blue.

warp   Another name for the *lengthwise grain*.

weaving   A finishing method in which pieces are butted together, a join is worked on the right side of the piece, and no visible seam appears.

weft   Another name for the *crosswise grain*.

whipstitch   A stitch that holds together two finished edges. The needle is inserted at a right angle to the edge through both fabrics, forming a slanted stitch.

whitework   The name given to any white embroidery used on a white ground fabric.

whole cloth quilt   A quilt top for a bed covering, made of one single piece of fabric.

wrong side (ws)   The side that faces inward in a knitted or crocheted item, such as the inside of a sweater.

yarn over (yo)   In knitting, winding the yarn around a knitting needle to increase one stitch and create a decorative hole in the fabric. In crochet, the movement of passing the hook under the yarn and then catching the yarn with the hook; this movement is fundamental to all crochet stitches.

yarn winder   A funky, two-piece tool that enables you to easily wind skeins of yarn into balls. Generally, only hardcore knitters and crocheters purchase yarn winders.

Yo-Yo quilt   A novelty bed covering made from small round pieces of fabric gathered to form a flat circle, many of which are then invisibly sewn together.

zigzag stitch   Just like it sounds—a zigzag stitch that's sewn as a seam finish to prevent unraveling or for stretchy fabrics because it has more "give" than a straight stitch.

Index

row-by-row sewing, quilts, 54-56

rubber cement, quilting, 14

ruffles, pillow project (quilting), 225-228

rugs
canvases, needlepoint, 317-318
wool, needlepoint, 320

rulers, quilting, 12, 18

running fabrics, 33

running stitches
embroidery, 254
hand stitching, 608

S

sable paintbrushes, cleaning embroidery projects, 301

samplers
embroidery, 277-278, 303-308
needlepoint, 352-354

sandpaper, quilting, 15

sashing (lattice strips), 173-176

satin stitches (embroidery), 256-257

sc (single crochet) stitches, 516-517, 524-525

scale of design, quilt fabrics, 29-30

scarf project (knitting), 441-442
checkerboard design, 442-444
modifications, 443-444
supplies, 442

scarves, sewing project, 717-719

scissors
dressmaker shears, 321
embroidery, 240, 321
quilting, 13

scroll stitches (embroidery), 268

seams
allowances (sewing), 617-620
crocheting, joining pieces, 579-587
lines, machine quilting, 206-207
pressing, 670-672
puckered, 154
quilts, 53-54
rippers, quilting, 15
sewing, 626
curved seams, 628-629
finishes, 623-626
flat-fell seams, 628
French seams, 626-627
mock French seams, 627
preparing pieces, 620-621
ripping out, 629-630
straight seams, 621-623
skipped stitches, 154
zippers
centered, 646-648
lapped, 649-651

securing embroidery thread, 247-248

securing stitches, hand quilting, 203-204

seed stitches
embroidery, 257-258
knitting, 432-433

selection
commercial patterns, 680
quilt fabric, 27-28

selvage (fabrics), 35, 612

selvage stitches (crocheting), 578-579

separating zippers, 644

sequins, embroidery beadwork, 284-285

sergers (sewing)
finishing seams, 626
machine feet, 605

setup, quilts, 6-7

sew-through (buttons), 632-634

sewing
aprons, 716-717
blocking fabrics, grainlines, 612-615
buttonholes, 638-640
cutting, 640-641
machine-sewn, 636
placement, 636-638
buttons, 631-632
button anchors, 634-635
hand stitching, 633-634
machine-sewn buttons, 635
sew-through, 632
shanks, 632
calibrating tension, 601-602
Christmas stockings, 721-722
commercial patterns, 679
catalogue, 680
envelopes, 682-683
fabric requirements, 681-682
instruction sheets, 683-685
recommendations, 682
selection, 680

Check Out These
Best-Selling
COMPLETE IDIOT'S GUIDES®

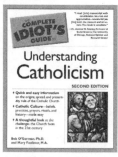

Understanding
Catholicism
SECOND EDITION

1-59257-085-2
$18.95

Learning
Spanish
THIRD EDITION

0-02-864451-4
$18.95

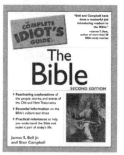

The
Bible
SECOND EDITION

0-02-864382-8
$18.95

Being a
Groom
SECOND EDITION

0-02-864456-5
$9.95

**Grammar
and Style**
SECOND EDITION

1-59257-115-8
$16.95

Playing the
Guitar
SECOND EDITION

0-02-864244-9
$21.95 w/CD

Personal Finance
in Your **20s & 30s**
SECOND EDITION

0-02-864374-7
$19.95

**Knitting and
Crocheting**
SECOND EDITION
Illustrated

1-59257-089-5
$16.95

The **Perfect
Resume**
THIRD EDITION

0-02-864440-9
$14.95

**Buying and
Selling a Home**
FOURTH EDITION

1-59257-120-4
$18.95

**Low-Carb
Meals**

1-59257-180-8
$18.95

Calculus

0-02-864365-8
$18.95

More than *450 titles* in *30 different categories*
Available at booksellers everywhere

ALPHA